Economics without Borders

If treated as a single economy, the European Union is the largest in the world, with an estimated GDP of over 14 trillion euros. Despite its size, European economic policy has often lagged behind the rest of the world in its ability to generate growth and innovation. Much of the European economic research itself often trails behind that of the United States, which sets much of the agenda in mainstream economics.

This book, also available as open access, bridges the gap between economic research and policy-making by presenting overviews of twelve key areas for future economic policy and research. Written for the economists and policy-makers working within European institutions, it uses comprehensive surveys by Europe's leading scholars in economics and European policy to demonstrate how economic research can contribute to good policy decisions, and vice versa, demonstrating how economics research can be motivated and made relevant by hot policy questions.

Economics without Borders

Economic Research for European Policy Challenges

Edited by

Richard Blundell
University College London

Estelle Cantillon
Université Libre de Bruxelles

Barbara Chizzolini
Università Commerciale Luigi Bocconi, Milan

Marc Ivaldi
Toulouse School of Economics, EHESS

Wolfgang Leininger
Technische Universität Dortmund

Ramon Marimon
European University Institute, Florence and Universitat Pompeu Fabra – Barcelona GSE

Laszlo Matyas (Lead Editor)
Central European University

Frode Steen
Norwegian School of Economics

CAMBRIDGE
UNIVERSITY PRESS

CAMBRIDGE
UNIVERSITY PRESS

University Printing House, Cambridge CB2 8BS, United Kingdom

Cambridge University Press is part of the University of Cambridge.

It furthers the University's mission by disseminating knowledge in the pursuit of education, learning, and research at the highest international levels of excellence.

www.cambridge.org
Information on this title: www.cambridge.org/9781316636398
http://dx.doi.org/10.1017/9781316636404

When citing this work, please include a reference to the DOI 10.1017/9781316636404

First published 2017

A catalogue record for this publication is available from the British Library.

ISBN 978-1-107-18515-9 Hardback
ISBN 978-1-316-63639-8 Paperback

Contents

Contents   vii

Contents   ix

Figures

Tables

Foreword

As the Chair of the Scientific Advisory Committee of the Cooperation on European Research in Economics (COEURE) project, I am pleased to present to the public this comprehensive and enlightening volume. The aim of the COEURE initiative is to take stock of current economics research and formulate an agenda for research funding in the field in Europe. From this point of view, the surveys collected in this book are written by top European economists who are intellectual leaders in their respective fields. These surveys identify both research areas that are particularly promising and their potential impact on policy in the European context.

European economics has made significant progress in recent decades. Before the late 1980s, European economics was very fragmented with very little interaction across national borders. Research was mostly published in national languages with very little communication and cross-country fertilization. However, a number of changes have taken place over the last 30 years. First of all, European-wide networks have started to develop. The European Economic Association was created in 1985 and has organized an annual Congress every year since then, partly in coordination with the Econometric Society. The Centre for Economic Policy Research (CEPR), founded by Richard Portes on the model of the US NBER, played a pioneering role in creating the first European-wide high-quality economic research network in Europe. It started selecting outstanding young researchers as Fellows and Affiliates, disseminating their work, organizing European-wide workshops and attracting some of the best US economists to them. Its emphasis on the policy relevance of research has been particularly important and has helped elevate the intellectual debate on all aspects of European integration. The most prominent economists of my generation acknowledge the key role played by the CEPR since the late 1980s and 1990s in internationalizing European economics. Several other cutting-edge European-wide networks have been created since. A good example is the Institute for the Study of Labor (IZA) in Bonn, led with great success by Klaus Zimmerman for the last 20 years. IZA has been very good at recruiting eminent young applied economists, partly because their horizon is not restricted to Europe.

Another important factor that has played a key role in promoting high-quality research is funding not only by the European Commission under various Framework Programmes, but also through Marie Curie fellowships in various European universities. These initiatives from the Commission have helped fund high-quality research networks, as well as the mobility of academics across Europe. The Marie Curie program has been very useful, because it has improved the European job market for economists. Until very recently, and still to a very large extent, we have seen in Europe an inefficient model for recruiting young professors. Universities established barriers to entry, favoring the recruitment of inhouse PhDs. As we know, this usually fosters mediocrity. In most good US universities, departments choose not to recruit even their very best students, because they think that they must first earn recognition in the wider profession, not just in their home university. European economics departments have increasingly adopted this approach and are active on the international job market.

Finally, a major milestone in the progress of research funding in Europe has been the establishment of the European Research Council (ERC) grants. ERC grants are recognized as a signal of excellent research, helping to thereby disseminate clear and unbiased signals of quality. The key aspect to the success of the ERC is that projects are selected by panels of peer researchers, usually highly distinguished senior researchers. Academics are better able to judge the quality of research than nonacademics are. Another aspect of the ERC organization is also important. Panels are large enough in their composition to prevent collusive deals from being made ('I agree to fund the candidate you support if you support mine'). ERC grants are therefore changing the landscape of European research, and universities and departments without ERC grants can no longer pretend that they represent the best of European research.

Despite the huge progress made in the last decades in European economics, there are still many problems. Too much academic work is done in national languages, funding of research is mostly at the national level and European universities often resist external competition in recruitment. In many universities, there is still virtually no research. Promotion is by seniority with no incentives to engage in productive research. The ERC only funds the very best projects and its vocation is purely scientific, not policy-oriented, as it should be. However, there needs to be a European conversation on research funding. Additionally, policy-makers do not necessarily like the findings, especially those of economic research. This is why research projects need to be independent and not subject to forms of political censorship.

While economic research in Europe has addressed many of the key policy issues specific to Europe, there is limited access to data and little availability of good databases on many important issues that need to be investigated. Data are therefore badly needed in many areas, especially for issues that are specific to Europe (like, for example, intra-European migration, regional trade and transport, the efficiency of European (co)financed infrastructure and development projects, or the indirect economic, social, or other effects of EU transfers in the receiving countries and so on). Europe needs to become a data powerhouse. This is particularly true for economic research where economists have developed sophisticated statistical tools that can better help guide policy.

The voice of the best European economists needs to be heard when it comes to how economics research should be funded. The volume presents not only the state of the art in particular domains of research, but also the various policy implications of this research, as well as the major research and policy questions that remain open. They give an idea of where European research stands with respect to the rest of the world and propose further avenues.

The Scientific Advisory Committee of COEURE that I have the honor to chair is composed of distinguished economists: Oriana Bandiera (London School of Economics), Richard Blundell (University College London), François Bourguignon (Paris School of Economics), Andreu Mas-Colell, Universitat Pompeu Fabra), Peter Neary (University of Oxford) and Marco Pagano (University of Naples Federico II). The Scientific Advisory Committee advises the executive Committee of COEURE as well as the authors of the reports for COEURE. Our focus is on the scientific quality of the work carried out.

European economics has made a lot of progress in the last decade, but it still faces many challenges. COEURE aims at helping to improve the effectiveness and quality of the funding of economic research at the European level. I am confident it will.

Gerard Roland
E. Morris Cox Professor of Economics
and Professor of Political Science
University of California, Berkeley
February 29, 2016

Contributors

ROBERTO BARCELLAN Eurostat, Luxembourg, roberto.barcellan@ec.europa.eu

THORSTEN BECK Cass Business School, City University London and CEPR, London, UK, Thorsten.Beck.1@city.ac.uk

RICHARD BLUNDELL University College London and Institute for Fiscal Studies, London, UK, r.blundell@ucl.ac.uk

PETER BØEGH NIELSEN Statistics Denmark, Copenhagen, Denmark, pbn@dst.dk

CHARLES BRENDON Faculty of Economics, University of Cambridge, Cambridge, UK, cfb46@cam.ac.uk

SIMON BURGESS University of Bristol, Bristol, UK, Simon.Burgess@bristol.ac.uk

CATERINA CALSAMIGLIA CEMFI, Madrid, Spain, calsamiglia@cemfi.es

COLIN CAMERER California Institute of Technology, Pasadena, CA, USA, camerer@hss.caltech.edu

ESTELLE CANTILLON Université Libre de Bruxelles, Brussels, Belgium, Estelle.Cantillon@ulb.ac.be

ELENA CARLETTI Bocconi University, CEPR and IGIER, Milan, Italy, carlettie@unibocconi.it

BARBARA CHIZZOLINI Bocconi University, Milan, Italy, barbara.chizzolini@unibocconi.it

GIANCARLO CORSETTI Faculty of Economics, University of Cambridge, gc422@cam.ac.uk

BRUNO CRÉPON CREST and JPAL, Paris, France, bruno.crepon@ensae.fr

CHRISTINE DE MOL Université libre de Bruxelles, Brussels, Belgium, Christine.De.Mol@ulb.ac.be

BRAM DE ROCK Université Libre de Bruxelles, ECARES, Brussels, Belgium, bderock@ulb.ac.be

JUAN J. DOLADO Department of Economics, European University Institute, Florence, Italy, juan.dolado@ui.eu

PAUL DRUMMOND UCL Institute for Sustainable Resources (UCL ISR), University College London, London, UK, p.drummond@ucl.ac.uk

CHRISTIAN DUSTMANN Department of Economics and Centre for Research and Analysis of Migration (CReAM), University College London, London, UK, c.dustmann@ucl.ac.uk

LIRAN EINAV Stanford and NBER, Stanford, CA, USA, leinav@stanford.edu

PAUL EKINS UCL Institute for Sustainable Resources (UCL ISR), University College London, London, UK, p.ekins@ucl.ac.uk

GIOVANNI FACCHINI School of Economics and GEP, University of Nottingham, Nottingham, UK, giovanni.facchini@nottingham.ac.uk

ERIC GAUTIER Toulouse School of Economics, Toulouse, France, eric.gautier@tse-fr.eu

DOMENICO GIANNONE Federal Reserve Bank of New York, New York, USA, Domenico.Giannone@ny.frb.org

ITAY GOLDSTEIN Wharton School, University of Pennsylvania, Philadelphia, PA, USA, itayg@wharton.upenn.edu

LÁSZLÓ HALPERN Hungarian Academy of Science, Budapest Hungary, halpern@econ.core.hu

CECÍLIA HORNOK Kiel Institute for the World Economy, Kiel, Germany, cecilia.hornok@gmail.com

MARC IVALDI Toulouse School of Economics, Toulouse, France, marc.ivaldi@tse-fr.eu

ARIE KAPTEYN University of Southern California, Los Angeles, CA, USA, kapteyn@dornsife.usc.edu

ASIM I. KHWAJA Harvard Kennedy School of Government, Cambridge, MA, USA, akhwaja@hks.harvard.edu

GEORG KIRCHSTEIGER Université Libre de Bruxelles, ECARES, Brussels, Belgium, georg.kirchsteiger@ulb.ac.be

MIKLÓS KOREN Central European University, HAS-CERS and CEPR, Budapest, Hungary, korenm@ceu.edu

VIGDIS KVALHEIM Norway Social Science Data Service, Bergen, Norway, vigdis.kvalheim@nsd.uib.no

JULIA LANE New York University, New York, USA, julia.lane@nyu.edu

WOLFGANG LEININGER TU Dortmund University, Dortmund, Germany, Wolfgang.Leininger@tu-dortmund.de

RAMON MARIMON European University Institute, Florence, Italy, Ramon .Marimon@eui.eu

LASZLO MATYAS Central European University, Budapest, Hungary, matyas@ceu.edu

MARKUS MOBIUS Microsoft Research, Cambridge, MA, USA, mobius@microsoft.com

SENDHIL MULLAINATHAN Harvard University, Cambridge, MA, USA, mullain@fas.harvard.edu

PETER BØEGH NIELSEN Statistics Denmark, pbn@dst.dk

STEF PROOST Department of Economics–KU Leuven, Leuven, Belgium, stef.proost@kuleuven.be

LUCREZIA REICHLIN London Business School, London, UK, lreichlin@london.edu

LUKE SIBIETA Institute for Fiscal Studies, London, UK, luke s@ifs.org.uk

CORA SIGNOROTTO DEMM, University of Milan Milan, Italy, cora .signorotto@unimi.it

FRODE STEEN Norwegian School of Economics, Bergen, Norway, Frode .Steen@nhh.no

JACQUES-FRANÇOIS THISSE Columbia University, CORE-Université catholique de Louvain and CEPR, Louvain-la-Neuve, Belgium, jacques .thisse@uclouvain.be

JOSEPH TRACY Federal Reserve Bank of New York, New York, USA, joseph.tracy@ny.frb.org

ALAIN TRANNOY Aix-Marseille University (Aix-Marseille School of Economics), CNRS and EHESS, Marseille, France, alain.trannoy@gmail.com

FREDERIC UDINA Idescat, Barcelona, Spain, fudina@idescat.cat

HERMAN VAN DIJK Erasmus University Rotterdam, Rotterdam, The Netherlands, hkvandijk@ese.eur.nl

NIKOLAOS VETTAS Athens University of Economics and Business and CEPR, Athens, Greece, nvettas@aueb.gr

JIM WATSON University of Sussex and UK Energy Research Centre, Brighton, UK, jim.watson@ukerc.ac.uk

GUGLIEMO WEBER University of Padua, Padua, Italy, guglielmo.weber@unipd.it

JEFFREY WOOLDRIDGE Michigan State University, East Lansing, MI, USA, wooldri1@msu.edu

LISA WRIGHT Bureau Van Dijk, Manchester, UK, lisa.wright@bvdinfo.com

Introduction

Richard Blundell, Estelle Cantillon, Barbara Chizzolini,
Marc Ivaldi, Wolfgang Leininger, Ramon Marimon,
Laszlo Matyas and Frode Steen

The European Union is the world's largest economic entity, yet its ability to design and implement effective economic policies is not commensurate with its size. It is lagging, for example, in terms of effective policies promoting productivity, growth, scientific research or technological innovation. The Eurozone debt crisis has provided a sharp and painful reminder that the European Union must adopt a new approach to designing its economic policies and coordinating them with the policies of its Member States.

At the same time, while the field of economics in Europe has seen impressive growth in terms of global impact, and in the number of researchers and funding, Europe still lags behind the US in terms of research productivity, and European research remains fragmented across its Member States. According to recent research, the share of articles in the top economics journals published by European researchers represents 34 per cent of the total production of articles in the world, while the US amounts to 53.5 per cent.[1] The contrast is even sharper when the citation impact of these publications is taken into account. In terms of share of citations, the US represents 70.8 per cent while the EU share is 28.4 per cent, which illustrates the considerably higher impact of US research in economics.

Developing a competitive and open European research area is essential for growth and to the progress of European integration, because research is a key factor of growth, and competition among researchers provide them with incentives for cooperating across borders. However, different languages, a diversity of academic traditions and a variety of informal barriers often inhibit the free flow of research funding, the mobility of academic talent and, as a result, the efficient allocation of research and development funding. In times of financial restraint the latter becomes particularly important. In this context, research grants, especially if they are allocated across national borders (e.g., by the European Research Council, ERC), can provide valuable tools to circumvent limits to integration and consequently to enhance the exchange of ideas. In fact, the relationship between openness and successful research funding is reciprocal and internationalization can benefit national and regional funding, by, for example, permitting the inflow of foreign resources. On the other hand, if not designed correctly, research funding can exacerbate existing fragmentation, for example by conditioning grants on nationalities and/or local use or by failing to retain and attract the most able researchers.

The COEURE Project

The COEURE (Cooperation for European Research in Economics) network brings together the key stakeholders in the European economic research space – scientists from the different strands of economic research in Europe, users of research in the policy community and the private sector, statistical offices and other data providers and funders of research. It has been financed by the European Commission within the Seventh Framework Programme. COEURE is based on a process of stocktaking, consultation and stakeholder collaboration that aims at the formulation of an 'Agenda for Research Funding for Economics in Europe'.[2]

This involves taking stock of the current state of research in key fields in economics. The fields cover the entire spectrum of economics, while addressing the most relevant thematic issues identified in Europe. The stock taking exercise is centred on a survey of each by distinguished scholars. Each survey has mapped out the policy issues with which Europe is currently dealing, the research frontier in the given field and the activities of European researchers working at the frontier. It identifies the key open research questions and suggests ways in which research on these issues should evolve over the medium term, notably to better address the policy challenges that Europe is currently facing and likely to be presented in the future.

The COEURE network originates from an initiative of the European Economic Association (EEA). Fondation Jean-Jacques Laffont – Toulouse School of Economics – is leading the network assembling a group of academic institutions, with the support of the EEA. The partner institutions are: Bocconi University, Université Libre de Bruxelles, Dortmund University, the European University Institute, Central European University, the Norwegian School of Economics and the Centre for Economic Policy Research.

Advances in Economic Research: Foundations for European Policies

Five clusters of European economic policy challenges have been identified as being of paramount importance:
1. Economics of research, education and innovation in a European and global context, including economics of smart specialization (Europe 2020, European Research Agenda).

2. Knowledge-based growth and employment; prioritization of policies in Europe, in particular, the need for short-term consolidation, long-term growth policies like fiscal consolidation and smart / sustainable growth (i.e., addressing poverty, gender, employment and environmental issues).
3. The link between monetary and fiscal policy in Europe and between fiscal and private debts; efficient use of unconventional monetary policies; insolvency problems and the management of rescue funds (addressing asset inflation, housing prices and market bubbles).
4. Cross-border spillovers, interdependencies and coordination of European policies across borders (addressing the questions of externalities, economies of scale, etc.).
5. Institutional and structural reforms in the Member States and associated countries concerning issues like ageing, health systems, energy and resources efficiency, transport or environment in the context of Europe 2020 and their budgetary and macroeconomic consequences.

In light of these challenges, twelve specific topics have been selected to address the current state of research and its relationship with policy:

1. R&D, innovation and growth;
2. Labour markets;
3. Population, migration, ageing and health;
4. Human capital and education;
5. Competition and regulation in markets for goods and services;
6. Trade, globalization and development;
7. Energy, environment and sustainability;
8. Cities, regional development and transport;
9. Fiscal and monetary policy;
10. Financial markets;
11. Inequality and welfare; and
12. Data and methods, a topic which cuts across most areas and policy issues, and covers current developments in data and research methods in economics.

For each of these topics, a survey was solicited and a workshop organized that brought together key researchers in the field, as well as leading European policy-makers. The workshops served as forums to discuss recent advances in our understanding of policy issues, open questions, developments in methods and challenges facing research in a given area.

The main objective of the surveys has been to identify the key research challenges pertaining to one broad area of policy and demonstrate how economic research contributes (or not) to the policy issues related to that area. Its originality lies in synthesizing insights from different fields of economics, rather than summarizing the results from the literature in a single field, as is often the case with surveys in the academic literature.

The surveys have been designed to address the following questions:

1. Why is the topic important, both in general and in the European economic policy context?
2. How can economics contribute to our understanding and analysis of this political and societal topic?
3. What are the key questions (both novel and long-standing) in the area? What do we know and not know about them? Do we need to better understand the facts or develop better theories?
4. What are the key points of agreement and disagreement in the academic literature on the subject? Where is the research frontier?
5. What are the key open questions, that is to say, new questions or old questions that have not been addressed in economic research but are of vital importance for policy-making in Europe?
6. Where does Europe stand in terms of research and expertise in this area compared to other contributors to research, in particular the US?
7. What is the role of scientific advice in EU policy decision-making (see, for example, the European Commission's 2001 White Paper on European governance)? How does it compare to US economic policy-making governance?
8. What is the research methodology currently used to address questions in this area?
9. What specific challenges do Europe-based researchers working in this area face (including data access, its availability or quality, methods, funding and any other relevant issue)?

This volume is the outcome of this process. As we will see, European researchers address most key European economic policy issues and challenges. The policy recommendations are plentiful, although not always politically correct or easily acceptable. Economic research is firmly grounded on facts, although data, while more and more developed, are not always accessible or available. The theoretical challenges and methodological difficulties that current research is facing begs for inter-European cooperation and cooperation with other fields and disciplines, while given its actual state or art, its own logic and approach should and can be preserved.

About the Chapters

The *first chapter* of the volume deals with innovation and growth, which have been central to European policy-making since at least the Lisbon Agenda. The chapter argues that the Schumpeterian paradigm provides a unifying framework to organize existing empirical evidence and think about R&D, innovation and growth policies. The authors show how the Schumpeterian framework sheds new light on ongoing policy debates such as the role of competition for innovation or the consequence of innovation on inequality, and they discuss the policy implications of recent advances in our understanding of these phenomena.

The Schumpeterian growth paradigm relies on three fundamental ideas. First, innovation (rather than simply the growth of capital or labour as in the classic growth models) drives long-term growth. These can be process innovations, which increase the productivity of existing assets or labour, product innovations or organizational innovations. Second, innovations result from investments by firms and entrepreneurs. This raises the question of the incentives for innovation, including the ability of firms and entrepreneurs to reap the benefits of their innovations. Third, new innovations tend to make old innovations, old technologies or old skills obsolete (creative destruction). Thus growth intrinsically involves a conflict between 'the old' and 'the new': the innovators of yesterday will tend to resist new innovations that render their activities obsolete. Creative destruction also explains why, in the data, higher productivity growth is associated with higher rates of firm and labour turnover.

Because firms and entrepreneurs are at its core, the Schumpeterian paradigm provides a natural link between micro phenomena, such as firm entry and exit, firm heterogeneity, firm organization, or job turnover, and macro phenomena, such as growth and inequality. In fact, the authors show how the Schumpeterian framework is able to explain a number of existing stylized facts about firm and job turnover, the size distribution of firms and the correlation between firm size and firm age, to name a few. They also show how the framework has been used to develop new predictions that have then been tested, using new micro datasets. The scope of applications is very large and this is an active field of research. For example, recent research has shown how the level of competition differentially impacts the incentives for innovation of firms that are close to the technology frontier of the economy and those that are furthest away. Other research has looked at the impact of market protection on innovation as a function of a country's distance to the world technology frontier.

A central message of the chapter is that institutions and policies that foster growth depend on where a country lies with respect to the world technology frontier. There is no one-size-fits-all. In advanced economies, competitive product markets, flexible labour markets, quality graduate education and developed equity-based financial markets form the four pillars of innovation-led growth: competition in product markets encourages innovation by firms seeking to escape the low margins of neck-to-neck competition; flexible labour markets ease the process of creative destruction; quality graduate education produces the research skills necessary for innovation; and equity-based financing is more receptive to the risk intrinsic to innovation. The chapter revisits the rationale and design of competition policy, the welfare state, macroeconomic policy and R&D policy in this light. It ends with a call for a new Growth Pact in

Europe, one that relies on structural reforms aimed at liberalizing product and labour markets, a renewed industrial policy and more flexible macroeconomic policies.

Chapter 2 focuses on the prevalence of 'dual labour markets' in the European Union. In the 1960s unemployment in Europe was no higher than in the US, but by the end of the twentieth century the 'European unemployment problem' was the code name for a widespread problem of inefficient allocation of human resources in Europe and in Continental Europe in particular. At the beginning of the twenty-first century the problem seemed to recede, with some countries undertaking critical labour reforms (e.g., Germany) and some of the 'high unemployment' countries showing very high rates of net job creation (e.g., Spain). Although still lower than in the US, European employment rates were not only higher on average but also less dispersed than in the recent past. However, with the financial and euro crises the problem took on a different dimension, that of a divided Europe (and Euro Area), with some countries exhibiting once again very high unemployment rates (mostly Southern EU), as a reflection of their deeply entrenched structural problems.

Chapter 2 provides an overview of the research – most of it by European labour economists – that focuses on this new version of the 'European unemployment problem'. The theoretical and empirical research provides a consensus view on who the culprit is: the 'duality' induced in labour markets by the existence of labour contracts with large differences in their implied employment protection legislation. In particular, this chapter describes the highly asymmetric employment protection that distinguishes permanent from temporary contracts, tracing their historical origins and institutional arrangements. In line with the most advanced literature, the chapter takes a general equilibrium perspective. The historical perspective explains why different European countries have followed different paths and why 'changing paths' has proven difficult. The theoretical, general equilibrium perspective reveals the side effects of such 'dualism' and why it cannot simply be identified with the coexistence of temporary and permanent contracts, which are used in all countries.

After World War I and up to the mid 1970s, many European countries experienced a significant increase in employment protection legislation. Spain, Italy, France and Portugal regulated their labour markets by imposing severance payments and restrictions on dismissals, among other measures. These laws made it costly for firms to adjust in response to a changing environment and once the oil crises hit in the 1970s, the need for higher flexibility became a more pressing priority on political agendas.

Nevertheless, dismantling the benefits that workers were entitled to was not politically feasible due to the large political influence of highly protected workers. Thus reforms were made at the margin, affecting new employees only. Specifically, the emergence of temporary contracts with a lower regulatory burden was the policy response to the quest for flexibility in labour markets. These reforms thus created a dual labour market by allowing for two types of contracts: temporary and permanent (open-ended). The former was designed to facilitate turnover and fast adjustments, while the latter represented the remains of stringent policies targeted at guaranteeing job and income stability.

The chapter describes how economic research – in particular, 'insider-outsider' theories – has helped to explain why dual labour markets have been a longstanding feature of many European economies. Insider-outsider models have set the framework for the analysis of the tensions between workers with permanent contracts (insiders) and the rest of the labour force (outsiders) when it comes to deciding on a reform. Beyond rationalizing the observed pattern in the creation of a dual labour market and its political sustainability, these models have extended our understanding of the interplay between the political decision-making process and real business-cycle (RBC) effects – e.g., why employment is so volatile in economies with 'dual markets' and how these RBC effects reinforce the lack of effective political support for labour market reforms.

Nevertheless, as the chapter emphasizes, the coexistence of temporary and permanent contracts is a desirable feature, as firms might have temporary or seasonal needs. Furthermore, a temporary contractual relationship can help workers gain experience or acquire human capital. In fact, in countries like Austria, Denmark or Sweden, temporary jobs are the first step into the labour market and are followed by a permanent contract. On the other hand, in southern European countries, temporary jobs have become 'dead-end' jobs. Workers tend to experience a sequence of fixed-term contracts and the dream of a transition to a permanent contract rarely comes true. The chapter documents this difference and reviews relevant research, showing that market dualism is due to the existence of large gaps in redundancy costs among permanent and temporary workers, combined with wage rigidity.

The general equilibrium formulations have helped to explain the pervasive effects of 'labour market duality' beyond its direct effects on the level and volatility of employment: First, its composition effect, in particular the high levels of youth unemployment and NEET ('not in education, employment or training'), second, the lower human capital accumulation, and third, how these labour supply effects have also shaped firms' demand for low-productivity jobs, low levels of innovation and, in particular, investment in sectors of low growth potential (e.g., construction) in times of low interest rates.

The chapter closes with a review and evaluation of the reforms that have been undertaken, or proposed, in different countries to overcome 'the duality disease', demonstrating how both empirical and theoretical research reveal the need for overall reforms of labour market regulations. In particular, the chapter discusses the possibility of a single/unified contract, both from a theoretical and a practical perspective. Finally, the survey identifies three main directions in which economic research can enrich the policy debate: (i) empirical work on the differential incentives and responses induced by the two types of contracts; (ii) analysis of the political feasibility of reforms within the current scheme and (iii) the role of labour market dualism in technology adoption by firms.

Chapter 3 deals with the problems of population, migration, ageing and health. World migration, and in particular net migration in the European Union, has been an extremely hot topic in the last few years, debated in the media as much as in the political arenas of each EU Member State and in the European Commission. A large part of the debate has, however, focused on how to deal with the current emergency inflow of undocumented migrants that are fleeing from war zones and natural disasters.

Not much is known and discussed about medium and long-run causes and effects of migration. For instance, one of the recognized structural motivations of migration is the contrast between the ageing population in most destination countries and the young, more fertile population of the countries of origin. Migrants are typically younger than the host country population when they arrive, and, as a result they contribute to rejuvenating the host country's labour supply in the short run. However, migrants age as well as natives, and it has also been shown that their fertility behaviour, and that of their descendants, tends to adapt in time to the pattern of behaviour of the host country. Is then migration a long-term solution to the ageing population problem of most Western European countries? Similarly, what are the long-run economic benefits and costs of migrant workers in the destination countries? Do the tax revenues and benefits to the economic activity due to changes in the composition of the working population exceed the welfare costs over the entire lifecycle of a cohort of immigrants? What determines exactly these benefits and costs? Which migration policies are more effective in fostering welfare enhancing migration patterns?

Looking instead at the countries of origin, can the 'brain drain' phenomenon be a problem? Is their growth potential impaired by the out-migration they experience? The chapter addresses these questions from an economics standpoint, with the explicit aim of suggesting clear migration policies and indications for future research.

The main message put forward by the authors is the need for a dynamic approach to simultaneously describe migration plans, human capital acquisition and labour supply, that evolve in time and that both affect and are affected by the social, economic and demographic structure of the host countries. The key issue, in this context, is the analysis of the choice between temporary and permanent migration. Data shows that the percentage of temporary migrants is much higher in Europe than in Anglo-America, Australia and New Zealand. Why is that? What are the determinants of return migration to the countries of origin? The literature is as yet only able to provide partial answers. It is, however, quite clear that the demographic, social and economic impacts of immigration vary depending on how long migrants stay in the destination countries.

As for the fiscal effects of migration, there is consensus on the finding that host countries experience a net gain from highly skilled, young, possibly temporary, workers; but effects are less clear-cut in the presence of low-skilled workers. In particular, the evidence collected in Norway by Bernt Bratsberg clearly outlines the tendency of low-skilled migrants to exit the labour force early and become social security dependents. In addition, migrant workers are more likely to suffer from macroeconomic downturns than natives. Nevertheless, there exists significant heterogeneity across destination countries and migrants' behaviour responds to incentives provided by the local welfare state, as well as to the local implementation of migration policies. Expanding on the latter issue, the effect of any migration policy depends strongly on the institutional setting: the evidence on the relative efficacy of immigrant driven versus employer driven policies in attracting the 'best' migrants is ambiguous. In both cases what makes the difference is the credibility of the State and the efficiency of local labour markets.

To conclude, the authors also emphasize the lack of data for certain types of studies. Analysis on the long-run causes and effects of migration require as yet unavailable long panels of information on migrants and their descendants. Even more relevant is the need to standardize and guarantee access to data across EU member states and to link EU Member States' Immigration Registries.

Moving to the next chapter, it is well understood that the process of globalization has reinforced the basic tenet of human capital theory, namely that the economic well-being of a society is determined not only by its stocks of financial capital, labour and natural resources but also – and ever increasingly so – the knowledge and skills of its individual members. Accordingly, already the 2000 Lisbon Agenda of the European Union set out the aim to turn Europe into the most competitive and dynamic knowledge-based economy in the world, capable of sustainable economic growth with more and better jobs and greater social cohesion.

Indeed, research results in the economics of education show that education has a considerable impact on economic growth. Simple qualitative measures for education such as indicators based on cognitive achievement of students turn out to be extremely good predictors for the long-run economic growth of nations. Plainly, enhancing the EU's average student performance using a test like PISA would yield substantial returns in the form of EU Member States' long-term economic growth.

From this economic perspective it appears that education systems 'produce' the human capital embodied in the workforce of a society. They are hence prime subjects for economic investigation. At the same time, educational attainment is an important determinant of equity and social cohesion in a society. This makes the search for educational policies and forms of political governance that influence the formation of human capital in a most favourable way, a particularly important one.

Chapter 4 surveys and organizes a huge body of mainly empirical work that addresses the question of how education policies can advance student attainment. To understand which policies work, education economists employ advanced micro-econometric methods to perform carefully designed quasi-experimental evaluations. The main emphasis is on the identification of *causal effects* from the data; these methods and set-ups may require new types of datasets which are not yet uniformly available across Europe. Consequently, the survey also draws heavily on studies and evaluations of the US educational system.

The chapter is organized around the economic paradigm of a more or less competitive 'market for education'. More precisely, this market takes the special form of a matching or assignment market as students and pupils on the demand side have to be 'matched' with schools and other institutions of the educational system on the supply side. How can such matching be accomplished as efficiently as possible if efficiency is measured by educational attainment? And what assignment methods are beneficial to what groups? The answers to these questions can be very surprising, if one also takes into account the reactions of the actors in this market, parents, pupils, schools, teachers etc. to the assignment mechanism chosen by society. The identification and assessment of such incentive effects is a hallmark of economic inquiry. The chapter performs this task for the most common assignment mechanisms: neighbourhood schooling (each pupil goes to the local school), tracking or elite schooling (schools are allocated on the basis of a test score), choice-based schooling (parental choice of school subject to a rationing mechanism) and income-based schooling (admission to private schools).

Another central concern is how the political governance of education systems affects educational success and equity. What makes an effective education system with good schools given an assignment mechanism? School accountability, i.e., the provision of rewards or sanctions for 'good' and 'bad' schools, is the key issue here, which – economically speaking – determines the degree of competition between schools. It can only be effective, if schools also have some autonomy and hence decision-making in the governance structure becomes decentralized. As a consequence, individual school leadership and management become more important. Indeed, the evidence shows that all three components – accountability, autonomy and management, each of which can take many forms – exert an influence on school and pupil achievements.

Knowledge of the patterns of *causal* dependencies between student attainment and these market *design* features of an educational system should be extremely useful for progressing along the strategic framework 'Education and Training 2020' adopted by the European Commission. It provides for some common ground to improve cooperation between the European Commission and its Members on educational matters while fully respecting Member States' competencies in the field of education and training.

Chapter 5 deals with the issues of competition and regulation in markets for goods and services. Competition policy has become an important tool in Europe's common work towards a more efficient and innovative economy. The major topics in competition policy and regulation are organized around four areas: collusion and cartels, abuse of dominance, merger controls and state aid. Policy and regulation have been guided by growing research in Industrial Organization (IO), both theoretically and empirically. The EU has built national and European structures to manage competition issues both through law and regulation and by strengthening regulative institutions' scope and capacity for governing competition and efficiency within- and across national markets.

A major new concern within both research and the implementation of policy is how markets work in the 'digitalized' economy and electronic trade. The efficient functioning of digital and online markets is crucial to welfare and is expected to become even more important in the near future. Already by 2020, more than half of total European retail sales are anticipated to be web-impacted.[3] The digitaliation of the economy challenges traditional competition and regulation tools as well as theory. Several issues distinguish digitalized markets; often such markets are two sided; search and transaction costs are different and significantly lower compared to traditional offline markets; the cost structure is tilted heavily towards the fixed cost component and not the marginal ones; there are challenges on how to protect intellectual property rights; and new privacy issues are in focus due to the increased availability of private information on market participants. For instance, a significant part of traditional competition regulation, and partly theory, relates to firm size, dominance and market definition. In the online economy, market borders are fluid, at best, and the competition is geared towards competition for the market, rather than competition in the market. The latter implies in its most liberal consequence that even monopolized online markets are not necessarily a problem as long as they are contestable and are exposed to continuous competitive pressure. The regulation and competition problem transfers to entry barrier questions rather than dominance as such.

The challenges we are facing can be seen through the policy questions and decisions that have been relevant in recent and ongoing competition cases. From these cases several questions emerge; the existence and the challenges with most favoured national (MFN) clauses (e.g., Amazon e-books and online travel agents), selective distribution (Adidas, ASICS and Casio), the usage of selective non-neutral price comparison algorithms (Google), cross-border rules on fees (MasterCard) and resale price maintenance (RPM) rules (Swedish sport nutrition products), to name a few.

This chapter shows that the policy-makers and courts take different stances due to different views on how to solve these issues: motivating a discussion on the difficult choices policy-makers now face between ex ante regulation (per se prohibition) and ex post regulation (rule of reason). It discusses the EU's digital single market imitative and some of the economic challenges we are facing on vertical relations and pricing. The IO literature offers both 'old' and new "wisdom" as regards how we can deal with these issues, still the chapter shows that there are both coexisting theories suggesting different outcomes with regards to efficiency and welfare, and several open questions that need answers. For instance, the way in which we are to deal with RPM rules are not obvious, neither in the offline, nor in the digitalized economy. Although RPM rules offer vertical related firms to facilitate pricing and increase competition, they also sometimes facilitate collusion. Likewise, it is unclear that not allowing any restrictions on cross-border online sales are enhancing welfare always and in all cases.

The chapter surveys the new literature on competition and digitalized markets, and clearly advocates more work. In particular, it shows that despite the increased data availability from the online economy, very few empirical studies exist. This is surprising since the theory typically generates ambiguous predictions that depend on the size of the effects at play when it comes to show how pricing arrangements affect equilibrium prices, profits and welfare.

Many of the issues that surface as important in 'digitalized' markets are also evident in more traditional markets. However, the systematic presence of some key new features like two-sidedness, cost structure and vertical pricing structures, significantly modifies the nature of the models that should be used. Overall, new research on this topic needs to balance the important central results from the existing IO literature, even if reorganized and reinterpreted, against new approaches required by the new features of the digitalized economy.

Chapter 6 deals with the problems of trade, globalization and development. It is well understood that the fortune of workers, consumers, firms, regions and countries increasingly depends on other regions and countries. This global interdependence is driven by the flow of goods, capital, information, ideas and people across them. An almost tautological conclusion of theory is that if countries choose to interact with one another, they have to be better off than being in isolation. While there are many quantifiable models to evaluate the gains from trade, the welfare gains from global production sharing, either via arm's length global value chains or via multinational production, are less clearly quantifiable. Better understanding how multinational firms operate is central to comprehend and estimate their contribution to the costs and benefits of globalization.

An overarching theme is that globalization benefits some more than others. In fact, some may even become worse off as their country becomes more open to the flow of goods, ideas and people. For example, workers in import-competing industries stand to lose when countries open up to trade. There is a need for better understanding the redistributional effects of globalization and to develop policies to mitigate the negative effects. Economists find it difficult to give definite answers to trade policy challenges, partly because the remaining policy barriers to cross-border transactions are difficult to quantify. There is broad-based evidence that these frictions are large, but many of them cannot be captured by taxes and quotas, which are the standard tools to model them for policy analysis. We need to better understand not only protectionist, but also precautionary motives for trade policy.

There are also important challenges in measurement. Recent initiatives to match data from various national sources are very promising, but the national fragmentation of data collection remains the primary data challenge facing analysts of globalization. To be more specific, the most relevant tasks in this area are to:

1. harmonize firm-level trade and balance sheet data across countries;
2. develop statistical methods and computational tools to work with multidimensional data;
3. develop new datasets on workers within firms, while ensuring privacy and consistency across studies;
4. build harmonized firm-level data on services trade;
5. collect data on buyer-supplier links within the EU;
6. link national administrative data, harmonize data collection and reporting;
7. synthesize research based on ad-hoc proprietary data; and
8. construct international input-output accounts from the ground up.

There are some important challenges for theory as well. We need to:

1. reeconcile model-based and reduced-form estimates of gains from trade;
2. identify losers from globalization and quantify their losses;
3. understand and quantify nontax, nonquota frictions in trade;
4. develop a toolbox for quantitative analysis of redistribution;
5. understand and quantify the effects of standards and harmonization on trade and welfare; and
6. develop a quantitative theory of supply-chain trade and of multinationals.

Chapter 7 deals with the economic approaches to energy, environment and sustainability. Different schools of economic theory hold differing views on the basic characteristics of the relationship between the economy and the environment. The two principal schools are 'environmental and resource economics', which considers environmental concerns as an aspect of broader economic issues to which the approaches of rationality, marginalism and efficiency may be suitably applied, and 'ecological economics', which considers the economy as a component of the global ecosystem, and employs 'methodological pluralism' to assess different aspects of what proponents view as a highly complex, multifaceted human–economy–environment interaction. These two opposing viewpoints produce different concepts of 'sustainability' and 'sustainable development', and different ways of measuring whether progress towards such states is being achieved. Environmental and resource economics takes the position of 'weak' sustainability, which advocates that as long as the total economic value of all capital stock (natural, human and man-made) can be maintained in real terms, regardless of the distribution, sustainability is achieved. The monetary valuation of natural capital and ecosystem services is a central tool in such analysis.

Ecological economics instead takes the position of 'strong' sustainability, which considers some natural capital to be 'critical' in that it makes a unique contribution to welfare or has intrinsic value, and cannot be substituted by manufactured or other forms of capital. The insights of institutional/evolutionary economics, and behavioural economics, are also important to our conception of the economy/environment relationship, and challenge the core tenets of neoclassical economics (upon which environmental and resource economics is based), including assumptions of rational, maximizing behaviour by all economic agents (individuals and firms) according to exogenous preferences, the absence of chronic information problems, the complexity and limits to cognitive capacity, and a theoretical focus on movements towards or attained equilibrium states of rest.

Although sometimes contradictory, these schools of thought are complementary in many respects, and bring different insights to bear on both the issues of sustainability (such as the 'wicked problem' of the 'Energy Trilemma'; decarbonizing the energy system whilst maintaining both energy security and energy access and affordability) and policy approaches to tackle issues that threaten it. Whilst the application of economic thought and methodological approaches has advanced our understanding of interactions within and between the human and natural world, many important areas of further theoretical, empirical and methodological research remain. These areas may be broadly delineated into four interrelated themes.

Basic characteristics of the economy–environment relationship. This concerns the notions of weak and strong sustainability, central to which is valuation of natural capital and ecosystem services. Particular areas of research should show how to include or mitigate the impact of behavioural and cognitive complexities on values elucidated, how nonmonetary valuation approaches may be integrated or made complementary to monetary valuation, whether monetary valuation, by framing the good or service in such terms, crowds out other forms of valuation, and the extent to and nature in which monetary valuation can and does impact decision- and policy-making (including the drivers and barriers involved). Another ongoing area for research should be the refinement of robust approaches to identifying 'critical' natural capital, in order to further define our 'safe operating space' within 'planetary boundaries' that are not open to meaningful monetary valuation.

'Natural' (nonpolicy) drivers of changes to this relationship. This contains two principal longstanding questions. The first concerns the validity of the Environmental Kuznets Curve hypothesis, which suggests that the relationship between resource depletion and pollution levels and income follows an inverted 'U'-shaped parabola; resource depletion and pollution levels increase with income until a given level of income is reached, after which environmental pressures decrease (driven by, rather than simply inversely correlated to, increasing income). Further research using structural equation models, along with an increased focus on the influence of economic and demographic structures and the political economy, is required. The second question surrounds approaches to the robust calculation of marginal social costs of pollution, and of CO_2 in particular. Alongside valuation of natural capital and ecosystem services (in addition to valuation of human health and comfort etc.), debates about appropriate social discount rates are central in this field.

The design and impact of policy interventions. Four principal, interrelated topics for further research are dominant. The first concerns the cost for firms of environmental policy of different designs (both individually and in a policy 'mix'), and the effect this has on competitiveness (and in particular 'carbon leakage'). The second surrounds the process, drivers and barriers to innovation and diffusion of innovations, and the development of innovation 'indicators'. The third topic concerns the role, nature and impact of institutions and behaviour in policy choice, design and impact. In terms of the 'energy trilemma', continued research into the availability of 'win–win' options, and options for reducing the risks surrounding the inherent uncertainty of future developments, would also be of substantial benefit. The fourth topic concerns issues of environmental justice and distributional impacts. Uncertainty surrounds whether instruments utilizing monetary valuation of natural capital and ecosystem services reduces or exacerbates preexisting economic and social inequalities, particularly at the local level. Further research is required to determine the distributional impacts of policy instruments, instrument mixes and their specific design.

Modelling approaches and techniques. Most models employed to assess the impact of environmental policy tend to focus on a particular component of the environmental-economic system. Although numerous Integrated Assessment Models (IAMs) attempt to link different components of the environment and economy, such dynamic links are usually relatively basic. Further research should be directed at improving such links. However, improvements to the individual components of such models are also required. For example, integration of the insights provided by behavioural and institutional economics in macroeconomic models is often poor, meaning that such models mischaracterize critical, 'real-life' dynamics. The improved incorporation of such insights into economic-environmental models should hold a high priority on the research agenda.

Chapter 8 provides a detailed account of the general economic principles governing regional growth. It starts from the very basics of spatial economics to progress to advanced econometric testing of predictions following from models based on New Economic Geography and New Trade Theory, both of which attach prominent roles to increasing returns and network effects occurring through complex 'linkages'. Mostly publicly provided infrastructure and transport networks are key drivers of these linkages.

The chapter provides sobering insights for advocates of clear, politically well-intentioned goals such as regional cohesion and (income) equalization in Europe. As shown, the authors' conclusions hold in particular against the background of decreasing transport and communication costs, which has recently given rise to popular catch-words like 'the death of distance' or 'the flat world'. The insinuated quasi-irrelevance of distance and location in space and markets and the intuition that this should foster more equal development across different regions *have no economic foundation.*

It appears that regional disparities are inevitable due to the economic forces of agglomeration and dispersion at work, and the complex ways they are reinforced or dampened by transport costs. Moreover, decreasing transport costs as well as the new transport infrastructure, which better links lagging regions to thriving markets in urban agglomerations, may work *against* the aimed convergence of income and living standards, if agglomeration forces become *relatively* stronger. There is ample evidence that this occurs at a European level. The crucial point to assess is economic agents' reaction to these changes, that is, how *firm and labour* mobility are affected. Results indicate that differences between regions matter less than differences between people living there. As a consequence, helping poor regions need not help poor people in that region. Thus, investments into training and human capital may be a better development strategy than additional transport infrastructure.

What are the consequences of these findings for the transport and infrastructure policy of the European Union? Firstly, the selection and assessment of large transport infrastructure projects must be improved. Standard piecemeal cost-benefit analysis does not suffice as system-wide consequences have to be accounted for. Secondly, the present use of the existing transport infrastructure in Europe has to be put to much better use. The EU does not do well in comparison to the US in using its rail and air transportation systems. Both suffer from the national fragmentation of regulations and operation standards as well as the 'protectionist' interests of large domestic firms. In particular, the proportion of rail transport of goods in the EU is very low compared to the US, as most goods are transported by trucks across Europe. Simple fuel taxes have given way to new distance-based 'truck taxes' imposed by countries with a high share in transit traffic, such as Germany or Austria. This instrument for more efficient pricing is very promising. The present implementation of distance charges, however, is suboptimal as distance-based charges for trucks have considerably lowered diesel taxes due to tax competition initiated by neighbouring countries. Moreover, distance is not necessarily a good proxy for the external costs of a road trip, which also depend on local conditions such as congestion, air pollution and accidents. Taking account of these factors in more sophisticated formulas for road pricing of trucks cannot ignore the impact of traffic by passenger cars. Already today the diesel tax is likely to be too low for passenger cars and too high (combined with distance charges) for trucks. The political shift in road pricing for trucks must also pave the way to a new system of road pricing for cars.

The treatment of urban development and spatial planning within the social sciences underplays the importance of economics in a serious way. This is mostly self-inflicted by the field, as Urban Economics has never formed a central part of mainstream economics. Originally, the development of spatial economic theory was almost exclusively driven by German contributors: Heinrich von Thünen, Wilhelm Launhardt, Alfred Weber, Walter Christaller and August Lösch. As there are no counterparts to them in the Anglo-Saxon tradition of economic theorizing, initially spatial economics was completely absent from neoclassical economics. Even today it is much less central to mainstream economics than it should be, because the introduction of space and land use into economic analysis brings about important ramifications. Space cannot be incorporated into the competitive general equilibrium model in a frictionless way as changing location incurs costs, especially *transport* costs. This fact lies at the heart of the phenomenon of agglomeration.

Chapter 9 convincingly argues that agglomeration drives economic growth and the social cohesion of a society in a fundamental way. This insight holds important lessons for policy-makers in the European Union: the single most important insight perhaps is that wealth is *increasingly* created in cities and metropolitan areas.

What are the economic driving forces behind this development? For consumers as well as firms, agglomeration produces increasing returns due to improved learning, sharing and matching opportunities in productive and social processes. Given consumers' preferences for affordable housing and dislike of commuting, cities emerge as the outcome of a trade-off between the gains and costs of agglomeration. The simultaneous spatial treatment of land use for housing and business and transportation in spatial theory is not easy. There are many externalities at work; for example, any person's decision to use a car or occupy a certain flat yields consequences for others who are deprived from using this particular space. Taking account of these externalities theoretically and estimating them empirically leads to another remarkable result: cities, in particular European cities, are likely to be too *small* rather than too large to reap the full benefits of agglomeration. The success of cities – much more so than that of regions – is instrumental for future growth in the European Union.

Improvements to the organization of metropolitan areas and big cities should hence focus on a reduction of agglomeration costs. Traffic and the transport of *people* as a main source of congestion in urban areas are prime targets in this regard. For example, the single most important external cost of car use in urban areas is congestion, *rather than* climate damage. However, much more public and political attention is paid to climate change than to congestions. The economic answer to the problem of congestion is the politically unpopular device of road pricing. Nevertheless, efficient pricing of congestion will bring about time and productivity gains, as well as generate valuable revenues. The need for congestion pricing is reinforced by the finding that *in the absence of road pricing* the public provision of expensive new infrastructure and transportation links will not alleviate the congestion problem. The authors present impressive evidence of the scope and implementation of smart pricing schemes that have consequences not only for the cost-benefit analysis of large transportation projects but also for public finance in general; for example, they suggest spending the revenues from congestion pricing on a reduction in labour taxes.

The bottom line is simple: the European Union needs the design of urban policies (on behalf of the European Commission and its Member States) similar in standing, importance and funding to its present design of regional policies.

Chapter 10 focuses on 'Fiscal and Monetary Policies after the Crises'. Historically, macroeconomic policy and research have always been intertwined, main policy and institutional designs have been rooted in economic analysis (price stability, Central Bank Independence, etc.) and, likewise, economic research has always been stimulated by macroeconomic events; especially negative ones. The financial and euro crises (2008–2013) – the Great Recession for many countries – have been no exception.

These have also been crises of confidence: for advanced societies, who viewed themselves in a sustainable growth path supported by the 'great macroeconomic moderation'; for policy-makers, who entertained similar self-views to those of Jean-Claude Trichet, president of the ECB, who wrote on the occasion of that Institution's 10th anniversary: 'The achievements of the past decade are due to the vision and determination of the Governing Council members, past and present, and due to the energy and efforts of all staff of the Eurosystem',[4] and also for the macroeconomic academic profession who, in the words of Nobel Laureate Robert E. Lucas Jr. at the dawn of this century, thought that 'macroeconomics in this original sense has succeeded: its central problem of depression prevention has been solved'.[5]

The chapter provides an overview of the up-growth of research in macroeconomics, in response to these severe shocks of the early twenty-first century. The debate about which instruments to use to stimulate economies in recession, and which stabilization policies should be pursued when traditional interest rate policies prove to be ineffective, have become the centre of attention in both academia and policy-making. The chapter shows how new research has contributed to clarify issues, assess new and old policies, and raise new questions.

The authors present the landscape that policy-makers and researchers faced after the recession by highlighting the trends observed in three economic aggregates: output, unemployment and inflation. Their attention then turns to analysing policy design in economies with low or negative output growth, low inflation, high unemployment and a binding zero lower-bound (ZLB) for interest rates. Part of the economics literature indicates that the driver leading an economy to hit the ZLB is a fall in the natural rate of interest. Taking this literature as a starting point, the chapter discusses both monetary and fiscal policy alternatives. In particular, three alternative monetary policies are discussed: forward guidance, quantitative easing and credit easing. On the fiscal side, the discussion focuses on research that has investigated the effectiveness of fiscal stimulus when the economy is near the ZLB, as well as on what the most effective instruments to be used are: labour taxes, consumption taxes and government expenditures, among others.

The scientific method has prevailed over the 'crisis of confidence'. That is, new theories and methods have been developed *which build on* the existing ones (not throwing them away as 'culprits of the crises', as it was often put in the media). For example, the authors show how different new contributions can be mapped into a key ingredient of dynamic macroeconomic models; how policies and frictions distort the intertemporal choices that households, and societies, make sense through *the Euler equation*. From how the fall in the natural rate is modelled, to how the different proposed policies provide incentives to escape from a recession at the ZLB, is better understood through the lens of the *Euler equation*. The results of this analysis indicate that most of the suggested policies work through 'the expectations channel'. More precisely, policies are effective if they increase expectations of future inflation and consequently lower the real interest rates. As the authors note, it remains a theoretical and empirical challenge to effectively assess the size and validity of 'the expectations channel' as the pivotal policy transmission mechanism at the ZLB.

In economic models, a fall in the natural interest rate is commonly modelled as an exogenous increase in the discount factor: consumers become more patient and want to save more. This is just a convenient modelling strategy rather than a fundamental explanation for the fall in the natural interest rate. One of the main concerns raised by the analysis is that most of the theories based on standard business cycle shocks only account for a short permanence of the economy at the ZLB. Contrary to this prediction, Europe has been experiencing this situation for over six years, and Japan for over 20 years. This has motivated the search for theories that can sustain the ZLB as a 'persistent' situation. The chapter discusses two such theories: secular stagnation and self-fulfilling recessions. As an alternative, it also illustrates how the seemingly temporary effects of business-cycle shocks could be highly persistent due to labour market frictions.

Some features of the financial crisis and recession are common to most of the advanced economies that have experienced them, but the euro crisis and its 'South recession' has some specific elements. For the European Monetary Union (EMU) the 'crisis of confidence' was the collapse of 'the convergence view' – that is, that the expectation that due to the common currency and the established fiscal and monetary policies, convergence among EMU countries would be relatively fast. The debt and banking crises and the divergence among Euro Area countries has added new challenges to EMU fiscal and monetary policies, and the chapter also discusses these issues, and some of the research that they have stimulated (most of it undertaken by researchers based in Europe). For instance, the chapter concludes with a section on risk-sharing and fiscal policy within a monetary union. The aim is to analyse how a system of conditional transfers can strengthen EMU, beyond what can be achieved through private insurance and ECB interventions, without needing a large 'federal budget' or becoming a 'transfer union'.

Chapter 11 deals with financial regulation in Europe. It has often been said that the recent economic crisis was mainly caused by worldwide interdependence and the excessively risky and apparently out-of-control behaviour of financial markets. This not entirely correct statement has once again brought to the forefront the debate on the need for coordinated intervention policies among European countries, and on the optimal degree of regulation in this vital and already highly regulated sector of the economy.

It is a known fact that it is extremely difficult to keep a balance between free market forces and regulation in order to both preserve the stability of the overall financial system and of the banking sector in particular, and enhance financial innovation, hence the efficiency of financial intermediation and ultimately the smooth working of real economic activity. Moreover, there exists a seemingly endless cycle, between regulators, reacting to the last crisis by imposing more and more sophisticated rules and financial intermediaries always finding new loopholes and side paths to avoid the regulating constraints.

The debate has been particularly intense in Europe, where economies are strongly bank-based and where some segments of financial markets, the private equity market for example, are not as developed as in other advanced economies. This implies that the efforts of both policy-makers and regulators have mainly been directed towards ensuring the stability of the banking sector using both micro and macro prudential regulation and enforcing the European Banking Union, a successful endeavour that still needs some finishing touches. The more recent focus of the financial community, which includes operators in the field as well as the European Commission, the European Central Bank, National Central Banks and Regulating Authorities, has also been the design and implementation of the Capital Markets Union.

This chapter is a comprehensive, clear and detailed review of what has happened and what was done during and after the crisis in Europe and what still needs to be done. It may well be considered a reference text to be kept very close and to be used by policy-makers, practitioners and students interested in understanding regulation and how it has been applied to European financial markets, in particular to the European Banking System.

The authors trace the struggle of 'complexity against simplicity' in regulation, they discuss the risks attached to financial crises, describe the rules that have been implemented and review the opinions of economists, both European and non-European, on the pros and cons of alternative policies. They show that further economic research is strongly needed. While the risks of a fragile financial system are well known and have been thoroughly studied by economists, there exists very little recent theoretical work on how to map basic failures into regulatory reforms. Most of the published contributions in the last decade are indeed applied *ex post* analyses of the effects of the enacted regulatory reforms, often with ambiguous results, maybe because of the restricted access to data that Central Banks and regulators in fact collect but are not as yet published.

This state of affairs may partially be the consequence of the particularly strong and productive interaction between economists, regulators and practitioners: most regulators are themselves economists, while economists that work in academia are often consultants to policy-makers and regulators. This implies not only that there is no overwhelming 'language problem', but also that regulators and policy-makers may request relatively quick operative answers to their questions, not leaving enough time for in-depth theoretical assessments by researchers. Nevertheless, the involvement of academics in policy-making, specific to this branch of economics, is extremely welcome and has been the main driver of the research on financial markets in the last few decades.

Chapter 12 deals with inequality and welfare, and asks whether Europe is special. Historically economists and politicians alike have been concerned with inequality and welfare. Recently the topic has regained focus, most notably due to the work by Thomas Piketty in his book, *Capital in the twenty-first*, where he shows that inequality, if anything, has increased in the last decades. It is not presumptuous to say that the question how inequality affects major topics such as education, health, migration, growth, technical progress and innovation and social security, to name a few, are at the very essence of how the European welfare state will develop.

Why is this regained focus both important, but also so difficult? First, the concept of both inequality and welfare have proven difficult to define and measure in a coherent and agreeable manner. Second, when considering the present empirics on inequality, most measures show a stark increase in inequality since the 1970–80s. Third, research has uncovered strong hysteresis effects in inequality development in the sense that the next generation will inherit much of the present pattern, suggesting that the situation will take many years to mend.

The situation in Europe seems to be less critical, at least at the average level. Whereas the US has experienced a 20 per cent-points increase in the top 10 per cent income share since 1970 (from an already high 30%+ level), Europe started on its own inequality-trip ten years later in the 1980s, increasing their top 10 per cent income share from 30 to 35 per cent from 1980 to 2010. However, when treating Europe as a unified country, inequality in Europe is as high as the inequality in the US.

Focusing on the country level, several patterns are visible. First, the Northern countries have very different inequality levels (lower) than the other countries. The UK defines the other side of the coin, with the highest inequality levels in Europe. Second, this heterogeneity is, however, decreasing over time. There is a clear pattern of convergence in inequality since 1985. Whereas the Northern countries, starting from a significantly lower inequality level, increase inequality over time, and more than all others (e.g., more than 25% in Sweden), the other countries have considerably flatter developments. Even in the UK, we find a flattening of the upward trend in inequality since 2000. Seen in the light of a common labour market with open borders and new migration streams, this suggests several potential explanations, one is a revealed preferences argument that points towards a more integrated Europe when it comes to the redistributive preferences across Europe.

A major challenge addressed also in other parts of this volume is migration. Partly migration seems to change political fundamental views, and partly it challenges the foundations of traditional welfare states. An example of how this challenge remains unresolved is Belgium. Two-thirds of the increase in poverty in Belgium in recent years is attributed to migrants, and at the same time Belgium is struggling with minority groups that are willing to engage in terror acts. This picture is not very different from several other EU countries. Some have even argued that this new development changes the fundamental political preferences, from earlier being one-dimensional (more or less welfare state) to a bi-dimensional political agenda where the second political axis is how open the society should be to people originating from other ethnicities. The choice along the second dimension interferes with the choice over the redistributive dimension and changes the equilibrium of the entire political game. Obviously, such changes bear consequences when it comes to future inequality acceptance and the welfare state's and not states political and economic fundaments.

At present, we do not know enough about peoples' acceptance towards inequality, though surveys show a large heterogeneity in views across Europe. For instance, on questions on why people are 'living in need', only around 20 per cent in countries such as Belgium, Netherlands and Sweden attribute this to 'laziness or lack of willpower', this in contrast to more than 50 per cent of Finnish and Austrian citizens. People from Finland and Austria, however, share views with many outside Europe and are quite representative of people living in countries such as the US, Canada and Japan. This heterogeneity partly implies that people seem to have very different acceptance towards ex ante and ex post inequality. Ex post inequality that is a direct result of people's own choices is generally much more accepted than ex ante inequality resulting from inherited economic situation and birth. Both new and comparable data on people's perceived welfare and happiness, as well as a new focus on research on fairness and preferences through experimental studies provide, and will continue to provide, new insight on these issues.

The European welfare state has other challenges related to these questions. Tax rules seem to change towards more favourable tax rates for firms in several countries, resembling a race to the bottom across countries, resulting in large corporations and firms moving to the most attractive locations. This in turn has consequences for where the smartest people move to work, and obviously also for inequality and how the welfare state is to be financed in the future.

Most of the above and several other questions are raised and discussed in this comprehensive chapter. It concludes with several areas where it is of vital importance for Europe to gain new knowledge. In particular, it has five clear research policy recommendations for Europe. It needs to:

1. build a network of researchers in economics and social sciences to understand the fabric of equality of opportunity: ex ante inequality is a major challenge for the foundations of the future welfare state;
2. build up a large panel of data specific to studying the dynamics of poverty, how people get in, how people get out;
3. undertake research to prepare the ground for a standing-up policy to fight poverty and promote equal opportunities;
4. look at the sustainability of national welfare states in an environment where capital and labour are mobile; and
5. further strengthen the research on the issues that lead to convergence of Southern societies to the social model of the Nordic societies.

The Relevance of Data and Methods

The last two chapters of this volume deal with developments in data and methods that cut across policy areas and fields. The past 20–30 years have witnessed a steady rise in empirical research in economics. In fact, the majority of articles published by leading journals these days are empirical. This evolution was made possible by improved computing power but, more importantly, thanks to an increase in the *quantity*, *quality* and *variety* of data used in economics.

This data revolution has led to significant intellectual breakthroughs in economics. Several chapters in this volume allude to the role that better data played in recent advances of our understanding in important economic issues, such as innovation and growth (Chapter 1), human capital and education (Chapter 4) or inequality and welfare (Chapter 12), among others. More and better data are sometimes even credited for changing the research paradigm in some fields, where data are no longer used as means for testing theory but as a *central* input to theory development, as in trade and globalization (Chapter 6 and Eaton and Kortum, 2010).[6]

Equally important, most chapters conclude that our ability to satisfactorily address the *remaining* open questions in key policy areas will hinge upon the availability of better, more comparable (i.e., across countries), or more accessible data.

Data do not, however, come for free: they need to be collected, checked, harmonized, and organized for easy retrieval and analysis. When they contain confidential information, access needs to be organized in a way that preserves the legitimate privacy concerns of data subjects. More fundamentally, data for economic research come from many different sources and involve many different producers: not only statistical agencies, but also public administrations and agencies, central banks, private firms, data vendors and, last but not least, researchers.

Chapter 13 brings together several actors and stakeholders of recent developments in data for economic research to discuss their drivers, their implications and the remaining challenges. The chapter starts with microdata, i.e., data at the individual, household, firm or establishment level, produced from surveys or collected for administrative reasons. Such data have been at the forefront of important new research insights. Administrative data in particular is now the new Eldorado for empirical work. The big issue here is access to these data for research purposes. Nordic countries are world leaders on this front. They combine some of the best and most comprehensive statistical systems in the world with some of the highest level of access. Access is often more difficult in other European countries. However, things are improving and the chapter outlines recent developments towards greater and easier access in the UK and Catalonia which are illustrative of the ways stakeholders can foster greater access despite less favourable contexts than those of the Nordic countries.

Another big issue for administrative data, especially when it comes to business data, is cross-country data harmonization and data linking (i.e., the ability to link data from different sources but corresponding to the same firm or statistical unit). Harmonized cross-country data are essential, as several chapters have outlined, to draw sound comparisons between countries and assess the scope for replicability across borders (e.g., whether the experience of one country is relevant for another). Moreover, we are living in a globalized world where firms operate across borders and we need statistical systems that reflect this reality. Until recently this was not the case. The 2008 economic crisis cast a crude light on the mismatch between existing data structures in official statistics (mostly organized along national lines) and the reality of global financial and economic markets. Two developments are taking place in reaction. At the international level, the G20 Data Gaps Initiative is bringing together Eurostat and other international organizations such as the Bank for International Settlements, the World Bank and the OECD to coordinate statistical issues and strengthen data collection to improve its alignment with economic realities. At the same time, a number of initiatives are under way among national statistical offices to improve data harmonization and data linking across national borders. Eventually, this is likely to contribute to improving access to harmonized cross-country datasets for researchers, even if the impetus for the current changes is mostly political and access to researchers is not a priority.

Of course, statistical offices are not the only producers of data. Private data firms have long been involved in harmonizing and linking firm data across borders. Their data are often used by researchers as a complement or a substitute to administrative data. A number of researchers are also involved in large-scale data collection or production efforts. The chapter describes three such researcher-led data initiatives that illustrate their advantages. First, the data are typically immediately and easily made accessible to researchers. Second, not being subject to the same operational constraints as statistical offices, the databases produced by these researchers often use innovative designs (such as internet surveys or automated reporting from handheld devices) that reduce costs and improve reliability. Third, unlike official data that are collected because there is a policy or administrative need, data collection can be more forward-looking and focus on issues and topics that might not yet be recognized as a policy issue. The Survey of Health, Ageing and Retirement in Europe is a perfect example. Funding, however, is a critical challenge that all such initiatives face.

Another type of data produced by researchers is data generated from economic experiments, either in the lab or in the context of randomized controlled trials. Both types of data have led to major advances in our understanding of human behaviour and the robustness of economic institutions, for the first one, and in our understanding of the impact of policies and the mechanisms underlying them, for the second. Both approaches are now well-established and registries have been set up to archive the data produced and ensure that it is accessible for researchers interested in replicating the results. The chapter describes recent developments, remaining challenges and outlook for each type of approach.

An emerging trend in economic research is the development of new forms of collaborations between researchers and private- and public-sector organizations. One form that such collaborations have taken is closer relationships with private firms for access to their proprietary data. A complementary form has been collaborations between researchers and policy-makers where the focus is not only on data, but also on helping design and recalibrating policy interventions. In both cases, these collaborations are providing researchers with unmatched data access and data quality, as well as opportunities to investigate novel research questions or existing research questions in new ways. The chapter illustrates the potential of these collaborations but also discusses their risks and their implications for how research is organized, evaluated and funded.

The chapter concludes that there is no single type of data that is superior to all others. Each type of data is unique and has advantages over the others for a given research question. It is important for economic research to acknowledge the benefits of variety and the potential complementarity among data producers, and for stakeholders to support – politically, legally, technically and financially – this diversity.

A benefit of the data revolution in economics is that researchers now have access to unprecedented amounts of data, a phenomenon that has been popularized under the name of 'Big Data'. The term itself is used to cover a variety of data-driven phenomena that have very different implications for empirical methods. Chapter 14 deals with some of these methods-related issues.

In the simplest case, 'Big Data' simply means a large dataset that otherwise has a standard structure. Administrative data, which cover *entire populations* rather than population samples, belong to this category. The large size of these datasets allows for better controls and more precise estimates and is a bonus for researchers. It may raise challenges for data storage and handling, but it does not raise any particularly heavy methodological issues.

But 'Big Data' often means more than just standard datasets of large sizes. First, large numbers of units of observation often come with large numbers of variables. To continue with the same example, the possibility of linking different administrative datasets increases the number of variables attached to each statistical unit. Likewise, business records typically contain all interactions of the customers with the business. This 'curse of dimensionality' challenges traditional econometric approaches because coefficients on explanatory variables may no longer be identified or only poorly so. Second, the term also covers new datasets that have a very different structure from the structures we are used to in economics. This includes web search queries, real-time geolocational data or social media, to name a few. This type of data raises questions about how to structure and possibly re-aggregate them. If economists want to be able to take advantage of the data revolution, they will need to be equipped with appropriate methods to deal with these new datasets and data structures.

Chapter 14 starts by describing standard approaches in statistics and computer science to overcome the curse of dimensionality. Such approaches usually take an agnostic stance on the data generation process when seeking to balance the goal of 'letting the data speak' with the need to generate stable estimators.

Economic problems and economic data have specificities, however, to which it is worthwhile to tailor solutions. One specificity of economic problems is that we are often interested in measuring a (causal) relationship between some variable of interest (for example, a policy) and its effects. In other words, there might be many variables, but one of them (the policy) is of special interest to the researcher. Recent research efforts seek to combine the power of 'standard approaches' in statistics and computer science with the ability to give, within the algorithms, a special status to one variable – the policy variable – which we are interested in identifying precisely.

Economic data also have their own specificities, which vary by context. For example, macroeconomic indicators tend to be serially correlated, are released nonsynchronously and with different frequencies. Recent research has shown that estimators that take these specificities into account outperform standard approaches in statistics and computer science for dealing with the curse of dimensionality. We are only at the beginning of these efforts, however, and much still needs to be done.

Another methodological challenge raised by 'Big Data' is the development of estimators that are computationally tractable for very large datasets (e.g., high-frequency trading data, browsing data, etc.). Indeed, despite recent progress in computing power and storage, these can be a constraint for such datasets. Estimation methods that take advantage of parallel computing offer a promising route.

In short, 'Big Data' is not only exciting for economics because of all the things we can learn from these new data, but it is also essential to make sure economists are equipped to take advantage of these opportunities. On this front, economists can learn a lot from recent and current research in statistics and computer science. It is, nevertheless, essential that methods be developed that account for the specificities of economic problems and data.

Overall, it can clearly be seen from all chapters that a large number of new results are based on new datasets across all fields of economics. An immense body of new knowledge has emerged from the analyses of newly collected/assembled datasets; and from new methods of using existing data. New questions have surfaced, and new answers have been given to long-standing questions. Europe could become the leader in the collection and linkage of new types of big data and related methods. There also seems to be a genuine need for the economics and policy interface to be strengthened. Unfortunately, few economic policy decisions are based on known and established economics results, and vice versa, not enough economics research is motivated by direct policy questions. Finally, it is also easy to spot that many new useful insights have been provided by the generalization of local (country-related and/or regional) knowledge into a more general EU-wise understanding, and vice versa, by the analysis of how general knowledge is interpreted or translated at the local level. It is fair to say that the critical mass of talented European-based researchers is available, and it clearly transpires through the chapters of this volume that they tend to work on problems, challenges and data covering Europe.

Acknowledgements

First of all, we would like to thank the authors of the volume for the excellent chapters produced from the original, much longer, COEURE surveys. We appreciate as well their patience in dealing with all requests of the Editors, especially the Lead Editor. Administrative support within the EU from Marianne Paasi (DG Research and Innovation) has been of great value during the complete project. Editorial assistance by Laszlo Balazsi (CEU), Robin Bellers (CEU) and Eszter Timar (CEU) added much to the quality of this volume and is kindly acknowledged. We would also like to thank Stefan Bergheimer (ULB), Melinda Molnar (CEU) and Luis Rojas (EUI) for the research assistance provided. Finally, we are grateful to Alessandra Contigiani (TSE) and Eunate Mayor (TSE) for their excellent administrative and scientific assistance in the management of the COEURE Project.

Notes

1. http://core.ac.uk/download/files/153/6369012.pdf or http://www.eco.uc3m.es/temp/09-55-34.pdf.
2. For more details, see www.coeure.eu.
3. According to Forrester Research (July 2015), 'Cross-channel' retail sales in Europe (i.e., purchases consumers begin using a digital channel, but do not complete online) are expected to reach € 704 billion by 2020, up from € 457 in 2015. Combined with online sales, total sales related to the web are expected to reach € 947 billion, or 53 per cent of total European sales by 2020.
4. '10th Anniversary of the ECB', European Central Bank Monthly Bulletin, 2008.
5. Lucas, Robert E. Jr. (2003). Macroeconomic Priorities. American Economic Review, 93(1): 1–14.
6. Eaton, J. and Kortum, S. (2011). The Contribution of Data to Advances in Research in International Trade: An Agenda for the Next Decade, in: Schultze, C.L., and Newlon, D.H. (eds), *Ten Years and Beyond: Economists Answer NSF's Call for Long-Term Research Agendas*, US National Science Foundation.

1   Innovation and Growth: The Schumpeterian Perspective

Philippe Aghion and Ufuk Akcigit

Abstract

This chapter shows how the Schumpeterian growth paradigm can be used both to shed light on various aspects of the growth process which cannot be easily understood using alternative paradigms, and also to think about policies to foster innovation-led growth in a developed economy. In particular it will: (i) look at the relationship between growth and competition; (ii) shed light on how growth relates to firm dynamics and the size distribution of firms; (iii) revisit the debate on how growth relates to income inequality and social mobility; and (iv) discuss the role of the state in fostering innovation-led growth, and question the design and limits of R&D subsidies, or the desirable scope for patent protection, or whether the government should provide sectoral state aids or instead limit itself to pure horizontal targeting.

1.1   Introduction

There is a broad consensus among most European leaders and in Brussels on the importance of structural reforms to foster innovation-based growth in Europe. However, this consensus has not reached the European public at large. One recent example is France, where the timid reforms proposed by the Economy Minister have met opposition from all political parties. So often do we hear that structural reforms amount to austerity, and therefore are detrimental to growth and employment. Similarly, a commonly held view is that going for supply side policies (structural reforms or fiscal devaluations aimed at fostering such reforms) necessarily means that we have decided to ignore the demand side. We also hear that a fiscal system conducive to innovation and entrepreneurship would necessarily aggravate inequality and reduce social mobility. The purpose of this chapter is twofold: first, to bring the reader up to speed with recent research in the Economics of Innovation and Growth; second, to provide the reader with the theoretical and empirical background to think about growth policy design in EU countries.

We should emphasize right away that this chapter is opinionated in the sense that it reflects our own biases and uses the lenses of our own work. However, the reader should feel free (and is welcome) to disagree and take issue with the models, analyses and statements outlaid in the next sections. Our main purpose is indeed to encourage debates and criticisms and to inspire future work on the subject, in particular contributions that involve creative destruction of our own work.

In particular, we will propose some answers to questions such as:

1. Why do we need competition policy for innovation-led growth?
2. How does growth relate to firm dynamics and the size distribution of firms?
3. Does growth increase or reduce unemployment?
4. What distinguishes innovation-led growth from other types of growth? What are the main drivers of innovation-led growth?
5. How can macroeconomic policy help sustain innovation-based growth? Should we oppose structural reforms and the need for (more flexible) macroeconomic policy to enhance innovation-led growth?
6. What is the relationship between innovation-led growth, inequality and social mobility?
7. Should this relationship lead us to dispense with patent protection: in other words, should we oppose patent protection and competition as potential drivers of innovation-led growth? Similarly, should the need for competition policy lead us to reject any form of sectoral (or industrial) policy?
8. How should we reform the welfare state in order to facilitate innovation-led growth?
9. Should governments subsidize R&D to foster innovation-led growth: is such government intervention necessary or sufficient?
10. What are the limits to patenting and intellectual property and why do we need academic freedom and openness?

The remaining part of this chapter will be organized as follows. Section 1.2 will succinctly present the main growth paradigms. Section 1.3 will present some of the main distinctive predictions of the Schumpeterian growth paradigm. Section 1.4 will discuss growth policy design in advanced countries. Section 1.5 will talk about technological waves and will touch upon the debate on secular stagnation. Section 1.6 will provide Schumpeterian insights into the design of R&D policy. Section 1.7 will analyse the role for openness and freedom in a multistage process of innovation. Section 1.8 will build on the policy discussion in this survey to revisit the issue of how to bring Europe back into a high growth path. Finally Section 1.9 will conclude the survey.

1.2   Looking for Growth Paradigms to Think about Growth Policy

Today's research on growth economics, with its double objective of improving our understanding of the growth process and of helping us think more systematically about growth policy design, uses essentially four leading growth paradigms.

1.2.1   The Neoclassical Growth Model

The primary reference in growth economics is the neoclassical paradigm. The success of this model first is due to its parsimony; the growth process is described by only two equations: (i) a production equation that expresses the current flow of output goods as a function of the current stocks of capital and labour:

$$Y = AK^{\alpha}L^{1-\alpha},$$

where A is a productivity parameter and where $\alpha < 1$ so that production involves decreasing returns to capital, and (ii) a law of motion that shows how capital accumulation depends on investment (equal to aggregate savings) and depreciation:

$$\dot{K} = sY - \delta K,$$

where sY denotes aggregate savings and δK denotes aggregate depreciation.

What also makes this model the benchmark for growth analysis is, paradoxically, its implication that, in the long run, economic growth does not depend on economic conditions. In particular, economic policy cannot affect a country's long-run growth rate. Specifically, per capita GDP Y/L cannot grow in the long run unless we assume that productivity A also grows over time, which Solow (1956) refers to as 'technical progress'. The problem is that in this neoclassical model, technical progress cannot be explained or even rationalized. Thus the model cannot explain long-run economic growth, it can just predict that faster capital accumulation (through increasing the savings rate) will boost growth temporarily.

To analyse policies for long-run growth, one needs a theoretical framework in which productivity growth is endogenous; that is, dependent upon characteristics of the economic environment. This framework must account for long-term technological progress and productivity growth, without which diminishing marginal productivity would eventually choke off all growth.

1.2.2   The AK Model

The first version of endogenous growth theory is the so-called AK theory,[1] which does not make an explicit distinction between capital accumulation and technological progress. In effect it just lumps together the physical and human capital whose accumulation is studied by neoclassical theory with the intellectual capital that is accumulated when technological progress is made. When this aggregate of different kinds of capital is accumulated there is no reason to think that diminishing returns will drag its marginal product down to zero, because part of that accumulation is the very technological progress needed to counteract diminishing returns. According to the AK paradigm, the way to sustain high growth rates is to save a large fraction of GDP, some of which will find its way into financing a higher rate of technological progress and will thus result in faster growth.

Formally, the AK model is the neoclassical model without diminishing returns. The theory starts with an aggregate production function that is linear homogeneous in the stock of capital:

$$Y = AK$$

with A a constant. If capital accumulates according to the same equation:

$$\dot{K} = sY - \delta K$$

as before, then the economy's long-run (and short-run) growth rate is

$$g = sA - \delta.$$

which is increasing in the saving rate s.

AK theory presents a '*one size fits all*' view of the growth process. It applies equally to countries that are at the leading edge of the world technology frontier and to countries that are far behind. Like the neoclassical model, it postulates a growth process that is independent of developments in the rest of the world, except insofar as international trade changes the conditions for capital accumulation. Yet, it is a useful tool for many purposes when the distinction between innovation and accumulation is of secondary importance.

1.2.3   The Product-Variety Model

The second wave of endogenous growth theory consists of so-called 'innovation-based' growth models, which themselves belong to two parallel branches. A first branch within this new class of endogenous growth models is the product variety model of Romer (1990), in which innovation causes productivity growth by creating new, but not necessarily improved, varieties of products. This paradigm grew out of the new theory of international trade, and emphasizes the role of technology spillovers.

It starts from a Dixit and Stiglitz (1977) production function of the form:

$$Y_t = \sum_0^{N_t} K_{it}^{\alpha} di$$

in which there are N_t different varieties of intermediate product, each produced using K_{it} units of capital. By symmetry, the aggregate capital stock K_t will be divided up evenly among the N_t existing varieties equally, which means we can re-express the production function as:

$$Y_t = N_t^{1-\alpha} K_t^\alpha.$$

According to this function, the degree of product variety N_t is the economy's aggregate productivity parameter, and its growth rate is the economy's long-run growth rate of per-capita output. Product variety raises the economy's production potential because it allows a given capital stock to be spread over a larger number of uses, each of which exhibits diminishing returns.

The fact that there is just one kind of innovation, which always results in the same kind of new product, means that the product-variety model is limited in its ability to generate context-dependent growth. In particular, the theory makes it difficult to talk about the notion of technology frontier and about a country's distance to the frontier, since all intermediate products are on a technological par.

Moreover, nothing in this model implies an important role for exit and turnover; indeed increased exit can do nothing but reduce the economy's GDP, by reducing the variety variable N_t that uniquely determines aggregate productivity. Thus there is no role for '*creative destruction*', the driving force in the Schumpeterian model to be discussed below.

1.2.4   The Schumpeterian Model

The second branch in this new wave of (innovation-based) endogenous growth models is the Schumpeterian paradigm (see Aghion and Howitt, 1992, 1998). This paradigm grew out of modern industrial organization theory and put firms and entrepreneurs at the heart of the growth process. The paradigm relies on three main ideas.

First idea: long-run growth relies on innovations. These can be process innovations, namely to increase the productivity of production factors (e.g., labour or capital); or product innovations (introducing new products); or organizational innovations (to make the combination of production factors more efficient).

Second idea: Innovations result from investments like research and development (R&D), firms' investments in skills, search for new markets, that are motivated by the prospect of monopoly rents for successful innovators. An important consideration for thinking about the role for public intervention in the growth process is that innovations generate positive knowledge spillovers (on future research and innovation activity), which private firms do not fully internalize. Thus private firms under laissez-faire tend to underinvest in R&D, training, etc. This propensity to underinvest is reinforced by the existence of credit market imperfections which become particularly tight in recessions.

Hence there is an important role for the state as a co-investor in the knowledge economy.

Third idea: creative destruction. Namely, new innovations tend to make old innovations, old technologies, old skills, become obsolete. Thus growth involves a conflict between the old and the new: the innovators of yesterday resist new innovations that render their activities obsolete. This also explains why innovation-led growth in OECD countries is associated with a higher rate of firm and labour turnover. And it suggests a second role for the state, namely as an insurer against the turnover risk and to help workers move from one job to another. More fundamentally, governments need to strike the right balance between preserving innovation rents and at the same time not deterring future entry and innovation. This is the paradigm that we find most useful, and it plays an especially important role throughout the book. We present it in Chapter 4 and then use it and extend it in the subsequent chapters of the book.

More formally, Schumpeterian theory begins with a production function specified at the industry level:

$$Y_{it} = A_{it}^{1-\alpha} K_{it}^{\alpha}, \qquad 0 < \alpha < 1.$$

where A_{it} is a productivity parameter attached to most recent technology used in industry i at time t. In this equation, K_{it} represents the flow of a unique intermediate product used in this sector, each unit of which is produced one-for-one by final output or, in the most complete version of the model, by capital. Aggregate output is just the sum of the industry-specific outputs Y_{it}.

Each intermediate product is produced and sold exclusively by the most recent innovator. A successful innovator in sector i improves the technology parameter A_{it} and is thus able to displace the previous product in that sector, until it is displaced in turn by the next innovator. Thus a first implication of the Schumpeterian paradigm, is that *faster growth generally implies a higher rate of firm turnover, because this process of creative destruction generates entry of new innovators and exit of former innovators.*

A first distinct prediction of Schumpeterian Growth Theory is therefore:

Prediction 1 *The turnover rate is positively correlated with the productivity growth rate.*

Another distinctive implication of the model is that *innovation-led growth may be excessive under laissez-faire.* Growth is excessive (respectively insufficient) under laissez-faire when the business-stealing effect associated with creative destruction dominates (respectively is dominated by) the intertemporal knowledge spillovers from current to future innovators.[2]

1.3 Some Main Applications and Extensions of Schumpeterian Growth Theory

1.3.1 Growth Meets IO

Both empirical studies[3] and casual evidence point to a positive correlation between growth and product market competition, which is at odds with what most growth models predict. The Solow and AK models assume perfect competition, thus by construction they cannot look at how growth is affected by changes in the degree of product market competition. In the product variety model, more product market competition corresponds to a higher degree of substitutability α between intermediate inputs, and therefore to lower rents for potential innovators. This in turn has a detrimental effect on R&D and therefore on growth.

While in Aghion and Howitt's (1992) model as well, more competition discourages innovation and growth, yet one can reconcile theory with evidence by allowing for *step-by-step innovation* in the Schumpeterian growth paradigm.[4] Namely, a firm that is currently behind the technological leader in the same sector or industry must catch up with the leader before becoming a leader itself. This step-by-step assumption implies that firms in some sectors will be *neck-and-neck*. In turn in such sectors, increased product market competition, by making life more difficult for neck-and-neck firms, will encourage them to innovate in order to acquire a lead over their rival in the sector. This we refer to as the *escape competition effect*. On the other hand, in *unleveled* sectors where firms are not neck-and-neck, increased product market competition will tend to discourage innovation by laggard firms as it decreases the short-run extra profit from catching up with the leader. This we call the *Schumpeterian effect*. Finally, the steady-state fraction of neck-and-neck sectors will itself depend upon the innovation intensities in neck-and-neck versus unleveled sectors. This we refer to as the *composition effect*.

The Schumpeterian growth framework with step-by-step innovation, generates three interesting predictions:

Prediction 2 *The relationship between competition and innovation follows an inverted-U pattern.*

Intuitively, when competition is low, innovation intensity is low in neck and neck sectors, therefore if we take a picture of the overall economy at any point in time, we will observe that most sectors in the economy are neck and neck; but precisely it is in those sectors that the escape competition effect dominates. Thus overall aggregate innovation increases with competition at low levels of competition. When competition is high, innovation intensity is high in neck and neck sectors, therefore if we take a picture of the overall economy at any point

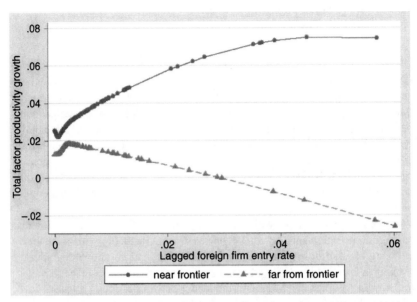

Figure 1.1 Entry effects near and far from the technological frontier (Aghion et al., 2009b).

in time we will see that most sectors in the economy are unleveled sectors, so that the Schumpeterian effect dominates overall. This inverted-U prediction is confirmed by Aghion et al. (2005a), using panel data on UK firms.

Prediction 3 *More intense competition enhances innovation in 'frontier' firms but may discourage it in 'nonfrontier' firms.*

Intuitively, a frontier firm can escape competition by innovating, unlike a nonfrontier firm who can only catch up with the leader in its sector. This prediction is tested by Aghion et al. (2009c) again using panel data of UK firms. Figure 1.1 below (from Aghion et al., 2009b) shows how competition (here measured by the lagged foreign entry rate) affects productivity growth in domestic incumbent firms. The upper curve shows averages among domestic firms that are closer to the technological frontier in their sector worldwide, compared to the median. We see that on average productivity growth in those firms responds positively to more intense competition. This reflects an '*escape competition effect*', that is, the fact that such firms innovate more to escape the more intense competition. In contrast, productivity growth, in firms that are farther below the technological frontier in their sector worldwide than the median, reacts negatively to more intense competition. This reflects a discouragement effect: firms far below the frontier know they have little chance to win against a potential entrant; thus the higher the entry rate, the more discouraged such firms are to invest in innovation and productivity growth. Now, the closer a country is to the world leading productivity level, the higher the fraction of firms close to the corresponding technological frontier, and therefore the more productivity-enhancing product market competition is.

Prediction 4 *There is complementarity between patent protection and product market competition in fostering innovation.*

Intuitively, competition reduces the profit flow of noninnovating neck-and-neck firms, whereas patent protection is likely to enhance the profit flow of an innovating neck-and-neck firm. Both contribute to raising the net profit gain of an innovating neck-and-neck firm; in other words, both types of policies tend to enhance the escape competition effect.[5] This prediction is confirmed by Aghion et al. (2013) using OECD country-industry panel data. This prediction cannot be generated by the product variety model where competition can only counteract the effects of better patent protection (the former reduces innovation rents, whereas the latter enhances those rents).

1.3.2   Schumpeterian Growth and Firm Dynamics

The empirical literature has documented various stylized facts on firm size distribution and firm dynamics using micro firm-level data. In particular: (i) the firm size distribution is highly skewed; (ii) firm size and firm age are highly correlated; and (iii) small firms exit more frequently, but the ones that survive tend to grow faster than the average growth rate.

These are all facts that non-Schumpeterian growth models cannot account for. In particular, the first four facts listed require a new firm to enter, expand, then shrink over time, and eventually be replaced by new entrants: these and the last fact on the importance of reallocation are all embodied in the Schumpeterian idea of '*creative destruction*'.[6]

However, the Schumpeterian model by Klette and Kortum (2004) can account for these facts. This model adds two elements to the baseline model: first, innovations come from both entrants and incumbents; second, firms are defined as a collection of production units where successful innovations by incumbents will allow them to expand in product space.[7]

This model allows us to explain the above stylized facts:

Prediction 5 *The size distribution of firms is highly skewed.*

Recall that in this model, firm size is summarized by the number of product lines of a firm. Hence, a firm needs to have succeeded many attempts to innovate in new lines and at the same time survived many attempts by potential entrants and other incumbents at taking over its existing lines, in order to become a large firm. This explains why there are so few very large firms in steady-state equilibrium, that is, why firm size distribution is highly skewed as shown in a vast empirical literature.

Prediction 6 *Firm size and firm age are positively correlated.*

In the model, firms are born with a size of 1. Subsequent successes are required for firms to grow in size, which naturally produces a positive correlation between size and age. This regularity has been documented extensively in the literature.[8]

Prediction 7 *Small firms exit more frequently. The ones that survive tend to grow faster than average.*

In the above model, it takes only one successful entry to make a one-product firm exit, whereas it takes two successful innovations by potential entrants to make a two-product firm exit. The fact that small firms exit more frequently and grow faster conditional on survival have been widely documented in the literature.[9]

The previous two sections have implications for how Schumpeterian growth theory can help bridge the gap between growth and development economics: first, by capturing the idea that growth-enhancing policies or institutions vary with a country's level of technological development; second, by analysing how institutional development (or the lack of it) affects firm size distribution and firm dynamics.

1.3.3   Growth Meets Development: Appropriate Institutions

In Section 1.3.1 above we mentioned some recent evidence for the prediction that competition and free-entry should be more growth-enhancing in more frontier firms, which implies that they should be more growth-enhancing in more advanced countries since those have a larger proportion of frontier firms. This idea can be extended to other aspects of growth policy design. Indeed, the Schumpeterian paradigm is flexible in modelling the contribution of past innovations. It encompasses the case of an innovation that leapfrogs the best technology available before the innovation, resulting in a new technology parameter A_{it} in the innovating sector i, which is some multiple γ of its preexisting value. And it also encompasses the case of an innovation that catches up to a global technology frontier $\overline{A}_t$ which we typically take to represent the stock of global technological knowledge available to innovators in all sectors of all countries. In the former case the country is making a leading-edge innovation that builds on and improves the leading edge technology in its industry. In the latter case the innovation is just implementing (or imitating) technologies that have been developed elsewhere.

One can thus naturally capture Gerschenkron's idea[10] of 'appropriate institutions'. Namely, far from the frontier a country will maximize growth by favouring institutions that facilitate implementation; however, as it catches up with the technological frontier, to sustain a high growth rate the country will have to shift from implementation-enhancing institutions to innovation-enhancing institutions as the relative importance of frontier innovation for growth is also increasing. Institutions which favour innovation-led growth include graduate schools, competition enforcement, labour market flexibility and financial sectors which emphasize equity financing.

Thus Acemoglu et al. (2006) (Acemoglu-Aghion-Zilibotti, henceforth AAZ), provide support to the following predictions using a cross-country panel of more than 100 countries over the 1960–2000 period. Using Frankel and Romer's (1996) measures of openness (namely exports plus imports divided by GDP and instrumented using geographical and regulatory variables), they show:

Prediction 8 *Average growth should decrease more rapidly as a country approaches the world frontier when openness is low.*

AAZ repeat the same exercise using entry costs faced by new firms instead of openness. They show:

Prediction 9 *High entry barriers become increasingly more detrimental to growth as the country approaches the frontier.*

These two empirical exercises point to the importance of interacting institutions or policies with technological variables in growth regressions: openness is particularly growth-enhancing in countries that are closer to the technological frontier; entry is more growth-enhancing in countries or sectors that are closer to the technological frontier.

Next, to the extent that frontier innovation makes greater use of research education than imitation, the prediction is:

Prediction 10 *The more frontier an economy is, the more growth in this economy relies on research education.*[11]

Finally, one can look at the relationship between technological development, democracy and growth. An important channel is Schumpeterian: namely, democracy reduces the scope for expropriating successful innovators or for incumbents to prevent new entry by using political pressure or bribes: in other words, democracy facilitates creative destruction and thereby encourages innovation.[12] To the extent that innovation matters more for growth in more frontier economies, the prediction is:

Prediction 11 *The correlation between democracy and innovation (or growth) is more positive and significant, the closer the country is to the frontier.*

This prediction is confirmed by Aghion et al. (2007) using employment and productivity data at industry level across countries and over time.

This dichotomy between catch-up growth and innovation-led growth explains why countries like China grow faster than all OECD countries: growth in China is driven by technological imitation, and when one starts far below the frontier, catching up with the frontier means a big leap forward. Second, it explains why growth policy design should not be exactly the same in developed and in less developed economies. In particular, an imitative economy does not require labour and product market flexibility as much as a country where growth relies more on frontier innovation. Also, bank finance is well adapted to the needs of imitative firms, whereas equity financing (venture capital, etc.) are better suited to the needs of an innovative firm at the frontier. Similarly, good primary, secondary and undergraduate education is well suited to the needs of a catching-up economy whereas graduate schools focusing on research education are more indispensable in a country where growth relies more on frontier innovations. This in turn suggests that beyond universal growth-enhancing policies such as good property right protection (and more generally the avoidance of expropriating institutions) and stabilizing macroeconomic policy (to reduce interest rates and inflation), the design of growth policy should be tailored to the stage of development of each individual country or region.

1.3.4   Growth Meets Development: Firm Dynamics in Developing Countries

Firm dynamics show massive differences across countries. In a recent work, Hsieh and Klenow (2014) show that while establishments grow 5 times relative to their entry size by the age of 30, Indian counterparts barely show any growth.

What are the aggregate implications of the lack of delegation and weakness of rule of law on productivity and firm dynamics? To answer this question, Akcigit et al. (2014b) (Akcigit-Alp-Peters, henceforth AAP) extend the firm dynamics model introduced in the previous section, by adding two major ingredients: (i) production requires managers and unless firm owners delegate some of the tasks, firms run into span of control problem as owners' time endowment is limited; and (ii) firm owners can be of two types, high or low. High-type firms are more creative and have the potential to expand much faster than low type firms. Whether this fast expansion is materialized or not depends on the return to expansion which itself depends on the possibility of delegation.

The predictions, both on the delegation margin and on the firm dynamics can be summarized as follows:

Prediction 12 *Everything else equal, the probability of hiring an outside manager and, conditional on hiring, the number of outside managers is increasing with firm size, and increasing with the rule of law.*

Larger firms operate with more product lines and hence have less time from the owner directly. Hence, the marginal contribution of an outside manager is much higher in larger firms. The second part relates the family size to delegation. If the owner has more time (due to larger family size, for instance), then the owner has already more time to invest in his business and this lowers the demand for outside managers. Finally stronger rule of law implies higher net return to delegation. AAP provide empirical support for these predictions using Indian manufacturing establishments.

Prediction 13 *Average firm size increases with the rule of law.*

Firm value is increasing with owner time and therefore the firms are willing to innovate and expand more when firm value is higher. The positive link between firm size and the rule of law has been extensively documented in the literature (see for instance Bloom et al. (2012) for a detailed discussion). Finally, AAP show that the link between firm size and family size is weaker in high-trust regions in India.

Prediction 14 *Firm growth decreases in firm size, and the more so when the rule of law is weaker.*

This prediction follows from the fact that in larger firms, the owner has less time to allocate to each product line and hence the frictions to delegate become much more important for large firms. Hence, when the rule of law is weak, larger firms have less of an incentive to grow, which means that the difference in growth incentives between large and small firms will be much more pronounced in weak rule of law countries or regions. AAP show that growth decreases faster in firm size in low-trust regions in India.

Prediction 15 *Everything else equal, creative destruction and the reallocation among firms will be much higher in economies where the rule of law is stronger.*

Clearly this latter prediction is in line with the main findings of Hsieh and Klenow's work, which showed the missing growth and reallocation in developing countries. Understanding the reasons behind the lack of reallocation and creative destruction is essential in designing the right development policies.

The Schumpeterian growth framework provides a useful framework to conduct counterfactual policy exercises which can shed light on this important debate.

1.3.5   Growth and Unemployment

Peter Diamond, Dale Mortensen and Christopher Pissarides received their Nobel Prize in Economics for their research on 'markets with search frictions'. Their research was centred on the idea that in markets, buyers and sellers or workers and firms do not find each other immediately and it takes time for them to match. This delay was broadly attributed to so-called *search and matching (S&M) frictions* that exist in those markets that prevent the matches from happening immediately. But search market frictions in turn imply that creative destruction and therefore the growth process should affect the unemployment rate.[13]

And indeed the Schumpeterian growth paradigm allows us to analyse the implications of frictional matching on the labour market for the relationship between innovation-led growth and unemployment. In particular, it points to three counteracting effects of growth through creative destruction on the equilibrium unemployment level. While it is leading to incumbents getting replaced by new entrants and therefore release the workers of the incumbent firm to the unemployment pool: hence a positive *creative destruction effect* of innovation-led growth on unemployment (i.e., a negative effect of innovation-led growth on the equilibrium employment rate). However, new firms entering the economy also create new jobs, hence a negative *job creation effect* of growth on unemployment (i.e., a positive effect of innovation-led growth on the equilibrium employment rate). In addition to these two effects, more creative destruction implies higher growth and therefore a higher discounted value for new firms entering the market: hence a negative *capitalization effect* of growth on entry. Whether this capitalization effect increases or reduces equilibrium unemployment depends upon which of the creative destruction and job creation effects dominates. If the creative destruction effect dominates, then the capitalization effect will reinforce the creative destruction effect. If the job creation effect dominates, then the capitalization effect will reinforce the job creation effect.

Now, when jobs can be destroyed for '*exogenous*' reasons, that is, for reasons that do not have to do with innovation, then innovation becomes more a source of new job creation than mainly a source of job destruction. More precisely, the Schumpeterian theory of growth and unemployment with search frictions, predicts that:

Prediction 16 *When the rate of exogenous destruction is small, the job destruction effect dominates the job creation effect and therefore growth and unemployment should be positively correlated.*

The intuition is simply that when the rate of job destruction is small, then innovation is the main source of job destruction and job destruction is immediate, whereas job creation happens later due to the labour market frictions.

Prediction 17 *When the rate of exogenous job destruction is high, then the relationship is negative growth and unemployment: in this case the job creation effect of innovation-led growth on unemployment dominates the job destruction effect.*

This framework is used by Aghion et al. (2015b) to analyse the relationship between innovation-led growth and well-being. On the one hand, more creative destruction implies more job destruction, which should reduce well-being of currently employed workers. On the other hand, more creative destruction implies both more new job creation and a higher growth rate, both of which should be welfare-enhancing.

1.4   Enhancing Productivity Growth in Advanced Countries

1.4.1   Pillars of Innovation-Led Growth

In the previous section we explained why institutions and policies to enhance productivity growth should differ between countries at the world technology frontier and countries that are farther behind the frontier. In particular we saw that competition is more growth enhancing in sectors or countries that are closer to the technological frontier. Similarly, Aghion et al. (2005b) show that more flexible labour markets (which facilitate the process of creative destruction) foster greater productivity growth in more advanced countries.

A third lever of productivity growth in advanced countries is graduate education: indeed frontier innovation requires frontier researchers and therefore good universities and research centres, whereas good undergraduate education is sufficient for imitation. Figure 1.2, drawn from Aghion et al. (2009c). Shows that research education enhances productivity growth more in more frontier US states, that is, in states with a higher per capita GDP (California, Massachusetts, ...): these are states where a higher fraction of firms are '*frontier-firms*', that is, firms with levels of productivity that are close to the best practice in the corresponding sector. On the other hand, two-year college education is what enhances productivity growth more in less advanced states (Alabama, Mississippi, ...): in those states, imitation (i.e., catch-up growth) is the main source of technological progress, and good undergraduate education enhances imitation. The same is true across countries: higher (and especially graduate) education enhances productivity growth more in countries with higher per capita GDP (see Vandenbussche et al., 2006).

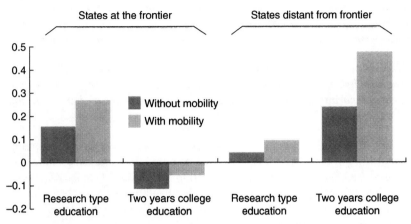

Figure 1.2 Long-term growth effects of $1000 per person spending on education, US states (Aghion et al., 2005b).

A fourth lever of productivity growth is the organization of the financial sector. As shown by Figure 1.3 below (drawn from Koch, 2014), choosing a bank based financial system enhances productivity growth more for less advanced countries, whereas choosing a more market-based financial system enhances productivity growth more in more frontier countries. The intuition is as follows: frontier-innovation that breaks new ground entails a higher level of risk than imitation activities, which are already well defined. But this in turn implies

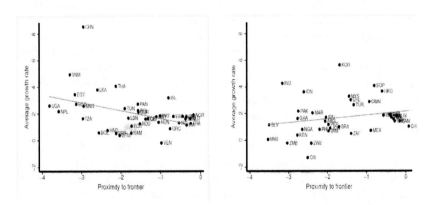

Figure 1.3 Average growth rate and proximity to the frontier for the bank-based (left) and market-based (right) countries (per capita GDP growth rate, Koch, 2014).

that outside financiers involved in frontier-innovation will ask for a higher share of upside revenues and also for higher control rights: hence the role of equity in financing frontier innovation.

1.4.2   Competition Policy against Industrial Policy

Should sectoral policies always be precluded if we (justifiably) believe in the virtues of competition for innovation-led growth? Our answer is that sectoral policy can be designed and governed in a way that reconciles it with the need for more product market competition.

Indeed, the 'pick winner' objection against sectoral policy loses bite when vertical targeting is properly designed and governed: in particular, when: (i) *the government chooses to pick activities, not particular firms*: indeed, while governments and policy-makers do not have all the knowledge and wisdom needed for proper vertical selection, identifying activities with high growth potential is presumably easier than selecting individual firms[14]; (ii) *the criteria underlying the selection of activities are clear and verifiable:* in particular, recent research[15] points at skill-intensity and the degree of product market competition as relevant selection criteria for vertical targeting; and (iii) *the vertical interventions are properly governed:* in particular, they should be governed in a way that preserves or even enhances product market competition in the corresponding sectors, and also in a way that guarantees exit from nonperforming activities.

First empirical support for rethinking sectoral policy is provided by Nunn and Trefler (2010). These authors use micro data on a set of countries to analyse whether, as suggested by the argument of 'infant industry', the growth of productivity in a country is positively affected by the measure in which tariff protection is biased in favour of activities and sectors that are '*skill-intensive*', that is to say, use more intensely skilled workers. They find a significant positive correlation between productivity growth and the '*skill bias*' due to tariff protection. Of course, such a correlation does not necessarily mean there is causality between skill-bias due to protection and productivity growth: the two variables may themselves be the result of a third factor, such as the quality of institutions in countries considered. However, Nunn and Trefler show that at least 25 per cent of the correlation corresponds to a causal effect. Overall, their analysis suggests that adequately designed (here, skill-intensive) targeting may actually enhance growth, not only in the sector which is being subsidized, but also the country as a whole.

More recently, Aghion et al. (2015c) argue that sectoral policy should not be systematically opposed to competition policy. They use Chinese firm-level panel data. More precisely, they use firm-level panel data from the Chinese

National Business Survey and regress productivity growth, patenting, or other measures of innovativeness and entrepreneurship, over various measures of sectoral intervention (subsidies, tariffs, etc.) interacted with the degree of competition in the sector, and also with the extent to which intervention in each sector is not concentrated on one single firm, but rather distributed over a larger number of firms. They show that Total Factor Productivity (TFP), TFP growth and product innovation (defined as the ratio between output value generated by new products to total output value) are all positively correlated with the interaction between state aid to the sector and market competition in the sector. Thus the more competitive the recipient sector, the more positive the effects of targeted state subsidies to that sector on TFP, TFP growth, and product innovation in that sector. Moreover, Aghion et al. (2015c), show that the interaction between state aid and product market competition in the sector is more positive when state aid is less concentrated.

And finally Acemoglu et al. (2013) extend the Klette-Kortum model of growth and firm dynamics to allow for high versus low R&D productivity firms. Their model implies that subsidizing incumbents' R&D inhibits the entry of high-efficiency firms, which in turn can be detrimental to growth and welfare. We get back to this paper in more details in Section 1.5 below.

Yet this does not address the issue of why vertical targeting would be at all needed. A main theoretical argument in support of vertical targeting, is the existence of knowledge spillovers. Thus, Aghion et al. (2015a) explore a cross-country panel dataset of patents in the automotive industry. They distinguish between '*dirty innovations*' which affect combustion engines, and clean innovations such as those on electric cars. Then they show that the larger the stock of past '*dirty*' innovations by a given entrepreneur, the '*dirtier*' current innovations by the same entrepreneur. This '*path dependence*' phenomenon, together with the fact that innovations have been mostly dirty so far, implies that in the absence of government intervention our economies would generate too many dirty innovations. Hence a role for government intervention to '*redirect technical change*' towards clean innovations. Indeed Aghion et al. (2015a) show that an increase in carbon price (e.g., through carbon taxes) induces firms to redirect innovation towards clean technologies (e.g., to develop electric cars).

A reinforcing factor is the existence of credit constraints which may further limit or slow down the reallocation of firms towards new (more growth-enhancing) activities. Now, one can argue that the existence of market failures on its own is not sufficient to justify vertical intervention. On the other hand, there are activities – typically high-tech activities – which generate knowledge spillovers on the rest of the economy, and where assets are highly intangible which in turn makes it more difficult for firms to borrow from private capital markets to finance their growth.

1.4.3   Reforming the State

Aghion and Roulet (2011) use Schumpeterian growth theory to discuss why and how the welfare state should be reformed in the process of making the transition to an innovation-led economy. One extreme view is that the state should remain organized as it was when European countries were in a catching-up phase (from 1945 to the early 1970s). Another extreme view is that the transition from catch-up growth to innovation-led growth, should lead to a radical reform of the state, with the state withdrawing from the economy almost completely, except when it comes to law and order, national security and defence, and basic public services.

However, we depart from these two extreme views on the following grounds. First, the transition to innovation-led growth, where frontier innovation is associated with creative destruction, that is, with the constant replacement of old activities by new activities, implies that the state must give up the old industrial policies based on the support of few national champions. Instead, the state must favour and accompany the process of creative destruction, and in particular implement sectoral policies that are competition-friendly. On the other hand, the existence of knowledge externalities (reinforced by the existence of credit constraints) implies that the state cannot completely withdraw from the economy. Thus one has to look for a third way between these two extremes. This is what we refer to as the '*strategic state*' or the '*smart state*'.

In particular a main issue facing countries in the euro area, particularly in its southern part, is how to reconcile the need to invest in the main levers of innovation-led growth with that of reducing public debt and deficits. To address the challenge of reconciling growth with greater budgetary discipline, governments and states must become strategic. This first means adopting a new approach to public spending: in particular, they must depart from the Keynesian policies aimed at fostering growth though indiscriminate public spending, and instead become selective as to where public funds should be invested. They must look for all possible areas where public spending can be reduced without damaging effects on growth and social cohesion: a good example is the potential savings on administrative costs: technical progress in information and communication makes it possible to decentralize and thereby reduce the number of government layers, for similar reasons as those that allowed large firms to reduce the number of hierarchical layers over the past decades. Decentralization makes it also easier to operate a high-quality health system at lower cost, as shown by the Swedish example.

Second, governments must focus public investments on a limited number of growth-enhancing areas and sectors: education, universities, innovative SMEs, labour market policies and support to labour and product market flexibility; industrial sectors with high growth potential and externalities as we argued above.

1.4.4   Macroeconomic Policy

Recent studies (see Aghion et al., 2009a, 2012) performed at cross-country/cross-industry level, show that more countercyclical fiscal and monetary policies enhance growth. Fiscal policy countercyclicality refers to countries increasing their public deficits and debt in recessions but reducing them in upturns. Monetary policy countercyclicality refers to central banks letting real short-term interest rates go down in recessions, while having them increase again during upturns. Such policies can help credit-constrained or liquidity-constrained firms to pursue innovative investments (R&D, skills and training, etc.) over the cycle in spite of credit tightening during recessions, and it also helps maintain aggregate consumption and therefore firms' market size over the cycle (see Aghion and Howitt, 2009, ch. 13). Both contribute to encouraging firms to invest more in R&D and innovation. This view of the role and design of macroeconomic policy departs both from the Keynesian approach of advocating untargeted public spending to foster demand in recessions, and from the neoliberal policy of just minimizing tax and public spending in recessions.

Note that such policies are complementary to the above-mentioned structural policies aimed at favouring innovation-led growth, namely product market liberalization, labour market flexibility and training, and higher education reform. As well argued by Mario Draghi in his Bretton Woods speech a year ago, quantity easing and other devices to increase the flexibility of macroeconomic policy in the Euro area, will have little effect on productivity growth if they are not accompanied by systematic structural reforms that make it easier for new firms to enter the product market and hire on the labour market.

1.4.5   Innovation, Inequality, and Social Mobility:
Making Growth Inclusive

Figures 1.4 and 1.5 below show innovation (measured by the flow of patents per 1000 inhabitants) and top income inequality (measured by the share of income accruing to the top 1% income earners) over the past 50 years, respectively for the US and for Sweden. In both cases, we see that innovation and top income inequality follow parallel evolutions, first essentially flat until the late 1970s and then sharply increasing since the early 1980s.

Does this mean that innovation necessarily leads to increased inequality? And what can governments do to reconcile innovation-led growth with the need to avoid excessive inequality and instead maintain social cohesion?

In recent work, Aghion et al. (2015d) use cross-US-state panel data on patenting and inequality over the period 1975–2010 to show that: (i) the top 1 per cent income share in the US state is positively and significantly correlated with the state's degree of innovativeness, that is, with the quality-adjusted

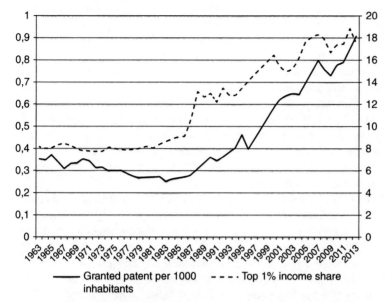

Figure 1.4 Evolution of the top 1 per cent income share and of the total patent per capita in the US (Aghion et al., 2015d).

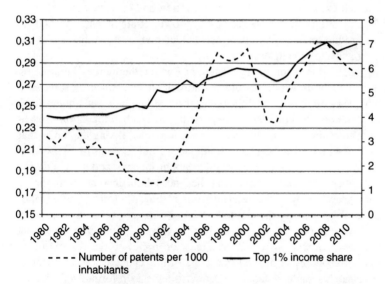

Figure 1.5 Evolution of the top 1 per cent income share and of the total patent per capita in Sweden (Aghion et al., 2015d).

amount of innovation in this country or state, which they measure by citation count; (ii) the effect of innovation on top income inequality is (at least partly) causal, from innovation to top income inequality[16] (iii) in cross-state panel regressions, innovativeness is less positively or even negatively correlated with measures of inequality which do not emphasize the very top incomes, in particular the top 2–10 per cent income shares (i.e., excluding the top 1%), or broader measures of inequality like the Gini coefficient. From cross-section regressions performed at the CZ level, Aghion et al. (2015d) also find that: (i) innovativeness is positively correlated with upward social mobility; and (ii) the positive correlation between innovativeness and social mobility, is driven mainly by entrant innovators and less so by incumbent innovators, and it is dampened in states with higher lobbying intensity.

In short, innovation tends to increase top income inequality, but not inequality at large.[17] And moreover, innovation appears to be positively correlated with social mobility. However, both entrant innovation and social mobility are dampened by lobbying activities.

What are the implications of these findings for policy design aimed at making growth more inclusive? Investing more and better in schools and universities, clearly has the effect of increasing growth, while also fostering social mobility. But what is more interesting in the sense that it goes against the popular view, is that structural reforms such as product and labour market liberalization, which enhance productivity growth as we have argued above, also increase social mobility to the extent that they favour innovation and creative destruction.[18] Thus the three pillars of an innovation-led growth strategy, namely (higher) education, product market flexibility, and labour market flexibility, lie at the heart of an inclusive growth strategy.

Now, what about taxation policy? There is a whole theoretical literature on how capital and labour income should be optimally taxed. However, somewhat surprisingly, very little has been done on taxation and growth, and almost nothing in the context of an economy where growth is driven by innovation. Absent growth considerations, the traditional argument against taxing capital is that this discourages savings and capital accumulation, and amounts to taxing individuals twice: once when they receive their labour income, and a second time when they collect revenues from saving their net labour income. Introducing endogenous growth may either reinforce this result (when the flow of innovation is mainly driven by the capital stock) or dampen it (when innovation is mainly driven by market size, which itself revolves around employees' net labour income). An analysis of optimal taxation policy in the context of an innovation-led economy is beyond the scope of this chapter and represents a huge new research agenda. Yet, one can learn from the tax reforms implemented in some developed countries during the past decades. In particular, it is widely acknowledge that by deciding to: (i) lower its maximum tax rate on labour income from around 90 per cent before 1991 to 57 per cent after 1991; and (ii) move from a progressive tax schedule on capital income with a maximum marginal tax rate at 72 per cent before 1991 to a flat rate of 30 per cent after 1991, Sweden has spurred innovation-led growth (as shown by the acceleration in patenting and in productivity growth after 1991), while still maintaining public services (health, schools and universities) of high quality and available to all for free. Moreover, Sweden remains the second least unequal country worldwide.

1.5   Technological Waves and the Debate on Secular Stagnation

1.5.1   The Debate

Based on the (apparent) slowing down of productivity growth in advanced countries since 2001, Gordon (2012, 2013) holds that the IT revolution is over and moreover, that the slowdown is there to last for a long period to come. His view is that: (i) the IT wave exhausted its growth-enhancing power; and (ii) several factors make the arrival of a new wave unlikely in the near future: in particular, the demographic transition, the limits in the growth of educational attainment, the rising income and wealth inequality resulting in mounting household debts that add to government debts. We disagree with this pessimistic view for at least three reasons. First, as pointed out by Dale Jorgenson and others, the IT revolution has durably changed the technology for producing ideas: in particular, it has made it easier for researchers to communicate and interact at long distance, which has certainly contributed to increasing the flow of new ideas. And we already see new ideas about to be implemented, which could revive the IT wave, such as 3D chips and 3D printing. Second, there is an obvious demand for new fundamental innovations, for example in renewable energies and in bio techs, both by individuals and by governments. Third, as stressed by Byrne et al. (2013), the apparent slowdown in the contribution of IT to productivity growth, can be due to measurement problems: in particular Byrne et al. (2013) make the argument that the BLS price index has not properly factored in the continuous progress in semi-conductor technology: the rate of decline in the price of semi-conductor embodying products has been underestimated according to these authors.

But there is another consideration, made by Bergeaud et al. (2014), which directly links to the focus of this chapter: the IT wave is diffusing with delays to countries other than the US, and the delay is most important in countries which have not yet fully implemented the structural reforms (university reform, product and labour market liberalization) required for a successful transition to innovation-based growth.

1.5.2   Historical Wave Patterns

In the remaining part of this section we take a brief look at technological waves and their diffusion from the US to other developed countries. In particular we will point at the relationship between structural reforms and a country's ability to take advantage of the new IT wave. We define a technological wave as the diffusion of new General Purpose Technologies (GPT).[19] General Purpose Technologies are defined as generic technologies which affect most sectors of the economy. Obvious examples include steam energy in the early and mid nineteenth century, electricity and chemistry in the early twentieth century, and the Information and Communication Technology revolution in the 1980s. While innovation-led productivity growth goes beyond the diffusion of these generic technologies, the speed at which a country adopts and diffuses a new General Purpose Technology, reflects the country's ability to innovate more generally. It is therefore of interest to compare the diffusion patterns of General Purpose Technologies across countries, especially when showing that lags in such diffusion reflect market or institutional rigidities which hamper innovation-led growth more generally.

Two Productivity Growth Waves

Using annual and quarterly data over the period 1890–2012 on labour productivity and TFP for 13 advanced countries (the G7 plus Spain, The Netherlands, Finland, Australia, Sweden and Norway) plus the reconstituted Euro area, Bergeaud et al. (2014) (BCL thereafter) show the existence of two big productivity growth waves during this period.

The first wave culminates in 1941, the second culminates in 2001. The first wave corresponds to the second industrial revolution: that of electricity, internal combustion and chemistry. The second wave is the ICT wave. This wave is of smaller magnitude than the first one, and a big question is whether it has ended in the US.

Diffusion Patterns

Figure 1.6 from Cette and Lopez (2012) shows that the Euro Area[20] and Japan suffer from a lag in the diffusion of technological waves compared to the US. Thus the first wave fully diffused to the current euro area, Japan and the UK only post World War II. As for the second productivity wave, so far it does not show up in the Euro Area or in Japan. Market rigidities contribute to explaining such delays.

And through an econometric analysis, Cette and Lopez (2012) show that this lag of ICT diffusion in Europe and Japan, compared to the US, is explained by institutional aspects: a lower education level, on average, of the working-age population and more regulations on labour and product

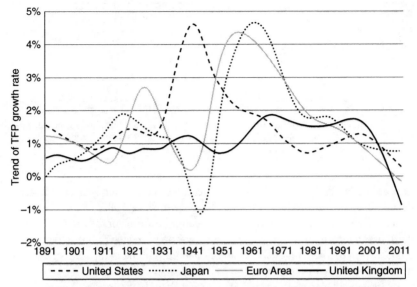

Figure 1.6 Delayed productivity growth waves in other countries. HP filtering of TFP growth with λ = 500 (Cette and Lopez, 2012).

markets. This result means that by implementing structural reforms, these countries could benefit from a productivity acceleration linked to a catch-up of the US ICT diffusion level. The lower quality of research and higher education in the Euro area and Japan compared to the US also appears to matter for explaining the diffusion lag.

Country-specific Shocks and the Role of Reforms

Figure 1.7 from Bergeaud et al. (2014) shows a positive break in labour productivity and in TFP growth in Sweden after 1990. This stands in contrast with

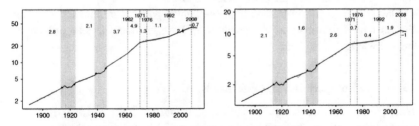

Figure 1.7 Productivity breaks: country-specific shocks (Sweden), labour productivity (left), total factor productivity (right). US $ PPP of 2005 (log scale). Areas in grey: war periods (Bergeaud et al., 2014).

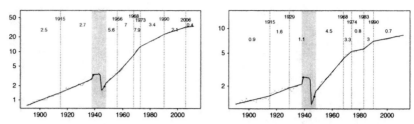

Figure 1.8 Productivity breaks: country-specific shocks (Japan), labour productivity (left), total factor productivity (right). US $ PPP of 2005 (log scale). Areas in grey: war periods (Bergeaud et al., 2014).

the case of Japan shown in Figure 1.8: there, we see no such break but instead decelerating labour productivity and TFP growth since 1980. Our explanation is that Sweden implemented sweeping structural reforms in the early 1990s: in particular a reform of the public spending system to reduce public deficits, and a tax reform to encourage labour supply and entrepreneurship. No significant reform took place in Japan over the past 30 years.

Let us consider from Bergeaud et al.'s (2014) study the four countries which are commonly presented as lead reformers over the past three decades. The reforms initiated in Sweden in the early 1990s made the rate of TFP growth increase from an average of 0.4 per cent over the period 1976–1992 to an average of 1.9 per cent over the period 1992–2008. Similarly, the 1982 reform (Wassenaard agreement) in the Netherlands is associated with a break from an average TFP growth rate of 0.5 per cent over the period 1977–1983 to an average TFP growth rate of 1.5 per cent over the period 1983–2002. The reforms initiated in the early 1990s in Canada are associated with a break from an average TFP growth rate of 0.3 per cent over the period 1974–1990 to an average rate of 1.1 per cent over the period 1990–2000. Finally, the reforms initiated in the early 1990s in Australia are associated with a break from an average TFP growth rate over the period 1971–1990 of 0.4 per cent to an average growth rate of 1.4 per cent over the period 1990–2002.

These findings are in line with cross-country panel regressions suggesting that structural reforms play a key role in speeding up the diffusion of technological waves.

1.6   Schumpeterian Insights into R&D Policy

How should the optimal R&D policy be designed? This question is at the heart of any policy debate which targets technological progress through R&D and innovation. Many governments are providing massive subsidies to foster innovation. As an example, the US spends more than $130 billion per year at the federal level to support innovation (NSF + NIH + Army Research Office + R&D tax credit).[21] The proponents of R&D subsidy have argued that R&D has spillovers that are not internalized by the innovating firms. The opponents claim that product market competition already provides sufficient incentives to firms and that any additional subsidy would be wasteful.

In this section, summarizing the findings from recent research on R&D policy from the Schumpeterian growth viewpoint, we argue that there are at least two new and important aspects that the design of optimal R&D policy should consider: namely, firm selection and the distinction between basic and applied research. The former implies that R&D policy could affect firm survival and consequently resource reallocation between more productive and less productive firms, or between incumbent and entrant firms. The latter relates to the fact that different types of research, in this case basic and applied, could have different spillovers and R&D policy should take into account its impact on the distinct types of research.

1.6.1   R&D Policies and Firm Selection

The goal of R&D policies is to incentivize firms to undertake greater R&D investment, produce more innovations, increase productivity, and create more jobs. However, these policies do not affect every firm in the economy in the same way. For instance, Criscuolo et al. (2012) have shown that large incumbents are better at obtaining government subsidies. Therefore one can argue that R&D subsidies to incumbents might be inefficiently preventing the entry of new firms and therefore slowing down the replacement of inefficient incumbents by more productive new entrants. The turnover and factor reallocation between incumbents and entrants is an important source of productivity growth. Foster et al. (2000, 2006) have shown empirically that the reallocation of factors across firms accounts for more than 50 per cent of productivity growth in the US. Given the empirical importance of this reallocation margin, it is necessary that R&D policy takes into account the interaction between innovation and factor reallocation. This is our focus in Acemoglu et al. (2013).

Recent literature has emphasized the importance of firm size and age for firm level heterogeneity that are observed in the data (Akcigit and Kerr, 2015). In particular Acemoglu et al. (2013) use data from the Census Bureau's Longitudinal Business Database and Census of Manufacturers, the National Science Foundation's Survey of Industrial Research and Development, and the NBER Patent Database. Their analysis focuses on innovative firms that are in operation during the 1987–1997 period. If we define small and large firms by their size relative to the median employment in the sample by year, and we define young and old firms by whether or not the firm is older than ten years, then the evidence points to small and young firms being both more R&D intensive and growing faster.[22] It then follows that industrial policies that discourage the reallocation of resources towards younger firms might indeed be costly in that they slow the movement of R&D resources from less efficient innovators (struggling incumbents) towards more efficient innovators (new firms).

Acemoglu et al. (2013) extend the Klette-Kortum model of growth and firm dynamics considered above by allowing for high versus low ability firms, that is, firms with more versus less efficient R&D technologies. Then they calibrate their model by matching empirical moments capturing key features of firm-level R&D behaviour, shipments growth, employment growth and exit, and the variation of these moments with size and age. Finally, they use the estimated model as a lab to run counterfactual experiments and test the impacts of various R&D policy designs on economic growth and welfare. The policies that we consider include a subsidy to new entrants, a subsidy to R&D by incumbents, and a subsidy for the continued operation of incumbents.

Their main findings can be summarized as follows. First, subsidizing incumbents reduces the equilibrium growth rate and welfare decrease. The reason is that this may prevent low-ability incumbents from exiting, thereby inhibiting the entry of high-ability firms. Solving for the optimal policy, the authors find that it involves a substantial tax on the operation of incumbents, combined with an R&D subsidy to incumbents. The reason for this result is that taxing operations makes it harder for low-type firms to survive and forces them to exit. This way the freed-up factors of production are reallocated to high-type firms, which make use of them much more effectively.

Overall, this general equilibrium analysis, which incorporates both reallocation and selection effects, highlights the fact that the economy in equilibrium might contain too many low-type firms and policies that ignore the selection effect might help low-type firms survive. Another point that is highlighted is the fact that intertemporal spillovers are sizable and the overall R&D investment is too little. Therefore a combination of R&D subsidies and taxes on firm operations could be an effective way of providing innovation incentives to firms, while also leveraging the selection margin in the economy.

1.6.2   Basic versus Applied R&D

In many countries national funds allocated to basic research have been among the top items in governments' policy agendas. For instance, in a recent report by the US Congress Joint Economic Committee, it is argued that despite its value to society as a whole, basic research is underfunded by private firms precisely because it is performed with no specific commercial applications in mind. The level of federal funding for basic research is deemed 'worrisome' and it is claimed that it must be increased in order to overcome the underinvestment in basic research (Joint Economic Committee (JEC), 2010). However the report also complains about the lack of research studies that actually quantify the extent of this underinvestment and about the lack of data.[23]

For similar reasons governments introduce programmes to promote collaboration between basic academic researchers and private firms, with the hope that synergies generated from these interactions could lead to breakthrough technological advances. For instance, the US government has aggressively promoted collaboration between universities and industrial researchers through specific funding programmes. Among many others, the National Science Foundation (NSF) sponsors the Fundamental Research Program for Industry-University Cooperative Research (FRP), the Industry-University Cooperative Research Centers Program (I/UCRC) and Grant Opportunities for Academic Liaison with Industry (GOALI).

Although the different characteristics of basic and applied research on the one hand, and academic and corporate research on the other hand have been widely recognized to be of first-order importance by policy-makers, these issues have received insufficient attention in the economic literature on productivity and economic growth. In particular, the endogenous growth literature has mainly considered a uniform type of (applied) research and overlooked basic research investment by private firms.

What are the key roles of basic and applied research for productivity growth? How should R&D policy be geared towards basic versus applied research? What are the incentives of private firms to conduct basic research? How does academic research contribute to innovation and productivity growth? Akcigit et al. (2014a) provide a first attempt at answering these questions. In order to understand the potential inefficiencies involved in different types of research investments and to design appropriate industrial policies to address them, it is necessary to adopt a structural framework that explicitly models the incentives for different types of research investments by private firms. Akcigit et al. (2014a) take an important step towards developing this theoretical framework, identifying the potential spillovers, and studying their macroeconomic implications for innovation policy.

Their analysis starts from the observation that countries allocate a significant share of their GDP to R&D (around 2–3%). The question then is: which fraction of it goes to basic versus applied research? The interesting fact is that almost half of overall spending goes into basic research.[24]

Akcigit et al. (2014a) first test Nelson's (1959) view that 'firms which support research towards the basic-science end of the spectrum are firms that have *fingers in many pies*'. According to this argument, as the range of its products and industries gets more diversified, a firm's incentive for investing into basic research relative to applied research should increase due to better appropriability of potential knowledge spillovers. To measure multi-industry presence, the authors count how many distinct SIC codes a firm is present in.

Using microlevel data on French firms, they plot average basic research intensity against the total number of distinct 1 digit SIC codes in which the firm is present. And they find a positive and statistically and economically significant relationship between multi-industry presence and basic research spending. A broader technological base is associated with higher investment in basic research relative to applied research. Thus the authors support Nelson's hypothesis about the link between multi-industry presence and relative research incentives. These correlations are robust to a large variety of potential confounding factors. This result suggests that cross-industry spillovers are sizable and using the variation in firms' technology base, we can estimate the cross-industry spillovers associated with basic research.

In order to study the policy implications of these spillovers, Akcigit et al. (2014a) build a general equilibrium, multi-industry framework with private firms and a public research sector. Firms conduct both basic and applied research, whereas the public sector focuses exclusively on basic research. In their model, basic research generates fundamental technological innovations and generates spillovers, both within and across industries, that affect subsequent applied innovations.[25] In line with the '*Ivory Tower*' theory of academic research, basic research by private firms in this model will turn into consumer products faster than that undertaken by public research labs. Applied research, on the other hand, will be done only by private firms and will generate follow-on innovations building on the existing basic knowledge stock.

The authors then undertake a quantitative investigation of the impacts of various innovation policies on the aggregate economy. They first estimate the model by targeting some of the key moments in the data, especially public and private spending on basic and applied research in France. Then they use the estimated model to assess the extent of inefficiencies in basic and applied research and to study the implications of several important innovation policies.

Their main results can be summarized as follows. First, a large fraction of spillovers from basic research across industries are not internalized. As a result, there is a dynamic misallocation of research efforts, which reduces welfare significantly. One striking result is that the decentralized economy and the social planner's economy are using overall the same level of resources for research. However, the composition of the total research effort is very distinct. While the social planner is allocating more resources to basic research, it allocates less resources to applied research. This implies that the dominant misallocation here is not that between production and research, but among the various types of research activities, in this case, applied and basic research. There is actually *overinvestment* in applied research in the decentralized economy because of product market competition, whereas there is underinvestment in basic research due to uninternalized within-industry and cross-industry spillovers.

This raises an important question: to what extent can public policies address this inefficiency? The first policy we analyse is a uniform research subsidy to private firms. In this environment, subsidizing overall private research is ineffective since this will oversubsidize applied research, which is already excessive due to product market competition. Therefore, the welfare improvement from such a subsidy is limited, unless the policy-maker is able to discriminate between types of research projects at the firm level, a difficult task in the real world.

The authors then analyse another policy tool: the level of funding for public research labs. We show that due to the Ivory Tower nature of public basic research, allocating more money to the academic sector without giving property rights to the researchers (ownership over their inventions) is not necessarily a good idea. To demonstrate this, they simulate a policy similar to the Bayh-Dole Act enacted in the US in 1980. They consider alternative scenarios in which public researchers have no property rights, then 50 per cent and 100 per cent property rights. And they find a complementarity between the level of property rights and the optimal allocation of resources to academic research. The optimal combination turns out to grant full property rights to the academic researcher and allocating a larger fraction of GDP to public research. This reduces the welfare gap significantly.

1.7 The Role of Freedom and Openness in the Innovation Process

How do incentives and organizations affect the probability and nature of innovation? As well explained by Pierre Azoulay in his lecture notes, providing incentives for producing ideas is problematic for at least three reasons. First, ex ante it is difficult to describe the innovation in advance. Second, ex post property rights on innovations may be difficult to enforce (for example, how do we enforce patent breadth). Third, innovation efforts are hard to observe and verify.

In short, a contract for future innovation is bound to be an incomplete contract, one whereby the contracting parties allocate property rights on the realized innovation and/or decision rights on the innovation process, leaving much of the revenue sharing to expost bargaining.[26]

In this section we explore one particular implication of contractual incompleteness, namely the issue of how to allocate control rights on the choice of research agenda in the context of multistage research lines. This leads us to revisit the role of intellectual property (IP) versus academic freedom and openness in the innovation process.

1.7.1 The ADS Framework and the Role of Academic Freedom

The incentives of academics are known to be different from those of private researchers (see Dasgupta and David, 1990). Building on an emerging body of research in the new economics of science (Dasgupta and David, 1994), Aghion et al. (2008) (Aghion-Dewatripont-Stein, henceforth ADS) emphasize the role of intellectual freedom: granting control rights to allow researchers to select their own research agenda.

More formally, ADS consider a multistage research line. The line starts with an initial idea. Then the idea is elaborated upon in stages, until it leads to a marketable product. Each stage on the research line requires one researcher, and that researcher succeeds with some probability p if she follows a (success-maximizing) practical strategy at that stage. Instead of the practical strategy, the researcher may choose to follow an 'alternative' strategy which yields a zero probability of success. One interpretation is that the alternative strategy may be the one that the researcher enjoys more, even though it does not pay off in monetary terms. Another interpretation is that the alternative strategy may help initiate new lines but does not generate progress on the initial line.

There is an infinite supply of researchers at each stage, each of whom has an outside option R that she can obtain by working in another profession. After being exposed to the idea from the previous stage, each researcher decides whether she would better enjoy following the practical strategy or the alternative strategy. If she is able to undertake her favoured strategy, she suffers no disutility from working. However, if the researcher has to undertake the strategy that she likes less, she suffers a positive disutility. ADS assume that the choice of the practical vs. the alternative strategy is ex ante noncontractible. In other words, one cannot write a contract that promises a bonus for following the practical strategy, because the nature of the work that the strategy entails cannot be adequately described ahead of time.

If the researcher is employed by a university which leaves her with full control rights over the choice of research strategy (the '*researcher-freedom*' regime), in equilibrium, she is paid the reservation wage and she always works on her preferred strategy. This implies that with positive probability the scientist will not work on the practical strategy, but on the alternative strategy.

Suppose instead that the researcher is employed by a centralized firm who has full control rights on the choice of research agenda. Then, ex-post, the manager has the authority to force the researcher to work on the practical strategy. Anticipating this, the researcher will demand a higher wage in order to work under this '*manager-control*' regime. The researcher's markup over the researcher-freedom regime represents compensation for loss of creative freedom – the fact that the researcher now must always adopt the practical strategy, whether this turns out to coincide with her preferences or not.

ADS show that it is optimal to allocate control rights on the research agenda (i.e., to grant academic freedom) in early stages of the research line, as this reduces the cost of research, whereas for later stages in the research line focus on the practical strategy becomes paramount, so that it is optimal to have research performed within a firm.

More generally, whether the researcher will or will not enjoy control rights – that is, real authority – over her research agenda, will depend upon how strongly she is monitored by the firm that employs her.

It is easy to show that: (i) the more the researcher is being monitored by the firm, the higher the wage the researcher will ask to compensate for her loss of control rights; and (ii) it is optimal to grant more freedom to the researcher in the earlier stage of the research process. In other words, research firms endogenously become more hands on in later stages of research projects as the value of focus increases as one moves down the research line closer to the commercialization stage.

1.7.2   Freedom and Openness

Another implication of the ADS framework, is that openness should play an important role in early stage research, whereas later stages in the research process are bound to be more 'proprietary'. Indeed, when granted academic freedom, researchers are free to explore alternative strategies which may lead to the creation of new research lines that those researchers may not pursue. Then there is value in having other researchers freely access the knowledge that will enable them to pursue these new research lines. Openness is less justified in later stages of the research process when research is more focused and also closer to commercialization. However, openness has no value when the firm owner controls the researcher's agenda, since the researcher is always forced to work on the practical strategy in that case.

1.7.3   Evidence on the Limits of IP and the Role of Openness and Freedom

The above model generates the following predictions:

Prediction 18 *Earlier stages of research should be managed in a more decentralized way, leaving more freedom to researchers.*

There is some empirical research speaking to this prediction, although indirectly. For example, using French and British firm-level data, Acemoglu et al. (2008) show that firms that encounter newer problems to solve tend to be more decentralized. This includes firms in more heterogeneous industries (where it is harder to learn from others), firms closer to the technological frontier (so that there are fewer other firms to learn from) and younger firms (thus with less experience to learn from their own mistakes). That more frontier firms should delegate more may also explain why subsidizing higher education, in particular graduate education, is more likely to be innovation-enhancing if universities are more decentralized (as shown for example by Aghion et al. (2010), using cross-US-state panel data). Incidentally, universities are a sector in which formal delegation can be more easily enforced.

Prediction 19 *More openness: (i) enhances research freedom; (ii) enhances the creation of new lines and (iii) enhances basic research.*

Murray et al. (2015) test the prediction that in a research setting characterized by a high level of intellectual freedom, greater openness does not only increase the flow of research, but also increases the diversity of new research discoveries. More precisely, they consider the following natural experiment in openness: NIH agreements in the late 1990s that reduced the costs of accessing information on genetically engineered mice.[27] Using a sample of engineered mice linked to specific scientific papers, some of which were affected by the NIH agreements and some were not, Murray et al. (2015) evaluate how the level and nature of follow-on research changes after the NIH-induced increase in openness. They find that increased openness encourages entry by new researchers and the exploration of more diverse research lines.

Particularly influential has been Heidi Williams's contribution to the field. In particular, Williams (2013) uses a fascinating dataset on the sequencing of the human genome to analyse the impact of the IP restrictions imposed by the private firm Celera until 2003, on subsequent innovation. The author finds that these restrictions have indeed negatively affected subsequent scientific research and product innovation.

Both Williams (2013) and Murray et al. (2015) have in common that they both analyse the impact of nonpatent IP restrictions on subsequent innovation. More recently, Sampat and Williams (2015) have looked at the potential impact of gene patents on subsequent innovation on human genes. Somewhat surprisingly, using USPTO data on human genes the authors find that gene patents have no systematic effect on subsequent innovation.

1.8   Towards a New Growth Pact in Europe

The above discussion suggests some directions for a new growth package for EU and in particular countries in the Euro area: (i) structural reforms starting with the liberalization of product and labour markets: here we will argue that an important role can be played by structural funds provided the targeting and governance of these funds is suitably modified; (ii) industrial investments along the lines suggested by our above discussion on vertical targeting; and (iii) more flexible macroeconomic policies (budgetary and monetary) at EU level.

1.8.1   *Structural Reforms and the Role of Structural Funds*

There is a broad consensus among European leaders regarding the importance of structural reforms, in particular product and labour market liberalization and higher education reform, to foster long-run growth in Europe. In this section we first assess the potential increase in growth potential from having all Eurozone countries converge fully or partly to the best standards with regard to product or labour market liberalization, and also with regard to higher education. In the second part of the section we discuss the role that structural funds might play in encouraging such reforms.

Assessing the Growth Effects of Structural Reforms

As in Aghion et al. (2005b) one can look at the effect of structural policies using cross-country panel regressions across 21 European countries. Our structural indicators are the following: For higher education system: the share of the 25–64-year-old population having completed tertiary education (SUP); for product market: an OECD index assessing product market regulation (PMR); for labour market: an OECD index assessing the strictness of employment protection (LPE). In fact we focus on the interaction between these two rigidities, namely the variable PMR × LPE, in the analysis of labour and product market reforms. Indeed, there are good reasons to believe the effects of liberalizing product markets are complementary to those of liberalizing labour markets: for example, making entry in a new activity easier is of lesser value to an entrepreneur if she cannot hire new employees to work on that activity.

We can look at the short- and long-run growth effects of converging towards the performance levels of '*target countries*'. The target groups include those countries which are found to be the 'best performers' in terms of education, product and labour market regulations. In order to determine these groups, we rank countries according to the variables SUP and PMR × LPE and we come up with two target groups: Non-European target group: USA and Canada; European target group: UK, Ireland and Denmark. The advantage of these two target groups is that they allow comparisons between countries within the European Union as well as with non-European counterparts. Interestingly, we found the same target groups both for the higher education and the labour and product market regulation. Then we can assess the average effect of converging towards best practice for the eurozone (EMU) as a whole. Our results are that converging towards the best practice in terms of product and labour market liberalization generates a growth gain of between 0.3 and 0.4 already in the short run. Converging towards the best practice in terms of higher education enrollment generates a growth gain which is initially smaller (if we take the UK, Ireland and Denmark as the reference countries), but grows up to 0.6 by 2050. Altogether, a full percentage point in growth can be gained through structural convergence towards those three countries.

Rethinking the Role and Design of Structural Funds

Here we argue that structural funds can be partly reoriented towards facilitating the implementation of structural reforms. So far, these funds have been used mainly to finance medium-term investment projects and to foster socio-economic cohesion within the EU. Moreover, these funds are allocated ex ante based on recipient countries' GDP relative to the EU average, population and surface.

We argue in favour of an alternative approach to the goals, targeting and governance of Structural Funds. On the goals of Structural Funds: these funds should become transformative, in other words they should help achieve structural reforms in the sectors they are targeted to. In our above discussion, we identified some main areas where structural reforms are needed: labour markets, product markets and education. Structural funds should aim at facilitating changes in the functioning of these sectors in the various countries. The allocation of funds should generally be made on an individual basis; in other words, they should mainly target schools, employment agencies, individual workers, not so much countries except for infrastructures that help enhance competition. The funds would help finance transition costs. The allocation of funds should be to well-specified deliverables (provision of better tutorship in education, improvements in the organization of employment agencies, transition to portable pension rights across two or more countries, setting up of diploma equivalence for service jobs, etc.) and should be also conditional upon the country or region not having put in place a general policy that contradicts the purpose of the fund allocation.

Regarding the governance of Structural Funds, the allocation of funds should be made by European agencies on the model of the European Research Council: bottom up approach with peer evaluation ex ante and ex post.

1.8.2   *Rethinking Industrial Policy in the EU*

Growth in the EU also requires adequate vertical targeting, both by member states and at EU level. In the previous sections we have emphasized the view that horizontal targeting should be given priority: basic and applied research, higher education, labour mobility. But, in light of our discussion in the previous sections, we also believe that well-governed vertical targeting by member states and at EU level can help foster growth further within the EU.

At EU level, infrastructure investments in transportation, energy and broadband networks should greatly contribute to increasing product market competition in local markets. In other words, proper vertical targeting at EU level can help enhance horizontal policies in member states. Another justification for privileging vertical targeting at EU level, is that targeting at this level is more likely to preserve product market competition when the targeted activities involve important fixed costs. What we mean here, is that subsidizing activities with high fixed costs at local level (i.e., at the level of one particular country) often boils down to subsidizing one particular firm, which in turn defeats the purpose of reconciling industrial policy with the need to enhance product market competition. This consideration becomes less binding when vertical targeting is done at EU level, since at EU level it is easier to find more than one potential recipient of vertical subsidies, including for activities involving high fixed costs.

But EU policy with regard to vertical targeting goes beyond EU level investments; it also concerns the attitude of the European Commission with regard to sectoral policies by member states. These are currently perceived by European authorities as a threat to European integration, which in turn explains the fussy checks by European competition authorities of all devices supporting industrial activities. Here, let us mention a remarkable work on state aid in Europe, Japan and the US by Pierre-André Buigues and Khalid Sekkat, which identifies false debates and arguments against industrial policy. These authors find a general tendency in Europe towards lowering state aid (Germany being an exception, although mainly since the past ten years with the integration of the Eastern landers). This in turn suggests that the Commission has been remarkably effective in limiting the scope of state aid. What we recommend is to have the Commission become less a priori biased against the use of state aid, while at the same time setting new and clear guidelines for the allocation and governance of that aid. In other words, the Commission should move from an *ex ante*, legalistic, approach to sectoral state aid to an *ex post*, pragmatic, approach where state aid is sanctioned only when it can be proved that it resulted in lowering product market competition in the corresponding activity.

Whether at EU level or by member states, vertical targeting should be adequately designed and governed. In the previous section we mentioned the recent paper by Nunn and Trefler (2010), suggesting that sectoral aid is more likely to be growth-enhancing if it targets sectors with higher growth potential, one measure of it being the extent to which various industries are skill-biased. We also mentioned the work by Aghion et al. (2013) suggesting that vertical targeting is more growth-enhancing if it targets activities with higher degree of product market competition and enhances product market competition within the sector.[28]

1.8.3 More Flexible Macroeconomic Policies at EU Level

In previous sections we have argued that more countercyclical macroeconomic policies can help (credit-constrained) firms maintain R&D and other types of innovation-enhancing investments over the business cycle. One implication of this for European growth policy design, is that all the debt and deficit targets (both in the short and in the long term) should be corrected for cyclical variations, in other words they should always be stated in structural terms. Thus, for example if a country's current growth rate is significantly below trend, then the short-run budgetary targets should be relaxed so as to allow this country to maintain its growth enhancing investments. However, while the fiscal compact specifies long-term objectives that are stated in structural terms, the short and medium term targets agreed between the European Commission and member states last year, are in nominal terms. This inconsistency is damaging to growth.

1.9   Conclusion

In this chapter we have tried to show how theoretical models of growth and innovation can deliver testable predictions and also policy recommendations. Our emphasis has been on the Schumpeterian approach where each innovation not only induces positive knowledge spillovers on subsequent research but also destroys rents from previous innovations.

Where do we see the research on R&D, innovation and growth being pushed over the next years? A first direction is to look more closely at how growth and innovation are affected by the organization of firms and research. Thus over the past five years Nick Bloom and John Van Reenen have popularized fascinating new datasets that allow us to look at how various types of organizations (e.g., more or less decentralized firms) are more or less conducive to innovation. But firms' size and organization are in turn endogenous, and in particular they depend upon factors such as the relative supply of skilled labour or the nature of domestic institutions.

A second and related avenue for future research is to look in more detail at innovation-led growth, firm dynamics and reallocation in developing economies. Recent empirical evidence (see Hsieh and Klenow, 2009, 2012) has shown that misallocation of resources is a major source of productivity gap across countries. What are the causes of misallocation, why do these countries lack *creative destruction* which would eliminate the inefficient firms? Schumpeterian theory with firm dynamics could be an invaluable source to shed light on these important issues that lie at the core of the development puzzle.

A third avenue is to look at the role of finance in innovation-led growth. Recent studies point at equity finance being more growth-enhancing in more frontier economies. More generally, we still need to better understand how different types of financial instruments map with different sources of growth and different types of innovation activities. Also, we need to better understand why we observe a surge of finance during the acceleration phase in the diffusion of new technological waves, and also how financial sectors evolve when the waves taper off.

A fourth avenue is to analyse in greater depth the relationship between innovation, income inequality and social mobility, and to gather new data on individual patenting and revenues to look at how taxation policy affects the flow and nature of innovation and the mobility of innovators. These and many other microeconomic aspects of innovation and growth await further research.

Acknowledgements

This is the final version of the survey on R&D, innovation and growth for the COEURE Coordination Action. The authors are grateful to the participants at the associated COEURE workshop in Brussels in June 2015 for useful comments and suggestions.

Notes

1. A precursor version of the AK model is the Harrod-Domar model (see Aghion and Howitt, 1998). Frankel (1962) developed the first version of the AK model as we know it, i.e., with Cobb-Douglas production functions (in capital and labour) for firms and knowledge externalities driven by capital accumulation by firms. Romer (1986) developed an AK model similar to Frankel but where savings are determined by intertemporal utility maximization instead of just being a constant fraction of final output as in Frankel (1962).
2. Which of these effects dominates will depend in particular upon the size of innovations. Assessing the relative importance of these two effects in practice, requires estimating the structural parameters of the growth model using micro data (see footnote 9).
3. E.g., see Blundell et al. (1995).
4. See Aghion et al. (1997, 2001).
5. That competition and patent protection should be complementary in enhancing growth rather than mutually exclusive is at odds with Romer's (1990) product variety model, where competition is always detrimental to innovation and growth (as we discussed above) for exactly the same reason that intellectual property rights (IPRs) in the form of patent protection are good for innovation: namely, competition reduces post-innovation rents, whereas patent protection increases these rents. See Acemoglu and Akcigit (2012) for a general analysis of optimal patent protection in Schumpeterian models with step-by-step innovation.
6. In the product variety model, exit is always detrimental to growth as it reduces product variety.
7. Various versions of this framework have been estimated using micro-level data by Lentz and Mortensen (2008), Acemoglu et al. (2013), Garcia-Macia et al. (2014) and Akcigit and Kerr (2015).
8. For recent discussions, see Haltiwanger et al. (2010) and Akcigit and Kerr (2010).
9. See Akcigit and Kerr (2010) and Aghion et al. (2014) for references. In a recent work, Acemoglu et al. (2013) analyse the effects of various industrial policies on equilibrium productivity growth, including entry subsidy and incumbent R&D subsidy, in an enriched version of the above framework.
10. See Acemoglu et al. (2006) for a formalization of this idea.
11. Aghion et al. (2005b) show that research-type education is always more growth-enhancing in US states that are more frontier, whereas a bigger emphasis on

two-year colleges is more growth-enhancing in US states that are farther below the productivity frontier. Similarly, using cross-country panel data, Vandenbussche et al. (2006) show that tertiary education is more positively correlated with productivity growth in countries that are closer to the world technology frontier.

12. Acemoglu and Robinson (2006) formalize another reason, also Schumpeterian, as to why democracy matters for innovation: namely, new innovations do not only destroy the economic rents of incumbent producers, they also threaten the power of incumbent political leaders.

13. See Aghion and Howitt (1994) and Mortensen and Pissarides (1998).

14. Activities that come to mind when talking about vertical targeting most often pertain to the same four or five sectors, namely energy, biotech, ICT, transportation, etc.

15. E.g., by Nunn and Trefler (2010), and Aghion et al. (2015c) which we summarize below.

16. They establish this result by instrumenting for innovativeness following two different strategies, first by using data on the appropriation committees of the Senate, and second by relying on knowledge spillovers from the other states.

17. In Sweden for example, the Gini has not increased over the past 25 years, whereas both patenting and top income inequality have.

18. See Aghion and Roulet (2014).

19. See Bresnahan and Trajtenberg (1995).

20. The Euro Area is here the aggregation of Germany, France, Italy, Spain, The Netherlands, Austria and Finland. These seven countries represent together, in 2012, 88.5 per cent or the total GDP of the Euro Area.

21. http://www.whitehouse.gov/sites/default/files/microsites/ostp/Fy%202015%20R&D.pdf.

22. Likewise Akcigit and Kerr (2015) regress firm growth on log firm size and find an estimate of -0.04 and innovation intensity (number of innovations relative to the firm size) on log firm size and find an estimate of -0.18.

23. http://jec.senate.gov/public/?a=Files.Serve&File_id=29aac456-fce3-4d69-956f-4add06f111c1.

24. See Akcigit et al. (2014a) for references.

25. By fundamental innovation, we mean major technological improvements that generate larger than average contributions to the aggregate knowledge stock of society. In addition, these will have long-lasting spillover effects on the size of subsequent innovations within the same field.

26. Of course, the monetary incentives for innovation are not only determined by ex post bargaining: ex post monetary rewards through prizes, as well as ex ante financing of R&D as part of research grants or procurement contracts, also play an important role in inducing innovation.

27. Specifically, in 1998 and 1999, the National Institutes of Health negotiated two Memoranda of Understanding with the firm DuPont, which granted academic researchers low-cost, royalty-free and independent access to both the use of DuPont's methods and to the transgenic mice associated with them through the Jackson Laboratory, a nonprofit research mice repository.

28. While it is part of the EU mission to promote product market competition, at the same time, natural monopolies are prevalent in network sectors, and having too many networks, may result in Europe becoming underequipped in the field of

broadband optics and more generally disadvantaged in digital industry activities. This consideration should of course be also taken into account when designing vertical targeting at EU level.

References

Acemoglu, D., and Akcigit, U. 2012. Intellectual Property Rights Policy, Competition and Innovation. *Journal of the European Economic Association*, **10**, 1–42.

Acemoglu, D., and Robinson, J. 2006. Economic Backwardness in Political Perspective. *American Political Science Review*, **100**, 115–131.

Acemoglu, D., Aghion, P., and Zilibotti, F. 2006. Distance to Frontier, Selection, and Economic Growth. *Journal of the European Economic Association*, 37–74.

Acemoglu, D., Aghion, P., Lelarge, C., Van Reenen, J., and Zilibotti, F. 2008. The Unequal Effects of Liberalization: Evidence from Dismantling the License Raj. *American Economic Review*, **94**, 1397–1412.

Acemoglu, D., Akcigit, U., Bloom, N., and Kerr, W. 2013. *Innovation, Reallocation and Growth*. NBER Working Paper 18993.

Aghion, P., and Howitt, P. 1992. A Model of Growth through Creative Destruction. *Econometrica*, **60**, 323–351.

Aghion, P., and Howitt, P. 1994. Growth and Unemployment. *Review of Economic Studies*, **61**, 477–494.

Aghion, P., and Howitt, P. 1998. *Endogenous Growth Theory*. MIT Press.

Aghion, P., and Howitt, P. 2009. *The Economics of Growth*. MIT Press.

Aghion, P., and Roulet, A. 2011. *Repenser l'Etat*. Editions du Seuil.

Aghion, P., and Roulet, A. 2014. *Structural Reforms and Social Mobility*. Mimeo Harvard.

Aghion, P., Harris, C., and Vickers, J. 1997. Competition and Growth with Step-by-Step Innovation: An Example. *European Economic Review, Papers and Proceedings*, 771–782.

Aghion, P., Harris, C., Howitt, P., and Vickers, J. 2001. Competition, Imitation and Growth with Step-by-Step Innovation. *Review of Economic Studies*, **68**, 467–492.

Aghion, P., Bloom, N., Blundell, R., Griffith, R., and Howitt, P. 2005a. Competition and Innovation: An Inverted-U Relationship. *Quarterly Journal of Economics*, **120**, 701–728.

Aghion, P., Boustan, L., Hoxby, C., and Vandenbussche, J. 2005b. *Exploiting States' Mistakes to Identify the Causal Effects of Higher Education on Growth*. Harvard mimeo.

Aghion, P., Alesina, A., and Trebbi, F. 2007. *Democracy, Technology, and Growth*. NBER Working Paper No. 13180.

Aghion, P., Dewatripont, M., and Stein, J. C. 2008. Academic Freedom, Private-Sector Focus, and the Process of Innovation. *RAND Journal of Economics*, **39**, 617–634.

Aghion, P., Hemous, D., and Kharroubi, E. 2009a. Countercyclical Fiscal Policy, Credit Constraints, and Productivity Growth. *Forthcoming in the Journal of Monetary Economics*.

Aghion, P., Askenazy, P., Bourles, R., Cette, G., and Dromel, N. 2009b. Education, Market Rigidities and Growth. *Economics Letters*, **102**, 62–65.

Aghion, P., Blundell, R., Griffith, R., Howitt, P., and Prantl, S. 2009c. The Effects of Entry on Incumbent Innovation and Productivity. *Review of Economics and Statistics*, **91**, 20–32.

Aghion, P., Dewatripont, M., Hoxby, C., Mas-Colell, A., and Sapir, A. 2010. The Governance and Performance of Universities: Evidence from Europe and the US. *Economic Policy*, **25**, 7–59.

Aghion, P., Farhi, E., and Kharroubi, E. 2012. Monetary Policy, Liquidity and Growth. *Harvard mimeo*.

Aghion, P., Howitt, P., and Prantl, S. 2013. *Patent Rights, Product Market Reforms and Innovation*. NBER Working Paper 18854.

Aghion, P., Akcigit, U., and Howitt, P. 2014. What Do We Learn from Schumpeterian Growth Theory? In *Handbook of Economic Growth*, 2, Elsevier, pp. 515–563.

Aghion, P., Dechezlepretre, A., Hemous, D., Martin, R., and Van Reenen, J. 2015a. Carbon Taxes, Path Dependency and Directed Technical Change: Evidence from the Auto Industry. *forthcoming, Journal of Political Economy*.

Aghion, P., Akcigit, U., Deaton, A., and Roulet, A. 2015b. *Creative Destruction and Subjective Wellbeing*. NBER Working Paper No. 21069.

Aghion, P., Dewatripont, M., Du, L., Harrison, A., and Legros, P. 2015c. *Industrial Policy and Competition*. Harvard mimeo.

Aghion, P., Akcigit, U., Bergeaud, A., Blundell, R., and Hemous, D. 2015d. *Innovation and Top Income Inequality*. Harvard mimeo.

Akcigit, U., and Kerr, W. 2010. *Growth through Heterogeneous Innovations*. NBER Working Paper 16443.

Akcigit, U., and Kerr, W. 2015. *Growth through Heterogeneous Innovations*. PIER Working Paper 15-020.

Akcigit, U., Hanley, D., and Serrano-Velarde, N. 2014a. *Back to Basics: Basic Research Spillovers, Innovation Policy and Growth*. NBER Working Paper 19473.

Akcigit, U., Alp, H., and Peters, M. 2014b. *Lack of Selection and Limits to Delegation: Firm Dynamics in Developing Countries*. Working Paper.

Bergeaud, A., Cette, G., and Lecat, R. 2014. *Productivity Trends from 1890 to 2012 in Advanced Countries*. Banque de France, Working Paper No. 475, February.

Bloom, N., Sadun, R., and Van Reenen, J. 2012. Americans Do I.T. Better: US Multinationals and the Productivity Miracle. *American Economic Review*, **102**, 167–201.

Blundell, R., Griffith, R., and Van Reenen, J. 1995. Dynamic Count Data Models of Technological Innovation. *Economic Journal*, **105**, 333–344.

Bresnahan, T., and Trajtenberg, M. 1995. General Purpose Technologies: Engines of Growth? *Journal of Econometrics*, **65**, 83–108.

Byrne, D., Sichel, D., and Oliner, S. 2013. Is the Information Technology Over? *International Productivity Monitor*, **25**, 20–36.

Cette, G., and Lopez, J. 2012. ICT Demand Behavior: An International Comparison. *Economics of innovation and New Technology, Taylor and Francis Journals*, **21**, 397–410.

Criscuolo, C., Martin, R., Overman, H., and Van Reenen, J. 2012. *The Causal Effects of Industrial Policy*. CEP Working Paper 1113.

Dasgupta, P., and David, P. A. 1990. *The New Economics of Science*. High Technology Impact Program Working Paper, Center for Economic Policy Research, Stanford University.

Dasgupta, P., and David, P. A. 1994. Toward a New Economics of Science. *Policy Research*, **23**, 487–521.

Dixit, A. K., and Stiglitz, J. E. 1977. Monopolistic Competition and Optimum Product Diversity. *American Economic Review*, **67**, 297–308.

Foster, L., Haltiwanger, J., and Krizan, C. 2000. Aggregate Productivity Growth: Lessons from Microeconomic Evidence. In: *New Developments in Productivity Analysis*. University of Chicago Press.

Foster, L., Haltiwanger, J., and Krizan, C. 2006. Market Selection, Reallocation, and Restructuring in the U.S. Retail Trade Sector in the 1990s. *Review of Economics and Statistics*, **88**, 748–758.

Frankel, J., and Romer, D. 1996. *Trade and Growth: An Empirical Investigation*. NBER Working Paper No. w5476.

Frankel, M. 1962. The Production Function in Allocation of Growth: A Synthesis. *American Economic Review*, **52**, 995–1022.

Garcia-Macia, D., Hsieh, C., and Klenow, P. J. 2014. *How Destructive is Innovation?* Working paper.

Gordon, R. 2012. *Is U.S. Economic Growth Over? Faltering Innovation Confronts the Six Headwinds*. NBER Working Paper 18315.

Gordon, R. 2013. US Productivity Growth: The Slowdown Has Returned after a Temporary Revival. *International Productivity Monitor*, **25**.

Haltiwanger, J., Jarmin, R., and Miranda, J. 2010. *Who Creates Jobs? Small vs. Large vs. Young*. NBER Working Paper 16300.

Hsieh, C., and Klenow, P. 2009. Misallocation and Manufacturing TFP in China and India. *Quarterly Journal of Economics*, **124**, 1403–1448.

Hsieh, C., and Klenow, P. 2012. *The Life Cycle of Plants in India and Mexico*. NBER Working Paper 18133.

Hsieh, C., and Klenow, P. J. 2014. The Life Cycle of Plants in India and Mexico. *The Quarterly Journal of Economics*, **129**, 1035–1084.

Joint Economic Committee (JEC). 2010. *The 2010 Joint Economic Report*. Tech. rept. Washington, DC: Government Printing Office.

Klette, T., and Kortum, S. 2004. Innovating Firms and Aggregate Innovation. *Journal of Political Economy*, **112**, 986–1018.

Koch, W. 2014. *Does Financial Structure Matter for Economic Development*. Mimeo UQAM.

Lentz, R., and Mortensen, D. 2008. An Empirical Model of Growth Through Product Innovation. *Econometrica*, **76**, 1317–1373.

Mortensen, D., and Pissarides, C. 1998. Technological Progress, Job Creation, and Job Destruction. *Review of Economic Dynamics*, **1**, 733–753.

Murray, F., Aghion, P., Dewatripont, M., Kolev, J., and Stern, S. 2015. Of Mice and Academics. *American Economic Journal, Micro, forthcoming*.

Nelson, R. 1959. The Simple Economics of Basic Research. *Journal of Political Economy*, **67**, 297–306.

Nunn, N., and Trefler, D. 2010. The Structure of Tariffs and Long-Term Growth. *American Economic Journal: Macroeconomics*, **2**, 158–194.

Romer, P. 1986. Increasing returns and long-run growth. *Journal of Political Economy*, **94**, 1002–1037.

Romer, P. 1990. Endogenous Technical Change. *Journal of Political Economy*, **98**, 71–102.

Sampat, B., and Williams, H. 2015. *How Do Patents Affect Follow-on Innovation? Evidence from the Human Genome*. NBER working paper 21666.

Solow, R. M. 1956. A Contribution to the Theory of Economic Growth. *The Quarterly Journal of Economics*, **70**, 65–94.

Vandenbussche, J., Aghion, P., and Meghir, C. 2006. Growth, Distance to Frontier, and Composition of Human Capital. *Journal of Economic Growth*, **11**, 97–127.

Williams, H. 2013. Intellectual Property Rights and Innovation: Evidence from the Human Genome. *Journal of Political Economy*.

2 European Union Dual Labour Markets: Consequences and Potential Reforms

Juan J. Dolado

Abstract

This chapter provides an overview of a growing literature on the emergence of dual labour markets and their persistence in some EU countries, as well as the impact that dualism has on a large range of labour market dimensions including, among others, job and worker flows, (overall and youth) unemployment, wage setting, training, labour mobility, household formation, and technology adoption. A distinctive feature of the chapter is that it places the accumulated evidence on these issues in a general equilibrium framework, which helps understand why dual labour markets have performed so poorly since 2008, and also to identify promising avenues of research for the near future. The chapter also evaluates recent reforms and reform proposals (single and unified labour contracts) to eliminate the undesirable consequences of excessive dualism in the labour market.

2.1 Introduction

This COEURE Survey deals with the consequences of dual labour markets, namely labour markets where workers are entitled to different employment protection depending on the contract they hold, and where these differences are large. The effect of dualism on several labour-market dimensions has been widely analysed in the literature but many of these issues have strongly re-emerged during the recent crisis due to the poor performance of countries subject to strong dualism. In this survey we review the main lessons drawn from past experience with these labour market regimes, where they originate from, why they are so difficult to change, why they have failed during the Great Recession and the subsequent sovereign crisis, what reform proposals have been posed and which ones are more likely to work. In addition to reviewing the accumulated stock of knowledge on these issues, we place them in a general equilibrium framework to understand which ones constitute the most promising avenues of research for the near future. The rest of the survey is organized as follows. Section 2.2 deals with the historical origins of dual labour markets. Section 2.3 considers conditions under which labour contracts become too different, leading to optimal versus nonoptimal arrangements of stability and flexibility in the labour market. Section 2.4 looks at the performance of dual labour markets since the onset of the Great Recession. Section 2.5 documents the case of Spain, as an epitome of a dual labour market. Section 2.6 discusses the effects of dualism on youth labour market outcomes. Section 2.7 critically evaluates different proposals to abolish inefficient dualism. Finally, Section 2.8 provides some concluding remarks. An Appendix summarizes the main features of different proposals for the introduction of Single/ Unified labour contracts.

2.2   The Emergence of Dual Labour Markets in Europe

Since the oil crisis in the 1970s, the fight against unemployment in Europe has centred on allowing more flexibility in the labour market. In line with this goal, employment protection legislation (EPL) has been subject to frequent policy changes in many EU countries.[1] Although in several instances EPL reforms have taken place across the board, this has not always been the case. A well-known example is provided by labour market reforms in the Southern Mediterranean countries of the Euro Zone (EZ) where, until recently, rules for regular open-ended contracts have hardly been modified. Instead, changes in EPL regulations have mostly affected new hires, either through the introduction of a large spectrum of flexible fixed-term contracts or by expanding the opportunities to use existing temporary contracts (probation, replacement, training, internships, etc.) for regular economic activities. As a result, strong differences in the degree of employment protection between workers hired on permanent/open-ended (PC) and temporary/fixed-term (TC) contracts have emerged as the most salient feature of the so-called *dual* labour markets (see Booth et al., 2002a).

Not surprisingly, segmented labour markets have been hotly debated in academic circles and the policy arena over the last few years. After all, they have been largely responsible for the disappointing performance of employment and unemployment in Europe since the onset of the Great Recession (GR), as reflected by the large differences in labour market outcomes between the North/Centre and the South/Periphery during the crisis.

Following seminal work by Saint-Paul (1996, 2000), the political economy of these two-tier reforms has received a lot of attention over the past couple of decades. In particular, this literature has shed light on the determinants and timing of different types of EPL reforms. Among the relevant issues analysed from this viewpoint, the following stand out:
1. identifying the median voters in union elections (typically middle-aged middle-skilled workers with PC) as a key element in the development of insider-outsider models,

2. characterizing the cyclical properties of EPL reforms where rules pertaining to PC have been liberalized (these reforms are typically approved in recessions rather than in expansions because protected workers face higher exposure to job losses in the former business cycle phase),
3. analysing the dynamics of insiders and outsiders (driven by the pressure placed on union decisions by a growing share of unemployed or workers under nonregular contracts), etc. (cf. Boeri, 2010 and Bentolila et al., 2012a).

Following these two-tier reforms, the use of temporary workers has increased in total dependent employment, especially in those countries where EPL for permanent workers was higher to start with. For instance, this was the case of the olive-belt countries (Greece, Italy, Portugal and Spain) as well as in France. The reason why labour law was stricter in the first set of countries has to do with the fact that, in different periods of the twentieth century, they experienced transitions from authoritarian dictatorships to democratic regimes. In effect, though EPL regulations were mostly approved in the aftermath of World War I (see Table 2.1 for a chronology of these rules; Aleksynska and Schmidt, 2014), social pressure in military regimes with low productivity and wages (typical of autarkies) was kept under control by means of very stringent rules regarding worker dismissals, in conjunction with the ban of most trade unions. When democracy was restored and unions became legalized, upward wage pressure in collective bargaining took place but the prevailing rigid employment protection was kept fairly unaltered in order to get the support of unions.

As regards France, the origin of the implementation of stringent EPL can be traced back to the 1960s, when large migration inflows, especially from the Maghreb, led to downward pressure on wages (see Comte, 2015). As is well known, stagnating wages and deteriorating working conditions resulted in French wage earners' revolt in May 1968. The crisis was solved through a sharp increase in the minimum wage and its reassessment mechanisms (with the creation of SMIC in the 1970), which, from 1968 to 1982, almost tripled in real terms. The role of such an aggressive policy was to establish a barrier to downward wage pressure driven by increasing competition from migrant workers. The high minimum wage initially caused the ousting of less skilled migrant workers and a slight increase in the share of native's wages. However, after a while, the continuous rise in labour costs led to a surge of unemployment, especially among the youth. As a result, French unions successfully pushed for stricter conditions for dismissals and higher protection of the regular employment contract.

Yet, regardless of differences in the historical origins of EPL in the Southern Mediterranean area, the loss of competitiveness associated with upward pressure on wages in the context of the large adverse supply shocks of the 1970s and the increasing global trade competition in the 1980s called for drastic reforms

Table 2.1 *Chronology of EPL reforms in EU countries (Aleksynska and Schmidt, 2014)*

Area of regulation/country	FRA	GBR	ITA	ESP	GRC	PRT
Employment protection legislation						
Maximum trial period	–	–	1919	1976	1920	1969
Regulation of fixed-term contracts	1890[a]	1963	1919[b]	1926	1920[a]	1969
Obligation to provide reasons to the employee	1973	1975	1966	1956	–	–
Valid grounds (justified dismissal)	1973	≈ 1963[c]	1966	1926	–	–
Prohibited grounds (unfair dismissal)	1910	1971	1966	1931	1920	1933
Workers enjoying special protection	1910	–	1919	1931	1928	1933
Notification requirements	1958	–	–	1956	1930	1969
Notice period	1928	1963	1919	1931	1920	1969
Severance/redundancy pay	1967	1965	1919	1972	1930	1969
Compensation for unfair dismissal	1890	1975	1950	1926	–	1969
Procedure of reinstatement	1973	1975	1950	1931	–	–
Court procedure (preliminary mandatory conciliation, competent court(s), existing arbitration, time limits)	1941	1918	1919	1926	1920	1933
Regulation of collective dismissals	1975	–	–	1972	1934[d]	1974
Unemployment insurance	1905[e]	1911	1919[f]	1919	1945	1979

[a] Recognition of the use of temporary contracts as the laws on contracts of employment are only applicable to indefinite contracts.

[b] The law acknowledges the existence of such contracts and provides an attempt to regulate them.

[c] Case law.

[d] Only applicable to public utility undertakings with more than 50 employees.

[e] This very first unemployment insurance system was founded by Decree of September 9, 1905 and consisted of state support to provincial syndicates that established sectorial unemployment benefits schemes for their members.

[f] The Legislative Decree as of 1919 contains information on the Decree No. 670 as of April 29, 1917 introducing a general compulsory unemployment insurance.

of the existing EPL schemes in all these countries. With labour relations still dominated by highly protected workers affiliated to unions (the median voter in union elections) and by firms pushing for a quick implementation of cost-saving policies, the only politically feasible way of allowing for internal and external flexibility in firms' adjustment to demand/supply shocks was through reforms at the margin, that is, only applicable for newcomers. The typical reform made it easier for firms to use fixed-term contracts or TC with low firing costs, without significantly changing the protection of open-ended or PC (see Figure 2.1 where time patterns of OECD indices of EPL strictness are displayed). This resulted in a rapid increase of the share of fixed-term contracts, to the point of eventually representing virtually all hires. Furthermore, subsequent reforms have also

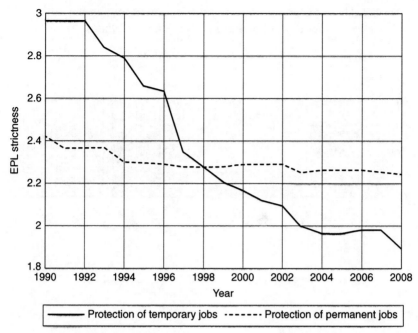

Figure 2.1 Time trends in EPL for permanent and temporary jobs, 1990–2008 (OECD, 2008).

blurred the boundary between dependent employment and self-employment, as illustrated by the growing use of nonregular forms of employment regulated by commercial laws, like freelance work contracts in Italy or contracts for services in Poland (see Bertola et al., 2000, OECD, 2014).

2.3   Temporary Contracts: Stepping Stones or Dead Ends?

It should be evident that temporary work is a key element in the good functioning of any labour market because it is tailor-made to cope with seasonal
changes in demand or other activities of a fixed-term nature (e.g., project-
related, replacement and substitution contracts). On top of that, TC can provide a useful device for employers in screening the quality of job matches,
especially with young inexperienced workers, as well as ease the transition of
entrants towards better stable employment. Indeed, whereas in some countries
(Austria, Denmark, Sweden, UK and US), these jobs become '*stepping stones*'
(see Holmlund and Storrie, 2002, Booth et al., 2002b, Heinrich et al., 2005)[2] to
more stable jobs, the key issue is why they have become '*dead-end*' jobs and a
source of excessive labour market volatility in others (see Boeri and Garibaldi,

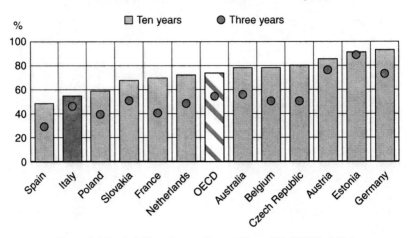

Figure 2.2 Probability of upgrading a TC to a PC (OECD, 2014).

2007). As Figure 2.2 shows, the probability of reaching a PC ten years after entering the labour market with a TC is lower than 60 per cent in countries like Italy or Spain, whereas is close to 100 per cent in Germany. After all, the conventional justification of all these nonregular contracts is to improve the labour market outcomes of disadvantaged workers in countries where employment protection is stringent.

But are temporary contracts really so helpful? In theory, by decreasing firing costs, they can help some workers to accumulate human capital and/or job experience. Yet, in parallel, there is the danger that they may end up moving from one fixed-term contract to another, leading to lower employment stability and no transition towards better jobs (see Blanchard and Landier, 2002, and Cahuc and Postel-Vinay, 2002). Indeed, it has been argued that the large discontinuity created by two-tier EPL schemes (i.e., the so-called EPL gap) in dual labour markets has negative consequences on unemployment, human capital accumulation and innovation. This is so because a large gap in redundancy pay leads to excessive worker turnover. In effect, given this discontinuity in EPL and the lack of wage flexibility, firms prefer to use TC in sequence rather than converting them into PC. The reason is that in case of dismissal, the latter become much more expensive, and wage rigidity prevents offsetting transfers from workers to firms in exchange for being insured against job losses (see Lazear, 1990). As a result, as the expected duration of temporary jobs gets

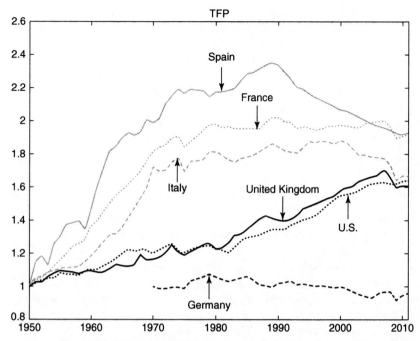

Figure 2.3 TFP in some OECD countries (Index 1950 = 1, Fernández-Villaverde and Ohanian, 2015).

shorter, firms become more reluctant to invest in workers' training because they can benefit less from this investment in human capital.

By the same token, temporary workers may lack the right incentives to improve on their job performance through exerting more effort and accumulating better productive capabilities. Further, given that these skills are important determinant of multifactor productivity, this mechanism may have played a relevant role in explaining the unsatisfactory development of TFP growth in EU countries with segmented labour markets, as depicted in Figure 2.3.

The empirical evidence about the impact of temporary work on labour market outcomes shows that, in general, it could be beneficial in unified labour markets (*stepping stones*) while it is unambiguously detrimental in dual labour markets (*dead ends*). As mentioned above, this is especially the case when wage bargaining is ruled by an insider-outsider model which prevents wages to offset labour turnover costs. For example, Zijl et al. (2004) and Dolado et al. (2015a) find that TC do not improve access to PC. Furthermore, they create excessive wage pressure (see Bentolila and Dolado, 1994), lead to low firms' training investments on workers (see Cabrales et al., 2014, OECD) and incentivize the adoption of mature rather than innovative technologies (see Saint-Paul, 2000, Bassanini et al., 2009, Garcia-Santana et al., 2015). Thus, it is quite well established that the coexistence of workers with quite different seniority rights could have important undesirable consequences for wage setting, human capital accumulation and even for the political economy of labour market reforms (see Saint-Paul, 1996). For example, given than the median voter in union elections is often a worker with a PC, reforms entailing cuts in EPL will take place in recessions, when this type of workers feel the risk of losing their jobs, instead of in expansions, when the benefits of higher contractual flexibility would translate into higher job creation rather than job destruction (Wasmer, 1999).

2.4   Dual Labour Markets Before and After the Great Recession

Overall, the Great Moderation and GR periods have shown that economies with higher segmentation in the labour market exhibited most of the following salient features:
1. A growing specialization in low value-added sectors (such as construction, tourism or personal services) as the engine of rapid output and employment growth during expansions, followed by very dramatic negative adjustments during recessions,
2. A significant productivity (TFP) slowdown,
3. A high dropout rate both in secondary and tertiary education, together with an increasing degree of over-education among college graduates,
4. Large immigration inflows,
5. A very large cyclical volatility in the labour market.

There is an extensive literature analysing the developments of these economies from the early 1990s to the mid-2000s, before the onset of the GR (Dolado et al., 2002, OECD, 2004, and Boeri, 2010). However, a common feature of these studies is that they address the above-mentioned salient features separately or, at best, they treat them from a partial equilibrium viewpoint. For example, there are studies dealing with the rise of the construction sector and its complementarities with the immigration (see Gonzalez and Ortega, 2011), as well as with innovation deficit and specialization in low-value added sectors (see Cingano et al., 2010). Given this background, it would be advisable for future research to unify all these themes under the umbrella of a single (general equilibrium) framework. This could be useful to understand the course of events, which has led to the current recession, as well as to draw policy lessons for subsequent recovery. The basic roadmap guiding this unifying approach could be as follows:
1. Following large cuts in real interest rates, as a result of the Great Moderation period in general and of accession to the EZ in particular, future profitability of mid- and long-run investment projects experienced a large boost in

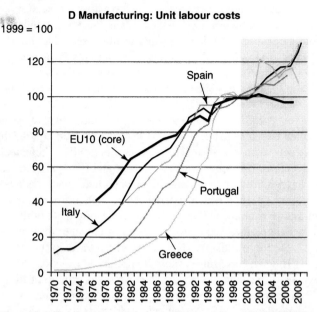

Figure 2.4 Unit labour costs in some EU countries, 1970–2008 (Eurostat).

several EU countries, especially in those with high inflation whose nominal interest rates became assimilated to the German ones. In countries with dual EPL, for reasons spelled out in the next paragraph, cheap credit fuelled job creation through flexible TC in less skilled labour-intensive sectors. These were fixed-duration jobs which are much cheaper to open and destroy than permanent jobs (leading to the so-called '*honeymoon effect*'; cf. Boeri and Garibaldi, 2007). The fact that the latter were subject to high statutory and red-tape dismissal costs inhibited job creation either through PC or conversion of TC into PC. That initial surge in job creation led to a rise in school drop-out rates and to lower on-the-job training. As regards the first phenomenon, high wages paid in the growing industries meant larger opportunity costs for youth staying in school. With regard to the second feature, it was due to the fact that in most of these countries neither temporary workers nor firms creating these jobs had incentives to accumulate and provide much human capital, as reflected by the low rate of conversions from temporary to permanent jobs (see Dolado et al., 2015a, and Cabrales et al., 2014). This hampered TFP growth and increased unit labour costs (as a result of the high demand for real estate), reinforcing the choice of retarded technologies (see Figure 2.4). For example, employment in the construction sector reached levels close to 15 per cent of overall employment. Furthermore, the widespread use of temporary contracts led to a huge workers' turnover rate, which increased labour market risk impinging negatively on labour mobility, household formation decisions and fertility (see Ahn and Mira, 2001, and Becker et al., 2010). Not surprisingly, this *'job-bust, baby-bust'* phenomenon, with negative consequences for the sustainability of pay-as-you-go pension systems, has been further aggravated during the GR (see Figure 2.5).

2. As mentioned earlier, these mechanisms implied a relative abundance of less-skilled labour which favoured large investments in nontradable industries like construction and some service sectors (tourism, hotel and catering etc.), as well as in the public sector (Greece and Portugal). Notice that this did not happen in other countries with more unified labour markets (and better education systems) which experienced similar cuts in real interest rates. A well-known example is Finland, which in the aftermath of the collapse of its main trade partner, the USSR, invested in IT rather than in *'bricks and mortars'*. On top of this, the dual nature of contracts in the labour market induced a rigid wage-setting system (Bentolila and Dolado, 1994) making it inadequate to specialize in more innovative sectors: more flexibility would have been required to accommodate the higher degree of uncertainty associated with producing riskier higher value-added goods (see Saint-Paul, 1997 and Beaudry et al., 2010). In parallel, the size of the cohorts entering the labour market (e.g., someone born in 1980 and entering the labour market in 1996 after completing or dropping out of compulsory lower-secondary education), proved to be too small for the needs of the highly labour-intensive sectors where entrepreneurs had targeted their investment. As a result, large inflows of less-skilled immigrants were attracted, as in Italy or Spain (see Figure 2.6). The rapid increase in the population of these countries meant an additional increase in the demand for residential housing, which was further reinforced by the higher demand of youth workers, stemming from an increasing home-leaving rate resulting from the high employment growth process fuelled by the booming sectors. Thus, *'Say's law'* got resurrected in labour markets subject to strong search frictions: supply created its own demand and mortgage loans soared.

3. Since the industrial structure chosen in some of the Southern-European countries had favoured the expansion of small- and medium-sized firms, which heavily relied on cheap credit, the financial crisis hit these companies hard, leading to bank failures and the burst of housing bubbles (see Bentolila et al., 2014). The large gap between the firing costs of permanent and temporary workers and the lack of response of insider-dominated bargained wages led to a free fall of employment where flexible TC bore most of the burden and the unemployment rate surged. Moreover, the uncertainty surrounding TC as *stepping stones* to indefinite contracts gave rise to

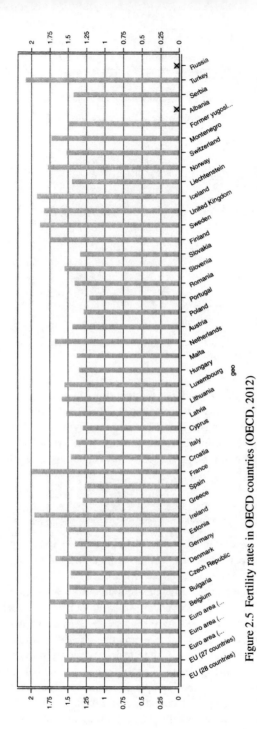

Figure 2.5 Fertility rates in OECD countries (OECD, 2012)

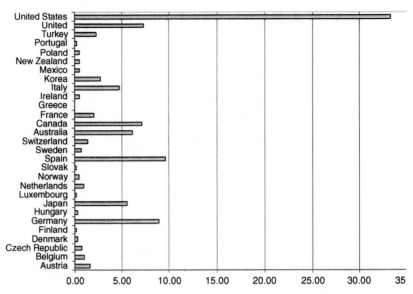

Figure 2.6 Immigration inflows in some OECD countries (2000–2007).

very low geographical mobility and therefore a higher mismatch (the Beveridge curve shifts outwards in countries like France and Spain, whereas it shifts inwards in countries like Germany; see Figure 2.7). Higher mismatch reinforces higher equilibrium unemployment via a reallocation shock compounded with the initial aggregate financial shock (see Carrillo-Tudela and Visschers, 2014).

2.5   Lessons from Spain

Having become the epitome of a dual labour market, Spain provides the best illustration of the pervasive effects that temporary contracts may have in the long run. For almost three decades (see Figure 2.8), about one-third of employees worked on this type of contracts, although currently the rate of temporariness has gone down to about 25 per cent since temporary workers have suffered massive layoffs during the GR and the subsequent sovereign debt crisis. Thus, without any substantial changes, it seems that TC will remain the predominant entry route to employment as the Spanish economy starts recovering (see Caggese and Cunat, 2010). This seems to be the case in 2014 and 2015 when temporary employment is shooting up again and conversion rates remain low.[3] In a recent paper using Spanish social security data, García-Pérez et al. (2014) find that cohorts of native male high-school dropouts who entered the labour

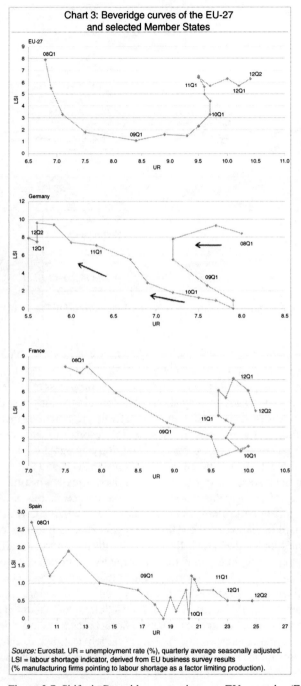

Figure 2.7 Shifts in Beveridge curves in some EU countries (Eurostat).

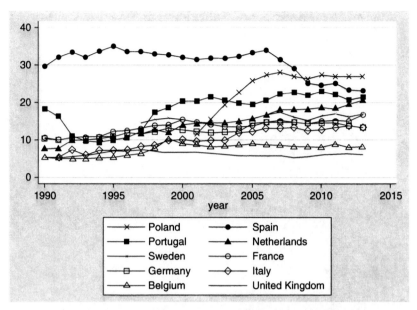

Figure 2.8 Share of temporary work in EU countries (OECD, 2014).

market just after the total liberalization of TC in Spain in 1984, experienced worse labour market outcomes than cohorts that had just preceded them.

Specifically, they spent 200 days at work (i.e., a 7% drop) less than the control group, whereas their wages drop by about 22 per cent in the long run. Lacking any major changes in EPL legislation, these effects are bound to materialize again in the future. Yet, the negative side of TC becomes especially marked once the economy enters a recessionary period. Relying again on the Spanish experience, employment fell by 18 per cent between 2007 and 2013, making it evident that the inadequate design of Spanish labour market institutions and their pervasive effect on industrial specialization are key factors in explaining this extremely volatile employment scenario. In effect, as shown in Figure 2.9, the standard deviation of the (HP filter) cyclical component of employment in Spain doubles the one in the US, but with the important difference that inefficient churning in Spain is mostly borne by one-third of the employees, namely those on temporary contracts, rather than by the whole population. Coupled with a rigid collective bargaining system at the sectoral/provincial level (also anchored in the needs of a rapid transition to democracy in the late 1970s), the dysfunctional design of hiring and firing procedures in Spain forces firms to use external adjustment mechanisms (via job destruction) rather than internal adjustment mechanisms (via wage moderation or reduction in working

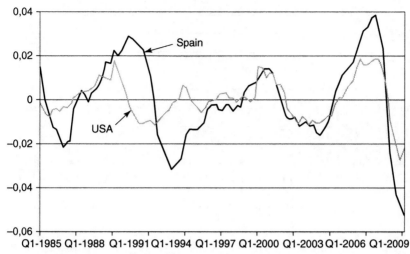

Figure 2.9 Standard deviation of cyclical employment (Spain and US; HP filter, Bentolila et al., 2012a).

time) when hit by adverse shocks. The same happened in Portugal and Greece prior to the GR, before their dual EPL systems were dismantled as part of their memorandums of understanding with the Troika. In contrast, some other EU countries, like, for example, Germany or UK, with similar or greater declines in economic activity, suffered considerably smaller reductions in employment over the GR, basically because of their much lower EPL gaps, higher wage flexibility and less dependent sectoral specialization on low-value added industries. Indeed, before 2010, the EPL gap in Spain between the severance pay of workers with PC (typically 45 days of wages per year of seniority (d.w.y.s) for unfair dismissals) and TC (8 d.w.y.s. or even zero in some cases) was quite substantial. For example, a firm deciding whether to hire a worker on a permanent contract for five years or five workers on fixed-term contracts of one-year each, would pay 225 d.w.y.s. ($= 5 \times 45$) in the first case and 40 ($= 5 \times 8$) in the second case. Furthermore, were the firm to promote a temporary worker to a permanent position after two years, it would bear again a cost of 225 d.w.y.s. in case of dismissal in the fifth year, since the corresponding redundancy pay scheme for PC after the third year also applies to the initial two-year period on TC. Thus the EPL gap would rise to slightly above half a year of wages ($225 - 40 = 165$ days) making the firm reluctant to upgrade temporary contracts. To those gaps, one should add sizeable red-tape cost stemming from the frequent appeals to labour courts by workers dismissed for fair (economic) reasons to get higher mandatory redundancy pay for unfair reasons (see Galdon-Sánchez and Güell,

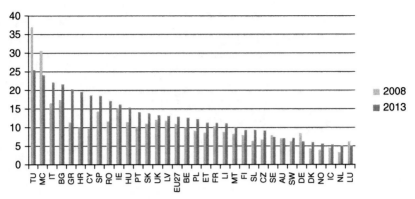

Figure 2.10 Share of temporary work in OECD countries (OECD, 2014).

2003). In this respect, there is concluding evidence showing that almost 45 per cent of the astonishing surge of the Spanish unemployment rate (from 8% to 23%) over 2007–2011 could have been avoided had the EPL gap in red-tape cost been halved to reach the levels in other countries with milder segmentation, as is the case of France (see Bentolila et al., 2012b).[4]

2.6   Dual Labour Markets and Youth Unemployment

It is not surprising that that the countries with the highest youth unemployment and NEET ('not in education, employment, or training') rates in the EU are the olive-belt countries (see Figures 2.10 and 2.11). Greece is a case apart because of its dramatic real GDP contraction of 29 per cent between 2008 and 2013, a fall about five times greater than that experienced in the other three laggard economies (−4.7% in Italy, −6.5% in Portugal and −6.4% in Spain). Yet, Italy, Portugal and Spain share segmented labour markets. Introducing TC for regular activities was key in reducing youth unemployment in otherwise rigid labour markets, since the low employment protection for these contracts made them useful in creating (and destroying) jobs. However, as discussed earlier, the high EPL gap in these countries has led to excessive churning, underemployment and poor training, especially among youth, as reflected by NEET rates among the 15–24 population exceeding 20 per cent in some instances. Yet, there are interesting differences among these countries. Figure 2.12 displays the ratios between youth (15–24) and adult (25–54) unemployment rates as of 2013. As can be observed, the reported ratios are above 3.5 in Italy (also in Sweden and the UK) and close to 3.0 in Portugal, while they lie between 2.0 and 2.5 in Greece and Spain. Notice also that countries with strong dual vocational training systems – like Austria, Germany and Switzerland – exhibit the

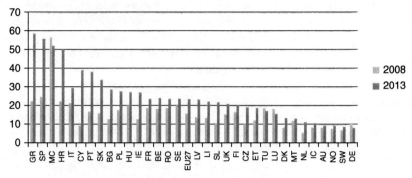

Figure 2.11 NEET rates in OECD countries (OECD, 2014).

lowest ratios. Thus, a lesson to be drawn from this evidence is that in some countries youth labour market problems just reflect general difficulties (Greece and Spain), while in others there is a specific issue about youth (Italy and Portugal).

At any rate, all of the olive-belt countries share a poorly designed vocational training (VT) system. A large share of small firms hinder the use of apprenticeships, lack pre-apprenticeship tracks and the use of Active Labour Market Policies (ALMP) based subsidized permanent contracts is widespread. This has limited impact due to the large substitution effects suggesting that the

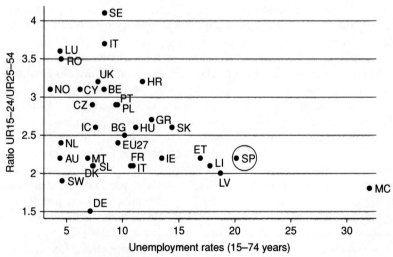

Figure 2.12 Ratio of youth to adult unemployment rates in EU countries (own ellaboration from EU LFS data).

scarring consequences of the GR for youths in these countries are bound to be long-lasting. Further, the recent strong signs of recovery in the Portuguese and Spanish economies have been mostly based on the creation of temporary and part-time jobs so that one cannot discard that in a few years we may observe a repetition of some of the episodes of the past.

The concern that there may be a lost generation led the European Commission to launch the Youth Guarantee (YG) scheme in 2013 as a pledge by member states to ensure that youths under 25 (whether or not they are registered in the public employment services, PES) receive an offer of employment, continued education, an apprenticeship or training within four months of becoming unemployed or leaving formal education. Relying on the successful experiences of some Nordic countries, the YG aims to combine early intervention with activation policies, involving public authorities and all social partners, in order to improve school-to-work transition and the labour market outcomes of youths, especially in the crisis-ridden countries. The EU will top up national spending on YG schemes through the European Social Fund earmarked to help NEETs in regions with youth unemployment exceeding 25 per cent. In comparison with the annual needs, this is clearly an insufficient amount. Yet, as in the case of the Junker Plan for investment in infrastructure, the hope is that the leverage multipliers will be large.

It is too early to evaluate the effects of the YG, but past experience of similar schemes in Scandinavia and elsewhere (Card et al., 2010, 2015) indicates that the expected gains from its introduction are not too large, at least in the short run and in the absence of an agenda to stimulate growth in Europe. Further, there is a risk that the introduction of the YG may delay the adoption of more politically sensitive reforms, such as measures to reduce labour market dualism in the peripheral countries.

Nevertheless, the YG contains elements that may improve the labour market outcomes for youths in Europe. The most important of these is having a specific target in the form of NEETs, rather than a blurred target. The lessons drawn from some successful experiences in Scandinavian countries should be applicable to the rest of Europe. Some will be easier to implement, like the introduction of pre-apprenticeship tracks in the education system or a fruitful collaboration between the PES and private agencies. In exchange for reasonable fees for each difficult NEET that receives one of the above-mentioned offers, the latter could help PES (dealing with the easier cases) in achieving training and job sustainability, initially for disadvantaged young people but later also for older starters. What the YG should definitely avoid is providing unlimited subsidies to firms that rarely translate into stable jobs and lead to a lot of churning due to their deadweight and substitution effects (see García-Pérez and Rebollo, 2009). It should also avoid handing control of training funds over to trade unions and employer associations without strict surveillance by public authorities. As proven in Spain, where there have been several big scandals relating to the mishandling of these funds, this is not a good strategy. Further, the difficulty in implementing apprenticeships and traineeships in small firms could be circumvented by encouraging large (and profitable) firms to support this type of action targeted at small firms.

Finally, a drastic reform of EPL in dual labour markets is paramount. As mentioned earlier and as will be further discussed in the next section, marginal reforms do not seem to work, and the introduction of a single/unified contract with severance pay smoothly increasing with job tenure (up to a cap), or the combination of this and a so-called '*Austrian capitalization fund*' (i.e., workers' notional accounts involving a few percentage points of payroll taxes, which can be used along the lifecycle and not necessarily when a dismissal takes place) should be prioritized before the YG funds reach the countries concerned. The recent approval in Italy in December 2014 of a draft law involving a single open-ended contract shows that the usual excuses from other governments for blocking its introduction – under the claim that it is against their constitutions are not justified. A few fixed-term contracts (e.g., replacement contracts) should be allowed to persist, since they may play a role in rapid job creation when the economy picks up speed (Lepage-Saucier et al., 2013). Even in countries that signed Convention C158 of ILO requiring a cause for termination of employment at the initiative of employers there could be two different profiles of SOEC: one related to economic dismissals and another to unfair dismissals with minimal intervention by judges.

2.7   How to Dismantle Dual Employment Protection Legislation

2.7.1   Recent EPL Reforms

Given the pervasive effects of large EPL gaps documented above and the weakness of dual labour markets during recessions, there has been a growing pressure to close the gap between the severance payments of permanent and temporary contracts.[5]

For example, this was the basic strategy adopted in the last labour market reform in Spain in early 2012, and the recent ones in Greece and Portugal following the intervention of these last two countries by the Troika.[6] In Greece, recent legislation has abolished PC for new employees in all public enterprises and entities though it still needs to rebalance employment protection for different occupations, in particular reduce high severance costs for white-collar workers, in order to bring them in line with those for blue-collar workers.

As for Portugal, the severance payments for PC have been aligned to those of TC (20 d.w.y.s., with a cap of 12 months in total), while a mutual fund to partly finance severance payments has been created. Redundancy pay for the new open-ended contracts has been reduced from 30 to 10 d.w.y.s. plus 10 additional days to be paid by the mutual fund. The preexisting minimum redundancy allowance of three months is eliminated. Total severance pay for fixed-term positions has been reduced from 36 to 10 d.w.y.s for contracts shorter than 6 months and from 24 to 10 d.w.y.s. for longer contracts, again with an additional 10 days from the mutual fund. Finally, in consultation with social partners, the definition of fair individual dismissals for economic reasons has been eased, and the reform of severance payments has been extended to all current contracts, without reduction of accrued-to-date rights.[7]

With regard to Italy, Article 18, which required employers with at least 15 employees to reinstate permanent employees whose employment had been unlawfully terminated, has been changed in the recent Jobs Act reform. Now reinstatement only applies to employees who are dismissed for discriminatory reasons. In contrast, those subject to other unlawful terminations (e.g., due to economic reasons), will only be entitled to mandatory redundancy pay (60 d.w.y.s., with a min. of 4 months' salary and a max. of 24 months), not reinstatement. In addition, project-based employment contracts (co-co-co's), which were often misused by employers, are now prohibited. Finally and foremost, a new type of open-ended employment contract has been introduced including gradual protections for new employees that increase with the employee's job tenure. This contract will be subject to further discussion below.

In Spain, besides other important changes regarding unemployment benefits and collective bargaining, reforms have tried to reduce the EPL gap. However, the gap continues being quite substantial: after the approval of the latest labour market reform in 2012, compensation for end of fixed-term contracts is currently 12 d.w.y.s. (8 d.w.y.s. before), while the mandatory cost of unfair dismissals for all new permanent contracts was set equal to 33 d.w.y.s. (45 d.w.y.s. before), while the cost of fair dismissals remained the same (20 d.w.y.s.). Existing permanent contracts keep the accrued-to-date rights up to the implementation of the 2012 reform, with a cap of 720 d.w.y.s., and the new one afterwards. Additionally, a new PC has been designed for firms with below 50 employees (entrepreneurship contracts) with a probationary period of one year during which firms can lay off workers without a cause and at zero cost. Beyond that period, workers are entitled to the same redundancy payments as workers on ordinary open-ended contracts. The flaw in the design of this contract is the fact that dismissal costs are effectively zero during the first twelve months. This means that the discrete jump in employment protection after twelve months is bigger than the EPL gap between PC and TC. Moreover, this probation period may come after several years of employment on fixed-term contracts, implying that many workers may still be trapped during extended periods on precarious contracts. Overall, this reduction in the gap has not been large enough and the incentive of employers to hire on a permanent contract is still very low (only 8.1% of all contracts signed in 2014 in Spain have been permanent).

2.7.2   Single/Unified Contracts in Theory

As mentioned earlier, the alternative to partial reforms could be to achieve a full convergence through the elimination of most fixed-term contracts and the introduction of a *single open-ended contract* (SOEC) with termination costs smoothly increasing with job tenure (up to a cap) and applied to all workers in line with the Portuguese reform. In principle, the level of termination costs could be chosen in a way that matches each country's social and political preferences for worker protection, thus not necessarily implying convergence towards low degrees of employment protection.[8]

One of the first proposals in this vein was made by a group of Spanish economists (see Andrés et al., 2009 and Dolado, 2012) where they asked for a drastic simplification of the available menu of labour contracts in Spain (more than 40 types) and the implementation of a SOEC with the characteristics listed above. The Spanish proposal is an example of an *extended single contract with reduced dismissal requirement* but with stringent rules for the use of fixed-term contracts. These are allowed for replacements and to contract workers from a temporary work agency. Agency contracts can be used to cover peaks in demand, but the contract between the worker and the TWA would be subject to the same restrictions as the ordinary employment relationships between a firm and its employees. These contracts can also serve to cover seasonal fluctuations in labour demand, but if the firm wishes to hire the same worker several years in a row, they should use what is called a discontinuous open-ended contract that allows for interruptions. Finally, the regulation should include the possibility of training contracts for labour market entrants.

Its basic goal was to prevent massive redundancies before the deadline when firms face the decision of converting TC into PC (between the second and the third year in Spain, depending on the contract type). To avoid legal uncertainty, they propose creating a SOEC with two scales of compensation – corresponding to fair and unfair dismissals (see Bentolila and Jansen, 2012). In particular, they suggest that compensation for TCs should be higher than at present and grow at a moderate rate until it reaches a value similar to the average severance pay in EU countries (around 21 d.w.y.s.). Furthermore, in order to maximize the social and economic benefits of the introduction of the SOEC, they argued that a high degree of legal certainty should be reached in dismissal procedures. Finally, this contract could be part or full-time and should be the basic hiring contract for all firms (some other contracts could also be needed: for example a well-designed training contract and an interim contract that could cover most of the companies' needs to train and/or replace workers). Firms could use Temporary Help Agencies, which should also hire their workers under this SOEC to accommodate their short-term hiring needs. Figure 2.13 presents an example for a SOEC which begins with severance payments as it is currently the case for a TC in Spain (12 days) after seven years, and ends up with the same rate

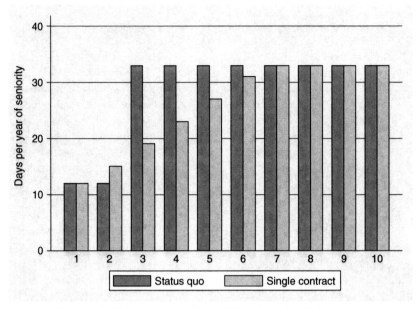

Figure 2.13 Severance pay in Spain (Bentolila et al., 2012a).

as it is currently the case for permanent contracts, under unfair dismissals (33 days).

García-Pérez and Osuna (2014) have recently quantified the steady-state effects of introducing a similar SOEC in Spain. In particular, they simulate the effects of the so-called '12–36 Single-Contract' (12–36 SOEC), where compensation starts as before from 12 d.w.y.s. and smoothly increases by 2 days for each additional year of tenure, until it reaches a cap of 36 d.w.y.s. (see Figure 2.12).[9] The main goal of this simulation is to compare the steady-state effects of introducing this SOEC with the EPL rules prevailing in Spain until 2012 (status quo), when a new EPL reform was implemented (see further below in this section). The main findings are that both unemployment (by 21.0%) and the job destruction rate (by 28.0%) decrease substantially with the introduction of the aforementioned SOEC. What is most interesting is that the tenure distribution could be smoother than under the status quo, as 22.5 per cent more workers could have job tenures exceeding three years, whereas there would be 38.5 per cent fewer one-year contracts. The insight for these results is that the job destruction rate of the TC rate was still rather high under the status quo because the EPL gap induced massive firings at the beginning of the fourth year in order to prevent the high future severance costs of PCs in the event of a contract conversion. Under the proposed SOEC, however, the probability of being fired on contracts with tenure equal to or below three years is reduced substantially (from 26.7% to 6.1%) because, with the smoother tenure profile of redundancy pay, the pervasive incentives to destroy jobs at the termination of fixed-term contracts (beginning of fourth year) are largely diminished.

Regarding welfare consequences, see García-Pérez and Osuna (2014), a transition exercise is also presented that shows that the SOEC would be highly beneficial for the majority of workers, especially for the unemployed, because their prospective job stability increases quite substantially. According to their calculations, less than 5.5 per cent would experience reduced tenure as a result of this reform, while 24.6 per cent would not be affected, ending up with the same severance payments and tenure as if the system remained unchanged. For firms, this contract would not necessarily increase the average expected severance cost because job destruction is lower than under current legislation. In fact, the average compensation (weighted by the job destruction rate for any duration) decreases by 9.1 per cent. Another advantage from the firms' point of view would be the reduction in the degree of uncertainty due to the much simpler schedule of dismissal costs under a SOEC. However, for this to be true, it would also be necessary to redefine the legal reasons for firing so that uncertainty over the type of firing and over the official decision on its fairness is reduced.

There have been similar proposals for introducing SOEC in France (see Blanchard and Tirole, 2004, and Cahuc and Kramarz, 2005), Italy (see Boeri and Garibaldi, 2008 and Garibaldi and Taddei, 2013), Poland (see Arak et al., 2014) and Portugal (see Portugal, 2011). Although the details vary (see next section), most basic features are common. First, the distinction between a fixed-term and an open-ended contract in terms of workers' protection disappears and, secondly, the tenure profile of compensations under the SOEC increases gradually rather than abruptly.

However, it is interesting to distinguish three types of single-contract proposals.[10] A first type would consist of introducing a new open-ended contract for new hires with an '*entry*' phase (say 4 years), during which worker entitlements in the case of dismissal are reduced and identical in the case of both fair and unfair dismissal, and a '*stability*' phase, during which the worker would obtain the standard PC with no changes in his/her rights in case of termination.[11] As explained in OECD (2014), the main problem of this proposal resides in the difficulty of eliminating the discontinuity induced by passing from the '*entry*' to the '*stability*' phase, to the extent that worker rights in current open-ended contracts are different in the case of fair and unfair dismissal. Therefore, employers would generally face a strong disincentive to keep their employees beyond the '*entry*' phase.

A second type of single-contract, like the one advocated by Andrés et al. (2009) explicitly aims at avoiding discontinuities in severance payments and, thus, proposes a smooth increase of the job tenure profile coupled with a redefinition of unfair dismissal, which should be restricted only to cases of discrimination and prohibited grounds. One shortcoming of this type of proposals is that, by tying workers' rights to the firm where they are working, it is likely to reduce efficient turnover and prevent mobility across jobs. In order to address this problem, the idea of a SOEC based on experience-increasing rights to severance pay has also been explored (Lepage-Saucier et al., 2013). In this case, for the whole duration of the employment relationship, employers would pay additional social security contributions into a fund tied to the worker, as the one in place in Austria since 2003, which could be carried across jobs when the worker changes employers. Then if the worker is dismissed, the fund would finance his/her severance pay. However, as explained in Blanchard and Tirole (2008), this system may create excessive firing (i.e., inducing a social cost), which could be prevented by financing unemployment benefits by layoff taxes (as in the US experience-rate system) deposited in a Mutual Fund. An alternative based on a mixed model where severance payments and a capitalization fund coexist has been proposed for Spain by Conde-Ruiz et al. (2011). The main objective here is to restrict the standard application of LIFO (*last in, first out*) rules in the firms' firing decisions by reducing the marginal cost of dismissal for all workers, thus making continuation easier in the firm, especially for younger workers.

An important caveat in the aforementioned proposals is that suppressing all fixed-term contracts would run the risk of introducing excessive rigidity in hiring decisions and could lead to less employment growth, especially during recovery upturns, given that not all temporary jobs would be substituted by permanent ones. Furthermore, it may also foster the use of other types of atypical contracts, as the ones mentioned above, that is an even less protected form of employment. In this case, an alternative could be what Cahuc (2012) calls a *unified contract* with the same termination costs applying to all contracts, except in cases of discrimination and prohibitive grounds, irrespectively of whether they are TC or PC but embedded in a unified contract. In other words, the new contract can be formalized as a fixed-term contract or a regular open-ended contract, and upon termination the firm needs to pay redundancy pay to the worker and a solidarity contribution to the state. This layoff tax would yield resources to mutualize the reallocation costs of displaced workers and induce firms to internalize the social cost of dismissals, without any need of reinstating workers, if set at a sufficiently high level (Cahuc and Zylberberg, 2008). Payment of the solidarity contribution frees the firm from the obligation to offer reintegration or outplacement services to dismissed workers. These costs are mutualized and the assistance to the unemployed is provided by the PES. The unified contract combines essential features of the existing fixed-term and open-ended positions in France. Firms that sign fixed-term contracts are committed to pay the wages until the pre-fixed end of the contract. This means that an employer must pay the employee until the end of the contract in case of a premature termination (except in case of *force majeure*). Moreover, French employers are obliged to pay workers on fixed-term contracts a bonus equal to 10 per cent of the worker's gross salary at the moment of termination to compensate the employee for the instability of the relationship.

Relying on these ideas, recent research by Dolado et al. (2015b) develops an equilibrium search and matching model to investigate the effects of introducing a SOEC in a labour market subject to EPL discontinuities, such that its tenure profile is chosen according to some pre-specified welfare function. A distinctive feature of this model is that workers are risk averse and therefore demand insurance to smooth out consumption in the presence of productivity shocks. In addition, their model has a lifecycle structure where young and older workers coexist in the labour market. Both receive severance pay but differ as regards the use they can make of this compensation. While young workers are modelled as living from hand to mouth, and therefore consume dismissal compensation upon reception (say, because of binding credit constraints associated to lower job stability), older workers are allowed to buy annuities in order to smooth out their consumption until retirement. The latter feature captures the fact that older workers often have a hard time re-entering the labour market close to retirement. In this way, job security provided by EPL can play an important role in bridging the gap until full retirement.

Optimality is defined in terms of the welfare (defined in terms of consumption-equivalent units) of a newborn in a steady state but the average welfare across the current population at the time of the EPL reform is also considered when taking into account the transition from a dual EPL system to the chosen SOEC. In particular, during the transition workers with existing matches have redundancy pay according to the accrued-to date rights until the date when the reform is approved, while later on the new redundancy profile applies. For illustrative purposes, the model is calibrated to the Spanish labour market before the GR, at a time when the unemployment rate in this country was similar to the EU average rate, namely about 8.5 per cent, which seems to be a reasonable estimate for a steady-state equilibrium. An alternative insurance mechanism to SOEC is provided by an unemployment insurance (UI) system that is financed through social security contributions. Using conventional values for the coefficient of risk aversion, UI replacement rates, quit rates (not entitled to EPL) and share of red-tape costs, they find that an initial '*entry*' phase of one year (with no redundancy pay in case of termination) and a slope of 14 d.w.y.s. maximize the chosen welfare criterion. Figure 2.14 shows the status quo (cumulated) tenure profile in 2008 (8 d.w.y.s. for the first two years and 45 d.w.y.s. later on, with a cap of 42 months),[12] at the onset of the GR, and the optimal SOEC.

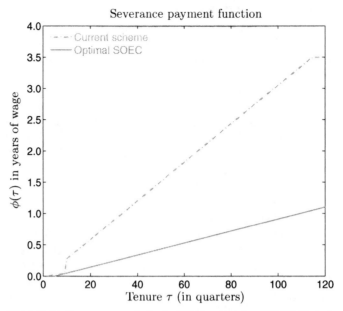

Figure 2.14 Severance pay in Spain (2008) and optimal SOEC (Dolado et al., 2015b).

This profile is rather robust to the above-mentioned parameter values, except when risk aversion increases and the slope becomes 11 d.w.y.s. or when quits or the share of red-tape costs increase, in if which case the slope goes down up to 4 or 5 d.w.y.s. Compared to the status quo in a steady state, this SOEC implies an increase in welfare of 2.8 per cent, an increase in output of 1.1 per cent and, foremost, a reduction in the job destruction rate of about 1 percentage point (pp.) and a rise in the job creation rate of around 3 pp. It is worth noticing that during the transition, job destruction increases initially due to the lower slope of the SOEC but then converges to a lower steady-state value after two years (see Figure 2.15).[13] By contrast, the job finding rates immediately jumps to a much higher steady-state value (see Figure 2.16).[14] Overall, youth unemployment and the nonemployment of older workers go down by about 10 and 15 per cent, respectively. Furthermore, using the welfare function for the whole population at the time of the reform, Table 2.2 shows the fraction of each group of workers (defined by age and labour market status) who would benefit from the implementation of this SOEC and who therefore would be in favour, against or indifferent to this EPL reform.

Finally, a comparison is made between the welfare gains of implementing SOEC and the reduction of the gap in severance pay that took place in the 2012

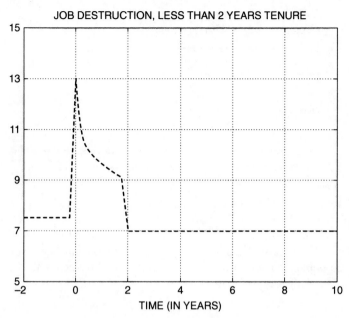

Figure 2.15 Job destruction rate during transition (Dolado et al., 2015b).

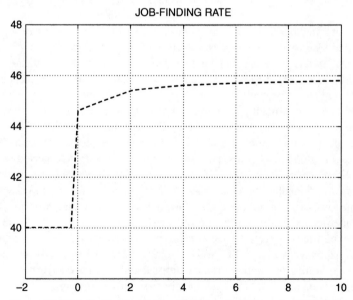

Figure 2.16 Job finding rate during transition (Dolado et al., 2015b).

Table 2.2 *Political support for transition to SOEC*
(Dolado et al., 2015b)

		Pro	Con	Indiff
Young workers	Employed	100[a]	0	0
	Not employed	100	0	0
Older workers	Employed	31.7	68.3	0
	Not employed	0	0	100
Overall		79.7	10.2	10.1

[a] All numerical entries refer to population measures in per cent.

EPL reform, when EPL for unfair dismissals of workers on PC went down from 45 d.w.y.s. to 33 d.w.y.s, whereas compensation for nonrenewal of TC went up gradually from 8 d.w.y.s. to 12 d.w.y.s. The main finding is that while SOEC will bring in a welfare gain (in terms of consumption equivalent units for the current population at the time of the reform) of 1.93 per cent, the 2012 reform would imply half of that gain.

2.7.3   Single/Unified Contracts in Practice

Nonetheless, a key requirement of all these proposals is the restriction of the definition of unfair dismissal to false reasons, discrimination and prohibited grounds. In other words, any economic motive or personal reason related to the worker's performance (such as reduction of individual productivity or unsuitability) would be a fair and justified reason for dismissal, with the judicial review of courts restricted to just assessing that the purported reason is not in fact masking prohibited grounds. However, implementing this requirement might be very difficult in countries whith a long tradition of judicial review of employers' decisions (see Ichino et al., 2003 and Jimeno et al., 2015).[15] For this reason, since the aim of SOEC is to ensure that open-ended contracts become the default option of firms, they should include a probation period to screen applicants, as Dolado et al. (2015b) suggest. The objective is not to eliminate short-duration jobs, but rather to avoid the rotation of temporary workers on the same job as a means to save costs. Nonetheless, it is clear that the termination of an open-ended contract is more costly and/or time-consuming for the firm than the expiration of a fixed-term contract. This is true even if redundancy pay were equalized across TC and PC. Workers on PC must receive an advance notification explaining the motive for the dismissal and they have a right to challenge this decision in court. Moreover, the dismissal of several workers within a short time may entitle the worker to higher compensation or additional services as part of a collective dismissal procedure. None of these obligations exists in case of fixed-term positions when the relationship is terminated at the scheduled date or in accordance with the predetermined conditions for termination. Hence proposals that advocate the abolishment of most TC and their replacement by a SOEC with increasing severance pay at ever slower rates would face the problem that almost any worker could appeal to labour courts, so that the labour market would end up being run by judges making it more rigid rather than more flexible.

One solution to this problem may be provided by the introduction of a new open-ended contract with slowly increasing redundancy pay in the recent Jobs Act reform in Italy (see Ichino, 2014). The Jobs Act comes on top of two earlier reforms that restricted the application of the right to reinstatement (Article 18) and that exempted firms from the obligation to state a cause for the temporary nature of the employment relationship. The main advantage of the newly created contract is the fact that it eliminates the discrete jump in dismissal payments for unfair dismissals. After the Monti-Fornero reform in 2012, firms had to make redundancy payment between 12 and 24 for months for an unfair dismissal for economic motives. The Jobs Act replaces this severance pay with a smooth schedule and introduces a fast-track settlement. While a legal decision entitles the worker to redundancy pay of 60 d.w.y.s. (min. 4 months and max. 24 months) subject to income taxation, the *fast-track* settlement guarantees redundancy payment of 30 d.w.y.s. (min. 2 months and max. 18 months) exempted of income taxation. Figure 2.17 illustrates the job tenure profiles of the two modalities of single contract in terms of monthly wages. Furthermore, offering this single contract for new hiring entails a reduction of employers' social security contribution for three years (with a cap of € 8,060). Besides new hiring, the new contract can be offered to workers after conversion from a TC. In parallel, fixed-term contracts entail no redundancy pay to workers upon termination of the contract. One could argue that this is equivalent to a unified contract as firms are not obliged to pay an indemnity in case of a fair dismissal either, but the fast-track settlement may lead to a situation in which firms prefer to pay an indemnity after any dismissal to avoid the cost and uncertainty associated with lengthy legal procedures. If so, then the economic costs of terminations are clearly not equalized across all contingencies.

A similar contract to the Italian '*fast track*' has been used in Spain since 1980 under the slightly different labelling of '*express dismissal*'. In order to avoid lengthy legal processes in labour courts and the associated payment of interim wages, firms in Spain can deposit the mandatory amount of compensation for unfair dismissal (33 d.w.y.s. nowadays and 45 d.w.y.s. before the 2012 reform) in the labour court within two days of the redundancy and, in case of withdrawing this deposit, the worker is not be entitled to appeal to a labour court. A noticeable difference with the fast-track contract is that the two tenure profiles in Figure 2.16 would be reduced to a single profile in Spain, namely, one that

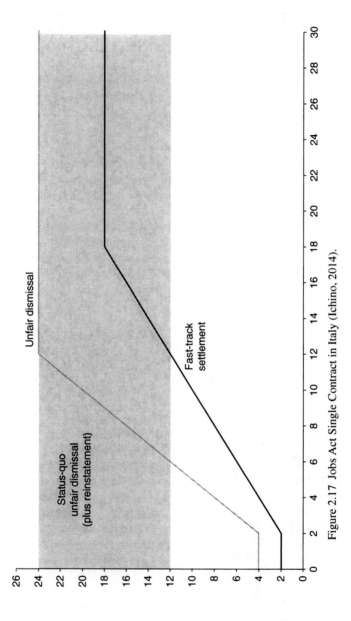

Figure 2.17 Jobs Act Single Contract in Italy (Ichino, 2014).

involves the highest redundancy pay. Although Spanish employers could avoid paying expected red-tape costs in case of appeal, the *'express dismissal'* led them to layoffs for unfair reasons even in the deepest troughs of the business cycle; for example above two-thirds of individual dismissals in Spain during the GR were filed under this category, although it was a period where redundancies for economic reasons should have been the norm rather than the exception.

The Italian *'fast-track'* contract avoids this shortcoming by both cutting the firm's conventional costs of unfair dismissals and benefiting workers, since the after-tax *'fast-track'* compensation is likely to be more attractive than the gross mandatory one, at least for workers with long tenures.[16] Yet, in light of the results in Dolado et al. (2015b), albeit in a model calibrated for Spain, the mandatory severance pay in both options of the unified contract seems excessive: 30 d.w.y.s. in the *'fast track'* is about the same as the unfair dismissal rate in Spain after 2012 (33 d.w.y.s.). Yet, it reaches a cap of 12 months after 18 years while in Spain the cap of 24 months is reached after 22 years. By the same token, a rate of 60 d.w.y.s. for the conventional unfair-dismissal option is about twice the corresponding rate in Spain, but again the cap of 24 months is reached much earlier (in 12 months) than in Spain. At any rate, recent evidence on the Italian unified contract is positive: the share of PC in all contracts signed each month has doubled since its implementation, going up from 17 per cent to 35 per cent. In contrast, the corresponding share in Spain still remains below 10 per cent.

In addition, as in Spain, the new contract in Italy is heavily subsidized in the first three years. Though it is still too early to evaluate its success, a key question is whether its promising start in early 2015 will continue once the subsidies are phased out. The conclusive evidence in Spain about considerable substitution (employees with nonsubsidized contracts replaced by others with subsidized contracts) and deadweight (employers would have hired workers irrespectively of the subsidies) is likely to apply to Italy as well, given the step tenure profile of redundancy pay chosen for the new contract. Moreover, the Jobs Act does not involve any employer's contribution to a capitalization fund, as in Austria, to inhibit the low labour mobility in this country. In this respect, a potentially good idea for countries with high youth unemployment and NEET could be that a fraction of redundancy pay should go to financing training courses. This amount should be transferred to a notional account in the name of the dismissed worker and its availability to the worker should be conditional on having found a job. In this way, there would be an incentive for job search so as to maximize the remaining balance in the notional account that the worker could receive in cash (see Garcia-Perea and Molinas, 2015).

A final issue to consider is the role that higher wage flexibility may bring about in reducing the employment turnover effects of dual EPL. Reforms following the crisis in southern European countries have made wages much more flexible than before. Even if the scars of the GR have made individuals more risk averse than in the past, it may be conjectured that EPL in general and dual EPL in particular may have smaller real effects than in the past.

2.8   Conclusions

This chapter has tried to show how both theoretical models and good empirics can help identify the features of labour market models with contractual diversity that push them to become dual labour markets, and the pros and cons of dualism. Our emphasis has been on how a combination of historical facts, politico-economic models and search and matching models can deliver testable predictions and also policy recommendations which help describe the past in a coherent way and improve the future. Where do we see the research on Dual Labour Markets moving over the near future? A first direction is to have better datasets combining information reflecting incentives for temporary and permanent workers. For instance, there are no longitudinal datasets on the relative productivity of workers under PC and TC, nor on the probability of the latter being upgraded. This is important because, according to that view, TC is a screening device and tournament considerations should be quite relevant. For example, temporary workers could end up exerting more effort than permanent workers, and employers may react by offering them more training, like in the *stepping stone* hypothesis. Having this data available would help understand how multiple equilibria can arise and identify the best possible way of transiting from a bad equilibrium (dead end) to a good one (springboards).

A second avenue of research is to investigate further the dynamics of social partners. How do the characteristics of pivotal workers in trade unions and employer associations' election change with the business cycle or with reforms entailing more or less duality? In this way, we would be able to characterize the dynamics of political support to different types of reforms, we would know when are they triggered and who the winners and losers are.

A third avenue of research is to dig deeper into the role of labour market dualism into technology adoption. It is often argued that temporary contracts arise because of the sectoral composition of some economies (e.g., those where the weather is better and tourism or construction is a leading sector) but, as argued above, maybe causality is also relevant the other way around: EPL regulations provide incentives to invest in specific sectors which are profitable in the short run but may be more vulnerable in the medium and longer runs.

Finally, we need more theoretical work to evaluate the different proposals in relation to single/unified contracts in setups where workers can have insurance against job losses through a variety of mechanisms: savings, unemployment insurance, EPL, etc.

Acknowledgements

This chapter is based on a survey prepared for presentation at the COEURE workshop on Dual Labour Markets, Brussels, June 2015. I am grateful to all participants in this workshop for valuable ideas and suggestions that helped improve a preliminary draft. Part of the ideas contained in this chapter stem from joint research and endless discussions with Samuel Bentolila, Florentino Felgueroso, Marcel Jansen and Juan Jimeno, whose inputs are gratefully acknowledged.

Appendix

Summary of Proposals

Single Contract

Spain

The original Spanish proposal Andrés et al. (2009), known under the name of Contrato Unico or Contrato de Igualdad de Oportunidades, contemplated the introduction of a single contract with a unique severance pay schedule for economic dismissals that increases gradually with tenure, starting at a level comparable to the one that firms in Spain need to pay upon termination of a fixed-term position and ending at a level somewhere in between the costs associated with fair (20 days of salary p.y.o.s) and unfair dismissals (45 days of salary) for the existing open-ended contracts.[17] This first proposal suppressed the distinction between fair and unfair dismissals for economic dismissals. As this suppression could be interpreted as a violation of the right to legal protection against unfair dismissals, a later version proposed separate schedules for fair and unfair dismissals (Bentolila and Jansen, 2012). Under the legal fast track that existed at the time (despido expres Law 45/2002), employers could opt to pay the indemnity associated with unfair dismissals to bypass legal control on the economic causes of the dismissal. In practical terms, the two proposals therefore had the same implications.

Italy

Boeri and Garibaldi (2008) launched an alternative proposal for a single contract with an extended trial period known under the name of Contratto Unico a Tiempo Indeterminato. Their proposal is an example of a single contract with an extended trial period. An employment relationship would start with an entry stage of up to three years in which workers would only be entitled to a redundancy payment in case of an unfair dismissal, equal to 5 days of salary per month of work (60 days of wages p.y.o.s) and a maximum of six months of salary (180 days). After this entry phase, the contract enters the stability phase in which the worker is entitled to the full employment protection of the existing open-ended contracts. At the time, this included the right to reinstatement after an unfair dismissal for economic motives if the worker was employed in a firm with more than 15 employees (Art. 18). This discontinuity would have induced a strong discontinuity in the level of protection that would probably have caused considerable churning around the three year threshold as it is comparable to the costs associated in Italy with the conversion of fixed-term into open-ended contract. However, it should be stressed that the right to reinstatement has been severely limited in Italy since the adoption of the Monti-Fornero reform in 2012.

The proposal of Boeri and Garibaldi (2008) does not foresee the elimination of fixed-term contracts or freelance contracts, but rather than specifying specific tasks or contingencies for the use of nonregular contracts, their use is restricted on the basis of salary thresholds. Fixed-term contracts would be allowed in jobs with an annual gross salary above € 20,000 and freelance contracts for workers who earn more than € 30,000 per year. In other words, Boeri and Garibaldi propose the introduction of a single contract for low-paid workers as these are the workers that are most exposed to the risk of lengthy periods of employment in precarious contracts. By contrast, for skilled workers the proposal preserves the choice between fixed-term and open-ended positions.

It is clear from the above discussion that the Italian proposal is more conservative than the Spanish one. In part this can be explained by the much higher incidence of fixed-term contracts in Spain since their use was liberalized in 1984. Moreover, workers in Spain are not entitled to reinstatement after an unfair dismissal for economic motives and the fast track mentioned above offered a secure (but expensive) procedure for dismissals.

Unified Contract

France

Economists in France have formulated several proposals for the introduction of a unified contract. The most recent and detailed proposal is the recent proposal for a unified contract by Cahuc (2012). It is based on a 2005 proposal of Francis Kramarz and Pierre Cahuc. Cahuc proposes the introduction of a new contract in which the legal cost of termination depends exclusively on seniority. The new contract can be formalized as a fixed-term contract or a regular open-ended contract, and upon termination the firm needs to pay a redundancy compensation to the worker and a solidarity contribution to the state. Payment of the solidarity contribution frees the firm from the obligation to offer reintegration or outplacement services to dismissed workers. These costs are mutualized under Cahuc's proposal and the assistance to the unemployed is provided by the Public Employment Services.

The unified contract combines essential features of the existing fixed-term and open-ended positions in France. Firms that sign fixed-term contracts are committed to pay the wages until the pre-fixed end of the contract. This means that an employer must pay the employee until the end of the contract in case of a premature termination (except in case of *force majeure*). Moreover, French employers are obliged to pay workers on fixed-term contracts a bonus equal to 10 per cent of the worker's gross salary at the moment of termination to compensate the employee for the instability of the relationship.

By contrast, workers on open-ended contracts are entitled to redundancy pay for tenures above 18 months. The unified contract combines both monetary compensations in a single redundancy pay schedule for economic dismissals. During the first 18 months of any contract the worker is entitled to a redundancy payment of 10 per cent of the gross wages and from then onwards the redundancy payment grows at the same rate as in the existing open-ended contracts (20% of a monthly salary for each year of service until 10 years of tenure and a third of a month salary per year of service for job tenures above 10 years). Moreover, after any separation the firm has to pay a solidarity contribution which equals 1.6 per cent of the total wage sum.

The proposal creates a single redundancy pay schedule without any breaks as the difference between fair and unfair dismissals for economic motives is suppressed. In Cahuc's proposal, the redundancy payment is the only legal protection against dismissals for economic reasons. Together with the solidarity contribution, they force firms to internalize the social costs of a dismissal, and the legal intervention of judges should therefore be restricted to avoid violations of fundamental rights. Similarly, there is no distinction between the level of protection between individual and collective dismissals. The costs of outplacement services are mutualized through the solidarity contribution, and the assistance to displaced workers is provided by the public employment services.

Italy

In the case of Italy, the best-known example of unified contract proposal is the one formulated by labour law expert Pietro Ichino. His proposal is part of a wider legal initiative to simplify the Italian labour code (see Ichino (2014)). Ichino's proposal foresees the introduction of a new open-ended contract with gradually increasing employment protection that firms can use in future hiring. The contract starts with a probation period of six months. After that time, the right to reinstatement (Art. 18) applies to dismissals due to discrimination, disciplinary motives (when proved unfounded) and dismissals due to other illicit motives. Only economic dismissals entitle the worker to an economic compensation.

The economic motives for dismissals are unified. During the first two years of an employment relationship, being either of a temporary or permanent nature, the worker is entitled to a redundancy payment of one month of salary per year of service. In addition, in case of a dismissal due to economic reasons beyond the third year the worker is entitled to an additional contribution on top of the redundancy payment and the statutory unemployment benefits introduced after the Monti-Fornero reform. This additional component is supposed to bring the replacement rates of the worker during the first months of unemployment to levels comparable to the level prevailing in a country like Denmark, but this point is not essential.

The true value of Ichino's proposal is his defence of redundancy pay as a valid legal instrument against unfair dismissal. The costs associated with dismissals prevent that firms dismiss a worker without some ground and the intervention of the judges should be limited to preventing that these grounds are illicit, that is, judges should not be asked to perform an in-depth review of the economic motives for a dismissal. Thus his views are close to the view of economists who interpret firing costs as a Pigouvian tax that helps to align the private and social costs from separation.

Ichino's proposal does not include outright restrictions on the use of fixed-term contracts. After the introduction of severance pay obligations for fixed-term contracts, the new open-ended contract should offer sufficient advantages to employers and workers to become the voluntary default option in the vast majority of hirings. In that sense, the proposal is less ambitious than the one formulated by Boeri and Garibaldi. By contrast, Ichino is in favour of much stronger limitations on the interventions of judges.

Notes

1. EPL is multidimensional and includes regulations pertaining to severance pay and advance notice of layoffs, restrictions on valid reasons for individual and collective dismissals, rules governing the use of fixed-term contracts, and restrictions concerning temporary work agencies. EPL may affect labour cost directly (via mandated severance pay) or indirectly via red tape costs.
2. See Autor and Houseman (2010) for a more negative view on the role of temporary help-jobs relative to jobs placements through direct-hire employers in the US.
3. Almost 92 per cent of all new hires in Spain over the last two years have relied on temporary contracts. The same happens in Italy (83.4% in 2013 according to Garibaldi and Taddei, 2013).
4. According to the Spanish Labour Force Survey, two-thirds of workers dismissed during that period in Spain had a TC.
5. The evidence offered in García-Pérez and Rebollo (2009) shows that five years of seniority and more than seven contracts were required on average until the year 2008

to earn a PC. Furthermore, almost 40 per cent of the workers who have a TC at the age of 20 still have one at the age of 40.

6. The Netherlands is another EU country where there is widespread use of atypical contracts and which is moving towards a unified contact. The last initiative in this respect is the Wet Werk en Zekerheid (Law on Employment and Security) that became effective on July 2015. This country has traditionally counted on two separate dismissal procedures: (i) administrative approval with no right to redundancy pay, and (ii) dismissals approved in court with a right to redundancy pay according to a pre-established formula ('*kantonrechtersformule*'). The most recent reform creates a single route for all economically motivated dismissals and entitles all workers, irrespective of the fixed-term or open-ended nature of their contracts, to redundancy payment (*transitievergoeding*/transition compensation).

7. The definition of economic dismissals in Portugal has been broadened to include 'unsuitability of the worker'. The latter implies that fair dismissals are not limited to situations of the firm's economic difficulty. Workers may be laid off if they are no longer suited to perform their task. The latter comes very close to the definition of fair dismissals in the UK.

8. In the Annex, we provide further details on the different proposals.

9. There exists a maximum compensation of two years of wages.

10. The following classification is due to Chapter 4 in OECD (2014), where all single contract proposals have been precisely surveyed.

11. This is the proposal Boeri and Garibaldi (2008) made for Italy.

12. For example, the red line in Figure 2.14 indicates that a worker suffering an unfair dismissal after 10 years (40 quarters) of job tenure in a firm, would get a severance package of 1.23 his/her yearly wages ($= 45 \times 20/365$), etc.

13. In the horizontal axis of Figure 2.15 there is time in years prior to the SOEC reform ($t < 0$), at the time of the reform ($t = 0$) and after the reform ($t > 0$). The vertical axis displays job destruction rates in percentage.

14. The meaning of the horizontal axis in Figure 2.16 is as in Figure 2.15. The vertical axis displays job finding rates in percentage.

15. For example, some of the provisions in this respect in the 2012 labour reform in Spain have been restated by some recent court decisions.

16. Assuming an average income tax of 30 per cent, the '*fast track*' compensation would be preferable to the '*unfair*' dismissal compensation when a worker exceeds 16.8 years of employment($= 24$ years $\times 0.7$). Before that it is doubtful unless other administrative costs associated with the appeal, and borne by the worker in case of losing are large.

17. Most of this Appendix has been drafted by Marcel Jansen to whom I am very grateful.

References

Ahn, N., and Mira, P. 2001. Job Bust, Baby Bust: Evidence from Spain. *Journal of Population Economics*, **14**, 505–521.

Aleksynska, M., and Schmidt, A. 2014. *A Chronology of Employment Protection Legislation in Some Selected European countries*. ILO – Conditions of Work and Employment Series No. 53.

Andrés et al. 2009. *A Proposal to Restart the Spanish Labour Market*. Grupo de Discusin de Economía Laboral. FEDEA. http://crisis09.es/economialaboral.

Arak, P., Lewandowski, P., and Zakowieck, P. 2014. *Dual Labour Market in Poland Proposals for Overcoming the Deadlock*. IBS Policy Paper 01/2014.

Autor, D., and Houseman, S. 2010. Do Temporary Help Jobs Improve Labor Market Outcomes for Low-Skilled Workers? Evidence from 'Work First'. *American Economic Journal: Applied Economics*, **2**, 96–128.

Bassanini, A., Nunziata, L., and Venn, D. 2009. Job Protection Legislation and Productivity Growth in OECD Countries. *Economic Policy*, **24**, 349–402.

Beaudry, P., M., Doms, and Lewis, E. 2010. Endogenous Skill Bias in Technology Adoption: City-Level Evidence from the IT Revolution. *Journal of Political Economy*, **118**, 988–1036.

Becker, S., Bentolila, S., Fernandes, A., and Ichino, A. 2010. Youth Emancipation and Perceived Job Insecurity of Parents and Children. *Journal of Population Economics*, **23**.

Bentolila, S., and Dolado, J. 1994. Labour Flexibility and Wages: Lessons from Spain. *Economic Policy*, **18**, 55–99.

Bentolila, S., and Jansen, M. 2012. Un Primer Análisis Económico de la Reforma Laboral de 2012. *Actualidad Laboral*, 15–16.

Bentolila, S., Dolado, J., and Jimeno, J. F. 2012a. Reforming an Insider-Outsider Labor Market: The Spanish Experience. *IZA Journal of European Labor Studies*, **1**.

Bentolila, S., Cahuc, P., Dolado, J., and Barbanchon, T. Le. 2012b. Two-tier Labour Markets in the Great Recession. *The Economic Journal*, **122**, 155–187.

Bentolila, S., Jansen, M., Jimenez, G., and Ruano, S. 2014. *When Credit Dries Up: Job Losses in the Great Recession*. Cemfi, mimeo.

Bertola, G., Boeri, T., and Cazes, S. 2000. Employment Protection in Industrialized Countries: The Case for New Indicators. *International Labour Review*, **139**, 57–72.

Blanchard, O. J., and Landier, A. 2002. The Perverse Effects of Partial Labor Market Reform: Fixed Duration Contracts in France. *The Economic Journal*, **122**, 214–244.

Blanchard, O. J., and Tirole, J. 2004. Contours of Employment Protection Reform. In: Fitoussi, J.P., and Velupillai, K. (eds), *Macroeconomic Theory and Economic Policy: Essays in Honor of Jean-Paul Fitoussi*. 4887, London: Routledge.

Blanchard, O. J., and Tirole, J. 2008. The Optimal Design of Unemployment Insurance and Employment Protection: A First Pass. *Journal of the European Economic Association*, **6**, 45–77.

Boeri, T. 2010. Institutional Reforms and Dualism in European Labor Markets. In: Ashenfelter, O., and Card, D. (eds), *Handbook of Labor Economics*. Elsevier.

Boeri, T., and Garibaldi, P. 2007. Two Tier Reforms of Employment Protection Legislation: A Honeymoon Effect? *The Economic Journal*, **117**, F357–F385.

Boeri, T., and Garibaldi, P. 2008. *Un Nuovo Contratto per Tutti*. Chiarelettere, Torino.

Booth, A., Dolado, J., and Frank, J. 2002a. Introduction: Symposium on Temporary Work. *The Economic Journal*, **112**, 181–189.

Booth, A., Francesconi, M., and Frank, J. 2002b. Temporary Jobs: Stepping Stones or Dead Ends. *The Economic Journal*, **112**, 189–213.

Cabrales, A., Dolado, J., and Mora, R. 2014. Dual Labour Markets and (Lack of) On-the-Job Training: PIAAC Evidence from and other EU Countries. *CEPR DP* 10246.

Caggese, A., and Cunat, V. 2010. Financing Constraints and Fixed-Term Employment Contacts. *The Economic Journal*, **118**, 2013–2046.

Cahuc, P. 2012. For a Unified Contract. *European Labour Law Journal*, **3**, 191–206.

Cahuc, P., and Kramarz, F. 2005. *De la précarité à la mobilité, vers une sécurité sociale professionnelle*. Paris: La Documentation Francaise.

Cahuc, P., and Postel-Vinay, F. 2002. Temporary Jobs, Employment Protection and Labor Market Performance. *Labour Economics*, **9**, 63–91.

Cahuc, P., and Zylberberg, A. 2008. Optimum Taxation and Dismissal Taxes. *Journal of Public Economics*, **92**, 2003–2019.

Card, D., Kluve, J., and Weber, A. 2010. Active Labour Market Policy Evaluations: A Meta-Analysis. *The Economic Journal*, **120**, 452–477.

Card, D., Kluve, J., and Weber, A. 2015. *What Works? A Meta Analysis of Recent Labor Market Program Evaluations*. IZA DP 236.

Carrillo-Tudela, C., and Visschers, L. 2014. *Unemployment and Endogenous Reallocation over the Business Cycle*. IZA DP 7124.

Cingano, F., Leonardi, M., Messina, J., and Pica, G. 2010. The Effect of Employment Protection Legislation and Financial Market Imperfections on Investment: Evidence from a Firm-Level Panel of EU Countries. *Economic Policy*, **25**, 117–163.

Comte, E. 2015. *The Origins of the May 1968 Labour Crisis in France*. EUI-MW DP 2015/13.

Conde-Ruiz, J. I., Felgueroso, F., and Perez, J. I. Garcia. 2011. El Fondo de Capitalización a la Austriaca. *Moneda y Credito*, **233**, 7–44.

Dolado, J. 2012. The Pros and Cons of the Latest Labour Market Reform in Spain. *Spanish Labour Law and Employment Relations Journal*, **1**, 22–30.

Dolado, J., García-Serrano, C., and Jimeno, J. F. 2002. Drawing Lessons from the Boom of Temporary Jobs in Spain. *The Economic Journal*, **112**, 270–295.

Dolado, J., Ortigueira, S., and Stucchi, R. 2015a. Does Dual Employment Protection Affect TFP? Evidence from Spanish Manufacturing Firms (forthcoming, *Journal of the Spanish Economic Association*, 2016).

Dolado, J., Lalé, E., and Siassi, N. 2015b. *Moving Towards a Single Labour Contract: Transition vs. Steady State*. EUI mimeo.

Fernández-Villaverde, J., and Ohanian, L. 2015. *The Political Economy of European Stagnation*. University of Pennsylvania (mimeo).

Galdon-Sánchez, and Güell. 2003. Dismissal Conflicts and Unemployment. *European Economic Review*, **47**, 127–139.

Garcia-Perea, P., and Molinas, C. 2015. Acabar con el Paro: Queremos Podremos. *Fundacion de Estudios Financieros no. 55*.

García-Pérez, J. I., and Osuna, V. 2014. Dual labour markets and the tenure distribution: reducing severance pay or introducing a single contract. *Labour Economics*, **29**, 1–13.

García-Pérez, J. I., and Rebollo, Y. F. 2009. The Use of Permanent Contracts across Spanish Regions: Do Regional Wage Subsidies Work? *Investigaciones Económicas*, **33**, 97–130.

García-Pérez, J. I., Marinescu, I., and Vall-Castello, J. 2014. *Can Fixed-Term Contracts Put Low-Skilled Youth on a Better Career Path?* FEDEA Working Paper No. 2014-08.

Garcia-Santana, M., Benito, E. Moral, Pijoan-Mas, J., and Ramos, R. 2015. *Growing Like Spain: 1995–2007*. Cemfi (mimeo).

Garibaldi, P., and Taddei, F. 2013. *Italy: A Dual Labour Market in Transition*. ILO Employment WP, **144**.

Gonzalez, L., and Ortega, F. 2011. How Do Very Open Economies Absorb Large Immigration Flows? Evidence from Spanish Regions. *Labour Economics*, **18**, 57–70.

Heinrich, C., Mueser, P., and Troske, K. 2005. Welfare to Temporary Work: Implications for Labor Market Outcomes. *Review of Economics and Statistics*, **87**, 154–173.

Holmlund, B., and Storrie, D. 2002. Temporary Work In Turbulent Times: The Swedish Experience. *Economic Journal*, **112**, 245–269.

Ichino, A., Polo, M., and Rettote, E. 2003. Are Judges Biased by Labor Market Conditions? *European Economic Review*, **47**, 913–944.

Ichino, P. 2014. Disegno di Legge per la Transizione a un Regime di Flexicurity. n. 1481, 25 March. Synthesis in English at http://pietroichino.it/wp-content/uploads/2014/05/Warsaw.29V14.def2.pdf.

Jimeno, J. F., Martínez-Matute, M., and Mora-Sanguinetti, J. S. 2015. *Employment Protection Legislation and Labor Courts' Activity in Spain*. Bank of Spain WP 1507.

Lazear, E. 1990. Job Security Provisions and Employment. *Quarterly Journal of Economics*, **105**, 699–726.

Lepage-Saucier, N., Schleich, J., and Wasmer, E. 2013. *Moving Towards a Single Labour Contract: Pros, Cons and Mixed Feelings*. OECD Working Paper No. 1026.

OECD. 2004. *Employment Outlook*. Paris.

OECD. 2008. *Employment Outlook*. Paris.

OECD. 2012. *Employment Outlook*. Paris.

OECD. 2014. Non Regular Employment, Job Security and the Labour Market Divide. *Employment Outlook*. Chapter 4. Paris.

Portugal, P. 2011. Mercado de Trabalho. In: *Memorandum of Economic and Financial Policies*. NOVA School of Business & Economics.

Saint-Paul, G. 1996. *Dual Labor Markets*. The MIT Press.

Saint-Paul, G. 1997. Is Labour Rigidity Harming Europe's Competitiveness? The Effect of Job Protection on the Pattern of Trade and Welfare. *European Economic Review*, **41**, 499–506.

Saint-Paul, G. 2000. *The Political Economy of Labour Market Institutions*. Oxford University Press.

Wasmer, E. 1999. Competition for Jobs in a Growing Economy and the Emergence of Dualism in Employment. *The Economic Journal*, **109**, 349–371.

Zijl, M., Berg, G. Van Den, and Heyma, A. 2004. *Stepping Stones for the Unemployed: The Effect of Temporary Jobs on the Duration until Regular Work*. IZA Discussion Paper 1241.

3 Population, Migration, Ageing and Health: A Survey

Christian Dustmann, Giovanni Facchini
and Cora Signorotto

Abstract

We review the literature on recent demographic changes in Europe, focusing on two of the main challenges brought about by an ageing population: severe labour shortages in many sectors of the economy and growing pressures on both health and welfare systems. We discuss how and to what extent migration can contribute to addressing these challenges both in a short and a long-term perspective. Finally, we identify several areas in which more research is needed to help devise more effective policies to cope with a greying society.

3.1   Introduction

As European countries experience rapidly ageing populations, two major challenges have emerged for policy-makers. First, the decline in the size of the domestic labour force implies severe shortages in the availability of key skills needed in several sectors of the economy.[1] Possible consequences are reduced productivity growth and decline in global competitiveness. Second, the increase in life expectancy will typically imply longer periods spent in retirement, generating pressures on the sustainability of existing pension systems, as well as new needs to provide care for a growing elderly population.

Immigration is often referred to as a possible response to address both of these challenges. Young foreign workers can fill some of the short-term skill shortages that have emerged and contribute in the medium and long run to reversing the trend towards population stagnation. At the same time, cultural differences and the common perception that foreigners might be a threat for the domestic population, in conjunction with the large migrations required to counter demographic developments in many European countries, suggest that migration can only be part of a broader mix of interventions.

The goal of this survey is to provide a systematic overview of the literature that has analysed the interplay between population dynamics, ageing, health and migration, aimed at offering policy-makers a sound understanding of the state of the art in this important research area. At the same time, we will identify key issues where more research is needed both to foster our knowledge, as well as to provide guidance for effective policy interventions. The review is carried out from the perspective of the economics literature, but given the complexity of the question we also refer to relevant studies carried out by demographers and sociologists.

Following an initial description of the main stylized facts on population ageing, migration and health in Section 3.2, the survey focuses on current demographic developments and fertility trends among the migrant and native populations in destination countries (Section 3.3) and on the length of the migration spell (Section 3.4). We then review the main findings in the literature on the fiscal effects of migration in European countries and the US (Section 3.5) and describe the role that migration can play in addressing skill and labour shortages (Section 3.6). Section 3.7 analyses the health care sector, focusing on shortages of health care workers in European countries and the international migration of health professionals. Finally, we present the main findings from the very recent literature on amenity-driven migration of retirees from Northern European countries towards Mediterranean coastal regions (Section 3.8). Section 3.9 summarizes our main conclusions and policy implications.

3.2   Main Stylized Facts

Europe's population is ageing rapidly[2] and, as shown in Figure 3.1, the most recent forecasts suggest that the phenomenon is likely to become more severe over the next 45 years (see European Commission, 2014a). By 2060, less than 57 per cent of the population is expected to belong to the economically active group.

There are two main reasons why a population ages. First, a decline in overall fertility rates. Second, an increase in life expectancy. Considering the 28 current members of the EU, average total fertility rates were on a steady downward path over the period from 1960 to 2005. While in 1960 the average European woman was expected to give birth to 2.67 children, this number dropped to only 1.49 children by 2005. There was a slight improvement in total fertility over the last decade, with fertility reaching 1.56 by 2012. This basic trend conceals important differences across countries, however. For instance, while fertility rates in Ireland have been consistently higher than in the rest of the EU, countries like Portugal or Spain had substantially higher fertility rates than the EU average in the 1960s, 1970s and even 1980s, but then saw them drop below the EU average starting in 1990. Other countries like France have been able, through a series of targeted policies, to maintain fertility rates close to the replacement rate of 2.1 children per woman (see Figure 3.2). The most recent forecasts indicate that we should expect a slight improvement over the next 45 years, with total fertility

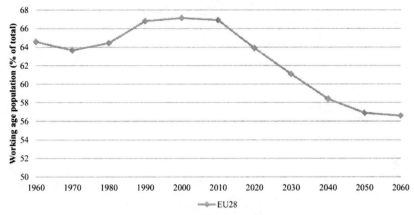

Figure 3.1 Working age population in the EU28: Past trends and projections (European Commission, 2014a, p. 409). Figures always refer to the same group of countries.

rates reaching 1.76 children by 2060, a figure that is still substantially short of the natural replacement rate (see European Commission, 2014a).

Over the same period, life expectancy has increased dramatically. The European Commission Ageing Report (2014a) shows that the average man born in an EU country in 1960 is expected to live 66.9 years, whereas the average woman lives 72.3 years. By 2010 these figures had increased dramatically to 75.6 years for men and 82 years for women, that is, by a staggering 13 per cent (see Figure 3.3), and life expectancy is forecast to continue to rise. By 2060

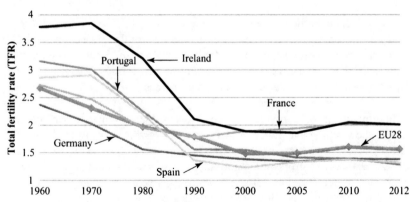

Figure 3.2 Past trends in total fertility rates (TFR), 1960–2012: Selected EU countries (European Commission, 2014a, p. 9).

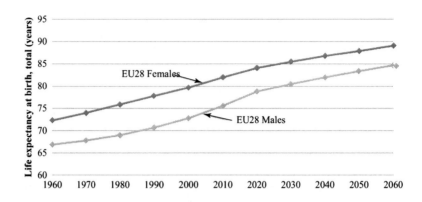

Figure 3.3 Life expectancy at birth in the EU28: Past trends and projections (European Commission, 2014a, pp. 12–13). Figures always refer to the same group of countries, with the exception of 1960, when no data are available for Cyprus and Romania, and 1970, when no data are available for Cyprus.

it is expected to reach 84.7 years for males and 89.1 years for females (see European Commission, 2014a).

Population ageing will generate growing pressures on welfare states, adding strains to existing pension systems, which might no longer be able to guarantee adequate living standards in old age. Similarly, health systems are expected to require more resources and to adapt to an increased demand for long-term care (LTC) for a growing elderly population.

In fact, as pointed out by the European Commission (2015), the expected gross replacement rate of public pensions has declined in all EU countries. Furthermore, the burden of health and long-term care (LTC) on public finances is expected to increase. Figure 3.4 reports forecasts for the EU Health and LTC expenditures as a percentage of GDP for the next 45 years. Health expenditures will reach 7.9 per cent of GDP by 2050 and level off the following decade, while spendings on LTC services are predicted to increase by 1.1 percentage points by 2060 (European Commission, 2015).

In principle, immigration can help offset these trends by increasing both the size of the working age population and the total fertility rate. Considering the EU, a positive net inflow[3] has been consistently observed since the second half of the 1980s (see European Commission, 2014a). In particular, new arrivals peaked in 2003, averaging well over a million per year. Following a sharp drop during the global economic crisis, net migration flows picked up once again after 2011 and reached pre-crisis levels by 2013 – the last year for which data are available (see Figure 3.5[4]).

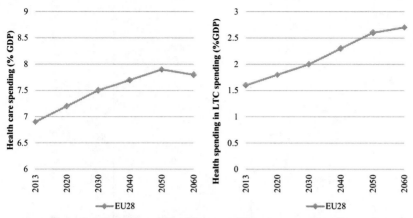

Figure 3.4 Projections of health care and long-term care spending as percentage of GDP for EU28 countries (European Commission, 2015, pp. 265, 271).

According to the most recent projections,[5] between 2013 and 2060 cumulated net inflows to the EU are expected to reach 55 million. The main destination countries will be Italy, the United Kingdom, Germany, and Spain, with a forecasted cumulated net inflow of 15.5 million, 9.2 million, 7 million and 6.5 million migrants respectively (see European Commission, 2014a).

Whether migrants help rejuvenate Western countries ultimately depends on their age structure and fertility behaviour. In the next section, we will review the main differences in fertility patterns among the migrant and native populations, and discuss the extent immigration represents a viable solution to the host countries' ageing workforce.

3.3 Migration and Demographic Developments

Migrants are typically younger than natives when they arrive, and in the short run they contribute to rejuvenating the host country's labour supply. In the medium to long run, migrants will age as well, and new immigration will be required to counteract population ageing. One key factor determining to what extent the host country's age structure is affected by immigration in the medium or long term is the relative fertility of the immigrant compared to the native population.

To understand the importance of immigration in shaping future population dynamics, Table 3.1 (taken from Sobotka, 2008) displays the share of total births accounted for by immigrant women in eleven European countries. Almost all countries in the table have experienced a steady increase in the share of births to immigrant women since the mid-1990s. Southern European

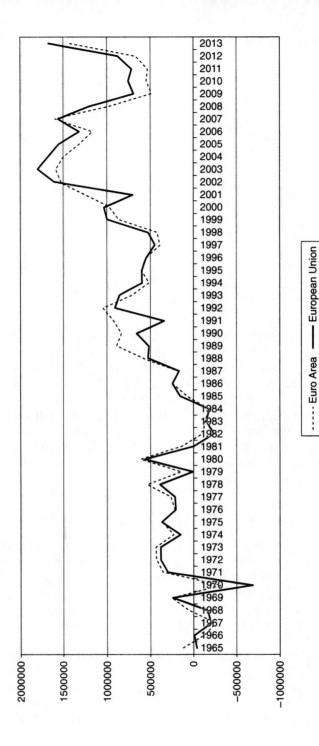

Figure 3.5 Net migration flows, 1965–2013 (European Commission, 2014a, p. 14). Figures always refer to the same group of countries.

- - - - Euro Area ——— European Union

Table 3.1 *Births to immigrant parents (Sobotka, 2008, p. 230)*

Country[a]	Period	Births to immigrant women (%)	Births to immigrant women, 1st + 2nd gen. (%)	Births to mothers with foreign nationality (%)	At least one parent foreign national (%)
Austria	2000			13.5	
	2005			11.7	
Belgium (Flanders)	2003–04	16.8		12.4	
Denmark	1999–03	13.5		11.1	
England and Wales	1980	13.3			
	1995	12.6			
	2005	20.8			
	2006	21.9			
France	1991–98	12.4			
	1998		21		14.5
	2004	15		12.4	18.2
Germany	1980			15	
	1985			11.2	
	1995			16.2	
	2004			17.6	
Italy	1999			5.4	
	2004			11.3	
	2005			12.2	
The Netherlands	1996	15.5	21		
	2005	17.8	25.5		
Spain	1996			3.3	4.5
	2000			6.2	7.9
	2004			13.7	16.9
	2006			16.5	
Sweden	2005	19.5		11.8	
Switzerland	1980			15.3	
	2000			22.3	
	2005			26.3	

[a] Notes: Country data sources: Austria: Kytir (2006); Belgium: VAZG (2007); Denmark: Statistics Denmark (2004); England and Wales: ONS (2006), ONS (2007), Schoorl (1995); France: Héran and Pison (2007), Prioux (2005), Toulemon (2004), Tribalat (2005); Germany: Schoorl (1995), Statistisches Bundesamt (2006); Italy: ISTAT (2007); Netherlands: CBS (2006); Spain: INE (2006), INE (2007), Roig Vila and Martín (2007); Sweden: Statistics Sweden (2006); Switzerland: Coleman (2003), SFSO (2006).

countries in particular report a sharp increase in fertility, which is at least partly due to the high immigration inflows they experienced in the 1990s and early 2000s.

Three main mechanisms affecting migrants' fertility behaviour have been studied in detail: selection, disruption and adaptation (for a comprehensive overview, see Adserà and Ferrer (2015). In the remainder of this section we will consider each one of them in turn.

3.3.1   The Selection Hypothesis

The first hypothesis we consider suggests that immigrant women are a self-selected sample of the country of origin's population in terms of their level of education, potential income, age, etc. This may make them different from women left behind when it comes to fertility and childbearing behaviour.

Kahn (1988) is one of the first systematic analyses of fertility differentials between native and foreign born women, and in particular of the role played by selection into emigration. Using individual level data from the 1980 US Census and aggregate data from origin countries, she performs a simple covariance analysis, highlighting the role of sending-country fertility levels in determining migrants' fertility behaviour. Migrants from high-fertility countries report, on average, higher fertility once in the host country compared to migrants from lower fertility countries. This positive relationship, however, is partly offset by self-selection: when immigrants are positively selected in terms of education, the influence of the high-fertility source-country norms is weaker and their fertility tends to be lower. Kahn also examines the fertility behaviour of child and adult immigrants separately and finds that adult immigrants have higher mean levels of fertility. This is partly explained by the fact that the latter tend to be older and somewhat less educated than child immigrants.

Using data from the 1970 and 1980 US Census and focusing on high fertility sending countries located in the Middle East, Asia, Latin America and the Caribbean, Blau (1992) finds evidence of a broadly similar fertility behaviour between immigrant and native women. In particular, her results indicate that immigrant women observed in 1970 have slightly fewer children than their native counterparts. She explains this finding by the positive selection of immigrants with regard to education, and by the fact that highly educated immigrant women tend to have fewer children than native women with comparable characteristics. Blau also finds indirect evidence of a higher demand for child quality among immigrant than among native women. In a more recent paper, Avitabile et al. (2014) use German data to show that the acquisition of citizenship rights is likely to reinforce migrants' preferences for child quality rather than quantity and reduce immigrants' fertility.

Evidence of migrants' positive selection on education is also reported by Choi (2014). The novelty of her study lies in combining nationally representative datasets from Mexico and the US: the 2002 Mexican Family Life Survey and the 2002 and the 2006–2010 US National Survey of Family Growth. The rich dataset built by the author allows her to identify a disruption in fertility in anticipation of migration, but a resumption of pre-migration fertility patterns and partial compensation for the earlier fertility loss after migration. Interestingly, she also finds that fertility levels among Mexican-Americans decrease both within and across generations, as increasingly educated immigrants adopt the fertility patterns of white Americans. Still, the data show that Mexican-American fertility has not yet fully converged to that of white Americans.

3.3.2   The Adaptation Hypothesis

Even if migrants are a selected group relative to both the source and destination country populations, their behaviour is likely to change once they settle in the new country. Immigrants may adapt and adjust their initially higher fertility rate to that of the native population over time. Research on fertility assimilation processes has addressed the issue following three different approaches: by distinguishing between first and second generation immigrants (Stephen and Bean, 1992, Parrado and Morgan, 2008, Dubuc, 2012), by focusing on foreign born migrants who migrated as children (see e.g., Kahn, 1988, Bleakley and Chin, 2010, Adserà et al., 2012), or by studying the impact and strength of cultural and ethnic 'ties' over time (Fernández and Fogli, 2009, Blau et al., 2013).

The findings in the literature indicate that second generation and child immigrants' fertility behaviour is closer to that of the native population. Country of origin characteristics, like language and cultural heritage, may also contribute to the gap between immigrants and natives, and to the pace of assimilation.

For the US, Parrado and Morgan (2008) assess the fertility assimilation hypothesis for Hispanic and Mexican immigrants. They estimate fertility by computing the average number of children ever born for three immigrant generations of Hispanic and Mexican women born between 1885 and 1964. Their cohort and generational analysis reveals a declining trend in immigrants' fertility, which is consistent with the assimilation hypothesis. Mexican immigrant women are found to have significantly lower fertility levels than nonmigrant Mexican women. Evidence of convergence to the fertility of white women across immigrants' generations is also found.

Using data from the 1970 and 1980 US Census, Stephen and Bean (1992) likewise focus on Mexican women's fertility trends in the US, considering both first and second generation migrants. The authors report evidence consistent with assimilation across generations to non-Spanish-origin white women's fertility patterns: US-born Mexican immigrants have lower fertility rates than the first generation born in Mexico.

Evidence of fertility assimilation emerges also from European studies. Dubuc (2012) analyses fertility rates of second generation immigrants in the UK and compares them to those of their parents and to those of recent immigrants from the same ethnic group. While she finds evidence of fertility differentials by ethnic groups, she uncovers at the same time a convergence towards lower UK average fertility levels. The decrease in the fertility gap over time is found to be the result of both a decline in fertility of immigrants originating from high-fertility countries and lower fertility rates of second generation immigrants.

In an interesting paper, Adserà et al. (2012) focus on the fertility behaviour of women who migrated as children to Canada, the UK and France. Focusing on adaptation mechanisms, they perform a Poisson regression analysis to estimate the main determinants of the number of live births per woman. Their results are consistent with the assimilation hypothesis. They also illustrate a considerable heterogeneity in the effect of time spent in the destination country on the fertility of immigrants who are from different origin countries.

The heterogeneity in fertility behaviour driven by differences in migrants' countries of origin has been explained in the literature by the cultural and linguistic characteristics of the sending countries. Bleakley and Chin (2010) investigate the interrelation between English proficiency and social integration of immigrants in the US using microdata from the 2000 Census and exploiting information on immigrants' age at arrival and on whether they were born in an English-speaking country. Interestingly, they find evidence that immigrants who are more fluent in English have fewer children than less fluent immigrants.

Besides language, immigrants' cultural heritage may alter or delay the process of fertility assimilation through the intergenerational transmission of fertility behaviour. Fernández and Fogli (2006) try to disentangle the effects of personal-family related experiences (e.g., the number of a woman's siblings) from those driven by source country heritage. Their findings indicate a positive and significant impact of both family fertility experience and cultural heritage on fertility behaviour of US-born immigrant women. In a related paper, Fernández and Fogli (2009) use data from the 1970 US Census and find a similar effect of the migrants' culture of origin on the fertility behaviour of second generation immigrants.

Blau et al. (2013) extend Fernández and Fogli's analysis and allow the cultural heritage to vary across birth cohorts of second generation immigrants in the US. To this end, they combine information on second generation women immigrants taken from the 1995–2006 March Current Population Survey with parental characteristics constructed using the 1970, 1980, 1990 and 2000 Censuses. The authors are in particular interested in studying the transmission of first-generation immigrants' education, fertility, and labour supply to second-generation women labour supply and fertility behaviour. Their rich dataset allows them to separately study the effect of each parent's (mother and father) characteristics. Their results indicate that second-generation women's education, fertility and labour supply are positively affected by the corresponding immigrant generation's characteristics, even within an overall pattern of assimilation. Moreover, fertility and labour supply behaviours appear to be more strongly influenced by the fertility and labour supply characteristics of the mother's country of birth, whereas educational attainment is more strongly influenced by the norm prevailing in the father's country of birth.

3.3.3   The Disruption Hypothesis

The decision to migrate might affect reproductive behaviour, for instance, because a migrant decides to postpone childbearing after arrival into the new country due to a temporary negative income shock. Migrants may also be forced to postpone childbearing due to separation from the spouse around the time of migration (see Blau, 1992).

Disruption mechanisms can be observed when a decline in fertility occurs right before or right after migration, which may or may not be followed by a catchup. Assessing the disruption hypothesis empirically presents significant challenges as it requires information on pre-migration fertility patterns and because the migrant population is likely to be a nonrandomly selected subgroup (Adserà and Ferrer, 2015). US studies report evidence of migrants interrupting fertility around the time of migration, while results for European countries vary substantially by destination.

In an early study, Kahn (1994) exploits information from the 1980 US Census and the 1986 and 1988 June Current Population Surveys on the actual number of children ever born and the number of children women expect to have in the future. In particular, she runs a synthetic cohort analysis to trace the fertility pattern of a fixed cohort of immigrants in the 1980s and then compares the results with migrants' fertility expectations. The observed increase in the immigrant-native fertility gap in the 1980s is explained as a consequence of a sharp decrease in natives' fertility compared to immigrants' rather than a rise in migrants' fertility. The fertility gap is mainly explained by socio-economic and demographic differences between the migrant and native populations in terms of skills, income and ethnicity. However, the synthetic cohort analysis reveals that part of the fertility differential is driven by a disruption followed by catchup in fertility behaviour. Kahn's analysis of fertility expectations confirms this result: while recent immigrants are found to have had lower than average fertility compared to older immigrants' cohorts and natives, they are also found to compensate for this gap by expecting to have more children in the future. Blau (1992) also finds evidence of disruption in the fertility profiles of US immigrants, and attributes it to demographic factors such as delayed marriages or spouses' temporary separation due to migration, rather than to economic factors such as spouses' temporary income loss. Focusing on Mexican immigrants to the US, Choi (2014) finds evidence of disruption in fertility right before migration. Migrants seem to partially make up for the initial loss in fertility once they are in the destination country, but she finds evidence of a long-term effect of the initial shock.

In Europe, Andersson (2004) uses Swedish longitudinal register data and finds evidence of a before-migration disruption in fertility, which is followed by a right-after-migration catchup. Toulemon (2004) and Toulemon et al. (2008) also find evidence of disruption patterns in fertility for immigrants to France. Different results emerge instead in a study carried out by Garssen and Nicolaas (2008) on migrants to the Netherlands. Using information from Dutch municipal population registries for 2005, they find that Turkish and Moroccan women display higher fertility rates than those reported in their country of origin, and argue that migration for family formation reasons might explain this trend. Female migration from Turkey and Morocco, in fact, is mainly motivated by family reunification, given the traditional role of women in these source countries. Similar results are obtained also by Mayer and Riphahn (2000) in their analysis of assimilation and/or disruption patterns in the fertility of immigrants to Germany.

Open Issues

Data limitations is one of the main difficulties researchers face when studying immigrant fertility. In particular, detailed information on immigrants' lifetime events such as age at migration, complete birth histories (i.e., before and after migration), return migration and the socio-demographic characteristics of their families of origin would allow for a more comprehensive analysis of migrants' demographic trends.

Overall, and despite current limitations in fertility estimates and projections, the evidence we have reviewed suggests that migrants tend to assimilate to the destination country's fertility patterns. Immigrants' younger age and initially higher fertility rates may help rejuvenate the host countries' populations in the short run. However, migrants' assimilation to the host country fertility patterns implies that such rejuvenation will largely have to rely on a continuous inflow of immigrants. Therefore, migration alone is unlikely to compensate for the ageing workforces in European countries.

3.4   Permanent versus Temporary Migration

To fully understand the demographic and fiscal impact of immigration on the host countries, we must consider whether migrations are permanent or temporary, and more generally what their durations are. If immigration is predominantly permanent, older migrants will contribute to the ageing of the host country population in the longer run, and to an increase in the demand for health and long-term care services. If, however, most migrations are temporary, immigrants may contribute to rejuvenating the existing workforce and contribute in terms of taxes, and will burden the host country to a lesser extent in old age. Also, as immigrants are heterogeneous, it is important to understand whether those who leave the host country are systematically different from those who remain in terms of skill level and labour market outcomes. Temporary migrations can take different forms. They may be return migrations, where migrants return permanently to their countries of origin after a period in the host country; they may be circulatory migrations, with migrants migrating back and forth between origin- and destination country; or they may be transient migrations, where individuals move from country to country before reaching a final destination (see e.g., Nekby, 2006; see Dustmann and Görlach, 2016 for a discussion).

Nonpermanent migration plays an important role in many destination countries. Figure 3.6 – taken from Dustmann and Görlach (2016)[6] – plots the estimated share of immigrants who leave the host country against the number of years since migration. The figure illustrates that European countries display significantly higher outmigration rates compared to the more traditional destination countries. In particular, almost 50 per cent of immigrants to Europe have already left their first destination country ten years after arrival, while this is true for only about 20 per cent of immigrants to Anglo-America, Australia and New Zealand. These figures are in line with other studies that quantify the extent of return migration for specific countries. For instance, Dustmann and Weiss (2007) report that in the UK, more than 40 per cent of each arrival cohort has left the country after about 5 years.

Starting in the late 1980s, scholars began to investigate why migrants outmigrate from destination countries, and who the return migrants are, addressing the selectivity in the return migration decision and its effects on the host economy (see early papers by Dustmann, 1995, 1997, 2003, Borjas and Bratsberg, 1996 and Dustmann et al., 2011).[7]

3.4.1   Why Do Migrants Return?

In simple neoclassical models the migration decision only depends on differences in relative wage levels net of relocation costs, and on expectations of higher earnings in the country of destination. Within this framework, the individual migrates assuming to remain permanently in the destination country. Return migration in this setting is the result of mistaken expectations, meaning that the migrant assessed the benefits of migration inaccurately. More recent contributions, however, have introduced models of endogenous return migration decisions. In a recent paper, Dustmann and Görlach (2016) discuss different factors that may contribute to a migrant's return decision, such as a higher preference for consumption in the country of origin than in the host country, a lower price level in the migrant's origin country compared to the host country, and the possibility for the migrant to accumulate human capital faster in the

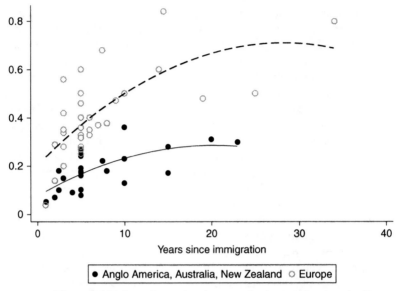

Figure 3.6 Estimated outmigration rates by host region (y-axis, Dustmann and Görlach, 2016).

host than in the origin country. Dustmann and Görlach (2016) develop a general dynamic framework within which return and circulatory migrations can be studied, and discuss various extensions, such as the introduction of shocks to earnings and preferences. The authors emphasize that many choices and decisions of immigrants, such as human capital investment, labour supply or savings, depend on the expected duration of the migration, and that such decisions should therefore be jointly modelled with migration and re-migration decisions.

Structural dynamic models of migrants' decision problems have been developed, for instance, by Colussi (2003), Thom (2010) and Lessem (2013), in which time varying location preferences determine location choices. See also Kennan and Walker (2011) for a dynamic model of internal migration decisions.

3.4.2   Who Are the Return Migrants?

The second important question that needs to be addressed is whether there are systematic differences between permanent and temporary migrants. This potential heterogeneity is particularly relevant as it might have important consequences for the host country's demographic and fiscal trends. In particular, several papers have emphasized that, if outmigration is selective, it may affect the analysis of immigrants' earnings assimilation in the host country (see e.g.,

Borjas, 1989, Borjas and Bratsberg, 1996, Lubotsky, 2007, Dustmann and Görlach, 2015).

Borjas and Bratsberg (1996) use a one-dimensional Roy model to explain selective outmigration. There are two reasons for return migration: human capital that has a higher return in the home country is accumulated faster in the host country, and there are unforeseen shocks that result in lower than expected earnings in the host country. The main prediction of the model is that selection of return migrants accentuates the original selection of immigrants to the destination country. In particular, if immigrants are positively selected, then those who stay are likewise positively selected, while if immigrants are negatively selected, then those who remain end up being the worst of the worst.

While Borjas and Bratsberg (1996) implicitly assume a fixed migration duration for all temporary migrants, Dustmann and Görlach (2015) extend the model by allowing a migrant's gain in human capital to vary with the time spent in the host country, and study the implications for the length of migrations. Dustmann et al., 2011 introduce instead a dynamic multidimensional Roy model with return migration, where migrations may occur for the purpose of skill accumulations, or because earnings are higher in the host country, of which the Borjas and Bratsberg (1996) model is a special case.

Some recent data sources report retrospective histories of immigrants (e.g., the Mexican Migration Project dataset). Further, administrative data, especially in Nordic European countries, often include information on year of emigration, the countries of destination, and the migration trajectories back and forth from these countries over time (see Dustmann and Görlach, 2015, for a survey of available data sources).

Evidence on outmigration patterns and selectivity has shown that differences in the probability to return depend on migrants' country of origin, and on the different motives to migrate, that is, whether the focus is on labour migrations, asylum seekers or family migrants (see e.g., Jasso and Rosenzweig, 1982 and Bijwaard, 2010). For instance, using combined Dutch register data at the national and municipal level, Bijwaard (2010) finds that non-Dutch labour migrants display a higher probability of leaving the host country compared to family migrants.

The literature also reports evidence on the relation between educational attainment and the propensity to outmigrate. Using German data from the German Socio-economic Panel (GSOEP) and IAB data on Turkish migrants in Germany, Dustmann (1996) finds that years of schooling increase the probability that a migration is intended to be permanent. However, higher education decreases the residual time spent in the country for those who intend to return. Constant and Zimmermann (2011) claim that more than 60 per cent of the migrants belonging to the countries with which Germany had guest-worker agreements in place engage in repeat and circular migration, and that being highly educated reduces the number of exits, while being a male and owning a German passport positively affects the number of exits from Germany.

Reagan and Olsen (2000), using instead longitudinal data from the 1979 cohort of the US National Longitudinal Survey, show that migrants with a higher earnings potential are less likely to outmigrate, though obtaining a college degree increases the possibility of return. Moreover, the authors find that time since migration has a negative effect on the probability of return, while the opposite is true for age at migration.

The nonrandom selection of return migrants has important consequences for their performance in the host country's labour market and for their likely impact on the host country's welfare state. Borjas (1989) uses information from the 1972–1978 Survey of Natural and Social Scientists and Engineers to estimate outmigration rates from the US and finds evidence of lower average earnings of return migrants in comparison with permanent migrants to the US. Lubotsky (2007) takes a more systematic perspective linking information from administrative sources, that is, the US Social Security records, to data from the US Survey of Income and Program Participation and to the Current Population Survey to construct migrants' employment and earnings histories. He finds evidence of both selective return migration and circular migration to and from the US. His results indicate that returnees are characterized by lower than average earnings, and that ignoring selective outmigration leads to an upward bias in the estimates of immigrant earning assimilation.

Open Issues

The temporariness of migration and the potential selectivity of outmigration opens up a multitude of future research avenues. One recently emerging stream of literature investigates immigrants' assimilation paths in destination countries and models migrants' migration plans in conjunction with their economic decisions, including labour supply and human capital investments (Adda et al., 2015, Dustmann and Görlach, 2016). Such approaches coupled with more and better data will help to push future research in this important area.

3.5   The Fiscal Effect of Immigration

Demographic developments (see Section 3.3), as well as the mobility of immigrant populations (see Section 3.4) must be taken into account when studying the fiscal impact of immigration on the host country. This topic has received considerable attention over the past few decades, and the recent financial crisis has contributed to making this debate even more controversial.

The characteristics and preferences of a country's citizens determine its public budget constraint via tax rates corresponding to different levels of government spending (Preston, 2014). Immigration may also impact public finances of the host country by increasing a country's workforce and changing the age composition of the population. The fiscal system may not only benefit from immigrants' tax contributions, but may also face a rise in the demand for public services. The literature on migrants' potential fiscal effects on Western countries has followed a variety of different methodologies. Two broad groups of studies can be identified, depending on whether they followed a 'static' or a 'dynamic' approach. In this section we briefly review each of them in turn.

3.5.1   Static Frameworks

Static analyses allow us to answer questions such as 'What is the net fiscal contribution of immigrants who arrived after year X, compared to natives?' This is a politically important question. The approach essentially compares the immigrants' and natives' utilization of public services, and contrasts this to tax revenues collected from the two groups. This is achieved by combining public accounts information on expenditures and tax revenues with microdata that allow constructing group specific weights for each public account item, so that these can be allocated to different demographic groups, such as immigrants and natives.[8]

We briefly report the main findings from some studies for European countries characterized by different welfare systems, such as Norway, Sweden and Germany. We also review some evidence from the analysis of the overall fiscal effects of immigration to the US, the UK and Sweden.

Bratsberg et al. (2010) use longitudinal administrative register data on male immigrants who arrived in Norway from developing countries between 1971 and 1975, and follow their employment history over time. They report a significant drop in labour market participation rates ten years after arrival, much larger than the decline estimated for the native reference group. The authors also find evidence of high social security dependency rates for those migrants who exit the labour market. Their analysis is extended in Bratsberg et al. (2014) to a larger set of migrant entry cohorts. Unlike immigrants from developing countries, immigrants from Western countries exhibit lifecycle patterns in terms of employment, earnings and welfare dependence that resemble those of natives.

Using a different methodology, Hansen and Lofstrom (2003) study differences in welfare utilization between immigrants and natives in Sweden over the period 1990–1996. Their findings suggest that migrants' welfare benefit utilization patterns become more similar to those of natives as they spend time in the host country. Despite evidence of assimilation, Hansen and Lofstrom (2003) report persistently higher dependency rates for immigrants and a gap that does not disappear even after 20 years spent in the host country.

Evidence from Germany shows that foreign households display a lower probability of welfare utilization than natives, after controlling for observable socio-economic and demographic characteristics such as a household's head labour force status, family composition and home ownership (Riphahn, 2004). Using several waves of the German Socioeconomic Panel (1984–1996), Riphahn finds that higher take-up rates for foreign born families are driven by differences in socio-economic characteristics between native and foreign households. She also uncovers a positive trend in welfare take-up by the immigrant population, indicating that welfare utilization increases with time spent in the new country.

Another stream of research uses cross-sectional data to estimate immigrants' net contribution to the fiscal system by simultaneously considering the expenditures and revenues side of the government budget. Drawing information from the 1990 US Census, Borjas (1994) calculates the annual net fiscal contribution of immigrants in the US and finds that they are net contributors to US public government finances. For the UK, Dustmann et al. (2010a) assess the net fiscal contribution of immigration from Central and Eastern European countries (the A8 countries) that joined the EU in 2004 and show that they are not only less likely than natives to receive welfare benefits and to live in social housing, but they are also more likely to be net contributors to the UK public finances, due to higher participation rates in the labour market and lower benefit transfers. Dustmann and Frattini (2014) estimate the net fiscal contribution of immigrant arrival cohorts to the UK since 2000. Overall, immigrants are found to be less likely than natives to receive welfare state benefits or tax credits, and make a positive net fiscal contribution over that period. Ruist (2014) performs a similar analysis for European A10 accession migrants to Sweden and finds results close to those in Dustmann et al. (2010a).

3.5.2   Dynamic Models

Dynamic analyses are 'forward looking', computing the net present fiscal contribution of a particular arrival cohort (i.e., the net present value of the stream of future taxes and expenditures over the entire lifecycle corresponding to a given cohort or flow of immigrants). This requires strong assumptions regarding future fertility, employment, government tax rates and expenditures patterns (Rowthorn, 2008). Typical examples of this approach are two papers by Storesletten (2000, 2003), which consider the fiscal impact of immigration on the US and Sweden.

Storesletten (2000) develops and calibrates a general equilibrium overlapping generation model to compute the net present value (NPV) to the government of admitting one additional immigrant to the US. The model allows for return migration, which is assumed to depend on the time spent in the host country, but is not endogenously determined,[9] and for the portability of social insurance benefits from the host to the source country in case of return. When comparing an initial situation which allows for migrants' return to the case of no outmigration, the model predicts an increase in government's NPV profiles when admitting highly skilled migrants who are less than 49 years old, while reducing the NPV in the case of other migrant groups (old, unskilled etc.). The intuition for this result is that young, highly skilled workers are net contributors to the welfare state, and restricting their mobility will increase their overall fiscal contribution to the destination country.

Storesletten (2003) extends the analysis focusing on Sweden. He uncovers also in this case potential gains from migration. While the qualitative effects of immigrant's fiscal impact on the host country finances are similar for the US and Sweden, the size of potential benefits from high-skilled migration to Sweden is much smaller than in the US, reflecting important differences between the two countries in terms of labour market outcomes, fiscal burden and size of the welfare state.

A second approach applied to study the long-term effect of immigration is based on the generational accounting technique. This methodology assesses the redistribution of the tax burden across generations by taking into account the lifecycle contributions made by current and future generations; it allows for an in depth analysis of the costs and benefits of immigration in terms of revenues and expenditures and for a comparison of the potential fiscal effects of alternative migration policies. The information needed, however, is substantial and involves reliable demographic forecasts, as well as data on the tax and transfers structure for each demographic group, detailed data and projections on government expenditures, information on the initial stock of public debt etc.

Findings from the numerous papers that have applied this methodology indicate a net fiscal gain if immigrants are highly skilled and relatively young, but the magnitude of the effects depends on institutional features of the destination countries. Auerbach and Oreopoulos (1999, 2000) study the fiscal effects of immigration to the US. They find little evidence of either a positive or negative effect of changes in the overall level of immigration on public finances. Only when looking at the impact of skilled immigration do they obtain clear-cut results: an increase in the share of skilled immigrants unambiguously improves the US fiscal position. Chojnicki (2013) carries out a similar exercise focusing on France. His findings indicate a slight positive effect in the long run, mainly driven by the continuous inflows of working age migrants and by the net positive contribution of the descendants of first-generation immigrants. The net gain from immigration is larger if the immigrants entering the country are highly qualified. However, the magnitude of the effects is not large enough to significantly reduce government fiscal imbalances. A more sizable positive fiscal effect of immigration is found by Collado et al. (2004) for Spain, and by Mayr (2005) for Austria.

The immigrants' impact on the government budget in the host country might have important policy consequences, which have also received some attention in the literature. Razin and Sadka (1999, 2000) develop an overlapping-generation model where each generation lives for two periods, two types of skills coexist, and a pay as you go pension system is in place, which requires the young generation in employment to finance retirement benefits for the elderly through income taxes. Under the assumption of free capital mobility,[10] the model predicts a net gain from migration for both low and high income groups and young and old age groups of individuals living at the time of the immigrant flow. This is possible since, in an everlasting economy, the potential net burden immigrants impose on the native population may be indefinitely shifted onwards to the next generation. This result crucially depends on the assumption of free capital mobility, which ensures that factor prices are unaffected. If this assumption is relaxed, Razin and Sadka (2000) show that an anti-immigration sentiment may arise and weaken or even overturn the positive effects of migration: the migrants' net contribution may turn into a loss for some native income groups of both current and future generations.

Open Issues

The analysis of the fiscal impact of immigration in destination countries still does not systematically include return or circular migration when modelling migrants' net contributions to the host country public finances. Moreover, the assumptions needed for dynamic models of the fiscal impact of immigration, especially in the generational accounting context, are very strong, and predictions are highly sensitive to small changes in these assumptions. For example, in a recent study Bonin et al. (2014) show that the findings of traditional generational accounting exercises are significantly affected when the impact of business cycle fluctuations is taken into account. The more robust approach, with minimal data requirements and at the same time answering politically important questions, is developed by Dustmann and Frattini (2014).

3.6   Migration and Skill Shortages

Immigration can – at least partially – offset the effects of a shrinking population. In this section we review research concerned with how the inflow of foreign workers can help to fill labour shortages and bring about skills that are in short supply in destination countries, thus relaxing important bottlenecks leading to inefficiencies in the production of goods and services.[11]

Even if the notions of labour and skill shortages are extensively used by economists and policy-makers, there is no consensus over a universal definition of 'shortage' (see UK Migration Advisory Committee – MAC, 2008, 2010 and Dustmann et al., 2010b). From a theoretical perspective, a shortage arises when supply and demand for a given type of worker are not in equilibrium and the demand is greater than the supply.[12] In this context, a shortage of workers is resolved if wages increase to balance demand and supply. Labour market failures, however, may generate shortages due to factors unrelated to the economic cycle and, although wage increases may affect native population skill-specific human capital investments in the long run, it may take several years before the economy reaches the equilibrium. Moreover, labour market imperfections such as wage rigidities in specific sectors (e.g., the public sector) may make equilibrium adjustments harder and lead to persistent shortages of workers in specific occupations (see MAC, 2010).

Two major approaches have been adopted to identify and measure shortages: a microeconomic perspective focuses on the employers' viewpoint, whereas a macroeconomic approach relies on aggregate indicators such as wages (see MAC, 2008). Current methodologies to identify and forecast labour and skill shortages often use a combination of the two, relying on macro-level model-based projections, on sectoral and occupational studies and on stakeholder surveys.

Descriptive findings from Europe reveal shortages in various occupations, across a broad spectrum of skill levels. Table 3.2 ranks occupations according to the 'bottleneck' vacancies[13] reported by employers in European countries,[14] and summarized in a recent study carried out by the European Commission (European Commission, 2014b). Among the most affected groups, we have both occupations which require a highly qualified workforce, such as cooks or engineering and health professionals,[15] as well as low-skilled occupations, such as waiters and heavy truck and lorry drivers. Occupations experiencing shortages are not only those characterized by growing employment, but also those in sectors which have been severely hit by the recent economic crisis, such as manufacturing and construction.

In order for a migration policy to be effective in addressing a labour market shortage, policy-makers should be able to design and develop a selection process able to attract the required type of migrants in a sufficiently short time, and to direct foreign workers towards the parts of a country where they are mostly needed (International Organization for Migration, 2012). Countries that have in place specific policies to attract skilled workers employ a wide array of instruments, which can be broadly classified as 'immigrant driven' or 'employer driven' (Chaloff and Lemaitre, 2009), and which focus on addressing temporary or permanent needs. In an 'immigrant driven' system, a foreigner is admitted without necessarily having a job offer in hand, and the selection is based upon a set of desirable attributes. In an 'employer driven' system, on the other hand, the worker must have already received a job offer in order to gain admission.

'Immigrant driven' systems use 'point assessment' to determine how desirable a foreign national is. This type of framework was first used in Canada in 1967, followed by Australia in 1989 and New Zealand in 1991 and more

Table 3.2 *Top 20 bottleneck vacancies in European countries (European Commission, 2014b, p. 9)*

Rank	Specific occupation
1	Cooks
2	Metal working machine tool setters and operators
3	Shop sales assistants
4	Nursing professionals
5	Heavy truck and lorry drivers
6	Welders and flamecutters
7	Mechanical engineers
8	Software developers
9	Specialist medical practitioners
10	Carpenters and joiners
11	Commercial sales representatives
12	Electrical engineers
13	Waiters
14	Civil engineers
15	System analysts
16	Primary school teachers
17	Plumbers and pipe fitters
18	Accountants
19	Building and related electricians
20	Health care assistants

recently by the UK, Denmark and, to a lesser extent, the Netherlands. The selection process is based on the stipulation of a '*pass rate*' and points are attributed based on a set of five main criteria: occupation; work experience; education; destination country language proficiency and age. A second set of criteria might also be used, including: employer nomination/job offer; prior work in the destination country; education obtained in the destination country; settlement stipulations; and presence of close relatives and prior earnings (Facchini and Lodigiani, 2014).[16]

Broadly speaking, two different economic models lie behind the attribution of 'points' to the first set of criteria. On the one hand, we have a short-term approach, which emphasizes the need to fill current gaps in the destination country's labour market. In this framework, the applicant's recent occupation and work experience are particularly highly rewarded. On the other hand, we have a longer term approach, that is, a model based on the earnings capacity of immigrants, where education, age and official language proficiency are the main focus.

In '*employer driven*' skilled immigration systems – like the US H1-B visa system or the current UK Tier 2 system – the focus is typically on temporary work permits,[17] and employers play a key role. They offer the migrant a job, sponsor his/her application and often carry out a 'labour market' test, whose purpose is to establish that the vacancy advertised cannot be filled by a local worker. The stringency of such tests varies substantially depending on an array of country specific factors.

Even if selection based on skill involves only a limited share of the total number of migrants admitted by Western destination countries, the existing literature suggests that migrant-driven schemes have been successful in rasing the skill level of the average migrant (Aydemir and Borjas, 2007, Aydemir, 2011). However, the evidence on employer driven schemes is ambiguous. Some countries have successfully deployed these frameworks to retain the best and brightest foreign students, graduating from their universities. The U.S. US H1-B scheme is a well-known example, and the literature has emphasized the role of immigrants admitted through this programme in promoting innovation (Kerr and Lincoln, 2010). As for other destinations less successful in attracting foreign students, such as some continental European countries, the employer-driven model has shown important limits, in particular when it comes to the identification of suitable candidates (Facchini and Lodigiani, 2014).

Over the past several years, the EU has become increasingly aware of the role that high-skilled migration may play in addressing labour market shortages. To systematically regulate and promote high-skilled migration by allowing access to the EU wide labour market, the European Council has introduced in 2009 a Directive on 'the conditions of entry and residence of third-country nationals for the purpose of highly qualified employment' (Directive 2009/50/EC), but its effect has not yet been thoroughly investigated (Facchini and Lodigiani, 2014).

Labour and skill shortages are often geographically localized, as destination countries face a population concentration in urban centres and depopulation in rural areas. Immigration may thus help to balance geographical mismatches within national labour markets, but the results have been mixed (International Organization for Migration, 2012). At the same time, some evidence indicates that by being more geographically mobile within the destination country, migrants might help address local labour shortages. For instance, Borjas (2001) emphasizes the 'greasing' effects that immigration may have in the wheels of the labour market by bringing a workforce that is highly responsive to different wages and economic opportunities across regions. Interestingly, empirical evidence for the US indicates that foreign migrants do play an important role in speeding up the process of wage convergence and in helping the national labour market reach an efficient allocation of resources. Similar evidence has been uncovered by Dustmann et al. (2010b) for the UK.

One important caveat to bear in mind when addressing shortages via migration, is that there might be potentially negative effects in the long run. In particular, complete reliance on foreign workers may lead to dependence on them and generate perverse effects. For example, employers might end up adopting less advanced, labour intensive technologies, and in order to remain competitive they will continue to require migrants in the future, contributing to the creation of new shortages (see e.g., Martin and Ruhs, 2011, International Organization for Migration, 2012).

Open Issues

Better tools, based on robust conceptual models, are needed to identify and measure labour and skill shortages at both the national and subnational level. Better data will certainly help. The development of effective policies to address shortages requires understanding the short- and the long-term effects of international migrants' recruiting and how they compare with available alternatives. Much more work is needed in this area.

3.7   International Migration and the Health Care Sector

In the previous section, we have argued that migration can be a short-term solution to skill shortages affecting destination countries' labour markets. We now turn to two specific sectors, health care and old age care. We start by investigating the role of immigrants as suppliers of those services (Subsections 3.7.1 and 3.7.2), and turn next to considering their impact on the demand side of this market (Subsection 3.7.3).

3.7.1   *International Migration of Health Care Professionals*

Migrant workers play an increasingly important role in the health care sector. Immigration is often seen as the quickest and cheapest solution to perceived short-term shortages in the availability of medical staff. Foreign trained workers may also be important in addressing local shortages in underserved and/or rural areas or in case of shortages in specific medical specialties, for example, those related to an ageing population. Moreover, Western countries are starting to use foreign health care professionals to address the needs of an increasingly diverse population whose health needs may be more efficiently met by an ethnically diverse medical staff (see Grignon et al., 2013 for a recent review).

Major suppliers of health-care workers are African countries, India and the Philippines, whereas destination countries who have historically recruited large numbers of foreign trained health professionals are Australia, Canada, the UK and the US (Bach, 2003). Recent data collected by the World Health Organization (WHO, 2014) show that employing immigrants in the health industry[18] is becoming more widespread (Table 3.3). By 2008, almost half of the nurses employed in Ireland were foreign trained, and the same is true for over a third of the doctors registered there. In New Zealand, almost 39 per cent of the doctors are foreign trained, and so are almost a quarter of the nurses. At

Table 3.3 *Foreign-trained (or foreign) nurses and doctors in selected OECD countries, based on professional registries (WHO, 2014, p. 87)*

	Year[a]	Number	Share (%)
Nurses			
Foreign-trained			
Finland	2008	530	0.5
Netherlands	2005	3479	1.4
Sweden	2007	2585	2.6
US	2004	100791	3.5
Denmark	2005	5109	6.2
Canada	2007	20319	7.9
United Kingdom	2001	50564	8
New Zealand	2008	9895	22.1
Ireland	2008	37892	47.1
Foreign			
Belgium	2008	2271	1.5
France	2005	7058	1.6
Portugal	2008	2037	3.6
Italy	2008	33364	9.4
Doctors			
Foreign-trained			
Poland	2005	734	0.6
Austria	2008	1556	4.1
France	2005	12124	5.8
Denmark	2008	1282	6.1
Netherlands	2006	3907	6.2
Belgium	2008	289	6.7
Finland	2008	2713	11.7
Canada	2007	14051	17.9
Sweden	2007	6034	18.4
Switzerland	2008	6659	22.5
US	2007	243457	25.9
United Kingdom	2008	48697	31.5
Ireland	2008	6300	35.5
New Zealand	2008	4106	38.9
Foreign			
Slovak Republic	2004	139	0.8
Japan	2008	2483	0.9
Greece	2001	897	2.5
Italy	2008	14747	3.7
Germany	2008	21784	5.2
Portugal	2008	4400	11.1
Norway	2008	3172	15.9

[a] Notes: Country data sources: Austria: Austrian Medical Chamber; Belgium: Federal Public Service Health, Food Chain Safety and Environment; Canada: CIHI Workforce Trends of Regulated Nurses in Canada, SMDB Scott's Medical Database; Denmark: Labor Register for Health Personnel, National Board of Health, Nursing Adviser; Finland: National Supervisory Authority for Welfare and Health (Valvira); France: ADELI, DREES, Ordre des Médecins; Germany: Bundesärztekammer; Greece: General Secretariat of the National Statistical Service of Greece; Ireland: An Bord Altranais, Irish Medical Council; Italy: AMSI Associazione Medici di Origine Straniera, based on ENPAM, Federazione Ipasvi; Japan: Statistic Bureau, Ministry of Internal Affairs and Communication; Netherlands: BIG Register (Beroepen in de Individuele Gezondheidszorg); New Zealand: Ministry of Health, Information Directorate, Nursing Council of New Zealand; Norway: Den Norske Legeforening; Poland: Polish Chamber of Physicians and Dentists; Portugal: ACIDI, I.P., Immigration Observatory, Ordem dos Enfermeiros; Slovak Republic: Ministry of Health of Slovak Republic; Sweden: Swedish National Board of Health and Welfare; Switzerland: FMH Swiss Medical Association; UK: General Medical Council, Nursing and Midwivery Council; US: American Medical Association, National Council of State Boards of Nursing (NCSBN).

the same time, the US continues to remain the main destination of medical professionals, with over 100,000 foreign trained medical doctors and almost a quarter of a million foreign trained nurses. Important differences exist though among the OECD countries for which data are available. In particular, Nordic European countries report very small numbers of registered foreign medical professionals, and in many Eastern European countries the number of foreign trained professionals is negligible.

The arrival of foreign medical professionals has both short- and long-term consequences on the host country's labour market. In particular, it may affect the employment and wages of natives in the sector and, importantly, it might have a significant impact on the overall quality of the health care services provided.

Most of the existing evidence comes from the US. Combining data from the National Survey of Registered Nurses and data from the Current Population Survey for the period 1995–2008, Schumacher (2011) studies earnings differentials between foreign-born/trained and native nurses and the effects of foreign nurses' immigration on natives' wages. He finds evidence of a negative wage gap only for recent immigrants and of a very small, if any, negative effect of immigration on native wages. Cortés and Pan (2014) also analyse the labour market impact of foreign health professionals. Following Card's (2001) spatial correlation approach, they exploit the variation in the distribution of foreign nurses across US cities and across labour market experience groups within cities. They find a large displacement of native nurses and provide evidence that the crowding out is due to natives changing occupation or to individuals deciding not to enter the nursing profession at all. The overall wage effect is instead negligible even if immigration might lead to a deterioration in working conditions.

Given the specific status of the health-care industry, a particularly important question often at the heart of the debate on the migration of health care professionals concerns the 'quality' of human capital supplied by migrants. Dustmann and Frattini (2011) find that immigrants employed in the public sector in the UK have on average more years of education than natives, which suggests that immigrants may positively affect the 'quality' of public services provided.

Cortés and Pan (2015) tackle this important issue by comparing foreign educated and native born nurses in the US. Interestingly, they find a positive wage gap for Filipino nurses, whereas no significant wage premium is found for nurses educated in other countries. Moreover, the positive wage gap for Filipino nurses cannot be explained by socio-demographic or economic characteristics, thus suggesting that it is driven by unobserved positive human capital attributes. Cortés and Pan (2015) conclude that the 'high quality' of Filipino nurses is likely to be driven by a strong positive selection into the profession in the country of origin.

Besides selection in the country of origin, the high 'quality' of foreign health care professionals is likely to be driven also by the strict rules put in place in immigrant destination countries, which severely limit access to health-care professions and often discriminate against foreigners. Several papers have tried to study the extent these policies are in place to respond to legitimate public concerns, or rather respond to pressures by native physicians to limit competition in the sector. Also in this case, the main evidence comes from the US.

Glied and Sarkar (2009) focus on the institutional factors affecting the size of the International Medical Graduate (IMG) population in the US, and assess the medical profession's role in shaping it. To this end, they construct estimates of the stringency of the tests required for foreign educated professionals over time and combine it with evidence on the underlying IMG cohort characteristics taken from Census data. They then investigate the quality of different cohorts of foreign graduates and construct an indicator for the 'rate of return' to the investment in human capital in the medical profession over time. Interestingly, their analysis suggests that in setting the pass rate for the medical licensing examination required for the IMGs, the medical profession tries to maintain a constant rate of return to the human capital investment of domestic doctors.

The role of medical associations in shaping access to the profession has been investigated also in a recent paper by Peterson et al. (2014), exploiting US cross-state variation in licensing requirements for foreign educated physicians over the period 1973–2010. The authors find that states with self-financing – rather than state government – funded medical boards end up with stricter rules for migrant licensing, and in particular foreign trained doctors require lengthier residency training in the US in order to gain access to the profession. The role of relicensing requirements in creating rents for native health professionals is also analysed by Kugler and Sauer (2005) using quasi-experimental data from Israel.

The migration of health care professionals has received considerable attention also in the development literature, and much has been written to assess whether it creates a '*brain drain*' or a '*brain gain*' for the source country. While this issue is very important, it goes beyond the scope of this survey and we refer the interested reader to the excellent review by Docquier and Rapoport (2012).

3.7.2   International Migration of Old Age Carers

Population ageing in Europe is expected to significantly increase the demand for long-term care (LTC). While the international flow of highly skilled health professionals has received a lot of attention in the literature, much less is known about the migration of old-age care workers.

Employment in the LTC sector continues to be female-dominated in most EU Member States (Bettio and Verashchagina, 2012). However, different patterns in the division of care work between the state, the private market and the family have given rise to a variety of models of care, in which foreign migrants play a very different role.

In what follows, we provide an overview of the different long-term care regimes, and compare their main features, focusing on the role of migrants and their employment conditions. While little is known of the direct effect of immigrant workers on natives employed in the same sector, a few studies have highlighted the impact of migration on the labour supply decisions of younger and possibly better educated Europeans, who would otherwise have been in charge of caring for their elderly family members.

Models of Long-Term Elderly Care

Migrants' role in LTC provision varies with the destination country traditions and institutional contexts. Three main arrangements have been identified in the literature.

Broadly speaking, a 'migrant in the family' model characterizes Southern European countries. In this context, care for the elderly is typically not delegated to private or public institutions, remaining instead the responsibility of the family (see Bettio et al., 2006). Italy is a fitting example of this tradition. A large demand for care workers, and a limited supply of native providers, has led many Italian families to rely heavily on migrant workers to manage family care needs. The majority of workers in this sector come from Eastern Europe (Van Hooren, 2012). They are typically middle-aged females, with children and family left in their origin country. This type of migration is often temporary or rotational, with migrant women regularly visiting their origin country to maintain ties with their families left behind (Bettio et al., 2006). Migrants' employment conditions vary substantially, and are highly sensitive to their legal status (Van Hooren, 2012).

Two additional models of care are common in other Western European countries. The United Kingdom represents the so-called 'migrant in the market' case, where access to publicly provided services is means-tested and high-income people often have to purchase care services on the market. Within this framework, migrants are often employed in the private formal sector, rather than in the informal or public sectors. Foreign workers' employment conditions, however, are found to be on average worse than those of natives and carers employed in the public sector. In particular, migrants are more likely than natives to work longer hours and do night shifts (Van Hooren, 2012). The last model is prevalent in the Netherlands and in Nordic countries, where citizens are entitled to publicly financed services. Care services are provided by private organizations, working in close collaboration with the government. In this context, the proportion of immigrants is much lower than in the other two regimes and their employment conditions are typically comparable to those of native workers.

Care Workers and Highly Skilled Natives' Labour Supply

Besides directly addressing specific needs for long-term elderly care, the availability of immigrant care workers – and more generally of low-skilled domestic workers – is likely to impact the native labour supply and, in particular, the employment decision of highly skilled women. The available empirical evidence, building both on US and European data, indicates a positive impact of low-skilled immigration on the labour supply of highly skilled native women.

Cortes and Tessada (2011) provide evidence from the US, using data from the 1980, 1990 and 2000 Census. In particular, they find a positive effect of low skilled immigration on the number of hours worked per week by women in the top quartile of the female wage distribution. They also show that this positive effect decreases in size and significance for women at lower points of the wage distribution, becoming insignificant for those with wages below the median. Importantly, immigration affects mainly the intensive margin, that is, the number of hours worked, whereas no significant effect is found on the extensive margin, that is on the probability to enter the labour market. The former effect is particularly large for occupations demanding long hours of work, like law, medicine and research. Similar results have been found, using Italian data, by Barone and Mocetti (2011) and using Spanish data by Farré et al. (2011).

3.7.3   Immigrants' Demand for Health Care

As migrants represent an increasing proportion of the European population, we need a better understanding of their health patterns and their access to health care. For many European health systems, equity in access remains a fundamental objective, and understanding the impact of immigrant flows on the sustainability of existing public health care systems is an important policy priority.

Traditional models for the demand for health care have highlighted the main factors able to explain differences in access to health services by groups of individuals. Predisposing characteristics (such as socio-demographic status and health beliefs), enabling factors (such as personal/family and community characteristics like income and health insurance systems), need variables (both perceived and assessed needs) and characteristics of the health care system have been identified as the main drivers of the demand for health services.

Health care demand is a derivative of migrants' health. Many studies report that immigrants have a good health status at their arrival in the host country (see e.g., Kennedy et al., 2006, Fennelly, 2007). The so-called '*healthy migrant effect*', however, tends to disappear once individuals' demographic characteristics such as age are accounted for. Moreover, once in the host country, immigrants' exposure to risk factors such as poverty and exclusion may deteriorate their mental and physical health status (see WHO, 2010).

Evidence on immigrants' health is scarce, given the lack of exhaustive and cross-country comparable data on health status (see e.g., Ingleby, 2009, Nielsen et al., 2009). Where data are available, large heterogeneity is found in migrants' health depending on age, gender, country of origin, legal status and economic wellbeing (see Rechel et al., 2011). Overall, however, migrants appear to be particularly vulnerable to communicable diseases (see Carballo, 2009a), report higher rates of accidents at work and work-related diseases (see Carballo, 2009b) and a higher incidence of mental illnesses (see Ingleby, 2008) compared to the native population. Evidence of higher maternal and infant mortality is also found in some destination countries (see the overview by Bollini et al., 2009, Carballo, 2009b). The migrants' higher vulnerability to specific diseases can be partly explained by migration-related traumatic events, health conditions in the country of origin and migrants' over-representation in occupations characterized by low wages and poor working conditions (see the overview by Gushulak et al., 2010).

The empirical literature also emphasizes a substantial heterogeneity in access to health care across countries, with much emphasis on the provision model. In the US, where health care is dominated by the private sector and traditionally health insurance coverage has not been universal, the empirical literature has looked at both differences in health insurance takeup between migrants and natives, and at their respective use of health care services. In an interesting study, Akresh (2009) examines the utilization patterns of Asian and Hispanic immigrants included in the 2003 New Immigrant Survey (NIS) and finds that duration of residence, knowledge of host country language, and being insured increase immigrants' access to health care services. This evidence confirms previous findings by Leclere et al. (1994), using data from the 1990 National Health Interview Survey.

Unlike in the US, health care provision in Europe is dominated by a model based on universal coverage. Most EU Member States extend health coverage to third country nationals, but the empirical evidence suggests that inequalities in access and health status between migrants and natives are pervasive also in Europe (see e.g., Ingleby et al., 2005, Mladovsky, 2007), even though the patterns differ substantially across countries.

Solé-Auró et al. (2012) carry out a cross-country analysis of the patterns of utilization of health services among elderly migrants and natives and find that immigrants significantly over-utilize health care services compared to natives, even after controlling for socio-economic and demographic characteristics.

Other studies focus on specific types of health services. The evidence on the usage of general practitioners' health care services does not exhibit a clear pattern: some papers emphasize a over-utilization by the immigrant or minority ethnic population (see e.g., Smaje and Le Grand, 1997, Reijneveld, 1998, Winkelmann, 2002, Morris et al., 2005, Uiters et al., 2006), which is almost completely explained though by gender and health status, whereas other researchers find no significant differences in primary care use between migrants and nonmigrants (see e.g., Antón and De Bustillo, 2010, Wadsworth, 2013) or even under-utilization of primary health care services by migrants (see e.g., Gimeno-Feliu et al., 2013). Overall, these studies suffer from a lack of detailed, comparable data across countries. A similar inconclusive picture emerges from the study of the usage of specialist and hospitalization services. However, a consistent pattern emerges when it comes to access to preventive care. Women and undocumented migrants appear to face significant barriers. In particular, migrant and ethnic minority women are found to have difficulties in accessing prenatal care services, as well as cancer screenings (see e.g., Webb et al., 2004, Wolff et al., 2008, McCormack et al. (2008), Moser et al. (2009), Price et al., 2010). Similarly, the existing evidence indicates that migrants tend to over utilize emergency services compared to natives (see Dyhr et al., 2007 for Denmark and Cots et al., 2007 for Spain).

Open Issues

The studies we have reviewed highlight that we have a good understanding, at least for some countries, of the effect of immigration on the supply of skilled health care professionals, and on how they impact the destination country's labour market.

More work is needed to understand the impact of LTC workers. In particular, we need better individual level data on both the migrants themselves and the native households benefiting from their services. Given the often informal nature of work arrangements in this area, collecting these data will not be an easy task.

As for the analysis of the impact of migration on the demand side of health care services, a large array of studies exist, but there is clearly a need to improve the cross-country comparability of the data used in the analyses, to better understand the sources of the significant differences reported in the various studies we have reviewed.

3.8   The Floridization of Europe: Old Age North–South Migration

The relatively recent phenomenon of amenity led migration of retirees from Northern European towards Mediterranean coastal areas is likely to have important consequences on the demographic structure, health care demand and provision and more generally the working of welfare states in both source and destination countries.

Little systematic evidence exists on intra-European old age migration, but several studies have considered late-age migration within the US. We will review this evidence, which will help identify the important questions that need to be addressed in the European context. In Section 3.8.1 we consider the existing evidence on the drivers of old age migration. We turn next to considering the effects of retirement migration on destinations (Section 3.8.2).

3.8.1   Determinants of Old Age Migration

A useful conceptual framework to understand the main forces at play in shaping old age migration decisions has been developed by Litwak and Longino (1987). Three main stages are identified: the first occurs at retirement, and the migration decision is driven by the maximization of utility, which depends upon environmental and lifestyle amenities. At this stage migrants are likely to be married, in good health and wealthy. The second stage is characterized by a decline in the health status and the potential loss of the spouse. Migration is mainly driven by the need to migrate back to the origin country to be close to the family. Finally, in the last stage the migrant needs permanent care, the health status has declined and the individual moves into structures providing formal care to the elderly.

Conway and Houtenville (1998) develop a theoretical model for the migration of the elderly, which takes into consideration the role of government policies, with a focus on state or local fiscal policies. By estimating out-migration and in-migration equations using US data, the authors conclude that state government public expenditures on education, as well as crime levels and taxation on property and income are important determinants of elderly migration behaviour. Gale and Heath (2000) extend Conway and Houtenville's model by decomposing state revenues and spending. Interestingly, they find that elderly migrants are more likely to move towards states where the costs of public government policies are mainly borne by individuals who are still active in the labour market. The composition of local revenues and spending is found to play an important role also at the county level (Duncombe et al., 2001).

In order to analyse the role of age-related heterogeneous effects, some empirical studies divide the elderly population into subgroups. Conway and Houtenville (2003) examine patterns of elderly migration by age groups using data from the 1990 US Census. Younger elderly migrants' location decisions are mainly affected by characteristics such as the presence of specific amenities, climate and government fiscal policies; older migrants are more likely to react to push factors driving them out of their origin state, such as income and property taxes and the cost of living in their origin country.

Among the main determinants of elderly migration, the portability of social security benefits[19] between source and destination countries is likely to play a key role in affecting, for instance, how return migration (see Section 3.4) impacts the fiscal cost of ageing in destination countries (see Section 3.5). While this question is receiving growing attention in the literature (see Holzmann and Koettl, 2015), our understanding of the actual role of portability is limited, even though 'bad experiences' with the portability of welfare benefits have been found to reduce the likelihood to move abroad for professional reasons, whereas 'good experiences' tend to increase it (d'Addio and Cavalleri, 2015). To understand the main difficulties involved in transferring across borders social security entitlements, note that social security benefits are characterized by both a pre-funded and a redistributive component. The latter is particularly important for European countries, where the welfare state is also relatively more generous compared to other immigrant destinations. The separation and identification of each component of a benefit is fundamental in order to make the pre-funded component readily transferable across countries, and informs also the need to set up bilateral or multilateral agreements to coordinate the mobility of the redistributive component.

The existing arrangements imply that international migrants who move for work reasons and then decide to retire in the host country have their portability rights more clearly regulated and are in a better position than those who decide to migrate after retirement (see e.g., Ackers and Dwyer, 2004, Dwyer and Papadimitriou, 2006). Under EU regulation, migrants' social status and rights to claim welfare benefits in the host country strongly depend on their relations with the host country labour market. In particular, economically inactive individuals' right to reside in the host country is constrained by a 'resources requirement'[20] according to which migrants must provide proof that they have sufficient resources not to become a burden on the host country welfare state. At the same time, elderly migrants' decision to return home after some time spent in the host country may not entitle them to the rights they could have enjoyed in their origin country before departure, since entitlement to specific benefits may require proof of habitual residence (Dwyer and Papadimitriou, 2006). This translates into large numbers of migrant retirees who do not regularize their position since they fear there might be difficulties if at some point they decide to migrate back to their origin country. Moreover, elderly migrants fear that by regularizing their position they may lose some of the benefits they would otherwise be entitled to (see Dwyer, 2000, Legido-Quigley and La Parra, 2007).

3.8.2   Effects on Host Country Economy

Late-age migration flows might have significant effects on the host country economy, but little systematic evidence exists on this issue, and most of the existing studies focus on the US.

Overall, late-age migration appears to have positive effects on the destination's economy, at least in the short run, and some US sunbelt and coastal states have progressively adopted aggressive policies to attract wealthy and relatively young retirees (Haas and Serow, 2002). The positive effects for the host communities are mainly associated with the increases in overall demand and tax payments. However, in the long run, migrant retirees may increase the demand for health care and long-term care services. The net effect on the destination's public finances has not yet been exhaustively studied, even though some attempts have been made, by separately considering old age and young age retirees. In particular, using data from the Bureau of Labor Statistics' Consumer Expenditure Survey, Stallmann et al. (1999) find an overall positive fiscal impact of both young and old elderly migrants, with the rise in local government expenditures being covered by the increased revenues, even in the case of older elderly.

To reach more general conclusions on the long-term economic effect of retirement migration, further research is needed. In particular, more information should be made available and included in the analysis of whether elderly migrants return back to their origin country once they have to rely on family or formal assistance.

Open Issues

Even if most observers expect intra-EU amenity-led migration to become increasingly important over the coming decades, very little is known about who migrates and about the effects of elderly European migration on the destination countries. Much of our ignorance is due to the lack of systematic data in this area so more efforts should be devoted to fill this gap.

3.9   Conclusions

Demographic developments in Europe and beyond, the rapid increase in population flows, both within Europe and between Europe and the rest of the world, and their consequences for the provision of health care services raise a host of vitally important policy questions reviewed in this survey. Several elements emerge from our discussion.

First, existing work addresses most of the issues we have discussed in isolation. Only few papers have attempted to develop general frameworks to capture the interactions between demographic changes, migration and health care provision. More work is required to develop richer theoretical models and empirical analysis to understand the interplay between these different forces, taking into account that they are intrinsically dynamic in nature.

Second, on the measurement side, our analysis has identified several key critical areas where more research is needed. Our current understanding of migration and population dynamics is shaped by our limited ability to systematically track individuals over time and across different countries. Existing administrative data sources allow in principle to trace individuals across national borders, but few efforts have been made to link them. When complemented by cross-border surveys, linked individual level administrative data would enable tremendous progress in the study of migration movements both towards and within the EU. Overcoming data limitations should be a priority if we want to better understand the issues covered in our survey.

Third, our analysis has argued that immigration plays a key role in providing a flexible response to short-term skill shortages, and in particular, for the health care sector and for long-term care services. While progress has been made in understanding the impact of foreign care workers on the destination country's labour force, the existing evidence is still rather sparse, and more work is needed to assess the impact and future importance of migration on the health sector and care services.

Finally, population ageing in a common market where people are free to move is likely to lead to migrations of individuals looking for better amenities while retired. The phenomenon has been ongoing for several decades in the US, and we have some basic understanding of the drivers and consequences of old age migration for the sun-belt states. However, little is known about the European context, where the flows of elderly migrants to the Mediterranean is increasing. More work is needed in this area, and data allowing us to capture individual level migration histories would greatly facilitate the analysis.

Acknowledgements

We would like to thank Laurent Aujean, Bernt Bratsberg, David Coleman, Patricia Cortes, Tommaso Frattini, Libertad Gonzales, Alessandra Venturini and Philip Verwimp for their comments on previous drafts. We would also like to thank Barbara Chizzolini, Marc Ivaldi and Marianne Paasi for their encouragement and the organization of the COEURE workshop, and acknowledge funding by the FP7/320300 grant under the FP7 SSH research programme.

Appendix

Glossary of Terms

- **Brain drain** is defined as the reduction in the per capita human capital in the emigration country (see Dustmann et al., 2011).
- **Circular/repeat migration** refers to the systematic and regular movement of migrants back and forth from their country of origin towards foreign countries.

- **Destination/host country** refers to the place where the migrant has settled.
- **Immigrants** are identified as individuals born in a different country from the one they live in.[21]
- **Net migration** is the difference between the inflow and the outflow of individuals over a given period. In most official statistics, inflows and outflows include both the native born and the foreign born.
- **Origin/source country** refers to a migrant's country of birth.
- **Outmigration** refers to migrants moving out of the host country either to return to their country of origin (return migration) or to move onwards towards a third destination.
- **Replacement (fertility) rate** is the total fertility rate per woman which generates the stability of a population under the hypothesis of no migration flows and unchanged mortality rates. This is estimated by the literature at about 2.1 children per woman for most countries, although it may vary slightly with mortality rates.
- **Return migration** refers to re-migration from the host country back to the country of origin by the migrant's own choice (see Dustmann, 2000).
- **Total fertility rate** is an indicator of the level of fertility calculated by summing age-specific birth rates over all reproductive ages. In a specific year, it refers to the number of children that would be born to a woman if she were to live to the end of her fertile years and if throughout her life she were subject to the age-specific fertility rates observed in a given year.

Notes

1. Germany is a leading example of this phenomenon, as pointed out by *The Economist on 15 June, 2013*. For more details, see http://www.economist.com/news/special-report/21579148-overcome-its-skills-shortage-germany-needs-remodel-its-society-erasmus-generation.
2. We follow most of the existing literature in measuring ageing by looking at the evolution of the share of the population aged 15–64 in the total. For an alternative definition, see Sanderson and Scherbov (2010).
3. The figure includes both immigrants born in other EU/Euro member countries and immigrants born elsewhere.
4. Net migration is measured as the difference between the total population on 31 December and 1 January for a given calendar year, minus the difference between births and deaths (or natural increase).
5. Projection estimates are carried out starting from the EUROPOP2013 demographic projections by Eurostat.
6. See the original paper for the sources of the data used to produce the figure.
7. Migration policies play an important role in shaping the length of the migration spell. For more on this, see Section 3.6.
8. See Dustmann and Frattini (2014) for an application, and a detailed explanation of this approach.

9. See Kirdar (2012) for an extension of the model in which outmigration is endogenized.

10. This assumption ensures that factor returns are not affected by migration.

11. One important caveat to bear in mind though is that – as pointed out by the OECD (2014) and the European Commission (2014b) – less than 40 per cent of the migrants coming to the EU from outside the area gain access to it for work related reasons. The most important channel is instead family reunification.

12. Shortages are therefore the result of a disequilibrium condition in which a labour market does not clear.

13. Bottleneck occupations are defined at the ISCO 4 digit level and are 'occupations where there is evidence of recruitment difficulties, that is, employers have problems finding and hiring staff to meet their needs' (European Commission (2014b) Report on 'Mapping and Analysing Bottleneck Vacancies in EU Labour Markets', p. 7).

14. The sample includes EU Member States, Iceland, Liechtenstein and Norway.

15. See Section 3.7 for a detailed analysis of the health sector.

16. For a recent proposal on the construction of an 'optimal' point-based system, see by McHale and Rogers (2009).

17. Change of status is often allowed though, as in the case of the US H1-B visa programme.

18. Information is available for foreign trained and foreign citizen registered workers.

19. Holzmann and Koettl (2015) define portability as a mechanism to grant and transfer social security rights independently of an individual's country of residence, citizenship status or current or previous occupation.

20. Article 1 of the European Union Council Directive 90/365 limits economically inactive persons' right to reside by two important conditions: ' … [that they] are covered by sickness insurance … [and] … have sufficient resources to avoid becoming a burden on the social assistance system of the host Member State during their period of residence.'

21. An alternative definition used by some researchers is based on citizenship.

References

Ackers, L., and Dwyer, P. 2004. Fixed Laws, Fluid Lives: The Citizenship Status of Post-retirement Migrants in the European Union. *Ageing and Society*, **24**, 451–475.

Adda, J., Dustmann, C., and Görlach, J. S. 2015. Migrant Wages, Human Capital Accumulation and Return Migration. Unpublished manuscript.

Adserà, A., and Ferrer, A. 2015. Immigrants and Demography: Marriage, Divorce, and Fertility. In: Chiswick, Barry R., and Miller, Paul W. (eds), *Handbook of the Economics of International Migration*, vol. 1A. North-Holland, pp. 315–374.

Adserà, A., Ferrer, A., Sigle-Rushton, W., and Wilson, B. 2012. Fertility Patterns of Child Migrants: Age at Migration and Ancestry in Comparative Perspective. *The ANNALS of the American Academy of Political and Social Science*, **643**, 160–189.

Akresh, I. R. 2009. Health Service Utilization among Immigrants to the United States. *Population Research and Policy Review*, **28**, 795–815.

Andersson, G. 2004. Childbearing after Migration: Fertility Patterns of Foreign-born Women in Sweden. *International Migration Review*, **38**, 747–774.

Antón, J. I., and De Bustillo, R. M. 2010. Health Care Utilisation and Immigration in Spain. *The European Journal of Health Economics*, **11**, 487–498.

Auerbach, A. J., and Oreopoulos, P. 1999. Analyzing the Fiscal Impact of US Immigration. *American Economic Review*, **89**, 176–180.

Auerbach, A. J., and Oreopoulos, P. 2000. The Fiscal Impact of US Immigration: A Generational Accounting Perspective. In: Poterba, James (ed), *Tax Policy and the Economy*, vol. 14. MIT Press, Cambridge, 123–156.

Avitabile, C., Clots-Figueras, I., and Masella, P. 2014. Citizenship, Fertility, and Parental Investments. *American Economic Journal: Applied Economics*, **6**, 35–65.

Aydemir, A. 2011. Immigrant Selection and Short-term Labor Market Outcomes by Visa Category. *Journal of Population Economics*, **24**, 451–475.

Aydemir, A., and Borjas, G. J. 2007. Cross-country Variation in the Impact of International Migration: Canada, Mexico, and the United States. *Journal of the European Economic Association*, **5**, 663–708.

Bach, S. 2003. *International Migration of Health Workers: Labour and Social Issues*. International Labour Office, Geneva.

Barone, G., and Mocetti, S. 2011. With a Little Help from Abroad: The Effect of Low-skilled Immigration on the Female Labour Supply. *Labour Economics*, **18**, 664–675.

Bettio, F., and Verashchagina, A. 2012. *Long-term Care for the Elderly: Provisions and Providers in 33 European Countries*. Publications Office of the European Union, Luxembourg.

Bettio, F., Simonazzi, A., and Villa, P. 2006. Change in Care Regimes and Female migration: The 'Care Drain' in the Mediterranean. *Journal of European Social Policy*, **16**, 271–285.

Bijwaard, G. E. 2010. Immigrant Migration Dynamics Model for the Netherlands. *Journal of Population Economics*, **23**, 1213–1247.

Blau, F. D. 1992. The Fertility of Immigrant Women: Evidence from High-fertility Source Countries. In: Borjas, George J, and Freeman, Richard B (eds), *Immigration and the Workforce: Economic Consequences for the United States and Source Areas*. University of Chicago Press, pp. 93–134.

Blau, F. D., Kahn, L. M., Liu, A. Y. H., and Papps, K. L. 2013. The Transmission of Women's Fertility, Human Capital, and Work Orientation across Immigrant Generations. *Journal of Population Economics*, **26**, 405–435.

Bleakley, H., and Chin, A. 2010. Age at Arrival, English Proficiency, and Social Assimilation among US Immigrants. *American Economic Journal: Applied Economics*, **2**, 165.

Bollini, P., Pampallona, S., Wanner, P., and Kupelnick, B. 2009. Pregnancy Outcome of Migrant Women and Integration Policy: A Systematic Review of the International Literature. *Social Science & Medicine*, **68**, 452–461.

Bonin, H., Patxot, C., and Souto, G. 2014. Cyclically-Neutral Generational Accounting. *Fiscal Studies*, **35**, 117–137.

Borjas, G. J. 1989. Immigrant and Emigrant Earnings: A Longitudinal Study. *Economic Inquiry*, **27**, 21–37.

Borjas, G. J. 1994. The Economics of Immigration. *Journal of Economic Literature*, **32**, 1667–1717.

Borjas, G. J. 2001. Does Immigration Grease the Wheels of the Labor Market? *Brookings Papers on Economic Activity*, **1**, 69–119.

Borjas, G. J., and Bratsberg, B. 1996. Who Leaves? The Outmigration of the Foreign-Born. *The Review of Economics and Statistics*, **78**, 165–76.

Bratsberg, B., Raaum, O., and Røed, K. 2010. When Minority Labor Migrants Meet the Welfare State. *Journal of Labor Economics*, **28**, 633–676.

Bratsberg, B., Raaum, O., and Røed, K. 2014. Immigrants, Labour Market Performance and Social Insurance. *The Economic Journal*, **124**, F644–F683.

Carballo, M. 2009a. Communicable Diseases. In: Fernandes, Ana, and Miguel, José Pereira (eds), *Health and Migration in the European Union: Better Health for All in an Inclusive Society*. Instituto Nacional de Saúde Doutor Ricardo Jorge, Lisbon, pp. 53–69.

Carballo, M. 2009b. Non-communicable Diseases. In: Fernandes, Ana, and Miguel, José Pereira (eds), *Health and Migration in the European Union: Better Health for All in an Inclusive Society*. Instituto Nacional de Saúde Doutor Ricardo Jorge, Lisbon, pp. 71–78.

Card, D. 2001. Immigrant Inflows, Native Outflows, and the Local Labor Market Impacts of Higher Immigration. *Journal of Labor Economics*, **19**, 22–64.

CBS. 2006. Internet Database of the Centraal Bureau voor de Statistiek. CBS Statline. Statistics Netherlands. Voorburg. http://statline.cbs.nl.

Chaloff, J., and Lemaitre, G. 2009. Managing Highly-Skilled Labour Migration: A comparative Analysis of Migration Policies and Challenges in OECD Countries. Working Paper No. 79. OECD Social, Employment and Migration. OECD Publishing.

Choi, K. H. 2014. Fertility in the Context of Mexican Migration to the United States: A Case for Incorporating the Pre-migration Fertility of Immigrants. *Demographic Research*, **30**, 703.

Chojnicki, X. 2013. The Fiscal Impact of Immigration in France: A Generational Accounting Approach. *The World Economy*, **36**, 1065–1090.

Coleman, D. 2003. Mass Migration and Population Change. *Zeitschrift für Bevölkerungswissenschaft*, **28**, 183–215.

Collado, M. D., Iturbe-Ormaetxe, I., and Valera, G. 2004. Quantifying the Impact of Immigration on the Spanish Welfare State. *International Tax and Public Finance*, **11**, 335–353.

Colussi, A. 2003. *Migrants' Networks: An Estimable Model of Illegal Mexican Migration*. Mimeo, University of Pennsylvania, Philadelphia.

Constant, A. F., and Zimmermann, K. F. 2011. Circular and Repeat Migration: Counts of Exits and Years Away from the Host Country. *Population Research and Policy Review*, **30**, 495–515.

Conway, K. S., and Houtenville, A. J. 2003. Out with the Old, In with the Old: A Closer Look at Younger Versus Older Elderly Migration. *Social Science Quarterly*, **84**, 309–328.

Conway, K. S., and Houtenville, A. J. 1998. Do the Elderly 'Vote with their Feet?'. *Public Choice*, **97**, 663–685.

Cortés, P., and Pan, J. 2014. Foreign Nurse Importation and the Supply of Native Nurses. *Journal of Health Economics*, **37**, 164–180.

Cortés, P., and Pan, J. 2015. Relative Quality of Foreign Nurses in the United States. *Journal of Human Resources*, **50**(4), 1009–1050.

Cortes, P., and Tessada, J. 2011. Low-skilled Immigration and the Labor Supply of Highly Skilled Women. *American Economic Journal: Applied Economics*, **3**, 88–123.

Cots, F., Castells, X., García, O., Riu, M., Felipe, A., and Vall, O. 2007. Impact of Immigration on the Cost of Emergency Visits in Barcelona (Spain). *BMC Health Services Research*, **7**, 9.

d'Addio, A. C., and Cavalleri, M. C. 2015. Labour Mobility and the Portability of Social Rights in the EU. *CES Ifo Economic Studies*, **61**, 346–376.

Docquier, F., and Rapoport, H. 2012. Globalization, Brain Drain, and Development. *Journal of Economic Literature*, **50**, 681–730.

Dubuc, S. 2012. Immigration to the UK from High-Fertility Countries: Intergenerational Adaptation and Fertility Convergence. *Population and Development Review*, **38**, 353–368.

Duncombe, W., Robbins, M., and Wolf, D. A. 2001. Retire to Where? A Discrete Choice Model of Residential Location. *International Journal of Population Geography*, **7**, 281–293.

Dustmann, C. 1995. Savings Behaviour of Migrant Workers – A Life Cycle Analysis. *Zeitschrift fuer Wirtschafts- und Sozialwissenschaften*, **4**, 511–533.

Dustmann, C. 1996. Return Migration: The European Experience. *Economic Policy*, **11**, 213–250.

Dustmann, C. 1997. Return Migration, Uncertainty and Precautionary Savings. *Journal of Development Economics*, **52**, 295–316.

Dustmann, C. 2000. Temporary Migration and Economic Assimilation. *Swedish Economic Policy Review*, **7**, 213–244.

Dustmann, C. 2003. Return Migration, Wage Differentials, and the Optimal Migration Duration. *European Economic Review*, **47**, 353–369.

Dustmann, C., and Frattini, T. 2011. *The Impact of Migration on the Provision of UK Public Services*. Report for the Migration Advisory Committee.

Dustmann, C., and Frattini, T. 2014. The Fiscal Effects of Immigration to the UK. *The Economic Journal*, **124**, F593–F643.

Dustmann, C., and Görlach, J. S. 2015. Selective Out-Migration and the Estimation of Immigrants' Earnings Profiles. In: Chiswick, Barry R., and Miller, Paul W. (eds), *Handbook of the Economics of International Migration*, vol. 1A. North-Holland, pp. 489–533.

Dustmann, C., and Görlach, J. S. 2016. The Economics of Temporary Migrations. *Journal of Economic Literature*, **54**(1), 98–136.

Dustmann, C., and Weiss, Y. 2007. Return Migration: Theory and Empirical Evidence from the UK. *British Journal of Industrial Relations*, **45**, 236–256.

Dustmann, C., Frattini, T., and Halls, C. 2010a. Assessing the Fiscal Costs and Benefits of A8 Migration to the UK. *Fiscal Studies*, **31**, 1–41.

Dustmann, C., Frattini, T., and Preston, I. 2010b. *Can Immigration Constitute a Sensible Solution to Sub-national and Regional Labour Shortages?* Report for the Migration Advisory Committee.

Dustmann, C., Fadlon, I., and Weiss, Y. 2011. Return Migration, Human Capital Accumulation and the Brain Drain. *Journal of Development Economics*, **95**, 58–67.

Dwyer, P., and Papadimitriou, D. 2006. The Social Security Rights of Older International Migrants in the European Union. *Journal of Ethnic and Migration Studies*, **32**, 1301–1319.

Dwyer, P. J. 2000. Movements to Some Purpose? An Exploration of International Retirement Migration in the European Union. *Education and Ageing*, **15**, 353–377.

Dyhr, L., Andersen, J. S., and Engholm, G. 2007. The Pattern of Contact with General Practice and Casualty Departments of Immigrants and Non-immigrants in Copenhagen, Denmark. *Danish Medical Bulletin*, **54**, 226–229.

European Commission. 2014a. The 2015 Ageing Report: Underlying Assumptions and Projection Methodologies. *European Economy*, **8/2014**.

European Commission. 2014b. *Mapping and Analysing Bottleneck Vacancies in EU Labour Markets*. EC Overview Report Final.

European Commission. 2015. The 2015 Ageing Report: Economic and Budgetary Projections for the 28 EU Member States (2013–2060). *European Economy*, **3/2015**.

Facchini, G., and Lodigiani, E. 2014. Attracting Skilled Immigrants: An Overview of Recent Policy Developments in Advanced Countries. *National Institute Economic Review*, **229**, R3–R21.

Farré, L., González, L., and Ortega, F. 2011. Immigration, Family Responsibilities and the Labor Supply of Skilled Native Women. *The BE Journal of Economic Analysis & Policy*, **11**, Article 34.

Fennelly, K. 2007. The 'Healthy Migrant' Effect. *Minnesota Medicine*, **90**, 51–53.

Fernández, R., and Fogli, A. 2006. Fertility: The Role of Culture and Family Experience. *Journal of the European Economic Association*, **4**, 552–561.

Fernández, R., and Fogli, A. 2009. Culture: An Empirical Investigation of Beliefs, Work, and Fertility. *American Economic Journal: Macroeconomics*, **1**, 146–177.

Gale, L. R., and Heath, W. C. 2000. Elderly Internal Migration in the United States Revisited. *Public Finance Review*, **28**, 153–170.

Garssen, J., and Nicolaas, H. 2008. Fertility of Turkish and Moroccan Women in the Netherlands: Adjustment to Native Level Within One Generation. *Demographic Research*, **19**, 1249.

Gimeno-Feliu, L. A., Magallón-Botaya, R., Macipe-Costa, R. M., Luzón-Oliver, L., Cañada-Millan, J. L., and Lasheras-Barrio, M. 2013. Differences in the Use of Primary Care Services between Spanish National and Immigrant Patients. *Journal of Immigrant and Minority Health*, **15**, 584–590.

Glied, S., and Sarkar, D. 2009. The Role of Professional Societies in Regulating Entry of Skilled Immigrants: The American Medical Association. In: Bhagwati, Jagdish, and Hanson, Gordon (eds), *Skilled Migration: Problems, Prospects, and Policies*. Oxford and New York: Oxford University Press, pp. 184–206.

Grignon, M., Owusu, Y., and Sweetman, A. 2013. The International Migration of Health Professionals. In: Chiswick, Barry R., and Miller, Paul W. (eds), *International Handbook on the Economics of Migration*. Edward Elgar, Cheltenham, UK, and Northampton, USA, pp. 75–97.

Gushulak, B., Pace, P., and Weekers, J. 2010. Migration and Health of Migrants. In: Koller, T (ed), *Poverty and Social Exclusion in the WHO European Region: Health Systems Respond*. WHO Regional Office for Europe, Copenhagen, pp. 257–281.

Haas, W. H., and Serow, W. J. 2002. The Baby Boom, Amenity Retirement Migration, and Retirement Communities: Will the Golden Age of Retirement Continue? *Research on Aging*, **24**, 150–164.

Hansen, J., and Lofstrom, M. 2003. Immigrant Assimilation and Welfare Participation: Do Immigrants Assimilate Into or Out of Welfare? *Journal of Human Resources*, **38**, 74–98.

Héran, F., and Pison, G. 2007. Two Children per Woman in France in 2006: Are Immigrants to Blame? *Population and Societies*, **432**.

Holzmann, R., and Koettl, J. 2015. Portability of Pension, Health, and Other Social Benefits: Facts, Concepts, and Issues. *CESifo Economic Studies*, **61**, 377–415.

INE. 2006. Vital Statistics 2005. Definitive data. Instituto National de Estadística. Madrid. http://ine.es/inebmenu/indice.htm.

INE. 2007. Movimiento natural de la población. Resultados provisionales 2006. Instituto National de Estadística. Madrid. http://ine.es/inebmenu/indice.htm.

Ingleby, D. 2008. *New Perspectives on Migration, Ethnicity and Schizophrenia*. Willy Brandt Series of Working Papers in International Migration and Ethnic Relations No. 1/08, Malmö University.

Ingleby, D. 2009. *European Research on Migration and Health*. Background paper for AMAC project. International Organization for Migration, Brussels.

Ingleby, D., Chimienti, M., Hatziprokopiou, P., Ormond, M., and De Freitas, C. 2005. The Role of Health in Integration. In: Fonseca, Maria Lucinda, and Malheiros, Jorge (eds), *Social Integration and Mobility: Education, Housing and Health*. IMISCOE Cluster B5 State of the art report. Estudos para o Planeamento Regional e Urbano no 67, Centro de Estudos Geográficos, Lisbon, pp. 89–119.

International Organization for Migration. 2012. *Labour Shortages and Migration Policy*. In: A. Platonova and G. Urso (eds). IOM LINET, Brussels.

ISTAT. 2007. Natalità e fecondità della popolazione residente: Caratteristiche e tendenze recenti. Anno 2004. Istituto nazionale di statistica. Roma. http://istat.it.

Jasso, G., and Rosenzweig, M. R. 1982. Estimating the Emigration Rates of Legal Immigrants Using Administrative and Survey Data: The 1971 Cohort of Immigrants to the United States. *Demography*, **19**, 279–290.

Kahn, J. R. 1988. Immigrant Selectivity and Fertility Adaptation in the United States. *Social Forces*, **67**, 108–128.

Kahn, J. R. 1994. Immigrant and Native Fertility during the 1980s: Adaptation and Expectations for the Future. *International Migration Review*, **28**, 501–519.

Kennan, J., and Walker, J. R. 2011. The Effect of Expected Income on Individual Migration Decisions. *Econometrica*, **79**, 211–251.

Kennedy, S., McDonald, J. T., and Biddle, N. 2006. *The Healthy Immigrant Effect and Immigrant Selection: Evidence from Four Countries*. Social and Economic Dimensions of an Aging Population Research Papers No. 164. McMaster University, Hamilton.

Kerr, W. R., and Lincoln, W. F. 2010. The Supply Side of Innovation: H-1B Visa Reforms and US Ethnic Invention. *Journal of Labor Economics*, **28**, 473–508.

Kirdar, M. G. 2012. Estimating the Impact of Immigrants on the Host Country Social Security System when Return Migration is an Endogenous Choice. *International Economic Review*, **53**, 453–486.

Kugler, A. D., and Sauer, R. M. 2005. Doctors without Borders? Relicensing Requirements and Negative Selection in the Market for Physicians. *Journal of Labor Economics*, **23**, 437–465.

Kytir, J. 2006. *Demographische Strukturen und Trends 2005*. **9**, 777–790.

Leclere, F. B., Jensen, L., and Biddlecom, A. E. 1994. Health Care Utilization, Family Context, and Adaptation among Immigrants to the United States. *Journal of Health and Social Behavior*, **35**, 370–384.

Legido-Quigley, H., and La Parra, D. 2007. The Health Care Needs of UK Pensioners Living in Spain: An Agenda for Research. *Eurohealth*, **13**, 14–17.

Lessem, R. 2013. *Mexico-US immigration: Effects of Wages and Border Enforcement.* Working paper. Carnegie-Mellon University, Tepper School of Business, Pittsburgh.

Litwak, E., and Longino, C. F. 1987. Migration Patterns among the Elderly: A Developmental Perspective. *The Gerontologist*, **27**, 266–272.

Lubotsky, D. 2007. Chutes or Ladders? A Longitudinal Analysis of Immigrant Earnings. *Journal of Political Economy*, **115**, 820–867.

MAC. 2008. *A Review of Labour Shortages, Skills Shortages and Skill Gaps.* Migration Advisory Committee, London.

MAC. 2010. *Skilled, Shortage, Sensible. Review of Methodology.* Migration Advisory Committee, London.

Martin, P., and Ruhs, M. 2011. Labor Shortages and US Immigration Reform: Promises and Perils of an Independent Commission. *International Migration Review*, **45**, 174–187.

Mayer, J., and Riphahn, R. T. 2000. Fertility Assimilation of Immigrants: Evidence from Count Data Models. *Journal of Population Economics*, **13**, 241–261.

Mayr, K. 2005. The Fiscal Impact of Immigrants in Austria: A Generational Accounting Analysis. *Empirica*, **32**, 181–216.

McCormack, V. A., Perry, N., Vinnicombe, S. J., and dos Santos Silva, I. 2008. Ethnic Variations in Mammographic Density: A British Multiethnic Longitudinal Study. *American Journal of Epidemiology*, **168**, 412–421.

McHale, J., and Rogers, K. 2009. *Selecting Economic Immigrants: A Statistical Approach.* Working Paper No. 0145. National University of Ireland, Galway.

Mladovsky, P. 2007. *Migration and Health in the EU.* Research note. European Commission, Brussels.

Morris, S., Sutton, M., and Gravelle, H. 2005. Inequity and Inequality in the Use of Health Care in England: An Empirical Investigation. *Social Science & Medicine*, **60**, 1251–1266.

Moser, K., Patnick, J., and Beral, V. 2009. Inequalities in Reported Use of Breast and Cervical Screening in Great Britain: Analysis of Cross Sectional Survey Data. *British Medical Journal*, **338**, 1480–1484.

Nekby, L. 2006. The Emigration of Immigrants, Return vs Onward Migration: Evidence from Sweden. *Journal of Population Economics*, **19**, 197–226.

Nielsen, S. S., Krasnik, A., and Rosano, A. 2009. Registry Data for Cross-country Comparisons of Migrants' Healthcare Utilization in the EU: A Survey Study of Availability and Content. *BMC Health Services Research*, **9**, 210.

OECD. 2014. *OECD Factbook 2014: Economic, Environmental and Social Statistics.* OECD Publishing. http://dx.doi.org/10.1787/factbook-2014-en.

ONS. 2006. *Birth Statistics. Review of the Registrar General on Births and Patterns of Family Building England and Wales, 2005.* Series FM1. No. 34. Office of National Statistics. London.

ONS. 2007. *Fertility Rate is Highest for 26 Years.* News release, 7 June 2007. Office of National Statistics. London.

Parrado, E. A., and Morgan, S. P. 2008. Intergenerational Fertility among Hispanic Women: New Evidence of Immigrant Assimilation. *Demography*, **45**, 651–671.

Peterson, B. D., Pandya, S. S., and Leblang, D. 2014. Doctors with Borders: Occupational Licensing as an Implicit Barrier to High Skill Migration. *Public Choice*, **160**, 45–63.

Preston, I. 2014. The Effect of Immigration on Public Finances. *The Economic Journal*, **124**, F569–F592.

Price, C. L., Szczepura, A. K., Gumber, A. K., and Patnick, J. 2010. Comparison of Breast and Bowel Cancer Screening Uptake Patterns in a Common Cohort of South Asian Women in England. *BMC Health Services Research*, **10**.

Prioux, F. 2005. Recent Demographic Developments in France. *Population–E*, **60**, 371–414.

Razin, A., and Sadka, E. 1999. Migration and Pension with International Capital Mobility. *Journal of Public Economics*, **74**, 141–150.

Razin, A., and Sadka, E. 2000. Unskilled Migration: A Burden or a Boon for the Welfare State? *The Scandinavian Journal of Economics*, **102**, 463–479.

Reagan, P. B., and Olsen, R. J. 2000. You Can Go Home Again: Evidence from Longitudinal Data. *Demography*, **37**, 339–350.

Rechel, B., Mladovsky, P., Devillé, W., Rijks, B., Petrova-Benedict, R., and McKee, M. 2011. Migration and Health in the European Union: An Introduction. In: Rechel, Bernd, Mladovsky, Philipa, Devillé, Walter, Rijks, Barbara, Petrova-Benedict, Roumyana, and McKee, Martin (eds), *Migration and Health in the European Union*. Open University Press McGraw-Hill Education. UK.

Reijneveld, S. A. 1998. Reported Health, Lifestyles, and Use of Health Care of First Generation Immigrants in The Netherlands: Do Socioeconomic Factors Explain Their Adverse Position? *Journal of Epidemiology and Community Health*, **52**, 298–304.

Riphahn, R. T. 2004. Immigrant Participation in Social Assistance Programs: Evidence from German Guestworkers. *Applied Economics Quarterly*, **50**, 329–362.

Roig Vila, M., and Martín, T. Castro. 2007. Childbearing Patterns of Foreign Women in a New Immigration Country: The Case of Spain. *Population–E*, **62**, 351–380.

Rowthorn, R. 2008. The Fiscal Impact of Immigration on the Advanced Economies. *Oxford Review of Economic Policy*, **24**, 560–580.

Ruist, J. 2014. Free Immigration and Welfare Access: The Swedish Experience. *Fiscal Studies*, **35**, 19–39.

Sanderson, W. C., and Scherbov, S. 2010. Remeasuring Aging. *Science*, **329**, 1287–1288.

Schoorl, J. 1995. Fertility Trends of Immigrant Populations. *Proceedings of the Symposium, NIAS, Wasenaar, 27–29 September 1990*. Report No. 44. The Hague: NIDI.

Schumacher, E. J. 2011. Foreign-born Nurses in the US Labor Market. *Health Economics*, **20**, 362–378.

SFSO. 2006. Statistique du mouvement naturel de la population. Résultats définitifs 2005. Swiss Federal Statistical Office. Neuchâtel. http://bfs.admin.ch/.

Smaje, C., and Le Grand, J. 1997. Ethnicity, Equity and the Use of Health Services in the British NHS. *Social Science & Medicine*, **45**, 485–496.

Sobotka, T. 2008. The Rising Importance of Migrants for Childbearing in Europe. *Demographic Research*, **19**, 225–248.

Solé-Auró, A., Guillén, M., and Crimmins, E. M. 2012. Health Care Usage among Immigrants and Native-born Elderly Populations in Eleven European Countries: Results from SHARE. *The European Journal of Health Economics*, **13**, 741–754.

Stallmann, J. I., Deller, S. C., and Shields, M. 1999. The Economic and Fiscal Impact of Aging Retirees on a Small Rural Region. *The Gerontologist*, **39**, 599–610.

Statistics Denmark. 2004. *Befolkningens bevaegelser 2003*. (Vital statistics 2003). Danmarks Statistik. Copenhagen.

Statistics Sweden. 2006. *Tabeller över Sveriges befolkning*. Statistics Sweden. Statistiska centralbyrán Stockholm.

Statistisches Bundesamt. 2006. *Statistisches Jahrbuch 2006*. Statistisches Bundesamt. Wiesbaden. https://destatis.de/DE/Startseite.html.

Stephen, E. H., and Bean, F. D. 1992. Assimilation, Disruption and the Fertility of Mexican-Origin Women in the United States. *International Migration Review*, **26**, 67–88.

Storesletten, K. 2000. Sustaining Fiscal Policy through Immigration. *Journal of Political Economy*, **108**, 300–323.

Storesletten, K. 2003. Fiscal Implications of Immigration: A Net Present Value Calculation. *The Scandinavian Journal of Economics*, **105**, 487–506.

The Economist. 2013, June 15th. Erasmus Generation: To Overcome Its Skills Shortage, Germany Needs to Remodel Its Society. http://economist.com/news/special-report/21579148-overcome-its-skills-shortage-germany-needs-remodel-its-society-erasmus-generation.

Thom, K. 2010. *Repeated Circular Migration: Theory and Evidence from Undocumented Migrants*. Mimeo, New York University.

Toulemon, L. 2004. Fertility among Immigrant Women: New Data, a New Approach. *Population and Societies*, 1–4.

Toulemon, L., Pailhé, A., and Rossier, C. 2008. France: High and Stable Fertility. *Demographic Research*, **19**, 503–556.

Tribalat, M. 2005. *Fécondité des immigrées et apport démographique de l'immigration étrangère*. vol. 2. UDEP / IEDUB, Bordeaux.

Uiters, E., Deville, W. L. J. M., Foets, M., and Groenewegen, P. P. 2006. Use of Health Care services by Ethnic Minorities in The Netherlands: Do Patterns Differ? *The European Journal of Public Health*, **16**, 388–393.

Van Hooren, F. J. 2012. Varieties of Migrant Care Work: Comparing Patterns of Migrant Labour in Social Care. *Journal of European Social Policy*, **22**, 133–147.

VAZG. 2007. Tables on Births in Flanders Provided by the Flemish Healthcare Agency. Vlaams Agentschap Zorg en Gezondheid. http://zorg-en-gezondheid.be/topPage.aspx?id=684.

Wadsworth, J. 2013. Mustn't Grumble: Immigration, Health and Health Service Use in the UK and Germany. *Fiscal Studies*, **34**, 55–82.

Webb, R., Richardson, J., Esmail, A., and Pickles, A. 2004. Uptake for Cervical Screening by Ethnicity and Place-of-birth: A Population-based Cross-sectional Study. *Journal of Public Health*, **26**, 293–296.

WHO. 2010. *How Health Systems Can Address Health Inequities Linked to Migration and Ethnicity*. World Health Organization Regional Office for Europe, Copenhagen.

WHO. 2014. *Migration of Health Workers: WHO Code of Practice and the Global Economic Crisis.* World Health Organization Report, Geneva.

Winkelmann, R. 2002. *Work and Health in Switzerland: Immigrants and Natives.* Working Paper No. 0203, Socioeconomic Institute-University of Zurich.

Wolff, H., Epiney, M., Lourenco, A. P., Costanza, M. C., Delieutraz-Marchand, J., Andreoli, N., Dubuisson, J. B., Gaspoz, J. M., and Irion, O. 2008. Undocumented migrants Lack Access to Pregnancy Care and Prevention. *BMC Public Health*, **8**.

4   Education Systems: Assignment, Admissions, Accountability and Autonomy

Simon Burgess

Abstract

This chapter focuses on education market systems, as one of the key issues for policy in education. Research suggests that a coherent market structure for schools is very important for attainment. The key elements are: assignment of pupils to schools and admissions policies, and school accountability and autonomy. The central element of the market structure is the assignment mechanism, which allocates each child to a school. There are different such mechanisms available: school choice, neighbourhood schooling and elite schooling or 'tracking', which assigns pupils on the basis of an exam. Other key elements include governance rules and hierarchy: school accountability and school autonomy. Finally, the nature of school leadership is tied up with the degree of autonomy – leaders are far more important in autonomous schools.

4.1   Introduction

Education is crucially important for many of the policy outcomes that citizens and politicians care about. At an individual level, your education affects your earnings, your employability and your chance of succeeding in life starting from a disadvantaged neighbourhood. It also affects your health, future family structure, intellectual fulfilment and other aspects of a good life. At a national level, a country's stock of skills matters hugely for its prosperity and growth rate. The distribution of skills is a big determinant of inequality, and the relationship of a person's skills to their background is central to the degree of social or intergenerational mobility.

Providing education costs a lot: on average in 2011 OECD countries spent over 6 per cent of their GDP on educational institutions; and it accounted for almost 13 per cent of total public spending in the OECD (http://www.oecd.org/edu/Education-at-a-Glance-2014.pdf), so governments are keen to make it as productive as possible. And schooling takes up a lot of time in young lives – if you're under 20 years old, being at school, thinking about school and doing school work take up a huge fraction of your time awake, on average perhaps around 10,000 hours in school over the OECD. And in older lives too, parents of school-age children also spend a lot of time, energy and stress worrying about their child's education.

Unsurprisingly then, there has been a lot of research on education. A lot of progress has been made, there are a number of things researchers are now fairly confident about. But there are also many open questions, and no doubt new questions yet to be asked, so a great deal of research is still needed. One of the corollaries of this is that more and different datasets are needed. New knowledge has been gained by using traditional surveys, including the difference in earnings that people receive for having higher skills. But increasingly, new data types are being exploited in this field and it is often these that are yielding the current big breakthroughs.

I take 'human capital' to mean the stock of skills, traits and knowledge that an individual possesses. It is important to be clear that there are multiple valuable skills, and that human capital does not just mean IQ. It is really only relatively recently that researchers have begun to map out the range of skills that can be considered part of human capital and we cannot yet determine precisely which types of human capital matter most in particular areas and contexts. Like other capital, human capital grows through being invested in, and that investment is called education. Not all education is done in schools; families are a very important part of the process. But education in schools is perhaps the primary lever for policies on human capital.

The full review as a whole aims to describe the research frontier on human capital and education in economics research. It delineates what is known and largely agreed, and what the most promising lines for future research are.[1]

In this chapter, I focus on education market systems, as one of the key issues for policy in education. A coherent market structure for schools to operate in is very important for attainment, as cross-country comparisons suggest. The central element of the market structure is the assignment mechanism, which allocates each child to a school. There are different such mechanisms available: school choice, neighbourhood schooling and elite schooling or '*tracking*', which assigns pupils on the basis of an exam. Other key elements include governance rules and hierarchy: school accountability and school autonomy. Finally, the nature of school leadership is tied up with the degree of autonomy – leaders are far more important in autonomous schools. The evidence reviewed in this chapter will chiefly consist of research that identifies causal effects.

Education policy-making in the European Union happens on different levels. Policy is determined at a national level,[2] but the European Commission offers support to its members addressing common educational challenges, primarily focussing on skills deficits. The relevant framework is 'Education and training 2020'.[3] ET2020 has four common EU objectives: enhancing lifelong learning;

improving the quality and efficiency of education; promoting equity and social cohesion; and enhancing creativity, innovation and entrepreneurship. In 2015, the EU set new priorities for education again around promoting employability and skills, increasing social mobility, but also this time aiming to counteract '*fanaticism*' and promote democracy.

4.1.1 What Can Economics Contribute to the Study of Education?

The decisions by families and individuals on how much to invest in human capital are the standard types of decisions that economics can fruitfully analyse. They involve trade-offs between current costs and future benefits, interrelated dynamic decisions and risk. The education system has actors with goals and constraints who interact in an allocative mechanism. This is well-suited to an economic analysis. Researchers are using the tools of industrial economics to understand the incentives and constraints of all the different players in the market, and to analyse their interactions. Typically in Europe and the US, education does not function as a straightforward marketplace, so there has been interest in other forms of accountability to replace pure market discipline.

Another key contribution of economics is a strong quantitative approach. The majority of research in the economics of education is empirical, and uses a range of techniques including computable general equilibrium models and programme evaluation (see Meghir and Rivkin, 2011 for a review of methods in the field). However, perhaps the most important feature is an emphasis on trying to estimate causal relationships. Causality is not everything and descriptive studies can be extremely useful, for example in identifying need for action, but a policy discussion can really only take off from causal studies.

Of course, other disciplines also bring insights to education. In recent years, economists have started to combine effectively with psychologists and neuroscientists in the study of the development of cognitive and noncognitive abilities and traits (for example, Cunha et al., 2006), with geneticists in studying the origins of traits and abilities (Benjamin et al., 2012) and also with behavioural scientists in trying to understand motivations and the best way to design incentives (for example Levitt et al., 2012).

4.2 The Aims of Education: Rates of Return, Inequality and Social Mobility

Education is central to three very important policy domains. First, human capital and education are key, causal, drivers of growth and prosperity. Second, the distribution of human capital across people is an important determinant of income inequality, ever more important with a high wage premium for skills. Third, with higher inequality has come a renewed interest in social mobility, and the relationship between a person's human capital and their background is a major determinant of social mobility.

Starting with growth, Goldin and Katz (2008) write simply that higher levels of education lead to higher labour productivity, and that higher aggregate levels of education in a country support faster national economic growth. They explain why: 'Economic growth ... requires educated workers, managers, entrepreneurs, and citizens. Modern technologies must be invented, innovated, put in place and maintained' (pp. 1–2). Recent cross-country analysis bears this out. Hanushek and Woessmann (2012) show that measures of cognitive skills are strongly associated with economic growth. Previous research had found mixed evidence of a role for education in influencing growth, but Hanushek and Woessmann argue that this previous research used the wrong measure of attainment, and that completed years of schooling or national enrolment rates in education do not capture skills. Instead, they use direct measures of cognitive skills from international tests of maths and science abilities among pupils in 50 countries. The effect size is not trivial, since even small additions to a long-run growth rate are valuable. A quarter of a standard deviation rise in the cognitive skill score implies a higher growth rate of 0.3 to 0.5 percentage points; for comparison, the authors note that the difference between the US's PISA performance and the top performers is 40 per cent of a standard deviation.

To establish that the relationship is causal, Hanushek and Woessmann implement an instrumental variables strategy and use school institutional features (the presence of external exit exams, the share of privately operated schools, and the centralization of decision-making) as instruments. The implication is therefore that these policies are effective drivers of growth. They have since expanded the argument at greater length in Hanushek and Woessmann (2015), and quantified the very high cost of low skills to national income in Hanushek and Woessmann (2010).

Turning to inequality, Goldin and Katz (2008) argue that we can think of earnings inequality and growth as the outcomes of a 'race' between education and technology. When the education system produces skilled people at a fast rate (at least keeping up with the increasing demand for skills from technological advance) then average income rises and inequality falls. For example, they argue that this picture characterizes the US for the first three-quarters of the twentieth century. But when the supply of skill slows behind technological advance, then inequality rises, distinguishing the time since the 1980s. They say 'the skill bias of technology did not change much across the century, nor did its rate of change. Rather, the sharp rise in inequality was largely due to an educational slowdown' (p. 8). A lot of the foundational work understanding the sharp rise in inequality was carried out by Katz and co-authors, summarized in Katz and Autor (1999). It has been established that the higher inequality is largely accounted for by a rising premium for skills, for education, from the 1970s. Whilst a lot of the early discussion focussed on technological change, it is now clear that the return to skills depends on both demand ('technology') and supply ('education').

One of the enduring concerns in developed economies is the question how you get on in life. Getting an education has always been part of the answer, evidenced by innumerable stories from around the world. At an individual level, education can be seen as a way out of an unpromising start in life, an escape route. Over the last decade, policy-makers have focussed on this, and comparing rates of intergenerational mobility between countries (Jäntti et al., 2006). Intergenerational mobility or social mobility is about where you end up in an economy relative to where you started; basically a correlation between the income of the present generation and their parents' income.

Black and Devereux (2011) see a substantial shift in emphasis in economists' studies of intergenerational mobility over the previous decade, away from refining measures of persistence towards understanding the underlying mechanisms that generate that persistence. Education, skills and (natural) abilities are at the heart of this. A very useful simple model by Solon (2004) considers intergenerational transmission as depending on parents passing on genetic endowments and investing in the education of their children, on the return to that education, and on the progressivity of government policy on education. Since heritability is fixed, Black and Devereux note that we can best understand differences in intergenerational mobility by focussing on 'differences in the returns to skills ...and differences in government investments [in education]' (p. 1500). Evidence from international cross-sections (Ichino et al., 2009) and across US states (Mayer and Lopoo, 2008) backs up the idea that social mobility is higher when public education is better funded. Recently, Chetty et al. (2014) have used administrative data to characterize cities in the US as having high or low intergenerational mobility; they show considerable variation across the country, and one of the correlated factors is the quality of primary education. Gregg et al. (2013) in an international comparison stress variations in the return to education as a driver of differences in intergenerational income persistence. A much more focussed version of essentially the same question is put by Dobbie and Fryer (2011a) and Fryer and Katz (2013): is a high-quality school enough to break out of a cycle of intergenerational poverty? Focussing on the Harlem Children's Zone schools and using quasi-experimental methods, they answer optimistically.

So education matters centrally in many of the biggest economic policy debates. Before moving on, it is worth noting that education has been shown to have impacts on other outcomes too: health, crime, household structure and happiness. Last in this list, but first for some people, it is a source of personal fulfilment and inspiration.

4.3   Education Systems: Assignment, Admissions, Accountability and Autonomy

The processes underlying the formation of human capital, the delivery of effective education, and the returns to schooling form the 'fundamentals' of human capital. The systemic issue is to design an education system that facilitates the best outcome given these fundamentals. The important role of the family in early education suggests that an education system could be construed in a very broad sense to include areas of social policy. However, that is beyond the scope of this chapter and this section relates to the education system as typically understood, relating to schools and higher education.

4.3.1   Assignment Mechanisms

At the heart of every school system is a set of rules to assign pupils to schools. Consider one city; there is a set of pupils with particular characteristics (location, parental background, ability) and a set of school places with characteristics (for example, a highly effective school or an ineffective school, a particular specialism, location). Assuming that there are enough places overall, the question is: which pupil goes to which school? What is required is a mapping that assigns each pupil to a school based on her characteristics and its characteristics. The dependence on characteristics can be null – for example, a simple lottery over all pupils into all schools. Or the function might assign pupils purely on location, or on ability, and so on. Another mechanism is choice: families list their preferred schools and this plus school priorities, determines the assignment.

The assignment mechanism constitutes the main element in the '*rules of the game*' in the education market. As such, it is part of the incentive structure of all the players, families and pupils, and schools. Different assignment mechanisms will generally yield different outcomes for a range of measures of interest: mean attainment, variation in attainment, school sorting, social mobility and inequality.

The most common assignment mechanisms are: neighbourhood schooling (each pupil goes to her local school); tracking or elite schooling (schools are allocated on the basis of a test score); and choice-based schooling (school assignment depends on parental choice and school capacity). I also consider assignment based directly on income – the role of the private sector interacting with state schools. I discuss these in turn, and the evidence on how they affect outcomes. But first, I review evidence on parents' preferences for schools.

What Are Parental Preferences for Schools?

Preferences matter most obviously under a regime of school choice. But they also matter whatever the assignment mechanism, as there will in general be

strategies available to parents to raise their chance of getting their most preferred school. This includes moving house under a neighbourhood schooling
rule, and intensive additional coaching under an exam-based assignment rule.

There are a number of empirical challenges in estimating preferences for
schools, particularly around identification. It is generally impossible to know
the pool of schools that parents consider when making their choice, so this
has to be estimated. Also, given that admissions to popular schools have to
be rationed, it can be difficult to disentangle parental preferences from school
priorities. Finally, as I discuss below, it is not always optimal to put down the
truly preferred school as the top choice and this also complicates the analysis.

Hastings et al. (2008) use school choice data from Charlotte-Mecklenburg,
North Carolina, to estimate a mixed-logit demand model for schools. They
find that parents value school–home proximity and academic attainment highly.
They also find considerable heterogeneity in preferences and for example show
that the preference attached to a school's mean test score increases with household income and with the child's academic ability. They use their model to estimate the elasticity of demand for each school with respect to mean test scores in
the school. They find that demand at high-performing schools is more responsive to increases in mean test scores than demand at low performing schools.
Their model also implies a 'mobile', more affluent group of families exerting
pressure on school performance, and a less mobile, less affluent group essentially going to the local school.

Hastings and Weinstein (2008) make an important distinction between a family's preferences for school characteristics and the information they are able to
access about the schools. Using a mix of field and natural experiments, they
show that the provision of additional information on school characteristics does
change school choices, particularly for disadvantaged families.

Burgess et al. (2015a) estimate the preferences of parents for schools in the
UK, as a function of the school–home distance, the academic performance of
the school, school composition in terms of socio-economic status and ethnicity, and whether it is a faith school. They pay attention to the key method
for rationing access to over-subscribed schools (distance) and define a set of
schools for each family in the data that they could almost surely access. They
also find academic performance and proximity to be highly valued; social composition is also valued, but ethnic composition has no effect. By comparing
schools that are feasible by distance and the subset to which the family has
almost-sure access, they show that the use of the distance rule for rationing
access has strong regressive effects.

There are a few other studies using different techniques. Schneider and Buckley (2002) use an online schools database in Washington, DC to track parent
search behaviour for schools as an indicator of parent preferences. They find
that patterns of search behaviour depend on parent characteristics, and find a

strong interest in the demographic composition of a school. Rothstein (2006) adopts a more indirect approach to evaluate the relative weight parents place on school effectiveness and peer group and finds little evidence that parents focus strongly on school effectiveness.

Pupil Assignment by School Choice

School choice has been much studied, principally, but not only, in the US. It is seen as a way 'out': a way of escaping a low-quality local school and attending a better school further away. It is also seen as the basis of school competition, raising standards in all schools. Research has considered the outcome of this process, for individual pupils as well as at a systemic level.

It is useful to distinguish two senses of 'school choice': as a systemic market rule for assigning all pupils to schools; and as a specific individual entitlement to attend a different school to your current one, rather like a voucher. I deal with the systemic market rule first.

Does School Choice as a Systemic Market Rule Raise Attainment?

The claim is that school choice induces competitive pressure on low-performing schools to improve (Hoxby, 2003b). If parents value academic attainment and have the information to recognize it in a school, if their choices make a difference to the allocation, and if schools benefit and expand with greater demand, then the market should operate to raise the attainment. Low-performing schools lose pupils, lose funding and so work to reverse this by raising their performance. A counter-claim is that enhanced choice results in greater sorting or stratification across schools in poor and affluent neighbourhoods. Academic and policy debates on school choice remain controversial and unresolved. A recent contribution from Avery and Pathak (2015) reminds us of the complexities of school choice programmes when residence is a choice variable, and that the distributional consequences can be surprising.

Research in this field proceeds by defining some measure of the degree of choice that families have, and relating this measure to attainment scores. As always, the key issue is to identify a causal effect; there are many studies reporting associations between the two (reviewed in Belfield and Levin, 2003), but plausibly exogenous differences in competition are much harder to find.

A market for school places is inherently spatial – you have to actually be in the school all day, so measures of competition are about geography. This includes the number of different school districts that are close together (so could be chosen whilst working in the same job for example), the number of schools within a short drive from home and so on. For example, a number of studies use the HHI (Herfindahl-Hirschman Index) of local districts as proxies for competition (Hoxby, 2000, for example). Alternatively, Burgess et al. (2007) combine school locations with a complete road map to define 10-minute drive time zones around each school, and then for each school count the number of other schools in the zone. Feasible school choice is almost always going to be higher in densely populated urban areas, which are, of course, different in many ways from rural or suburban areas. Consequently, simple associations between this measure of choice and attainment are likely to be biased by confounding variables.

The best known attempt to establish causality is Hoxby (2000), who uses natural landscape features to instrument for historical school district boundaries and the HHI. She shows that areas with more school districts – higher competition – raise attainment. The findings have been strongly questioned by Rothstein (2007), however, arguing that they are not robust to simple changes in data coding; taking these into account he finds no impact of competition. A more structural econometric approach is taken by Bayer and McMillan (2010), who adopt an equilibrium sorting model between neighbourhoods (see Bayer et al., 2007) and use the slope of the school's demand curve to measure the degree of competition each school faces. They find that a one standard-deviation increase in competition leads to a 0.1 standard-deviation improvement in attainment.

In the UK, there have been two attempts to estimate a causal effect, both yielding low to zero impacts of competition. Gibbons et al. (2010) use the distance of a school from its nearest local authority boundary to instrument the amount of competition it faces; they find no overall effect of choice or competition on school performance. Burgess and Slater (2006) use the administrative boundary change of 1998 that split Berkshire into six local authorities to estimate the impact on pupil progress of possible falls in competition across the new boundaries. They also find no significant impact of these boundary changes on pupil achievement.

School choice as a systemic rule has a long history in the Netherlands and in Denmark, and something of a history in Sweden since 1992. A number of studies of the Swedish system are discussed below. In the Netherlands, parental choice of school has been in place since the early twentieth century. Dijkgraaf et al. (2013) find that increases in competition as measured by the HHI are associated with a small decrease in attainment, but this is not a causal study. Competition specifically from Catholic schools also appears not to have an impact. de Haan et al. (2011), using a law change for identification, find a negative effect from a city having more but smaller schools, although the effect disappears once school size is controlled for.

Lavy (2010) considers a school reform in Tel Aviv that switched from an inter-district bussing programme to a school choice system. As this is not experimental variation, Lavy uses alternative identification strategies and comparison groups and shows that the choice system increases school completion and raises cognitive achievement (it also raises students' satisfaction with the school).

Choice as a Voucher

The idea of an educational voucher is that it entitles a child to go to a different school than her default or 'normal' school. Details vary hugely by scheme, but in essence it is seen as an 'escape' from a low-quality local school. This is generally a specific entitlement (for example, Figlio and Page, 2002 consider a scheme in Florida in which students in 'failing' schools are given vouchers, which they can use to move to an alternative school) rather than a system-wide assignment mechanism, although it is sometimes combined in system-wide reforms as in Sweden. The outside option school can be a private school (as in Sweden, though with capped fees) or a charter school as is often the case in the US. The biggest voucher programmes are in Chile and Colombia (see Bettinger et al., 2011, for a survey) but they are also part of the system in Sweden and the Netherlands; and of course in the US.

In all of these cases, there are two main research and policy questions: what is the impact of the voucher on the individual who receives it? And what is the impact on the system as a whole, on those '*left behind*' in the low-performing schools? There are also complex general-equilibrium theoretical issues in voucher schemes that are summarized by Epple and Romano (2012).

There still appear to be no definitive answers to the two core empirical questions. In a substantial recent review, Epple et al. (2015) argue that the bulk of the findings suggest no significant effect, yet 'multiple positive findings support continued exploration'. The task now seems to be to understand the role of the context in determining the variation in outcomes. In surveying work outside the US, Bettinger et al. (2011) argue that evidence from Columbia on the impact on the voucher-user is possibly the strongest, but it may not be causal. On the second question, there is some evidence that the system improved in Sweden (for example, Björklund et al., 2004 and Böhlmark and Lindahl, 2007) but it is difficult to single out the voucher component as many reforms were introduced together in 1992. More recently Böhlmark and Lindahl (2012) now find small positive results from competition and choice, ten years after the reform.

Evidence from the US is also complex and contested, and generalizing is difficult given the differences in design (Ladd, 2002) and in some cases small numbers. The evidence on the impact on the voucher-using student is mixed. Peterson et al. (2003), for example, examine data from three privately funded school voucher programmes in New York, Washington DC and Dayton, Ohio. In all three schemes, a lottery is used to allocate vouchers among eligible (low income) families, and the voucher does not cover full costs. Test-score gains from switching to private schools are evident for African-Americans but not for students from other ethnic backgrounds. Hoxby's (2003b) review of the evidence from recent studies using randomized control groups of students from lottery allocation mechanisms shows the same. Cullen et al. (2006) collect data from the lotteries used to allocate students to oversubscribed schools in the Chicago Public School (CPS) system; arguably in the CPS choice is essentially systemic as over half the pupils do not attend their default school. Cullen et al. (2006) find that winning a lottery has no impact on test scores at ninth or tenth grade. They speculate why this might be, but it is not because the treatment had no effect, as the lottery winners did attend schools that are better across several dimensions. Nor is it that winners had longer school commutes and more disruption to their friendship groups. It is true that lottery winners have lower in-school rank than the losers, which may be a factor in greater school drop-out. They do find positive effects on nonacademic outcomes and consider that this might be the reason that parents enter school lotteries rather than for attainment improvements. Howell's (2004) work on New York City also cautions that the final users of targeted vouchers may differ significantly from the average intended user: among targeted voucher schemes, those actually using them tend to be the better off in the group.

Turning to the question of the systemic impact, Hoxby (2003c) investigates the causal impact of three school choice reforms: vouchers in Milwaukee, charter schools in Michigan and charter schools in Arizona. In each case, state schools responded to competition from the choice programme by raising the achievement levels of their remaining students. This increase was sufficient to outweigh any negative allocation effects. Hoxby's analyses are not unchallenged, Ladd and Fiske (2003) noting that the Milwaukee programme was part of a broader package. Bettinger (2005) challenges the findings for Michigan, and Bifulco and Ladd (2006) find negative impacts in North Carolina.

Does Choice Raise Sorting?

Analysis of choice and sorting is complex with theoretical analysis as well as empirical work contributing insights. Hoxby (2003a) argues that there are no general theoretical predictions about student sorting with choice. In particular, she argues that 'cream skimming' (schools actively selecting high ability students) is not a general prediction, but is more likely with broad eligibility for vouchers and a uniform value of vouchers; if vouchers are targeted, this will necessarily reduce sorting. Nechyba (2003a,b, 2006) uses a theoretical approach to explore the complex 'spillover' effects of school choice and sorting. For example, Nechyba (2003b) shows that a pure state school system leads to more spatial segregation than a private system. Nechyba (2006) summarizes work on income and ability sorting, discussing different channels of sorting. Similarly, Epple and Romano (2003) analyse three different student assignment regimes: neighbourhood schooling (a strict residence requirement for admission); school choice with no choice costs; and choice over many school districts and show that different public policy regimes have dramatic effects on the nature of sorting. Neighbourhood schooling leads to strong income stratification across neighbourhoods, whereas costless, frictionless choice equalizes peer groups across schools. Much of this theoretical work, however, analyses a system where individual schools can grow or shrink costlessly to accommodate the outcome of parents' choices; this flexibility is often lacking, in which case the theory is not so useful a guide.

Evidence from England, New Zealand, Sweden and the US suggests that the degree of choice does influence the degree of sorting. For example, Burgess et al. (2007) analyse student-level data from England, and show that the degree of student sorting in terms of ability and socio-economic status varies considerably across the country. Looking at choice, they measure the degree of choice as the number of schools that can be reached within a particular drive time and show that school sorting relative to residential sorting is considerably higher in areas where there is more choice. Cullen et al. (2006) show that in the Chicago state school system, the exercise of parental choice leads to an increase in sorting by ability, although Hoxby (2003b) argues that Chicago does not have pure school 'choice' as money does not follow students, and schools cannot expand or contract much in response to the demand. Again it is worth noting that the last feature is not uncommon. Soderstrom and Uusitalo (2010) analyse student level data from Sweden, and compare student sorting before and after a significant reform to the school admission process in Stockholm, switching from a predominantly residence-based admissions system to an explicitly ability-based system. Unsurprisingly, they find a significant increase in ability sorting in schools, but no change in residential sorting.

Overall, the evidence suggests that, compared with neighbourhood schooling, parental school choice with supply-side flexibility reduces sorting. Parental choice plus poor flexibility on the supply side means that schools have to use some criteria to choose students. The evidence from a number of countries suggests that this combined process of choice by parents and proximity rationing schools leads to greater sorting.

What Are the Best (Truth-revealing) Market Mechanisms to Implement Choice?

Allocations based on school choice need a way of aggregating parental choices and school priorities to yield an assignment. In turn, the nature of the mechanism will affect parents' school nominations (Roth, 1984). Ideally, that mechanism should have optimal properties, for example including the Pareto characteristic that there is no other assignment preferable to all; and whether it elicits parents' true preferences. Abdulkadiroğlu and Sonmez (2003) set out the mechanism design approach to school assignment, and Abdulkadiroğlu et al. (2005a,b) apply this approach to the Boston and NYC school districts respectively, and Pathak and Sonmez (2008) and Abdulkadiroğlu et al. (2009b) subsequently update the design. These papers determine the properties of particular assignment mechanisms and whether they elicit true preferences from the participants. Revealing true preferences is a weakly dominant strategy in two common mechanisms, Student Proposing Deferred Acceptance (SPDA, Gale and Shapley, 1962, also called Student Optimal Stable Matching) and Top Trading Cycles. More recent refinements, for example restricting the number of schools that parents are allowed to nominate, show that when parents can make only limited nominations, truth telling is not optimal in some circumstances even with an SPDA mechanism (Haeringer and Klijn, 2009 and Calsamiglia et al., 2010).

What is the Effect of Tracking and Selective Schools on the Distribution of Attainment?

An alternative way to assign pupils to schools is by a measure of ability, typically by setting an exam. This is the way that the school system works in a number of European countries. The public school system in Germany is tracked, with entry to the Gymnasium schools determined by exam performance. In the Netherlands, Switzerland and France (from age 15) too, pupils are assigned to different curricula based on their ability or attainment. In some cases these are different curricula within the same school, and in others, different schools; I return to this issue below. This was also the case in England and the Nordic countries until a wave of comprehensive reforms were adopted from the 1950s through the 1970s. In the US, elite '*exam schools*' in New York or Boston are accessed by taking a competitive exam.

The two main questions that researchers have asked are: What is the impact on the system as a whole in terms of inequality and social mobility, and what is the benefit to the student of attending the elite schools? Again the empirical concerns are around dealing with the selection issues inherent in the problem and identifying a causal effect. A theoretical contribution from Brunello (2004) sets out the trade-off in designing an optimal tracked system, differentiating vocational and general education in terms of required labour market skills.

There are two core distributional questions on tracking. Using cross-country evidence and a difference-in-difference methodology, Hanushek and Woessmann (2006) show that it raises inequality. Brunello and Checchi (2007) show that tracking from an early age across schools reinforces the impact of family background on attainment and labour market outcomes and so reduces social mobility. On the other hand, they report more nuanced results of tracking on the scope to access vocational training. The overall level of attainment is lower under tracking and it seems plausible that some families and pupils might reduce their investment in schooling if they know that they cannot go on to higher education. Atkinson et al. (2006) use NPD data to compare value-added attainment across selective and nonselective school districts in England. They use matched selective and nonselective districts and show that grammar-educated children in selective districts outperform similar children in nonselective districts on average, while nongrammar-educated children in selective districts underperform compared to similar children in nonselective districts. This fits well with the results of Burgess et al. (2014), which show that earnings inequality among children growing up in selective areas is greater than that of similar children growing up in nonselective areas.

Major systemic school reforms took place in Sweden in the 1950s and Norway in the 1960s. These raised the school-leaving age so that mandatory schooling was extended by two years and the system became comprehensive so that all students followed the same track. These have been studied by Meghir and Palme (2005) and Aakvik et al. (2010). Both studies found a weakening of the influence of family background, and Meghir and Palme (2005) show a causal impact of increased earnings among pupils from disadvantaged families. Pekkarinen et al. (2009) exploit a similar reform in Finland in the 1970s and show that the elimination of tracking reduced the intergenerational elasticity of income very substantially.

Students in the elite schools may benefit in many ways, as Brunello and Checchi (2007) describe: pupil peer effects, more effective teachers and possibly greater resources. Estimating the gain to the marginal student of attending an elite school, Clark (2010) uses access data from a district in England to estimate the causal impact of attending a grammar school. He finds small effects of grammar schools on test scores at 16 but larger effects on longer-run outcomes such as taking more advanced courses and more academic courses. Clark and Del Bono (2014) implement a regression discontinuity design to assess the impact of attending a grammar school for a cohort of young people born in Aberdeen in the 1950s. They find large effects on educational attainment, and for women there are long-run impacts on labour market outcomes and reduced fertility. For men no long-term impacts were identified. In the US, Abdulkadiroğlu et al. (2011) and Dobbie and Fryer (2011b) assess the effect of attending elite exam schools in Boston and New York on attainment and test scores. Both studies find limited impacts on student achievements, though Dobbie and Fryer (2011b) find positive effects on the rigour of the courses taken.

The top-level distinction is between comprehensive and tracked systems. As with the discussion of peer groups above, the key trade-off is between the unequalizing effect of differential peer groups (and potentially lower overall investment) in tracking, against the potentially more efficient teaching possible from more homogenous classes that tracking brings. There is also an important distinction between within-school tracking and between-school tracking; the former meaning different curricula, different tracks, offered within the same school, and the latter meaning different schools. Here the issues are about the difficulty of rectifying incorrect assignment of children to schools, versus the cost and practicality of running many curricula within the same school. It seems that the slowly increasing age of tracking and the greater frequency of within-school tracking suggests that the latter is less of a problem.

What Are the Effects of Neighbourhood Schooling Assignment Rules?
Neighbourhood schooling means that every child goes to her neighbourhood school. This is well illustrated by Fack and Grenet (2010) for Paris: 'During the period under study (1997–2004), primary and middle school assignment was purely residence-based. It was also "strict" in the sense that each school catchment area contained one school only, which means that in principle parents had no control over the choice of their child's public school' (p. 62) and 'School catchment areas are released every school year in the form of booklets that indicate, for each street section, the assigned public middle school' (p. 63).

What are the implications of this? It does not make families into passive players in the school choice process; it simply turns the school choice into a choice of residence. Given parents' preferences for schools discussed above and a rule that you gain access to a certain school by living in a certain place, popular schools imply popular neighbourhoods. This affects housing demand and so house prices.

There is a substantial literature trying to estimate the true house price premium arising from a popular local school. An influential study is that of Black (1999), in which she adopts a regression discontinuity approach, comparing house prices either side but very close to a school assignment boundary to model the impact of school quality on house prices. She finds that families paid 2 per cent more on the value of the house for a 5 per cent increase in academic quality measured by test scores. Gibbons and Machin (2003, 2006) carry out a similar analysis for primary schools in England, with similar results. The literature as a whole has been summarized by Black and Machin (2011): 'parents are prepared to pay substantial amounts of money to get their children educated in better performing schools. ...A not unreasonable benchmark summary of the magnitude of the average causal impact is that a one standard deviation increase in test scores raises house prices by around 3%'.

This has implications for schools and for neighbourhoods themselves. These are principally around sorting or segregation as discussed above; there are subtle externalities and dependencies at work. Nechyba (2003b) and Epple and Romano (2003), among others, have shown that neighbourhood schooling in a model with peer effects implies income and residential sorting in equilibrium. One of these models' key parameters is the valuation of school performance by parents: the higher this parameter, the higher the level of sorting. It is important to stress that, far from producing an even mix of students (no sorting), neighbourhood schooling produces strong sorting of students by income and ability. This is because parents take steps to achieve their chosen school through other means – by choosing where they live. So the level of sorting in the absence of choice is potentially quite high.

This sorting produces very heterogeneous income-segregated neighbourhoods, which may matter for reasons beyond education. For schools, this will affect the distribution of attainment if peer groups are important in the education production function. But it also matters for inequality in access to the best schools. The high house prices exclude access to the highest-performing schools. Note that this also applies to choice-based schooling when the proximity criterion is used for rationing places under choice rules (see Burgess and Briggs, 2010 and Burgess et al., 2015b, for estimates of this effect).

Assigning by Income: Private Schools and the State Sector

A fourth mechanism for assigning children to schools is by income and choice, to private, fee-paying schools. There is huge variation across the OECD in the fraction of pupils attending private schools, see OECD, 2012, p. 21. This variation arises in part exogenously from different national laws and regulations, and in part endogenously from the attractiveness of free state schools. There are different dimensions of 'private' schooling. This includes the degree of public/private funding and also whether the school is privately managed (again see OECD, 2012, pp. 19–21). An alternative way of thinking about this is whether private schools fees' are unregulated (for example in England) or are capped at the level of state funding (for example in the Netherlands and Sweden), in which case the 'private' aspect is in the operations and management of the school, and the system is more akin to a voucher scheme.

What are the implications of these schools for the national education system? Focussing first on the pupils themselves, since attending these schools is a proactive choice, the revealed preference suggests that the parents are happy with the outcome relative to the marginal state school (for example, Green et al., 2012, track the changing earnings return to a private school education in England). As Brunello and Rocco (2008) note, this outcome may not always be the level of attainment, but may be the ability to cope with difficult-to-teach children.

The main question is about the systemic impact, and the interaction between state and private sectors. Epple et al. (2004) set out a model of price-setting by private schools faced by state schools in the same market. Fack and Grenet (2010) discuss interaction in admissions – the impact of a local private school on admissions in an otherwise neighbourhood schooling scheme. The OECD (2012) shows that socio-economic stratification across schools is not associated with the prevalence of privately managed schools in a country, but is associated with the level of public funding to those schools. For example, in Sweden, Germany, Belgium, the Netherlands and Ireland, over 80 per cent of school funding for privately managed schools comes from the government. By contrast, in the

United Kingdom and Greece 1 per cent or less of funding for privately managed schools comes from the state. In those countries where privately managed schools receive higher proportions of public funding, there is less stratification between publicly and privately managed schools. Green et al. (2008) consider competition between state and private schools in the market for teachers. They show that private schools are increasingly recruiting teachers from the state sector. Teachers in the private sector report greater job satisfaction; while this may be causal, it may well be about selection into sector and a better worker–job match.

4.3.2 Accountability, Autonomy and Regulation

Schools are given two very valuable resources by the government – a large amount of public money and, far more valuable, the future skills of the nation's children. Schools should be accountable for how they deal with these resources. This accountability is enacted in different ways and to differing extents in countries around the world. The implications of this are discussed below.

Accountability makes most sense when those being held accountable can actually make a difference to the outcome – that is, have some autonomy in the running of their schools. Strong accountability mechanisms seem inefficient and unfair without autonomy. Evaluating school autonomy is a relatively recent topic of research generating interest in the US and the UK in particular, and this is reviewed below. Studies using international comparative tests suggest that market features enabling school accountability and autonomy are important for student performance (e.g., Woessmann, 2007).

School Accountability

The essence of school accountability is the provision of rewards or sanctions attached to the test performance of pupils in the school. The sanctions or rewards can be explicit, such as the replacement of school leaders, or implicit, such as good performance raising applications to the school. The theoretical argument basis for the accountability system is a principal-agent model; the publication of school performance data helps to monitor the output of the school. These tables might be scrutinized by parents, who could react by avoiding low-performing schools and/or by the education authorities, who may take action against such schools.

What Effects Does the Accountability System Have on Pupil Performance?

Researchers face two main difficulties in trying to establish the impact of accountability systems on pupil performance. Figlio and Ladd (2008) note that typically a multifaceted performance management reform is introduced all at once, removing the possibility of evaluating an individual component; and that finding an adequate control group for the counter-factual is often hard.

Causal evidence on this comes from changes in accountability systems. Burgess et al. (2013) are able to exploit a policy experiment that changed school accountability in Wales but not in England. Following a referendum, power over education policy was devolved to the Welsh Assembly Government, which immediately stopped publication of school performance tables. This event is useful for analysis as it sidesteps the two issues raised above. First, we have a ready-made control group of students in England as the education systems of the two countries were practically identical until that point. Second, there were no other major changes to the education system in Wales at the same time. Using a difference-in-difference analysis, Burgess et al. (2013) find significant and robust evidence that this reform markedly reduced school effectiveness in Wales. The impact is sizeable, 0.23 of a (school-level) standard deviation, equivalent to 0.09 of a pupil-level standard deviation. In this study, the significant heterogeneity shows a much stronger effect on attainment of low-achieving pupils.

Two other recent studies have evaluated the introduction of school accountability in Portugal and the Netherlands. In Portugal, Reis et al. (2015) show that the publication of school rankings makes a significant difference to parents' choice of schools and to schools' enrolment. Koning and van der Wiel (2012) show that once school quality scores are published (following campaigning by a newspaper), the lowest ranked schools raised performance substantially.

Much of the available evidence uses the introduction in the US of a mandatory school accountability system under the No Child Left Behind (NCLB) Act in 2002; this evidence is usefully summarized in Figlio and Loeb (2011). Dee and Jacob (2009) use the federal introduction of NCLB to estimate its effect on school performance, comparing states that had implemented a system of school accountability before NCLB as the control group. They found that NCLB had no impact on reading scores and a 0.15 pupil-level standard deviation impact on maths scores. Wong et al. (2009) triangulate their evidence using different approaches, essentially by defining different control groups; they find a positive impact of the introduction of accountability in both approaches on both the fourth and eighth grades. Hanushek and Raymond (2005) actually use state-level accountability, pre-NCLB, and adopt a state-level fixed effects model to identify the introduction of NCLB and find a positive effect of around 0.2 of a (state-level) standard deviation on test scores. Other studies exploit discontinuities in school accountability ratings and adopt a regression discontinuity approach. They show that schools receiving low ratings subsequently showed positive conditional impacts on pupil achievement gains, with strong and substantial effects (for example, Figlio and Rouse, 2006, Chiang, 2009, Rockoff and Turner, 2010 and Rouse et al., 2013).

There is consensus that accountability measures raise performance, and typically more for low-performing pupils. There are fewer studies showing how this is achieved. Rouse et al. (2013) show that schools do change their teaching practices, for example spending more of the school day on instruction; Reback et al. (2014) show that teachers work harder but also narrow the curriculum; and Craig et al. (2015) show that school district administrators reinforce the effect of the ratings, rewarding high-performing schools by allocating them more funds.

To date there have been few studies of the long-run consequences of accountability; Deming et al. (2013) find substantial positive long-run effects of accountability pressure on high-ability pupils, but find equally substantive negative effects for low-ability students.

What About Gaming, Unintended Consequences and Cheating?

Whilst one of the main issues in this literature is the impact of accountability on attainment, the other main focus is quantifying the strategies that schools undertake to game the system. These behaviour distortions can take many forms, from a particular concentration of teacher time and effort, to outright cheating in the exams.

It has been generally established that schools will tend to focus their resources on whatever is tested: the subjects that are tested, the topics within subjects that are tested, the topics in which scores can be increased most easily, the school grades that are tested, and on the pupils who may be pivotal in reaching a threshold. Figlio and Loeb (2011) summarize all this evidence, and Rouse et al. (2013) also review evidence on a range of responses by schools. Whether this focus on the things tested is a bad thing depends on the tests: this focus may in fact be what society wants and intends, and if the test is well-designed it may be wholly appropriate. Conversely, if the high-stakes tests are not well-designed, then the lack of broader knowledge and skills can be deleterious.

Boyd et al. (2008) also show that high-stakes testing also altered the allocation of teachers to grades in New York. Relatedly, teachers face greater work pressure from accountability. Reback et al. (2014) show that accountability pressure from NCLB lowers teachers' perceptions of job security and causes untenured teachers in high-stakes grades to work longer hours than their peers.

One way of gauging the degree of '*teaching to the test*' is to compare performance on high-stakes tests with that on low-stakes tests covering the same material. Jacob (2005) compared test score gains in maths in high stakes tests to those on comparable, but low-stakes, tests; he shows that the gains for eighth graders were confirmed in the low-stakes tests, but that those for fourth-grade pupils were not. Similarly, Figlio and Rouse (2006) find a smaller impact of accountability on low-stakes tests than on high-stakes tests.

Beyond focussing school resources on a subset of subjects, topics and pupils, researchers have documented other practices which, while not illegal, are certainly not what the accountability systems' designers would have had in mind as appropriate tactics. Figlio and Winicki (2005) show that schools change their lunch menus at the time of the tests, 'substantially increasing calories in their menus on testing days'; Bokhari and Schneider (2009) show that pupils in schools under stronger accountability threat 'are more likely to be diagnosed with Attention Deficit/Hyperactivity Disorder (ADHD) and consequently prescribed psychostimulant drugs'; and Anderson et al. (2011) find that pupils in such schools have a higher chance of being obese, with one of the channels they cite being less exercise in school.

Finally, there is straightforward cheating on the test by teachers or school administrators. Jacob and Levitt (2003) show that the frequency of cheating appears to respond strongly to relatively minor changes in incentives, such as those implied by school accountability measures. Bertoni et al. (2013) also implicitly detect cheating by noting that test scores in Italy are lower when external monitoring of tests takes place.

Of course, the existence of these inappropriate behaviours does not mean that accountability measures should be abandoned; the costs need to be weighed against the benefits. There are also implications for the design of the tests underlying the system and perhaps for the monitoring of the testing system.

What Is the Best Content for an Accountability System?

A subsidiary, but important question, is the nature of the performance data to be included in the accountability system. One key issue is whether it should be based on the level of student performance, or the per-pupil change in test score, also called value-added. The former is certainly of interest to policy-makers and parents, but the latter is fairer to the schools in that it takes account of prior attainment. An excellent early analysis of the statistical issues involved for the implementation of NCLB is in Kane and Staiger (2001). Allen and Burgess (2011) and Allen (2013) use the long run of pupil-level data available in England to model different possibilities. There is a trade-off between functionality (whether the data actually help parents to identify high-performing schools) and comprehensibility (whether the presentation is straightforward enough to make sense).

There is reasonable consensus that test-based school accountability measures raise pupil attainment, sometimes substantially. It is also clear that schools can be very sophisticated in designing strategies to game the metrics; some of these are arguably positive or benign (such as assigning strong teachers to the key classes), while others are strongly negative (risking pupil obesity, or cheating). Research priorities in this field include further exploration of the long-run impacts of schooling under strong accountability, and the impact of introducing accountability systems in a number of other countries, including Australia, Poland and Spain.

School Autonomy

There are two introductory questions to answer: why autonomy and autonomy from what? The basic concept behind the attraction of school autonomy is a simple one and a familiar one in economics: the people best placed to make 'production' decisions are those with most information, those closest to the process. This means teachers and school leaders; it follows that they should be able to implement those decisions, free from constraints from higher up the hierarchy. The argument is that school autonomy will therefore raise attainment, which is the empirical question I discuss below. The constraints placed on schools vary over time and countries. Typically, autonomy involves schools being able to determine all or some of: their own curriculum; hours and days of teaching; pedagogy and general approach; hiring and firing of teachers, and teachers' pay.

Does School Autonomy Raise Pupil Attainment?

The main cases of experimentation in school autonomy are Academies in England, Free Schools in Sweden (and more recently in England, too) and Charter schools in the US. Of these, the most secure evidence comes from recent quasi-experimental studies of the US case.

In England, there have been many new school 'types' tried over the past three decades, some introduced as offering more autonomy. One of these was Grant Maintained (GM) schools, studied by Clark (2009). These schools were able to opt out of the control of local government, and given control of teacher contracts and admissions. This reform is particularly susceptible to evaluation because the conversion to GM status required a vote of parents, and Clark is therefore able to do a like-for-like comparison between schools that just voted to convert and those that just voted not to (a regression discontinuity design). Attainment in the GM schools rose substantially, by about a quarter of a school-level standard deviation. Clark notes that GM schools were also more generously funded and he cannot rule out that this contributed to the rise in attainment. Looking at a more recent reform and schools with similar types of 'freedoms', Foundation schools, Allen (2013) repeats the regression discontinuity approach and finds little evidence for improved attainment having taken account of a rich set of pupil characteristics.

Academy schools are the latest type of school offered much greater freedoms in England. Machin and Vernoit (2011) evaluate the impact on attainment of attending such schools, updated in Eyles and Machin (2015). This analysis provides the most robust evidence on Academies but was undertaken early in the Academy programme and relates to the schools set up under the Labour government before 2010, not those set up under later governments under very different criteria. There is no natural identification structure so the authors compare early converters to similar late converters. They find positive effects on attainment, of around 18 per cent of a school-level standard deviation. The effect appears to be stronger the greater the increase in autonomy, either because of simply more time as an academy, or because of switching from a school with the lowest initial degree of autonomy.

The establishment of Free Schools followed a 1992 reform in Sweden, allowing schools with great operational and strategic autonomy to compete with state schools for pupils and funding. The evidence is mixed and studies vary in finding no, small or large effects. Because of the data they assemble, Böhlmark and Lindahl (2007, 2008) is possibly the most persuasive approach (see Allen, 2010, for a useful summary). They find a small positive impact of municipality-level free school growth on municipality-level academic performance for 16-year-olds, though this dissipates by age 19. Again, the larger positive effect is on higher ability pupils. Using siblings data, Bohlmark and Lindahl show that this improved performance is due in part to the greater effectiveness of the free schools, but that competitive threat played a bigger role. Other studies include Ahlin (2003), Björklund et al. (2005) and Sandström and Bergström (2005).

However, it is not clear that these results can be attributed to increased school autonomy itself, as that reform was introduced alongside others (as documented in Björklund et al., 2005) and the increased autonomy is confounded with increased parental choice.

Turning to the US, Charter schools have much more autonomy than regular state schools, and there are now many thousands of such schools since the first in 1992. Whether this improves the attainment of pupils is a controversial question. A comprehensive study of Charter schools across 16 states is published in CREDO (2009). The authors use matching techniques (creating a '*virtual twin*' for each Charter school pupil based on demographics and poverty status) to compare the outcomes for pupils in Charter schools and regular schools. They find that about half the Charter schools do no better for their pupils, 17 per cent of Charter schools perform better and the remaining 37 per cent perform worse than the comparator regular school. Epple et al. (2015) provide a wide-ranging survey of the Charter movement as it approaches its 25th anniversary. They concur that the impact of Charters on pupil performance is very variable: some produce dramatically higher performance, but most are about the same, a bit worse or a bit higher.

More recently, an important set of studies has used an experimental approach to isolate the role played by Charter schools. The key is that some Charter schools that are over-subscribed use random chance, lotteries, to determine which of the applicants are given a place. This means that among the set of applicants to a school, Charter attendance is exogenous. While these studies are small-scale, this may be appropriate: charter schools are very heterogeneous, so charter school treatment effects are also likely to be heterogeneous. On the other hand, the very fact that the schools are over-subscribed suggests that they are likely to be at the higher end of the outcome distribution rather than representative. Hoxby and Rockoff (2004) is an early example, studying the Chicago Public School system. They find that pupils who win the lottery and enroll in lower elementary grades have higher subsequent attainment than students who are lotteried-out, but find no effect for pupils joining in the upper elementary grades. Using the same methodology, Hoxby and Murarka (2009) find positive and significant effects of charter school attendance in New York City charter schools, with the impact increasing for each additional year spent at a charter school. Sticking with New York, Dobbie and Fryer (2011a) focus on the charter schools associated with the Harlem Children's Zone (HCZ). They too find significant increases in attainment in both maths and English, for pupils of all abilities. Likewise, in Boston, Abdulkadiroğlu et al. (2009a) also using assignment lotteries find large and significant gains in attainment for lottery winners in both middle school and high school. In a related paper, Angrist et al. (2010) focus on a school belonging to the largest charter group, the Knowledge is Power Program (KIPP), a strong advocate of the *'No Excuses'* approach to public education. This means they have a long school day and a long school year, highly selective teacher hiring, strict rules for behaviour and a focus on traditional learning. The lottery methodology shows huge gains in attainment: 0.35 standard deviations in maths and 0.12 standard deviations in reading for each year spent at KIPP Lynn.

The comparison of winners and losers within lotteries only provides a causal effect for charter school applicants, who might be very different to nonapplicants. Abdulkadiroğlu et al. (2014) study a case in which regular public schools are taken over by charter schools so the pupils are not as selected a group as lottery applicants. They confirm substantial test score gains for these pupils too, suggesting that there is something in the schools that substantially and significantly raises attainment. Discovering what that something is, is clearly a question of the first importance. Dobbie and Fryer (2013) and Angrist et al. (2013) make a start on explaining this, and Fryer (2014) reports the impact of attempting to introduce those practices into regular public schools.

What Aspects of Autonomy Are Crucial?

Given that autonomy matters, what sorts of 'freedoms' matter for attainment? The main evidence on this comes from Abdulkadiroğlu et al. (2009a) who are able to compare regular charter schools with Boston Pilot schools: 'These schools have some of the independence of charter schools, but operate within the school district, face little risk of closure, and are covered by many of the same collective bargaining provisions as traditional public schools.' The same lottery methodology that found large effects for the regular charter schools found small and insignificant effects for the Pilot schools.

Reviewing this evidence, the results from Sweden are mixed, but are somewhat difficult to evaluate as the increased school autonomy coincided with other major changes to the school system. In England, this was not the case and the increased autonomy was legislated within a settled system of parental choice. However, the way that academies were introduced means that the identification of a robust causal effect is difficult. The best evidence to date is from the lottery-based studies of US charter schools. There are two caveats here, however. First, the effect is identified among applicants to charter schools, so it is not clear how the findings will carry over to the wider population of pupils, although as discussed Abdulkadiroğlu et al. (2014) find similar nonexperimental results. Second, as is widely noted, charter schools are very heterogeneous, and lottery-based results necessarily imply that these are very popular schools.

The stand-out results are for '*No Excuses*' schools, both the HCZ schools and the KIPP schools, which bring very substantial causal impacts on attainment. Dobbie and Fryer (2011a, 2013) make a start on understanding what it is about these schools that works, but this is surely a key endeavour for future research. We cannot necessarily expect similar results for all charter schools, and so from a systemic perspective, the rules on monitoring performance and awarding and removing autonomous status are likely to be very important.

School Leadership

The nature of school leadership varies directly with the level of school autonomy. In a system of tight central control, school leaders are middle managers, line-managing teachers and implementing policies from the centre. The commitment to a centrally run system means that the values and beliefs of any one headteacher should not impact on the education outcomes for her pupils. In a decentralized model, the system needs good and great leaders, since there is much less central direction on how to run a school.

Policy-makers seem to set great store by the idea of transformational school leadership. The changing of headteachers or principals is taken very seriously as a school improvement policy. There are plenty of stories of how charismatic headteachers have turned failing schools into beacons of achievement. Grissom and Loeb (2011) and Branch et al. (2012) both document prior research, much of it qualitative, associating excellent school leadership with positive school outcomes.

But this is a hard arena in which to do quantitative research, and very hard to robustly identify causal effects. Changes in school leadership are rarely exogenous, and policy-makers are unlikely to be keen on randomizing high- and low-quality principals across schools. Typical changes in school leadership may occur when a school is under-performing, for example, making it difficult to disentangle other compensatory responses, as well as mean-reversion from the leadership change.

While there is now a small literature on what effective schools do (for example Dobbie and Fryer, 2013 and Angrist et al., 2013), this has yet to be linked across to research on what effective or indeed transformative principals do.

Recent research on school leadership can be split roughly into papers attempting to measure the effectiveness of principals; papers looking at the career path or turnover history of principals and an association with school effectiveness; and a set of papers on what principals do, or the management of schools.

The Effectiveness of Principals

Grissom et al. (2015) set the scene by highlighting some of the problematic issues involved in using test score data to estimate principal effectiveness, and setting out a series of models to capture different ways of thinking about what principals do. This useful foundational work shows that the choice of model matters as different approaches can yield very different results, ranging from 18 per cent of a standard deviation to 5 per cent using the same data. They also compare the results with other school outcomes including administrative evaluations, although this yields some puzzling results.

Going down the same track, Coelli and Green (2012) can identify principal effects using a dataset in which principals were rotated amongst schools by districts (using Rivkin et al.'s 2005 approach) and assuming constant effectiveness within-school. They find substantial effects, with one standard deviation of principal effectiveness implying 33 per cent of a school-level standard deviation in graduation rates. Branch et al. (2012) also find large variation in principal effects; they also show greater variation for schools in disadvantaged neighbourhoods. They also note that schools with ineffective principals are estimated to have higher than average teacher turnover, and that this might be a mechanism through which low effectiveness affects school performance.

A different approach to estimating the importance of principals is taken by Lavy (2008). He exploits an experiment in Israel giving a very large pay rise (50%) to school principals. He finds statistically significant but quantitatively modest effects on attainment, probably insufficient to justify an expensive treatment.

Principals' Careers and School Effectiveness

Béteille et al. (2012) provide an overview of principals' career paths, and document substantial turnover rates: more than a 20 per cent annual separation rate for principals. A typical path is to use a low-attaining, disadvantaged school as a stepping-stone to a more preferred school. They show that high principal turnover rates are generally associated with lower school performance: 'The departure of a principal is associated with higher teacher turnover rates and lower student achievement gains' (p. 905) and that this negative relationship is stronger in more disadvantaged neighbourhoods. Because of the interlocking issues of principal's desired career paths, endogenous principal mobility and school performance, robustly attributing causality to this is likely to be difficult. All of this research paints a picture of schools in disadvantaged neighbourhoods underperforming and struggling to hire principals, struggling to keep them, and struggling to hire effective principals.

Clark et al. (2009) try to characterize what effective principals look like in terms of observable characteristics. As with teachers, they find little evidence for a role for the principal's own academic record, nor for their pre-principal experience. Again as with teachers, there is evidence of learning through experience, particularly steep in the early years. By contrast, Grissom and Loeb (2011) try to characterize what effective principals do, combining survey responses with administrative data. They isolated five skill categories – instruction management, organization management, administration, internal relations and external relations. The results suggest that only organization and management skills are consistently associated with school performance across different outcome measures and sources.

School Management

This stress on organizational management ties in well with the findings of Loeb et al. (2010), who document principals' time use and relate that to school outcomes including student attainment, but also teacher and parental assessments. They show that time spent on organizational management is associated with positive outcomes.

Bloom et al. (2014) collect data on management practices in nearly 2000 schools (educating 15-year-olds) in eight countries. They show that higher management quality is strongly associated with better educational outcomes, and in particular that autonomous public schools have significantly higher management scores than regular government schools and private schools. They highlight the role of the principal, assigning a high fraction of the effect to differences in leadership and governance. Consistent with the evidence above on the connection between ineffective principals and high staff turnover, Bloom et al. (2014) note that schools are generally weak in people management practices.

A big part of what principals need to do well is the selection of teachers. Jacob and Lefgren (2008) show that principals can generally identify teachers at the extremes of the distribution of effectiveness, but are much less able to distinguish teachers in the middle of the distribution. In a companion piece, Jacob (2010) shows that principals do weight measures of teacher effectiveness when firing probationary teachers, but only alongside demographic factors.

4.3.3 Education Market Structure: Policy Summary

Two notes of caution are needed before offering a policy summary. As has been evident throughout this chapter, much of the research in the economics of education is about policy. However, it should be clear that we are nowhere near, for example, an engineering level of precision in policy discussion. An engineer could say 'if you want the bridge $x\%$ longer it will need $y\%$ more concrete and be subject to $z\%$ more stress'. As education economists we cannot equivalently say: 'if you reduce the schools budget by $x\%$ by raising class sizes and put that money into $y\%$ more child care, then end-of-schooling attainment will rise by $z\%$'. Secondly, European countries differ in very many ways, including in their education systems,[4] both in terms of the overall system and in the detail, so it is impossible to describe the ways in which specific policies might work in each country.

This is the industrial organization approach to schools, determining the market rules and the market incentives. There are a number of interlocking factors that create an effective school system. Accountability matters for schools' performance, even relatively low-stakes accountability (Reis et al., 2015). Accountability requires some common and consistent form of assessment, typically centralized external exit exams. Accountability also makes more sense if schools have autonomy in their operations. All of these factors have been robustly shown to raise school performance and pupil attainment. Such a policy also leads to a focus on two other things. First, if schools are held to account on a specific assessment basis, then this is undoubtedly what schools will focus on. So governments need to take care that the assessment is well designed, and that it does indeed test the skills that society wants pupils to have. Teaching to the test is detrimental if a test is badly designed. Second, publication of rankings showing schools are better performing can in principle increase socio-economic sorting of pupils, though the evidence on this is mixed. Whether it does so depends on the admissions process to schools and whether this is manipulable by parents. While the broad characteristics of a successful market structure are reasonably clear, the details of any implementation will vary according to existing institutional arrangements.

Acknowledgements

I would like to thank a number of people for their comments and suggestions. Most thanks of all to Susanna Loeb, who was particularly helpful and made a number of great suggestions to improve the first draft. Many thanks also to Paolo Battaglia, Lex Borghans, Gabriella Conti, Neil Davies, Matt Dickson, Emla Fitzsimons, Robin Naylor, Kjell Salvanes, Ismael Sanz, Paolo Sestito, Helen Simpson, Eleanor Stringer and Anna Vignoles. I would also like to thank

Julia Belau, Marc Ivaldi and Wolfgang Leininger for comments and for organizational support. All errors and omissions are my own.

Notes

1. The full review is available at http://www.coeure.eu/wp-content/uploads/Human-Capital-and-education.pdf; for space reasons, only a portion can be included here.
2. See https://webgate.ec.europa.eu/fpfis/mwikis/eurydice/index.php/Countries for levels of devolution.
3. ET2020; http://ec.europa.eu/education/policy/strategic-framework/index_en.htm.
4. See https://webgate.ec.europa.eu/fpfis/mwikis/eurydice/index.php/Countries.

References

Aakvik, A., Salvanes, K., and Vaage, K. 2010. Measuring Heterogeneity in the Returns to Education Using an Education Reform. *European Economic Review*, **54**, 483–500.

Abdulkadiroğlu, A., and Sonmez, T. 2003. School Choice: A Mechanism Design Approach. *American Economic Review*, **93**, 729–747.

Abdulkadiroğlu, A., Pathak, P., Roth, A. E., and Sonmez, T. 2005a. The Boston Public School Match. *American Economic Review*, **95**, 368–71.

Abdulkadiroğlu, A., Pathak, P. A., and Roth, A. E. 2005b. The New York City High School Match. *American Economic Review*, **95**, 364–367.

Abdulkadiroğlu, A., Angrist, J., Dynarski, S., Kane, T., and Pathak, P. 2009a. Accountability and Flexibility in Public Schools: Evidence From Boston's Charters and Pilots. *National Bureau of Economic Research Working Paper 15549*.

Abdulkadiroğlu, A., Pathak, P. A., and Roth, A. E. 2009b. Strategyproofness versus Efficiency in Matching with Indifferences: Redesigning the NYC High School Match. *American Economic Review*, **99**, 1954–1978.

Abdulkadiroğlu, A., Angrist, J., Dynarski, S., Kane, T., and Pathak, P. 2011. Accountability and Flexibility in Public Schools: Evidence from Boston's Charters and Pilots. *The Quarterly Journal of Economics*, **126**, 699–748.

Abdulkadiroğlu, A., Angrist, J., Hull, P., and Pathak, P. 2014. *Charters without Lotteries: Testing Takeovers in New Orleans and Boston*. National Bureau of Economic Research Working Paper 20792.

Ahlin, Å. 2003. *Does School Competition Matter? Effects of a Large-scale School Choice Reform on Student Performance*. Department of Economics, Uppsala University Working Paper No.2.

Allen, R. 2010. Replicating Swedish 'Free School' Reforms in England. *Research in Public Policy*, **10**. http://bristol.ac.uk/media-library/sites/cmpo/migrated/documents/allen10.pdf.

Allen, R. 2013. Measuring Foundation School Effectiveness using English Administrative Data, Survey Data and a Regression Discontinuity Design. *Education Economics*, **21**, 431–446.

Allen, R., and Burgess, S. 2011. Can School League Tables Help Parents Choose Schools? *Fiscal Studies*, **32**, 245–261.

Anderson, P., Butcher, K., and Schanzenbach, D. M. 2011. *Adequate (or Adipose?) Yearly Progress: Assessing the Effect of 'No Child Left Behind' on Children's Obesity*. NBER Working Paper No. 16873.

Angrist, J., Dynarski, S., Kane, T., Pathak, P., and Walters, C. 2010. *Who Benefits from KIPP?* NBER Working Paper No. 15740.

Angrist, J., Pathak, P., and Walters, C. 2013. Explaining Charter School Effectiveness. *American Economic Journal: Applied Economics*, **5**, 1–27.

Atkinson, A., Gregg, P., and McConnell, B. 2006. *The Result of 11 Plus Selection: An Investigation into Equity and Efficiency of Outcomes for Pupils in Selective LEAs*. CMPO DP no. 06/150.

Avery, C., and Pathak, P. 2015. *The Distributional Consequences of Public School Choice*. NBER Working Paper No. 21525.

Bayer, P., and McMillan, R. 2010. *Choice and Competition in Local Education Markets*. ERID Working Paper Number 48.

Bayer, P., Ferreira, F., and McMillan, R. 2007. A Unified Framework for Measuring Preferences for Schools. *Journal of Political Economy*, **115**, 588–638.

Belfield, C. R., and Levin, H. 2003. The Effects of Competition on Educational Outcomes: a Review of US Evidence. *Review of Educational Research*, **72**, 279–341.

Benjamin, D., Cesarini, D., Chabris, C., Glaeser, E., and Laibson, D. 2012. The Promises and Pitfalls of Genoeconomics. *Annual Review of Economics*, **4**, 627–662.

Bertoni, M., Brunello, G., and Rocco, L. 2013. When the Cat is Near the Mice Won't Play: the Effect of External Examiners in Italian Schools. *Journal of Public Economics*, **104**, 65–77.

Béteille, T., Kalogrides, D., and Loeb, S. 2012. Stepping Stones: Principal Career Paths and School Outcomes. *Social Science Research*, **41**, 904–919.

Bettinger, E. 2005. The Effect of Charter Schools on Charter Students and Public Schools. *Economics of Education Review*, **24**, 133–147.

Bettinger, E., Kremer, M., and Saavedra, J. 2011. How Do Vouchers Work? Evidence from Colombia. *Economic Journal*, **546**, F204–F228.

Bifulco, R., and Ladd, H. F. 2006. The Impacts of Charter Schools on Student Achievement: Evidence from North Carolina. *American Education Finance Association*, **1**, 50–90.

Björklund, A., Edin, P.-A., Fredriksson, P., and Krueger, A. 2004. Education, Equality and Efficiency: An Analysis of Swedish School Reforms during the 1990s. *IFAU report*, **1**.

Björklund, A., Clark, M., Edin, P.-A., Fredriksson, P., and Krueger, A. 2005. *The Market Comes to Education in Sweden: An Evaluation of Sweden's Surprising School Reforms*. Russell Sage Foundation: New York.

Black, S. 1999. Do Better Schools Matter? Parental Valuation of Elementary Education. *Quarterly Journal of Economics*, **114**, 578–599.

Black, S., and Devereux, P. 2011. Recent Developments in Intergenerational Mobility. In: *Handbook of Labor Economics*, vol. 4B. Elsevier B.V., pp. 1487–1541.

Black, S., and Machin, S. 2011. Housing Valuations of School Performance. In: Hanushek, E. A., Machin, S., and Woessmann, L. (eds), *Handbook of the Economics of Education*, vol. 3. Elsevier B.V.

Bloom, N., Lemos, R., Sadun, R., and Van Reenen, J. 2014. *Does Management Matter in Schools?* NBER Working Paper No. 20667.

Böhlmark, A., and Lindahl, M. 2007. *The Impact of School Choice on Pupil Achievement, Segregation and Costs: Swedish Evidence.* IZA Discussion Paper No. 2786.

Böhlmark, A., and Lindahl, M. 2008. *Does School Privatization Improve Educational Achievement? Evidence from Sweden's Voucher Reform.* IZA Discussion Paper No. 3691.

Böhlmark, A., and Lindahl, M. 2012. *Independent Schools and Long-run Educational Outcomes: Evidence from Sweden's Large Scale Voucher Reform.* IFAU Working Paper 2012:19.

Bokhari, F. A. S., and Schneider, H. 2009. School Accountability Laws and Consumption of Psychostimulants. *Journal of Health Economics*, **30**, 355–372.

Boyd, D., Lankford, H., Rockoff, J., Loeb, S., and Wyckoff, J. 2008. The Narrowing Gap in New York City Teacher Qualifications and its Implications for Student Achievement in High-poverty Schools. *Journal of Policy Analysis and Management*, **27**, 793–818.

Branch, G., Hanushek, E., and Rivkin, S. 2012. *Estimating the Effect of Leaders on Public Sector Productivity: The Case of School Principals.* Working Paper 17803. National Bureau of Economic Research.

Brunello, G., and Checchi, D. 2007. Does School Tracking Affect Equality of Opportunity? New International Evidence. *Economic Policy*, **22**, 781–861.

Brunello, G., and Rocco, L. 2008. Educational Standards in Private and Public Schools. *Economic Journal*, **118**, 1866–1887.

Brunello, G. Giannini, M. 2004. Stratified or Comprehensive? The Economic Efficiency of School Design. *Scottish Journal of Political Economy*, **51**, 173–193.

Burgess, S., and Briggs, A. 2010. School Assignment, School Choice and Social Mobility. *Economics of Education Review*, **29**, 639–649.

Burgess, S., and Slater, H. 2006. *Using Boundary Changes to Estimate the Impact of School Competition on Test Scores.* CMPO DP 06/158. CMPO.

Burgess, S., McConnell, B., Propper, C., and Wilson, D. 2007. The Impact of School Choice on Sorting by Ability and Socioeconomic Factors in English Secondary Schools. In: Woessmann, L., and Peterson, P. (eds), *Schools and the Equal Opportunity Problem.* MIT Cambridge.

Burgess, S., Wilson, D., and Worth, J. 2013. A Natural Experiment in School Accountability: The Impact of School Performance Information on Pupil Progress. *Journal of Public Economics*, **106**, 57–67.

Burgess, S., Dickson, M., and Macmillan, L. 2014. *Selective Schooling Systems Increase Inequality.* CMPO Discussion Paper 14/323, CMPO, University of Bristol.

Burgess, S., Greaves, E., Vignoles, A., and Wilson, D. 2015a. What Parents Want: School Preferences and School Choice. *The Economic Journal*, **125**, 1262–1289.

Burgess, S., List, J., Metcalfe, R., and Sadoff, S. 2015b. *Using Behaviour Incentives to Improve Performance on High Stakes Tests: Evidence from a Field Experiment.* Mimeo, CMPO.

Calsamiglia, C., Haeringer, G., and Klijn, F. 2010. Constrained School Choice: An Experimental Study. *American Economic Review*, **100**, 1860–1874.

Chetty, R., Hendren, N., Kline, P., and Saez, E. 2014. Where is the Land of Opportunity? The Geography of Intergenerational Mobility in the United States. *The Quarterly Journal of Economics*, **129**, 1553–1623.

Chiang, H. 2009. How Accountability Pressure on Failing Schools Affects Student Achievement. *Journal of Public Economics*, **93**, 1045–1057.

Clark, D. 2010. Selective Schools and Academic Achievement. *B.E. Journal of Economic Analysis and Policy*, **10**, 1935–1682.

Clark, D., and Del Bono, E. 2014. *The Long-Run Effects of Attending an Elite School: Evidence from the UK*. ISER Working Paper No. 2014-05.

Clark, D., Martorell, P., and Rockoff, J. 2009. *School Principals and School Performance*. CALDER Working Papers. Center for Analysis of Londitudinal Data in Education Research.

Coelli, M., and Green, D. 2012. Leadership Effects: School Principals and Student Outcomes. *Economics of Education Review*, **31**, 92–109.

Craig, S., Imberman, S., and Perdue, A. 2015. Do Administrators Respond to Their Accountability Ratings? The Response of School Budgets to Accountability Grades. *Economics of Education Review*, **49**(C), 55–68.

CREDO. 2009. *Multiple Choice: Charter Performance in Sixteen States*. Tech. rept. Center for Research on Education Outcomes, Stanford University. http://credo.stanford.edu/reports/MULTIPLE_CHOICE_CREDO.pdf.

Cullen, J., Jacob, B., and Levitt, S. 2006. The Effect of School Choice on Participants: Evidence from Randomized Lotteries. *Econometrica*, **74**, 1191–1230.

Cunha, F., Heckman, J., and Navarro, S. 2006. Counterfactual Analysis of Inequality and Social Mobility. Chap. 4 of: Morgan, S., Grusky, D., and Fields, G. (eds), *Mobility and Inequality: Frontiers of Research in Sociology and Economics*. Stanford University Press, Palo Alto.

de Haan, M., Leuven, E., and Oosterbeek, H. 2011. *Scale Economies Can Offset the Benefits of Competition: Evidence from a School Consolidation Reform in a Universal Voucher System*. CEPR Discussion Papers 8272.

Dee, T., and Jacob, B. 2009. *The Impact of No Child Left Behind on Student Achievement*. NBER Working Paper No. 15531, NBER: Cambridge MA.

Deming, D. J., Cohodes, S., Jennings, J., and Jencks, C. 2013. *School Accountability, Postsecondary Attainment and Earnings*. NBER Working Paper No. 19444.

Dijkgraaf, E., Gradus, R. H. J. M., and de Jong, M. 2013. Competition and Educational Quality: Evidence from the Netherlands. *Empirica*, **40**, 607–634.

Dobbie, W., and Fryer, R. 2011a. Are High Quality Schools Enough to Close the Achievement Gap? Evidence from a Social Experiment in Harlem. *American Economic Journal: Applied Economics*, **3**.

Dobbie, W., and Fryer, R. 2011b. *Exam High Schools and Academic Achievement: Evidence from New York City*. NBER WP no. 17286.

Dobbie, W., and Fryer, R. 2013. Getting beneath the Veil of Effective Schools: Evidence from New York City. *American Economic Journal: Applied Economics*, **5**, 28–60.

Epple, D., and Romano, R. 2003. Neighbourhood Schools, Choice, and the Distribution of Educational Benefits. In: Hoxby, C. (ed), *The Economics of School Choice*. Chicago: University of Chicago Press.

Epple, D., and Romano, R. 2012. Economic Modeling and Analysis of Educational Vouchers. *Annual Review of Economics*, **4**, 159–184.

Epple, D., Figlio, D., and Rockoff, J. 2004. Competition between Private and Public Schools: Testing Stratification and Pricing Predictions. *Journal of Public Economics*, **88**, 1215–1245.

Epple, D., Romano, R., and Zimmer, R. 2015. *Charter Schools: A Survey of Research on Their Characteristics and Effectiveness.* NBER Working Paper No. 21256.

Eyles, A., and Machin, S. 2015. *The Introduction of Academy Schools to England's Education.* CEP Discussion Paper No 1368.

Fack, G., and Grenet, J. 2010. When Do Better Schools Raise Housing Prices? Evidence from Paris Public and Private Schools. *Journal of Public Economics*, **94**, 59–77.

Figlio, D., and Ladd, H. 2008. School Accountability and Student Achievement. In: Ladd, H., and Fiske, E. (eds), *Handbook of Research in Education Finance and Policy.* London: Routledge.

Figlio, D., and Loeb, S. 2011. School Accountability. In: Hanushek, E., Machin, S., and Woessmann, L. (eds), *Handbook of Economics of Education*, vol. 3. Amsterdam: North-Holland.

Figlio, D., and Page, M. E. 2002. School Choice and the Distributional Effects of Ability Tracking: Does Separation Increase Inequality? *Journal of Urban Economics*, **51**, 497–514.

Figlio, D., and Rouse, C. E. 2006. Do Accountability and Voucher Threats Improve Low-performing Schools? *Journal of Public Economics, Elsevier*, **90**, 239–255.

Figlio, D., and Winicki, J. 2005. Food for Thought: The Effects of School Accountability Plans on School Nutrition. *Journal of Public Economics, Elsevier*, **89**, 381–394.

Fryer, R. 2014. Injecting Charter School Best Practices into Traditional Public Schools: Evidence from Field Experiments. *Quarterly Journal of Economics*, **129**, 1355–1407.

Fryer, R., and Katz, L. 2013. Achieving Escape Velocity: Neighborhood and School Interventions to Reduce Persistent Inequality. *American Economic Review (Papers and Proceedings)*, **103**, 232–237.

Gale, D., and Shapley, L. S. 1962. College Admissions and the Stability of Marriage. *The American Mathematical Monthly*, **69**, 9–15.

Gibbons, S., and Machin, S. 2003. Valuing English Primary Schools. *Journal of Urban Economics*, **53**, 197–219.

Gibbons, S., and Machin, S. 2006. Paying for Primary Schools: Admission Constraints, School Popularity or Congestion. *Economic Journal*, **116**, 77–92.

Gibbons, S., Machin, S., and Silva, O. 2010. Choice, competition, and pupil achievemnet. *Journal of the European Economic Association*, **6**, 912–947.

Goldin, C., and Katz, L. 2008. *The Race between Education and Technology.* Cambridge, MA: Harvard University Press.

Green, F., Machin, S., Murphy, R., and Zhu, Y. 2008. Competition for Private and State School Teachers. *Journal of Education and Work*, **21**, 385–404.

Green, F., Machin, S., Murphy, R., and Zhu, Y. 2012. The Changing Economic Advantage from Private Schools. *Economica*, **79**, 658–79.

Gregg, P., Jonsson, J., Macmillan, L., and Mood, C. 2013. *Understanding Income Mobility: The Role of Education for Intergenerational Income Persistence in the US, UK and Sweden.* Tech. rept. DoQSS DP 13-12, UCL Institute of Education.

Grissom, J., and Loeb, S. 2011. Triangulating Principal Effectiveness: How Perspectives of Parents, Teachers, and Assistant Principals Identify the Central Importance of Managerial Skills. *American Educational Research Journal*, **48**, 1091–1123.

Grissom, J., Kalogrides, D., and Loeb, S. 2015. Using Student Test Scores to Measure Principal Performance. *Education Evaluation and Policy Analysis*, **37**, 3–28.

Haeringer, G., and Klijn, F. 2009. Constrained School Choice. *Journal of Economic Theory*, **144**, 1921–1947.

Hanushek, E., and Raymond, M. 2005. Does School Accountability Lead to Improved Student Performance? *Journal of Policy Analysis and Management*, **24**, 297–327.

Hanushek, E., and Woessmann, L. 2006. Does Educational Tracking Affect Performance and Inequality? Differences-in-Differences Evidence across Countries. *Economic Journal*, **116**, C63–C76.

Hanushek, E., and Woessmann, L. 2010. *The High Cost of Low Educational Performance: The Long-run Economic Impact of Improving PISA Outcomes*. Tech. rept. OECD.

Hanushek, E., and Woessmann, L. 2012. Do Better Schools Lead to More Growth? Cognitive Skills, Economic Outcomes, and Causation. *Journal of Economic Growth*, **17**, 267–321.

Hanushek, E., and Woessmann, L. 2015. *The Knowledge Capital of Nations: Education and the Economics of Growth*. Cambridge, MA: MIT Press.

Hastings, J., and Weinstein, J. 2008. Information, School Choice, and Academic Achievement: Evidence from Two Experiments. *Quarterly Journal of Economics*, **123**, 1373–1414.

Hastings, J., Kane, T., and Staiger, D. 2008. *Heterogeneous Preferences and the Efficacy of Public School Choice*. Combines and replaces National Bureau of Economic Research Working Papers No. 12145 and 11805. http://aida.econ.yale.edu/~jh529/papers/HKS_Combined_200806.pdf.

Howell, W. G. 2004. Dynamic Selection Effects in Means-tested, Urban School Voucher Programs. *Journal of Policy Analysis and Management*, **23**, 225–250.

Hoxby, C. 2000. Does Competition among Public Schools Benefit Students and Taxpayers? *American Economic Review*, **90**, 1209–1238.

Hoxby, C. 2003a. Introduction. In: Hoxby, C. (ed), *The Economics of School Choice*. Chicago: University of Chicago Press.

Hoxby, C. 2003b. School Choice and School Competition: Evidence from the United States. *Swedish Economic Policy Review*, **10**, 11–67.

Hoxby, C. 2003c. School Choice and School Productivity: Could School Choice Be a Tide that Lifts All Boats? In: Hoxby, C. (ed), *The Economics of School Choice*. Chicago: University of Chicago Press.

Hoxby, C., and Murarka, S. 2009. *Charter Schools in New York City: Who Enrolls and How They Affect Student Achievement*. NBER Working Paper 14852.

Hoxby, C., and Rockoff, J. 2004. *The Impact of Charter Schools on Student Achievement*. Mimeo, Harvard.

Ichino, A., Karabarbounis, L., and Moretti, E. 2009. *The Political Economy of Intergenerational Income Mobility*. Discussion paper no. 4767, Institute for the Study of Labor (IZA), Bonn.

Jacob, B. 2005. Accountability, Incentives and Behavior: The Impact of High-stakes Testing in the Chicago Public Schools. *Journal of Public Economics*, **89**, 761–796.

Jacob, B. 2010. *Do Principals Fire the Worst Teachers?* NBER Working Paper No. 15715.

Jacob, B., and Lefgren, L. 2008. Can Principals Identify Effective Teachers? Evidence on Subjective Performance Evaluation in Education. *Journal of Labor Economics*, **25**, 101–136.

Jacob, B., and Levitt, S. 2003. Rotten Apples: An Investigation of the Prevalence and Predictors of Teacher Cheating. *The Quarterly Journal of Economics*, **118**, 843–877.

Jäntti, M., Bratsberg, B., Røoed, K., Raaum, O., Naylor, R., Eva, O., Björklund, A., and Eriksson, T. 2006. *American Exceptionalism in a New Light: A Comparison of Intergenerational Earnings Mobility in the Nordic Countries, the United Kingdom and the United States*. Discussion paper no. 1938, Institute for the Study of Labor (IZA), Bonn.

Kane, T., and Staiger, D. 2001. *Improving School Accountability Measures*. NBER Working Paper No. 8156.

Katz, L., and Autor, D. 1999. Changes in the Wage Structure and Earnings Inequality. In: Ashenfelter, O., and Card, D. (eds), *Handbook of Labour Economics*, vol. 3A. North-Holland: Amsterdam.

Koning, P., and van der Wiel. 2012. School Responsiveness to Quality Rankings: An Empirical Analysis of Secondary Education in the Netherlands. *De Economist*, **160**, 339–355.

Ladd, H. 2002. School Vouchers: A Critical View. *Journal of Economic Perspectives*, **16**, 3–24.

Ladd, H., and Fiske, E. 2003. Does Competition Improve Teaching and Learning? Evidence from New Zealand. *Educational Evaluation and Policy Analysis*, **25**, 97–112.

Lavy, V. 2008. Does Raising the Principal's Wage Improve the School's Outcomes? Quasi-experimental Evidence from an Unusual Policy Experiment in Israel. *Scandinavian Journal of Economics*, **110**, 639–662.

Lavy, V. 2010. Effects of Free Choice among Public Schools. *Review of Economic Studies*, **77**, 1164–1191.

Levitt, S., List, J., Neckermann, S., and Sadoff, S. 2012. *The Behavioralist Goes to School: Leveraging Behavioral Economics to Improve Educational Performance*. NBER Working Paper 18165.

Loeb, S., Horng, E., and Klasik, D. 2010. Principal's Time Use and School Effectiveness. *American Journal of Education*, **116**, 491–523.

Machin, S., and Vernoit, J. 2011. *Changing School Autonomy: Academy Schools and Their Introduction to England's Education*. CEE Discussion Paper 123.

Mayer, S. E., and Lopoo, L. M. 2008. Government Spending and Intergenerational Mobility. *Journal of Public Economics*, **92**, 139–158.

Meghir, C., and Palme, M. 2005. Educational Reform, Ability, and Family Background. *American Economic Review*, **95**, 414–424.

Meghir, C., and Rivkin, S. 2011. Econometric Methods for Research in Education. In: Hanushek, E., Machin, S., and Woessmann, L. (eds), *Handbook of the Economics of Education*, vol. 3. North-Holland Amsterdam.

Nechyba, T. 2003a. Introducing School Choice into Multi-district Public School Systems. In: Hoxby, C. (ed), *The Economics of School Choice*. Chicago: University of Chicago Press.

Nechyba, T. 2003b. School Finance, Spatial Income Segregation and the Nature of Communities. *Journal of Urban Economics*, **54**, 61–88.

Nechyba, T. 2006. Income and Peer Quality Sorting in Public and Private Schools. In: Hanushek, E., and F., Welch (eds), *Handbook of Economics of Education*. Amsterdam: North Holland.

OECD. 2012. *Public and Private Schools: How Management and Funding Relate to their Socio-economic Profile.* OECD Publishing, http://dx.doi.org/10.1787/9789264175006-en.

Pathak, P. A., and Sonmez, T. 2008. Levelling the Playing Field: Sincere and Sophisticated Players in the Boston Mechanism. *American Economic Review*, **98**, 1636–1652.

Pekkarinen, T., Uusitalo, R., and Kerr, S. 2009. School Tracking and Intergenerational Income Mobility: Evidence from the Finnish Comprehensive School Reform. *Journal of Public Economics*, **93**, 965–973.

Peterson, P., Howell, W. G., Wolf, P. J., and Campbell, D. E. 2003. School Vouchers: Results from Randomized Experiments. *The University of Chicago Press*, 107–144.

Reback, R., Rockoff, J., and Schwartz, H. 2014. Under Pressure: Job Security, Resource Allocation, and Productivity in Schools under NCLB. *American Economic Journal: Economic Policy*, **6**, 207–241.

Reis, A., Nunes, L., and Seabra, C. 2015. The Publication of School Rankings: A Step Toward Increased Accountability? *Economics of Education Review*, **49**, 15–23.

Rivkin, S., Hanushek, E., and Kain, J. 2005. Teachers, Schools, and Academic Achievement. *Econometrica*, **73**, 417–458.

Rockoff, J., and Turner, L. 2010. Short Run Impacts of Accountability on School Quality. *American Economic Journal: Economic Policy*, **2**, 119–147.

Roth, A. E. 1984. The Evolution of the Labor Market for Medical Interns and Residents: A Case Study in Game Theory. *Journal of Political Economy*, **92**, 991–1016.

Rothstein, J. 2006. Good Principals or Good Peers? Parental Valuation of School Characteristics, Tiebout Equilibrium, and the Incentive Effects of Competition among Jurisdictions. *American Economic Review*, **96**, 1333–1350.

Rothstein, J. 2007. Does Competition among Public Schools Benefit Students and Taxpayers? A Comment on Hoxby (2000). *American Economic Review*, **97**, 2026–2037.

Rouse, C., Hannaway, J., Goldhaber, D., and Figlio, D. 2013. Feeling the Florida Heat? How Low-Performing Schools Respond to Voucher and Accountability Pressure. *American Economic Journal: Economic Policy*, **5**, 251–281.

Sandström, F., and Bergström, F. 2005. School Vouchers in Practice: Competition Will Not Hurt You. *Journal of Public Economics*, **89**, 351–380.

Schneider, M., and Buckley, J. 2002. What Do Parents Want from Schools? Evidence from the Internet. *Educational Evaluation and Policy Analysis*, **24**, 133–144.

Soderstrom, M., and Uusitalo, R. 2010. School Choice and Segregation: Evidence from an Admission Reform. *Scandanvian Journal of Economics*, **112**, 55–76.

Woessmann, L. 2007. International Evidence on School Competition, Autonomy, and Accountability: A Review. *Peabody Journal of Education*, **82**, 473–497.

Wong, M., Cook, T., and Steiner, P. 2009. *No Child Left Behind: An Interim Evaluation of its Effects on Learning Using Two Interrupted Time Series each with Its Own Non-equivalent Comparison Series.* Northwestern University Institute for Policy Research, Northwestern University, Working Paper Series WP-09-11.

5 Competition and Regulation in Markets for Goods and Services: A Survey with Emphasis on Digital Markets

Nikolaos Vettas

Abstract

In the last couple of decades, competition policy has been receiving increasing attention and has obtained a central role in microeconomic policy in Europe. Ensuring that markets work as competitively as possible is viewed as key for economic growth and welfare. While much progress has been made in the research that studies and shapes competition policy, the nature of competition in markets is also evolving and new issues are emerging. An important novel feature is related to the increase in the size of the digital sectors of the economy and especially to the way that digital technologies and e-commerce practices revolutionize essentially all other sectors of the economy. These developments represent some new challenges for research. One key issue is that with digital markets and technologies we are more likely to have intense competition *'for the market'*, rather than competition *'in the market'*. It follows that we need models that are more dynamic and incorporate to a larger extent network effects, other increasing returns to scale and uncertainty. At the same time, it is important that one does not ignore the lessons of the earlier and current literature, especially in core areas like pricing and vertical relations. On the empirical research side, the availability of relevant data can be expected to increase exponentially, due to the fact that electronic transactions can be recorded almost automatically. The need and opportunity for new empirical studies, given the nature of available data, thus emerges. New technologies also tend to minimize the distances between buyers and sellers in markets and facilitate information flows; *'single market'* issues therefore come to the forefront and their analysis can be controversial. This challenge becomes a clear priority since the Digital Single Market is a stated objective of the European Commission.

5.1 Introduction

Competition and innovation can be identified as the two, closely interrelated, pillars of long-run growth. Over the last decades, in particular, economic policy

194

has focused systematically and as a priority on how to protect and strengthen the factors that facilitate both competition and innovation. Importantly, the relevant policy design has to take into account that the relation between the two economic forces is complex and typically not monotonic. From a static view, competition among firms allows consumers to have access to goods that are less expensive and of higher quality, while overall reducing profit levels. From a more dynamic perspective, however, it is exactly the profit motive that makes firms proceed in their innovative activities, either in product innovation (that is, offering new and better products) or in process innovation (that is, producing goods more efficiently).

Policy at the European Union (EU) level has made the more efficient functioning of products' markets a clear priority. Worldwide, in the last couple of decades we have also seen very important progress both on the competition policy and the innovation policy fronts. This has led to a more systematic, clear and consistent approach to the design and application of policy, to some convergence of views, and in particular to bringing the legal and the economics-based approaches of the issue closer to each other, with the goal of contributing to a more efficient functioning of markets and to increases in social welfare. In fact, how structural reforms that improve the functioning of markets can lead to sustainable growth is the focus of the modern economics of growth (see e.g., Aghion and Akcigit, 2015).

Regarding competition policy itself, it has grown from an area that was peripheral, of secondary importance and perhaps relatively more important only in the US (building on the more than century-long tradition that followed the Sherman Act of 1890), into one of the most active and important areas in micro-economic policy. In particular, starting in the mid-1980s, the explosion of important research in industrial organization (IO) economics has been gradually and naturally blended with developments in competition policy and law. This research in IO, directly linked to developments in game theory and information economics (with its first wave of key contributions reflected in Tirole, 1988), has contributed towards narrowing the gap between the more formalistic and the '*Chicago school*' approaches, and has proved fruitful.[1] Overall, progress in competition policy in the EU has been made, on a number of important fronts, both at the level of the European Commission (DG-Competition) and the more decentralized level of the National Competition Authorities (NCAs). Recently, a set of new and important challenges have appeared for the application of competition policy, specifically in the context of how markets work in the '*digitalized*' economy and electronic trade.[2]

The efficient functioning of the digital and online markets is of high importance for welfare and is expected to become increasingly so in the near future; therefore progress in the related research and policy areas should be of high priority. Importantly, not only is it true that digital markets, more narrowly defined, are an increasingly larger part of the economy, but also that the new technologies tend to change in important ways how all other markets essentially work.[3] For instance, 'cross-channel' retail sales in Europe (that is, purchases that consumers begin using a digital channel, but do not complete online) are expected to reach €704 billion by 2020, up from €457 billion in 2015; combined with online sales, these cross-channel sales are expected to reach €947 billion, with the result that 53 per cent of total European retail sales over the next five years will be web-impacted.[4] This chapter focuses, therefore, on how the literature examines some issues related to the economic phenomena that become important due to the development of digital markets, and shape the basis for competition policy. On this policy front, we have seen a series of recent and high-profile cases at the EC against the largest companies in the digital or high-technology sectors.

From an economics perspective, a key distinguishing feature of trade in the digitalized world is the ability of sellers and buyers to access some important information about their trading partners in ways that, for practical reasons, are essentially impossible in traditional markets. As a result, with constraints and incentives for the market participants becoming significantly modified, equilibrium strategies and outcomes are expected to change. In turn, competition policy also has to take a stand on a number of issues that were not present in traditional markets or were much less important.[5]

More specifically, one of the main new areas that pose challenges in their analysis is related to the significantly enhanced ability that firms have to price differently to different clients and under different conditions in a digitalized environment. Possible competition restrictions in e-commerce include geographical targeting both for the digital content and for the online sale of goods. Online sellers may sell goods to different countries using terms that may differ substantially across countries. This also includes the frequent practice of directing buyers from different areas to different websites and also blocking digital content, such as sports or movies. Often an important part of the online distribution of digital content takes place through licensing arrangements that include explicit territorial restrictions.

Related to the above matters are also 'parallel trade' restrictions, in e-commerce and otherwise, that prevent a distributor from selling a good outside a particular country. It is often the case in practice that retailers are prevented from distributing a service or a good in a certain territory as a result of a silent understanding, or of a particular contractual restriction. A related recent phenomenon of increasing importance is that of imposing limitations on the sales through third party platforms (or *'marketplaces'*). These limitations include the sale through websites that operate in different countries and the application of *'most favoured nation'* (MFN) clauses.

More broadly, pricing restrictions and other vertical restraints, such as resale price maintenance (RPM) and types of MFN clauses, have emerged as quite important in competition policy practice. In fact, NCAs in different EU member states have reached decisions that appear to be moving in opposite directions, especially in the area of vertical pricing practices, indicating that a more solid scientific basis would be useful for the comprehension and analysis of such cases.

In addition to competition policy objectives, a stated core goal in the EU is the promotion of the 'single market'.[6] This objective is often served by the application of competition and other policy measures, however, it is often viewed as a goal in itself. It can be interpreted in a narrower or a broader way. The narrower way is that all buyers should have access to products and services on the same terms, regardless of the member state where they reside. In close relation to the topic of this chapter, the Single Digital Market objective has been set by the European Commission (EC) as one of its top priorities, as also detailed in its May 2015 Communication,[7] while the Commission launched at the same time an antitrust competition inquiry into how the e-commerce sector functions in the EU. The inquiry, as already announced by Competition Commissioner Margrethe Vestager in March, will allow the Commission to identify possible competition concerns affecting European e-commerce markets.[8] While making this issue a priority appears a reasonable policy choice, interpreting the single market objective as a way to eliminate all price discrimination practices is likely too narrow an approach and not based on solid economic principles. Economic analysis does not always offer clear predictions about the welfare effects of price discrimination. If the single market objective is understood to mean uniform prices across all EU areas, then that would be an extreme view; after all, prices are not typically the same even within the same country. Prohibiting price discrimination may not lead to everyone having access to the goods or services at the lower possible price, which is often implicitly assumed. Instead it is possible that it may lead to some markets not being served at all, which would be contrary to the single market principle.

Overall, while in this chapter we are motivated by some important recent cases and emphasize new aspects of how markets work and the need for new research, we also wish to stress the *continuity* that should exist both in the economics analysis and in competition policy: when moving forward to applications in new markets, ignoring past research is not an appropriate way to proceed. Many of the issues that surface as important in digital markets are not absent in other markets and therefore (should) have also already been studied in some way. However, the difference in scale is often so dramatic that from a practical viewpoint the priorities for what matters, the nature of how the market forces interact and the application of policy analysis, is often perceived as a completely different market environment. The challenge therefore is to try to identify the new elements that play the key role for each case. Online travel agencies, for example, make searching for a hotel reservation a very different activity than it used to be. However, we could in principle have had (and we did have) travel agents before the Internet and also we could have (and we sometimes still have) online searches without online platforms to act as intermediaries.

To argue that the new markets require a whole new set of research that would make the existing one obsolete would not necessarily be a reasonable way to proceed. Instead, the key is how to use existing results, to refine, extend and enrich them in the context of digital markets. In particular, there are at least two important literatures within IO that are relevant here and, by their nature, necessarily closely related to the currently open issues. These refer to the study of vertical relations (integration and vertical restraints) and to pricing practices: in particular, price discrimination and nonlinear pricing. We sketch some of the progress that has been made in areas that are still open and important. The challenges faced by researchers in these areas are not trivial. The study of vertical relations necessarily finds in its way the issue of bargaining between vertically-linked firms. Such firms act both as collaborators, since they trade goods and services with each other, and at the same time as competitors, since they compete in sharing the joint surplus.

Pricing itself has naturally been a core issue in economics. However, we may not have a full understanding of how pricing functions when there is price discrimination and various types of nonlinear pricing under oligopoly competition, when there are vertical relations, or what the welfare implications are of the various restrictions, especially under important dynamic effects.

It is beyond the scope of this chapter to discuss in depth the important related competition cases that have been recently examined or are under examination. Instead, we use these as a motivation to focus on some related ideas and results from the relevant literature. We also discuss areas and topics where further research would be useful and possibly important for policy. This refers both to more basic research (that could be useful across a number of competition policy issues and other cases) and to research that is motivated by specific competition cases.

The remainder of this chapter is organized as follows. The next section starts with a general perspective on competition policy in the EU, before turning to some recent developments there. We discuss digital markets and differentiate according to the features of the goods supplied and other dimensions, since the digital nature of each market does not have to be the same. Then we discuss some recent competition cases in Europe (including e-books and online travel agencies) that can serve as leading examples for the analysis and relate to the Commission's Single Digital Market initiative. We close this section with a comparison between online and offline trade. Section 5.3 sketches some selected results from the IO literature, looking at pricing (with a focus on price discrimination) and at vertical relations (with a focus on restraints). Section 5.4

turns to research that is motivated specifically by recent and current competition issues, such as how to treat online and offline sales, geographical and other pricing restrictions and *'most favoured nation'* clauses. Section 5.5 discusses the main challenges that economics research is facing when analyzing and supporting competition policy in digital markets. Section 5.6 concludes.

5.2   A View on Competition Policy Developments in Europe

5.2.1   Competition Policy: The General Context

Policy at the EU level has made the more efficient functioning of product and services markets a priority. Related policy is organized around four areas, collusion and cartels, abuse of dominance, merger control and state aid. Activity has been high in each of these areas, as is also manifested by the several high-profile cases examined and by the increasing level of fines imposed. In terms of the foundations for policy, significant progress has been made in a number of important fronts; the challenges, however, have not been trivial.

A central issue has been the tension between following an economics-based and a more formalistic approach in policy, a distinction that often expresses itself as a choice between a more effects-based and a per se approach to competition. While there has been progress on this front, the matter is not resolved and will likely remain a core element of the debate about competition policy for the decades to come. Industrial organization economists have studied systematically topics directly or indirectly related to competition policy, while some policy-makers have appeared open to receiving guidance for their decisions by economic analysis.[9] The primary area where economic analysis has contributed significantly in the last few years in European policy-making is in identifying economic *efficiencies* and the related trade-offs of policy actions. This was primarily effective in the areas of vertical relations, as well as in mergers and in state aid. However, certainly not everyone agrees on the importance of the progress economic analysis has made, or even how important a role economics could or should play in competition policy decisions in any event.[10]

A second important area where progress has been made is in defining the limits of the application of competition policy. The main issue here is the relation between the competition policy principles (which typically refer to ad hoc and ex post interventions) and sectoral regulation (which typically aims to establish economic efficiency by ex ante and often comprehensive interventions). Where should one draw the line between the two approaches and how can one facilitate the transition from a more regulation-based to a more 'free-market' operation, that is, without systematic regulation but with an application of competition law when this is needed? This question is central in many markets including telecoms, energy, transport and banking and, of course, affects the relation between DG-Competition and the other Directorates in the Commission. A related important challenge has been the gradual harmonization of policy between countries, especially with the US and also within the EU.

A third challenge has been to clarify the relation between competition policy and other policy areas. In relation to innovation policy, such as in intellectual property protection, the central question is to understand how static efficiency (where high profit is often a measure of market inefficiency) and dynamic efficiency (where it is exactly the prospect of profit that may drive innovation) are related. Related key challenges have been made evident by the recent financial and macroeconomic crisis. Should one think differently about the application of competition law, especially in the areas of merger control and state aid, when important firms (including banks) or even entire sectors face distress, or is the importance of the rules exactly to offer guidance at the more difficult times, even if this means that a significant part of economic activity will be eliminated?

Overall, and looking across the four core areas (cartels, abuse of dominance, mergers and state aid), the amount of work that has been put in place in the EU over the recent years has been significant, although the issues described above are too deep and complex to be fully resolved. A useful summary of the economic analysis used in DG-Comp in recent years, including both cases based on some innovative economic analysis and new issues, can be found in a sequence of articles: Neven and Albæk (2007); Neven and de la Mano (2009, 2010); Kühn et al. (2011, 2012); Buettner et al. (2013), and Buehler et al. (2014).[11]

5.2.2   Digital Trade and Online Markets

While it is now commonplace for economists and business people to concern themselves with the issues that the digital economy brings, it is important to try to clarify what the term 'digital markets' really means and what (if anything) is really fundamentally new there and in online trade (or electronic-trade, e-trade). One way to approach and organize the various aspects of the issue is as follows.

1. A first category refers to cases where *the Internet is used so that the end user has access to a good that is being offered (online) in digital form.* This includes movies, music, news, e-books, scientific articles, and various other such types of goods that would typically have informational or entertainment value. The user goes online and can obtain access directly. Some remarks for this case:

    i. Goods in this category can typically also be supplied in some other form, through some alternative channel. Access to them in digital form could be made without the Internet (i.e., by using a CD, DVD or some other such medium). They could also be used in a nondigital form, but in other traditional ways: *Casablanca* was being watched by large audiences years before the digital format became possible; the *New York Times* was published only in paper format for decades. In many cases the two channels, digital and traditional, coexist in the market either complementing or competing with each other.

ii. Users of these goods obtain access to them typically by paying directly online and this payment could take the form of either paying for each item separately, or by purchasing a subscription. Some other times the end user could have access to the good without making any payment and the supplier only benefits indirectly.[12]

iii. How convenient and secure the payment is can be crucial for the efficient operation of such markets. Therefore, the development of electronic payments systems is complementary to such markets.[13]

2. A second category involves markets where the end good that will be consumed is *not* in digital form and instead the online operation *merely facilitates search and purchasing*. In cases such as searching or booking for hotel stays, travel, car rentals, housing, clothes or theaters, the Internet can be used either for providing information about the good (directly from the supplier or indirectly through other sources) or by proceeding to a booking and possibly payment. The actual consumption in all of these cases is not made online but in the 'real' world. In this sense, digital markets can affect literally any other market and they are offering a complementary good, which is the facilitation of the contact between the supplier and the potential buyer.

- One possibility in this case is that online search could only serve comparison purposes, without completing the actual transaction. The search would typically be about information for the goods' characteristics and prices. It may include access to information that is not only provided by the supplier, but also by past users or by third-party experts. For the search to be more useful, at some level some comparison should be possible between alternative purchases and substitute goods.

- Another possibility is that, in addition to the information provided, a booking or a full purchase is made online. In this case, and depending on the physical nature of the good, the actual consumption will then take place either with the end-user travelling to it (visit a hotel or a theatre) or with the final good being transferred to the user (e.g., clothes shipped to home). Some comments for this case follow:

i. The sale could be made online through a website that is operated exclusively by the supplier. In the same way that the selling company could have a traditional brick-and-mortar store, it may (also) have an online store.

    ii. The online sale could also be made through a platform which allows the comparison and sale of goods offered by several competing brands and items. In this case, the platform plays the role of an intermediary, a type of 'online shopping mall'. The platform acts as an agent for the various suppliers and would typically charge a fee for the service. The delivery of the actual good could be the responsibility of either the platform (e.g., Amazon shipping a book) or the supplier (a hotel providing services purchased through Booking.com).

3. A third category may involve digital markets only at the wholesale level (B2B). These may take various forms (e.g., they may be exclusive, or open, with or without paying a subscription fee) and their goal is to facilitate trade between businesses, such as suppliers and distributors. Many of these markets do not employ the Internet but other internal electronic systems. Several also existed independently and before the explosion of online trade at the retail level.[14]

4. Online auctions (at the retail or wholesale level) are also a distinct category. Auctions, even when organized offline, are market activities that operate on the basis of some clear and precise rules, and their conduct online mainly provides some gains in terms of lower transaction costs. However, the changes that are being introduced relatively to the traditional format are in general less important than in other markets, where the rules are initially less formal in the traditional format.[15]

Given the above categorization and description of characteristics, it would be useful to make some initial remarks. A key feature of digital markets from an economics viewpoint is the much lower search and transaction costs, relative to how these markets tend to operate offline. At the same time, suppliers and intermediaries have much easier access to potential buyers than before and also to key data about their characteristics. Issues related to vertical restraints and price discrimination become central.[16] In many cases we tend to have two-sided market features. In addition, whether content is sold online, or the online nature simply is confined to facilitating trade, intellectual property issues become very important and an analysis of the effects of patents and copyrights may be necessary. This feature becomes even more important due to the cost structure, which is tilted heavily towards the fixed components and not the marginal ones. Finally, whoever controls pricing and access to the means via which trade takes place is important, including the question of pricing internet access.

The nature of the concerns that competition authorities express in recent cases in this broad digital context varies. In the electronic-books markets (e.g., Apple, Amazon), the main concern is about the format in which pricing takes place (e.g., wholesale pricing vs. agency); in the online travel agency cases (e.g., HRS) the concern has been about 'best price' (or MFN) clauses in contracts between the platform and the hotels. In distribution cases (e.g., Adidas or Asics) the main concern is if it could make economic sense for a supplier not to allow some broader platform to offer their products. We turn next to a description of some recent cases.

5.2.3   Some Recent Competition Cases

A number of high-profile competition cases have been recently examined or are currently open in Europe and are related, directly or indirectly, to online trade and similar issues. While the details in each case are different, online pricing raises issues of possible abuse of a firm's dominant position: a theme that often emerges is that of pricing restrictions that tend to exclude some suppliers or distributers, or tend to discriminate among categories of buyers.

MasterCard: Cross-border Rules and Inter-regional Interchange Fees

In July 2015, the EC sent a Statement of Objections to MasterCard, expressing the view that MasterCard's rules prevent banks from offering lower interchange fees to retailers based in other Member States, where interchange fees may be higher. This follows a series of important previous actions on interchange fees, while there is also an on-going investigation into Visa Inc.'s interregional interchange fees policy.[17]

According to the preliminary view of the EC, retailers cannot benefit from lower fees in other areas and cross-border competition between banks may be restricted. It is also stated that MasterCard's interchange fees for transactions in the EU using MasterCard cards issued in other regions of the world (e.g., in the US or Russia) breach European antitrust rules by setting an artificially high minimum price for processing these transactions. It is further explained that payments by card play a key role in the Single Market, both for domestic purchases and for purchases across borders, or over the Internet. Banks use MasterCard to set on their behalf the interchange fees that apply between them. The Commission takes the preliminary view that the practices outlined violate Article 101 of the Treaty on the Functioning of the European Union (TFEU) that prohibits cartels and other anticompetitive business practices.

Two interrelated concerns were raised in the statement. First, interchange fees vary considerably from one Member State to another. MasterCard's rules prevent retailers in a high-interchange fee country from benefitting from lower interchange fees offered by an acquiring bank located in another Member State. A second concern is about the high levels of MasterCard's 'inter-regional interchange fees'. These fees are paid by an acquiring bank for transactions made in the EU with cards issued in other regions of the world. High interregional fees may increase prices for retailers and may in turn lead to higher prices for products and services for all consumers, according to the EC.

This case follows recent important developments in the markets for digital payments and, in particular, regarding how market competition is related to the appropriate regulation of interchange fees.[18] The more controversial part of the new case may be that, under the current practice, banks in one EU Member State are prevented from offering lower interchange fees to a retailer in another EU country where interchange fees may be higher. If this practice is found to violate the law, a move towards high concentration is expected to be observed. In particular, banks from all Member States may move towards acquirers in other Member States where, because of their currently larger volume of transactions, fees can be set at lower rates. This possibility generates an interesting tension for policy-makers. On the one hand, the single market initiative should allow any agent to have access to lower prices at any level and available anywhere in the EU. On the other, in a market where a large installed base plays a crucial role and smaller players cannot survive, removing all barriers may lead to greatly increased concentration and ultimately to lower welfare, at least for consumers in some Member States.

Amazon: e-books

In June 2015, the EC opened an investigation into Amazon's electronic book contracts with publishers in the EU. According to the announcement, the main concern is about clauses requiring publishers to inform Amazon of terms with its competitors that may be more favourable, known as *'most favoured nation'* (MFN) clauses. The view of the EC is that the use of such clauses may make it more difficult for other e-book distributors to compete with Amazon by developing new and innovative products and services.[19] It is stated that certain clauses included in Amazon's contracts with publishers concerning such e-books could constitute a breach of EU antitrust rules that prohibit the abuse of a dominant market position and restrictive business practices. In particular, the investigation focuses on clauses which may shield Amazon from competition from other e-book distributors, such as clauses granting it the right to be informed of more favourable or alternative terms offered to its competitors or the right to terms and conditions at least as good as those offered to its competitors.

MFN clauses were at the centre of the ruling against Apple and five major US publishers in 2013. Apple settled a big e-book antitrust case in the US that was driven in part by Amazon's complaints over Apple's deals with publishers. In December 2011, the EC had also opened proceedings in the sector, because it had concerns that Apple and five international publishing houses (Penguin Random House, Hachette Livres, Simon & Schuster, HarperCollins and Georg von Holtzbrinck Verlagsgruppe) may have colluded to limit price competition at the retail level for e-books. In December 2012 and July 2013, respectively, the companies offered a number of commitments, to make changes to their contracts with Apple, which addressed the Commission's concerns. Overall, the significant increase in e-book reading in Europe has drawn the attention of the EC. The new case will focus mainly on the largest markets for books, in English and German.

Cross-border Provision of Pay-TV Services

In July 2015, the EC sent a Statement of Objections to Sky UK and six major US film studios (Disney, NBC Universal, Paramount Pictures, Sony, Twentieth Century Fox and Warner Bros). The Commission's preliminary view is that the studios and Sky UK have bilaterally agreed to put in place contractual restrictions that prevent Sky UK from allowing EU consumers located elsewhere to access, via satellite or online, pay-TV services available in the UK and Ireland. Without these restrictions, Sky UK would be free to decide on commercial grounds whether to sell its pay-TV services to such consumers requesting access to its services, taking into account the regulatory framework including, as regards online pay-TV services, the relevant national copyright laws.[20]

US film studios tend to license audio-visual content to a single pay-TV broadcaster in each Member State (or combined for a few Member States with a common language). The investigation identified clauses in licensing agreements between the six film studios and Sky UK which require Sky UK to block access to films through its online pay-TV services ('geo-blocking') or through its satellite pay-TV services to consumers outside its licensed territory. Such clauses may restrict Sky UK's ability to accept unsolicited requests for its pay-TV services from consumers located abroad, that is, from consumers located in Member States where Sky UK is not actively promoting or advertising its services ('passive sales'). Some agreements also contain clauses requiring studios to ensure that, in their licensing agreements with broadcasters other than Sky UK, these broadcasters are prevented from making their pay-TV services available in the UK and Ireland. As a result, these clauses grant 'absolute territorial exclusivity' to Sky UK and/or other broadcasters. They eliminate cross-border competition between pay-TV broadcasters and partition the internal market along national borders.[21]

In related cases, the EC currently investigates licensing agreements between the film studios and other major European broadcasters (Canal Plus of France, Sky Italia of Italy, Sky Deutschland of Germany and DTS of Spain). In its October 2011 ruling on the Premier League / Murphy cases, the EU Court of Justice addressed the issue of absolute territorial restrictions in licence agreements for broadcasting services. The Court held that certain licensing provisions preventing a satellite broadcaster from providing its broadcasts to consumers outside the licensed territory enable each broadcaster to be granted absolute territorial exclusivity in the area covered by the licence, thus eliminating all competition between broadcasters and partitioning the market in accordance with national borders.

Google: Online Comparison Shopping

In April 2015, the EC sent a Statement of Objections to Google concerning its comparison shopping service. The allegation is that the company is abusing its dominant position in the market for general internet search services by systematically favouring its own comparison shopping product in its general search results pages. The view expressed is that such conduct infringes EU antitrust rules, because it stifles competition and harms consumers.

According to the EC, comparison shopping products allow consumers to search for products on online shopping websites and compare prices between different vendors. The preliminary conclusion of the Commission is that Google gives systematic favourable treatment to its own product 'Google Shopping', for example, by showing Google Shopping more prominently on the screen. It may therefore artificially divert traffic from rival comparison shopping services and hinder their ability to compete on the market. The Commission is concerned that users do not necessarily see the most relevant results in response to queries – this is to the detriment of consumers, and stifles innovation. Further, the Commission's preliminary view is that to remedy such conduct, Google should treat its own comparison shopping service and those of rivals in the same way.

Online Marketplaces and Selective Distribution

Some important cases in Germany, in July 2014, considered the terms of distribution via online marketplaces. The German Federal Cartel Office (*Bundeskartellamt*, or BKartA) and the Schleswig Court of Appeals (*Oberlandesgericht*, or OLG Schleswig) have held that Adidas, ASICS and Casio must allow their approved resellers to use internet auction sites and online marketplaces to resell their goods. These cases suggest that a supplier may not prohibit, but merely regulate, such online resale by way of a selective distribution system in which requirements and restrictions on online sales do not exceed similar obligations imposed on resellers for other, namely offline, distribution channels.

These cases, as well as the ruling of the Berlin Court of Appeals (*Kammergericht*, KG) in 2013, on Scout satchels (Case 2 U 8/09 Kart), suggest that a supplier may only restrict the use of internet platforms and marketplaces in a selective distribution system in which the criteria imposed on online sales are at least overall equivalent to criteria imposed for other sales channels, for example, sale in physical shops, as explained in the Guidelines of the European Commission on vertical restraints.

In a statement relating to the Adidas case, BKartA took the view *'that the trading possibilities offered by the Internet create new challenges for both manufacturers and retailers'* and that it is its *'task to keep markets and opportunities open for the benefit of retailers and consumers'*. The statement continues, *'It goes without saying that manufacturers can select their distributors according to certain quality requirements. However, both under European and German competition law they are prohibited from largely eliminating a principal distribution channel such as the web.'*

5.2.4   Online Travel Agencies and MFNs

In a series of cases across Europe, competition authorities have looked at MFN clauses and other pricing restrictions in relation to the operation of online travel agencies. In January 2015, the Düsseldorf Higher Regional Court rejected the appeal of Robert Ragge GmbH's Hotel Reservation Service (HRS) against the decision of the Federal Cartel Office (*Bundeskartellamt*) of December 2013. In its decision, the authority had prohibited HRS from continuing to apply its 'best price' clause and at the same time initiated proceedings against the hotel booking portals, Booking.com and Expedia, for applying similar clauses in their contracts with their hotel partners. Under the 'best price' clauses the hotels are obliged to always offer the hotel portal their lowest room prices, maximum room capacity and most favourable booking and cancellation conditions available on the Internet.

The Düsseldorf Higher Regional Court decision has confirmed that HRS's 'best price' clauses restrict competition to such a degree that they cannot be exempted under the TFEU Block Exemption Regulation, or as an individual exemption. The Federal Cartel Office originally issued a statement of objections against HRS in early 2012 focusing on the company's policy which bans hotels from offering better deals to customers who book directly through the hotel or through another booking platform. The concern was that, while the clauses used (also by other travel websites) may appear to benefit consumers, in reality they may eliminate competition for lower room prices between the hotel booking portals. Consumers are worse off because they cannot get a better price or better quality service conditions by exploring alternative reservation paths.[22]

Several other competition authorities in Europe have also recently conducted similar investigations against hotel booking platforms in relation to their 'best price' clauses. These include the UK's Office of Fair Trading case against Expedia Inc. and Booking.com in coordination with InterContinental Hotels Group PLC and the Swiss Competition Commission's case against several online travel agencies, including Booking.com, Expedia and HRS.[23]

How competition policy should treat the employment of MFN clauses (by online platforms or otherwise) is not a simple matter and how economic analysis can help the formulation of policy will be discussed in subsequent parts of the chapter. Many interesting applied policy analyses have also appeared; for example, P. Akman in a July 2015 article considers the acceptance of commitments offered by Booking.com to the French, Swedish and Italian competition authorities.[24] She argues that these commitments may represent at best an ineffectual solution to any problem existing on the relevant market.[25] Booking.com has agreed not to use the 'broad' MFN clauses in its contracts with its hotel partners for a period of five years, from 1 July 2015. As a result, Booking.com can no longer require hotels to offer Booking.com the best price across platforms or the best price that the hotel charges through its offline channels. Yet, the commitments do not stop Booking.com from imposing MFN clauses to the extent that the clause seeks parity between the prices on Booking.com and the prices on the hotel's online channels such as the hotel's own website. This commitment is different from the infringement decision taken by the Bundeskartellamt in the HRS case and does not prevent Booking.com from seeking parity between prices on Booking.com and the hotel's online channels, whereas the Bundeskartellamt's infringement decision prohibited all types of MFN clauses.

Resale Price Maintenance

Resale price maintenance (RPM) is a common vertical restraint which has received much attention in competition policy. The view is often adopted that minimum RPM or fixed RPM, since it is a restraint, is bad for competition and violates the law. In particular, in a recent series of cases, some NCAs find that fixed price or minimum RPM directly violates the law, even when the market shares of the related firms are low, focusing, in other words, only on contractual freedom and without a reference to efficiencies and other economic implications. In other cases, some NCAs have recently taken a different route. In particular, in October 2014, the Swedish Competition Authority adopted a reasoned priority decision not to pursue the investigation of a complaint regarding RPM.[26] In April 2015, the Dutch Competition Authority published a paper setting out its strategy and enforcement priorities relating to vertical agreements. It confirms its relatively lenient economic approach towards vertical restraints and assumes that vertical restraints are generally pro-competitive in the absence of market power. This claim includes typical hard-core restraints, such as resale price maintenance.[27]

5.2.5   *The Digital Single Market Initiative*

Partly motivated by some cases like the ones described above, the EC considers that too many barriers still block the flow of online services and entertainment across national borders. The Digital Agenda is set to update the EU Single

Market rules for the digital era and creating a Digital Single Market is stated as one of the priorities of President Juncker.[28] According to the EC, its Digital Agenda is one of the seven pillars of the Europe 2020 Strategy. The Digital Agenda proposes to better exploit the potential of Information and Communication Technologies in order to foster innovation and growth. The main objective is to develop a digital single market in order to generate *'smart, sustainable and inclusive growth'* in Europe and is made up of seven pillars. A key consideration towards achieving the digital single market goal is that internet access should not 'stop' at Member States' borders. Instead it becomes a goal that consumers should 'benefit from the best content, deals and services, wherever we are in the EU, without being geo-blocked. Businesses should be able to market and share their bright ideas across the EU.'

The associated Sector Inquiry, announced in May 2015 by the EC, could help reveal possible problems with competition in digital markets in Europe and where interventions may be warranted at present or future times. This could become an important document, if it is guided by sound and state of the art economic analysis. It should be noted, however, that the Single Market objective does not always coincide with the application of competition principles as understood by economists, in particular welfare maximization, especially when it comes to enforcing uniformity of market outcomes across Member States.[29]

5.2.6 Distinguishing Features of Digital Markets

While there are differences between how markets operate and should be regulated in the digital world and in the 'traditional' context, there are also of course similarities. All markets share some common features and more traditional economic analysis never relied on the assumption that sellers and buyers would meet at the same physical space. Frictions, search costs and asymmetries in information have always been part of how economists would analyze a market. So what may be the distinguishing features of digital markets? Are there characteristics that may make our current understanding of how markets work obsolete?

It would be useful to distinguish some of the main features, also building on some previous approaches. Lieber and Syverson (2012), for example, offer a review of the basic facts, as well as a related analysis.[30] One could attempt to present the following list.

1. The supply of digital products typically involves a specific cost structure: fixed costs tend to be high while the marginal cost of supply can be trivial (often practically zero).
2. When it comes to the production of content (news, scientific, entertainment, etc.) this fixed cost is typically sunk when the market operates. In

this sense, copyrights and other forms of intellectual property protection are essential for the functioning of many digital markets.

3. When selling nondigital products online, distribution and storage costs are typically much lower than when selling through traditional 'brick-and-mortar' stores.

4. Search costs for buyers, at least in reference to prices, can be much lower than through traditional stores where a physical visit would be required.

5. Distance (the ability to have contact only online) makes it difficult for buyers to inspect some products, with respect to some important characteristics. Therefore, asymmetric information may be high. Reputation and having the trust of the buyers is essential for the success of any firm selling online, often much more that a firm selling through traditional stores, where physical inspection is possible.

6. When selling physical goods online, delivery will take some time; having a large enough size that allows economies of scale and scope in delivery could be important.

7. Online sellers could collect key data for their potential buyers, either by tracing their past browsing and purchasing history, or from other sources. These data may be valuable when designing pricing strategies, in particular for price discrimination. Data collection and processing may often represent a market opportunity in itself.

8. Significant privacy issues may be raised that may concern online buyers. Personal data protection is important.

9. Services are often provided by multi-sided platforms. Size may play an important role, and often competition *for the market* may be more relevant than competition *in the market.*

10. Online and offline sale activities could be substitutes but also often complements.

We next briefly turn to the IO literature, which is important and relevant, even when not produced only having competition policy in digital market issues in mind. Subsequently, in Section 5.4, we review some work that has been motivated by specific aspects of how competition policy should approach digital markets.

5.3   Approaches in Industrial Organization

There are at least two important related literatures within IO that by their nature are closely related to the currently open competition issues. These refer to the study of vertical relations (integration and vertical restraints) and to pricing practices, in particular, price discrimination and nonlinear pricing. We sketch some of the issues that have been analyzed in these areas and discuss some open topics in relation to policy.

5.3.1   Pricing

Pricing is naturally an important concern in economics. However, we may not yet have a complete understanding of how pricing functions when there is price discrimination and various types of nonlinear pricing under oligopoly competition, when there are vertical relations, and what the welfare implications are of the various related restrictions, especially when we may have important dynamic effects. Overall, a key challenge is how to determine the welfare effects of (direct or indirect) price discrimination or of price restrictions, especially in rich environments where the technology significantly facilitates the identification of buyers or groups of buyers by (some of) the sellers and where the technology may make possible (often inexpensive or automatic) price comparison practices (e.g., through websites). The matter is complex and, not surprisingly, the literature is not conclusive.

An obvious starting point for the review of the broad issues in price discrimination is Tirole (1988, Ch. 3), Varian (1989) and Armstrong (2008b) and on nonlinear pricing, Wilson (1993) and Armstrong (2015). Prices play two interrelated roles in economics: they determine how surplus is divided between buyers and sellers, for a trade that takes place and, at the same time, what trades will and what will not take place. With price discrimination, two identical (in practice, 'similar') products have the same marginal cost to produce but are sold by a seller at different prices. This definition is generalized to cover the case of different costs: then the proportional mark-ups should not be different. The impact that price discrimination has on consumers' surplus, rival firms and welfare is mixed. In general, price discrimination will tend to allow more trades to take place, but at the same time allows the sellers that employ this practice to capture more of the surplus created (see e.g., Varian, 1985).

Price discrimination is important for competition policy for at least three reasons (see Armstrong, 2008a). First, one may consider price discrimination as part of an 'exploitative' abuse by a dominant firm. However, in practice and probably for good reasons, this path is only rarely followed by most competition authorities, although the legal framework in Europe may allow it. Second, as also discussed earlier in this text, promoting the single market across the EU is stated as an independent objective by the EC. It is often expressed in practical terms as not allowing firms to set different prices across regions, or at least to not prevent arbitrage across regions that would tend to indirectly equalize prices. Third, and a matter that has received much attention from competition authorities, price discrimination can be used by a dominant firm to *'exclude'* (or weaken) actual or potential rivals. The question that arises is in which cases price discrimination can be an effective way to put rivals at a disadvantage so as to make them exit the market or compete less aggressively.

For price discrimination to be possible and effective, three factors are known to be important and required, (and are all related, in fact, to the study of digital markets). First, pricing firms have to have some market power (otherwise they will have to be price takers). In digital markets, we typically have one, and sometimes two firms with significant market power (or at least with high market shares), and these could in principle price discriminate, while some other players are too small for that. Second, there has to be some information about buyer values (either directly or indirectly, e.g., through past sales or some other correlated characteristic of the buyer population). In digital markets, information about the identities of actual or prospective buyers tends to be much easier to obtain (e.g., through web-browser cookies or the exact purchasing history of end users), and this is why price discrimination comes to the centre of the picture in the analysis. At the same time, 'geo-blocking', where access to content can be allowed to users residing only in some areas, even though technologically a wider access would be very easy is an important issue. Third, there have to be restrictions on arbitrage, which would otherwise tend to undo the effect of discrimination. Some vertical restraints and other pricing restrictions are very important in this regard.

That new technologies allow firms to have detailed digital information about their customers, whether they are returning or new, is an important feature which provides mechanisms for price discrimination. When firms can have reliable information about consumers' previous buying behaviour at low costs, they would benefit from using this information to offer different prices or products to consumers with different purchase histories. With web-browser cookies and other technologies firms can collect and process important information about consumers, and can affect the prices and products offered to them, individually or as groups.[31]

In terms of some fundamental results, Hart and Tirole (1988) have considered the problem of pricing over time when consumer valuations are not changing across periods, and a monopoly seller can trace the identity (although not the exact reservation value) of those who have bought in the past. Competition has been introduced into this problem by Villas-Boas (1999) and Fudenberg and Tirole (2000), where firms learn both about the values of the buyers that buy from them but also from rivals. Chen and Pearcy (2010) extend the theory model by allowing variation of values across time periods. Buyers may also wish to act strategically, as in Villas-Boas (2004). The more relevant part of this literature perhaps is when learning about consumers' values may be active, that is the firms strategies include how much information about key buyer characteristics they may obtain. Relevant two sided market issues can be found, for example, in Armstrong (2006) and subsequent work.

Geographical restrictions imposed by firms are an application of price discrimination strategies in order to separate across market segments where demand elasticities may differ. Parallel trade, in turn, is a way to seek alternative channels, so that the buyers can seek the most favourable price or product characteristics, in the context of arbitrage that would tend to undo price discrimination. Parallel trade specifically has been studied among other work in Ahmadi and Yang (2000), also by Valletti and Szymanski (2006), while an early paper on 'most favoured nation' clauses across markets is by Akman and Hviid (2006).

5.3.2 Vertical Relations

Along a 'vertical chain' there is a need to analyse the relation between a wholesaler and a retailer, or more abstractly an 'upstream' and a 'downstream' firm. Vertical chains differ in many ways: how many stages there are before reaching the final consumer, whether firms are vertically separated (independent) or vertically integrated (one firm that operates both upstream and downstream) and whether trade is exclusive (with an exclusive supplier or exclusive buyer or both). Any study of vertical relations necessarily finds in its way the issue of the distribution of power across vertically linked firms and possibly of bargaining among them. An excellent starting point for the review of the broad issues in vertical relations and in particular of vertical restraints are the analyses and reviews of Motta (2004, Ch. 6), Rey and Tirole (2008), Rey and Vergé (2008) and Lafontaine and Slade (2008).

Under vertical separation and linear pricing, when we have a constant price for each additional unit sold, vertical separation leads to higher final product prices than those we would have under vertical integration (VI). This 'double marginalization' is a fundamental result in the literature (Spengler, 1950). It relies on each firm acting independently from the others, in the sense that it seeks to maximize its own profit and not that of the entire chain. It implies prices for the final consumers that are *higher* than the prices that would emerge under vertical integration. In this sense, vertical separation with linear pricing can hurt both the consumers and the firms, because independent firms fail to internalize the vertical externality between them. Thus, one solution to this problem would be vertical integration.[32] However, the problem can also be eliminated or greatly minimized if alternative pricing schemes are used instead, like two-part tariffs. Under such arrangements, and in the absence of uncertainty, if the per-unit price is set at the competitive level (cost) and the fixed fee is set just a little lower than the total monopoly profit, the monopoly solution can be recovered, without having formally a vertical integration arrangement. Another way to address the double marginalization problem would be some vertical restraint, in particular a RPM that would fix the final market price at the monopoly level. Importantly, the outcome depends on the distribution of bargaining power across the chain. If, for example, we allow the downstream firm to have the price setting power, against both the final consumers and the upstream firm, only one profit margin can be applied and there is no additional distortion relative to the standard monopoly. Finally, when the downstream firm is able to participate in setting the price at which it transacts with the upstream firm, the formal or informal bargaining procedure that is expected to take place between the upstream and the downstream firm would restrict the market power of the upstream firm and would lead to the internalization, at least partially, of the final market price considerations. As a result, the final price will be *lower* in the equilibrium of the game when the bargaining power is balanced between the upstream and the downstream firm, or when the downstream firm is more powerful than the upstream firm.

In a typical market, of course, one encounters much richer vertical structures than the simple one-supplier-one-distributor chain. Thus, in addition to the basic vertical double marginalization effect, there may also be horizontal externalities in the competition among wholesalers or among retailers, a phenomenon that we could call 'intra-brand' competition. In such cases, it is not only the vertical strategic interaction between suppliers and distributors that matters, but also all the horizontal relations.[33] In cases where only intra-brand competition downstream is important, nonlinear pricing schemes or other vertical restraints could be effective in 'softening' the competition in the final market and, by implication, maximizing the suppliers' (upstream) profits. With a two-part tariff, the wholesale price can control the horizontal externality and soften competition between the distributors, while profit may be shifted upstream in the form of a fixed fee. RPM, or other resale restrictions set by the supplier, such as restrictions on the retailers' discretion to set a price, or restrictions imposing that each retailer only deals with a part of the final demand, in a territorial or other sense, could also lead to higher downstream prices and higher profit for the entire chain.[34] Rey and Vergé (2008) provide an excellent analysis of how vertical restraints operate and a review of recent work in the area, focusing on the horizontal externalities that such constraints may affect along with the vertical contracting issues.[35]

Resale price maintenance is a common vertical restraint which has received much attention in competition policy. The economics literature finds that there are both anti-competitive and pro-competitive effects from the use of RPM.[36] On the one hand, a possible anti-competitive effect could be related to the solution of the 'commitment problem' of a monopolist, which would impede even a monopolistic supplier from enjoying full monopoly profits. This is because this supplier would have the temptation to reduce the wholesale price set to one distributor to allow that distributor to expand its market share, even when this hurts rival distributors (see Hart et al., 1990). A market-wide RPM, if credible to all parties, could solve this problem because it could prevent the opportunistic behaviour on the part of the supplier. RPM may also soften competition when two or more suppliers sell their products to two or more distributors ('interlocking relationships'). RPM might also facilitate collusion, either among suppliers or among distributors (see e.g., Jullien and Rey, 2007). In particular, collusion among suppliers may be easier to achieve because RPM can help offer a superior monitoring of deviations from the collusive agreement. On the other hand, however, there may be very important pro-competitive effects, since RPM may help protect necessary 'specific investments' by preventing opportunistic or free-riding behaviour among distributors. It may also help by signalling the quality of products, or help establish a price reputation and the overall brand image for the supplier's product.

The publication of the Commission Regulation No 2790/1999, on the application of Article 81(3) of the Treaty to certain categories of vertical agreements and concerted practices,[37] was an important development in the area of vertical relations. This 'Block Exemption Regulation' (BER) was intended to provide a 'safe harbour' to firms with less than a 30 per cent market share and was accompanied by the relevant Guidelines on Vertical Restraints.[38] The BER was viewed as the first of a new generation of block exemption regulations and guidelines, inspired by an 'effects-based' approach, where economic analysis should play an important role and it has been followed by similar reforms in other areas of competition policy. The core of this approach is that, in order to reach an assessment about a given vertical agreement, the precise potential effects of the agreement on the market should be analyzed, thus moving away from the old formalistic approach. The 1999 BER established that article 81(1) (now article 101 TFEU) did not apply to vertical agreements in which the supplier does not hold more than 30 per cent market share, since vertical agreements are likely to harm welfare only if the firms using them possess substantial market power. In addition, in its Article 4, it also stated that the exemption should not apply to some vertical agreements that the Commission considered harmful. These 'blacklisted' or 'hardcore' clauses include in particular RPM (more precisely resale price fixing and minimum resale price) and vertical clauses, which aim at restricting 'active' sales from one territory to the other.[39]

The revised BER, No 300/2010 of April 2010, still contains a list of restrictions that are 'blacklisted', including RPM and other (that is, nonprice) resale restrictions.[40] The view is still taken that there should be a presumption in the EC law that they should be prohibited. Specifically, according to Paragraph 47 of the Guidelines, if an agreement contains a 'blacklisted' restriction, the agreement presumptively falls within the scope of prohibited agreements under Article 101(1) as having actual or likely negative effects, and it presumptively does not satisfy the justification standards of Article 101(3). It follows that once a hardcore restriction is established, the agreement is presumptively both anti-competitive and unjustifiable. Nevertheless, it is recognized that this double presumption is rebuttable and the parties can bring forward evidence that the positive effects of the agreement under examination outweigh the presumed negative effects. Regarding minimum price and fixed price RPM, in particular, the Guidelines offer a detailed exposition about evidence that could be put forward in RPM cases.[41] However, a restriction on passive sales (responding to 'unsolicited' requests from customers outside the specified territory or consumer group) would be considered a hard-core restriction. Regarding selective distribution, the BER allows suppliers to have a selective distribution system, where distributors are selected according to some specified criteria.[42] On the basis of academic research, many economists would not necessarily agree with the approach taken by the EC Guidelines regarding the treatment of RPM and would favour a less formalistic approach that recognizes efficiencies.

Perhaps one of the important areas where research can offer greater clarity is the more detailed definition and study of online sales. Treating all online sales as 'passive', and with restrictions on these not being allowed, the assessment of practically any restriction of cross-border online sales is a one way street which does not necessarily lead to a correct assessment. Resale price maintenance is also an important topic for further research, with part of the relevant economic approaches not being always aligned with the direction of the Guidelines or with some recent policy practice. Naturally, especially with the presence of both online and offline sales, when competition is examined, it is also important to examine the relevant *investment incentives* by the suppliers, since quality improvement may often be at least as important an issue as pricing.

5.4   Recent Research on Competition Issues Related to Digital Markets

Some recent work specifically considers the effects that the ability to price discriminate or restrictions to this ability (because of strategic or regulatory reasons) may have on markets with vertical relations. In particular, Edelman and Wright (2015) examine the implications of 'price coherence', the constraint that the purchase from an intermediary has to occur at the same price as the purchase of the same good directly from the initial supplier or through some alternative, competing, intermediary. This pricing practice is often used in payment card systems, travel reservation systems, rebate services and other related services. It differs from some other vertical restraints like RPM. RPM would restrict the absolute prices (not necessarily at the same level for every intermediary), while price coherence restricts relative price differences.

In the Edelman and Wright (2015) model, an intermediary provides a benefit to buyers when they purchase from sellers using the intermediary's technology, relative to the possibility of a direct purchase. They show that the intermediary would want to restrict sellers from charging buyers more for transactions that it intermediates. With this restriction, an intermediary can profitably raise demand for its services by eliminating any extra price that the buyers may face for purchasing through the intermediary. The authors show that this leads to inflated retail prices, excessive adoption of the intermediaries' services, over-investment in benefits to buyers, and a reduction in consumer surplus and even sometimes welfare. Since there is no surcharge for the services of the intermediary, consumers tend not to consider the cost of the intermediary's services and thus consumers tend to use more such services. This allows the intermediary to extract more fees from sellers than what would be the case without price coherence. In equilibrium, prices are higher under price coherence, ultimately harming consumer welfare. Competition among intermediaries intensifies these problems by increasing the magnitude of their effects. In a setup with price coherence, competition among intermediaries is focused on offering more benefits, such as rebates etc., to consumers, rather than reducing costs. As a result, prices increase further, to cover the higher benefit offers. Nevertheless, the model discussed by the authors only fully applies to cases where buyers tend to rely on a single intermediary, while sellers can join many intermediaries to reach buyers. Moreover, the model does not account for the potentially beneficial effects of price coherence, as a tool to address the problem of consumers using the intermediary's services to identify or test a product, and then buy the product directly from the seller (the problem of 'showrooming').

There are now also several papers motivated by the Apple e-books case and other related cases in markets where content providers supply content via online platforms.[43] We review some representative ones.[44] Several analyses compare, in different models, standard wholesale pricing schemes, where the upstream firm (say a publisher, or other content provider) charges a wholesale price for the good to the downstream retailer, who then sets a final price for the good, to agency contracts. In agency contracts, in contrast, the retailer sets a percentage commission that he will collect from the sales of the good, and the upstream firm is free to set the good's final price. Effectively, via the agency model, upstream firms choose the retail prices of their products (that is, we have effectively RPM) subject to a fixed revenue-sharing rule. The matter has received significant attention, with competition policy-makers being generally adverse to the agency model.

Johnson (2013) contrasts wholesale and agency agreements. The paper extends standard models of product differentiation (spatial competition) to incorporate bilateral oligopoly in order to investigate the agency model of pricing when there is consumer lock-in. For example, in the e-book market lock-in may exist because a consumer becomes accustomed to using, for example, Amazon's e-book store or e-book reading app. The equilibrium analysis shows that the agency model raises prices initially, but lowers them in the future. The author points out that in markets where consumers are locked in a particular retailer's platform, wholesale agreements, in letting retailers determine prices, allow retailers to exert market power in the long run, ultimately harming consumer surplus. In a market with significant consumer lock-in, under wholesale agreements retailers would compete intensely in early periods, lowering prices, in order to lock in more consumers, so that these consumers may be harvested in the future. In contrast, under agency agreements suppliers have no such incentive to subsidize early consumption, as suppliers sell through many retailers. However, in later periods, agency agreements ensure that robust competition exists between suppliers, leading to lower prices. Suppliers setting prices and selling through many retailers are not influenced by consumer lock-in in either retailer. In contrast, wholesale agreements allow retailers in later periods to internalize competition between suppliers and further harvest consumers. Therefore, while price increases are a natural consequence of the transition from the wholesale to the agency model, it is not correct to conclude that consumers are worse-off overall. Indeed, consumers are better off under agency agreements, despite price increases in the early stages following the move to the agency model, as they benefit from competition between suppliers in the long run.

In a related model, Johnson (2014) focuses on the use of MFN clauses and their impact under both agency and wholesale agreements. The author finds that the agency pricing model does not eliminate double marginalization. The reason is that the revenue-sharing contracts that the retailers select distort the perceived marginal cost of suppliers. Under revenue-sharing, the supplier receives only a fraction of the sold product's price. This has similar effects to an increase in the supplier's marginal cost. When retailers compete in revenue shares, however, adopting the agency model lowers retail prices and industry profit, while retailers' profits increase, compared with the wholesale model. MFN clauses that impose retail price parity can facilitate the emergence of high industry prices, as retail price parity eliminates retailer competition on revenue shares. Without price parity, a retailer offering his suppliers a lower revenue share, will induce a higher perceived marginal cost to the supplier, resulting in higher prices for that retailer, relative to his competitors. Retail price parity eliminates this downside. However, in some cases it may also raise market-entry incentives and in this way eventually benefit consumers. These results provide an explanation for why many online retailers have adopted both the agency model and MFN clauses.

Abhishek et al. (2015) study entry and compare equilibrium outcomes under wholesale and agency agreements when a monopolist producer sells online goods through two competing distributors (e-retailers). They find that when sales in the electronic channel lead to substantial stimulation of demand in the traditional channel, e-retailers prefer reselling. Under the agency model, in the presence of such positive cross-effects on demand, a producer would set low prices in the e-channel, in order to benefit from increased demand in the traditional channel. Yet, this would trim the e-retailer's profits, hence the e-retailer prefers reselling. Conversely, when the e-channel has a negative cross-effect on demand in the traditional channel, it is optimal for the e-retailers to adopt the agency selling agreement. The authors also find that as the intensity of competition among e-retailers increases, they prefer agency selling over reselling. Using the agency model and thus letting the producer set retail prices, allows e-retailers to mitigate retail competition. In addition, under an agency arrangement, e-retailers set the agency fees first and the producer then sets prices. Therefore e-retailers under agency are in a sense Stackelberg leaders, enjoying the strategic advantage that goes with being an early mover. Furthermore, the authors find that agency selling is beneficial for consumers, as prices are lower under agency selling and consumer surplus is higher.[45]

Foros et al. (2014) also study the equilibrium properties of the agency pricing model and the impact of market competition at both the retailing and the publishing (upstream) level. They study a set of alternative assumptions, depending on how intense competition is at each stage and on how contract terms are selected. They show that employing the agency pricing model leads to higher prices if the competitive pressure is relatively higher downstream than upstream. The authors also demonstrate that upstream firms earn positive surplus even when platform providers have all the bargaining power. In addition, with asymmetric business formats, that is when only some platform providers use the agency model, an MFN clause at the retail level leads to retail prices that resemble the outcome under industry-wide RPM.

Gaudin and White (2014) study more closely the effects of Apple's entry into the e-book market in 2010 and the related equilibrium pricing incentives. Like the work of Foros et al. (2014), they contrast agency and wholesale vertical agreements. The model equilibrium is characterized both in the presence and in the absence of an 'essential device' sold by the retailer. This part of the model corresponds to the fact that, before the Apple entry, Amazon, who was a dominant retailer, controlled an essential access device (the Kindle) while agreements regarding e-book pricing followed wholesale pricing. Subsequently, two distinct changes took place, first no device was any longer essential (with the introduction of the iPad) and second Amazon's pricing agreements with publishers took the agency form. The novel aspects of the model are the interaction between the device and pricing contracts (with the device prices endogenous in the analysis) and also that properties of the downstream demand favouring one or the other pricing arrangement are identified. There are two main results. First, the comparison between price levels arising under agency and wholesale contracting arrangements hinges crucially on whether one of the firms controls a complementary market (that is, the device). Second, a demand feature is identified (loosely, that demand does not become too convex too quickly – more formally that the elasticity of demand strictly decreases as quantity increases, up to the point where marginal revenue reaches zero) as the key for the pricing comparison. The basis for the first main result is that, when the good can be consumed without using the essential device (or equivalently when there is competition among substitute devices), there is double marginalization under both forms of pricing. Moreover, the authors' model shows that an increase in e-book prices can be explained by heightened competition for reading devices. Depending on the shape of demand, final prices under wholesale may be higher than under agency.

Condorelli et al. (2013) also study alternative pricing terms when the downstream firm has more information about the final demand than the upstream firm. The analysis provides a justification for the prevalence of the agency model in online markets. In the model, a seller has an object for sale and can reach buyers only through intermediaries, who also have private information about buyers' valuations. Intermediaries can either mediate the transaction by buying the object and reselling it, or refer buyers to the seller and release information for a fee, the agency model. The merchant model suffers from double marginalization. The agency model suffers from adverse selection, since intermediaries would like to refer low-value buyers, but retain high-value ones and make profits from resale. In equilibrium, intermediaries specialize in agency. Joint profits equal the seller's profits when he has access to all buyers and all intermediaries' information and the division of profits depends on seller's and intermediaries' relative bargaining power.

Kwark et al. (2015) demonstrate that the choice of pricing model, wholesale or agency, can serve as a strategic tool for online retailers, allowing them to benefit from third-party information, such as product reviews posted online and used by consumers to help them make more informed decisions. Consumers collect third-party information both regarding the quality of products and regarding the extent to which products are fit for their individual needs and tastes. When product quality is more important than fit to particular consumer tastes, reliable third-party information regarding product quality intensifies upstream competition. When upstream competition is strong, retailers benefit from the wholesale model of pricing. Conversely, when product fitness is relatively more important than quality, third-party information regarding product fitness heterogenizes consumers' estimated fit to the products, thus softening upstream competition. Under such circumstances, retailers benefit from agency pricing.

Lu (2015) compares the wholesale and the agency pricing models in the setup of a bilateral duopoly with differentiation at both the upstream and the downstream level. The author finds that suppliers benefit from the wholesale model and retailers benefit from the agency model, so long as upstream differentiation is sufficiently high. Under the wholesale structure, high upstream differentiation benefits suppliers and harms retailers and, similarly, high downstream differentiation benefits retailers and harms suppliers. However, under the agency structure the incentives of suppliers and retailers are better aligned. The author stresses that if the degree of differentiation at both levels is high enough, agency is a more efficient business format.

Wang and Wright (2014) examine why platforms, such as Amazon or Visa, rely predominantly on fees proportional with transaction prices (ad-valorem fees), rather than fixed fees per transaction, despite facing small per-transaction costs. The authors demonstrate that ad-valorem fees serve as tools that allow efficient price discrimination, when the costs and valuations of the goods a platform deals with vary widely. A fixed per-transaction fee would result in a disproportionate amount being charged on low-cost, low-value goods, and thus demand elasticity for such goods being too high, compared to high-cost, high-value goods. Nevertheless, the authors show that ad-valorem fees can also lead to higher welfare, and argue that welfare did increase due to the use of such fees in the cases of Amazon and Visa.

Wirl (2015) compares the wholesale and agency pricing models in a setup with an upstream oligopoly and Bertrand competing retailers, where retailers can increase demand by incurring a cost and thus the retailers' efforts matter (the model was inspired by the e-book market). Wholesale pricing can be preferable to agency pricing, despite double marginalization, because wholesale pricing can help incentivize retailers to exert effort and increase demand (or equivalently add value to the product).

Adner et al. (2015) study how platforms decide to make their content available to the users of competing platforms. In the authors' setup, designed to describe the e-book market, two competing platforms generate profits both through royalties from content sales and through hardware sales. Depending on what the primary source of profit for each platform is, incentives may arise to establish one-way compatibility. One-way compatibility leads to greater social welfare and in some circumstances, one-way compatibility may be more profitable for both platforms than incompatibility.[46]

Finally, some work studies pricing in payment systems or other platforms. For example, Bourguignon et al. (2014) study the incentives of merchants to differentiate price based on the payment method used. Assuming that consumers are imperfectly informed about the merchants' payment policy (cash only, credit card acceptance etc.), the authors identify the conditions under which merchants, concerned about missed sales, will be willing to accept card payments and examine how cash discounts, card surcharges and platform fees are set. The authors find that a ban on surcharges for card payments intensifies merchants' incentives to accept card payments. Furthermore, platforms tend to charge higher fees for credit cards than for debit cards and merchants always prefer to apply a card surcharge than to offer a cash discount.

In another study on card payment platforms, Ding and Wright (2014) examine a monopolist card platform that can price discriminate, setting different interchange fees (fees a merchant's bank pays to the card-holder's bank) for different types of retailers. The authors find that the platform would tend to set interchange fees too high, resulting in low fees for card usage and excessive usage of cards. Compared to the case where only a single interchange fee can be set, price discrimination by the platform can result in a lower average interchange fee, but also in lower welfare.

One of the main issues in digital markets is the use of personal data and related privacy issues. Access to data about buyers (e.g., from past purchases) can be used by the buyers themselves, however such datasets certainly have a value and, depending on the legal restrictions, could be transferred to third parties.[47] Spiegel (2013) examines how privacy issues are related to the choice between selling new software commercially and bundling it with ads and distributing it for free. The willingness of buyers to offer access to personal data may also be dependent on their understanding of the market and legal environment. See Cabral and Hortaçsu (2010) and Cabral (2012) for reputation issues and Belleflamme and Peitz (2012) for digital piracy. The matter is also related to behavioral approaches to markets and competition (see e.g., Eliaz and Spiegler, 2008, Acquisti, 2010, Zhang, 2011 and Koszegi, 2014).

The work reviewed above is on the theory side of the analysis. Viewed as a set, the results obtained in this recent literature generally cast doubt on the view that one pricing model leads to higher prices or lower welfare compared to another and in particular to the standard wholesale pricing model. The analyses are conducted with different model specifications, such as with buyers' switching costs, asymmetric information, complementary goods, and demand interaction between online and traditional sales. It follows that competition policy may need to seek more guidance when it comes to banning pricing according to the agency model.

On the empirical side, there is still only very little work on the topic of how different pricing arrangements affect equilibrium prices, profits and welfare. This is despite the fact that the theory analysis offers mixed results, as explained above, with the outcomes depending crucially on some parameters; therefore the empirical guidance towards the formulation of policy would be very useful. One notable study on the empirical side is by De los Santos and Wildenbeest (2014). They perform a difference-in-differences analysis to estimate the impact of the switch from the agency agreements to wholesale pricing on e-book prices. The dataset used in the analysis contains daily prices of e-books for a large number of titles, collected in the US across some major online retailers. The analysis exploits cross-publisher variation in the timing of the return to the wholesale model to estimate its effect on retail prices. It is found that e-book prices for titles that were previously sold using the agency model on average decreased – by 18 per cent at Amazon and 8 per cent at Barnes & Noble. The results illustrate a case where upstream firms prefer to set higher retail prices than retailers. In this way, the analysis helps clarify some of the conflicting predictions in the theory work described above.

The authors also investigate the pricing strategies of the retailers and publishers in some greater depth, examining some alternative theories. The data shows that due to the relatively higher commission kept by the retailers, on average e-book profit margins for the publishers were lower during the agency period than afterward. The analysis does not provide evidence that the pricing strategies of the retailers are primarily intended to lock-in consumers, as argued in the analyses by Johnson (2013) and Gaudin and White (2014) sketched above. In particular, Amazon's retail prices decreased after it regained the ability to set retail prices, and have remained consistently low despite having reduced means to leverage the Kindle platform due the availability of Kindle apps for mobile phones etc. The paper therefore characterizes as likely that other factors explain the publishers' adoption of the agency model, such as fears that lower e-book prices may cannibalize print book sales or diminish the perception of the books' value. Another important effect may be the one examined by Jullien and Rey (2007), where upstream firms may engage in RPM at high retail prices as part of a collusive upstream agreement that prevents them from engaging in secret wholesale price cuts. Yet the analysis does not find any indication that wholesale prices went up, even though publishers' coordinated move towards the agency model raised retail prices. Clearly, more empirical studies of other related cases would be extremely useful.

Baye et al. (2015) study empirically how different online platforms that consumers use to search for books and booksellers operate. They find that the use of these platforms is shifting over time. The data they present suggest that, as a result of digitization, consumers are increasingly conducting searches for books at retailer sites and closed systems and not so much in general search engines. This paper also identifies and discusses some areas where more work would be needed in relation to the pricing of e-books and digital media but also specific challenges that will make it difficult for researchers to measure internet-based search behaviour in the future.[48]

5.5   Challenges for Research on Competition Issues in Digital Markets

It is useful to discuss here the main novel challenges that research has to face in order to analyze and support the design of competition policy in digital markets. These markets tend to be characterized by strong network effects:

platforms provide the basis for aggregating and delivering content and services, acting as intermediaries between providers and end users; the related network effects, direct or indirect, will tend to promote high concentration, consumers may be locked-in and first mover advantages may be of critical importance. Service providers may have different interrelated routes for delivering digital services, with some key market positions being contestable – one may expect that *'tipping'* is a frequent phenomenon following some innovation. Combining the above features, it is crucial for competition policy to prevent the creation or reinforcement of entry barriers: it is not actual competition that matters so much, but making sure that entry is allowed for efficient and innovating new players. As a result, the more traditional analysis of competition policy, even when proceeding to market definition and measuring market shares, may face significant difficulties, since the boundaries are fluid. It is, in fact, important to understand the underlying dynamics of the market in terms of technology and strategic incentives.

Access to end user data is valuable since it may greatly facilitate price discrimination and also versioning according to individual needs. Established, large players in the market will tend to obtain a very significant advantage through the access to such data relative to newcomers. In addition, by proceeding to the combination of user data from multiple platforms, an owner of such multiple platforms will tend to be able to offer a more valuable service. The much enhanced ability to sell to wider sets of diverse buyers makes price discrimination, or blocking access to content, or other services, a higher concern relative to traditional markets. In particular, such practices that fragment the markets, pose, almost by definition, challenges to the single market goal. However, neither the literature nor practice necessarily suggests that imposing price or content uniformity across all areas is necessarily the optimal policy. Instead, imposing uniform prices and qualities across otherwise different areas too soon, may prove an obstacle for market development.

Suggestions about how research can proceed could be organized around four distinct themes. *First*, 'digital' markets may be different but they are still markets and some of the issues arising in 'digital' markets can be found, in some form, even if less systematically, in other markets. Therefore, the stock of knowledge from the existent IO literature is valuable. This statement may be obvious, but the temptation may emerge to ignore economic principles altogether and to follow a completely formalistic approach, using the idiosyncrasies of these new markets as a pretext.[49]

What economics analysis has to offer is primarily the identification of efficiencies that should be considered. Placing the maximization of economic welfare as an anchor, it ensures that there is some consistency in legal approaches that may otherwise run the risk of becoming too formalistic. Especially with market shares that tend to be quite high, it may be too easy for competition policy to position itself against pricing and other strategies of large firms that may not be viewed as safe, simply because they are not well-enough understood.

Second, while the application of competition policy should be characterized by continuity whenever possible, the coexistence of some systematic characteristics implies that there are some high challenges that the digital economy poses, which at least require a change in focus and priorities. So the creation of some fundamental new theory is most likely needed. When network effects and economies of scale or scope are very strong, the analysis of equilibrium in markets and of the optimum economic welfare becomes more challenging. 'Standard' economic models often rely on optimization over 'concave sets' or proceed by ruling out local deviations. Under conditions such as the ones that digital technologies imply, the optimum may in principle involve large market shares by firms, or even 'near monopolies'. This is for two reasons, both so that economies of scale are adequately exploited and as a reward to successful (but costly and risky) innovative activity.

In terms of theory, in digital markets we are more likely to see competition *'for the market'* (and races where the occasional winner 'takes it all') rather than competition *'in the market'*. This feature, in turn, has two implications. First, that in the application of competition policy, more attention should be given to ensure that innovative activity is high and entry barriers (including, of course, those created strategically by rivals) are as low as possible. This appears to be the first-order effect, while any other within market conduct effects are of second order. Second, the economic models for analyzing the matter need to be more dynamic. Naturally this comes at a cost. Increased complexity is an important issue, especially when the results and model implications eventually need to be informing policy-making and legal documents and decisions. A related problem will likely be the lack of robustness. Moreover, in other fields in economics, where dynamic analysis is the norm, like in macroeconomics, it is only rarely the case that analytical model results can be obtained and often the situation is understood through numerical simulations. It is unclear if the profession (e.g., in terms of publication standards for IO work in top journals) and policy-makers are fully ready to accept such a shift in emphasis and in modelling approaches. Currently, at any rate, it appears that there is a gap in the literature, since essentially no IO approaches on which competition policy builds put the emphasis on a fully dynamic analysis of the relevant markets.

Nonetheless, the above analysis strongly suggests that, quite likely, we do not currently have the suitable theory background to deeply understand how policy should proceed in markets with many of the features that we encounter in digital markets. The challenge for economic theory is significant – perhaps the building of some new 'price theory' is indeed needed to understand how product markets work.[50] The general foundation for economic research in competition policy has been the fundamental price theory analysis in general equilibrium theory and the associated welfare analysis. Under certain conditions regarding technology and consumers' preferences, a competitive equilibrium exists and is efficient. Competition policy starts from this point and attempts to correct or prevent local deviations. In other words, the role of competition policy has been viewed as trying to bring markets as close as possible to the competitive equilibrium benchmark. However, when the fundamentals of markets are very different from the generally accepted assumptions (and this does happen when we have network externalities, significantly increasing returns to scale in production and competition for the market), a competitive equilibrium may not exist or may not be efficient. Thus, the need to fully rethink and characterize what we consider as the optimum in markets emerges as a priority. With the characteristics of digital markets, it is not obvious if the way that these markets work fits the standard microeconomic paradigm. It may even be that temporary monopolies, especially when they respond to competition for their markets by other firms who are attempting to replace them, represent the optimal organization in markets. In this light, competition policy has to be extra careful to find some solid ground on which to base its arguments so that it does not risk doing more harm than good.

Third, there are also important implications for empirical current research. Empirical research that can inform competition policy, and such research in industrial organization more generally, has been constrained by the limited availability of data. In addition, the particular techniques developed have also been developed partly to respond to this limitation. This is in contrast to other fields, like in financial economics or labor economics where some important data is easier to find. With digital markets becoming the norm, this picture may become quite different, since retail transactions may become much easier to record. In principle, a researcher can have access to a wealth of data that do not refer only to the prices and quantities in each market transaction, but also key characteristics of the buyers and sellers, like their age, past purchases, or location. As a result, the opportunity arises for new methods to be developed and for a sequence of important empirical papers to be written that would shed significant light on how markets work in practice.

Fourth, with online sales, *'single market'* issues emerge as even more important than before. Online sellers could, in principle, reach buyers across geographical and perhaps language barriers, typically without a significant additional cost. This is a development consistent with the notion of a single market, which is central in EC policies. The idea is to allow buyers and sellers to have market access regardless of their location or other characteristics. However, it is not clear what such a development could imply for pricing and investment incentives. A standard result from economics research is that if a 'single market' is understood to imply uniform pricing, the implications for the market participants and for welfare will tend to be mixed. Removing the ability to price discriminate from the toolkit of firms, will tend to raise the price for some buyers (or to prevent them from having access at all) and may reduce social welfare, especially if it leads to a reduction in traded volume. This observation is important and very relevant because if the objective of the Single Digital Market currently pursued by the EC is viewed as a way to impose price uniformity across all areas and market participants, the implications may not be positive. Further, price discrimination may be a mechanism to ensure the profit level required for the necessary initial investments to be made, thus in its absence a market may not operate efficiently. Some of the competition cases that are currently open in Europe, such as the cross border pay-TV cases, primarily have such a 'single market' character.[51]

5.6   Conclusion

Despite the important progress that has been made in academic research and in competition policy itself, developments that modify the way that markets work are calling for additional work and a modification of the approaches that should be used. New issues, related to the size increase in the digital sectors of the economy, and especially the way that digital technologies and e-commerce practices revolutionize essentially all other sectors of the economy, imply some new and important challenges for academics and policy-makers. Many of the issues that surface as important in 'digital markets' are not absent in more traditional markets. However, the systematic presence of some key new features significantly modifies the nature of the models that should be used.

Overall, research on the topic has to achieve a delicate balance. On the one hand, important central results from the existing industrial organization research have to be used, even if reorganized, reinterpreted and understood under some new light. On the other hand, the problems studied often call for some completely new approaches, where the analysis should focus on the strong economies of scale and scope, network effects and other features that create nonconvexities in the models and imply that some assumptions underlying parts of our standard analysis are not valid. Overall, competition becomes more dynamic and often more discontinuous in nature than we currently recognize in standard models and incorporate in our intuition when designing and applying policy.

It would certainly be misguided to argue that the shift to digital markets makes old results in economics research obsolete and that only a formalistic approach to the application of competition policy could work well. Such an approach would be especially wrong if it is accompanied by a tendency to block innovative strategies employed by firms in their effort to be more competitive. While these may not fall directly in the range that competition policy typically understands as pro-competitive, they may very well lead to significant welfare improvements via innovation. This can be done by offering new services to consumers or by leading to significant efficiencies. Especially with strong network effects and economies of scale and scope present, and a tendency for high market concentration and strong positive cross-market effects, what becomes relatively more important is to ensure that innovation is possible and attractive for businesses and that any unnecessary entry barriers are removed. The benefits from innovation, even if they tend to be high to successful innovators themselves and imply high market shares and profits, can also be equally high for the consumers. These benefits can often be much higher than the static benefits one might expect from the application of standard price competition arguments. It follows that economic analysis has to incorporate to a much greater extent dynamics in order to be more useful for the understanding and formulation of competition policy. Competition policy itself, in turn, should have as a prime objective to ensure that firms have the incentive and the room to innovate, offer new products and open new markets. In digital markets, in particular, this not only means innovation on the technology side, but often in experimenting with new approaches about how various needs of consumers can be served. Overall, the ground that has to be covered is significant, and the research prospects appear quite exciting.

Acknowledgements

This chapter was prepared in the context of the COEURE Coordination Action, funded by the European Commission's FP7 SSH Programme and aiming at evaluating European research in economics from the perspective of its contribution to key EU economic policy issues. The author is grateful to Jacques Crémer, Marc Ivaldi, Kai-Uwe Kühn, Damien Neven, Lars Sørgard, Yossi Spiegel, Frode Steen, and other participants in the September 2015 COEURE workshop in Brussels for their very helpful ideas, suggestions, comments and criticism. All omissions, misrepresentations and other shortcomings, however, are exclusively the responsibility of the author.

Notes

1. This earlier work is summarized in relevant chapters in Schmalensee and Willig (1989). More recent texts, like Belleflamme and Peitz (2010), nicely blend new contributions into the past stock of knowledge in IO, while how developments in IO theory have shaped competition policy can be found in texts like Motta (2004).
2. See e.g., Italianer (2014), summarizing the relevant issues.
3. See e.g., Cohen et al. (2004).
4. According to a survey by Forrester Research published in July 2015. It is also expected that northern European countries will see more of their total retail sales

impacted by the web compared with southern European markets, while the UK will have the largest proportion of web-impacted sales by 2020.

5. On recent issues in the development of digital markets, see also Ng (2014).
6. See http://ec.europa.eu/internal_market/20years/singlemarket20/facts-figures/what-is-the-single-market_en.htm.
7. See http://ec.europa.eu/priorities/digital-single-market/index_en.htm.
8. Some first results would be expected in 2016 – http://europa.eu/rapid/press-release_IP-15-4921_en.htm.
9. See Motta (2004) for an overview that connects the policy and the economic analysis sides of this relation.
10. A case to be noted is Intel, which has been considered as a critical test for the EC effects-based approach in abuse of dominance cases, as set out in its 2009 Guidelines. This approach was in contrast to the prior case law which was form-based and left little room for an analysis of the competitive nature of potentially exclusionary conduct. In a key recent (June 2014) General Court judgment, the EC 2009 Intel decision was confirmed. In particular, the 2009 decision had found the computer-chip producer to infringe competition rules by granting anti-competitive rebates to computer manufacturers in an attempt to exclude its rival AMD from the market. The General Court's Intel judgment holds that the Commission rightly found that the chip producer breached competition rules. Importantly, however, the judgment also notes that the effects-based analysis was redundant given the particular form of rebates used. Thus, from a policy perspective, the Court re-asserts the form-based standard and finds that effects-based analysis is largely unnecessary for these types of rebates. See http://europa.eu/rapid/press-release_MEMO-14-416_en.htm.
11. There is now a number of high-quality competition policy textbooks and handbooks with articles describing the progress in specific areas, see, for example, Buccirossi (2008).
12. Some 'hidden costs' of free goods, and associated antitrust implications, are examined in Gal and Rubinfeld (2015).
13. See, for example, Bolt and Chakravorti (2012).
14. See, for example, Garicano and Kaplan (2001) and Jullien (2012).
15. See, for example, Bajari and Hortaçsu (2004).
16. See Fudenberg and Villas-Boas (2006).
17. See http://europa.eu/rapid/press-release_IP-15-5323_en.htm.
18. In September 2014, the European Court of Justice upheld a 2007 decision by the EC that MasterCard's multilateral interchange fees on cross-border transactions breached competition rules. Overall, through a sequence of decisions, caps have been placed in EU Member States to interchange fees of 0.3 per cent of the value of credit-card transactions and 0.2 per cent for debit-card transactions.
19. See http://europa.eu/rapid/press-release_IP-15-5166_en.htm.
20. See http://europa.eu/rapid/press-release_IP-15-5432_en.htm.
21. Broadcasters also have to take into account the applicable regulatory framework beyond EU competition law when considering sales to consumers located elsewhere. This includes, for online pay-TV services, relevant national copyright laws, a matter related to EC's proposal to modernize EU copyright rules, as part of its Digital Single Market Strategy.
22. According to a statement in 2013 by FCO President Andreas Mundt, 'Such clauses make the market entry of new suppliers offering innovative services, such as

last-minute offers via smartphone, considerably more difficult, as these new competitors are not able to offer hotel rooms at better rates.' 'The competition between the hotels is also hindered because they are not free to set their prices independently and cannot respond flexibly to new competition developments.'

23. Booking.com is currently the largest online hotel agency in the world. Expedia Inc., including Expedia.com, Hotels.com and Venere, ranks second. HRS is a Germany-based travel agency.

24. The French, the Italian and the Swedish Competition Authority coordinated their investigations and on 21 April 2015 adopted parallel decisions accepting identical commitments from the market-leading online travel agent Booking.com and making them binding in their respective jurisdictions. The EC assisted the authorities in coordinating their work. In the course of the investigations, Booking.com conducted a customer survey of 14,000 consumers in 9 Member States and produced economic papers to argue that parity between room prices in hotels' own sales channels and prices offered on Booking.com's platform is important in preventing free-riding on Booking.com's investments and ensuring the continued supply of search and comparison services free of charge to consumers. The adopted commitments prevent Booking.com from requiring hotels to offer better or equal room prices via Booking.com than they do via competing online travel agents. In addition, Booking.com cannot prevent hotels from offering discounted room prices provided that these are not marketed or made available to the general public online. The discounted prices can be offered online to members of a hotel's loyalty scheme or via offline channels.

25. See *'Are the European Competition Authorities making a less anticompetitive market more anticompetitive? The Booking.com saga,'* Competition Policy Centre, University of East Anglia, *Competition Policy Blog*, 8 July, 2015.

26. The case concerned the market for the manufacture and sale of sports nutrition products such as protein and carbohydrate-based products and other performance enhancing products. The authority was informed that 13:e Protein Import AB, a manufacturer of sports nutrition products under the brand 'SELF Omninutrition', had sent a minimum resale price list for protein powder products to its online buyers, asking them not to adopt prices below the prices on the price list. The preliminary investigation indicated that 13:e Protein Import AB had a low market share, below 3 per cent, in the upstream market for the manufacture of protein powder products. The findings indicated that both the upstream and downstream markets for protein powder products were highly fragmented. Based on these facts, the Authority concluded that the case did not merit prioritization.

27. See https://www.acm.nl/en/publications/publication/14226/ACMs-strategy-and-enforcement-priorities-with-regard-to-vertical-agreements/.

28. See https://ec.europa.eu/digital-agenda/en/digital-single-market.

29. A Study conducted for the DG for Internal Policies, *A Digital Single Market Strategy for Europe*, see European Commission (2015) was published in July 2015. It describes the challenges for competition policy in relation to the digital economy and also some neighboring policy areas such as intellectual property and data protection. Another useful and relevant policy paper was published by the German Monopolies Commission in June 2015 (Competition policy: The challenge of digital markets, pursuant to Section 44(1)(4) ARC, 1 June 2015, see Monopolkommission, 2015). The report puts emphasis on the analysis of markets in which services are provided by multi-sided platforms. This set includes search engines, social

networks, and some areas of e-commerce. It takes the view that the multi-sided nature of services and the importance of data must be taken into account to a more significant extent by competition policy.

30. See also Smith et al. (2000) for an earlier review.

31. See, for example, Fudenberg and Villas-Boas (2012) for a rich analysis of the main forces in terms of theory.

32. See Riordan (2008), for a review of the issues related to vertical integration.

33. See Bonanno and Vickers (1988), for strategic delegation issues in the context of vertical separation.

34. Mortimer (2008) examines related issues in the context of the video rental industry.

35. Mathewson and Winter (1984, 1988), Shaffer (1991), Martin et al. (2001), Marx and Shaffer (2004, 2007), Dobson and Waterson (2007) are among the main contributions. For some recent applications see Asker and Seitz (2013) and Asker and Bar-Isaac (2014).

36. See e.g., the analysis in the EAGCP report by Motta et al. (2009) prepared in the context of the revision of the verticals BER.

37. Official Journal L 336, 29.12.1999, pp. 21–25.

38. Official Journal C 291, 13.10.2000, pp. 1–44.

39. Vertical agreements containing such hardcore restrictions were not exempted from the application of Article 81(1), even if the firms concerned had an arbitrarily small market share, since the *de minimis* Notice (2001/C 368/07) does not apply to such hardcore restrictions. According to the Guidelines, paragraph 46, 'Individual exemption of vertical agreements containing such hardcore restrictions is also unlikely', thus implying a regime which is in practice very close to *per se* prohibition for these black-listed restrictions.

40. See also Vettas (2010).

41. Paragraph 224 of the Guidelines describes various possible ways in which RPM may restrict competition, while Paragraph 225 states that justifications will be considered and that the possible efficiencies will be assessed under Article 101(3). Similar to RPM, the BER generally does not cover agreements that restrict the buyer's ability to sell in some territories or to some consumers the goods or services that the agreement refers to. However, there are a number of important exceptions, where such restrictions are not considered hard-core, with the most important ones being systems of 'exclusive distribution' and 'selective distribution'.

42. The revised BER pays particular attention to the matter of online (internet) sales, since the Resale Restrictions' rules apply to both online and (traditional) store sales. Once distributors have been authorized, they must be free to sell on their websites as they do in their traditional shops and physical points of sale. For selective distribution, this means that manufacturers cannot limit the quantities sold over the Internet or charge higher prices for products to be sold online.

43. Nocke et al. (2007) examine the impact of different platform ownership structures as this also depends on the strength of the underlying two-sided network effects.

44. For a discussion of recent developments in the e-books market, including sales trends, impact on traditional booksellers, the implications of the complementarity between e-books and e-readers, a discussion on Amazon's monopsony power and publishers' strategies to confront it and the implications of Apple's entry into the market and of the recent antitrust cases against Apple and publishers, see Gilbert (2015).

45. See Jin and Kato (2007) for an analysis of dividing online and offline sales, also, see Loginova (2009).
46. Baye and Morgan (2002) study firms that pay a fee to list prices at a price comparison site and can price discriminate between consumers who do and don't use the site. They show that prices listed at the site are dispersed but lower than at the firms' websites.
47. See Taylor (2004) and Acquisti and Varian (2005) for early approaches to the issue and Acquisti et al. (2015) for a comprehensive survey.
48. See also Clay et al. (2001) and Chevalier and Goolsbee (2003) for empirical approaches to price dispersion.
49. A related misguided approach was used in the 90s, when some finance analysts evaluating internet industries claimed that the laws of economics need not apply to the dot.coms, contributing to the creation of a bubble.
50. This paragraph includes some ideas that Jacques Crémer presented at the COEURE September 2015 workshop in Brussels. I am grateful for his insights, though responsible for any misinterpretations.
51. See also Langus et al. (2014).

References

Abhishek, V., Jerath, K., and Zhang, Z. J. 2015. Agency Selling or Reselling? Channel Structures in Electronic Retailing. *Management Science*, **62**(8), 2259–2280.

Acquisti, A. 2010. *Privacy and Behavioral Economics: The Paradox of Control and Other Studies*. Conference Presentation. Paduano Symposium, Heinz College / CyLab, Carnegie Mellon University.

Acquisti, A., and Varian, H. R. 2005. Conditioning Prices on Purchase History. *Marketing Science*, **24**, 367–381.

Acquisti, A., Taylor, C., and Wagman, L. 2015. The Economics of Privacy. *Journal of Economic Literature*, **54**(2), 442–492.

Adner, R., Chen, J., and Zhu, F. 2015. *Frenemies in Platform Markets: The Case of Apple's iPad vs. Amazon's Kindle*. Working Paper 15-087. Harvard Business School.

Aghion, P., and Akcigit, U. 2015 (June). *Innovation and Growth: The Schumpeterian Perspective*. Draft Survey for Discussion. COEURE Coordination Action, Harvard University and University of Chicago.

Ahmadi, R., and Yang, R. B. 2000. Parallel Imports: Challenges from Unauthorized Distribution Channels. *Marketing Science*, **19**(3), 279–294.

Akman, P., and Hviid, M. 2006. A Most-Favoured-Customer Clause with a Twist. *European Competition Journal*, **2**(1), 57–86.

Armstrong, M. 2006. Competition in Two-Sided Markets. *RAND Journal of Economics*, **37**(3), 668–691.

Armstrong, M. 2008a. Interactions between Competition and Consumer Policy. *Competition Policy International*, **4**(1), 97–147.

Armstrong, M. 2008b. Price Discrimination. In: Buccirossi, P. (ed), *Handbook of Antitrust Economics*. Cambridge, Massachusetts: The MIT Press, pp. 433–468.

Armstrong, M. 2015. *Nonlinear Pricing*. Working Paper. Department of Economics, University College London.

Asker, J., and Bar-Isaac, H. 2014. Raising Retailers' Profits: On Vertical Practices and the Exclusion of Rivals. *American Economic Review*, **104**(2), 672–686.

Asker, J., and Seitz, S. 2013. Vertical Practices and the Exclusion of Rivals Post Eaton. *CPI Antitrust Chronicle*, **2**(July).

Bajari, P., and Hortaçsu, A. 2004. Economic Insights from Internet Auctions. *Journal of Economic Literature*, **42**(2), 257–286.

Baye, M. R., and Morgan, J. 2002. Information Gatekeepers and Price Discrimination on the Internet. *Economics Letters*, **76**(1), 47–51.

Baye, M. R., De los Santos, B., and Wildenbeest, M. R. 2015. Searching for Physical and Digital Media: The Evolution of Platforms for Finding Books. In: Goldfarb, A., Greenstein, S., and Tucker, C. (eds), *NBER Book Economic Analysis of the Digital Economy*. University of Chicago Press, pp. 137–165.

Belleflamme, P., and Peitz, M. 2010. *Industrial Organization. Markets and Strategies*. Cambridge: Cambridge University Press.

Belleflamme, P., and Peitz, M. 2012. Digital Piracy: Theory. In: Peitz, M., and Waldfogel, J. (eds), *The Oxford Handbook of the Digital Economy*. Oxford University Press.

Bolt, W., and Chakravorti, S. 2012. Digitization of Retail Payments. In: Peitz, M., and Waldfogel, J. (eds), *The Oxford Handbook of the Digital Economy*. Oxford University Press.

Bonanno, G., and Vickers, J. 1988. Vertical Separation. *Journal of Industrial Economics*, **36**, 257–265.

Bourguignon, H., Gomes, R. D., and Tirole, J. 2014 (October). *Shrouded Transaction Costs*. Discussion Paper DP10171. CEPR.

Buccirossi, P. (ed). 2008. *Handbook of Antitrust Economics*. Cambridge, Massachusetts: The MIT Press.

Buehler, B., Koltay, G., Boutin, X., and Motta, M. 2014. Recent Developments at DG Competition: 2013-2014. *Review of Industrial Organization*, **45**, 399–415.

Buettner, T., Federico, G., Kühn, K.-U., and Magos, D. 2013. Economic Analysis at the European Commission 2012-2013. *Review of Industrial Organization*, **43**, 265–290.

Cabral, L. 2012. Reputation on the Internet. In: Peitz, M., and Waldfogel, J. (eds), *The Oxford Handbook of the Digital Economy*. Oxford University Press.

Cabral, L., and Hortaçsu, A. 2010. The Dynamics of Seller Reputation: Evidence from eBay. *Journal of Industrial Economics*, **58**(1), 54–78.

Chen, Y., and Pearcy, J. A. 2010. Dynamic Pricing: When to Entice Brand Switching and When to Reward Consumer Loyalty. *RAND Journal of Economics*, **41**, 674–685.

Chevalier, J., and Goolsbee, A. 2003. Measuring Prices and Price Competition Online: Amazon and BarnesandNoble.com. *Quantitative Marketing and Economics*, **1**, 203–222.

Clay, K., Krishnan, R., and Wolff, E. 2001. Prices and Price Dispersion on the Web: Evidence from the Online Book Industry. *Journal of Industrial Economics*, **49**(4), 521–539.

Cohen, D., Garibaldi, P., and Scarpetta, S. (eds). 2004. *The ICT Revolution. Productivity Differences and the Digital Divide*. Oxford: Oxford University Press.

Condorelli, D., Galeotti, A., and Skreta, V. 2013 (May). *Selling through Referrals*. Working Paper 2451/31774. NYU.

De los Santos, B., and Wildenbeest, M. R. 2014 (December). *E-book Pricing and Vertical Restraints*. Working Paper. Kelley School of Business, Indiana University.

Ding, R., and Wright, J. 2014 (March). *Payment Card Interchange Fees and Price Discrimination*. Working Paper. NUS.

Dobson, P., and Waterson, M. 2007. The Competition Effects of Industry-Wide Vertical Price Fixing in Bilateral Oligopoly. *International Journal of Industrial Organization*, **25**(5), 935–962.

Edelman, B., and Wright, J. 2015. Price Coherence and Excessive Intermediation. *Quarterly Journal of Economics*, **130**(3), 1283–1328.

Eliaz, K., and Spiegler, R. 2008. Consumer Optimism and Price Discrimination. *Theoretical Economics*, **3**(4), 459–497.

European Commission. 2015 (July). *A Digital Single Market Strategy for Europe*. Communication from the Commission to the European Parliament, the Council, the European Economic and Social Committee and the Committee of the Regions. Study prepared by Nicolai Van Gorp and Olga Batura.

Foros, Ø., Kind, H. J., and Shaffer, G. 2014. *Turning the Page on Business Formats for Digital Platforms: Does Apple's Agency Model Soften Competition?* Working Paper 06/14. NHH, Norwegian School of Economics.

Fudenberg, D., and Tirole, J. 2000. Customer Poaching and Brand Switching. *RAND Journal of Economics*, **31**, 634–657.

Fudenberg, D., and Villas-Boas, J. M. 2006. Behavior-Based Price Discrimination and Customer Recognition. Chap. 7 of: Hendershott, T. (ed), *Handbooks in Information Systems: Economics and Information Systems*. Amsterdam, The Netherlands: Elsevier.

Fudenberg, D., and Villas-Boas, J. M. 2012. Price Discrimination in the Digital Economy. In: Peitz, M., and Waldfogel, J. (eds), *The Oxford Handbook of the Digital Economy*. Oxford University Press.

Gal, M. S., and Rubinfeld, D. L. 2015. *The Hidden Costs of Free Goods: Implications for Antitrust Enforcement*. Working Paper 403. Law and Economics Working Papers, New York University.

Garicano, L., and Kaplan, S. N. 2001. The Effects of Business-to-Business E-Commerce on Transaction Costs. *Journal of Industrial Economics*, **49**(4), 463–485.

Gaudin, G., and White, A. 2014 (September). *On the Antitrust Economics of the Electronic Books Industry*. Working Paper 147. Dusseldorf Institute for Competition Economics.

Gilbert, R. J. 2015. A Tale of Digital Disruption. *Journal of Economic Perspectives*, **29**(3), 165–184.

Hart, O., Tirole, J., Carlton, D. W., and Williamson, O. E. 1990. Vertical Integration and Market Foreclosure. *Brookings Papers on Economic Activity. Microeconomics*, 205–286.

Hart, O. D., and Tirole, J. 1988. Contract Renegotiation and Coasian Dynamics. *Review of Economic Studies*, **55**, 509–540.

Italianer, A. 2014. *Competition Policy in the Digital Age*. Conference Presentation. 47th Innsbruck Symposium 'Real Sector Economy and the Internet – Digital Interconnection as an Issue for Competition Policy', Innsbruck, March 7.

Jin, G. Z., and Kato, A. 2007. Dividing Online and Offline: A Case Study. *Review of Economic Studies*, **74**(3), 981–1004.

Johnson, J. P. 2013 (March). *The Agency Model and Wholesale Models in Electronic Content Markets.* Working Paper. Johnson Graduate School of Management, Cornell University.

Johnson, J. P. 2014 (January). *The Agency Model and MFN Clauses.* Working Paper. Johnson Graduate School of Management, Cornell University.

Jullien, B. 2012. Two-Sided B to B Platforms. In: Peitz, M., and Waldfogel, J. (eds), *The Oxford Handbook of the Digital Economy.* Oxford University Press.

Jullien, B., and Rey, P. 2007. Resale Price Maintenance and Collusion. *RAND Journal of Economics*, **38**(4), 983–1001.

Koszegi, B. 2014. Behavioral Contract Theory. *Journal of Economic Literature*, **52**(4), 1075–1118.

Kühn, K.-U., Albæk, S., and de la Mano, M. 2011. Economics at DG Competition, 2010-2011. *Review of Industrial Organization*, **39**, 311–325.

Kühn, K.-U., Lorincz, S., Verouden, V., and Wilpshaar, A. 2012. Economics at DG Competition, 2011-2012. *Review of Industrial Organization*, **41**, 251–227.

Kwark, Y., Chen, J., and Raghunathan, S. 2015. *Platform or Wholesale? A Strategic Tool for Online Retailers to Benefit from Third-Party Information.* Working Paper. University of Texas at Dallas.

Lafontaine, F., and Slade, M. 2008. Exclusive Contracts and Vertical Restraints: Empirical Evidence and Public Policy. In: Buccirossi, P. (ed), *Handbook of Antitrust Economics.* Cambridge, Massachusetts: The MIT Press, pp. 391–414.

Langus, G., Neven, D., and Poukens, S. 2014 (March). *Economic Analysis of the Territoriality of the Making Available Right in the EU.* Technical Report. European Commission DG-MARKT. Charles River Associates Report, prepared for the EC DG-MARKT.

Lieber, E., and Syverson, C. 2012. Online versus Offline Competition. In: Peitz, M., and Waldfogel, J. (eds), *The Oxford Handbook of the Digital Economy.* Oxford University Press.

Loginova, O. 2009. Real and Virtual Competition. *Journal of Industrial Economics*, **57**(2), 319–342.

Lu, L. 2015. *A Comparison of the Wholesale Structure and the Agency Structure in Differentiated Markets.* Working Paper 15-7. Centre for Competition Policy, School of Economics, University of East Anglia.

Martin, S., Normann, H.-T., and Snyder, C. 2001. Vertical Foreclosure in Experimental Markets. *RAND Journal of Economics*, **32**, 466–496.

Marx, L., and Shaffer, G. 2004. Opportunism in Multilateral Vertical Contracting: Nondiscrimination, Exclusivity, and Uniformity; Comment. *American Economic Review*, **94**, 796–801.

Marx, L., and Shaffer, G. 2007. Upfront Payments and Exclusion in Downstream Markets. *RAND Journal of Economics*, **38**(3), 823–843.

Mathewson, F., and Winter, R. 1984. An Economic Theory of Vertical Restraints. *RAND Journal of Economics*, **15**, 27–38.

Mathewson, F., and Winter, R. 1988. The Law and Economics of Resale Price Maintenance. *Review of Industrial Organization*, **13**, 57–84.

Monopolkommission. 2015. *Competition Policy: The Challenge of Digital Markets. Special Report by the Monopolies Commission Pursuant to Section 44(1)(4) of the Act Against Restraints on Competition.* Special Report 28.

Mortimer, J. H. 2008. Vertical Contracts in the Video Rental Industry. *Review of Economic Studies*, **75**, 165–199.

Motta, M. 2004. *Competition Policy. Theory and Practice*. Cambridge: Cambridge University Press.

Motta, M., Rey, P., Verboven, F., and Vettas, N. 2009. *Hardcore Restrictions under the Block Exemption Regulation on Vertical Agreements: An Economic View*. Technical Report. Economic Advisory Group on Competition Policy, DG-Competition, European Commission.

Neven, D., and Albæk, S. 2007. Economics at DG Competition, 2006-2007. *Review of Industrial Organization*, **31**, 139–153.

Neven, D., and de la Mano, M. 2009. Economics at DG Competition, 2008–2009. *Review of Industrial Organization*, **35**, 317–347.

Neven, D., and de la Mano, M. 2010. Economics at DG Competition, 2009–2010. *Review of Industrial Organization*, **37**, 309–333.

Ng, I. C. L. 2014. *Creating New Markets in the Digital Economy. Value and Worth*. Cambridge: Cambridge University Press.

Nocke, V., Peitz, M., and Stahl, K. 2007. Platform Ownership. *Journal of the European Economic Association*, **5**(6), 1130–1160.

Rey, P., and Tirole, J. 2008. A Primer on Foreclosure. In: Armstrong, M., and Porter, R. H. (eds), *Handbook of Industrial Organization*, vol. 3. Elsevier.

Rey, P., and Vergé, T. 2008. Economics of Vertical Restraints. In: Buccirossi, P. (ed), *Handbook of Antitrust Economics*. Cambridge, Massachusetts: The MIT Press, pp. 353–390.

Riordan, M. H. 2008. Competitive Effects of Vertical Integration. In: Buccirossi, P. (ed), *Handbook of Antitrust Economics*. Cambridge, Massachusetts: The MIT Press, pp. 145–182.

Schmalensee, R., and Willig, R. D. (eds). 1989. *Handbook of Industrial Organization*. Vol. 1 and 2. Amsterdam: Elsevier.

Shaffer, G. 1991. Slotting Allowances and Resale Price Maintenance: A Comparison of Facilitating Practices. *RAND Journal of Economics*, **22**, 120–136.

Smith, M. D., Bailey, J., and Brynjolfsson, E. 2000. Understanding Digital Markets: Review and Assessment. In: Brynjolfsson, E., and Kahin, B. (eds), *Understanding the Digital Economy*. Cambridge, Massachusetts: The MIT Press, pp. 99–136.

Spengler, J. J. 1950. Vertical Integration and Antitrust Policy. *Journal of Political Economy*, **58**(4), 347–352.

Spiegel, Y. 2013. Commercial Software, Adware, and Consumer Privacy. *International Journal of Industrial Organization*, **31**, 702–713.

Taylor, C. R. 2004. Consumer Privacy and the Market for Customer Information. *RAND Journal of Economics*, **35**, 631–650.

Tirole, J. 1988. *The Theory of Industrial Organization*. Cambridge, Massachusetts: The MIT Press.

Valletti, T. M., and Szymanski, S. 2006. Parallel Trade, International Exhaustion and Intellectual Property Rights: A Welfare Analysis. *Journal of Industrial Economics*, **54**(4), 499–526.

Varian, H. R. 1985. Price Discrimination and Social Welfare. *American Economic Review*, **75**(4), 870–875.

Varian, H. R. 1989. Price Discrimination. Chap. 10 of: Schmalensee, R., and Willig, R. D. (eds), *Handbook of Industrial Organization*, vol. 1. Amsterdam: Elsevier, pp. 597–654.

Vettas, N. 2010. Developments in Vertical Agreements. *Antitrust Bulletin*, **55**(December), 843–874.

Villas-Boas, J. M. 1999. Dynamic Competition with Customer Recognition. *RAND Journal of Economics*, **30**, 604–631.

Villas-Boas, J. M. 2004. Price Cycles in Markets with Customer Recognition. *RAND Journal of Economics*, **35**, 486–501.

Wang, Z., and Wright, J. 2014 (May). *Ad-Valorem Platform Fees, Indirect Taxes and Efficient Price Discrimination*. Working Paper. NUS.

Wilson, R. 1993. *Nonlinear Pricing*. New York: Oxford University Press.

Wirl, F. 2015. Downstream and Upstream Oligopolies when Retailer's Effort Matters. *Journal Of Economics*, **116**(2), 99–127.

Zhang, J. 2011. The Perils of Behavior-Based Personalization. *Marketing Science*, **30**(1), 170–186.

6   Winners and Losers of Globalization: Sixteen Challenges for Measurement and Theory

Cecília Hornok and Miklós Koren

Abstract

The goal of this chapter is to summarize the state of the art in research in international trade and global production, and discuss issues relevant to European policymakers. Much of recent research on globalization is primarily empirical, owing to the proliferation of available data. We begin by discussing recent advances in measuring the causes and effects of globalization, and discussing the particular data challenges that have emerged. We then turn to theories of trade and global production, first summarizing the conclusions on which there is a broad consensus in the field. We discuss new insights that may be relevant for policy-makers, and open research questions.

6.1   Introduction

The fortune of workers, consumers and firms increasingly depends on other countries. This global interdependence is driven by the flow of goods, capital, ideas and people across countries. This chapter summarizes research about two aspects of globalization: international trade in goods and services, and the international fragmentation of production. We first summarize the overarching themes that are common to both topics. We conclude with a set of open questions, and propose an agenda for better connecting academic research with the needs of policy-making. We also discuss data challenges facing economists and policy-makers alike.

The primary motivation of theories of globalization is to explain how international interactions differ from domestic interactions, and why they occur in the first place. Why do countries trade goods with one another? Why do some companies locate part of their production abroad? Canonical models of trade and globalization explain the magnitude and patterns of cross-country movements, and their welfare implications. An almost tautological conclusion of these models is that if countries choose to interact with one another, they must be better off than being in isolation. Models may differ in the magnitude of the gains from trade they predict, but these gains are almost uniformly positive.

A central theme is that globalization benefits some more than others. In fact, some may even become worse off as their country becomes more open to the flow of goods, ideas, and people. For example, workers in import-competing industries stand to lose when countries open up to trade. These distributional effects of globalization are widely studied both theoretically and empirically.

Economists find it difficult to give definite answers to trade policy challenges partly because the remaining policy barriers to cross-border transactions are difficult to quantify. The standard economics toolbox works with taxes and quotas. Advances in measurement and unifying theories have made it possible to robustly quantify the effects of such taxes and quotas with minimal theoretical assumptions. Less is known, however, about the role of nontariff and nonquota barriers such as regulations and standards in limiting the side effects of globalization. We need to understand the costs of nontariff barriers in limiting international transactions, but also their potential benefits in solving market failures. For example, most analysis of the Transatlantic Trade and Investment Partnership (TTIP) and similar agreements can say little about the effect of harmonized regulation and the investment dispute settlement mechanism, the key ingredients of the TTIP and other such deep agreements.

Given the scope of the task, this survey is admittedly very selective. We have chosen topics that we think are both important for European policy and are well covered in academic research. We have omitted some basic research that may be very influential in shaping our views and future work, but that are not in the forefront of current policy debate in Europe. We also do not discuss the topic of financial integration and international migration, which are the subject of Chapter 3 and Chapter 11, respectively. Chapters 8 and 9 complement our chapter by studying agglomeration and location choices of firms, as well as intra-EU regional development.

Even among the topics we cover, our discussion can only scratch the surface of the academic debate. We did not intend to (and certainly could not) give a comprehensive survey in all the topics. Instead, we just summarized the consensus if there is one, and judiciously discussed the open questions. We have relied on several excellent recent surveys of the literature (O'Rourke and Williamson, 1999, Rauch, 2001, Anderson and Van Wincoop, 2004, Hoekman and Javorcik, 2006, Bernard et al., 2007, Goldberg and Pavcnik, 2007a, Harrison, 2007, Helpman et al., 2008b, Antràs and Rossi-Hansberg, 2009, Bernard et al., 2012c, Melitz and Trefler, 2012, Yeaple, 2013, Johnson, 2014, Gopinath et al., 2014). When necessary, we tried to highlight the key papers, but often just refer to the conclusions of these surveys. Readers who want to follow up on any of the academic topics should turn to these surveys.

6.2   Advances in Measurement and Data Challenges

Data on international transactions is collected differently from domestic data, which both helps and hurts empirical analysis. On the one hand, international transactions are often more likely to leave a paper trail than domestic ones. Historically, many countries relied on tariffs as an easy-to-collect source of government revenue, and built and maintained customs administrations to collect information about shipments and levy the appropriate taxes. This put unparalleled richness of data in the hands of governments, which then became available for economic research. On the other hand, the fact that customs administrations and statistical bureaus have no jurisdiction outside their sovereign borders limits their ability to collect good quality data on international flows.

6.2.1   *Recent Advances in Measuring the Causes and Effects of Globalization*

Firm-level Measurement of Trade Flows and Competitiveness
Firm-level data from balance sheets, earnings statements, customs records or surveys have become increasingly available in a number of countries throughout the past two decades. This led to a rich empirical literature, starting with the papers of Bernard et al. (1995); Bernard and Jensen (1999), on the performance distribution of firms within countries and industries and on how the performance of firms relate to international involvement through trade or FDI.

Most related research on European firms, a recent assessment of which is provided by Wagner (2012), feature data on individual countries. A more systematic approach is made by Mayer and Ottaviano (2007), who look at firm-level data from seven European countries. More recently, two EU-wide research projects (EFIGE, CompNet) generated internationally comparable data. Findings from the EFIGE firm-level survey in seven – mostly major – EU countries are assessed, for example, by Navaretti et al. (2011), while Berthou et al. (2015) discuss evidence from the CompNet firm-level panel of 15 EU countries.

The major findings prove to be remarkably robust across countries, industries and databases. First, firms are very heterogeneous in their performance measures even within narrowly defined industries. Second, this heterogeneity is to a significant extent explained by the international activity. Internationalized firms are larger both in terms of number of employees and sales, they are more productive and more capital and skill intensive than firms operating only on the domestic market. Third, the bulk of exports in any given country is usually generated by a handful of very big exporters, which at the same time also heavily import intermediate inputs.

Firm-level data is also increasingly used for policy analysis (Cernat, 2016). This is helpful not only to identify the heterogeneous effects of trade policy on individual firms, but also to better quantify the aggregate effects of policy. To understand aggregate effects, we need to rely on industry and macroeconomic models (discussed in Section 6.3).

Challenge 1 *Harmonize firm-level trade and balance sheet data across countries.*

Multidimensional Trade Data

Recent empirical work has used customs transactions data to analyse the patterns of trade. The availability of such data has opened up the possibility to ask questions beyond the volume of trade and its broad sectoral composition. A typical customs declaration (which serves as the primary unit of observation for most trade statistics) records the exporting and the importing firm, the precise classification of the product being shipped, the precise date of shipments, the mode of transport and many other logistical details about shipment. This has made it possible, for example, to study the distribution of trade across products, destination markets and firms.

Bernard et al. (2007) survey the empirical evidence on multi-product and multi-country traders. They find that although most exporters (40% of the total) sell only one product to one destination, most exports are done by large multi-product, multi-destination exporters. The number of products and firms shipping to a particular market increases with market size and decreases with distance. Similar patterns emerge for imports.

Armenter and Koren (2014) caution that patterns in multidimensional trade data may be difficult to interpret because such data is sparse. That is, there are few observations relative to the number of product, firm and country categories.

What is the quantitative relevance of the sparsity of trade data? Armenter and Koren (2014) build a statistical benchmark (which can be thought of as a special case of a wide class of economic models), in which trade shipments are 'randomly' assigned to trade categories. The randomness is conditional on the size distribution of firms, countries, and products, so it does not imply that exporters behave erratically. Such a '*balls-and-bins*' model can quantitatively fit many of the statistics reported about the number of exported products, exporting firms, and export destinations. Given that many models are consistent with the balls-and-bins framework, we cannot distinguish among them on the basis of such simple statistics.

We hence need new statistical methods to deal with large multidimensional trade datasets. Armenter and Koren (2014) do not offer a universal tool, but their reliance on the statistical properties of the multinomial distribution may be a useful starting point for further analysis. A more structural approach is followed by Eaton et al. (2012) and Armenter and Koren (2013), who build trade models with infrequent purchases.

The multidimensionality of most databases on international transactions (trade, investment, etc.) also poses a computational challenge in empirical applications. Panels of bilateral trade flows have at least three dimensions, while more detailed (micro) databases potentially more. Most empirical applications of the gravity equation on panel data, for example, include multiple sets of fixed effects to control for country, time, or country-pair unobservables. With large data, estimating out lots of fixed effects can become difficult or even practically impossible. To help overcome this problem Balázsi et al. (2015) derive, both for balanced and unbalanced data, the within transformations for several fixed effects models, while Mátyás et al. (2012) and Mátyás et al. (2013) propose random effects estimation and derive the appropriate estimators.

Challenge 2 *Develop statistical methods and computational tools to work with multidimensional data.*

Using Linked Employer-employee Data

The emergence of linked employer-employee datasets (LEEDs) (see Abowd and Kramarz, 1999) has spurred a fast-growing research on the effect of trade, FDI and other modes of globalization on worker-level outcomes, such as wages and employment probabilities. This is useful because it helps us understand the distributional effects of globalization more deeply.

The value added of LEEDs relative to firm-level studies is twofold. First, they help measure the heterogeneity of responses by different worker types. In a typical research design, some firms are exposed to globalization, some firms are not, and the researchers study the evolution of wages for different classes of workers within the firm. For example, Frias et al. (2012) estimate the effect of increased exports by Mexican firms after the 1994 peso devaluation on the wages of workers at these firms. They find that workers at the bottom of the wage distribution are not affected, but higher ranked workers see wage increases. That is, exports contribute to an increase in within-firm wage inequality. This would be impossible to measure with just firm-level data. See Schank et al. (2007), Krishna et al. (2011), Baumgarten (2013) and Hummels et al. (2014) for studies with similar designs.

A second contribution of LEEDs is that we can measure the exposure to globalization directly at the worker level. Koren and Csillag (2011) use a Hungarian LEED to estimate the effect of machine imports on the wages of machine operators. Crucially, knowing the precise product classification of machines and the precise occupation classification of workers, they can identify which workers are directly exposed to machine imports. For example, importing a new printing machine should affect the printing machine operator, but not the forklift driver. Koren and Csillag (2011) find that this is indeed the case and operators exposed to imported machines receive higher wages.

We expect that proprietary datasets within the firm will help us paint an even richer picture of the microeconomic effects of globalization.

Challenge 3 *Develop new datasets on workers within firms, while ensuring privacy and consistency across studies.*

Trade in Services

Services were earlier treated by economists as nontradables, as they typically require the physical proximity of the consumer and the service provider. Recent advances in information and communication technologies, however, have made several services 'disembodied' and enabled their cross-border trade. Where proximity is still important, international trade can take the form of sales through foreign affiliates or the (temporary) movement of persons.

Services are traded not only directly but also indirectly as components of traded manufactured products in the form of, for example, transport, telecommunication, banking or retail services. According to an OECD estimate, the services value added content of exported manufactured goods is 20–30 per cent. Hence, the liberalization of services trade, as long as it leads to cheaper, better quality services, can also improve the competitiveness of the manufacturing sector (see empirical evidence from Arnold et al., 2011 on the Czech Republic and Arnold et al., 2016 on India).

No distinct theory has been developed for understanding trade in services. Some argue that the existing theories of trade in goods and FDI can be applied to services trade as well, once we reinterpret transport costs as costs associated with the need for geographical proximity (Francois and Hoekman, 2010). The cost of this proximity burden in services is likely to be larger than the cost of distance in goods trade. Anderson et al. (2014) find that geographical barriers alone reduce international services trade seven times more than goods trade.

Recent firm-level studies on several large EU economies reveal important similarities between goods and services trade on the micro level (Breinlich and Criscuolo, 2011, Federico and Tosti, 2012, Kelle et al., 2013 and Temouri et al., 2013). Similar to trade in goods, trade in services is also concentrated among a small group of traders. These firms are typically larger, more productive and pay higher wages than other firms. The most productive service exporters tend to be parts of multinational enterprises and export via foreign affiliates. All this suggests that self-selection through productivity into trading and FDI is also present in trade in services.

An important difference between goods and services trade is that most barriers to services trade are of a regulatory nature. Service sectors are typically heavily regulated by national authorities (e.g., due to natural monopolies, asymmetric information or equity concerns). To the extent that these regulations are different across countries or discriminatory to foreign providers, they can act as barriers to all forms of services trade (cross-border, FDI or movement of people). Drawing on policy experience with the WTO's General Agreement on Trade in Services (GATS) and other bilateral liberalization efforts, Hoekman and Mattoo (2013) emphasize that services trade liberalization cannot be separated from regulatory reform and international regulatory harmonization.

During recent years much has been done to overcome the serious data limitations in the field of trade in services. Bilateral service flow data from several different sources have been consolidated in a global database (Francois et al., 2009). Firm-level data on services trade are available for more and more countries. Information on barriers to services trade are summarized in two large-scale projects, the World Bank's Services Trade Restrictions Database (World Bank, 2015, Borchert et al., 2012a,b) and the OECD's Services Trade Restrictiveness Index (OECD, 2015). Nevertheless, there is still a lot to be done in the future to build and maintain comprehensive and reliable databases in this field.

Challenge 4 *Build harmonized firm-level data on services trade.*

Matched Buyer-seller Data

Most theoretical frameworks, even when they deal with business-to-business transactions, treat one side of the market as anonymous. In these models, exporters sell to many anonymous buyers, and importers buy from many anonymous sellers. In reality, however, most firms are only linked to a few buyers and few suppliers.

Understanding the nature of buyer-supplier linkages is crucial for two reasons. First, firms differ in their set of buyers and set of suppliers, and this heterogeneity may contribute to heterogeneity in performance (Eaton et al., 2013). We want to understand how firms with few and many links behave differently. Second, the structure of the network may affect the behavior of the entire economic system (Acemoglu et al., 2012).

Bernard et al. (2014b) analyse a novel two-sided dataset on trade. Using transaction-level trade data from Norway, they identify buying and selling firms, and document a number of facts about the distribution of trade flows across buyers and sellers. First, there is substantial variation in the number of buyers per seller. Most firms sell to a single buyer, but large firms sell to many buyers. Second, the distribution of sales across buyers does not vary systematically with firm size. Third, larger sellers sell to, on average, smaller buyers.

Carballo et al. (2013) study a similar buyer–seller dataset for Costa Rica, Ecuador and Uruguay. They show how the number of buyers varies across destination markets. Firms have more buyers in large and close markets. In markets with tougher competition, the distribution of sales is more skewed towards the largest buyer. Carballo et al. (2013) also build a model to show that increased international openness to competition leads to selection and reallocation across buyer–supplier relationships, increasing productivity and welfare.

Data on buyer-supplier links is also (if not more) difficult to obtain for domestic transactions. Bernard et al. (2014a) work with a unique Japanese dataset, showing that the average firm has 4.9 suppliers and 5.6 (business) customers. They also study the geographic distribution of suppliers.

We discuss the theoretical questions raised by this new empirical work on buyer-supplier links in Section 6.3.3.

Challenge 5 *Collect data on buyer–supplier links within the EU.*

6.2.2 Data Challenges

Data Collection is Fragmented Across Countries

To study globalization, it is important to have internationally comparable data, and to follow transactions outside country borders. The European Union is closer to this ideal than other free trade areas would be, as Eurostat coordinates the development, production and dissemination of European statistics (Eurostat, 2011). However, most data wealth is still held by national statistical agencies.

There are several recent advances to improve data harmonization and data matching across countries. Lopez-Garcia et al. (2014) and Berthou et al. (2015) describe the CompNet project, which collects firm-level indicators of competitiveness across European countries in a harmonized manner. Researchers have also matched various datasets necessary for analysis. Bernard et al. (2012a,b) matched trade and production data for Belgium. Bernard et al. (2014b) identify individual buyers of all exporters and sellers of all importers in Norway, which could serve as a first step to match this data with statistics outside Norway. Carballo et al. (2013) similarly identify buyers of exporters in Costa Rica, Ecuador and Uruguay. However, such matched data is not widely available for research.

Challenge 6 *Link national administrative data, harmonize data collection and reporting.*

Collecting Data Within the Firm is Difficult

A large fraction of global transactions are carried out by multinationals (Yeaple, 2013). Correspondingly, economists have started to study the motivation of multinationals to keep production in house, rather than sourcing inputs at arm's length. (See Antràs and Rossi-Hansberg, 2009 for a review.) Understanding the behavior of multinationals demands access to within-firm data: where foreign affiliates are located, how much they sell in various markets, what their transactions are with the parents. We only know of a few such datasets.

First, confidential microdata collected by the US Bureau of Economic Analysis on Direct Investment and Multinational Enterprises is used by many researchers surveyed in Yeaple (2013). Second, the Deutsche Bundesbank collects and maintains the Microdatabase on Direct Investment of German parent companies (Lipponer, 2006). Third, proprietary datasets published by private-sector vendors have also been used in research: WorldBase published by Dun and Bradstreet (Alfaro and Chen, 2014), or Orbis, published by Bureau van Dijk (see Alfaro and Chen, 2012).

We expect more reliance on private-sector data and within-firm case studies to inform the theories of multinationals.

Challenge 7 *Synthesize research based on ad-hoc proprietary data.*

Measuring Trade and Competitiveness in Value Added Terms
The fragmentation of data collection across countries also makes it difficult to identify the real contribution of countries to global value added. The key challenge is that international trade is recorded in gross output terms, which do not necessarily reflect accurately the local contribution of a country. For example, a car assembly plant in Hungary might export to Germany. Exports are recorded as the total value of the car exported, whereas the Hungarian value added might be just a fraction of that value.

National statistical offices compile input–output tables to track how value is added along the supply chain within the country. Johnson (2014) summarizes recent efforts by researchers to estimate a similar global input–output table that also takes account of global trade flows. One such database is the GTAP (Global Trade Analysis Project) Database, which Koopman et al. (2014) used to break up country gross exports into value added components. A more recently compiled and publicly available database is the World Input Output Database (Stehrer et al., 2014), which also has a full time series dimension.

The basic fact is that trade in value added is about 25 per cent less than trade in gross output. Patterns of value added trade also differ in subtle ways from patterns of gross output trade. For example, in terms of value added, services are about as traded as products. In fact, the final price of many high end manufacturing products includes a substantial portion of services, such as design and marketing. Second, some countries add relatively more value to their exports than others. Taiwan's value added exports are about half of its gross exports, whereas for Brazil this ratio is 86 per cent (Johnson, 2014).

Timmer et al. (2013) discuss how measurement of value added trade affects our view on European competitiveness. They develop a measure of global value chain (GVC) income and GVC employment, as the value added that comes directly or indirectly from exporting manufactured goods, and the jobs that are directly or indirectly contributing to these goods. They show that GVC income grew slower in Europe than gross exports, that GVC income is biased towards services, increasingly over time, and that GVC jobs are increasingly higher and higher skilled.

Challenge 8 *Construct international input-output accounts from the ground up.*

6.3   Insights from Theories of Globalization

This section discusses the insights from theories of international trade and the international fragmentation of production. We first report broad lessons about the causes and effects of globalization, lessons in which there is a consensus among scientists, then discuss open questions.

6.3.1   Broad Lessons about the Causes and Effects of Globalization

Gains from Trade

Classical and neoclassical economics states that countries gain from trade because they can specialize according to their comparative advantage. If the country can produce more of what it produces cheaply, and consume more of what it produces expensively, its residents have to be better off.

This basic result in trade theory can be derived with minimal assumptions about the structure of the economy other than what is usual in neoclassical economics: perfect competition and constant returns to scale (see, for example, Dixit and Norman, 1980). Notably, it does not matter whether countries trade because they have access to different technologies, because they have different factor endowments, or because they differ in taste. Simply the fact that an open country finds prices different from its own in the world market establishes the gains from trade: it can sell whatever is more expensive abroad and buy whatever is cheaper.

New trade theory has provided new explanations for why countries trade. Krugman (1979, 1980) argues that even identical countries may gain from trade if firms exploit internal economies of scale. Such economies of scale may arise in high tech sectors, where costs of product development and marketing are large relative to actual production costs. Cars, computers and pharmaceuticals are prime examples.

In an open economy, each firm has an incentive to produce at bigger scale and economize on fixed costs. As a result, more firms will enter and consumers will have more variety at their disposal. To the extent that consumers value variety of choice, they will gain even by integrating with an identical economy. Such models are capable of explaining the large volume of trade between similar economies such as the EU and the US. They are also consistent with large volumes of simultaneous exports and imports of similar products ('*intraindustry trade*'). An additional prediction of the theory is that whenever trade is costly, producers will want to locate and bear the fixed cost close to their final consumers.

Davis and Weinstein (1999) and Head and Ries (2001) provide evidence for the qualitative conclusions of new trade theory. They find that industries subject to product differentiation are overrepresented in countries and regions with high local demand. Hanson and Xiang (2004) also find that industries with more product differentiation and with higher transport costs are overrepresented in large countries.

Broda and Weinstein (2006) quantify the gains from increased variety, which is at the heart of the gains from trade in models with economies of scale. They compute a variety-corrected import price index to account for the fact that consumers value goods from different countries differently. They estimate that US consumers gained 2.6 per cent of GDP from increased import variety between 1972 and 2001.

Old trade theory has been concerned mainly with aggregate trade patterns. New trade theory has focused instead on the export decision: Which firms export, how many products and destinations they serve. We have now finely disaggregated data to answer these questions. New trade theory offers the promise of building aggregate models from the bottom up. Melitz (2003) is the workhorse model in the new trade literature. The theory is built on two key blocks: Firm heterogeneity in productivity and economies of scale (fixed costs) in exporting. The model's tractability makes it possible to bring together micro facts and macro analysis.

The key mechanism of the model is selection: Fixed costs prevent many firms from exporting, and only the more productive firms can recover the fixed cost. In the model as in the data, exporters are few and larger than nonexporters. Selection is also at work on the key implication of Melitz (2003) in the event of a trade liberalization: Existing exporters will sell more (the intensive margin), new firms will start exporting (the extensive margin). Resources are reallocated from nonexporters to exporters and thus to the more productive firms, and the least productive nonexporters are driven out of business. This reallocation leads to gains in aggregate productivity.

Firms can also gain from engaging in other forms of international production. They can substitute export sales and economize on trade costs by setting up production affiliates abroad. The incentive to do such horizontal FDI is characterized by the '*proximity-concentration tradeoff*' (Brainard, 1997). Firms want to produce close to their consumers (proximity) to economize on trade costs, but also want to concentrate production to exploit economies of scale. A special case of horizontal FDI aims to serve other countries from the foreign production plant: export platform FDI. While there is empirical evidence that firms locate their production plants in response to export-platform, not just host country demand (Feinberg and Keane, 2001, Head and Mayer, 2004), a quantitative modelling of this channel has been lacking due to computational complexities. The question of where to optimally locate a number of production facilities given a distribution of consumers is a computationally difficult problem to solve. New approaches have been proposed by Arkolakis et al. (2013) and Tintelnot (2016).

Much of the trade literature focuses on gains accruing to final consumers. However, firms also source some of their inputs from abroad, so they also stand to gain with lower trade barriers (Hummels et al., 2001).

Grossman and Rossi-Hansberg (2008) build a theory of offshoring based on the idea that firms decide on the set of tasks they want to source from abroad. These tasks differ in their costs of offshoring. In the model, firms that offshore a wider range of tasks become more productive and will expand. Surprisingly, they may even increase their demand for local labour, if the productivity effect is large enough. Halpern et al. (2015) build a model of firms using imported inputs and quantify the productivity gains from the access to foreign inputs. Antràs et al. (2014) combine these theories in a general equilibrium setting, and characterize the complex sourcing strategy of firms.

Some of this input trade may take place within the firm. When a firm opens an affiliate abroad (typically in a low wage country, Yeaple (2013)) to produce some of its intermediate inputs, it engages in vertical FDI. Hanson et al. (2005) find that such vertical FDI is higher in low-wage countries that can be reached by lower trade costs. The growth of vertical production networks has spurred further research, and we return to it in Section 6.3.3.

Several recent studies have contributed to policy analysis with quantifiable models of the gains from trade. They simulate counterfactual scenarios by setting trade costs to prohibitively large (so that countries are in autarky), or setting them to zero (so that countries engage in free trade). These losses from autarky and gains from further trade liberalization are the easiest to compute, but concrete tariff scenarios have also been worked out.

Eaton and Kortum (2002) build a model with Ricardian motives for trade. That is, countries face different productivities. Trade is also subject to trade costs, which can vary across pairs of countries. They derive that the pattern of trade follows a gravity equation: large and close countries trade more with one another. They also highlight subtle trade diversion effects of trade costs, as in Anderson and van Wincoop (2003). Theirs is a multi-country general equilibrium model suitable for analysing the effects of bilateral and multilateral trade agreements, for example.

Alvarez et al. (2007) quantify the gains from trade in a calibrated general equilibrium Eaton-Kortum model. They estimate that eliminating all tariffs among the 60 largest economies would increase their GDP by 0.50 per cent, on average (Table 2, weighted average). This estimate is much smaller than those of the historical case studies and the reduced-form estimates discussed below.

In an important recent contribution, Arkolakis et al. (2012) show how to quantify the gains from trade in a wide class of models, which includes the Eaton-Kortum model of technology differences, the Krugman model of scale economies and increased varieties, and a variant of the Melitz model due to Chaney (2008). In these models, the gains from trade of a country can be summarized by two important statistics: the share of income it spends on domestic goods and services, and the elasticity of trade volumes to trade costs. Intuitively, spending much on imported goods (and correspondingly little on domestic goods) signals a high willingness to pay for imports, whether because of lower prices, increased variety or selection based on productivity.

This unifying framework is promising for policy analysis, because these statistics are easy to measure or estimate. For example, the US spent 7 per cent of its income on imports in 2000. Using the domestic share of 93 per cent and elasticities of trade between 5 and 10, Arkolakis et al. (2012) estimate that American consumers were 0.7 to 1.4 per cent better off in 2000 than in complete autarky. Relative to the likely disruptions that a complete cessation of American exports and imports would entail, this estimate seems incredibly low.

Existing quantifiable models estimate the gains from trade to be implausibly small. They find that the typical country of the global economy is only about 1 to 2 per cent richer due to trade than it would be in complete isolation. (For other calibrations with different treatments of heterogeneity, multiple sectors, and intermediates, see Ossa, 2015, Melitz and Trefler, 2012, Melitz and Redding, 2014, Costinot and Rodriguez-Clare, 2014.) This is at odds with global efforts to reduce trade barriers and increase trade among countries, such as the creation and expansion of the World Trade Organization and the recent agreement on trade facilitation in the Bali Package. It is also inconsistent with credible reduced-form estimates of the GDP-enhancing effects of openness to trade.

Feyrer (2009a,b) exploits natural experiments in the variation in trade costs between countries to estimate how trade affects income per capita. Feyrer (2009a) uses the closure of the Suez Canal between 1969 and 1975 to generate quasi-random variation in trade costs between countries that were not part of the Suez conflict. He finds that the most affected countries, for which the closure of the canal made sea shipping most expensive, witnessed declines in their volume of trade and smaller-than-average income growth. He estimates the elasticity of income to trade around 0.16, that is, a 10 per cent increase in trade volumes increases income per capita by 1.6 per cent. Feyrer (2009b) exploits variation in the relative cost of air and sea freight over time. Landlocked countries are now more accessible than they were before a dramatic fall in air transport costs. This made them (exogenously) more open to trade and have higher income. Feyrer estimates the elasticity of income to trade to be about twice as high in this study.

One potential reason is that airplanes made it easy to not only transport goods, but also people across countries.

We believe that the quantitative fit between model-based and reduced-form estimates of the gains from trade could be further improved.

Challenge 9 *Reconcile model-based and reduced-form estimates of gains from trade.*

Distributional Effects of Globalization

Almost any change in openness to global competition is going to create winners and losers. A reduction in import tariffs makes consumers better off, while import competing producers worse off. Eli Heckscher and Bertil Ohlin, the founders of a theory of trade based on factor endowment differences already highlighted the distributional effects of trade opening:

Australia has a small population and an abundant supply of land, much of it not very fertile. Land is consequently cheap and wages high, in relation to most other countries. […] Australian land is thus exchanged for European labour. […] Thus trade increases the price of land in Australia and lowers it in Europe, while tending to keep wages down in Australia and up in Europe. (Ohlin, 1924, quoted in O'Rourke and Williamson, 1999, pp. 57–58)

The result that trade leads to a convergence of factor prices, and thus benefits the abundant (and hence previously cheap) factor, is known as the Stolper-Samuelson theorem (Stolper and Samuelson, 1941). It identifies the winners of globalization as the factor in abundance in the country (land for Australia), and the losers as the scarce factor (labour for Australia, land for Europe), which previously commanded high prices.

O'Rourke and Williamson (1999) find evidence for this pattern of factor price convergence in the late nineteenth-century Atlantic economy. The ratio of wages to land rents has steadily increased for open European countries such as England, Denmark, Sweden and Ireland. Hence in these countries, landed interests lost at the expense of workers. The wage–rent ratio has fallen for new land abundant countries such as Australia, Argentina and the US. This confirms the original predictions by Heckscher, Ohlin, Stolper and Samuelson.

In the more recent wave of globalization, it is not as easy to identify the losers. Goldberg and Pavcnik (2007a) review the evidence on the distributional effects of globalization in several developing countries (Argentina, Brazil, Chile, Colombia, India, Hong Kong and Mexico) for the time period between the 1970s and the 1990s. All of these countries liberalized international trade some time in this period and saw a surge of both imports and exports. The countries also hosted increasing amounts of FDI. Goldberg and Pavcnik (2007a) study various measures of inequality, but the broad pattern is that inequality increased everywhere. It seems that the losers are the workers who already had lower wages. This is surprising given that such workers had supposedly been in abundance in developing countries. Goldberg and Pavcnik (2007a) investigate several explanations for this pattern, and we also discuss it in Section 6.3.3.

Focusing on the low end of income distribution, Harrison (2007) reviews both cross-country and within-country studies of how poverty is affected by globalization. They also find that '[t]he poor in countries with an abundance of unskilled labour do not always gain from trade reform' (Harrison, 2007). In fact, even among the poor, there are generally winners and losers. Topalova (2007) finds that rural districts in India with higher-than-average concentration of sectors exposed to import competition witnessed an increase in poverty. Among urban households in Colombia, there is weak evidence that working in an import-competing sector and lower tariffs are associated with higher poverty (Goldberg and Pavcnik, 2007b). In Mexico (Hanson, 2007) and Poland (Goh and Javorcik, 2007), however, higher exposure to trade was associated with lower poverty.

Models with increasing returns and firm heterogeneity also produce losers, not only winners. In Melitz (2003), a reduction in trade costs increases profit opportunities abroad. When exporting entails a fixed cost, only a subset of firms will be exporters who can capitalize on these profit opportunities. Their increased demand for local resources (such as labour needed for production and R&D) will hurt the smaller firms that only sell in the domestic market. They will either shrink or exit the market. Bernard et al. (2003) and Melitz and Ottaviano (2008) arrive at similar conclusions in different models of industry competition and trade. Such reallocation effects across firms have been empirically documented by Pavcnik (2002) and many authors since.

It is important to note that the redistribution effects of globalization are not secondary to the aggregate gain from trade. Often it is exactly the redistribution that brings about the overall gain. Given the amount of resources in the economy, an export sector cannot expand without an import sector shrinking. Similarly, large productive firms cannot grow without the small unproductive firms shrinking or exiting. For too long we have assumed these reallocations to be frictionless: workers fired in shrinking sectors and firms will instantaneously get rehired in expanding sectors and firms. We now have the theoretical tools and measurements to show that this is not the case.

One paper measuring reallocation costs is Artuç et al. (2010), who estimate a structural model of industry choice of workers with switching costs in US data. They build a model where workers pick an industry in order to maximize lifetime discounted income. If they switch to a different industry, however, they have to pay a fixed cost. Artuç et al. (2010) estimate the mean and variance of these fixed costs in a panel of workers from the Current Population Survey by matching both the number of workers that switch sectors and the sensitivity of cross-sector worker flows to wage gains. The estimates reveal very large switching costs, equivalent to between 4 and 13 years of wage income.

More recently, Dix-Carneiro (2014) refines the above model by, among others, incorporating worker heterogeneity and estimates the switching cost on Brazilian data. He finds that the median switching cost is 1.4–2.7 times the annual wage, but with a high dispersion across the population. He argues that in certain segments of the labour market the adjustment process after a trade liberalization can take a long time, which can significantly offset the gains from trade. On the same Brazilian data, Dix-Carneiro and Kovak (2015) show that the labour market outcomes of the most affected regions deteriorated compared to other regions for more than a decade before beginning to level off.

Antras et al. (2015) study the welfare implications of trade in an economy where redistribution is subject to information constraints. Their conclusion is that even though progressive taxation might mitigate the effects of trade on inequality, in general inequality will go up after opening up to trade.

In a sequence of papers, Helpman and Itskhoki (2010) and Helpman et al. (2010, 2016) develop a new framework to think about trade, unemployment and wage inequality.[1] The key result of Helpman et al. (2010) is that opening a closed economy to trade increases inequality as better-paying exporting firms expand. However, this effect turns around when almost all firms export, and their expansion also pulls up the bottom of the wage distribution. The response of unemployment to trade is ambiguous. Helpman et al. (2016) find that the model describes well the evolution of wage inequality in Brazil, and that trade can contribute to large increases in inequality.

Challenge 10 *Identify losers from globalization and quantify their losses.*

Cross-border Frictions are Large

The third broad lesson from research on international trade is that frictions that impede the flow of goods and other interactions are large. Some of these frictions are related to geography, but many of them are associated with crossing borders.

Anderson and Van Wincoop (2004) provide a survey of the estimated trade costs (see Table 6.1). They report three sets of estimates. The first includes direct measures of transaction costs, such as charges for freight, insurance, tariffs, as well as costs of distribution and local taxes. For the average country, these amount to 170 per cent of the value of international trade. Distribution costs also arise in domestic trade, so the cross-border component of costs is 'only' 74 per cent.

The second method to estimate trade costs exploits the cross-country disparity in prices. If the price of a good in the destination market is 4 per cent higher than in the source market, trade costs between these countries are at least 4 per

Table 6.1 *Percentage equivalents of trade costs. Source: Anderson and Van Wincoop (2004), p. 692*

Cost component	Percentage
Transportation	21
Policy barrier	8
Language barrier	7
Currency barrier	14
Information barrier	6
Security barrier	3
Total border costs	44
Distribution	55

cent.[2] Estimates of the dispersion of log prices across locations vary between 20 and 40 per cent (Anderson and Van Wincoop, 2004).

The third method infers trade costs from the volume of trade relative to a frictionless benchmark. This method has been immensely popular, relying mostly on the gravity equation as the benchmark trade model.[3]

Theories of the past decades have incorporated these frictions mostly as taxes or wedges on import prices. These are often modelled as an ad-valorem cost, following Samuelson (1954). Recently, other forms of trade costs have also been modelled and estimated: fixed entry costs of operating in a market, time costs associated with shipping, fixed costs accruing per shipment, and additive rather than proportional shipping charges. We will briefly discuss estimates of each.

Fixed Entry Costs

Entry costs are useful in explaining why many firms do not export. If a firm is too small, it would not find it profitable to bear the fixed costs associated with distribution in a given market. Das et al. (2007) estimate a structural model of exporters with sunk market entry costs, and find that these costs are substantial, of the order of $400,000. The primary fact identifying such large sunk costs is that many large firms seem to forego large profit opportunities in foreign markets and do not enter.

Helpman et al. (2008a) estimate a model of heterogeneous firms with fixed costs of market entry from macro data: the volume of trade between pairs of countries. Their estimation is based on the idea that only fixed costs can generate zero trade flows in the data, variable costs cannot. They show how fixed costs vary across countries, and that FTAs, a common language, and a common religion predominantly reduce the fixed costs of trade, not the variable cost.

Armenter and Koren (2015) emphasize that there is large heterogeneity in the market entry costs across firms. By matching the size distribution of firms and the number and average size of exporters, they estimate that the 75th percentile of fixed costs is 32 thousand times as much as the 25th percentile. This huge variation suggests that a simple fixed entry cost is not a suitable structural model of export entry.

Arkolakis (2010) develops a theory with convex market access cost. This model is consistent with the fact that some firms do not enter export markets (because the marginal market access cost is strictly positive), but fits the pattern of small exporters better than models with fixed costs.

Time Costs
Trading time, that is, the time it takes to send a shipment from the origin to the destination, represents another form of trade costs. Firms are willing to pay significantly above the interest cost to get faster deliveries. Hummels and Schaur (2013) estimate that US importers pay 0.6–2.3 per cent of the traded value to reduce trading time by one day. Other empirical studies that use different data and methodology also confirm the importance of time costs in trade (Djankov et al., 2010 and Hornok, 2012). Internationally fragmented production processes, which involve the multiple shipping of intermediate inputs, are especially sensitive to the length and variation of shipping time (Harrigan and Venables, 2006).

Per-unit Costs
Recent research emphasizes that part of international trade costs are additive costs, that is, fixed cost per unit traded (Hummels and Skiba, 2004 and Irarrazabal et al., 2015). These may include per-unit tariffs, quotas, or transport costs proportional to the physical quantity of the cargo. The magnitude of these costs is likely substantial. Irarrazabal et al. (2015) estimate it to be 14 per cent of the median product price, which is a lower bound estimate. The presence of additive costs can have important welfare implications. Compared to ad valorem trade costs, per unit costs may create additional welfare losses, as they distort the within-market relative prices and consumption of different product varieties ('*Alchian-Allen hypothesis*').

Per-shipment Costs
Other trade costs are fixed per shipment. They include the costs of the bureaucratic procedures of sending a shipment and the shipping time. According to direct cost measures from the World Bank's Doing Business database, these costs exceed 10 per cent of the value of a typical shipment (Hornok and Koren, 2015b). Alternatively, Kropf and Sauré (2014) infer per shipment costs from trade flows and find them to be broadly 1 to 5 per cent of the traded value.

Empirical evidence shows that trading firms facing these costs respond by sending fewer and larger shipments. This creates losses in the form of higher inventory expenses (Alessandria et al., 2010) or less consumer satisfaction (Hornok and Koren, 2015a).

Challenge 11 *Understand and quantify nontax, nonquota frictions in trade.*

6.3.2   Insights for Policy

Imports Are Important

Earlier empirical studies in trade discussed patterns of exports disproportionately more than patterns of imports. With the emergence of new firm-level data, it has become clear that imports are as important as exports, especially when we think of imports used by firms in their production. Bernard et al. (2007, 2009) show that importers are just as special as exporters: they tend to be larger and more productive than nontrading firms.

The bigger size and better performance of importers is not only due to self-selection into importing. Studies show that improved access to foreign inputs has increased firm productivity in several countries, including Indonesia (Amiti and Konings, 2007), Chile (Kasahara and Rodrigue, 2008), India (Topalova and Khandelwal, 2011) and Hungary (Halpern et al., 2015). Results are conflicting for Brazil: Schor (2004) estimates a positive effect, while Muendler (2004) finds no effect of imported inputs on productivity. And for Argentina, Gopinath and Neiman (2014) show that variation in imported inputs may have contributed to fluctuations in aggregate productivity.

To understand why importers are better, Halpern et al. (2015) formulate a model of firms who use differentiated inputs to produce a final good. Firms must pay a fixed cost each period for each variety they choose to import. Imported inputs affect firm productivity through two distinct channels: as in quality-ladder models they may have a higher price-adjusted quality, and as in product-variety models they imperfectly substitute domestic inputs. Because of these forces, firm productivity increases in the number of varieties imported. They estimate that importing all tradable inputs raises firm-level productivity by 22 per cent relative to not importing at all, about half of which is due to imperfect substitution between foreign and domestic inputs.

Multilateral Agreements Prevent Trade Wars

The canonical view of free trade agreements is that they provide reciprocal market access to countries participating in them (see Maggi, 2014 for a survey of theories of trade agreements). Theory provides three reasons why countries sign trade agreements. First, they want to internalize 'terms of trade externality'.

Binding trade agreements may stop trade partners from manipulating their terms of trade by restricting trade. Second, with imperfectly competitive industries, trade agreements also help stop a 'profit stealing externality'. Third, trade agreements may serve as a form of commitment guarding against lobbying of special interests.

Empirical work on trade agreements falls into two categories. There is reduced-form evidence on the effect of trade agreements on trade volumes and other economic outcomes (Subramanian and Wei, 2007, Liu, 2007, Dutt et al., 2013). The majority of papers (with the exception of Rose, 2004) finds positive association between trade agreements and trade flows, that is, trade flows increase after a trade agreement is signed.

A key challenge of these reduced-form studies is identification of causal effect. Countries signing trade agreements are also likely better integrated in other, unobserved ways. One way to get around this omitted variable bias is to use only the timing of trade agreements, and see how trade increases in the years following its implementation (Eicher and Henn, 2011).

A second group of studies try to identify the particular theoretical motivations behind why countries sign trade agreements. There is some supporting evidence for all three theories: terms-of-trade externalities (Broda et al., 2008, Ludema and Mayda, 2013, Bagwell and Staiger, 2011), profit-stealing externalities (Ossa, 2014) and domestic commitments (Handley and Limão, 2015, Handley, 2014).

While there are competing interpretations of how and why trade agreements work, one broad lesson is that without binding trade agreements, countries would be prone to occasional escalating trade wars. Ossa (2014) conducts counterfactual analysis with two scenarios. In the trade talks scenario, WTO members (modelled as seven countries and regions: Brazil, China, EU, India, Japan, US, and the rest of the world) come to an efficient agreement about further tariff reductions relative to the status quo in 2007. This would increase global welfare by $26 bn per year. In the trade wars scenario, members engage in escalated tariff wars. This would reduce global welfare by $340bn a year. Hence Ossa (2014) argues that the primary success of the WTO is preventing trade wars.

6.3.3   Open Questions

In this section we discuss the open questions of recent research in trade. These are questions in which the theories and the data are in apparent disconnect, in which competing theories disagree, or for which we lack compelling theories altogether.

How Big are the Redistributive Effects of Globalization?

Most models of the redistributive effects of globalization are way too stylized to be used for quantitative analysis. The usual approach posits two types of workers, skilled and unskilled and finds some empirical counterpart for these worker groups. In reality, there is a much larger heterogeneity of worker skills that needs to be captured in the model.

Capturing the large heterogeneity across firms has become quite standard after Melitz (2003) and Bernard et al. (2003) and many quantitative studies calibrate firm heterogeneity to the data when studying trade liberalization (Balistreri et al., 2011, Corcos et al., 2012, Breinlich and Cuñat, 2015). A similar approach at the worker level has been lacking.

Costinot and Vogel (2010) build a matching model of heterogeneous workers and sectors to study the evolution of inequality in various globalization scenarios. They work with a continuous distribution of worker skills, so they can study the changes along the entire wage distribution. Antras et al. (2015) also permit rich heterogeneity across economic agents.

Challenge 12 *Develop a toolbox for quantitative analysis of redistribution.*

What are the Side Effects of Globalization?

We have so far mostly discussed the pecuniary effects of globalization: how prices and incomes change, and who wins and who loses in terms of real income. The policy stance towards globalization, however, is often motivated by the presence of nonpecuniary externalities (Harrison and Rodríguez-Clare (2010)), what we colloquially term the '*side effects of globalization*'. Exposure to foreign trade and investment may bring about both positive and negative side effects. Below we discuss one example for each, namely productivity enhancements from knowledge spillovers, and environmental pollution. We note that, given the intense policy interest, this is a very active field which we anticipate will flourish in the future.

A body of literature documents the empirical connection between imported technology and productivity. For example, Coe and Helpman (1995) find that countries importing from R&D abundant trade partners are more productive (also see Coe et al., 1997 and Bayoumi et al., 1999), while Keller (2002), Keller and Yeaple (2009), and Acharya and Keller (2009) obtain similar findings at the industry level. Less is known, however, about the effects of technology imports on firm productivity. Firm-level evidence is useful because it can help isolate the effect of imported technology from other confounding factors such as investment or FDI, thus allowing us to identify the mechanism more directly.

Knowledge spillovers from multinationals to local suppliers are thought to be important for foreign knowledge to take hold in the host country (see Pack and Saggi, 2006 for a review of the case-study literature). There is, however, no consensus if and how these spillovers take place. Görg and Greenaway (2004) survey the evidence to date on spillovers from foreign investment, finding a mix of results with both positive and negative effects.

Arnold and Javorcik (2009) document that Indonesian firms taken over by multinationals improve their productivity after acquisition, which is suggestive of technology transfer from the parent company. Blalock and Gertler (2009) utilize the same dataset to show that firms, which do R&D themselves and employ skilled workers benefit more from FDI. Javorcik (2004) finds that multinationals entering Lithuania have a positive productivity effect on local firms in upstream sectors. In this study, buyer-supplier links are inferred from input–output tables (also see Bloom et al., 2013). Javorcik and Spatareanu (2009) use a survey in the Czech Republic to measure buyer-supplier links at the firm level, and also find positive effects. Guadalupe et al. (2012) show that Spanish subsidiaries innovate more after foreign acquisition.

Knowledge may also spill over to the host country via worker mobility. If the technological and organizational knowledge is not too specific to the firm, then a worker moving from a foreign-owned, foreign-managed, or import-intensive firm will also have a higher marginal product at the new firm. This can serve as an indirect channel through which domestic firms acquire foreign knowledge. Stoyanov and Zubanov (2012) find evidence in Danish data that workers moving from more productive firms tend to enhance the productivity of the host firm. Mion and Opromolla (2014) show that, in Portugal, managers leaving exporting firms take their exporting knowledge with them: the new host companies become more likely to export; they also reward the new managers for their export experience.

This body of literature, and further studies in this area, help both distinguish the particular channels of technology spillovers and identify the barriers of such spillovers.

Trade may also have negative side effects, for example via environmental pollution. It is a firmly established empirical relationship that environmental pollution depends on economic development in an inverted U-shape pattern ('*Environmental Kuznets Curve*' Grossman and Krueger, 1993). In the development process, pollution rises as the scale of activity increases, but above a certain income level the relationship reverses because the economy moves to more environmentally friendly technologies and sectors. Hence, to the extent that trade promotes economic growth, trade openness should eventually also contribute to better environmental quality.

International trade can also have direct effects on the environment, which may be negative or positive. A negative effect may occur if the global competitive pressure makes countries adopt looser environmental policies. In contrast, if globalization helps spread environmentally friendly technologies, rules and standards across the world, trade can lead to less pollution. An excellent review of the literature on trade, growth and the environment is provided in Ekins et al. in Chapter 7 of this volume.

An issue that received most attention recently is the distributional impact of globalization on pollution. Polluting activity is increasingly concentrated in some developing countries (*'pollution havens'*), and it is fleeing developed countries with stringent environmental regulation. An example is the so-called carbon leakage, when CO_2 emission targets lead firms to relocate from Kyoto countries. The consequence is the rise of pollution-embodying imports in the developed world, which has recently been documented in several empirical studies (Babiker, 2005, Kellenberg, 2009, Grether et al., 2010, Aichele and Felbermayr, 2015).

Challenge 13 *Understand and quantify the external effects of globalization.*

What are the Deep Causes of Cross-border Frictions?

The large estimates of cross-border frictions surveyed in Section 6.3.1 suggest that international transactions are hampered by more than transport costs. In fact, even after controlling for transport costs, crossing a country border is associated with a 44 per cent ad-valorem trade cost. Only 8 per cent of this is related to policy barriers (tariffs and quotas), the rest remain unexplained.

We need better theories and measurement of frictions that are neither a tax, nor a quota. One candidate is the limited access to information across border (Rauch (1999)).

Information Frictions

Allen (2014) builds a model of information frictions and trade, in which producers sequentially search for the best place to sell their product. Estimating the model on agricultural trade in the Philippines, he finds that about half of the price dispersion can be attributed to information frictions.

Chaney (2014) proposes a theory in which firms find new buyers via the network of their existing buyers. This assumption is motivated by the patterns of export market entry of French firms. The model predicts a relationship between international trade and distance, close to what we observe in the data.

There are also several empirical studies finding evidence for the qualitative conclusion that better access to information increases trade. The maintained assumption in many studies is that immigrants facilitate trade between their source and their host country. Rauch and Trindade (2002) exploit spatial variation in the number of Chinese immigrants, Cohen et al. (2012) use the placement of Japanese internment camps as a natural experiment, Felbermayr et al. (2010) extend the analysis to other ethnicities such as Polish and Mexican. The broad conclusion is that regions with a large share of immigrants trade more with their source country. More work is needed, however, on identifying the specific channels through which immigrant networks facilitate trade.

Local Infrastructure

Another recent strand of literature suggests that local transportation also matters for international trade and development. This has been documented for railroads in India (Donaldson, 2016) and the US (Donaldson and Hornbeck, 2016), roads in Peru (Volpe Martincus et al., 2017), Turkey (Cosar and Demir, 2016) and the US (Duranton et al., 2013), and bridges for Argentina and Uruguay (Volpe Martincus et al., 2014) and the US (Armenter et al., 2014). Felbermayr and Tarasov (2015) also show that there is underinvestment in transport infrastructure in the border regions of France.

Challenge 14 *Develop theories to better understand the deep causes of cross-border frictions.*

How Does Supply-chain Trade Differ from Traditional Trade?

An increasing share of international trade is in intermediates (see Hummels et al., 2001), owing to the increased international fragmentation of production. Companies break up their production process in smaller stages, and source from a larger number of suppliers both at home and abroad. The international trade associated with such production processes is termed '*supply-chain trade*'.

Baldwin (2006) and Baldwin and Lopez-Gonzalez (2014) describe the patterns of supply-chain trade across countries and over time. They use several measures of supply-chain trade, such as imported intermediate inputs, re-exports and re-imports and value added trade. They argue that supply-chain trade between technologically advanced and low-wage countries is a relatively recent phenomenon, taking off in the early 1990s. This is the '*second unbundling of globalization*', in which the technological and management expertise of developed countries is matched with cheap labour in developing ones (Baldwin, 2006).

Supply-chain trade tends to be very regional, potentially because the costs of coordinating production increase sharply with distance. There are regional production clusters around the US, within Europe, and, to a lesser extent, Japan. Data on re-exports and re-imports helps identify headquarter and production countries. Within Europe, Germany is clearly a headquarter economy, tightly linked with several low-wage EU members, but also with high-wage neighboring countries. Britain and France also act mostly as headquarters, the role of Italy is less clear.

Bernard et al. (2014a) study buyer–supplier links in data with a broad network coverage. Using data from a Japanese credit report agency, they show links are distributed across firms and over space. They build a model where firms choose the number of suppliers. More suppliers make the firm more productive, because they can use cheaper inputs (also see Eaton et al., 2013 for a similar model). Exploiting the spatial variation caused by a new high-speed rail line, they find that firms that could expand their supplier base have increased productivity and sales.

Understanding supply-chain trade better is important, because it has distinct implications for trade policy. Baldwin (2011) and Blanchard (2015) summarize the key policy challenges associated with supply-chain trade. First, there is a complementarity between liberalizing trade and liberalizing global production (foreign direct investment). When a multinational company invests in a host country, this raises the incentives of the source country to give preferential market access to the host country. Second, countries may opportunistically manipulate policies behind the border to shift rent from foreign investors. Some form of investor protection may be beneficial, but the current wave of bilateral and regional investment agreements may give excess powers to current technology leaders. Third, long supply chains magnify the effect of trade barriers, especially if regulations concerning international transactions are complex and not harmonized across countries.

Challenge 15 *Build a quantitative theory of supply-chain trade.*

What Do Multinational Firms Do?

Production can be shared internationally not only by shipping the final product, but also by carrying out (parts of) the production process abroad. The research on global production revolves around several key questions (Yeaple, 2013). Why do some firms open production facilities abroad? Where do these multinationals go? What determines whether firms source their inputs from independent suppliers, or whether they vertically integrate with their supplier?

A surprising fact is that most economic activity of multinationals is concentrated at their headquarters and regions close to the headquarter (Keller and Yeaple, 2013). Alfaro and Chen (2014) also find strong agglomeration of multinational plants. This is at odds with models of horizontal FDI, which would predict that multinational production is a way of getting around trade barriers, geographical or other. It is therefore important to understand what frictions multinationals are subject to.

Ramondo et al. (2013) study the trade flows between US multinationals and their foreign affiliates. Surprisingly, they find that the median affiliate does not sell to its parent. Across all affiliates, the average share of sales to the parent company is 7 per cent. This does not vary substantially with the degree of input–output linkages between the parent and the affiliate.

One limitation of the analysis is that the US is geographically isolated from most countries except Canada and Mexico, and supply-chain trade tends to be very regionalized (Baldwin and Lopez-Gonzalez, 2014). In this respect, it is not surprising that most US affiliates sell primarily to their host countries. However, the finding of Ramondo et al. (2013) is consistent with those of Atalay et al. (2014), who study domestic shipments of vertically integrated firms. They estimate an upper bound for the shipments from upstream plants to downstream plants within the same firm, and find this to be less than 0.1 per cent of all upstream sales for the median firm. They argue that firms share intangible assets among establishments.

Irarrazabal et al. (2013) estimate a model of multinational production in which the affiliates use an input provided by the parent company. Because of the above patterns in the movement of goods, it is best to think of these inputs as intangible inputs, yet they are subject to the same trade costs. Irarrazabal et al. (2013) estimate the share of these parental inputs in the production by matching the rate at which affiliate sales falls off with distance. They find that about 90 per cent of an affiliate's cost is spent on this parental input. The welfare implication of this is that multinational companies cannot jump trade barriers very effectively, since parental inputs are also subject to these barriers. That is, multinational production adds little welfare relative to trade.

Keller and Yeaple (2013) build a similar model of knowledge transfer within the multinational firm. Their model has the additional implication that affiliate sales should fall off with distance faster for knowledge-intensive goods. They confirm this and related predictions in the data.

We hence need a better understanding of what vertically integrated firms do, what supply chains are used for, and the potential interaction of these two questions.

Challenge 16 *Build a quantitative theory of multinationals.*

6.4 Conclusion

We surveyed the recent economics literature on international trade and global production. We identified four areas where further research would help policy-makers: gains from global production sharing, more quantitative analysis of the redistributive effects of globalization, a better understanding of cross-border frictions, and estimates of the side effects of trade. With the goal of providing a research agenda, we identified 16 specific challenges for measurement and theory, and look forward to future research on trade and globalization.

Acknowledgements

This survey has been funded by the European Union's Seventh Framework Programme (FP7/2007-2013) under the grant agreement no 320300 (COEURE).

Koren is also grateful for funding from the European Research Council Starting Grant no 313164 (KNOWLEDGEFLOWS). The views expressed are those of the author(s) and do not necessarily reflect the views of the European Commission. We thank Pinelopi Goldberg, Pascal Lamy, Jonathan Eaton, Russell Hillberry, Riina Kerner, Paola Conconi, Hylke Vandenbussche, Lothar Ehring, Marc Auboin, Lucian Cernat, Peter Egger, Beata Javorcik, Marcel Timmer, László Mátyás and participants at the COEURE workshop at the Universitè Libre de Bruxelles for helpful comments. We are grateful to Andrea Kiss for excellent research assistance.

Notes

1. Also see Egger and Kreickemeier (2009), Felbermayr et al. (2011), Amiti and Davis (2012) on trade, unemployment and wages.
2. In imperfectly competitive markets, the producer may be willing to swallow some of the trade costs by reducing its markup abroad. They would not charge higher markups abroad for fear of parallel imports.
3. See Anderson and van Wincoop (2003), Anderson and Van Wincoop (2004), Head and Mayer (2014), as well as Proost and Thisse (Chapters 8 and 9 of this volume).

References

Abowd, J. M., and Kramarz, F. 1999. The Analysis of Labor Markets Using Matched Employer-Employee data. Chapter 40 of: Orley C. Ashenfelter and David Card (ed), *Handbook of Labor Economics*, vol. Volume 3, Part B. Elsevier, pp. 2629–2710.

Acemoglu, D., Carvalho, V. M., Ozdaglar, A., and Tahbaz-Salehi, A. 2012. The Network Origins of Aggregate Fluctuations. *Econometrica*, **80**(5), 1977–2016.

Acharya, R. C., and Keller, W. 2009. Technology Transfer through Imports. *Canadian Journal of Economics/Revue canadienne d'économique*, **42**(4), 1411–1448.

Aichele, R., and Felbermayr, G. 2015. Kyoto and Carbon Leakage: An Empirical Analysis of the Carbon Content of Bilateral Trade. *Rev. Econ. Stat.*, **97**(1), 104–115.

Alessandria, G., Kaboski, J. P., and Midrigan, V. 2010. Inventories, Lumpy Trade, and Large Devaluations. *Am. Econ. Rev.*, **100**(5), 2304–2339.

Alfaro, L., and Chen, M. X. 2012. *Selection and Market Reallocation: Productivity Gains from Multinational Production!* Working Paper 18207. National Bureau of Economic Research.

Alfaro, L., and Chen, M. X. 2014. The Global Agglomeration of Multinational Firms. *J. Int. Econ.*, **94**(2), 263–276.

Allen, T. 2014. Information Frictions in Trade. *Econometrica*, **82**(6), 2041–2083.

Alvarez, F., Lucas, Jr., and Robert, E. 2007. General Equilibrium Analysis of the Eaton–Kortum Model of International Trade. *J. Monet. Econ.*, **54**(6), 1726–1768.

Amiti, M., and Davis, D. R. 2012. Trade, Firms, and Wages: Theory and Evidence. *Rev. Econ. Stud.*, **79**(1), 1–36.

Amiti, M., and Konings, J. 2007. Trade Liberalization, Intermediate Inputs, and Productivity: Evidence from Indonesia. *Am. Econ. Rev.*, **97**(5), 1611–1638.

Anderson, J. E., and van Wincoop, E. 2003. Gravity with Gravitas: A Solution to the Border Puzzle. *Am. Econ. Rev.*, **93**(1), 170–192.

Anderson, J. E., and Van Wincoop, E. 2004. Trade Costs. *J. Econ. Lit.*, **42**, 691–751.

Anderson, J. E., Milot, C. A., and Yotov, Y. V. 2014. How Much Does Geography Deflect Services Trade? Canadian Answers. *Int. Econ. Rev.*, **55**(3), 791–818.

Antràs, P., and Rossi-Hansberg, E. 2009. Organizations and Trade. *Annu. Rev. Econom.*, **1**(1), 43–64.

Antràs, P., Fort, T. C., and Tintelnot, F. 2014. *The Margins of Global Sourcing: Theory and Evidence from US Firms*. Tech. rept.

Antras, P., de Gortari, A., and Itskhoki, O. 2015. *Trade, Inequality and Costly Redistribution*. Tech. rept.

Arkolakis, C. 2010. Market Penetration Costs and the New Consumers Margin in International Trade. *J. Polit. Econ.*, **118**(6), 1151–1199.

Arkolakis, C., Costinot, A., and Rodríguez-Clare, A. 2012. New Trade Models, Same Old Gains? *Am. Econ. Rev.*, **102**(1), 94–130.

Arkolakis, C., Ramondo, N., Rodríguez-Clare, A., and Yeaple, S. 2013. *Innovation and Production in the Global Economy*. Working Paper 18972. National Bureau of Economic Research.

Armenter, R., and Koren, M. 2013. *Everything All the Time? Entry and Exit in US Import Varieties*. Tech. rept.

Armenter, R., and Koren, M. 2014. A Balls-and-Bins Model of Trade. *Am. Econ. Rev.*, **104**(7), 2127–2151.

Armenter, R., and Koren, M. 2015. Economies of Scale and the Size of Exporters. *J. Eur. Econ. Assoc.*, **13**(3), 482–511.

Armenter, R., Koren, M., and Nagy, D. K. 2014. *Bridges*. Tech. rept.

Arnold, J. M., and Javorcik, B. S. 2009. Gifted Kids or Pushy Parents? Foreign Direct Investment and Plant Productivity in Indonesia. *J. Int. Econ.*, **79**(1), 42–53.

Arnold, J. M., Javorcik, B. S., and Mattoo, A. 2011. Does Services Liberalization Benefit Manufacturing Firms?: Evidence from the Czech Republic. *J. Int. Econ.*, **85**(1), 136–146.

Arnold, J. M., Javorcik, B., Lipscomb, M., and Mattoo, A. 2016. *Services Reform and Manufacturing Performance: Evidence from India*. Economic Journal 126(590): 1–39.

Artuç, E., Chaudhuri, S., and McLaren, J. 2010. Trade Shocks and Labor Adjustment: A Structural Empirical Approach. *Am. Econ. Rev.*, **100**(3), 1008–1045.

Atalay, E., Hortaçsu, A., and Syverson, C. 2014. Vertical Integration and Input Flows. *Am. Econ. Rev.*, **104**(4), 1120–1148.

Babiker, M. H. 2005. Climate Change Policy, Market Structure, and Carbon Leakage. *J. Int. Econ.*, **65**(2), 421–445.

Bagwell, K., and Staiger, R. W. 2011. What Do Trade Negotiators Negotiate About? Empirical Evidence from the World Trade Organization. *Am. Econ. Rev.*, **101**(4), 1238–1273.

Balázsi, L., Mátyás, L., and Wansbeek, T. 2015. *The Estimation of Multi-dimensional Fixed Effects Panel Data Models*. Econometric Reviews, http://dx.doi.org/10.1080/07474938.2015.1032164.

Baldwin, R. 2006. *Globalisation: The Great Unbundling (s)*. Economic Council of Finland.

Baldwin, R., and Lopez-Gonzalez, J. 2014. Supply-chain Trade: A Portrait of Global Patterns and Several Testable Hypotheses. *The World Economy*, **38**(11), 1682–1721.

Baldwin, R. E. 2011. 21st Century Regionalism: Filling the Gap between 21st Century Trade and 20th Century Trade Rules. Staff Working Paper ERSD-2011-08. World Trade Organization.

Balistreri, E. J., Hillberry, R. H., and Rutherford, T. F. 2011. Structural Estimation and Solution of International Trade Models with Heterogeneous Firms. *J. Int. Econ.*, **83**(2), 95–108.

Baumgarten, D. 2013. Exporters and the Rise in Wage Inequality: Evidence from German Linked Employer–Employee Data. *J. Int. Econ.*, **90**(1), 201–217.

Bayoumi, T., Coe, D. T., and Helpman, E. 1999. R&D Spillovers and Global Growth. *J. Int. Econ.*, **47**(2), 399–428.

Bernard, A. B., and Jensen, J. B. 1999. Exceptional Exporter Performance: Cause, Effect, or Both? *J. Int. Econ.*, **47**(1), 1–25.

Bernard, A. B., Jensen, J. B., and Lawrence, R. Z. 1995. Exporters, Jobs, and Wages in US Manufacturing: 1976–1987. *Brookings Pap. Econ. Act.*, **1995**, 67–119.

Bernard, A. B., Eaton, J., Jensen, J. B., and Kortum, S. 2003. Plants and Productivity in International Trade. *Am. Econ. Rev.*, **93**(4), 1268–1290.

Bernard, A. B., Jensen, J. B., Redding, S. J., and Schott, P. K. 2007. Firms in International Trade. *J. Econ. Perspect.*, **21**(3), 105–130.

Bernard, A. B., Jensen, J. B., and Schott, P. K. 2009. Importers, Exporters and Multinationals: A Portrait of Firms in the US that Trade Goods. In: Timothy Dunne, J. Bradford Jensen, and Mark J. Roberts (ed), *Producer Dynamics: New Evidence from Micro Data*, pp. 513–552. nber.org.

Bernard, A. B., Blanchard, E., van Beveren, I., and Vandenbussche, H. 2012a (July). *Carry-Along Trade*. Tech. rept. 9067.

Bernard, A. B., van Beveren, I., and Vandenbussche, H. 2012b (Dec.). *Concording EU Trade and Production Data over Time*. Tech. rept. 9254.

Bernard, A. B., Jensen, J. B., Redding, S. J., and Schott, P. K. 2012c. The Empirics of Firm Heterogeneity and International Trade. *Annu. Rev. Econom.*, **4**(1), 283–313.

Bernard, A. B., Moxnes, A., and Saito, Y. U. 2014a. *Production Networks, Geography and Firm Performance*.

Bernard, A. B., Moxnes, A., and Ulltveit-Moe, K. H. 2014b. *Two-Sided Heterogeneity and Trade*. Tech. rept. 20136. NBER.

Berthou, A., Dhyne, E., Bugamelli, M., Cazacu, A.-M., Demian, C.-V., Harasztosi, P., Lalinsky, T., Meriküll, J., Oropallo, F., and Soares, A. C. 2015 (May). *Assessing European Firms' Exports and Productivity Distributions: The CompNet Trade Module*. Tech. rept. 282.

Blalock, G., and Gertler, P. J. 2009. How Firm Capabilities Affect Who Benefits from Foreign Technology. *J. Dev. Econ.*, **90**(2), 192–199.

Blanchard, E. J. 2015. A Shifting Mandate: International Ownership, Global Fragmentation, and a Case for Deeper Integration under the WTO. *World Trade Review*, **14**(01), 87–99.

Bloom, N., Schankerman, M., and Van Reenen, J. 2013. Identifying Technology Spillovers and Product Market Rivalry. *Econometrica*, **81**(4), 1347–1393.

Borchert, I., Mattoo, A., and Gootiiz, B. 2012a (1 June). *Guide to the Services Trade Restrictions Database*. Tech. rept. WPS6108. The World Bank.

Borchert, I., Mattoo, A., and Gootiiz, B. 2012b (1 June). *Policy Barriers to International Trade in Services: Evidence from a New Database.* Tech. rept. WPS6109. The World Bank.

Brainard, S. L. 1997. An Empirical Assessment of the Proximity-Concentration Trade-off between Multinational Sales and Trade. *Am. Econ. Rev.*, **87**(4), 520–544.

Breinlich, H., and Criscuolo, C. 2011. International Trade in Services: A Portrait of Importers and Exporters. *J. Int. Econ.*, **84**(2), 188–206.

Breinlich, H., and Cuñat, A. 2015. Tariffs, Trade and Productivity: A Quantitative Evaluation of Heterogeneous Firm Models. *The Economic Journal*, **126**(595), 1660–1702.

Broda, C., and Weinstein, D. E. 2006. Globalization and the Gains from Variety. *Q. J. Econ.*, **121**(2), 541–585.

Broda, C., Limao, N., and Weinstein, D. E. 2008. Optimal Tariffs and Market Power: The Evidence. *Am. Econ. Rev.*, **98**(5), 2032–2065.

Carballo, J., Ottaviano, G. I. P., and Martincus, C. V. 2013 (July). *The Buyer Margins of Firms' Exports.* Tech. rept. dp1234.

Cernat, L. 2016. Towards 'Trade Policy Analysis 2.0': From National Comparative Advantage to Firm-level Trade Data. In: Wignaraja, G. (ed.), *Production Networks and Enterprises in East Asia: Industry and Firm-level Analysis.* Springer Japan, Tokyo, pp 21–31.

Chaney, T. 2008. Distorted Gravity: The Intensive and Extensive Margins of International Trade. *Am. Econ. Rev.*, **98**(4), 1707–1721.

Chaney, T. 2014. The Network Structure of International Trade. *Am. Econ. Rev.*, **104**(11), 3600–3634.

Coe, D. T., and Helpman, E. 1995. International R&D Spillovers. *Eur. Econ. Rev.*, **39**(5), 859–887.

Coe, D. T., Helpman, E., and Hoffmaister, A. W. 1997. North-South R & D Spillovers. *Econ. J. Nepal*, **107**(440), 134–149.

Cohen, L., Gurun, U. G., and Malloy, C. J. 2012. *Resident Networks and Firm Trade.* Working Paper 18312. National Bureau of Economic Research.

Corcos, G., Del Gatto, M., Mion, G., and Ottaviano, G. I. P. 2012. Productivity and Firm Selection: Quantifying the New Gains from Trade. *Econ. J. Nepal*, **122**(561), 754–798.

Cosar, A. K., and Demir, B. 2016. Domestic Road Infrastructure and International Trade: Evidence from Turkey. *Journal of Development Economics*, **118**, 232–244.

Costinot, A., and Rodriguez-Clare, A. 2014. Trade Theory with Numbers: Quantifying the Consequences of Globalization. In: Elhanan Helpman, K. R., and Gopinath, G. (eds), *Handbook of International Economics*, vol. 4. Elsevier, pp. 197–261.

Costinot, A., and Vogel, J. 2010. Matching and Inequality in the World Economy. *J. Polit. Econ.*, **118**(4), 747–786.

Das, S., Roberts, M. J., and Tybout, J. R. 2007. Market Entry Costs, Producer Heterogeneity, and Export Dynamics. *Econometrica*, **75**(3), 837–873.

Davis, D. R., and Weinstein, D. E. 1999. Economic Geography and Regional Production Structure: An Empirical Investigation. *Eur. Econ. Rev.*, **43**(2), 379–407.

Dix-Carneiro, R. 2014. Trade Liberalization and Labor Market Dynamics. *Econometrica*, **82**(3), 825–885.

Dix-Carneiro, R., and Kovak, B. K. 2015. *Trade Reform and Regional Dynamics: Evidence from 25 years of Brazilian Matched Employer-Employee Data.* Working Paper 20908. National Bureau of Economic Research.

Dixit, A., and Norman, V. 1980. *Theory of International Trade: A Dual, General Equilibrium Approach.* Cambridge University Press.

Djankov, S., Freund, C., and Pham, C. S. 2010. Trading on Time. *Rev. Econ. Stat.,* **92**(1), 166–173.

Donaldson, D. 2016. Railroads of the Raj: Estimating the Impact of Transportation Infrastructure. *American Economic Review,* forthcoming.

Donaldson, D., and Hornbeck, R. 2016. Railroads and American Economic Growth: A 'Market Access' Approach. *Quarterly Journal of Economics,* forthcoming.

Duranton, G., Morrow, P. M., and Turner, M. A. 2013. Roads and Trade: Evidence from the US. *Rev. Econ. Stud.,* 6 Nov.

Dutt, P., Mihov, I., and Van Zandt, T. 2013. The Effect of WTO on the Extensive and the Intensive Margins of Trade. *Journal of International Economics,* **91**(2), 204–219.

Eaton, J., and Kortum, S. 2002. Technology, Geography, and Trade. *Econometrica,* **70**(5), 1741–1779.

Eaton, J., Kortum, S. S., and Sotelo, S. 2012. *International Trade: Linking Micro and Macro.* Working Paper 17864. National Bureau of Economic Research.

Eaton, J., Kortum, S., Kramarz, F., and Sampognaro, R. 2013. *Firm-to-Firm Trade: Imports, Exports, and the Labor Market.* Tech. rept.

Egger, H., and Kreickemeier, U. 2009. Firm Heterogeneity and the Labor Market Effects of Trade Liberalization*. *Int. Econ. Rev.,* **50**(1), 187–216.

Eicher, T. S., and Henn, C. 2011. In Search of WTO Trade Effects: Preferential Trade Agreements promote Trade Strongly, but Unevenly. *J. Int. Econ.,* **83**(2), 137–153.

Ekins, P., Drummond, P., and Watson, J. 2017. Economic Approaches to Energy, Environment and Sustainability. Chapter 7 in this volume.

Eurostat. 2011. *European Statistics Code of Practice.* Tech. rept.

Federico, S., and Tosti, E. 2012 (24 Oct.). *Exporters and Importers of Services: Firm-Level Evidence on Italy.* Tech. rept. 877. Banca d'Italia.

Feinberg, S. E., and Keane, M. P. 2001. U.S.-Canada Trade Liberalization And MNC Production Location. *Rev. Econ. Stat.,* **83**(1), 118–132.

Felbermayr, G., Prat, J., and Schmerer, H.-J. 2011. Globalization and Labor Market Outcomes: Wage Bargaining, Search Frictions, and Firm Heterogeneity. *J. Econ. Theory,* **146**(1), 39–73.

Felbermayr, G. J., and Tarasov, A. 2015. Trade and the Spatial Distribution of Transport Infrastructure. *sbb-lab.idt.unisg.ch.*

Felbermayr, G. J., Jung, B., and Toubal, F. 2010. Ethnic Networks, Information, and International Trade: Revisiting the Evidence. *Ann. Econ. Stat.,* 1 Jan., 41–70.

Feyrer, J. 2009a (Dec.). *Distance, Trade, and Income – The 1967 to 1975 Closing of the Suez Canal as a Natural Experiment.* Working Paper 15557.

Feyrer, J. 2009b (Apr.). *Trade and Income – Exploiting Time Series in Geography.* Working Paper 14910.

Francois, J., and Hoekman, B. 2010. Services Trade and Policy. *J. Econ. Lit.,* **48**(3), 642–692.

Francois, J., Pindyuk, O., and Woerz, J. 2009 (Aug.). *Trends in International Trade and FDI in Services: A Global Database of Services Trade*. Tech. rept. 20090802.

Frias, J. A., Kaplan, D. S., and Verhoogen, E. 2012. Exports and Within-Plant Wage Distributions: Evidence from Mexico. *Am. Econ. Rev.*, **102**(3), 435–440.

Goh, C.-C., and Javorcik, B. S. 2007. Trade Protection and Industry Wage Structure in Poland. In: *Globalization and Poverty*. University of Chicago Press, pp. 337–372.

Goldberg, P. K., and Pavcnik, N. 2007a. Distributional Effects of Globalization in Developing Countries. *J. Econ. Lit.*, **45**(1), 39–82.

Goldberg, P. K., and Pavcnik, N. 2007b. The Effects of the Colombian Trade Liberalization on Urban Poverty. In: *Globalization and Poverty*. University of Chicago Press, pp. 241–290.

Gopinath, G., and Neiman, B. 2014. Trade Adjustment and Productivity in Large Crises. *American Economic Review*, **104**(3), 793–831.

Gopinath, G., Helpman, E., and Rogoff, K. (eds). 2014. *Handbook of International Economics, Volume 4*. Elsevier.

Görg, H., and Greenaway, D. 2004. Much Ado about Nothing? Do Domestic Firms Really Benefit from Foreign Direct Investment? *World Bank Res. Obs.*, **19**(2), 171–197.

Grether, J.-M., Mathys, N. A., and De Melo, J. 2010. Global Manufacturing SO2 Emissions: Does Trade Matter? *Review of World Economics*, **145**(4), 713–729.

Grossman, G. M., and Krueger, A. B. 1993. Environmental Impacts of a North American Free Trade Agreement. In: Garber, P. M. (ed), *Mexican-U.S. Free Trade Agreement*. MIT Press, pp. 13–56.

Grossman, G. M., and Rossi-Hansberg, E. 2008. Trading Tasks: A Simple Theory of Offshoring. *Am. Econ. Rev.*, **98**(5), 1978–1997.

Guadalupe, M., Kuzmina, O., and Thomas, C. 2012. Innovation and Foreign Ownership. *Am. Econ. Rev.*, **102**(7), 3594–3627.

Halpern, L., Koren, M., and Szeidl, A. 2015. Imported Inputs and Productivity. *American Economic Review*, **105**(12).

Handley, K. 2014. Exporting under Trade Policy Uncertainty: Theory and Evidence. *J. Int. Econ.*, **94**(1), 50–66.

Handley, K., and Limão, N. 2015. Trade and Investment under Policy Uncertainty: Theory and Firm Evidence. *American Economic Journal: Economic Policy*, **7**(4), 189–222.

Hanson, G. H. 2007. Globalization, Labor Income, and Poverty in Mexico. In: *Globalization and Poverty*. University of Chicago Press, pp. 417–456.

Hanson, G. H., and Xiang, C. 2004. The Home-Market Effect and Bilateral Trade Patterns. *Am. Econ. Rev.*, **94**(4), 1108–1129.

Hanson, G. H., Mataloni, R. J., and Slaughter, M. J. 2005. Vertical Production Networks in Multinational Firms. *Rev. Econ. Stat.*, **87**(4), 664–678.

Harrigan, J., and Venables, A. J. 2006. Timeliness and Agglomeration. *J. Urban Econ.*, **59**(2), 300–316.

Harrison, A. 2007. Globalization and Poverty: An Introduction. In: *Globalization and Poverty*. University of Chicago Press, pp. 1–32.

Harrison, A., and Rodríguez-Clare, A. 2010. Trade, Foreign Investment, and Industrial Policy for Developing Countries. *Handbook of Development Economics*, **5**, 4039–4214.

Head, K., and Mayer, T. 2004. Market Potential and the Location of Japanese Investment in the European Union. *Rev. Econ. Stat.*, **86**(4), 959–972.

Head, K., and Mayer, T. 2014. Gravity Equations: Workhorse, Toolkit, and Cookbook. In: Gopinath, Gita, Elhanan Helpman, and Kenneth Rogoff (ed), *Handbook of International Economics*, vol. 4. Elsevier, pp. 131–195.

Head, K., and Ries, J. 2001. Increasing Returns versus National Product Differentiation as an Explanation for the Pattern of U.S.-Canada Trade. *Am. Econ. Rev.*, **91**(4), 858–876.

Helpman, E., and Itskhoki, O. 2010. Labour Market Rigidities, Trade and Unemployment. *Rev. Econ. Stud.*, **77**(3), 1100–1137.

Helpman, E., Melitz, M., and Rubinstein, Y. 2008a. Estimating Trade Flows: Trading Partners and Trading Volumes. *Q. J. Econ.*, **123**(2), 441–487.

Helpman, E., Marin, D., and Verdier, T. (eds). 2008b. *The Organization of Firms in a Global Economy*. Harvard University Press.

Helpman, E., Itskhoki, O., and Redding, S. 2010. Inequality and Unemployment in a Global Economy. *Econometrica*, **78**(4), 1239–1283.

Helpman, E., Itskhoki, O., Muendler, M.-A., and Redding, S. J. 2016. Trade and Inequality: From Theory to Estimation. *Review of Economic Studies (forthcoming)*

Hoekman, B., and Mattoo, A. 2013. Liberalizing Trade in Services: Lessons from Regional and WTO Negotiations. *International Negotiation*, **18**(1), 131–151.

Hoekman, B. M., and Javorcik, B. K. S. 2006. *Global Integration and Technology Transfer*. World Bank Publications.

Hornok, C. 2012. *Need for Speed: Is Faster Trade in the EU Trade-creating?* Tech. rept. 4. MNB Working Papers.

Hornok, C., and Koren, M. 2015a. Administrative Barriers to Trade. *J. Int. Econ.*, **96, Supplement 1**(0), S110–S122.

Hornok, C., and Koren, M. 2015b. Per-Shipment Costs and the Lumpiness of International Trade. *Rev. Econ. Stat.*, **97**(2), 525–530.

Hummels, D., and Skiba, A. 2004. Shipping the Good Apples Out? An Empirical Confirmation of the Alchian-Allen Conjecture. *J. Polit. Econ.*, **112**(6), 1384–1402.

Hummels, D., Ishii, J., and Yi, K.-M. 2001. The Nature and Growth of Vertical Specialization in World Trade. *J. Int. Econ.*, **54**(1), 75–96.

Hummels, D., Jørgensen, R., Munch, J., and Xiang, C. 2014. The Wage Effects of Offshoring: Evidence from Danish Matched Worker-Firm Data. *Am. Econ. Rev.*, **104**(6), 1597–1629.

Hummels, D. L., and Schaur, G. 2013. Time as a Trade Barrier. *Am. Econ. Rev.*, **103**(7), 2935–2959.

Irarrazabal, A., Moxnes, A., and Opromolla, L. D. 2013. The Margins of Multinational Production and the Role of Intrafirm Trade. *J. Polit. Econ.*, **121**(1), 74–126.

Irarrazabal, A., Moxnes, A., and Opromolla, L. D. 2015. The Tip of the Iceberg: A Quantitative Framework for Estimating Trade Costs. *The Review of Economics and Statistics*, **97**(4), 777–792.

Javorcik, B. S. 2004. Does Foreign Direct Investment Increase the Productivity of Domestic Firms? In Search of Spillovers through Backward Linkages. *Am. Econ. Rev.*, **94**(3), 605–627.

Javorcik, B. S., and Spatareanu, M. 2009. Tough Love: Do Czech Suppliers Learn from their Relationships with Multinationals?. *Scand. J. Econ.*, **111**(4), 811–833.

Johnson, R. C. 2014. Five Facts about Value-Added Exports and Implications for Macroeconomics and Trade Research. *J. Econ. Perspect.*, **28**(2), 119–142.

Kasahara, H., and Rodrigue, J. 2008. Does the Use of Imported Intermediates Increase Productivity? Plant-level Evidence. *J. Dev. Econ.*, **87**(1), 106–118.

Kelle, M., Kleinert, J., Raff, H., and Toubal, F. 2013. Cross-border and Foreign Affiliate Sales of Services: Evidence from German Microdata. *The World Economy*, **36**(11), 1373–1392.

Kellenberg, D. K. 2009. An Empirical Investigation of the Pollution Haven Effect with Strategic Environment and Trade Policy. *J. Int. Econ.*, **78**(2), 242–255.

Keller, W. 2002. Trade and the Transmission of Technology. *J. Econ. Growth*, **7**(1), 5–24.

Keller, W., and Yeaple, S. 2009. Multinational Enterprises, International Trade, and Technology Diffusion: A Firm-level Analysis of the Productivity Effects of Foreign Competition in the United States. *Rev. Econ. Stat.*, **91**(4), 821–831.

Keller, W., and Yeaple, S. R. 2013. The Gravity of Knowledge. *Am. Econ. Rev.*, **103**(4), 1414–1444.

Koren, M., and Csillag, M. 2011. *Machines and Machinists: Capital-skill Complementarity from an International Trade Perspective*. Tech. rept. CEPR.

Krishna, P., Poole, J. P., and Senses, M. Z. 2011. Trade Liberalization, Firm Heterogeneity, and Wages: New Evidence from Matched Employer-Employee Data. *World Bank Policy Research*, 30 June.

Kropf, A., and Sauré, P. 2014. Fixed Costs per Shipment. *J. Int. Econ.*, **92**(1), 166–184.

Krugman, P. 1980. Scale Economies, Product Differentiation, and the Pattern of Trade. *Am. Econ. Rev.*, **70**(5), 950–959.

Krugman, P. R. 1979. Increasing Returns, Monopolistic Competition, and International Trade. *J. Int. Econ.*, **9**(4), 469–479.

Lipponer, A. 2006. Microdatabase Direct Investment-MiDi. A Brief Guide. *Economic Research Centre, Deutsche Bundesbank, mimeo.*

Liu, T. 2007. The Impact of Regional Trade Agreements on Trade: The Case of China. *The Chinese Economy*, **40**(2), 70–96.

Lopez-Garcia, P., di Mauro, F., Benatti, N., Angeloni, C., Altomonte, C., Bugamelli, M., DAurizio, L., Navaretti, G. B., Forlani, E., Rossetti, S., Zurlo, D., Berthou, A., Sandoz-Dit-Bragard, C., Dhyne, E., Amador, J. a., Opromolla, L. D., Soares, A. C., Chiriacescu, B., Cazacu, A.-M., Lalinsky, T., Biewen, E., Blank, S., Meinen, P., Hagemejer, J., Tello, P., Rodriguez-Caloca, A., Cede, U., Galuscak, K., Merikyll, J., and Harasztosi, P. 2014 (Feb.). *Micro-based Evidence of EU Competitiveness: the CompNet Database*. Tech. rept. 1634.

Ludema, R. D., and Mayda, A. M. 2013. Do Terms-of-trade Effects Matter for Trade Agreements? Theory and Evidence from WTO Countries. *The Quarterly Journal of Economics*, **128**(4), 1837–1893.

Maggi, G. 2014. International Trade Agreements. In: Gopinath, G., Helpman, E., and Rogoff, K. (eds), *Handbook of International Economics, Volume 4*. Amsterdam: Elsevier.

Mátyás, L., Hornok, C., and Pus, D. 2012 (17 Feb.). *The Formulation and Estimation of Random Effects Panel Data Models of Trade*. Tech. rept. 36789. MPRA.

Mátyás, L., Hornok, C., and Pus, D. 2013 (25 Mar.). *The Formulation and Estimation of Random Effects Panel Data Models of Trade*. Tech. rept. 2012_1.

Mayer, T., and Ottaviano, G. I. P. 2007. *The Happy Few: The Internationalisation of European Firms*. Bruegel, Brussels.

Melitz, M. J. 2003. The Impact of Trade on Intra-industry Reallocations and Aggregate Industry Productivity. *Econometrica*, **71**(6), 1695–1725.

Melitz, M. J., and Ottaviano, G. I. P. 2008. Market Size, Trade, and Productivity. *Rev. Econ. Stud.*, **75**(1), 295–316.

Melitz, M. J., and Redding, S. J. 2014. New Trade Models, New Welfare Implications. *American Economic Review*, Aug.

Melitz, M. J., and Trefler, D. 2012. Gains from Trade when Firms Matter. *J. Econ. Perspect.*, **26**(2), 91–118.

Mion, G., and Opromolla, L. D. 2014. Managers' Mobility, Trade Performance, and Wages. *J. Int. Econ.*, **94**(1), 85–101.

Muendler, M.-A. 2004. Trade, Technology and Productivity: A Study of Brazilian Manufacturers 1986–1998. Unpublished.

Navaretti, G. B., Bugamelli, M., Schivardi, F., Altomonte, C., Horgos, D., and Maggioni, D. 2011. The Global Operations of European Firms – The Second EFIGE Policy Report. *Blueprints*.

OECD. 2015. *Services Trade Restrictiveness Index*. http://oecd.org/tad/services-trade/services-trade-restrictiveness-index.htm. Accessed: 2015-6-4.

Ohlin, B. 1924. The Trade Theory. In: Flam, Harry and Flanders, M. June (eds), *Heckscher-Ohlin Trade Theory*, MIT Press, 82–213.

O'Rourke, K. H., and Williamson, J. G. 1999. *Globalization and History*, MIT Press.

Ossa, R. 2015. Why Trade Matters After All. *Journal of International Economics*, **97**(2), 266–277.

Ossa, R. 2014. Trade Wars and Trade Talks with Data. *American Economic Review*, **104**(12), 4104–46.

Pack, H., and Saggi, K. 2006. Is There a Case for Industrial Policy? A Critical Survey. *World Bank Res. Obs.*, **21**(2), 267–297.

Pavcnik, N. 2002. Trade Liberalization, Exit, and Productivity Improvements: Evidence from Chilean Plants. *Rev. Econ. Stud.*, **69**(1), 245–276.

Proost, S., and Thisse, J.-F. 2017. Regional Disparities and Efficient Transport Policies (Chapter 8 of this volume); Skilled Cities and Efficient Urban Transport (Chapter 9 of this volume).

Ramondo, N., Rappoport, V., and Ruhl, K. J. 2013. Horizontal versus Vertical Foreign Direct Investment: Evidence from US Multinationals. *UC San Diego Typescript Manuscript*.

Rauch, J. E. 1999. Networks versus Markets in International Trade. *J. Int. Econ.*, **48**(1), 7–35.

Rauch, J. E. 2001. Business and Social Networks in International Trade. *J. Econ. Lit.*, **39**(4), 1177–1203.

Rauch, J. E., and Trindade, V. 2002. Ethnic Chinese Networks in International Trade. *Rev. Econ. Stat.*, **84**(1), 116–130.

Rose, A. K. 2004. Do We Really Know That the WTO Increases Trade? *Am. Econ. Rev.*, **94**(1), 98–114.

Samuelson, P. A. 1954. The Transfer Problem and Transport Costs, II: Analysis of Effects of Trade Impediments. *The Econ. Journal*, **64**(254), 264–289.

Schank, T., Schnabel, C., and Wagner, J. 2007. Do Exporters Really Pay Higher Wages? First Evidence from German Linked Employer–Employee Data. *J. Int. Econ.*, **72**(1), 52–74.

Schor, A. 2004. Heterogeneous Productivity Response to Tariff Reduction. Evidence from Brazilian Manufacturing Firms. *J. Dev. Econ.*, **75**(2), 373–396.

Stehrer, R., de Vries, G. J., Los, B., Dietzenbacher, H. W. A., and Timmer, M. 2014. *The World Input-Output Database: Content, Concepts and Applications*. Tech. rept. GD-144.

Stolper, W. F., and Samuelson, P. A. 1941. Protection and Real Wages. *Rev. Econ. Stud.*, **9**(1), 58–73.

Stoyanov, A., and Zubanov, N. 2012. Productivity Spillovers across Firms through Worker Mobility. *Am. Econ. J. Appl. Econ.*, **4**(2), 168–198.

Subramanian, A., and Wei, S.-J. 2007. The WTO Promotes Trade, Strongly but Unevenly. *J. Int. Econ.*, **72**(1), 151–175.

Temouri, Y., Vogel, A., and Wagner, J. 2013. Self-selection into Export Markets by Business Services Firms: Evidence from France, Germany and the United Kingdom. *Structural Change and Economic Dynamics*, Vol. 25, pp. 146–158.

Timmer, M. P., Los, B., Stehrer, R., and Vries, G. J. 2013. Fragmentation, Incomes and Jobs: An Analysis of European Competitiveness. *Econ. Policy*, **28**(76), 613–661.

Tintelnot, F. 2016. Global Production with Export Platforms. *The Quarterly Journal of Economics (forthcoming)*

Topalova, P. 2007. Trade Liberalization, Poverty and Inequality: Evidence from Indian Districts. In: *Globalization and Poverty*. University of Chicago Press, pp. 291–336.

Topalova, P., and Khandelwal, A. 2011. Trade Liberalization and Firm Productivity: The Case of India. *Rev. Econ. Stat.*, **93**(3), 995–1009.

Volpe Martincus, C., Carballo, J., and Cusolito, A. 2017 (March). Routes, Exports, and Employment: Evidence from a Developing Country. *Journal of Development Economics*, Vol. 125, pp. 21–39.

Volpe Martincus, C., Carballo, J., Garcia, P. M., and Graziano, A. 2014. How Do Transport Costs Affect Firms Exports? Evidence from a Vanishing Bridge. *Econ. Lett.*, **123**(2), 149–153.

Wagner, J. 2012. International Trade and Firm Performance: A Survey of Empirical Studies since 2006. *Rev World Econ*, **148**(2), 235–267.

World Bank. 2015. *Services Trade Dataset*. http://iresearch.worldbank.org/servicetrade/. Accessed: 2015-6-4.

Yeaple, S. R. 2013. The Multinational Firm. *Annu. Rev. Econom.*, **5**(1), 193–217.

7 Economic Approaches to Energy, Environment and Sustainability

Paul Ekins, Paul Drummond and Jim Watson

Abstract

We first present an overview of different conceptual views of the relationship between the economy and the environment, and on the 'sustainability' of the interaction between them, and how this may be measured. We then discuss the components of the '*Energy Trilemma*'; energy security, decarbonization, and energy access and affordability, before examining the policies required for advancing a green, low-carbon economy – including lessons from and priority research areas surrounding EU climate policy. Issues relating to the science-policy 'interface' are then presented, before priorities for research on energy, the environment and sustainability are summarized.

7.1 Introduction

The intertwined topics of energy, environment and sustainability have, perhaps, more than other topics, been treated from a variety of economic perspectives, and in an interdisciplinary way that is outside economics altogether. The structure of this chapter is as follows. Section 7.2 first outlines the different schools of economic thought that influence the way in which the economy, natural resources and the environment are conceptualized and are seen to influence each other. Section 7.3 then explores how these economic approaches have been applied to fashion the core concepts in contemporary environmental and development discourse, of sustainable development, and the distinct but related idea of sustainability. This then leads to considerations of principles of environmental sustainability and, more broadly, of the many different measures that have been applied to assess progress or otherwise towards sustainable development. Section 7.4 focuses on the issues and future requirements concerning the energy system and climate change mitigation, particularly through the lens of the '*energy trilemma*'. Section 7.5 then discusses the policies required to achieve these requirements, and for a broader '*green economy*'. Section 7.6 assesses the interface and interaction between scientific analysis of the issues, and practitioners, policy and policy-makers. Section 7.7 concludes, and summarizes priorities for research in the field.

7.2   Economic Approaches to the Environment

In any general overview of economic literature it is hard to avoid the conclusion that the economics of natural resources and the environment is usually regarded as a relatively unimportant topic. For example, the book by Canterbery (2011), entitled a *Brief History of Economics*, has no entry in the Index for 'resources', 'natural resources', or 'environment', although as Hueting (1980) recognized, natural resources and the environment, and the ecosystem goods and services they produce are scarce goods, they are subject to competition, and they contribute to human welfare. As such, they fall squarely within Robbins's (1935) definition of economics. The two principal schools of economic thought regarding natural resources and the environment (concerning both natural resources and pollution) are *'environmental and resource'* economics and *'ecological'* economics.

7.2.1   Environmental and Resource Economics

Environmental and resource economics broadly adopts the worldview of mainstream neoclassical economics, and considers environmental concerns an aspect of broader economic issues to which the approaches of methodological individualism (general equilibrium models), rationality, marginalism and efficiency may be suitably applied. In this view the focus of economic analysis is overwhelmingly on the economy depicted as a flow of money between firms, households and government. When the environment is considered at all, it is in terms of 'externalities', the phenomenon whereby a third party is affected positively or negatively by the economic activities of others. The most common example of a negative environmental externality is pollution of air, water or land, which affects others who are not part of the economic activity or transaction that created it. The term 'externality' conveys the fact that the impact on the environment is often external to the market or other economic activity that created it, and as a result is not included in the prices of, and is therefore not taken account of in, the relevant transaction or any calculus of the activity's social benefit. Such externalities are characterized as a market failure and the standard environmental economic prescription for the correction of a negative environmental externality is the levying of a *'Pigouvian tax'* at the rate equal to the marginal social cost of the externality at the point where this equals the marginal social benefit of the activity causing it. This prescription indicates a key characteristic and dominant method of welfare analysis applied in environmental and resource economics, namely the conversion of all impacts from the economy, market transactions and externalities, into monetary values so an economic optimum can be computed in a social cost benefit analysis. This analytic method derives from an assumption of 'weak' sustainability, which purports that different forms of capital (discussed in Section 7.3.2) are (often fully) substitutable. Methods for nonmarket valuation of externalities, including key issues raised by such approaches, are also discussed in Section 7.3.2.

7.2.2   Ecological Economics

In contrast to environmental and resource economics, ecological economics considers the human economy as a component of the global ecosystem, and employs '*methodological pluralism*' to assess different aspects of what proponents view as a highly complex, multifaceted human-economy-environment interaction (Venkatachalam, 2007). Ecological economics considers the human economy as subject to the laws of thermodynamics, extracting high-grade energy, materials and ecosystem services from the natural environment, and discharging low-grade energy and wastes back into it, with consequent degradation of the ecosystems that produce the services. As such, as economic activity expands, so too does the throughput of energy and materials (the *physical growth* of the economy). Broadly, ecological economics represents the idea of 'strong' sustainability (discussed in Section 7.3.2), which purports that different forms of capital are not fully (or even widely) substitutable. Another key difference between environmental and ecological economics is their view of human motivation and behaviour. Implicit in much of the environmental economics worldview and literature is the assumption of rational, self-interested, utilitarian behaviour (*homo economicus*), whilst ecological economics largely rejects this model and leans towards the assumption of co-operative actors capable of being motivated by improving their environment (*homo reciprocans*) (Jansen and Jager, 2000). The institutional, evolutionary and behavioural schools of economic thought, discussed in Section 7.2.3, concur with this rejection.

Over time, these different views have matured into 'a new substantive research agenda, straddling resource, environmental and ecological economics', that needs to be tackled in 'a pluralistic and multidisciplinary spirit of tolerance' (Turner, 2002, p. 1003). The agenda included 'questions about sustainability and the substitutability of different forms of capital, including natural capital; macro-environmental scale and thermodynamic limits in source and sink terms; future technological and other changes, together with the problems of novelty and "surprise"; ecosystem resilience, thresholds and chaos'. Other issues were 'more fundamentally contentious', and included 'value systems, philosophy and ethics and related policy prescriptions' (Turner, 2002, p. 1003). Many of these issues are discussed further in the sections that follow.

7.2.3 Institutional, Evolutionary, and Behavioural Economics

These three schools of economics are included here because each is relevant to ongoing efforts to understand how humans interact with the natural environment through the economy, and how these interactions change over time. Each also challenges the core tenets of neoclassical economics, including assumptions of rational, welfare-maximizing behaviour by all economic agents (individuals and firms) according to exogenous preferences, the absence of chronic information problems, complexity and limits to cognitive capacity, and a theoretical focus on movements towards or attained equilibrium states of rest (Hodgson, 1988, p. xviii).

Institutional economics emphasizes the importance of institutions to economic action. Hodgson described economic institutions as 'complexes of habits, roles and conventional behaviour' (Hodgson, 1988, p. 140), whilst John Commons, another early father of institutional economics, conceived of them as 'embodying collective action' (Rutherford, 1983, p. 722), and 'including the state, political parties, courts, unions, firms, churches, and the like . . . [with their] rules, regulations, customs, common practices and laws that regulate the actions of individuals and concerns' (Rutherford, 1983, p. 723). Many institutional economists have paid little attention to the natural environment, and even (Hodgson, 1988, Figure 1.2, p. 16) considers it outside 'the projected domain of institutional economic theory', although many have applied this school of thought to resources and the environment (a recent example of which is Bromley, 2014). Although the terms 'institutional' and 'evolutionary' economics are often used interchangeably, the more ecologically aware version of the latter conceives development as a co-evolutionary process between five dimensions of economic and ecological systems: values, knowledge, organization, technology, and the environment (Norgaard, 2010). Furthermore, many evolutionary economists have focused in particular on the important role of technical change and innovation in markets and in broader long-run changes in economies (e.g., Freeman (1992)).

Behavioural economics focuses on the behaviour of individuals, rather than the nature of the institutions that influence or constrain them. An extensive behavioural economics literature concludes that human behaviour is highly complex, and exhibits characteristics of both *homo economicus* and *homo reciprocans*, espoused by environmental/resource and ecological economics, respectively (Gsottbauer and van den Bergh, 2011). Glasser (2002) explores a number of moral considerations and other factors that can result in actual human behaviour departing from the narrow self-interested and static assumptions of much neoclassical consumer theory. Moreover, people have often been observed to seek equitable outcomes where self-interest would produce higher rewards (Fehr and Schmidt, 1999). While this evidence runs counter to the basic *homo economicus* model, other evidence suggests that the *homo recipro-cans* model is unlikely to be broadly applicable either. For example, Dohmen et al. (2006) suggest that cooperation, even when it produces short-term costs to those engaging in it, may be in their long-term self-interest under certain conditions. An ongoing subject for further research is how to integrate such complex behavioural issues into economic-environmental models (An, 2012). Other behavioural economics literature that departs from neoclassical assumptions regarding individual behaviour concern *'satisficing'* and *'bounded'* rationality (where decisions are constrained by cognitive processes and available information), the presence of hyperbolic or *'present-biased'* rather than exponential discount rates (Venkatachalam, 2007), and the practice of *'mental accounting'* (which suggests that the substitution functions between different environmental goods and services is not smooth) (Knetsch, 2005). Additionally, the experiments reported in Kahneman et al. (1982) suggest that under uncertainty people look to heuristics and norms based on notions such as anchoring, availability and representativeness to guide their decisions, and further investigation established that these norms can acquire moral connotations associated with judgements about 'fairness' (Kahneman et al., 1986).

7.3   Sustainability and Sustainable Development

It is common in the literature to see the concepts of 'sustainable development' and 'sustainability' used interchangeably. However the distinction between these two concepts has been developed in some detail in Ekins (2011), and is briefly described in this section. Linguistically, the idea of 'sustainability' denotes the capacity for continuance into the future, and immediately begs the question – continuance of what? That question has a number of answers in the context of the sustainability literature, three of which are sustainability of the environment (environmental sustainability), sustainability of the economy (economic sustainability) and the sustainability of society (social sustainability). The over-arching concept that contains these three ideas is sustainable development; development that has the capacity of continuing into the future.

7.3.1   Sustainable Development

Definitions
Since it was first brought to prominence by the Brundtland Report (World Commission on Environment and Development, WCED, 1987), the concept of sustainable development has achieved and maintained a high international profile. Most recently, in September 2015, the United Nations General Assembly convened to adopt a broad range of Sustainable Development Goals (SDGs), to replace the Millennium Development Goals (MDGs) adopted in 2000. The

unanimity of support for sustainable development may give the misleading impression that its meaning and implications are clear. In fact, as early as 1989, Pearce et al. (1989) were able to cite a 'gallery of definitions', and although absolute clarity of meaning remains lacking, progress has been made. For example, (Jacobs 1999, p. 25) lists six ideas that are fundamental to sustainable development: environment-economy integration, futurity, environmental protection, equity, quality of life, and participation. These concepts are repeated in all of the more extended definitions of sustainable development, including that in the Brundtland Report ('Sustainable development is development that meets the needs of the present without compromising the ability of future generations to meet their own needs', WCED, 1987, p. 7), which clearly encompasses the first four of the six points above.

However, the scope for controversy increases markedly with attempts to move beyond such definitions, to identify policy objectives. For example, given that 'quality of life' contains many different dimensions, what is the balance to be struck between them in situations where they conflict? And are environmental objectives really compatible with aspirations for indefinite economic growth, to which all countries remain absolutely committed? And, intergenerationally, what is the balance to be struck between present and future generations, between development now and environmental sustainability for the future? These are intractable questions, to which it is unlikely that there are generally accepted answers. Rather, the answers will have to be continually negotiated and renegotiated through political processes, with considerable scope for confusion, misunderstanding and conflict. It may, therefore, justifiably be asked why policy-makers persist with, and have given new importance to, the concept of sustainable development if it is so problematic in practice. To answer this question it is necessary to go back to why the concept of sustainable development was introduced in the first place. This was basically in response to two concerns: the pace and scale of environmental degradation and perceptions of potential limits to economic growth.

Environmental Degradation

The principal cause of the increasing realization that a new path of development had to be found was the growing scientific evidence over the 1970s and 1980s, that has further accumulated since, that the combination of economic and human population growth was inflicting damage on the environment that threatened to disrupt some of the most fundamental natural systems of the biosphere, with incalculable consequences. The most recent evidence of widespread environmental degradation comes from four large-scale reviews. The first, the Millennium Ecosystem Assessment (MEA), was the first comprehensive evaluation of the impact of human activities on the natural environment and the ecosystem functions it provides. It identified three main problems arising from these activities: the degradation or unsustainable use of approximately 60 per cent of the ecosystem services (defined in Section 7.3.2) it examined; evidence that changes being made in ecosystems were increasing the likelihood of nonlinear changes in ecosystems (including accelerating, abrupt, and potentially irreversible changes) that have important consequences for human well-being; and the fact that the negative results of environmental degradation were being borne disproportionately by the poor, 'contributing to growing inequities and disparities across groups of people, and sometimes the principal factor causing poverty and social conflict.' (MEA, 2005, pp. 1–2). Secondly, in 2009, Rockström et al. (2009) developed the concept of '*planetary boundaries*', which defined a '*safe operating space*' for humanity within the environment, and published evidence of human activities in relation to this space across nine environmental issues. Their work suggested that for biodiversity loss, climate change and the nitrogen cycle, human activities were already outside the safe operating space (with the phosphorus cycle fast approaching this condition).

Thirdly, the Fifth Global Environmental Outlook of the United Nations Environment Programme concluded that 'As human pressures within the Earth System increase, several critical thresholds are approaching or have been exceeded, beyond which abrupt and nonlinear changes to the life-support functions of the planet could occur. There is an urgent need to address the underlying drivers of the human pressures on the Earth System' (UNEP, 2012, p. 194). Finally, in 2013 the Intergovernmental Panel on Climate Change (IPCC), in its Fifth Assessment Report, gave its starkest assessment yet on the threats to humanity because of its continuing large-scale emission of greenhouse gases (GHGs), with five 'integrative reasons for concern', namely unique and threatened ecosystems; extreme weather events; distribution of impacts; global aggregate impacts, including extensive biodiversity loss; and large-scale singular events, with risks of '*tipping points*' (IPCC WGII, 2014, p. 12).

Limits to Growth

The first economist to make an unequivocal prognosis of the unsustainable nature of human development was Thomas Malthus (Malthus, 1798). To summarize drastically, he noted that human population had an exponential growth trajectory, that agricultural productivity had a linear growth trajectory, and that fertile land was absolutely limited. From this, he drew the conclusion that human population growth would be brought to a halt by a shortage of food, and that such population as remained would bump along between subsistence and famine, disease and war. He considered that technology might increase the productivity of land, but ruled out the possibility that it could do so sufficiently to negate for long the difference between rates of increase of human populations and agricultural production, which led him to his dismal conclusion. Malthus was wrong, but that does not mean that this basic insight – that the physical resources of the planet are finite, and that the indefinite expansion of human activities that use these resources will lead to catastrophe – will always prove wrong.

The most powerful expression of the Malthusian prognosis in modern times was from Meadows et al. (1972), with the famous Club of Rome report *Limits to Growth*, which concluded that growing population and economic activity would exhaust resources, and that this and the pollution from this activity would result in the '*overshoot and collapse*' of both human population and economic output. In contrast to that of Malthus, this prognosis has not yet been proved wrong, because the authors envisaged this outcome within 100 years – a period that is not yet half way through. Moreover, the same authors have issued periodic updates of their prognosis claiming that their original projections were either essentially on track, or even optimistic, and overshoot and collapse could occur earlier (Meadows et al., 2005). However, the great majority of economists reject these conclusions. They continue to hold to their critique of *Limits to Growth*, which was forcibly expressed at the time, and which held that scarcity would be expressed in markets through rising prices, and would stimulate substitution away from scarce to more abundant resources, while technological progress would continue to make resources more productive and control pollution, well before overshoot and collapse took place. In recent years, the debate between these opposing points has centred on the question of whether it is possible to 'decouple' economic growth from environmental constraints and pressures.

Decoupling and the Environmental Kuznets Curve

Decoupling is the term used to describe a situation in which some environmental pressure (resource depletion or pollution) grows less fast than the economic activity causing it (relative decoupling) or declines while the activity continues to grow (absolute decoupling). The latter concept is reflected by the Environmental Kuznets Curve (EKC) hypothesis. The EKC suggests that the relationship between income and resource depletion and pollution levels follows an 'n'-shaped parabola; resource depletion and pollution levels increase with income until a given level of income is reached, after which environmental pressures decrease, with the reductions driven by, rather than simply inversely correlated to, increasing income. The term is borrowed from the original Kuznets Curve idea, which concerns the relation between income and inequality (Franklin and Ruth, 2012). The EKC aligns with the environmental economics position, but is at odds with the ecological economics standpoint. The former tends to consider growth as neutral or even positive for the environment, as technological innovation and substitution, the level of human capital (discussed in Section 7.3.2) and economies of scale increase efficiency of resource use and reduce environmental impact (including pollution and other wastes). The latter considers population as the 'consuming unit' of natural resources, with growth in population, affluence and technology mutually reinforcing each other to produce a nonlinear negative impact on the environment (through both the use of natural resources and resulting pollution) (Venkatachalam, 2007).

A very substantial body of theoretical and empirical literature has investigated this hypothesis, with no consensus reached on its validity. Studies produce different conclusions for different pollutants into different media (including local, transboundary and global commons pollutants), across different spatial scales, from different sources and in different economies. Additionally, when studies may agree on the existence of the EKC for a given set of conditions, they often disagree on where the peak of the curve lies (Chowdhury and Moran, 2012; Franklin and Ruth, 2012). The first explanation for such varied results is methodological. Data availability and quality is often cited as an issue (Chowdhury and Moran, 2012), along with the high degree of statistical sensitivity of such data to the specific modelling approach employed (Harbaugh et al., 2002). Reduced-form models are often used, linking income and pollution levels directly and reducing the need for data collection on multiple variables, rather than structural equation models that are more able to characterize the nature of the links between these variables. The second explanation is simply that it is unlikely that the EKC hypothesis is applicable as a general theory.

The influence of political and institutional circumstances on the relationship between economic growth and environmental damage is undoubtedly significant. In fact, a common explanatory factor for the EKC, where evidence for it exists, is that with increasing prosperity, citizens pay increasing attention to noneconomic aspects of their living conditions. Such *'vigilance and advocacy'* is then reflected by the introduction of increasingly stringent environmental protection instruments (Torras and Boyce, 1998). However, where an increased vigilance and advocacy is found to exist, the causal relationship between this and the introduction of environmental protection depends on the extent to which public preferences are heard by governing institutions, and whether pressure to act upon them exists. Indeed, evidence suggests that in the long-run, the higher the 'democratic stock' of a nation (i.e., the accumulation and evolution of democratic institutions over time, and thus the representation of and pressure from public opinion), the higher the level of environmental quality with respect to some pollutants (Gallagher and Thacker, 2008), whilst Torras and Boyce (1998) find that political rights and civil liberties (in addition to literacy) have a particularly strong positive effect on environmental quality in low-income countries. In addition, López and Mitra (2000) find that where corruption is found, while it may coexist with an EKC, levels of pollution for any level of income are likely to be above the socially optimal level (including the apex of the EKC).

Generating further insights into the validity or otherwise of the EKC hypothesis will require improved data availability and modelling approaches, including improved characterization of the technological, institutional (and broader political economy), and behavioural phenomena highlighted in Section 7.2.3 (Chowdhury and Moran, 2012). An additional focus on economic and demographic structures, which has thus far received little attention in the EKC literature (Franklin and Ruth, 2012), would also be beneficial, along with further investigation into the Pollution Haven and Porter Hypotheses (discussed in Section 7.5.5). Such research would advance the ongoing search for a more nuanced theory (or theories) regarding the link between economic development and environmental degradation.

7.3.2   Environmental Sustainability

The Concept of Capital

Conceiving of sustainability as the capacity for continuance immediately suggests, to economists at least, its logical connection to the concept of capital, where capital is a stock, or asset, that has the characteristic of producing a flow of goods and services, which contribute to human well-being. In order to maintain or increase welfare, the quantity of capital stock must therefore be maintained or increased. Four different types of capital may be identified. The first is 'manufactured capital' (e.g., built infrastructure), the traditional focus of capital economics. The second is 'human capital' (e.g., knowledge, skills, health), which extends the traditional identification of labour as a factor of production (and is explored further in Chapter 4). The third and fourth categories are relatively new to the concept of capital; 'social capital', which includes insights from institutional economics regarding the importance in economic activity of relationships and institutions, and 'natural capital' (also called environmental or ecological capital). Environmental sustainability is clearly related to natural capital, a broad definition of which might be everything in nature (biotic and abiotic) capable of contributing to human welfare, either through the production process or directly.

Viewed in these terms, what needs to be kept for environmental sustainability to be achieved is the flow of benefits that humans derive from it. Such benefits derive from 'ecosystem services' that flow from stocks of natural capital. These functions or services may be grouped into three broad kinds: the provision of resources, the absorption and neutralization of wastes, and the generation of services ranging from life-support (such as the maintenance of a stable climate) to amenity and recreation (Pearce and Turner, 1990). These three sets of functions collectively maintain the biosphere, and contribute to the human economy, human health and human welfare. However, as noted above (Section 7.2.1), the economy's use of the environment can impact negatively on the biosphere, and thus on the welfare which other people derive from it, through negative externalities.

Because natural capital has featured regularly in various definitions of sustainability and sustainable development, more attention has been paid to the concept as sustainable development has risen up the public policy agenda. In this context, considerable efforts have been invested in developing and making environmental indicators operational (discussed in Section 7.3.3).

Weak and Strong Sustainability

Environmental economics traditionally considers environmental resource scarcity as a Ricardian 'relative scarcity' issue, where biophysical constraints on economic growth may be overcome by incurring additional cost in the economy in the short-term (through investment in innovative technology) (Venkatachalam, 2007). This derives from a view that human or manufactured capital can substitute almost entirely for natural capital and ecosystem services, leading to the *weak sustainability* conclusion that, as long as the total economic value of all capital stocks (natural, human and man-made) can be maintained in real terms, regardless of the distribution between the different types, sustainability is achieved. An important strand in the sustainability and sustainable development literatures has called these assumptions into question, particularly for natural capital. The idea of *strong sustainability*, more often espoused in ecological economics, considers that certain elements, aspects are characteristics of natural resources and the environment, such as uncertainty and the 'irreversibility' of some phenomena (e.g., an extinct species cannot be recovered) (Pelenc and Ballet, 2015) mean that some kinds of natural capital, which has been called 'critical' natural capital (CNC) (Ekins et al., 2003) makes a unique contribution to welfare or has intrinsic value and therefore cannot be substituted by manufactured or other forms of capital.

Despite the contrasting theoretical positions taken on these issues, there is increasing alignment on them in practice in the environmental and ecological economics literatures. For example, many environmental economists recognize issues of multi-functionality, irreversibility and uncertainties surrounding natural capital, and support the idea of maintaining the natural capital stock independently of man-made capital. Summarizing the literature on the debate between the validity of the weak or strong sustainability approaches, Dietz and Neumayer (2007, p. 619) list four reasons why the strong approach to sustainability may be preferred to the weak: risk and uncertainty, irreversibility, risk aversion and the ethical nonsubstitutability of consumption for natural capital. However, proponents of both paradigms appear to agree that it is unlikely to be possible to conclude which natural capital may be considered 'critical' over an indefinite time horizon (Illge and Schwarze, 2009). A key, long-standing question remains the extent to which these two concepts may be combined, and how, to be useful for policy-makers and other stakeholders. Numerous indicators and indices of sustainability exist, with varied approaches, producing equally varied results (Mayer, 2008). Positions could probably be further aligned through the development of a robust, common indicator for sustainability, or collection of indicators, as discussed in Section 7.3.3.

Principles of Environmental Sustainability

As discussed, environmental sustainability may be conceptualized as requiring the maintenance of benefits derived from environmental functions and the natural capital that generates them. The major factor in the operationalization of this definition is the process for identifying which benefits and associated environmental functions are important to maintain, and to use the terminology introduced above, which natural capital, and at what level of stock, is 'critical' for providing these functions.

de Groot et al. (2003) put forward the criteria of maintenance of human health, avoidance of threat and economic sustainability. On the basis of such criteria, a number of principles of environmental sustainability may be derived. These principles spring from the perception that, in order for the environment to be able to continue to perform its functions, the impacts of human activities on it must be limited in some ways. At the global level it would seem important not to disrupt the climate (discussed further in Section 7.4), deplete the ozone layer or significantly reduce biodiversity. For pollution generally, emissions should not exceed levels at which they cause damage to human health, or the critical loads of receiving ecosystems. Renewable resources should be renewed, and the development of renewable substitutes should accompany the depletion of nonrenewable resources. For each of these, quantitative standards describing the environmental states (e.g., concentrations of pollutants) and pressures (e.g., emissions of pollutants) that are consistent with the criteria defined by de Groot et al. (2003) may be readily derived (though not without a broad range of uncertainty in some cases) from environmental science; for resources, it is depletion (or nonrenewal) of renewable resources that is currently giving most cause for concern, especially with respect to biodiversity, many aspects of which cannot readily be reduced to the idea of 'resources' at all, so that identifying sustainability standards for biodiversity is likely to be especially challenging. Given the great uncertainty attached to many environmental impacts, and the possibility that some of these may give rise to very large costs, the Precautionary Principle should also be used as a sustainability principle.

Valuation of Natural Capital and Ecosystem Services

A major divergence between environmental and ecological economics concerns the view of and approach to the valuation of natural capital and ecosystem services. Environmental economics tends to adopt an anthropocentric, preference-based, 'instrumental' approach based on the calculation of the monetized value of natural resources and services, according to the economic welfare of individuals, and in line with the weak sustainability paradigm. Ecological economics rather promotes the notion of nonmonetized 'intrinsic', rather than monetary value (Venkatachalam, 2007), in line with the strong sustainability perspective. Despite these traditionally opposing views, ecological economists now widely use and promote the monetary valuation of natural capital and ecosystem services (to calculate both instrumental and intrinsic values), possibly driven by pragmatism, leading to monetary valuation as a social convention among researchers (Plumecocq, 2014). There are six primary natural capital and ecosystem service valuation methodologies: *avoided cost* (services that allow society to avoid costs in the absence of those services, such as waste treatment by wetlands avoids heath costs or treatment by artificial means), *replacement cost* (services could be replaced by manmade systems, such as natural waste treatment can be replaced with artificial treatment systems), *factor income* (services provide for the enhancement of incomes, such as water quality improvements increase commercial fisheries catch and incomes of fishermen), *travel cost* (service demand may require travel, whose costs can reflect the implied value of the service, such as recreation areas attract visitors whose value placed on that area must be at least what they were willing to pay to travel to it), *hedonic pricing* (service demand must be reflected in the prices people pay for associated goods, such as housing prices at beaches exceed prices of otherwise identical inland homes without such an amenity), and finally, *contingent valuation* (service demand may be elicited by posing hypothetical scenarios that involve some valuation of alternatives, such as people would be willing to pay for increased forest cover) (Farber et al., 2002).

Each technique has particular strengths and weaknesses, with the most appropriate approach (or combination of approaches) and specific design based on the stock or service of interest. Valuation methodologies have been applied extensively to land, freshwater and marine resources across the world, including an extensive assessment across the EU's Natura 2000 network, using a combination of the approaches listed above (European Commission, 2013). Four key areas for further research regarding natural capital and ecosystem service valuation present themselves in the literature. The first is how to include or mitigate the effects of behavioural and psychological phenomena, discussed in Section 7.2.3 (Scholte et al., 2015). Such issues contribute to the substantial difference in results produced by techniques that determine '*stated preferences*' and '*revealed preferences*', along with '*willingness to pay*' and '*willingness to accept (compensation)*' approaches (Venkatachalam, 2007). The second surrounds how nonmonetary valuation, such as social-cultural value, may be integrated or made complementary to monetary valuation (Scholte et al., 2015). The third is on how monetary valuation of natural capital and ecosystem services itself impacts behaviour. For example, whether monetary valuation crowds out other forms of valuation (by altering the 'framing' of the good or service) (Neuteleers and Engelen, 2014). The fourth key area, linked to the previous two in particular, is the extent to and nature in which ecosystem service valuation can and does impact decision- and policy-making, and why (Laurans and Mermet, 2014) – including whether 'commodification' in discourse leads to 'commodification' in practice (e.g., via the use of payments for ecosystem services, discussed in Section 7.5.3) (Neuteleers and Engelen, 2014). Additionally, whilst a significant body of literature has been published on the valuation of biodiversity, the majority of studies instead value individual species, habitats or ecosystem services, rather than biodiversity per se, largely due to a lack of consensus on how 'biodiversity' may be defined and measured (Beaumont et al., 2008). Such an issue is also a topic for ongoing research.

Marginal Costs of Environmental Degradation

Linked to the valuation of natural capital and ecosystem services themselves is the marginal social cost of their degradation through resource extraction and pollution. This is a focus particularly in environmental economics, which uses social cost-benefit analysis as a key tool to determine the 'optimal' level between mitigation of such degradation (through policy mechanisms), and maintenance of the degrading activity. However, calculation of these marginal social costs is complex, and highly dependent on the characteristics of the pollution or resource considered and circumstances of its production, release or extraction. Broadly, it may be argued that the difficulty and uncertainty of marginal social cost calculation increases with spatial impacts (e.g., whether the pollutant is largely local, such as PM_{10}, or impacts the global commons, such as CO_2), as the heterogeneity, complexity and dynamic interaction between impacts increases. A broad and expanding base of literature attempting to estimate the marginal cost of CO_2 emissions (or the 'Social Cost of Carbon', SCC), produces values spanning at least three orders of magnitude (Watkiss and Downing, 2008). Two principal drivers behind such disparity include different assumptions regarding behaviour of economic agents, and monetary valuation of nonmarket entities (including natural capital and ecosystem services, discussed above, but also human health, etc.) (Van den Bergh and Botzen, 2015). As such, continued research into and improvement of nonmarket valuation techniques (both broadly and as related to natural capital and ecosystem services), and the focussed inclusion of behavioural insights into economic modelling would improve the calculation of marginal costs of pollution (at all spatial scales).

Two further essential issues lie behind such a range of estimates. The first is the value of the social discount rate used to compute the present value of costs and benefits experienced in the future. Unfortunately there is little agreement as to what the appropriate discount rate, especially with respect to such long-term issues such as those raised by climate change, should be. This has important implications for intergenerational equity – a high (exponential) discount rate quickly places a low value on the costs and benefits of resource extraction, pollution damage (including climate impacts) and policy interventions impacting future generations. Van den Bergh and Botzen (2015) provide a recent overview of the literature on discounting as applied to SCC calculations, and highlight the specific points of contention. They also highlight the requirement for further research on how to reflect risk aversion and uncertainty (both about the future and about the true value and profile of social discount rates) in discount rates employed in cost-benefit analyses.

The second issue is the specific characteristics of the consequences of CO_2 emissions (i.e., climate change), specifically (a) the likely extent of the damage is very uncertain, but may be very large (even catastrophic), (b) it is likely to affect every aspect of human life: mortality, morbidity, migration, the provision of water, food and energy (which have come to be called the '*resource nexus*'), and cultural and spiritual values, (c) the results will play out over the very long term, and (d) the results may be irreversible. Techniques of environmental economic valuation are unable adequately to reflect such characteristics for a number of reasons, including those discussed in the subsection above, but also the nonmarginal, irreversible nature of the changes, and the lack of knowledge about the probabilities or even full range of possible outcomes. Weitzman (2007) highlighted that the combination of uncertain costs and uncertain probabilities of climate change damage produces '*fat tailed*' distributions, and potential costs that are conceptually infinite, rendering traditional cost-benefit methodologies inapplicable. He termed this his '*Dismal Theorem*'.

Environmental Justice

As noted in Section 7.3.1, it is widely accepted that a core conceptual component of sustainable development is equity, both within and between generations. When applied to environmental issues this idea is often framed in terms of environmental justice (or injustice), which Laurent (2011) conceived as composed of four broad aspects: *exposure and access* (the distribution of environmental quality between individuals and groups, either negative, such as exposure to environmental nuisances, risk and hazard, or positive, such as access to environmental amenities), *policy impact* (the impact of environmental policies between individuals and groups, such as the distributional implications of an environmental tax; this, along with '*exposure and access*', may be classified as '*distributive*' justice), *environmental impact* (the environmental impact of different individuals and groups, related to lifestyle, consumption patterns, etc.), and finally, *representation in policy-making* (the involvement and empowerment of individuals and groups in decisions regarding their (usually immediate) environment; this may be termed '*procedural*' justice).

As with (and linked to) views on other subjects, there are different approaches to inter- and intra-generational equity in the environmental and ecological economics literature. A broad environmental economics view is that income growth and improved resource use efficiency, along with reduced pollution and other wastes (according to the EKC hypothesis) will improve intra-generational equity, as the poorest in society generally exhibit the highest exposure to 'bads' and the least access to 'goods'. At the same time intergenerational equity may be ensured through the maintenance of the total capital stock over time (following the 'weak sustainability' paradigm) (Venkatachalam, 2007). In contrast, many ecological economists view distributional injustice as a driver of environmental deterioration, so that intra-generational equity, as a precondition, makes an important contribution to intergenerational equity (Illge and Schwarze, 2009), in that the transfer of resources to future generations is influenced by the endowment of property rights, income distribution and the preferences of the preceding generations (Venkatachalam, 2007). In this view, the value of social discount rates is also clearly of significant importance for intergenerational equity.

Questions of environmental justice have been largely peripheral to debates surrounding valuation of natural capital and ecosystem services, discussed above, and subsequent policy instrument design and implementation (Matulis, 2014). However, they are becoming increasingly salient (McDermott et al., 2013). In particular, there are disagreements and uncertainties surrounding whether instruments utilizing monetary valuation reduce or exacerbate preexisting economic and social inequalities – particularly at a local level (a question of policy impact) (Matulis, 2014, Cobera, 2015). This is linked to a currently poor understanding of the dynamic interaction between distributional justice and procedural justice, and 'contextual' justice, which considers preexisting conditions (including culture, beliefs, practices and institutions) that limit or facilitate access to decision-making and environmental exposure and access, and therefore receipt of benefits or costs of policy intervention. This is now a key area for future research (McDermott et al., 2013, Cobera, 2015), that may be linked to priority research subjects highlighted in previous sections, surrounding natural capital and ecosystem service valuation methodologies and consequences, and consideration of behavioural and institutional economics. Further understanding of this interaction may allow for the advancement of a sound conceptual basis upon which to further develop and monitor robust indicators of environmental justice in practice, which has proven a continual difficultly thus far, despite several efforts (McDermott et al., 2013). The further development of such indicators aligns to broader efforts for indicators of sustainable development.

7.3.3   Measurement and Indicators of Sustainable Development and Sustainability

Since the UN Conference on Environment and Development in 1992, which established the idea of sustainable development as an overarching policy objective, there has been an explosion of activity to develop sustainable development indicators (SDIs) in order to determine whether sustainable development is actually being achieved. Because the meaning of sustainable development was (and is still) not particularly clear (as discussed in Section 7.3.1), this activity was characterized by much experimentation. Many indicator sets were put forward by different bodies at different levels (international, national, regional, local), and substantial efforts have since been invested in seeking to rationalize these into 'core' sets that can be used for comparison and benchmarking, while the development of particular sets of indicators for specific purposes has continued to flourish.

There are two main approaches to constructing indicators of sustainable development. The first is the 'framework' approach, which sets out a range of indicators intended to cover the main issues and concerns related to sustainable development. In 1996 the UNCSD published its first set of SDIs, comprising 134 economic, social, and environmental indicators (UN, 1996). The indicators were structured in a matrix that related Driving Force, State, and Response indicators to the chapters in Agenda 21. Because not all the indicators were relevant for the European Union, EUROSTAT carried out a study using a subset of 36 of these indicators, publishing the results of the study in 1997 (EUROSTAT, 1997). UNCSD subsequently produced a 'core' set of 59 SDIs based on its original set, and EUROSTAT (2001) produced another study involving 63 indicators, which related closely to the UNCSD core set and showed the very wide range of issues that sustainable development is considered to cover. There are many other frameworks of SDIs. Internationally, one of the best known is that published by the Organisation for Economic Co-operation and Development (OECD) in 2000. This contained a set of 'possible core sustainable development indicators', a number of country case studies on different aspects of sustainable development indicators, and indicators for the major environmentally significant sectors. It also contained a new set of social indicators, with context indicators and structured according to the themes of promoting autonomy (or self-sufficiency), equity, healthy living (or just health), and social cohesion. Within the themes the indicators were grouped according to social status and societal response (OECD, 2000).

The most recent and, arguably, most influential, framework of sustainable development indicators to be constructed is the Sustainable Development Goals (SDGs),[1] which were agreed by the United Nations in September 2015. There are 17 broad goals, spanning the economic, social and environmental dimensions of sustainable development, and underpinned by more than 100 indicators.

A limitation of the framework approach to indicators is that unless all the indicators are moving in the same direction (i.e., all making development more, or less, sustainable), it is not possible to say whether, in total, the objective of sustainable development is being advanced. This limitation is addressed by the second main approach to SDIs, which seeks to express development-related changes in a common unit so that they can be aggregated. A number of such methods have been developed, including *aggregation into environmental themes* (the approach underlying the Netherlands National Environmental Policy Plan process, described in Adriaanse (1993)), *aggregation across environmental themes* (one method of doing this is to weight the different themes according to perceptions of environmental performance, such as in the Eco-points system developed by BRE, 2008), and *aggregating across environmental and other themes* (this may use multi-criteria analysis, or relate the themes to some concept such as Quality of Life or Human Development). Another common aggregation approach is to express the different environmental impacts in monetary form. Examples include the Index of Sustainable Economic Welfare (ISEW), first proposed by Daly and Cobb (1989), which starts from consumer expenditure and then adds various social or environmental impacts. ISEW has been calculated for a number of countries, and has been further developed into the Genuine Progress Indicator (GPI), which has also been calculated for a number of countries, US states, and other subnational entities (see Posner and Costanza (2011) for further discussion). Another influential application is what is now termed *'inclusive wealth accounting'* (UNU-IHDP and UNEP (2014)). The approach remains rooted in weak sustainability, with the issues surrounding nonmarket valuation discussed in Section 7.3.2 coming into play. With this approach, therefore, whilst the indicator may be expressed as a single number, the number may lack credibility.

A third approach, confined to assessing (strong) environmental sustainability, involves establishing standards of environmental sustainability and calculating the 'gap' between current environmental situations and these standards. This gap may be characterized as the *'sustainability gap'* (SGAP) (Ekins and Simon, 1999). The SGAP concept takes explicit account of critical natural capital and indicates, in physical terms, the degree of consumption of natural capital or pollution levels in excess of what is required for environmental sustainability. The concept may also be applied to examine the time required, on present trends, to reach the standards of environmental sustainability (*'Years-to-Sustainability'*). See Ekins and Simon (1999, 2003) for further discussion of the SGAP concept, including how the indicator may be derived. A strong sustainability approach is also taken by the framework developed by the European research project CRITINC, which sets out a classification of natural capital in input-output form, together with the various steps that need to be implemented in order to identify CNC and whether the environmental functions are being sustainably used (Ekins et al., 2003). Over recent years, there has been considerable development of physical I-O tables (PIOT), and environmentally extended input output (EEIO) accounting, to match the monetary I-O tables which are a standard feature of national economic accounting (see, for example, Vaze, 1998, Stahmer et al., 1998 and, for an application of multi-region EEIO, Wiedmann et al., 2013).

7.4   The Energy System and Climate Change Mitigation

Energy is essential to human life, civilization and development. Societies became industrialized through their greatly enhanced use of energy per person, enabled by the discovery of fossil fuels and the development of technologies that enable their exploitation at an increasing scale, from less accessible locations, and with increasing efficiency. They continue to satisfy the great majority of the world's demand for energy, and their use, on current trajectories, is likely to continue to increase to provide energy to drive the continued development of emerging economies and to satisfy the needs and desires of an increasing global population, and to provide modern energy services to the current population of 1.4 billion people without access to electricity and 2.7 billion people who rely on biomass for cooking and heating (GEA, 2012). However, fossil fuels are increasingly associated with problems that are becoming more prominent on the world stage. The first is local air pollution. The old industrial societies have already grappled with, and to a considerable extent resolved, the local air pollutants associated with fossil fuel combustion. Fast-growing emerging economies, especially those that burn a lot of coal, are now struggling with the same problems. To these local air pollution issues arising from fossil fuel use may be added the global problem of CO_2 emissions from fossil fuel combustion, and associated climate change. A link between the two issues is that some actions to address CO_2 emissions from the energy system can also have a beneficial effect in terms of the reduction of both indoor and outdoor local air pollution (GEA, 2012, NCE, 2014).

The multidimensional nature of energy policy is sometimes expressed through the '*Energy Trilemma*' concept, employed by the World Energy Council (WEC) to describe the three objectives that most current energy policies now tend to seek to achieve. The three objectives are energy security, environmental sustainability (defined here as reducing CO_2 emissions), and energy equity (including accessibility and affordability) (WEC, 2015). Each objective is discussed below.

7.4.1   Energy Security

Although without a single definition, '*energy security*' relates to the desire of governments, businesses and citizens to have access to energy services when, where and in the quantity that they need and want – and at an affordable price. The factors that influence energy security may be summarized and grouped in numerous different ways and through a variety of different lenses, depending on the specific definition employed and the purpose of the categorization. However, from a broad perspective, six interrelated dimensions may be described (Mitchell et al., 2013).

The first concerns the *nature of the energy resources* in question. Many oil and gas resources are highly concentrated, leading to security risks that may produce rapid and significant price fluctuations. Relatively short-term changes in demand due to, for example, cold winters, may produce similar effects to constraints on supply. In the long term, the challenge of decarbonization (discussed below, in Section 7.4.2) may have a substantial impact. For fossil fuel exporters, decarbonization may be economically deeply threatening. For importers, this may give an opportunity to diversify away from fossil fuels to renewable energy sources or to nuclear power (both of which have their own, different, implications and challenges), and to increase energy system efficiency, reducing demand for energy in the first place. Indeed, the *technical characteristics* of the energy system comprise the second key dimension of energy security. Whilst energy efficiency measures can reduce energy demand, changes to the availability and relative costs of key technologies may alter the dynamics of the energy resources used to satisfy the demand that remains. For example, the development of low-cost electricity storage could reduce the need for back-up electricity generation capacity (such as natural gas) to maintain adequate supply when intermittent renewables (such as wind and solar) are not sufficient. In the shorter-term, vulnerability to 'common mode' failures (e.g., overheating power station, transmission substation failure) and 'one-off' failures (e.g., oil tanker spillage) may produce substantial effects. Technological and infrastructure vulnerability to natural events such as earthquakes, but also the impacts of climate change, such as threats to coastal sites and the availability of water for cooling in thermal generation, may also be significant (Watson and Scott, 2006).

The third dimension of energy security is the influence of *governance*. This exhibits two broad aspects. The first concerns governance structures. Energy security requires governance at multiple levels of jurisdiction (e.g., local, national and in the case of the EU, supranational), and an important concern is the extent to which responsibilities of and arrangements between each level (and with nongovernmental parties, such as energy suppliers) are clear and appropriate to ensure adequate decision-making for short- and long-term management. This is linked to the second aspect; the presence of appropriate strategy and policy that ensures the stable, secure and efficient operation of the energy system (such as protocols for its automated control), along with instruments and regulations that may be in place to meet health standards, emissions reduction goals and ethical standards that may rule out the use of otherwise available resources (e.g., fossil fuels from particular regions of the world, such as the Arctic).

The fourth dimension of energy security is the effect of *culture, norms and behaviour* of individuals, society, organizations and governments. This dimension is particularly multifaceted. The culture and norms of a society and government may dictate what rules, regulations and other policy instruments are feasible to introduce, and what technologies may be deployed. For example, concerning the EU legislature, a 'consensus reflex' still dominates, despite the formal permissibility of qualified majority voting (Wurzel, 2008, p. 82). In many countries, the acceptability of nuclear power reduced substantially in the wake of the Fukushima disaster in Japan in 2011. Additionally, culture and norms may influence what energy security means in the first place. For example, a primary component for improving energy security in a particular nation may be the reduced dependence on a particular fuel from a particular region (e.g., reducing reliance on Russian natural gas in Eastern and Central Europe). The behaviour of individuals and (nongovernmental) groups may impact energy security both directly and indirectly. For example, domestic activism and terror attacks may have substantial direct impacts on energy supplies. Indirectly, behavioural responses to policy instruments such as carbon pricing, subsidies for renewables and energy efficiency incentives (discussed in Section 7.5), along with nonpolicy influences such as underlying fuel price changes, may have equally substantial impacts (or, alternatively, little impact) on energy security in the longer-term.

The final two dimensions of energy security are particularly cross-cutting. The first of these, the fifth overall, is *time and space*. The dimensions above may influence energy security from a matter of seconds (e.g., terrorist attack or technical failure) to decades (e.g., resource depletion), and may themselves be influenced over such differing timeframes (e.g., particular instruments and market rules may be introduced relatively quickly if conditions permit, whilst altering culture and norms may take a generation). In terms of space, the processes of globalization, both of energy systems but also more broadly, have complex implications for energy security. On the one hand, countries without their own indigenous energy resources are obviously dependent on imports, and the extension and liberalization of energy markets can increase their energy security and provide them with access to lower cost sources of energy. On the other hand, the increasing use of energy encouraged by these open markets may introduce new vulnerabilities (e.g., volatile prices), and a new dependence on their continued and orderly functioning (Wicks, 2009). There is no straightforward relationship between the energy security of a given country and its degree of dependence on imported energy (Mitchell et al., 2013). The sixth and final dimension is *uncertainty*, which permeates all assessments of how the dimensions discussed above may develop into the future, and how such aspects may directly and indirectly influence each other over different timescales. Whilst uncertainty may be reduced by ongoing research into the particular influences of the above dimensions (both individually and in combination), and how the risks they hold for energy security may be mitigated, and benefits they have enhanced, a level of uncertainty will always remain. This must be recognized and understood, with decision-making and policy frameworks taking this into account (discussed in Section 7.5.5).

7.4.2   Reducing CO_2 Emissions

The most recent report of the Intergovernmental Panel on Climate Change (IPCC) concluded that 'anthropogenic greenhouse gas emissions have increased since the pre-industrial era, driven largely by economic and population growth, and are now higher than ever. [Their effects], together with those of other anthropogenic drivers, have been detected throughout the climate system and are extremely likely to have been the dominant cause of the observed warming since the mid-20th century' (IPCC WGIII, 2014b, p. 4). They also conclude that 'in recent decades, changes in climate have caused impacts on natural and human systems on all continents and across the oceans' (IPCC WGII, 2014, p. 4). Limiting CO_2-equivalent concentrations in the atmosphere to 450ppm (parts per million) would 'likely' (i.e., with a probability of 66–90%) limit warming to 2°C over the twenty-first century, relative to pre-industrial levels. Such a limit has been broadly accepted, and adopted by the United Nations Framework Convention on Climate Change (UNFCCC), to be the limit at which 'dangerous' climate change may be avoided – although, as discussed under Section 7.3.2, this is by no means certain. However, for the purposes of this Chapter, the 2°C target is assumed to be the *'environmentally sustainable'* limit. Achieving this target would require 40–70 per cent reductions in global anthropogenic GHG emissions by 2050 compared to 2010 levels, with emissions levels near zero in 2100 (IPCC, 2014). However, annual GHG emissions have continued to climb year on year, with recent data suggesting that 2014 may have been the first year in which CO_2 emissions from the energy sector (the principal type and source of anthropogenic GHG emissions) remained stable, rather than growing (IEA, 2015).

7.4.3   Financial Requirements and Affordability

A reduction of CO_2 emissions from the energy system may be delivered through a combination of three things: reduced demand for energy services (e.g., lighting, heating and transport), improved efficiency in delivering these services, and a reduction in the CO_2 intensity of the energy used to satisfy the remaining demand. Each of these may be delivered through a range of technological and behaviour change options, in varied combinations, to deliver the low-carbon objective. A well-known example of an attempt to classify various CO_2

abatement options from each of these three categories in terms of both abatement potential and associated cost per unit of CO_2 reduced is the so-called McKinsey (2007) marginal abatement cost curve (MACC). This curve shows that, globally, $5GtCO_{2e}$ ($\sim$ 15% current CO_2 emissions from the energy system) can be abated at negative net cost, and a further $21GtCO_{2e}$ (65% current CO_2 emissions from the energy system) can be abated at a marginal cost of less than € 40/tonCO_{2e}.

Various estimates of the net additional annual investment cost to move from the current global emissions trajectory to one consistent with the 2°C limit exist; however a commonly cited figure is that produced by the IEA (IEA, 2012, p. 137), which calculates the need for an extra US \$36 trillion invested in the energy system by 2050 – roughly US \$1 trillion per year (a 35% increase from what would be required in the absence of the decarbonization imperative). With global GDP in 2012 at around US \$70 trillion, and under the assumption that average annual global economic growth is around 2 per cent, this additional investment is in the order of 1 per cent the global GDP. However, this is not necessarily the same as a 1 per cent cost to GDP, as these additional investments in the energy system contribute to economic activity, and depending on their specific nature, may increase or decrease economic growth. Investment in energy efficiency measures and technologies that are already cost effective would tend to increase GDP (as noted above, McKinsey (2007) suggests that such opportunities are considerable). However, many low-carbon technologies currently cost more, and in some cases significantly more, than their fossil fuel alternatives. Furthermore, apparently cost effective measures such as energy efficiency are seldom implemented at the scale suggested by McKinsey (2007), and often require significant up-front investment. Such investments would tend to reduce GDP. However, it is expected that their large-scale deployment would cause their cost to be reduced. A number of new low-carbon technologies for power generation have indeed experienced significant cost reduction as they have been progressively deployed (Stern, 2007), discussed further in Section 7.5.4.

It is the macroeconomic costs and benefits of such investments that are of interest in calculating the overall economic impacts of CO_2 mitigation. Over the last 20 years, there have been a very large number of macroeconomic modelling analyses of CO_2 abatement. Barker (2008) carried out a meta-analysis of four of the most important such exercises, taking into account hundreds of model runs, using different, but mainly computable general equilibrium (CGE) models, in order to estimate the GDP costs of different levels of decarbonization. The majority of the runs estimated that a 60–80 per cent reduction in CO_2 emissions would cost between 1 per cent and 4 per cent of GDP. The IPCC's Fifth Assessment Report in 2014 arrived at a similar assessment on the basis of more recent published evidence, summarizing thus the costs of mitigation to a rather lower GHG concentration level (450ppm): 'Most scenario studies collected for this assessment ... estimate that reaching about 450ppm CO_{2eq} by 2100 would entail global consumption losses of 1–4% in 2030 (median of 1.7%), 2–6% in 2050 (median of 3.4%), and 3–11% in 2100 (median of 4.8%) relative to what would happen without mitigation' (IPCC WGIII, 2014a, Ch.6, pp. 418–419).

It is important to note that none of the baselines in the studies above, with which the mitigation runs were compared, incorporated any projections of significant costs of damage from climate change. That is to say, the baselines simply assumed that, with no attempt to reduce GHG emissions, economic growth would simply continue into the future at historic rates. However, the 2007 Stern Review on the Economics of Climate Change estimated that unabated climate change could produce costs equivalent to reducing annual GDP by 5–20 per cent 'now, and forever' (Stern, 2007). Were such costs to be included in baselines for the studies above, then instead of showing costs, the modelled emission reductions would almost certainly result in net benefits to GDP. Although, because of the uncertainties of the extent of environmental impacts from climate change (including 'fat tailed' risks, discussed in Section 7.3.2), and the difficulties of modelling these impacts in macroeconomic models, formal analysis and modelling of such issues is still in its infancy.

A recent literature has also emerged concerning the 'co-benefits' associated with tackling GHG emissions. A recent example is the New Climate Economy (NCE) Report (NCE, 2014), which reworks the McKinsey marginal abatement cost curve into a marginal abatement benefits curve, considering potential co-benefits of low-carbon investment such as fairer distribution, greater resilience, stronger local communities, improved quality of life, including from reduced air pollution and less commuting, and an enhanced natural environment. The reworked curve suggests that GHG emissions could be reduced by more than 15 $GtCO_{2e}$ by 2030 at net benefit to GDP as conventionally measured, but that if the non-GDP benefits were also included more than 20 $GtCO_{2e}$ may be abated at a net-benefit.

Beyond energy, there are now many studies that suggest that strong actions and investments to increase resource efficiency can generate economic benefits over the short, medium and long terms. One estimate puts these benefits at US$ 2.9 trillion in 2030, of which 70 per cent have an internal rate of return on investment of more than 10 per cent (Dobbs et al., 2011, p. 70). At the European level, MECAMEC and BIO IS (AMEC and BIO IS, 2013, pp. 95–96) estimate that European businesses could reap net benefits from resource efficiency measures based on current prices and technologies of €603 billion. As with GHG emissions reduction, there is almost no evidence that wider policies for environmental sustainability would have a significant negative effect on economic growth rates, still less choke off economic growth altogether.

7.5   Policies for Energy, Climate Change Mitigation and a Green Economy

The literature contains a number of similar, but slightly different definitions of a '*green economy*'. However, the conclusion of Ekins et al. (2014) was that a green economy is more easily characterized than defined: it has very low levels of CO_2 and other emissions to the atmosphere, it does not pollute the land, fresh water or seas, and it delivers high levels of human value (measured in money or other terms), for low throughput of energy and material resources. Thus, the green economy is a description of a whole economy that is characterized by climate stability, resource security and environmental quality, each of which are likely to play an important role in underpinning future prosperity. '*Green growth*', which may also be characterized in many different ways but broadly embodies the 'decoupling' objective described in Section 7.3.1, is required to deliver a green economy (under the assumption that economic growth will remain a key objective of policy-makers). Heading in such a direction requires appropriate policy frameworks. Grubb (2014, p. 69) provides detailed theoretical and empirical foundations of the need for three, simultaneous '*pillars of policy*' in order to achieve a low carbon economy. Each pillar in turn corresponds to three different 'domains' of risk, economic theory and processes, and opportunity.

The three domains in turn broadly correspond to behavioural economics, which stresses limits to individual rational market behaviour, neoclassical economics, which tends to view markets as generally well-functioning, optimizing entities, and institutional/evolutionary economics, which focuses on how economies evolve and transform. The policy approaches, or 'pillars' (as he calls them) most relevant to these domains are respectively; 'standards and engagement' (which include regulation, the provision of information and voluntary agreements), resulting in cost-effective increases in efficiency; 'markets and pricing' (economic instruments), resulting in cleaner products and processes derived from price-induced changes in behaviour and technology; and 'strategic investment in innovation and infrastructure', which causes the economy to shift to a new production possibility frontier, resulting in this context in much lower CO_2 emissions. Both standards and engagement and strategic investment have a medium relevance in the delivery of cleaner products and processes, and markets and prices have some effect on smarter choices and innovation and infrastructure.

Beyond decarbonization, Ekins et al. (2014) consider that a shift to a green economy more broadly requires three major conceptual and practical pillars of public-private cooperation: the provision of information, which is relevant to both market functioning and behaviour change; and innovation and infrastructure (together with the associated investment), which obviously maps closely onto Grubb's third policy 'pillar'. Each of these pillars will now be explored in greater detail.

7.5.1   Standards and Engagement

Standards

Standards may take many forms. However, all act to 'push' a market, product or process to higher levels of efficiency (or lower levels of pollution or resource intensity), through regulation. Such regulations help to overcome market failures such as split-incentives, a prominent example of which is the '*landlord–tenant dilemma*', under which the interests of the landlord and tenants are misaligned. Whilst the installation of energy efficiency measures, for example, would benefit the energy bill-paying tenant, savings do not accrue to the landlord who would generally bear the cost of installing such measures, preventing their introduction. Instead, standards can require their installation, or other measures to induce the same effect. Such standards may be applied with a legal basis, or through the use of voluntary agreements.

7.5.2   Information

It is well recognized that adequate, timely and relevant information is essential for the understanding of the state of an economy and where it is headed. There is a need for a new information infrastructure about material and resource use that enables economic actors and policy-makers to understand and manage the resource and environmental basis of the economy and businesses. Two major extensions of national accounting approaches are required for this. The first is the construction of a system of natural capital accounts (SNCA) to increase understanding as to how and where natural capital should be maintained and augmented, and to act as an interface between the economy and the environment, to facilitate the detailed modelling of the impacts of the economy on the environment and the contribution of the environment, resources and ecosystem goods and services to the economy. The second is the construction of much more detailed material flow accounts for national economies that track the flow of different materials through the economy, to facilitate their retention of value and their appropriate management at the end of product lives, without which policy-makers will not be able to understand how resource use is developing, and how it should be managed.

This information may feed in to engagement processes, mechanisms and instruments for targeted communication and engagement between governments, organizations, communities and individuals, which may help to overcome issues of psychological distancing, motivational issues, split incentives and information asymmetry. Such instruments act to 'pull' the market towards higher efficiency, lower emissions and resource consumption, and greater resilience, and may include training and education campaigns, labelling and certification, public reporting and other information disclosure and transparency measures. All act to provide consumers and investors with information surrounding environmental performance of a product, service, process or organization at the point of use, or across the product lifecycle or organizational operations and supply chain, in order to make informed decisions regarding investments, purchases and other behaviour.

7.5.3   Markets and Pricing

Carbon Pricing

Perhaps the most commonly suggested policy prescription to address climate change is carbon pricing, whether through carbon taxes, tradable permits, or some combination of the two. Contrary to many perceptions, this is a prescription that has actually been implemented in a number of countries. Globally, 40 national and over 20 subnational jurisdictions have implemented carbon pricing, representing almost a quarter of global GHG emissions (with a value of around US $50 billion in 2015) (World Bank, 2015). Goulder and Schein (2013) conducted an assessment of the relative advantages and disadvantages of carbon taxes and emission trading systems. On a number of grounds carbon taxes seem to be preferred, one of the most important of which is that additional climate change mitigation policies do not reduce emissions in a cap-and-trade system (unless the cap is adjusted downwards, which then undermines the principal feature of an emissions trading system, which is that it gives assurance over the quantity of emissions), whereas under a carbon tax additional policies do reduce emissions further. This is an important consideration when policy mixes are employed. However, there are political advantages to emission trading systems, such as the ability to allocate emissions permits for free, which have led to them being introduced more frequently than carbon taxes, despite the theoretical advantages of the latter.

Environmental Tax Reform

The introduction of carbon pricing (or other environmental pricing instruments) may be part of an environmental (or ecological) tax reform (ETR), which is the shifting of taxation from 'goods' (like income, profits) to 'bads' (like resource use and pollution). ETR is often implemented, and is normally modelled, to be revenue-neutral (i.e., taxes on labour or businesses are reduced in line with the revenues from the environmental taxes, such that there is no change in the overall fiscal balance). The basic hypothesis of ETR is that it can lead to higher human well-being (or welfare) both by improving the environment, and by increasing output and employment, and potentially also by stimulating green innovation (discussed in Section 7.5.4). Andersen and Ekins (2009) present the results of an assessment of environmental and economic effects of ETRs that had been implemented in six EU countries (Denmark, Finland, Germany, Netherlands, Sweden, UK). As would be expected, the modelling suggested that environmental impacts in those countries were reduced, but perhaps more significantly, that these countries experienced slightly faster economic growth than they had without the ETR. Ekins and Speck (2011) present the results of a modelling investigation into the implications of a large-scale ETR in Europe, which used two European macro-econometric models, and explored six scenarios of a varied carbon price (with revenue neutrality achieved by reducing taxes on incomes and employers' social security contributions). Broadly, the study suggests that ETR is a very cost-effective way of reducing CO_2 emissions, with employment increasing in all instances.

Payments for Ecosystem Services

A broader concept than the pricing of negative market externalities is the concept of 'Payments for Ecosystem Services (PES)', which has received significant attention in the literature in recent years. Although various definitions exist, PES may be broadly defined as a voluntary transaction where ecosystem managers (e.g., land owners), are compensated through conditional payments by ecosystem beneficiaries (often governments, with the public being the beneficiary), for the additional cost of maintaining ecosystem services above legally required levels (or in the absence of such requirements) (Schomers and Matzdorf, 2013). It is clear that effective implementation of PES depends on the possibility of arriving at an agreed valuation of ecosystem services, the difficulties of which are discussed in Section 7.3.2. Despite their growing use around the world, few PES systems have undergone rigorous ex post analysis to determine their effectiveness (Engel et al., 2008). As such, there is scope for further research to evaluate existing PES instruments, particularly surrounding how institutional and governance structures (including property rights, transaction costs and monitoring and enforcement regimes) influence effectiveness, cost-efficiency and distributional impacts in practice (Schomers and Matzdorf, 2013). The conditions under which 'bundling' ecosystem services together in a single instrument (reducing transaction costs and raising price premiums) is beneficial, and which services may be bundled together without producing trade-offs and perverse incentives, is also a topic for further research (Farley and Costanza, 2010).

Environmentally Harmful Subsidies

Economic instruments may only reach their full potential if other market failures and distortions are minimized. Whilst instruments discussed in the other two pillars of policy aim to do this, the presence of environmentally harmful subsidies may continue to inhibit the effectiveness (and cost-efficiency) of a policy mix. Globally, fossil fuels continue to receive substantial subsidies; US $544 billion in 2012, more than five times the level of subsidy paid to renewables (IEA, 2013). Such subsidies distort the market, encourage the consumption of fossil fuels and make the deployment of low-carbon options more expensive in relative terms. As such, fossil fuel subsidies (for both consumption and production) should be reduced and removed where they occur. G20 countries have a commitment from 2009 to phase out 'inefficient' subsidies to fossil fuels in the medium term, but since then such subsidies have grown substantially, and with no definition as yet of the 'medium term', the commitment seems somewhat hollow. While the justification for fossil fuel subsidies is often that they give energy access to low-income households, in fact the IEA (IEA, 2013, pp. 93–98) reports that only 7 per cent of fuel subsidies in low-income countries go to the bottom 20 per cent of households, while 43 per cent go to the wealthiest 20 per cent. As such, removing such subsidies may have positive distributional effects, particularly if the additional revenue (or rather, subsidies foregone) are targeted to directly counter the effects of the increased fuel costs to those most affected (through, for example, energy efficiency measures, or other ETR approaches). Countering negative distributional effects is also essential in wealthy countries. '*Fuel (energy) poverty*', a condition in which individuals must spend a high proportion of their income in order to keep warm or cool, is a substantial (political) issue in many EU Member States. In the UK, for example, over 10 per cent of all households were considered to be in fuel poverty in 2013 (defined as the number of households with required fuel costs above the national required median level, and if they were to spend that amount, would be left with a residual income below the official poverty line) (DECC, 2015).

7.5.4   Strategic Investment

Infrastructure Provision

As has long been recognized, market actors are unwilling and unable to create the infrastructure that underpins national prosperity by themselves. There are important choices to be made in respect of infrastructures of supply and demand, of energy, water, construction and transport, and of the information and communications infrastructure that will to a large extent determine how they are operated. Government and public policy has a crucial role to play in all the important choices in this area if businesses and consumers are not to be locked in to high-carbon, resource-intensive patterns of economic activity that become a growing liability in a world increasingly concerned about, and feeling the effects of, climate change and escalating demands for resources of all kinds. To avoid lock-in to carbon-intensive infrastructure and resource-inefficient infrastructure in general, governments need to adopt a clearer approach to prioritization of low carbon infrastructure, perhaps through a strategic infrastructure plan that sets out the criteria that ensure that infrastructure investments are compatible with long-term green economy objectives. This would enable a prioritization of those infrastructures that are required for a green economy (such as sufficient transmission capacity to incorporate renewable electricity into the power system), '*smarter grids*' to facilitate its management, and materials management facilities to delay or prevent resources from becoming wastes.

A National Infrastructure Bank with green criteria embedded within its mandate, could finance large infrastructure and demonstration projects. In addition, the capacity of local authorities to drive green infrastructure locally could be bolstered by enabling the establishment of green municipal bonds and a collective municipal bond agency owned by participating local authorities.

Innovation

Change in the energy sector since the industrial revolution has been rapid and dramatic, with a huge range of energy demand technologies and associated energy consumption practices being invented, developed and adopted as new, more convenient and versatile energy sources became widely available and cheaper. The extent of cost-reducing innovation is often described through learning or experience curves, and associated 'learning rates', the percentage reduction in unit cost for each doubling of installed cumulative capacity. Azevedo et al. (2013 p. vii) give learning rates for different electric power generation technologies from a literature review of different studies. Nuclear and coal have relatively low learning rates (rates for the former technology have been negative), whilst of the renewables technologies, the narrowest range of estimates is for hydropower. High rates of learning have been estimated for natural gas, onshore wind, solar PV and bio-power. In future, further innovation in low-carbon energy supply technologies, particularly innovation that reduces their costs, will be crucial.

The literature often characterizes innovation as having several distinctive stages – from research and development (R&D) to prototyping, demonstration, commercialization and deployment. Early conceptions of innovation tended to emphasize a linear process of moving through these stages from R&D to deployment. However, this 'linear model' is now regarded as too simplistic. Models of innovation have therefore evolved to reflect empirical observations of innovation processes, including feedback between innovation stages (a process that is sometimes referred to as 'learning by doing'), and the increasingly networked character of innovation (including parallel activities by different functional departments within innovating firms, closer relationships between technology suppliers and customers, and a focus on speed and flexibility of product development to respond to changing needs). This increasingly sophisticated understanding of innovation is further enhanced by a recognition that the scale and scope of innovation varies widely (from '*incremental*' to '*radical*' innovations) (Freeman, 1992), that patterns of innovation are also shaped by national institutions (Freeman, 1987), and that innovation processes vary significantly between sectors (Pavitt, 1984). These and other insights have led to a number of standard rationales for government innovation policies, including financial support. Most of these rationales focus on the existence of market failures, two of which are most prominent in low-carbon innovation. The first is the market externality of CO_2 emissions, distorting the relative economics between high- and low-carbon technologies, and thus the market for the latter. The second is a tendency of the private sector to under-invest in R&D because individual firms cannot fully capture the returns from their investments ('*knowledge externalities*').

Beyond such market failures, an 'innovation systems' perspective also focuses on wider system failures. The adoption of some low-carbon (or enabling) technologies may require both technological and institutional change. Technologies and institutions co-evolve and are closely integrated (Weber and Hemmelskamp, 2005), and many of those that currently exist were designed for a fossil fuel-based energy system. For example, the diffusion of smart metering technology is not just a simple technical challenge but also implies a new approach to information provision to energy consumers and new information technology infrastructure. Others require new links between established but hitherto separate actors within the innovation system. For example, carbon capture and storage (CCS) technologies require new collaborations between utilities, oil and gas companies, and power equipment companies, and can also require amendments to previously-unrelated existing regulations (e.g., those that govern marine pollution or issues around liability).

These insights have informed policies to support innovation in more sustainable technologies in many countries. In many cases, broad 'horizontal' policies have been implemented such as generic tax credits for R&D (Owen, 2012). However, many policies have gone further than this, and have emphasized more tailored policies for particular sectors or technology families that take into account sectoral differences and characteristics. An important area of debate has focused on the extent to which more specific policies for innovation require a different modus operandi for governments. One view is that, rather than implementing generic policies and leaving decisions to market actors, a more 'hands on' approach from governments and their agencies is required. Mazzucato (2011) argued the case for an '*entrepreneurial state*' that works in partnership with the private and third sectors to foster innovation. The aim is to underwrite the specific risks of developing and commercializing new technologies, and to share the rewards. As part of this, she argues that there is a need for much greater emphasis within public institutions on experimentation and learning. Mazzucato cites US institutions such as ARPA-E as successful examples of translating these principles into practice. Issues surrounding innovation in relation to economic growth are further explored in Chapter 1.

Industrial Strategies

As Mazzucato's research suggests, green industrial strategies can guide innovation and strengthen a country's innovation system and secure comparative advantage in key sectors and areas of technology that enhance resource productivity. This can be delivered with both horizontal instruments that give the right incentives right across the economy, and targeted sector-specific policies that focus on the skills and supply chains required for greener products and processes. This would also require a clear approach to the selection of technology priority areas with explicit processes for review, and enhancement of 'mission-driven' R&D agencies, identifying where new ones may be necessary to drive core green economy technologies. Where possible, these should build on existing regional industrial and innovation strengths. Complementary policies can include the development of long-term patient-finance vehicles for green innovation, to invest and hold equity in technology-based firms developing new technologies; better alignment of downstream policies focused on supporting diffusion of core green technologies (i.e., deployment subsidies) with upstream funding support for technological innovation; and support for innovation in business models, including the provision of a small fund for proof-of-concept or feasibility studies for innovative business models. Establishing appropriate financial institutions for such a purpose may be required, such as the Green Investment Bank in the UK.

7.5.5   EU Energy and Climate Change Policy: Lessons and Priorities for Research

The evidence suggests that the climate policy mix in the EU has had a relatively significant impact on CO_2 emissions in recent years, although nonclimate policy and nonpolicy factors (such as the 2008 financial crisis) have also been highly influential (Drummond, 2014).

The EU Emissions Trading System

The EU Emissions Trading System (EU ETS), a cap-and-trade system applicable to the power and heavy industry sector across EU Member States (plus Norway, Iceland and Lichtenstein), is the cornerstone of the EU's climate policy landscape, and covers around 55 per cent of total CO_2 emissions. Although the primary objective of the EU ETS (i.e., to maintain obligated emissions under the level of the cap) has been and continues to be achieved, it is unlikely that the EU ETS has been a significant driver of CO_2 abatement. A primary factor for this is permit oversupply and consequential low carbon prices, first as a result of initial overestimation of CO_2 emissions from obligated sectors due to lack of prior data (in Phase 1, 2005–2007), and subsequently due to the reduced demand for electricity and industrial products stemming from the 2008 financial crisis (in Phase 2 (2008–2012), and continuing into Phase 3 (2013–2020)). Instead, parallel (largely regulatory) instruments such as renewable deployment targets for Member States (implemented most commonly through feed-in tariffs), CO_2-intensity regulation for cars and minimum energy performance standards for energy-using products have driven the majority of abatement attributable to climate policy in the EU (Drummond, 2014).

Carbon Leakage and the Pollution Haven Hypothesis

Prior to its introduction, much analysis projected that the EU ETS would induce 'carbon leakage', the CO_2-specific manifestation of the Pollution Haven Hypothesis (PHH). The PHH contends that increasing environmental regulation will raise costs for pollution-intensive industries and encourage their migration to regions without such costs to achieve a comparative advantage. This raises the possibility that the (absolute) decoupling of income from environmental degradation, where evidence for it exists, may be driven by the export of such activities, rather than genuine pollution abatement (Kearsley and Riddel, 2010). Thus far however, no evidence of a loss of competitiveness and 'operational' leakage (an induced shift in the use of existing production capacities from within to outside the EU ETS' jurisdiction) exists for key industry sectors as a result of the EU ETS (Kuik et al., 2013). However, there is not yet sufficient evidence to determine whether 'investment' leakage – an induced change in relative production capacities – has been induced (Branger and Quirion, 2013). Indeed, despite substantial research over recent years, largely focussed on inward foreign direct investment (FDI) and net imports to the USA, the empirical validity of the PHH continues to be a highly contentious issue, with some studies demonstrating small or insignificant impact from environmental regulations on trade flows, and others finding a more substantial relationship. Where supporting evidence for the PHH is found, it is 'footloose' rather than the most pollution-intensive industries, that appear most at risk (Kellenberg, 2009). Additionally, it often appears that other factors such as capital availability, labour force qualification, proximity to customers and infrastructure quality may be more significant factors in location decisions than the presence of environmental regulations. There is also evidence that enforcement of environmental regulation is a more important factor than stringency (Cole, 2004, Kellenberg, 2009, Kuik et al., 2013). Further work is required in order to determine the relative strength and characteristics of these different factors in determining the potential for migration for different industries (Cole (2004)), and to produce empirical evidence from a wider geographic range. Additionally, the literature does not sufficiently address the impact of a regulatory approach; the difference between market-based or command-and-control, or poor or well designed instruments (Ambec et al., 2013). Such insights would be highly valuable for policy-makers.

The Porter Hypothesis

Contrary to the PHH, the Porter Hypothesis suggests that 'properly designed environmental standards can trigger innovation that may partially or more than fully offset the costs of complying with them [and] can even lead to absolute advantages over firms in foreign countries not subject to similar regulations' (Porter and van der Linde, 1995). Jaffe and Palmer (1997) disaggregate this hypothesis into 'weak', 'strong' and 'narrow' versions. The 'weak' version states that properly designed environmental regulation may spur innovation. The 'strong' version states that in many cases such innovation more than offsets any additional regulatory costs, leading to an increase in competitiveness. The 'narrow' version states that flexible regulatory instruments (market-based instruments) give firms greater incentive to innovate, and are thus preferable to prescriptive regulation (command-and-control instruments) (Ambec et al., 2013). Ambec et al. (2013) find that the 'weak' version has relatively strong empirical support, whilst empirical evidence for the 'strong' version (at firm- and industry-level) is largely negative (evidence for the 'narrow' version is not addressed here, as evidence for this significantly pre-dates the Porter Hypothesis). However, the vast majority of studies reviewed employ cross-sectional (one-period) or two-period models. Longitudinal studies may generate new insights into the issue. Moreover, substantial issues surrounding data availability and quality, and methodological approaches (including the use of compliance cost as a proxy for regulatory stringency), make robust conclusions and comparisons between studies difficult. Further research to address and refine these issues, for example through regular structural surveys to collect time series data at the micro (e.g., firm), meso (e.g., sector) and macro (e.g., national) levels, would be beneficial (Ambec et al., 2013). However, the administrative feasibility of such a data collection exercise may require a more targeted approach.

Policy Mixes

Meyer and Meyer (2013) found that the combination of the EU ETS and renewable energy targets (and instruments deployed to achieve them), along with ETR measures in some Member States (discussed in Section 7.5.3), likely increased both GDP and employment at the EU level against the counterfactual, although much analysis suggests that many climate policy instruments (such as the EU ETS and feed-in tariffs) may have had negative distributional impacts (Branger et al., 2015). However, such analysis often examines the impact of one or two instruments, rather than an instrument mix as a whole. Further research is required to understand the impacts of individual instrument design, and how multiple instruments may interact in an instrument mix, before comprehensive conclusions on the effects of climate and energy policy, particularly on issues of competitiveness and distributional impacts, may be drawn. Such lessons would help inform, and be informed by, improved modelling techniques and characterization that take into account existing and improved insight into behavioural and institutional economics (discussed under Section 7.2.3), innovation processes (discussed in Section 7.5.4), discount rates (discussed in Section 7.3.2), and the components and associated value of marginal social costs of carbon (particularly impacts on human health).

Improved knowledge and analytical techniques would also allow for improved understanding of complex issues, such as the energy trilemma (discussed under Section 7.4), and policy mixes that may effectively enhance synergies and reduce trade-offs between the three aspects of the trilemma; for example, how support for the different stages of innovation (from basic research to deployment) may be balanced, how the micro and macroeconomic costs of CO_2 emission mitigation actions may be minimized and equitably distributed, or even how such actions may most effectively increase prosperity and equity. Such questions have yet to be given adequate attention in the literature (Falkner, 2014).

The identification of 'win–win' actions and instruments, those that advance more than one aspect of the trilemma (without inhibiting the other), should be a priority. A classic example of a 'win–win' strategy is that of increasing energy efficiency, although continued robust investigation is required to further define where and how such action, along with the instrument mix required to achieve it, is most (cost-) effectively targeted (Mitchell et al., 2013).

Living with the Trilemma

However, the energy trilemma is a '*wicked problem*'.[2] Efforts to improve the situation in respect of one component of the trilemma may make the others better or worse, in multidimensional ways that are hard to predict. As such, successfully negotiating it will prove extremely difficult. Additionally, even if apparently suitable pathways and approaches are found, efforts to implement them in a long term, consistent strategy may flounder against political, institutional and decision-making realities. In practice, the three components of the energy trilemma may be hierarchical in priority to decision-makers, and may rapidly change in response to short-term events and 'shocks'. For example, the EU 'Energy Union', as initially proposed in response to increasing fears over dependence on Russian gas in the wake of the conflict in Ukraine in April 2014, focused on (fossil fuel) energy security – arguably at the expense of the 'decarbonization' element of the trilemma (in particular). However, the concept has since evolved and broadened to explicitly refer to the three aspects of the trilemma, with the objective of 'ensur[ing] that Europe has secure, affordable and climate-friendly energy' (European Commission, 2015). Further research should be conducted to determine how the concept of the Energy Union may evolve over time to negotiate the elements of the trilemma, and remain robust in the face of potentially abrupt changes in EU and Member State level priorities (which are, and are likely to continue to be, substantially different).

A key element of the energy trilemma, as discussed in Section 7.4.1, is uncertainty. Decision-makers must plan, invest and introduce policy instruments to satisfy the energy trilemma in the face of a raft of unpredictable developments that may occur over subsequent years and decades (e.g., technological development, economic pressures, energy resource scarcity and prices, public preferences, etc.). Whilst some of these uncertainties may be reduced, others are likely to remain. Policies, policy mixes and strategies must therefore be flexible and able to deal with uncertainties when they arise, as far as they are able to, to prevent abrupt changes and maintain long-term credibility. Examples of flexibility mechanisms are the forthcoming *Market Stability Reserve* for the EU ETS (intended to reduce existing and reduce the risk of future permit oversupply), and 'degression' mechanisms for renewables' subsidies (i.e., an automatic change in subsidy levels based on deployment rates) to prevent unacceptably high costs. However, the occurrence of some uncertain or unexpected events may be beneficial. For example, the rapid fall in oil prices that began in August 2014 has facilitated the reduction of fossil fuel subsidies in many countries around the world (IEA, 2015), and if it continues, may facilitate the continued introduction of robust carbon pricing. This helps reduce market distortions and the relative cost of low-carbon alternatives, and thus subsidies for their deployment. The research priorities identified above would contribute to the continued identification of appropriate approaches for policy flexibility and resilience, and key options for reform that may be introduced when the political economy allows.

7.6   The Science-Policy Interface

Economic analysis of policies to address energy, environment and sustainability challenges plays a central role in the development and implementation of such policies in many countries – including in the European Union and EU Member States. This chapter has demonstrated that a number of different schools of economic thought tend to frame the relationship between the environment, energy and the economy differently. They also emphasize different theoretical frameworks and methods. As a result, there are often conflicting views in answer to important policy questions, such as the most cost-effective strategy for reducing GHG emissions in the EU. Additionally, many of the key questions faced by policy communities working in these fields require an interdisciplinary approach. Economic perspectives therefore need to be combined with perspectives from other disciplines, including engineering, physical sciences, natural sciences and other social sciences.

The Role of Scientific Advice

The interface between science and policy is often populated by a range of institutions that are designed to inform government policies and strategies. Wilsdon and Doubleday (2015) emphasize the diversity of approaches used in different countries, but nevertheless they identify four common approaches of 'high-level advisory councils', more specialist 'scientific advisory committees', 'chief scientific advisers' and 'national academies and learned societies'. They note that in many countries more than one of these approaches is used in parallel, and that countries differ significantly in the extent to which scientific advice is sought formally or informally. They also argue that scientific advice systems need to deal with the fundamental differences between the science and policy worlds: 'debates about scientific advice often focus on the "supply-side" of the science-policy interface. But the "demand-side" is equally important: advisory bodies need a sophisticated understanding of how policy-making processes work, and the pressures and constraints under which politicians, officials and decision makers operate' (Wilsdon and Doubleday, 2015). Whilst these institutions are largely populated by natural scientists and engineers, this is not exclusively the case, with economic expertise included in some scientific advisory structures. However, it is important to remember that economics expertise is already embedded in policy-making in a much broader way. This includes the use of specific bodies that are set up to provide economic advice – either inside government or independent from it. Perhaps more importantly, economics has a central role in government departments in many countries. The civil service often includes large numbers of economists, and economic tools such as cost benefit analysis are used routinely to support decision-making. These tools tend to be rooted in traditional neoclassical economics, and this extends to their treatment of environmental impacts and natural resources (see Section 7.2). It is less common for economic ideas from outside mainstream neoclassical economics to be represented and used, however there are some exceptions to this. For example, the UK government's Cabinet Office established a *'behavioural insights team'* (known more popularly as the 'Nudge Unit') in 2010, which applies behavioural economics to a range of policy questions, including how to improve the adoption of energy efficiency measures.

Scientific Advice Structures in the EU

The European Governance White Paper (2001) called for a number of reforms that aimed to make European institutions more responsive and accountable (European Commission, 2001). These included proposed reforms to the use and networking of expert advice, which the Commission argued had a tendency to be nationally oriented. This Communication was followed in 2002 by a more specific publication outlining approaches to the collection and use of expertise.[3] This issue has also been a focus of attention more recently, in 2005 and 2006, including the establishment of a register of the expert groups used by the Commission and the publication of guidelines for these groups. According to Metz (2013), the number of expert groups to the Commission grew steadily until the mid-2000s when there were well over a thousand in existence. She attributes their rise to an increase in Commission competencies and regulations–though many expert groups cover areas where competencies are shared between the Commission and Member States. She also observes that numbers have fallen since the mid-2000s, partly as a result of the new guidelines and register, and partly due to pressure for more transparency. A similar trend occurred in the US, where the number of expert committees has reduced from 3000 in the 1970s to around 1000 in recent years.

Metz (2013) also identifies three distinctive roles for expert groups: problem solving (in areas where the Commission uses external expertise to develop policies and regulations); substantiating (where expert positions are used to support Commission positions); and consensus building (for areas where there are significant areas of controversy). In the area of research and innovation policy, she argues that the second substantiating role has been particularly significant. Of particular relevance for this chapter are the advisory groups on research priorities under Horizon 2020. These groups tend to be technologically focused, but their remits also extend to societal issues, and therefore sometimes incorporate some social science and economics expertise. There are currently groups focusing on energy, climate change and transport. There have also been ad-hoc committees formed to advise on overall strategy. One notable example is a committee formed to advise the Commissioner on Energy on the EU Energy Roadmap to 2050 (European Commission, 2011). The committee included a number of prominent energy economists. In addition to expert groups, the Commission's Joint Research Centre (JRC) provides in-house research capabilities, with the status of a Directorate General. The JRC includes significant research capabilities in energy, environment and sustainability – much of which is technical in nature. However, there is also substantial economics expertise in relation to these fields. For example, the Institute for Prospective Technological Studies (IPTS) has expertise in the economic analysis of energy, transport and climate change. It also includes a science area on innovation and growth. The most recent addition to European Commission institutions at the science-policy interface was the creation in 2012 of a new position of chief scientific adviser to the President (Wilsdon and Doubleday, 2015). However, this position has not been renewed since the completion of the first incumbent's three-year term. In May 2015, the Commission announced that a new scientific advisory panel will be appointed instead of a single chief scientific adviser. At the time of writing, the plan is for a seven-member group that could include at least one social scientist and/or economist.

The system of scientific advice in the US has some similarities with the European system and some EU Member States. The US government has a chief scientific adviser who is also head of the Office of Science and Technology Policy in the White House. In addition to this, the US National Academies have a formal role in providing advice to the US government on science, engineering and medicine. In the US, it is also common for senior scientists to be appointed as government ministers, with recent appointments including academics from Stanford University and MIT.

7.7   Conclusions and Research Priorities

It is clear that whilst the application of economic thought and methodological approaches has advanced our understanding of interactions within and between the human and natural world, many important areas of further theoretical, empirical and methodological research remain. These areas may be broadly delineated into three interrelated themes; (i) the basic characteristics of the economy-environment interaction, including how the state of this interaction and changes to it can be measured, (ii) the 'natural' (nonpolicy) drivers of this change (both from economic activity on the environment, and environmental degradation on the economy), and (iii) the impact and design of policy interventions.

The first theme largely concerns the opposing notions of weak and strong sustainability, and associated concepts and approaches. Central to the operationalization of the weak sustainability approach is the valuation of natural capital and ecosystem services. Four areas for particular further research have been identified. The first is the ongoing question of how to include or mitigate the impact of behavioural and cognitive complexities on values elucidated. Such issues are well known and expressed in the literature, but remain a key methodological issue (particularly for stated preference approaches). The second is how nonmonetary valuation approaches, such as social and cultural value, may be integrated with or made complementary to monetary valuation. A clear avenue for research concerning both these issues is the continued development of multi-criteria analysis methodologies. The third area is whether monetary valuation, by framing the good or service in such terms, crowds out other forms of valuation. The fourth concerns the extent to and nature in which monetary valuation can and does impact decision- and policy-making (including the drivers and barriers involved), and leads to the introduction of instruments based upon the values derived. Alongside methodological improvements and assessment of the impact such approaches have, further research into how they may be applied to biodiversity, rather than individual species, habitats or ecosystem services, is required. This also includes the construction of a commonly accepted, functional definition of the term. Such research will also provide a more robust basis for the use of biodiversity offsets, the focus of increasing policy attention.

An ongoing area of strong sustainability research is the refinement of robust approaches to identifying critical natural capital, in order to further define environmental limits, in respect of which monetary valuation is inappropriate, too expensive or impossible. Advances in the natural sciences will contribute to improving knowledge in this area. Research into the above issues would advance the development and quality of indicators for sustainability, in respect of both strong and weak interpretations – an important area for continued research.

The second theme, on nonpolicy drivers of change, contains two principal longstanding questions. The first concerns the validity of the EKC hypothesis. Whilst a large body of literature has attempted to address this question, no consensus has been reached. Further research using structural equations, rather than reduced-form econometric models, is required, along with an increased focus on the influence of economic and demographic structures, and the political economy. However, this requires additional efforts in the generation and collection of the required data, and improvements to modelling techniques, discussed below. The second long-standing question surrounds the calculation of marginal social costs of pollution, and of CO_2 in particular. Continued research in the natural sciences on the impact of climate change will help advance this question, although in the economics sphere, alongside improvements to the valuation of natural capital and ecosystem services (in addition to valuation of human health and comfort, etc.), debates around discount rates are dominant. Whilst this topic is a key broad area for continued research, specific efforts may focus on how to reflect risk aversion, uncertainty and time variation in respect of the discount rate.

The third theme, on the impact of policy interventions and their design, contains four principal, interrelated topics for further research. The first concerns the cost for firms of environmental, energy and climate policies, and the effect this has on competitiveness. As with other subjects, the contentious Pollution Haven and Porter Hypotheses have received significant attention in the literature, but with consensus yet to emerge. For the former, two principal areas of recommended research arise. Firstly, determining the relative strength and characteristics of nonregulatory cost factors, such as capital availability, labour force qualification and infrastructure quality in determining the potential for migration for different industries. Secondly, the impact of specific regulatory approaches, such as the difference between market-based and direct regulatory instruments, and the specific design of instruments therein (including 'well'- and 'poorly'-designed instruments), both individually and in a policy mix, including through longitudinal studies is required. However, such research requires empirical evidence from a broader geographical scope as well as the availability (or production) of high-quality data for analysis, an issue that already presents a substantial challenge.

These issues (particularly the Porter Hypothesis) link directly with the second topic, which concerns issues of innovation. The development of robust approaches to measurement, and the development of indicators for innovation, is one particular area of ongoing research and policy interest. Another, broadly, surrounds the process, drivers and barriers of innovation and diffusion of innovations – including technological, organizational, social and institutional innovation – including the appropriate combinations of incentives and policy instruments, framework conditions and context, and the role of institutions and governance arrangements.

This leads to the third topic, which concerns the role, nature and impact of institutions and behaviour more broadly in policy choice, design and impact. Knowledge about the interaction between governance institutions and resource users and managers on institutional choices, and on the role of each in enhancing or preventing institutional change, is relatively sparse, and potentially a rich avenue for further research. This links to the selection of appropriate policy instruments, and how effective and cost-efficient they may be in practice (e.g., the presence of appropriate property rights, the information available to actors, the scale of transaction costs, etc.), particularly concerning the use of payments for ecosystem services.

In terms of the '*energy trilemma*', continued research into the availability of 'win–win' options, and options for reducing the risks surrounding inherent uncertainty of future developments, would also be of substantial benefit in maximizing achievements as far as the political economy allows.

The fourth topic concerns environmental justice and distributional impacts. For example, uncertainty surrounds whether instruments utilizing monetary valuation of natural capital and ecosystem services reduce or exacerbate pre-existing economic and social inequalities, particularly at the local level. This is linked to a currently poor understanding of the dynamic interaction between distributional justice, procedural justice and contextual justice (with includes institutional arrangements, but also culture, beliefs and practices). Further research into this interaction would help shape our understanding of environmental justice and policy interventions. As with the impact on competitiveness, further research is also required to determine the distributional impacts of policy instruments and their specific design, both individually and in a policy mix.

A research agenda that would advance knowledge in each of the above themes would allow for improved characterization of the relationships that operate within and across the economy–environment interface, and provide the basis for such characterization to be adapted into computational models. However, much of the existing state of knowledge surrounding the above topics is often not incorporated into such models as currently designed and employed, for various reasons, the most important of which is the predominantly qualitative nature of this knowledge. This in itself may act to inhibit research into many of the above topics. One conclusion is that theoretical, empirical and methodological research approaches must continue in parallel and inform each other in order to achieve effective progression.

Most models employed to assess the impact of environmental policy (or the absence of it) tend to focus on a particular component of the environmental-economic system. For example, energy system models deeply characterize technologies and costs, macroeconomic models characterize the complex dynamics of economic processes and interactions, whilst yet others characterize environmental systems and interactions. Numerous Integrated Assessment Models (IAMs) attempt to link (at least two of) these domains and their interactions. However, such dynamic links are usually characterized relatively basically. Further research and efforts should be directed at improving the interaction between domains in IAMs. This allows for improved assessment both of the impact of policy interventions, and the projection of appropriate baselines against which such assessments may be made. These need to include increasingly robust research into the micro and macroeconomic costs of local environmental degradation (such as local air pollution), which in turn allows for increasingly robust assessments of the macroeconomic costs and benefits of climate change and climate change policy interventions (coupled with advances in knowledge and methodological considerations provided by the above research themes). However, such improvements also rely on improvements to the individual components of such models. For example, integration of the insights provided by behavioural and institutional economics in macroeconomic models is often poor, meaning that processes of structural transformation and innovation and diffusion, along with nonrational, nonwelfare maximizing choices made by individual economic actors, are not well represented. The improved incorporation of such dynamics into economic-environmental models should hold a high priority on the research agenda. In addition to this, more emphasis should be placed on other, complementary modelling frameworks (e.g., simulation or agent based models) that do not rely as much on assumptions made in many energy and economic models such as rational decision making and perfect foresight. To some extent, existing optimization models can be adapted or further developed to address the shortcomings of such assumptions, for example to explore the impact of uncertainty.

Advancing the research frontiers above would enhance policy-makers' ability to tackle 'wicked' environmental problems, such as the energy trilemma. It would also contribute to and allow for further research into how to combine the three 'pillars of policy' to encourage a low-carbon, and broader green economy, an increasingly pressing priority in a world of growing environmental and resource pressures, and their effects on the economy. European researchers have made many important contributions to this research agenda, and are well placed to make more, through national and especially European research programmes. There is some urgency, however, to make faster progress on the answers, especially in respect of climate change, if they are to be relevant to the task of trying to keep within the 2°C average global warming limit.

Notes

1. The SDGs may be viewed at https://sustainabledevelopment.un.org/?menu=1300.
2. *'Wicked problems'* are characterized by incomplete or contradictory knowledge, different opinions, which may be based on different value systems, held by large numbers of people, substantial economic implications, and complexity, both internally and in their relationship with other issues. Such problems are not amenable to definitive solution, although some resolutions of them may be judged better than others.
3. http://ec.europa.eu/governance/docs/comm_expertise_en.pdf.

References

Adriaanse, A. 1993. *Environmental Policy Performance Indicators.* SDU, The Hague.
Ambec, S., Cohen, M. A., Elgie, S., and Lanoie, P. 2013. The Porter Hypothesis at 20: Can Environmental Regulation Enhance Innovation and Competitiveness? *Review of Environmental Economics and Policy,* **7**, 2–22.
AMEC, and BIO IS. 2013. *The Opportunities to Business of Improving Resource Efficiency.* Report to the European Commission, February, http://ec.europa.eu/environment/enveco/resource_efficiency/pdf/report_opportunities.pdf.
An, L. 2012. Modeling Human Decisions in Coupled Human and Natural Systems: Review of Agent-Based Models. *Ecological Modelling,* **229**, 25–36.
Andersen, M. S., and Ekins, P. (eds). 2009. *Carbon Taxation: Lessons from Europe.* Oxford University Press, Oxford/New York.
Azevedo, I., Jaramillo, P., Rubin, E., and Yeh, S. 2013. *PRISM 2.0: Modeling Technology Learning for Electricity Supply Technologies.* EPRI, Palo Alto, CA. 3002000871, http://epri.com/abstracts/Pages/ProductAbstract.aspx?ProductId=000000003002000871.
Barker, T. 2008. *The Macroeconomic Effects of the Transition to a Low-Carbon Economy.* Briefing Paper for The Climate Group, London, July, http://theclimategroup.org/_assets/files/Macroeconomics-effects-of-the-Low-Carbon-Economy.pdf.
Beaumont, L. J., Hughes, L., and Pitman, A. J. 2008. Why is the Choice of Future Climate Scenarios for Species Distribution Modelling Important? *Ecology Letters,* **11**, 1135–1146.
Branger, F., and Quirion, P. 2013. *Understanding the Impacts and Limitations of the Current Instrument Mix in Detail: Industrial Sector.* Paris, Centre International de Recherche sur l'Environnement et le Développement.

Branger, F., Lecuyer, O., and Quirion, P. 2015. The European Union Emissions Trading Scheme: Should We Throw the Flagship out with the Bathwater? *WIREs Climate Change*, **6**, 9–16.

BRE. 2008. *Statement on The Green Guide from BRE Global and The Construction Products Association*. http://bre.co.uk/news/Statement-On-The-Green-Guide-From-BRE-Global-And-The-Construction-Products-Association-524.html.

Bromley, D. (ed). 2014. *Institutions and the Environment*. Edward Elgar, Cheltenham.

Canterbery, E. R. 2011. *A Brief History of Economics: Artful Approaches to the Dismal Science*. World Scientific Publishing, Singapore.

Chowdhury, R. R., and Moran, E. F. 2012. Turning the Curve: A Critical Review of Kuznets Approaches. *Applied Geography*, **32**, 3–11.

Cobera, E. 2015. Valuing Nature, Paying for Ecosystem Services and Realising Social Justice: A Response to Matulis. *Ecological Economics*, **110**, 154–157.

Cole, M. A. 2004. Trade, the Pollution Haven Hypothesis and the Environmental Kuznets Curve: Examining the Linkages. *Ecological Economics*, **48**, 71–81.

Daly, H. E., and Cobb, J. 1989. *For the Common Good: Redirecting the Economy Towards Community, the Environment and a Sustainable Future*. Beacon Press, Boston (UK edition 1990 Green Print, Merlin Press, London).

de Groot, R., Van der Perk, J., Chiesura, A., and Van Vliet, A. 2003. Importance and Threat as Determining Factors for Criticality of Natural Capital. In: Ekins, P., de Groot, R., and Folke, C. (eds), *Identifying Critical Natural Capital, Special Issue of Ecological Economics*, vol. 44, pp. 187–204 .

DECC. 2015. *Annual Fuel Poverty Statistics Report*. Tech. rept. London, Department of Energy and Climate Change.

Dietz, S., and Neumayer, E. 2007. Weak and Strong Sustainability in the SEEA: Concepts and Measurement. *Ecological Economics*, **61**, 617–626.

Dobbs, R., Oppenheim, J., Thompson, F., Brinkman, M., and Zornes, M. 2011. *Resource Revolution: Meeting the World's Energy, Materials, Food and Water Needs*. Tech. rept. McKinsey Global Institute, http://mckinsey.com/features/resource_revolution.

Dohmen, T., Falk, A., Huffman, D., and Sunde, U. 2006. *Homo Reciprocans: Survey Evidence on Prevalence, Behaviour and Success*. Discussion Paper Series No. 2205, Bonn, IZA.

Drummond, P. 2014. *Understanding the Impacts and Limitations of the Current EU Climate Policy Instrument Mix*. London, University College London.

Ekins, P. 2011. Environmental Sustainability: From Environmental Valuation to the Sustainability Gap. *Progress in Physical Geography*, **35**, 633–656.

Ekins, P., and Simon, S. 1999. The Sustainability Gap: a Practical Indicator of Sustainability in the Framework of the National Accounts. *International Journal of Sustainable Development*, **2**, 32–58.

Ekins, P., and Simon, S. 2003. An Illustrative Application of the CRITINC Framework to the UK. *Ecological Economics*, **44** (2–3), 255–275.

Ekins, P., and Speck, S. (eds). 2011. *Environmental Tax Reform: A Policy for Green Growth*. Oxford University Press, Oxford.

Ekins, P., Simon, S., Deutsch, L., Folke, C., and de Groot, R. 2003. A Framework for the Practical Application of the Concepts of Critical Natural Capital and Strong Sustainability. *Ecological Economics*, **44**, 165–185.

Ekins, P., McDowall, W., and Zenghelis, D. 2014. *Greening the Recovery*. Tech. rept. the Report of the UCL Green Fiscal Commission, University College London, UCL, http://ucl.ac.uk/public-policy/Policy_Commissions/GEPC.

Engel, S., Pagiola, S., and Wunder, S. 2008. Designing Payments for Environmental Services in Theory and Practice: An Overview of the Issues. *Ecological Economics*, **65**.

European Commission. 2001. *European Governance – A White Paper*. Tech. rept. Communication from the Commission: COM(2001) 428 final, Official Journal C 287, European Commission, Brussels.

European Commission. 2011. *The Advisory Group on the Energy Roadmap to 2050: Final Report*. Tech. rept. SEC(2011) 1569 Final. European Commission, Brussels.

European Commission. 2013. *The Economic Benefits of the Natura 2000 Network*. Tech. rept. Brussels, European Commission.

European Commission. 2015. *Energy Union: Making Energy More Secure, Affordable and sustainable*. Tech. rept. [Online] Available at: http://ec.europa.eu/priorities/energy-union/index_en.htm [Accessed 23rd September 2015].

EUROSTAT. 1997. *Indicators of Sustainable Development*. Tech. rept. Office for Official Publications of the European Communities, Luxembourg.

EUROSTAT. 2001. *Measuring Progress Towards a More Sustainable Europe: Proposed Indicators for Sustainable Development*. Tech. rept. Office for Official Publications of the European Communities, Luxembourg.

Falkner, R. 2014. Global Environmental Politics and Energy: Mapping the Research Agenda. *Energy Research & Social Science*, **1**.

Farber, S. C., Costanza, R., and Wilson, M. A. 2002. Economic and Ecological Concepts for Valuing Ecosystem Services. *Ecological Economics*, **41**, 375–392.

Farley, J., and Costanza, R. 2010. Payments for Ecosystem Services: From Local to Global. *Ecological Economics*, **69**, 2060–2068.

Fehr, E., and Schmidt, K. M. 1999. A Theory of Fairness, Competition, and Cooperation. *The Quarterly Journal of Economics*, **114**, 817–868.

Franklin, R. S., and Ruth, M. 2012. Growing Up and Cleaning Up: The Environmental Curve Redux. *Applied Geography*, **32**, 29–39.

Freeman, C. 1987. *Technology and Economic Performance: Lessons from Japan*. London, Pinter.

Freeman, C. 1992. *The Economics of Hope*. London, New York, Pinter Publishers.

Gallagher, K. P., and Thacker, S. C. 2008. *Democracy, Income and Environmental Quality*. Working Paper Series Number 164, Amherst, MA., University of Massechussets Amherst Political Economy Research Institute.

GEA, (Global Energy Assessment). 2012. *Global Energy Assessment – Toward a Sustainable Future*. Cambridge University Press, Cambridge, UK and New York, NY, and the International Institute for Applied Systems Analysis, Laxenburg, Austria.

Glasser, H. 2002. Ethical Perspectives and Environmental Policy Analysis. Chap. 66 of: Van den Bergh, J. (ed), *Handbook of Environmental and Resource Economics*. Edward Elgar, Cheltenham, pp. 981-1000.

Goulder, L., and Schein, A. 2013. Carbon Taxes versus Cap and Trade: a Critical Review. *Climate Change Economics*, **4**.

Grubb, M. 2014. *Planetary Economics: Energy, Climate Change and the Three Domains of Sustainable Development*. Routledge, London/New York.

Gsottbauer, E., and van den Bergh, J. C. J. M. 2011. Environmental Policy Theory Given Bounded Rationality and Other-Regarding Preferences. *Environmental and Resource Economics*, **49**, 263–304.

Harbaugh, W. T., Levinson, A., and Wilson, D. M. 2002. Reexamining the Empirical Evidence for an Environmental Kuznets Curve. *The Review of Economics and Statistics*, **84**, 541–551.

Hodgson, G. 1988. *Economics and Institutions*. Polity Press, Cambridge.

Hueting, R. 1980. *New Scarcity and Economic Growth*. North Holland, Amsterdam (Dutch edition first published 1974).

IEA, (International Energy Agency). 2012. *Energy Technology Perspectives 2012*. Tech. rept. IEA, Paris.

IEA, (International Energy Agency). 2013. *World Energy Outlook 2013*. Tech. rept. IEA, Paris.

IEA, (International Energy Agency). 2015. *World Energy Outlook Special Report: Energy and Climate Change*. Tech. rept. IEA, Paris.

Illge, L., and Schwarze, R. 2009. A Matter of Opinion – How Ecological and Neo-classical Environmental Economists Think about Sustainability and Economics. *Ecological Economics*, **68**, 594–604.

IPCC. 2014. *Climate Change 2014: Synthesis Report. Contribution of Working Groups I, II and III to the Fifth Assessment Report of the Intergovernmental Panel on Climate Change* [Core Writing Team, R.K. Pachauri and L.A. Meyer (eds.)]. Tech. rept. IPCC, Geneva, Switzerland.

IPCC WGII, (IPCC Working Group II). 2014. *Summary for Policymakers*. Tech. rept. in: *Climate Change 2014: Impacts, Adaptation, and Vulnerability. Part A: Global and Sectoral Aspects. Contribution of Working Group II to the Fifth Assessment Report of the Intergovernmental Panel on Climate Change* [Field, C.B., V.R. Barros, D.J. Dokken, K.J. Mach, M.D. Mastrandrea, T.E. Bilir, M. Chatterjee, K.L. Ebi, Y.O. Estrada, R.C. Genova, B. Girma, E.S. Kissel, A.N. Levy, S. MacCracken, P.R. Mastrandrea, and L.L. White (eds.)]. Cambridge University Press, Cambridge, United Kingdom and New York, NY, USA, This and the full reports are at http://ipcc-wg2 .gov/AR5/report/.

IPCC WGIII, (IPCC Working Group III). 2014a. *Assessing Transformation Pathways*. Tech. rept. Ch.6 in IPCC, 2014, *Climate Change 2014: Mitigation of Climate Change. Contribution of Working Group III to the Fifth Assessment Report of the Intergovernmental Panel on Climate Change* [Edenhofer, O., R. Pichs-Madruga, Y. Sokona, E. Farahani, S. Kadner, K. Seyboth, A. Adler, I. Baum, S. Brunner, P. Eickemeier, B. Kriemann, J. Savolainen, S. Schlömer, C. von Stechow, T. Zwickel and J.C. Minx (eds.)]. Cambridge University Press, Cambridge/New York, http:// mitigation2014.org/report/final-draft/.

IPCC WGIII, (IPCC Working Group III). 2014b. *Summary for Policymakers*. Tech. rept. in: *Climate Change 2014, Mitigation of Climate Change. Contribution of Working Group III to the Fifth Assessment Report of the Intergovernmental Panel on Climate Change* [Edenhofer, O., R. Pichs-Madruga, Y. Sokona, E. Farahani, S. Kadner, K. Seyboth, A. Adler, I. Baum, S. Brunner, P. Eickemeier, B. Kriemann, J. Savolainen, S. Schlomer, C. von Stechow, T. Zwickel and J.C. Minx eds.)]. Cambridge University Press, Cambridge/ New York, http://report.mitigation2014.org/ spm/ipcc_wg3_ar5_summary-for-policymakers_approved.pdf.

Jacobs, M. 1999. Sustainable Development as a Contested Concept. In: Dobson, A. (ed), *Fairness and Futurity: Essays on Environmental Sustainability and Social Justice.* Oxford: Oxford University Press, pp. 21–45.

Jaffe, A. B., and Palmer, K. 1997. Environmental Regulation and Innovation: A Panel Data Study. *Review of Economics and Statistics*, **79**, 610–619.

Jansen, M. A., and Jager, W. 2000. The Human Actor in Ecological-Economic Models. *Ecological Economics*, **35**, 307–310.

Kahneman, D., Slovic, P., and Tversky, A. (eds). 1982. *Judgement under Uncertainty: Heuristics and Biases.* Cambridge University Press, Cambridge.

Kahneman, D., Knetsch, J., and Thaler, R. 1986. Fairness as a Constraint on Profit Seeking: Entitlements in the Market. *American Economic Review*, **76**, 728–741.

Kearsley, A., and Riddel, M. 2010. A Further Enquiry into the Pollution Haven Hypothesis and the Environmental Kuznets Curve. *Ecological Economics*, **69**, 905–919.

Kellenberg, D. K. 2009. An Empirical Investigation of the Pollution Haven Effect with Strategic Environment and Trade Policy. *Journal of International Economics*, **78**, 242–255.

Knetsch, J. L. 2005. Behavioural Economics and Sustainable Forest Management. In: Kant, S., and Berry, R. A. (eds), *Economics, Sustainability and Natural Resources: Economics of Sustainable Forest Management.* Netherlands, Springer.

Kuik, O., Branger, F., and Quirion, P. 2013. *CECILIA2050 Task 2.8: International Competitiveness and Markets.* Tech. rept. Amsterdam, Paris: Institute for Environmental Studies, Centre International de Recherche sur l'Environnement et le Développement.

Laurans, Y., and Mermet, L. 2014. Ecosystem Services Economic Valuation, Decision Support System or Advocacy? *Ecosystem Services*, **7**, 98–105.

Laurent, E. 2011. Issues in Environmental Justice within the European Union. *Ecological Economics*, **70**, 1846–1853.

López, R., and Mitra, S. 2000. Corruption, Pollution and the Kuznets Environment Curve. *Journal of Environmental Economics and Management*, **40**, 137–150.

Malthus, T. R. 1798. *An Essay on the Principle of Population.* available electronically at http://esp.org/books/malthus/population/malthus.pdf.

Matulis, B. S. 2014. The Economic Valuation of Nature: A Question of Justice? *Ecological Economics*, **104**, 155–157.

Mayer, A. L. 2008. Strengths and Weaknesses of Common Sustainability Indices for Multidimensional Systems. *Environment International*, **34**, 277–291.

Mazzucato, M. 2011. *The Entrereneurial State.* London, Demos.

McDermott, M., Mahanty, S., and Schreckenberg, K. 2013. Examining Equity: A Multidimensional Framework for Assessing Equity in Payments for Ecosystem Services. *Environmental Science and Policy*, **33**, 416–427.

McKinsey. 2007. A Cost Curve for Greenhouse Gas Reductions. *The McKinsey Quarterly, February, McKinsey, London.*

MEA, (Millennium Ecosystem Assessment). 2005. *Ecosystems and Human Well-being: Synthesis.* Tech. rept. Island Press, Washington DC.

Meadows, D. H., Meadows, D. L., Randers, J., and Behrens, W. 1972. *The Limits to Growth.* London: Pan Books.

Meadows, D. H., Meadows, D. L., and Randers, J. 2005. *The Limits to Growth: the 30-Year Update.* Earthscan, London.

Metz, J. 2013. Expert Groups in the European Union: A Sui Generis Phenomenon. *Policy and Society*, **32**, 267–278.

Meyer, B., and Meyer, M. 2013. *Impact of the Current Economic Instruments on Economic Activity: Understanding the Existing Climate Policy Mix*. Osnabruck, Gesellschaft fur Wirtschaftliche.

Mitchell, C., Watson, J., and Whiting, J. (eds). 2013. *New Challenges in Energy Security – The UK in a Multipolar World*. London, Palgrave Macmillan.

NCE, (New Climate Economy). 2014. *Better Growth, Better Climate: the New Climate Economy Report – The Synthesis Report*. Tech. rept. New Climate Economy, http://static.newclimateeconomy.report/wp-content/uploads/2014/08/NCE-SYNTHESIS-REPORT-web-share.pdf.

Neuteleers, S., and Engelen, B. 2014. Talking Money: How Market-Based Valuation can Undermine Environmental Protection. *Ecological Economics*, **177**, 253–260.

Norgaard, R. 2010. *A Coevolutionary Interpretation of Ecological Civilization*. Available at http://neweconomy.net/webfm_send/23.

OECD. 2000. *Towards Sustainable Development: Indicators to Measure Progress: Proceedings of the OECD Rome Conference*. Tech. rept. OECD, Paris.

Owen, G. 2012. *Industrial Policy in Europe since the Second World War: What Has Been Learnt?* ECIPE Occasional Paper No. 1/2012. Brussels, European Centre for International Political Economy.

Pavitt, K. 1984. Sectoral Patterns of Technical Change: Towards a Taxonomy and a Theory. *Research Policy*, **13**.

Pearce, D., and Turner, R. K. 1990. *Economics of Natural Resources and the Environment*. Harvester Wheatsheaf, Hemel Hempstead, Herts., UK.

Pearce, D., Markandya, A., and Barbier, E. 1989. *Blueprint for a Green Economy*. London: Earthscan.

Pelenc, J., and Ballet, J. 2015. Strong Sustainability, Critical Natural Capital and the Capability Approach. *Ecologic Economics*, **112**, 36–44.

Plumecocq, G. 2014. The Second Generation of Ecological Economics: How Far Has the Apple Fallen from the Tree? *Ecological Economics*, **107**, 457–468.

Porter, M. E., and van der Linde, C. 1995. Toward a New Conception of the Environment-Competitiveness Relationship. *Journal of Economic Perspectives*, **9**, 97–118.

Posner, S., and Costanza, R. 2011. A Summary of ISEW and GPI Studies at Multiple Scales and New Estimates for Baltimore Coty, Baltimore County, and the State of Maryland. *Ecological Economics*, **70**, 1972–1980.

Robbins, L. 1935. *The Nature and Significance of Economic Science*. 2nd edn. Macmillan, London.

Rockström, J., Steffen, W., Noone, K., øA. Persson, Chapin III, F. S., Lambin, E. F., Lenton, T. M., Scheffer, M., Folke, C., Schellnhuber, H. J., Nykvist, B., de Wit, C. A., Hughes, S., van der Leeuw, Rodhe, H., Sörlin, S., Snyder, P. K., Costanza, R., Svedin, U., Falkenmark, M., Karlberg, L., Corell, R. W., Fabry, V. J., Hansen, J., Walker, B., Liverman, D., Richardson, K., Crutzen, P., and Foley, J. A. 2009. A Safe Operating Space for Humanity. *Nature*, **461**, 472–475.

Rutherford, M. 1983. John R. Commons' Institutional Economics. *Journal of Economic Issues*, **XVII**, 721–744.

Scholte, S. S. K., van Teeffelen, A. J. A., and Verburg, P. H. 2015. Integrating Socio-Cultural Perspectives into Ecosystem Service Valuation: A Review of Concepts and Methods. *Ecological Economics*, **113**, 67–78.

Schomers, S., and Matzdorf, B. 2013. Payments for Ecosystem Services: A Review and Comparison of Developing and Industrialized Countries. *Ecosystem Services*, **6**, 16–30.

Stahmer, C., Kuhn, M., and Braun, N. 1998. *Physical Input-Output Tables for Germany, 1990*. Tech. rept. Report prepared for DGXI and Eurostat, Working paper No.2/1998/B/1. Brussels (European Commission).

Stern, N. 2007. *The Economics of Climate Change: The Stern Review*. Cambridge University Press, Cambridge.

Torras, M., and Boyce, J. K. 1998. Income, Inequality and Pollution: A Reassessment of the Environmental Kuznets curve. *Ecological Economics*, **25**, 147–160.

Turner, K. 2002. Environmental and Ecological Economics Perspectives. Chap. 67 of: Van den Bergh, J. (ed), *Handbook of Environmental and Resource Economics*. Edward Elgar, Cheltenham, pp. 1001–1033.

UN, (United Nations). 1996. *Indicators of Sustainable Development: Framework and Methodologies*. Tech. rept. UN, New York.

UNEP, (United Nations Environment Programme). 2012. *The Fifth Global Environmental Outlook: GEO-5*. Tech. rept. Geneva/Nairobi: UNEP.

UNU-IHDP, and UNEP. 2014. *The Inclusive Wealth Report: Measuring Progress Towards Sustainability*. Tech. rept. Cambridge University Press, Cambridge, http://mgiep.unesco.org/wp-content/uploads/2014/12/IWR2014-WEB.pdf.

Van den Bergh, J. C. J. M., and Botzen, W. J. W. 2015. Monetary Valuation of the Social Cost of CO_2 Emissions: A Critical Survey. *Ecological Economics*, **114**, 33–46.

Vaze, P. 1998. Environmental Input-Output Table for the United Kingdom. In: Vaze, P. (ed), *UK Environmental Accounts 1998*. London (The Stationery Office), pp. 125–146.

Venkatachalam, L. 2007. Environmental Economic and Ecological Economics: Where Can they Converge? *Ecological Economics*, **61**, 550–558.

Watkiss, P., and Downing, T. 2008. The Social Cost of Carbon: Valuation Estimates and Their Use in UK Policy. *The Integrated Assessment Journal*, **8**, 85–105.

Watson, J., and Scott, A. 2006. New Nuclear Power in the UK: A Strategy for Energy Security? *Energy Policy*, **37**, 5094–5104.

Weber, M., and Hemmelskamp, J. (eds). 2005. *Towards Environmental Innovation Systems*. Springer.

WEC. 2015. *Energy Trilemma Index*. Tech. rept. [Online] Available at: https://worldenergy.org/data/trilemma-index/ [Accessed 18th September 2015].

Weitzman, M. 2007. *Structural Uncertainty and the Value of Statistical Life in the Economics of Catastrophic Climate Change*. NBER Working Paper Series, Cambridge, MA., National Bureau of Economic Research.

Wicks, M. 2009. *Energy Security: a National Challenge in a Changing World*. August, DECC, http://130.88.20.21/uknuclear/pdfs/Energy_Security_Wicks_Review_August_2009.pdf.

Wiedmann, T. O., Schandl, H., Lenzen, M., Moran, D., Suh, S., West, J., and Kanemoto, K. 2013. The Material Footprint of Nations. *Proceedings of the National Academy of Sciences*, http://pnas.org/content/early/2013/08/28/1220362110.abstract.

Wilsdon, J., and Doubleday, R. 2015. *Future Directions for Scientific Advice in Europe*. Tech. rept. Cambridge, Centre for Science and Policy, University of Cambridge.

World Bank. 2015. *State and Trends of Carbon Pricing 2015*. Tech. rept. World Bank Group, Washington DC.

World Commission on Environment and Development (WCED). 1987. *Our Common Future (The Brundtland Report)*. Tech. rept. Oxford: Oxford University Press.

Wurzel, K. W. Rüdiger. 2008. Environmental Policy: EU Actors, Leader and Laggard States. In: Hayward, Jack (ed), *Leaderless Europe*. Oxford: Oxford University Press, pp. 66–88.

8   Regional Disparities and Efficient Transport Policies

Stef Proost and Jacques-François Thisse

Abstract

This chapter addresses the economics of regional disparities and transport policies in the European Union, offering an explanation for the uneven development of regions. We show that recent developments in spatial economics highlight the fact that trade is costly and location still matters. Since the drop in transport costs and the emergence of a knowledge-based economy, the proximity to natural resources has been replaced by new drivers of regional growth that rely on human capital and cognitive skills. Regions with a high market potential – those where demand is high and transport costs low – are likely to attract more firms and pay higher wages, which leads to sizable and lasting regional disparities. As a consequence, investments in interregional transport policies may not deliver their expected effects. In addition, new information and communication devices foster the fragmentation of the supply chain and the decentralization of activities.

8.1   Introduction

This chapter addresses the economics of regional disparities and regional policies in the European Union (EU). The fundamental challenge is to explain the uneven development of regions in both the EU and within EU member states. The purpose is not to delve into concrete regional policies and judge their results but rather to understand the main drivers of contemporary regional development. Earlier explanations evolved around natural resources and transport systems. But since the emergence of a knowledge-based economy, traditional location factors have been replaced with new drivers of regional growth that rely on human capital and cognitive skills. This chapter is organized in seven sections. In the second one, we focus on the concepts and tools of spatial economics that are necessary as a backdrop to regional economics. In the third section, we analyse the main forces driving the allocation of economic activity across regions: firms' market access and labour mobility. The fourth section examines these two forces to see whether they generate over or under-agglomeration. The fifth section is devoted to the effects of investments in interregional transport policies, while the sixth section briefly analyses current interregional transport policies. The seventh section concludes.

8.2   What Is Spatial Economics About?

The Industrial Revolution exacerbated regional disparities by an order of magnitude that was unknown before. The recent development of new information and communication technologies is triggering a new regional divide of which governments and the public should be aware. What economic tools can we use to understand those evolutions? As spatial economics deals with bringing location, distance, and land into economics, its aim is to explain where economic activities are located. This makes spatial economics one of the main economic fields that can be employed to understand how the new map of economic activities is being drawn. Yet, at first glance, the steady (actually spectacular) drop in transport costs since the mid-nineteenth century – compounded by the decline of protectionism post-World War II and, more recently, by the near-disappearance of communication costs – is said to have freed firms and households from the need to be located near one another. Therefore, it is tempting to foresee the *'death of distance'* and the emergence of a *'flat world'* in which competition is thought of as a race to the bottom, with the lowest-wage countries as the winners.

But – and it is a big but – while it is true that the importance of proximity to natural resources has declined considerably, this does not mean that distance and location have disappeared from economic life. On the contrary, recent work in regional and urban economics indicates that new forces, hitherto outweighed by natural factors, are shaping an economic landscape that, with its many barriers and large inequalities, is anything but flat. Empirical evidence shows that sizable and lasting differences in income per capita and unemployment rates exist. In brief, *the fundamental task of spatial economics is to explain the existence of peaks and valleys in the spatial distribution of wealth and people.* This is what we aim to accomplish in this chapter. Most graduate or undergraduate students in economics have barely come across the words 'cities', 'regions', and 'transport' during their studies. We therefore will define the basic concepts of spatial economics that are not part of the tool box of most economists. In particular, we show how the tools of modern economic theory can illuminate the main issues of spatial economics, and how modern empirical methods have helped measure them. Conversely, introducing space into economic modelling allows one to revisit existing theories and suggest new solutions to old problems. In particular, we highlight some of the findings that reveal the increased importance of space in the modern economy.

8.2.1   Location Does Matter

Why do economic activities cluster in a few places? There is no satisfactory answer to this question in the dominant paradigm of economic theory, which combines perfect competition and constant returns to scale. In the absence of scale economies, fragmenting production into smaller units at different locations does not reduce the total output available from the same given inputs, but transport costs decline. In the limit, if the distribution of natural resources is uniform, the economy is such that each individual produces for his or her own consumption. This strange world without cities has been called '*backyard capitalism*'. To put it differently, each location would become an autarky, except it is possible that trade between locations might occur if the geographic distribution of natural resources is uneven. Admittedly, different locations do not a priori provide the same exogenous amenities. However, using the unevenness of natural resources as the only explanation for the existence of large cities and for regional imbalance seems weak. Rather, as noted by Koopmans (1957) almost 60 years ago, *increasing returns are critical to understanding how the space-economy is shaped*.

A simple example will illustrate this fundamental idea. Suppose a planner has to decide where to locate one or two facilities to provide a certain good to a population of immobile users who are evenly distributed between two regions. Individual demands are perfectly inelastic and normalized to one; the marginal production cost is constant and normalized to zero. Consumers in the domestic region may be supplied at zero cost, whereas supplying those living in the foreign region entails a transport cost of T euros. If two facilities are built, the cost of building a facility is equal to F euros in each region. If only one facility is made available, the planner must incur cost F; if two facilities are built, the cost is $2F$. A planner who aims to minimize total costs will choose to build a facility in each region if, and only if, $F + T$ is more than $2F$, that is, $T > F$. This will hold when F is small, T is high, or both. Otherwise, it will be less expensive to build a single facility that supplies all people in both regions. In other words, weak increasing returns – F takes on low values – promote the scattering of activities, whereas strong increasing returns foster their spatial concentration. As a consequence, the intensity of increasing returns has a major implication for the spatial organization of the economy.

The first law of spatial economics: If many activities can be located almost anywhere, few activities are located everywhere.

It is in this sense that location matters: although a large number of activities become '*footloose*', a relatively small number of places in many countries account for a large share of the national value added, whereas many large areas account for no or little economic activity. The difficulty economists encounter when they take into account scale economies in general equilibrium theory probably explains why spatial economics has been at the periphery of economics for so long.

Nevertheless, it must be kept in mind that accounting for increasing returns often yields a message that differs from the standard neoclassical paradigm of perfect competition and constant returns to scale. Even though transport costs must be positive for space to matter, one should not infer from this observation that location matters less when transport costs decrease—quite the opposite. Spatial economics shows that lower transport costs make firms more sensitive to minor differences between locations. To put it another way, *a tiny difference may have a big impact on the spatial distribution of economic activity.*

8.2.2   Moving Goods and People is Still Costly

Transportation refers to the movement of people, goods, information, or anything else across space. Ever since the beginning of the Industrial Revolution, there has been spectacular progress in terms of the speed and cost for interregional *and* international transport. According to Bairoch (1997), 'overall, it can be estimated that, from 1800 to 1910, the decrease in (weighted) real average transport costs was on the order of 10 to 1'. For the US, Glaeser and Kohlhase (2004) observe that the average cost of moving a ton a mile in 1890 was 18.5 cents, as opposed to 2.3 cents today (in 2001 dollars). Yet, as will be seen, estimating the gravity equation reveals that distance remains a strong impediment to trade and exchange. What is more, the current concentration of people and activities in large cities and urban regions fosters steadily increasing congestion both in private and public transport as capacity is not easy to expand. In the regional context, transportation consists of interregional and international freight trips of inputs and outputs, as well as passenger trips. Unlike an urban environment, larger interregional passenger and freight flows tend to reduce rather than increase the average transport costs because of the presence of economies of density in scheduled transport and because capacity expansion (physical and/or frequency) is easier to implement. Therefore, transportation faces different challenges at the urban and interregional levels.

In the wonderful dimensionless world of some analysts and journalists, transport costs are zero, and thus any agent is equally connected to, or globally competes with, any other agent. If the monetary cost of shipping goods has dramatically decreased, other costs related to the transport of goods remain significant. For example, the opportunity cost of time rises in a growing economy, so that the time cost wasted in moving certain types of goods steadily rises. Similarly, doing business at a distance generates additional costs, even within the EU, due to differences in business practices, political and legal climates, or culture. One of the most robust empirical facts in economics is the Gravity Law: 'Holding constant the product of two countries' sizes, their bilateral trade will, on average, be inversely proportional to the distance between them' (Head and Mayer, 2013). To put it differently, distance between locations still matters because it affects the economic life under different disguises.

Doing a back-of-the-envelope calculation, Cheshire and Magrini (2006) find that despite smaller regional disparities and larger average distances in the US than in the EU, the net migration rate between areas having a comparable population size is almost 15 times higher in the US than in the EU. (The areas are the 50 US states plus Washington, DC versus the EU-12 large countries – France, Germany, Spain, and the UK – divided into their level 1 regions [in Germany, the Länder] and the EU's smaller countries, treated as single units.) These authors conclude that 'in Europe, urban population growth seems likely to be a rather imperfect signal of changes in welfare in cities'. This is to be contrasted with a recent macroeconomic study by Beyer and Smets (2015), who show that, once they control for country factors, labour mobility across 41 EU regions would account for almost 50 per cent of the long-run adjustment process to negative regional shocks, which is more or less the same as in the US where mobility has been decreasing since 1980. However, it takes much longer in Europe than in the US for this adjustment to unfold.

On the other hand, more disaggregate spatial studies strongly suggest that, even within European countries, migration is sluggish and governed by a wide range of intangible and time-persistent factors. For example, controlling for the geographical distance and several other plausible effects, Falck et al. (2012) show that actual migration flows among 439 German districts (the NUTS 3 regions) are positively affected by the similarity of dialects that were prevalent in the source and destination areas more than 120 years ago. In the absence of such dialects, which are seldom used today, internal migration in Germany would be almost 20 per cent higher than what it is. In the same vein, Dahl and Sorenson (2010) find that Danish scientists and engineers, who exhibit a more substantial sensitivity to wage differences than other Danish workers, have even stronger preferences for living close to their family and friends. Further evidence of the low mobility of workers is provided by Bosquet and Overman (2015). Using the British Household Panel Survey that involved 32, 380 individuals from 1991 to 2009, these authors observe that 43.7 per cent of workers worked only in the area where they were born. Among the unskilled workers, this share grows to 51.7 per cent but drops to 30.5 per cent for workers having a college degree. Such low lifetime mobility provides empirical evidence that migration costs are an important determinant of the space-economy. Furthermore, 44.3 per cent of the panel retirees live where they were born, revealing a high individual degree of attachment to their birthplace. Such studies suggest that labour markets operate at a local level, implying that even sizable wage differences between regions can persist for long periods of time.

To sum up, the transport of (some) goods remains costly, while many services used by firms and households are nontradable. Moreover, we will see that proximity remains critical for the diffusion of some information. European people are sticky; this means that the model widely used in the US to study urban and regional growth, which relies on the perfect mobility of people and the search for amenities, has very limited application within the EU, not to say within all European countries. These facts have a major implication for the organization of the (European) economic space:

The second law of spatial economics: The world is not flat because what happens near to us matters more than what happens far from us.

Combining the first and second laws of spatial economics leads us to formulate what we see as the fundamental trade-off of spatial economics:

The spatial distribution of activities is the outcome of a trade-off between different types of scale economies and the costs generated by the transfer of people, goods, and information.

We may thus already conclude that high transport costs promote the dispersion of economic activities, while strong increasing returns act as an agglomeration force, and the other way round. This trade-off is valid on all spatial scales (city, region, country, and continent), which makes it a valuable analytical tool. We will return to this in the next two sections.

At the interregional level, locations are aggregated into subnational units that are distant from each other. Regardless of what is meant by a region, the concept is useful if, and only if, a region is part of a broader network through which various types of interactions occur. In other words, any meaningful discussion of regional issues requires at least two regions in which economic decisions are made. Hence, space is the substratum of activities, but land is not a fundamental ingredient of regional economics. Furthermore, as repeatedly stressed by Ohlin (1967), if we do not want the analysis to be confined to trade theory, we must also account explicitly for the mobility of agents (firms and/or consumers) and for the existence of transport costs in trading commodities. However, how well a region does also depends on the functioning of its local markets and institutions. The surge of *new economic geography* (NEG) has allowed us to rethink regional economics by combining the trade of goods and the mobility of production factors. In NEG, a region is assumed to be dimensionless and is described by a node in a transport network. The objective of *regional economics* is then to study the distribution of activities across a regional system. Figure 8.1 shows the geographical distribution of the GDP per capita per NUTS 3 region in the EU. We note striking differences across countries but also within countries. Understanding these differences and what policies make sense is one of the principal motivations for this survey.

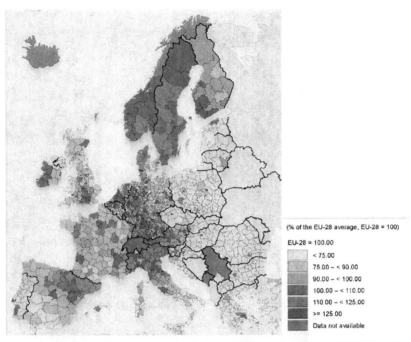

Figure 8.1 Geographical distribution of the GDP per capita per NUTS 3 region in the EU (Eurostat, 2015b).

Before proceeding, observe that the persistence of sizeable regional differences does not provide evidence of a lack of economic integration. Even in the world's largest and most integrated economy, 'local labour markets in the US are characterized by enormous differences in worker earnings, factor productivity and firm innovation' and these differences do not seem to go away (Moretti, 2011).

8.3   The Drivers of Regional Agglomeration

The EU has a wide diversity of cultures and a wide range of incomes at the inter-regional level. Cultural diversity is an asset that has its costs and benefits, but sizable income differences are a source of concern. Article 158 of the Treaty on European Union states that 'the Community shall aim at reducing disparities between the levels of development of the various regions and the backwardness of the least favoured regions or islands, including rural areas'. European integration is supposed to lead to the convergence of income levels across countries through more intense trade links. However, this process is slow and may be accompanied by widening interregional income gaps despite EU regional policy efforts.[1] The lack of regional convergence may lead to cohesion problems that, when combined with cultural differences, can contribute to secessionist tendencies and threaten the future both of countries and of their membership in the EU. Whether or not there is convergence across the European regional system remains a controversial issue that also raises various unsuspected methodological difficulties (Magrini, 2004).

The idea of spatial interaction is central to regional economics. Broadly defined, spatial interaction refers to a wide array of flows subject to various types of spatial frictions. Examples of these flows include traded goods, migration, capital, interregional grants, remittances, as well as the interregional transmission of knowledge and business-cycle effects. The bulk of NEG has been restricted to the movement of goods and production factors. NEG remains in the tradition of trade theory as it focuses on exchanges between regions to explain why some regions fare better than others. Furthermore, NEG models regions as dimensionless economies without land. In contrast, an approach that would build on urban economics would rather choose to focus on the internal functioning of a region. Both approaches are legitimate, but a full-fledged model of the regional system taking both into account is still missing.

The economic performance of regions is affected not only by their industrial mix and their relative position in the web of relations, but also by the interregional and international mobility of commodities and production factors (e.g., capital and labour). In particular, lowering transport and trade costs changes the incentives for both firms and workers to stay put or move to another location. Therefore, to assess the full impact of market integration and the monetary union, it is crucial to have a good understanding of how firms and workers react to lower trade and transport costs. In this respect, it should be stressed that European policy-makers often overlook the fact that market integration affects the locational choices of firms and households. In particular, as will be seen, NEG highlights the fact that a rising mobility of goods and people does not necessarily reduce spatial inequality. Even though regional development agencies typically think of spatial inequality as *temporary disequilibrium* within the economy, stable spatial equilibria often display sizable and lasting differences in income and employment, a fact that agrees with anecdotal evidence. Furthermore, we will see that regional disparities need not be bad because they can be the geographical counterpart of greater efficiency and stronger growth.

On interregional and international scales, accessibility to spatially dispersed markets drives the location of firms; this has long been recognized in both spatial economics and regional science (Fujita and Thisse, 2013). Accessibility is itself measured by all the costs generated by the various types of spatial frictions that economic agents face in the exchange process. In the case of goods and services, these frictions are called *trade costs*.[2] Spulber (2007) refers to them as 'the four Ts': (i) *transaction costs* that result from doing business at a distance due to differences in customs, business practices, as well as political and legal climates; (ii) *tariff and nontariff costs* such as different pollution standards, anti-dumping practices, and the massive number of regulations that still restrict trade; (iii) *transport costs* per se because goods have to reach their destination, while many services remain nontradable; and (iv) *time costs* because, despite the Internet and video-conferencing, there are still communication barriers across dispersed distribution and manufacturing facilities that slow down reactions to changes in market conditions. Because they stand for the cost of coordinating and connecting transactions between the supplier's and customer's locations, trade costs are crucial to the global firm and therefore are likely to stay at centre stage. The relative importance of the 'four Ts' obviously varies enormously from one sector to another, from one activity to another, from one commodity to another.

Anderson and van Wincoop (2004) provide a detailed estimate of trade costs, concluding that these costs would climb to approximately 170 per cent of the average mill price of manufactured goods, but the variance across goods is high. This estimate can be broken down as follows: 55 per cent internal costs, which include all logistics costs; and 74 per cent international costs ($1.7 = 1.55 \times 1.74 - 1$). International costs in turn are broken down as 21 per cent for transport costs and 44 per cent for costs connected with border effects ($1.74 = 1.21 \times 1.44$). Tariff and nontariff barriers account for 8 per cent of the border effects (exceptionally, this is 10 or 20 per cent in the case of developing countries); language difference, 7 per cent; currency difference, 14 per cent; and other costs, including information 9 per cent (all in all, $1.44 = 1.08 \times 1.07 \times 1.14 \times 1.09$). Therefore, it is not an exaggeration to say that the share of trade costs in the consumer price of several manufactured goods remains high. Note that there are also big differences from one trading area to another. For example, Head and Mayer (2004) convincingly argue that North American integration is significantly deeper than European integration.

8.3.1   The Home-Market Effect

The neoclassical theory of the mobility of production factors and goods predicts a market outcome in which production factors receive the same reward regardless of the place of operation. Indeed, when each region is endowed with the same production function that exhibits constant returns to scale as well as a decreasing marginal productivity, capital responds to market disequilibrium by moving from regions where it is abundant relative to labour and receives a lower return towards regions where it is scarce and receives a higher return. If the price of consumption goods were the same everywhere (perhaps because obstacles to trade have been abolished), the marginal productivity of both capital and labour in equilibrium would also be the same everywhere due to the equalization of capital – labour ratios. Therefore, the free mobility of goods and capital would guarantee the equalization of wages and capital rents across regions and countries. In this case, the size of markets would be immaterial to people's welfare.

However, we are far from seeing such a featureless world. To solve this contradiction, NEG takes a radical departure from the standard setting. NEG assumes that the main reason why there is no convergence is that firms do not operate under constant returns but under *internal* increasing returns. This point was made by Krugman (1980) in a paper now famous because it highlights how *market size* and *market accessibility* interact to determine the location of an industry. The idea that size matters for the development of a region or country was emphasized by the economic historian Pollard (1981) for whom 'it is obviously harder to build an industrial complex without the solid foundation of a home market'. In contrast, economic integration and regional trade agreements lower the importance of domestic markets and allow small regions and countries to supply larger markets.

Both economists and geographers agree that a large market tends to increase the profitability of firms established there. The idea is that locations with good access to several markets offer firms a greater profit because these locations allow firms to save on transport costs and lower their average production cost by selling more. In sum, firms would seek locations with the highest market potential where demand is high and transport costs are low. Most empirical works use the concept of *market potential*, introduced by the American geographer Harris (1954) and defined as the sum of regional GDPs weighted by the inverse of the distance to the region in question where the sum includes the region itself and its internal distance as a reduced-form expression derived from general equilibrium trade theory. Econometric studies suggest that market potential is a powerful driver of increases in income per capita (Mayer, 2008). In other words, larger and/or more centrally located regions or countries are, on average, richer than regions or countries with small local markets and few neighbours or neighbours that are also small.

Nevertheless, as firms set up in the large regions, competition is also heightened, thereby holding back the tendency to agglomerate. Indeed, revisiting Hotelling's (1929) pioneering work, d'Aspremont et al. (1979) show that *spatial separation allows firms to soften price competition*. However, by relaxing competition, product differentiation permits firms to seek the most accessible location. Consequently, the interregional distribution of firms producing a tradable good is governed by two forces that pull in opposite directions: the agglomeration force generated by firms' desire for market access, and the dispersion force generated by firms' desire to avoid market crowding. Thus, the equilibrium distribution of firms across regions can be viewed as the balance between these two forces.

The intensity of the agglomeration force decreases with transport costs, whereas the dispersion force gets stronger through tougher competition between regions. Although it is the balance of these forces that determines the shape of the spatial economy, there is no clear indication regarding their relative intensity as transport costs decrease. This is why the main questions that NEG addresses keep their relevance: When do we observe an agglomerated or a dispersed pattern of production at the interregional level? What is the impact of decreasing transport and trade costs on the intensity of the agglomeration and dispersion forces operating at that spatial scale?

Location and Market Size

The standard model involves two regions (North and South) and two production factors (capital and labour). The global economy is endowed with K units of capital and L units of labour. Each individual is endowed with one unit of labour and K/L units of capital. Capital is mobile between regions and capital owners seek the higher rate of return; the share $\lambda \geq 1/2$ of capital located in the North is endogenous. Labour is immobile between regions but perfectly mobile between sectors; the share of workers located in the North is exogenous and equal to $\theta \geq 1/2$. Both regional labour markets are perfect. Capital and labour are used by firms that produce a CES-differentiated product under increasing returns and monopolistic competition (Dixit and Stiglitz, 1977). Let $f > 0$ be the fixed capital requirement and $c > 0$ the marginal labour requirement needed for a firm to enter the market and produce one variety of the differentiated good. Capital market clearing implies that the number of firms is exogenous and given by K/f. Finally, shipping the differentiated good between the two regions is costly.

The above system of push and pull reaches an equilibrium when the capital return is the same in both regions. In this event, *the North hosts a more-than-proportionate share of firms*, a result that has been labeled the '*home-market effect*' (HME).[3] Since the North is larger in terms of population and purchasing power, it seems natural that North should attract more firms than the South. What is less expected is that the initial size advantage is magnified, that is, the equilibrium value of λ exceeds θ. What the HME shows is that the market-access effect dominates the market-crowding effect. Since $(\lambda - \theta)K > 0$ units of capital move from the South to the North, capital does not flow from the region where it is abundant to the region where it is scarce.

How does a lowering of interregional transport costs affect this result? At first glance, one could expect the market-access effect to be weaker when transport costs are lower. In fact, the opposite holds true: more firms choose to set up in the North when it gets cheaper to trade goods between the two regions.

This somewhat paradoxical result can be understood as follows. On the one hand, lower transport costs makes exports to the smaller market easier, which allows firms to exploit their scale economies more intensively by locating in the North; on the other hand, lower transport costs also reduce the advantages associated with geographical isolation in the South where there is less competition. These two effects push towards more agglomeration, implying that, as transport costs go down, the smaller region becomes deindustrialized to the benefit of the larger one. The HME is thus prone to having unexpected implications for transport policy: *by making the transport of goods cheaper in both directions, the construction of new infrastructure may induce firms to pull out of the smaller region.* In other words, connecting lagging regions to dynamic urban centres may weaken their industrial base. This result may come as a surprise to those who forget that highways run both ways. What is more, the intensity of competition in domestic markets matters for trade. Since large markets tend to be more competitive, penetrating such markets is more difficult than exporting to small regions, making the former regions even more attractive than the latter. But how robust is the HME?

Wages and Market Size

Although it is convenient to assume equal wages across regions because this allows the impact of falling transport costs to be isolated, the assumption clashes with anecdotal evidence. How wages vary with firms' location is best studied in a full-fledged general equilibrium model where wages are endogenous. As firms congregate in the larger region, competition in the local labour market intensifies, which should lead to a wage hike in North. Since consumers in the North enjoy higher incomes, local demand for the good rises and this makes the North more attractive to firms located in the South. However, the wage hike associated with more firms establishing in the North generates a new dispersion force, which lies at the heart of many debates regarding the deindustrialization of developed countries, that is, their high labour costs. In such a context, firms are induced to relocate their activities to the South when the lower wages in the South more than offset the lower demand. Takahashi et al. (2013) have shown that the equilibrium wage in the North is greater than the equilibrium wage in the South. Furthermore, the HME still holds. In other words, although the wages paid in the North exceed those paid in South, market access remains critical when determining the location of firms.

Furthermore, if the size of the larger region grows through the migration of workers from the South to the North, the interregional wage gap widens. Therefore, *fostering the mobility of workers could well exacerbate regional disparities.* Nevertheless, Takahashi et al. (2013) showed that the magnification of the HME discussed above no longer holds: as transport costs steadily decrease, both the equilibrium wage and manufacturing share first rise and then fall because competition in the larger labour market becomes very strong. Despite this caveat, market integration and factor mobility favour the agglomeration of activities within a small number of large regions.

It is commonplace in macroeconomics and economic policy to think of unemployment as a national problem, the reason being that labour market institutions and demographic evolutions are often country-specific. Yet empirical evidence reveals the existence of a strong correlation between high unemployment rates and a low GDP per capita, and the other way round, across regions belonging to the same EU country. This should invite policy-makers to pay more attention to the regional aspects of unemployment. In particular, is higher interregional labour mobility the right solution for large regional employment disparities? Not necessarily. As migrants get absorbed by the labour market of the core region, the agglomeration economies discussed in the companion chapter come into play, which reduces the number of job seekers. Such a scenario is more likely to arise when migrants are skilled. In contrast, the opposite evolution characterizes the lagging region, which loses its best workers. Epifani and Gancia (2005) illustrate this contrasting pattern by introducing job search frictions à la Pissarides in a standard NEG set-up and conclude that 'migration from the periphery to the core may reduce unemployment disparities at first, but amplify them in the long run'. This result clashes with the widespread idea that geographical mobility is the solution to regional unemployment disparities. Even though it would be daring to draw policy recommendations from a single paper, it is clear that more research is needed to fully understand the impact of labour mobility on the functioning of local labour markets when market size and agglomeration economies are taken into account.

Heterogeneous Firms

The evidence is mounting that firms differ vastly in productivity. This is reflected in their ability to compete in the international marketplace. For example, Mayer and Ottaviano (2007) observe that the top 1 per cent of European exporters account for more than 45 per cent of aggregate exports, while the top 10 per cent of exporting firms account for more than 80 per cent of aggregate exports. In short, a few firms are responsible for the bulk of exports. Having such numbers in mind, it is thus legitimate to ask what the HME is when firms are heterogeneous and also when they are, or are not, sorted out across regions according to their productivity. So, it is legitimate to ask what the HME becomes when firms are heterogeneous.

Heterogeneous workers are sorted between cities along educational lines (see Chapter 9). A comparable process is at work in the case of heterogeneous firms: *the more productive firms locate in the larger region*, whereas the less productive firms seek protection against competition by setting up in the smaller region (Nocke, 2006). Furthermore, despite the greater competition in the North, the

HME still holds. Nevertheless, the mechanism that selects firms differs from the sorting of workers. Indeed, the gathering of the more productive firms renders competition very tough in the North, which leads inefficient firms to locate far apart to avoid the devastating effects of competition with efficient firms. This sparks a productivity gap between regions, which is exacerbated when the size difference between regions increases. Using US data on the concrete industry, Syverson (2004) observes that inefficient firms barely survive in large competitive markets and tend to leave them. This result is confirmed by the literature that follows Syverson.

To sum up, *large markets tend to offer more and better opportunities to firms and workers*.

Care is Needed

Can the HME help explain strong regional disparities? First of all, the above results were obtained using specific models so their robustness remains an open question. Second, the share of the manufacturing sector has shrunk dramatically in developed economies. So one may wonder what the HME becomes when we consider the location of nontradable services. In this case, the HME still holds if the North is sufficiently large to overcome the competition effect. Otherwise, the larger region no longer provides a sufficiently big outlet to host a more-than-proportionate share of firms. In this case, the smaller region accommodates a larger share of firms (Behrens, 2005).

Third, and last, the HME is studied in a two-region setting. Unfortunately, it cannot readily be extended to multi-regional set-ups because there is no obvious benchmark against which to measure the *'more-than-proportionate'* share of firms. A multi-regional setting brings about a new fundamental ingredient – the variability in regions' accessibility to spatially dispersed markets. In other words, the relative position of a region within the network of exchanges (which also involves cultural, linguistic, and political proximity) matters. Any global (local) change in this network, such as market integration or the construction of major transport links, is likely to trigger complex effects that vary in nontrivial ways with the properties of the graph representing the transport network (Behrens and Thisse, 2007). For example, in a multi-regional setting, the greater specialization of a few regions in one sector does not necessarily mean that this sector becomes more agglomerated, and vice versa. Therefore, it is hardly shocking that empirical evidence regarding the HME is mixed (Davis and Weinstein, 2003, Head and Mayer, 2004).

However, intuitively, it is reasonable to expect the forces highlighted by the HME to be at work in many real-world situations.[4] But how can we check this? There are two possible ways. First, since there is no hope of deriving general results for multi-regional economies, it is reasonable to try to solve numerically spatial general equilibrium models where transport networks are selected randomly. For this, one needs a mathematical framework that is tractable but yet rich enough to analyze meaningful effects. Working with a NEG model that encompasses asymmetric regions, costly trade, and transport tree-networks that are generated randomly, Barbero et al. (2015) confirm that local market size (measured by population) and accessibility (measured by centrality in the trading network) are crucial in explaining a region's wage; the authors also confirm that local market size (measured by industry expenditure share) explains well the location of firms. Using Spanish data and computed transport costs, Barbero et al. (2015) find that the model is good at predicting the location of industries but less accurate concerning the spatial pattern of wages. The authors also observe that, after three decades of major road investments, the distribution of industries had not changed much in Spain. This might suggest that, once a few key connections exist, the supply of transport links obeys the law of decreasing returns.

The second method is to study empirically the causality between market access and the spatial distribution of firms. There is plenty of evidence suggesting that market access is associated with firms' location, higher wages, and employment. Starting with Redding and Venables (2004), various empirical studies have confirmed the positive correlation between the economic performance of territories and their market potential. Redding and Sturm (2008) exploit the political division of Germany after World War II as a natural experiment to show how the loss of market access for cities in West Germany located close to the border made these cities grow much less. After a careful review of the state of the art, Redding (2011) concludes that 'there is not only an association but also a causal relationship between market access and the spatial distribution of economic activity'. For example, one of the more remarkable geographical concentrations of activities is what is known as the '*manufacturing belt*' in the US. This 'belt' accommodated around four-fifths of the US manufacturing output for a century or so within an area that was one-sixth of the country's area. Klein and Crafts (2012) conclude that 'market potential had a substantial impact on the location of manufacturing in the USA throughout the period 1880–1920 and ...was more important than factor endowments'. In the same vein, Head and Mayer (2011) summarize their analysis of the relationship between market proximity and economic development over 1965–2003 by saying that 'market potential is a powerful driver of increases in income per capita'.

All of this only seems a paradox: inexpensive shipping of goods makes competition tougher, thus firms care more about small advantages than they did in a world in which they were protected by the barriers of high transport costs. In other words, *even at the interregional level, proximity matters*, but the reasons for this are not the same as those discussed in Chapter 9. However, both sets of results hinge on the same principle: *small initial advantages may be translated into large ex post advantages once firms operate under increasing returns.*

The HME explains why large markets attract firms. However, this effect does not explain why some markets are bigger than others. The problem may be tackled from two different perspectives. First, the two regions are supposed to be the same size and the internal fabric of each region (e.g., the magnitude of agglomeration economies) determines the circumstances in which a region accommodates the larger number of firms. Second, workers are allowed to migrate from one region to the other, thus leading to some regions being larger than others. The former case – when the two regions are a priori identical – is studied below, while the latter case is investigated in Section 8.3.3 because the mobility of labour generates effects that differ from those observed under the mobility of capital.

8.3.2 Agglomeration Economies and the Emergence of Asymmetric Clusters

According to Porter (1998), the formation of industrial clusters depends on the relative strength of three distinct forces: the size of intrasectoral agglomeration economies, the intensity of competition, and the level of transport costs. Despite the existence of a huge empirical – and inconclusive – literature devoted to industrial clusters, how the three forces interact to shape the regional economy has been neglected in NEG. This is probably because working with a model that accounts for the main ingredients of urban economics and NEG seems out of reach. Yet the formation of clusters can be studied by adopting a 'reduced-form' approach in which a firm's marginal production cost in a region decreases with the number of firms locating in the region. In doing this, one captures the effect of agglomeration economies and can study how agglomeration economies operating at the local level interact with the dispersion force generated by market competition in the global economy through lower trade costs (Belleflamme et al., 2000). In a spatial equilibrium, firms earn the same profits. However, if firms observe that one region offers higher potential profits than the other, they want to move to that region. In other words, the driving force that sustains the relocation of firms is the profit differential between the North and the South.

To show why and how a hierarchy of clusters emerges, we look at the interplay among the above three forces as a *symmetry-breaking device*. Therefore, we start with a perfectly symmetric set-up in which firms and consumers are evenly dispersed between the North and the South. When trade costs start decreasing, trade flows grow but, in the absence of agglomeration economies, firms stay put because spatial separation relaxes competition between firms. Things are very different when agglomeration economies are at work. In this case, when trade costs fall enough, some firms choose to produce in the North, say rather than in the South in order to benefit from a lower marginal cost while maintaining a high volume of export. As trade costs keep decreasing, a growing number of firms choose to set up in the North where the marginal cost decreases further. Note that firms tend to gather in one region despite the fact that the two markets where they sell their output are the same size. What now drives firms' agglomeration is no longer the size of the product market but the endogenous level of agglomeration economies.

But where does agglomeration occur? Will it be in the North or in the South? Consider an asymmetric shock that gives a region a small initial advantage. If this shock remains fixed over a long period, firms will attune their behaviour accordingly. The region benefiting from the shock, however small, will accommodate the larger cluster. Hence, *regions that were once very similar may end up having very different production structures* as market integration gets deeper. Once more, lowering trade costs drives the economy toward more agglomeration in one region at the expense of another.

Are growing regional disparities necessarily bad in this context? The answer is no. A planner whose aim is to maximize global efficiency sets up more asymmetric clusters than the market delivers. To explain, at the first-best optimum prices are set at the marginal cost level while locations are chosen to maximize the difference between agglomeration economies and transport costs. In contrast, at market equilibrium, firms take advantage of their spatial separation to relax price competition and do not consider the positive externalities associated with their location decision. So the optimal configuration tends to involve a more unbalanced distribution of firms than the market outcome. If agglomeration economies become increasingly important in some sectors, their uneven geographical distribution need not signify a wasteful allocation of resources. On the contrary, *the size of the clusters could well be too small*. However, the region with the larger cluster benefits from lower prices through larger agglomeration economies, more jobs, and a bigger fiscal basis.

8.3.3   The Core–Periphery Structure

The mobility of capital and the mobility of labour do not obey the same rules. First, while the movement of capital to a region brings with it production capability, the returns to capital do not have to be spent in the same region. In contrast, when workers move to a new region, they take with them *both their production and consumption capabilities* (putting aside remittances). As a result, migration affects the size of the labour and the product markets in both the origin and the destination regions. Second, while the mobility of capital is driven by differences in nominal returns, workers care about their *real wages*. In other words, differences in costs of living matter to workers but not to capital owners.

The difference in the consequences of capital and labour mobility is the starting point of Krugman's celebrated 1991 paper that dwells on the idea that the interregional economy is replete with *pecuniary externalities* generated by the mobility of workers. Indeed, when some workers choose to migrate, their move affects the welfare of those who stay behind because migration affects the size of the regional product and labour markets. These effects have the nature of pecuniary externalities because they are mediated by the market, but migrants do not take them into account when making their decisions. Such effects are of particular importance in imperfectly competitive markets as prices fail to reflect the true social value of individual decisions. Hence, studying the full impact of migration requires a full-fledged general equilibrium framework, which captures not only the interactions between product and labour markets, but also the double role played by individuals as workers and consumers.

To achieve his goal, Krugman (1991) considers the classical $2 \times 2 \times 2$ setting of trade theory. There are two goods, two types of labour, and two regions. The first type of labour (workers) is mobile and the only input in the first (manufacturing) sector, which operates under increasing returns and monopolistic competition; shipping the manufactured good is costly. The second type of labour (farmers) is immobile and the only input in the second (farming) sector, which produces a homogeneous good under constant returns and perfect competition; shipping the agricultural good incurs no cost. What drives the agglomeration of the manufacturing sector is the mobility of workers. For this, Krugman considers a setting in which both farmers and workers are symmetrically distributed between the North and the South and asks when this pattern ceases to be a stable spatial equilibrium.

Two main effects are at work: one involves firms, and the other workers. Assume that the North grows slightly bigger than the South. At first, this increase in market size leads to a higher demand for the manufactured good, thus attracting more firms. The HME implies that the hike in the number of firms is more than proportional to the increase in market size, thus pushing nominal wages upward. In addition, the presence of more firms means that a greater number of varieties are produced locally, so prices are lower in the North because competition there is tougher. As a consequence, real wages rise so that the North should attract a new flow of workers. Therefore, there is *circular cumulative causation* à la Myrdal in which these two effects reinforce each other. This snowball effect seems to lead inevitably to the agglomeration of the manufacturing sector in the North, which then becomes the core of the global economy.

But the snowball may not form. Indeed, the foregoing argument ignores several other effects triggered by the migration of workers. On the one hand, the increased supply of labour in the North tends to push wages down. On the other hand, since new workers are also consumers, there will be a hike in local demand for the manufactured good, which leads to a higher demand for labour. But this is not yet the end of the story. As more firms enter the local market, there is increased competition to attract workers, so the final impact of migration on nominal wages is hard to predict. Likewise, there is increased competition in the product market, as well as greater demand. Combining these various effects might well lead to a '*snowball meltdown*', which results in the spatial dispersion of firms and workers.

Krugman's (1991) great accomplishment has been to integrate all these effects within a single framework and to determine precisely the conditions under which the above prediction holds or not. Starting from an arbitrarily small difference between regions, Krugman singles out the cases in which there is agglomeration or dispersion of the manufacturing sector. He shows that the value of transport costs is again the key determining factor. If transport costs are sufficiently high, the interregional shipment of goods is low. In this event, firms focus on regional markets. Thus the global economy displays a symmetric regional pattern of production. In contrast, when transport costs are sufficiently low, then all manufacturers will concentrate in the North; the South will supply only the agricultural good and will become the *periphery*. In this way, firms are able to exploit increasing returns by selling more in the larger market without losing much business in the smaller market. Again, lowering trade costs fosters the gathering of activities. The core–periphery model therefore allows for the possibility of *convergence* or *divergence* between regions, whereas the neoclassical model based on constant returns and perfect competition in the two sectors predicts only convergence. Consequently, Krugman presents a synthesis of the polarization and neoclassical theories. His work appeals because the regional disparities associated with the core–periphery structure emerge as a *stable equilibrium* that is the involuntary consequence of decisions made by a large number of economic agents pursuing their own interests.[5]

Despite its great originality, the core–periphery model has several shortcomings. The following list, while not exhaustive, covers a fair number of issues. (i) The model overlooks the various congestion costs and agglomeration economies generated by the concentration of activities, discussed in Chapter 9. (ii) It only accounts for two sectors and two regions. (iii) The agricultural sector is given a very restricted role, its job being to guarantee the equilibrium of the trade balance. Along the same line, it is hard to see why trading the agricultural good costs nothing in a model seeking to determine the overall impact of trade costs. All these features have attracted a lot of attention, but the '*dimensionality problem*' is the most challenging one.

Having said that, we must stress the work by Helpman (1998) who argues that decreasing freight costs may trigger the dispersion, rather than the agglomeration, of economic activities when the dispersion force lies in the supply of nontradable services (housing) rather than immobile farmers. In this case, various congestion and market-crowding effects put a brake on the agglomeration process, and thus *Krugman's prediction is reversed*. The difference in results is easy to understand. Commuting and housing costs rise when consumers join the larger region/city, which strengthens the dispersion force. Simultaneously, lowering transport costs facilitates interregional trade. By combining these two forces, we see why dispersion arises. In other words, *land use appears to be a major dispersion force in the making of the space-economy*.[6] By neglecting the fact that the agglomeration of activities typically materializes in the form of cities where competition for land acts as a strong dispersion force, the core–periphery model remains in the tradition of trade theory. Therefore, conclusions drawn from this model are, at best, applicable only to very large areas.[7]

The econometric analysis undertaken by Crozet (2004), together with the observations made in Section 8.2, suggests that the low mobility of European workers makes the emergence of a Krugman-like core–periphery structure within the EU very unlikely. Therefore, moving beyond the Krugman model in search of alternative explanations appears to be warranted in order to understand the emergence of large industrial regions in economies characterized by a low spatial mobility of labour – such as the EU. A second shortcoming of the core-periphery model is that it ignores the importance of intermediate goods. Yet the demand for consumer goods does not account for a very large fraction of firms' sales, often being overshadowed by the demand for intermediate goods.[8]

8.3.4   Input–Output Linkages and the Bell-Shaped Curve of Spatial Development

The agglomeration of economic activities also arises in contexts in which labour mobility is very low, as in most European countries. This underscores the need for alternative explanations of industrial agglomeration. One strong contender is the presence of *input–output linkages between firms*: the output of one firm can be an input for another, and vice versa. In this case, the entry of a new firm in a region not only increases the intensity of competition between similar firms; it also increases the market of upstream firm-suppliers and decreases the costs of downstream firm-customers. This is the starting point of Krugman and Venables (1995).

Their idea is beautifully simple and suggestive: *the agglomeration of the final sector in a particular region occurs because of the concentration of the intermediate industry in the same region, and conversely*. Indeed, when firms belonging to the final sector are concentrated in a single region, the local demand for intermediate inputs is very high, making this region very attractive to firms producing these intermediate goods. Conversely, because intermediate goods are made available at lower prices in the core region, firms producing final goods also find that region very attractive. Thus, a cumulative process may develop that leads to industrial agglomeration within the core region.

In this alternative setting, new forces arise. Indeed, if firms agglomerate in a region where the supply of labour is inelastic, then wages must surely rise. This in turn has two opposite effects. On the one hand, *consumers' demand for the final product increases because they have a higher income*. This is again a market expansion force, now triggered by higher incomes rather than larger populations. On the other hand, such wage increases also generate a dispersion force. When the wage gap between the core and the periphery becomes sufficiently large, some firms will find it profitable to relocate to the periphery, even though the local demand for their output is lower than in the core. This is especially true when transport costs are low, because asymmetries in demand will then have a weaker impact on profits.

The set of equilibrium patterns obtained in the present setting is much richer than in the core–periphery model. In particular, if a deepening of economic integration triggers the concentration of industrial activities in one region, then beyond a certain threshold, an even deeper integration may lead to a reversal of this tendency. Some firms now relocate from the core to the periphery. In other words, *the periphery experiences a process of re-industrialization and, simultaneously, the core might start losing firms, thus becoming deindustrialized.* As Fujita et al. (1999) put it, 'declining trade costs first produce, then dissolve, the global inequality of nations'.

Therefore, economic integration would yield a *bell-shaped curve of spatial development*, which describes a rise in regional disparities in the early stages of the development process, and a fall in later stages (Williamson, 1965, Puga, 1999). Such a curve may be obtained in several extensions of the core-periphery model – surveyed in Fujita and Thisse (2013) – and seems to be confirmed by several empirical and historical studies.[9] However, owing to differences in data, time periods, and measurement techniques, it is fair to say that the empirical evidence is still mixed (Combes and Overman, 2004). Furthermore, this self-correcting effect can take too long in the face of some regions' urgent economic and social problems and the time horizon of policy-makers, which leads them to look for policies whose effects are felt more rapidly.

Note that the following coordination failure may prevent the redistribution of activities: many prices are not known in advance in the South. Lack of adequate information may then prevent the development of a network of service and intermediate goods suppliers, which leads to a vicious circle and persistent underdevelopment. In the presence of external effects, this problem is particularly acute. One solution is to have an agent who 'internalizes' the various costs and benefits arising during the first stages of the take-off process and who plays an entrepreneurial role facilitating individual decisions, so that a cluster in the South can form en masse.

8.3.5   Communication Costs and the Relocation of Plants

A major facet in the process of globalization is the *spatial fragmentation* of a firm associated with vertical investments. Vertical investments arise when firms choose to break down their production process into various stages spread across different countries or regions. Specifically, the modern firm organizes and performs discrete activities in distinct locations, which together form a *supply chain* starting at the conception of the product and ending at its delivery. This spatial fragmentation of the firm aims to take advantage of differences in technologies, factor endowments, or factor prices across places. We now turn our attention to this problem.

Besides transport costs, spatial separation generates another type of spatial friction, namely *'communication costs'*. Indeed, coordinating activities within the firm is more costly when the headquarters and its production plants are physically separated because the transmission of information remains incomplete and imperfect. Furthermore, more uncertainty about production plants' local environment is associated with conducting a business at a distance. Again, this implies higher coordination costs, hence higher communication costs between the headquarters and its plants. In the same vein, monitoring the effort of a plant manager is easier when the plant is located near the headquarters than across borders. Lower communication costs make the coordination between headquarters and plants simpler and therefore facilitate the process of spatial fragmentation.

For the international/interregional fragmentation of firms to arise, the intra-firm coordination costs must be sufficiently low so the operation of a plant at a distance is not too expensive; at the same time, transport costs must decrease substantially to permit the supply of large markets at low delivery costs from distant locations. To make low-wage areas more accessible and attractive for the establishment of their production, firms need the development of new information and communication technologies, as well as a substantial fall in trade costs. In this case, a certain number of firms choose to go *multinational*, which means that their headquarters are located in prosperous areas where they find the skilled workers they need and their plants are set up in low-wage areas, whereas the other firms remain spatially integrated (Fujita and Thisse, 2013).

Manufacturing firms started to relocate their production plants to regions where labour and land are cheaper than in large cities long ago (Henderson, 1997, Glaeser and Kohlhase, 2004). However, transport and communication costs for a long time imposed a limit to the distance at which plants could operate. The ongoing revolution in information and communication technologies freed some firms from this constraint, thus allowing them to move their plants much further away to countries where wages are a lot lower than in the peripheral regions where they used to establish their plants. Hence, the following question: *Which 'South' can accommodate firms' activities that are being decentralized?*

8.4   Does the Market Yield Over or Under-agglomeration?

Whether there is too much or too little agglomeration is unclear. Yet speculation on this issue has never been in short supply and it is fair to say that this is one of the main questions that policy-makers would like to address. Contrary to general beliefs, the market need not lead to the over-agglomeration of activities as competition is a strong dispersion force. We have discussed above two basic mechanisms that may outweigh this force and lead to the spatial clustering of activities. The former is the home-market effect (HME), which points to the relative agglomeration of firms in the large regions. The latter is related to the joint concentration of firms and workers in a few regions to form big markets. Since the mobility of capital and labour is driven by different forces, there is no reason to expect the answer to the question 'Does the market yield over or under-agglomeration?' to be the same.

8.4.1   *Does the Home-Market Effect Generate Excessive Agglomeration?*

Because spatial separation relaxes price competition, everything else being equal, firms earn higher profits by locating in different geographical markets. What the HME tells us is that the size of markets may outweigh this effect, leading to the concentration of firms in a few regions. When firms move from one region to another, they impose negative pecuniary externalities on the whole economy. More precisely, firms ignore the impact of their move on product and input markets in both destination and origin regions. The social surplus is lowered because location decisions are based on relative prices that do not reflect the true social costs. However, the inefficiency of the market outcome does not tell us anything about the excessive or insufficient concentration of firms in the big regions. In fact, *the HME involves too many firms located in the larger region*. The intuition is easy to grasp. A profit-maximizing firm chooses the location that minimizes its transport costs to serve foreign markets. Therefore, since firms absorb more freight when exporting from the smaller to the larger region than vice versa, they are incentivized to locate in the larger region. Tougher competition there holds back the agglomeration process, but this dispersion force is not strong enough for a sufficiently large number of firms to set up in the smaller region. However, it is worth noting that the first-best distribution of firms still involves a share of firms exceeding the relative size of the larger region (Ottaviano and van Ypersele, 2005).

8.4.2   Is the Core-Periphery Structure Inefficient?

Thus far, NEG has been unable to provide a clear-cut answer to this fundamental question. However, a few results seem to show some robustness. In the core–periphery model, the market outcome is socially desirable when transport costs are high or low. In the former case, activities are dispersed; in the latter, they are agglomerated. In contrast, for intermediate values of these costs, the market leads to the over-agglomeration of the manufacturing sector (Ottaviano and Thisse, 2002). Furthermore, when transport costs are sufficiently low, agglomeration is preferred to dispersion in the following sense: people in the core regions can compensate those staying in the periphery through interregional transfers, whereas those staying in the periphery are unable to compensate those workers who choose to move to what becomes the core regions (Charlot et al., 2006). This suggests that interregional transfers could be the solution for correcting regional income disparities. It is worth stressing that such transfers do not rest here on equity considerations, but only on efficiency grounds. However, implementing such transfers, paid for by those who reside in the core regions, may be politically difficult to maintain in the long run. In addition, they may give rise to opportunistic behaviour in the periphery.

Tackling this issue from a dynamic perspective sheds additional light on the problem. It has long been argued that growth is localized, the reason being that technological and social innovations tend to be clustered while their diffusion across places would be slow. For example, Hirschman (1958) claimed that 'we may take it for granted that economic progress does not appear everywhere at the same time and that once it has appeared powerful forces make for a spatial concentration of economic growth around the initial starting points'. And Hohenberg and Lees (1985) argued similarly that, 'despite the rapid growth of urban industries in England, Belgium, France, Germany and northern Italy after 1840 or so, economic development was a spatially selective process. Some regions deindustrialized while others were transformed by new technologies'.

Fujita and Thisse (2013) revisit the core–periphery model in a set-up combining NEG and endogenous growth theory; the high-skilled, who work in the R&D sector, are mobile whereas the low-skilled, who work in the manufacturing and agricultural sectors, are immobile. These authors show that the growth rate of the global economy depends positively on the spatial concentration of the R&D sector. Furthermore, the core–periphery structure in which both the R&D and manufacturing sectors are agglomerated is stable when transport costs are sufficiently low. This result gives credence to the idea that global growth and agglomeration go hand in hand. But what are the welfare and equity implications of this geography of innovative activities? The analysis undertaken by Fujita and Thisse supports the idea that the additional growth spurred by agglomeration may lead to a Pareto-dominant move: when the growth effect triggered by the agglomeration of the R&D sector is strong enough, even those who live in the periphery are better off than under dispersion.

It is worth stressing that this Pareto-optimal move does not require any inter-regional transfer; it is a pure outcome of market interaction. However, the gap between the unskilled who live in the core and those who live in the periphery enlarges. Put differently, the rich get richer and so may the poor, but without ever catching up. The welfare gap between the core and the periphery expands because of the additional gains generated by a faster growth spurred by the agglomeration of skilled workers. This in turn makes the unskilled residing in the core region better off, even though their productivity is the same as the productivity of those living in the periphery.

8.5   Do EU Interregional Transport Investment Policies Fulfil their Role?

This question may seem odd because the absence of good transport infrastructure is known to be one of the main impediments to trade. This is why international organizations such as the European Commission and the World Bank have financed a large number of transport projects. As the key objective of the EU is deeper market integration among member countries, the construction of big and efficient transport infrastructures was seen as a necessary step towards this goal. However, this does not mean that one should keep increasing the supply of transport infrastructure: its economic performance can be improved by selecting investments more carefully and by using the existing infrastructure better. Whether interregional transport infrastructure is beneficial in terms of welfare and whether it generates economic growth at the macroeconomic level are two different issues.

Another important question often forgotten in the debates over the interregional effects of a new transport infrastructure is that the development of new transport technologies has vastly changed the way in which distance affects transport costs. This history is briefly as follows. The long period during which all movement was very costly and risky was followed by another one during which, thanks to technological and organizational advances, ships could cross longer distances in one go, thus reducing their number of stops. On land, it was necessary to wait for the advent of the railroad for appreciable progress to occur, but the results were the same. In both cases, long-distance journeys became less expensive and no longer demanded the presence of relays or rest areas. This evolution has favoured places of origin and destination at the expense of intermediate places. In other words, *increasing returns in transport explain why places situated between large markets and transport nodes have lost many of their activities* (Thomas, 2002). Having this in mind, it is hardly shocking that not much happened in those transit regions, despite the high expectations of the local populations.

The policy intervention also involved the design of pricing and regulation policies for interregional transport. All this has led to an appreciable increase in the volume of both freight and passenger transport. Nevertheless, transport policies are still formed by individual member countries. Using a NEG set-up in which transport costs between regions of the same country differ from trade costs between countries, Behrens et al. (2007) show that the welfare of a country increases when its internal transport costs are lowered because domestic firms increase their market share at the expense of foreign firms, while the foreign trading partner is affected adversely for the same reason. As a consequence, we have something like a *'fortress effect'* in that *accessing the increasingly integrated national market becomes more difficult*, which may generate conflicts of interest between member countries.

In the EU, transport policy has two main objectives. The first is to decrease trade costs as the aim of transport policy is to build the EU internal market. The second objective is to promote the economic development and structural adjustment of lagging regions. Arbitrage possibilities arising from competition and factor mobility are expected to generate greater-than-average growth in lagging regions. Having the economic engine in a higher gear would eventually make these regions reach the standard of living realized elsewhere. Where convergence does not arrive quickly, an insufficient stock of public infrastructure is often blamed. The EU and national governments have responded by pouring huge quantities of concrete in lagging regions.

The EU has sent rather mixed signals in terms of transport policy. In the first phase, the integration of markets for goods was the priority; later, the emphasis shifted to environmental and resource efficiency. As a result, the development of rail and waterways was favoured over road and air transport. Yet road freight transport in the EU remains by far the dominant mode; the EU has a very different modal split from that in the US. International freight in the EU relies on road transport for 45 per cent of traffic, on sea transport for 37 per cent, on rail transport for 11 per cent, and on inland waterways and pipeline transport for the remainder. In the US, rail transport at 41 per cent is more important than road transport (32 per cent), followed by pipeline (15 per cent), and inland waterways. International passenger transport inside the EU also has a different modal split from that in the US. The US relies on car and air transport, while the EU also relies on high-speed rail (HSR). Thus, in the US, rail has an important share of the freight market while, in Europe, rail is more important for the passenger market.

Assessing the benefits of transport investments is difficult both ex ante and ex post, for two reasons. First, transport investments have a multitude of effects. They reduce trade barriers and so affect the pattern of trade for both freight and for services (via lower costs for business and tourism trips). As seen above, the outcome of a transport investment is difficult to predict ex ante in a world where economic activities are increasingly footloose. Second, the effect of an investment is also difficult to evaluate ex post because there is no obvious counterfactual. A transport investment is often located where decision makers expect it to produce the largest benefits. But then it becomes unclear whether it is the transport investment itself or the favourable pre-conditions that cause the observed effects.

As performance of transport infrastructure is an empirical question, we have chosen to discuss both ex ante and ex post methods. In particular, we consider three approaches: the econometric approach, the model-simulation approach, and the case-study approach.

8.5.1   Assessing Transport Investments Using Econometric Models

In the post-Reagan period, public investments were expected to stimulate economic growth. In an influential paper, Aschauer (1989) used a reduced-form estimation and found high rates of return for public investments. This was the start of a series of macroeconomic studies that produced fairly mixed evidence about the impact of transport investments on national growth (Gramlich, 1994). Melo et al. (2013) conducted a meta-analysis of the existing empirical literature on the output elasticity of transport infrastructure. They show that the productivity effects of transport infrastructure vary substantially across industries, tend to be higher in the US than in the EU, and are higher for roads compared with other transport modes of transport. The variation in estimates of the output elasticity of transport is also explained by differences in the methods and data used in the various studies. Failing to control for unobserved heterogeneity and spurious correlations tends to result in higher values, while failing to control for urbanization and congestion levels leads to omitted variable bias. In addition, Puga (2002) highlights several pitfalls of an aggregate approach. First, it could well be that transport investments happen just because economic growth allows the government to spend more money on infrastructure, not the other way around. Second, the first links of a transport network could well be very productive, whereas the productivity of adding new links decreases strongly.

Redding and Turner (2015) develop a general equilibrium framework in the spirit of Helpman to assess the effects of transport investments on the location of production and population, as well as on variables such as wages and prices. This framework allows the authors to construct the necessary counterfactuals to assess the effects of new transport investments. They find only limited evidence on the effect of interregional investments in the EU. Ahlfeldt and Feddersen (2015) study the impact of HSR on a corridor in Germany by comparing the effects on smaller towns with a HSR stop and those without such a stop. They find that, as HSR decreases the cost of human interaction but trade costs remain unchanged, this type of project has another effect on the core-periphery balance. Peripheral regions tend to experience negative effects through projects that reduce freight costs via a trade channel, as in NEG, but could benefit from HSR projects via Marshallian externalities.

Comparing the impact of transport investments in different and non-EU parts of the world, Redding and Turner find that, across a range of countries and levels of development, new transport infrastructures seem to generate similar effects. First, population density falls between 6 and 15 per cent with a doubling of the distance to a highway or railroad, while highways decentralize urban populations and, to a lesser extent, manufacturing activity. Second, different sectors respond differently to different transport modes. Another forceful piece of evidence is Faber (2014) who shows that the construction of new highways in China decreased trade costs but, as suggested by NEG, reinforced the core cities at the expense of the periphery.

One limitation of the econometric assessment approach is that transport investments are chosen in a political process, which may lead to the selection of poor investments. For example, Knight (2004) has found that, for the US Federal Highway Fund, about half of the investment money was wasted. Therefore, any econometric ex post assessment has the tough task of distinguishing between poor political selection mechanisms and the potential effects of a well-selected transport investment.

8.5.2   Assessing Transport Investments Using Model Simulations

When a reliable multi-regional simulation model is available, one can simulate the effects of transport investments and discriminate between the effects of the selection process and the productivity of a transport infrastructure. Only a handful of such models exist in the world. To this end, the European Commission has developed a spatial computable general equilibrium model (SCGE), RHOMOLO, where different policy shocks can be simulated at the regional level to obtain an ex ante impact assessment. The spatial implications of the general equilibrium approach followed in RHOMOLO have been investigated by Di Comite and Kancs (2015) who describe how the main agglomeration and dispersion forces of NEG enter the model: agglomeration is driven by increasing returns to scale, the use of intermediate inputs, and localized externalities; dispersion is driven by costly trade and locally produced varieties entering consumer utility asymmetrically (calibrated on observed trade flows). Capital and labour are mobile, and vertical linkages are accounted for using regionalized international input-output matrices. The model is implemented for the 267 NUTS 2 regions of the EU and used to assess the effect of investments that reduce trade costs. The properties of this model are tested by simulating the impact of planned Cohesion Policy investments in infrastructure, whose main targets are the poorer, peripheral regions. The aim of the exercise is to isolate the effect of the different economic mechanisms identified in Section 8.3, for which three scenarios are simulated.

Scenario 1: Isolating the Effect of Capital Mobility
By switching capital mobility on and off, allowing savings in one region to be invested in other regions, the authors find that the tendency toward the equalization of the rates of return on investments spreads the growth effects of the transport investments more equally. This is the home-market effect at work: although the poorer (peripheral) regions received a larger share of the transport investment, the relocation of capital leads to more growth in other EU regions.

Scenario 2: Isolating the Effect of Labour Mobility
By switching labour mobility on and off, allowing workers to relocate where their real wages are higher according to estimated elasticities, the authors find that the region receiving the initial investment will benefit from a lower cost of living. This attracts more workers and increases the size of the region, its production, and its consumption, which should foster agglomeration. However, since consumer tastes are calibrated in each region based on the observed trade flows in the base year, the growing regions also demand more from the peripheral regions, which bids up prices and prevents a strong agglomeration effect. The cost-of-living effect is found to be stronger than the labour market-crowding effect, thus magnifying the beneficial effect of local investments and making the lagging region better off, but the effect is very localized.

Scenario 3: Isolating the Effect of Vertical Linkages
By switching interregional consumption of intermediates on and off, it can be noted that higher demand for intermediate goods in regions with improved accessibility attracts producers of intermediate goods, which lowers the production costs for the producers of the final goods. In the absence of vertical linkages, the benefits of Cohesion Policy investments are more localized. However, when vertical linkages are allowed, the productivity improvements in one region spread to all the regions using its output as an input in their productive processes. Therefore, the benefits of allocating resources to a region are felt beyond its borders.

These models are powerful tools to check ex ante the potential effects of different transport policies. However, they suffer from several shortcomings. First, the model is calibrated but not econometrically tested. Second, the mechanisms are so complex and the model so big that it is impossible to isolate and identify the drivers of agglomeration and dispersion when all the features are included together. Last, the way workers' mobility is modelled is critical as European workers are very sticky, while mobility habits may change over time and respond to specific policies (which are impossible to capture accurately in the model). It should also be noted that the administrative capacity of local authorities and the quality of planned investments are key determinants of the success of a policy, but these aspects cannot be captured in a general equilibrium model. For this reason, the following approach should complement the ones based on econometric analysis and model simulations.

8.5.3 Assessing Transport Investments Using Case Studies

In the late 1990s, the EU selected a priority list of transport investments – the 'Trans European Network' investments – whose total value accounted for some € 600 billion. These investment projects are the first that should receive European subsidies. In an attempt to assess the benefits of the 22 priority freight projects, Bröcker et al. (2010) developed a model in the tradition of the new trade theories with 260 European regions. In this model, firms produce a differentiated good and operate under increasing returns and monopolistic competition; interregional trade is costly while capital and labour are immobile. Since production factors are immobile, one major ingredient of NEG is missing, that is, the endogenous formation of clusters. A particular transport investment decreases transport costs between specific regions, which translates into changes in production activities, trade patterns, and ultimately the welfare level of consumers residing in different regions.

There are three main findings for this first round of EU transport priority projects (Proost et al., 2014). First, *only 12 of the 22 projects pass the cost-benefit analysis test*. Second, most projects benefit only the region where the investment takes place, so that the *'EU value added'* – or the positive spillover argument – does not seem to warrant the investment. Finally, the projects do not systematically favour the poorer regions. These findings illustrate the role of political economy factors in the selection of projects. Knight's (2004) study suggests that substantial amounts money are spent inefficiently on interregional transport infrastucture. To avoid such a waste of resources, the EU should rely on independent project assessment. There has been great progress in this area over the last decade. The group of countries with a strong tradition of independent project assessment (Netherlands, Sweden, and the UK) has been widened and the methods are being refined to allow for relocation effects.

A second round of EU transport priority projects was approved in 2015. The selection of the projects is based on expert judgments, which refer to a wide range of objectives, but it is not clear how many projects would pass the cost-benefit-analysis test. In total, 276 proposals were recommended for funding.

When it comes to passenger transport, *the EU has put a strong emphasis on HSR investments*. This contrasts with the choice made in the US where air transport for medium to long-distance travel is used much more, but where HSR projects have never taken off. On average, Americans travel almost 3000 km a year by air inside the US, while the average EU citizen travels slightly more than 1000 km per a year by air inside Europe and some 200 km by HSR (Eurostat, 2015a). Both Americans and Europeans also make long-distance trips by car, but Europeans clearly have a lower demand for long-distance trips than Americans.

The EU probably opted for HSR because of the presence of strong (public) national railway companies wanting to preserve their market share. Air transport has grown robustly, and the liberalization of passenger air transport has led to lower prices, higher frequencies, and the loss of market share for rail. HSR networks require a large upfront investment in infrastructure (tracks, locomotives). Compared with air transport, HSR has high fixed costs, while infrastructure construction is almost fully subsidized. Maintenance and operation are supposed to be paid for by passenger fares. More investment subsidies are spent on rail than on roads, so it is crucial to have a good ex ante appraisal of the different transport modes.

De Rus and Nombela (2007) use standardized cost-benefit estimates to determine the level of demand that is needed to make a HSR link socially beneficial. They find that *a link needs some* 10 *million passengers a year and many new HSR links do not meet this target*. Adler et al. (2010) use a full-network model where EU passengers have the choice between HSR, air, and car for medium to long-distance trips. The reactions of the air transport sector are taken into account in order to avoid the mistake made when the Channel Tunnel was assessed without anticipating the reaction of competing ferries. When HSR has to cover all its costs, these authors have found that there will be an insufficient number of passengers for the project to be economically viable. When trips are priced at marginal cost, the HSR has a better chance of passing the cost-benefit test. But charging the marginal cost requires high government subsidies. In addition, the government must be able to pick the right project and cannot serve all regions equally. France and Spain have the largest HSR networks, and part of their network would probably not pass the cost-benefit test. The UK and the Netherlands have almost no HSR network. Finally, the EU defends HSR projects on environmental grounds, but sensitivity analysis shows that one needs extremely high carbon values to make HSR better than air transport on these grounds.

8.6   Is the EU Moving to a Better Utilization of Its Existing Transport Policy?

8.6.1   Competition on Diesel Fuel Taxes Leads EU Countries to Revise Their Pricing of Road Freight

Trucks are responsible for climate damage, conventional air pollution, accidents, congestion and road damage. The main determinant of road damage is the axle weight of a truck. In Europe, trucks pay for the use of roads via excise taxes on diesel fuel but this is changing fast as a result of intense fuel tax competition. Because trucks can cover 1000 to 2000 km with a single tank of fuel, countries or regions engage in fuel tax competition. The difference in distances covered implies that tax competition is much more important for trucks than for cars. Within the EU, some small countries (Luxemburg being the most obvious example) choose a strategy of low diesel excise tax rates to make international haulers fuel up in their country, generating large excise tax revenues for these countries. This strategic behaviour has prompted the EU to negotiate a minimum level of excise taxes.

New pricing technologies have allowed countries with a lot of transit traffic, such as Switzerland (2001), Austria (2004), Germany (2005), the Czech Republic (2007), Slovakia (2010), Poland (2011), and Belgium (2016), to introduce distance-based charging. The vignette system (a low fixed annual fee) is then replaced by a kilometre tax that charges trucks much more than before.

Replacing diesel taxes by distance charges is not necessarily welfare-improving (Mandell and Proost (2016)). When a country uses distance charges, it can replace part of the diesel fuel tax by a distance charge. In this way, it undercuts the diesel tax of its neighbours and increases its revenues. As a consequence, the neighbouring countries also have to implement a distance charge if they want to preserve their tax revenues. The end result will be low diesel taxes and high distance charges. Furthermore, when passenger cars also use diesel fuel, taxes are too low for diesel cars while diesel taxes and distance charges are too high for freight transport. Accounting for the inefficient levels of taxes and charges and for the high implementation costs of distance charges, tax competition could lead to a less efficient equilibrium than the fuel tax equilibrium. So the revolution in truck taxes, which is a priori an instrument for more efficient pricing, may end up with massive tax exporting.

To some extent, the EU has anticipated that the introduction of distance charges in countries with transit freight traffic may lead to charges that are too high. The EU constitution does not allow discriminatory charges, but this is no guarantee against too high truck charges in transit countries. It therefore requires distance charges for trucks to be based on external costs. This may be viewed as a principal–agent problem in which the EU is the principal, and the country is the agent with better information about external costs. For this reason, distance charges are capped by the EU on the basis of average infrastructure costs. Interestingly, this turns out to be a smart policy: when road congestion is an important share of external costs, and road building is governed by constant returns, this cap can guarantee efficient pricing, and there is no need for the regulator to know the external congestion costs (Van der Loo and Proost, 2013). Distance charges for trucks have, up to now, been used chiefly as a simple distance toll with some environmental differentiation. However, the charges can become much more efficient when they are more closely geared to the external costs such as congestion, local air pollution, and accidents. The current revolution in the pricing of trucks may pave the way for a very different charging system for cars.

Finally, we observe that this evolution in the pricing of trucks is largely a European phenomenon. In the US, the 'stealing' of fuel tax revenues from neighbouring states is avoided by a complex system of regularization payments among states, which allows the US to function as an efficient trade zone.

8.6.2   Europe Does Not Make the Best Use of Its Rail and Air Transport System

The EU is still confronted with an archaic rail and air transport system. For rail, there are powerful national regulators and powerful national companies. Rail freight activity has been more or less stable but rail passenger activity has been decreasing substantially over the last 20 years. Rail freight could play a bigger role in freight transport; its market share is 11 per cent compared with 41 per cent in the US. There are probably two reasons for this difference: the lack of consolidation among national companies, and the lack of harmonization in operation. Ivaldi and McCullough (2008) study the integration of freight activities in the private US rail market and found that this leads to an important gain in consumer surplus. In the EU, together with the lack of consolidation, there is a lack of harmonization in the rail business. Harmonization of operating standards is an extremely slow process as the national producers all want to protect their own rail and equipment market.

In the air space, similar mechanisms are at work. In the US, there is a single regulator for the management of air space while in Europe, there are 37 national, and partly regional, monopolies managing air traffic. All regional monopolies function under a cost-plus rule, but an effort is being made to shift to a price-cap system. As a result, costs are almost twice as high as they are in the US.

Consolidation of different air traffic control zones is possible, which should also lead to important cost reductions. However, it is blocked by the national monopolies.

8.7   What Have We Learnt?

1. Owing to the strength of market forces shaping the spatial economy, regional development is inevitably unequal. Given the first law of spatial economics, not all regions may have a large market populated by skilled workers employed in high-tech industries. To a large extent, the unevenness of regional development may be viewed as the geographical counterpart of economic growth, which is driven mainly by large and innovative cities. The cumulative nature of the agglomeration process makes the resulting pattern of activities particularly robust to various types of shocks, thus showing why it is hard to foster a more balanced pattern of activities. Regions may be similar at the outset, but they can diverge considerably later on. What makes the agglomeration forces so powerful is the combination of a drastic fall in transport and communication costs, together with the cumulative nature of the agglomeration process to give rise to a new type of economic geography in which space is '*slippery*', whereas locations are '*sticky*'. Affluent regions enjoy the existence of agglomeration rents that single-minded policies cannot easily dissipate. Consequently, if the aim of the European Commission is to foster a more balanced distribution of economic activities across European regions, it should add more instruments to its policy portfolio.

2. We show in Chapter 9 that people comprise a significant part of the wealth of regions. As a consequence, training people and investing in human capital are often better strategies than building new transport infrastructure, for this heightens the probability of individuals finding a job, maybe in places other than their region of origin. As observed by Cheshire et al. (2014), *regional disparities are driven more by differences between individuals than by differences between places*, although worker and place characteristics interact in subtle ways that require more investigation. After all, Toulouse initially did not seem a great place for the creation of a top school in economics. So there is hope for many places to develop new and creative activities.

If some regions are richer, it follows that others are less rich or poorer. Thus, at first sight, it seems logical to make spatial equity a criterion of economic policy. However, the underlying principles of spatial equity are ambiguous vis-à-vis the principles of social justice. Interpersonal inequality is often larger than interregional inequality. *Helping poor regions does not necessarily mean helping poor people*. The poor or unemployed in major urban areas today probably have more right to assistance than the inhabitants of poorer regions with a substantially lower cost of living. The job of the welfare state is to reduce interpersonal inequalities that run counter to the principles of social justice, and these principles do not refer to particular spatial entities.

3. A key difficulty highlighted by NEG is that small differences may be sufficient to trigger regional divergence. This leads to the following question: *When do small differences matter?* As pointed out by Duranton et al. (2010), great places are great because 'they have managed to periodically reinvent themselves after losing an important part of the economic fabric'. Since the reasons for the success of these cities are often region or country-specific, it would be futile to seek a universal recipe. Yet a few general principles may serve as a guide. The historical and social background of a region, its economic strengths and weaknesses, its education system, and its portfolio of amenities are the fundamental ingredients to be accounted for when designing local development policies.

Very much like firms that differentiate their products to relax competition, regions must avoid head-to-head (fiscal) competition with well-established areas. Instead, regional development strategies should identify areas of specialization that exploit local sources of uniqueness. The aim of these strategies is to strengthen regions' comparative advantages and to give priority to finding sustainable solutions to regions' weakest links. For example, by differentiating the infrastructure services they provide, regions can create niches that make them attractive to a certain type of firms, which need not be high-tech firms. The scope for such a strategy is increasing as the revolution in information and communication technology has shifted firms' needs towards more specialized inputs. Implementing such a policy requires precise assessments of the strengths and weaknesses of the regional socio-economic and political fabric. For this to be possible, better data must be made available at various levels (regional, local, household).

4. One should also bear in mind that *a spray-gun distribution of increasing-returns activities results in high investment expenditure and/or underutilization of infrastructure and facilities.* Spatial dispersion of public investments is often inefficient because it prevents activities from reaching the critical mass needed to be efficient enough to compete on the national or international marketplace. What is more, for infrastructures to have an impact on the space-economy, they must be available in only a few places. Once they become widespread across locations, their impact is negligible because they no longer matter when firms and workers compare different locations. This is one more reason for giving up spray-gun policies. Regional policies fail to recognize that regional income differences are often the result of scale economies. To a certain extent, this explains the disillusion regarding the effectiveness of policies that aim for a more balanced distribution of activities across the EU, which in turn affects the credibility of the EU.

A related and unsolved question is the lasting decay that characterizes several regions that used to be the engines of the Industrial Revolution. All industries must one day decline, and examples abound in Europe of old industrialized regions that have succeeded in attracting sizable subsidies to finance inefficient firms. These regions have thus delayed any possibility of the region finding a new niche in which to specialize. Polése (2009) uses the expression 'negative cluster' to describe situations where the (regional) government is essentially captured by a declining cluster dominated by a few big employers and trade unions. In addition, it is well documented that the performance of regions in a country also depends on institutions that may be deeply rooted in the past. This leads Polése (2009) to write 'It is not by accident that the traditional European centres of coal and steel became strongholds of socialist and sometimes communist parties. The era of violent social conflict and divisive labour disputes is today – hopefully – over. But that era has left a legacy from which some regions have found it more difficult to escape than others. ...I can find no other explanation of why seemingly well-located regions in northern France and in southern Belgium – in the European heartland – should continue to perform so poorly.' This is a strong claim but part of the story. However, as convincingly argued by Breinlich et al. (2014), we still have a poor understanding of *regional decline* as it *is not the mirror image of regional growth.*

5. One would expect the market-access effect to be weaker when transport costs are lower. But the opposite often holds true: more firms choose to set up in the large markets when it gets cheaper to trade goods between regions. Lower transport costs render competition tougher, leading firms to pay more attention to small differences between locations. They also make exports to small markets easier, which allows firms to exploit their scale economies more intensively by locating in large markets. Finally, lower transport costs reduce the advantages associated with geographical isolation in small markets where there is less competition. These various effects push toward more agglomeration. Hence, *connecting lagging regions to dynamic urban centres may weaken the lagging regions' industrial base.* This result may come as a surprise to those who forget that highways run both ways.

6. Regarding transport investment, there are at least three main research questions that are unsolved. First, given a major transport project, what share of the benefits is triggered by the resulting interregional shift in economic activity – and when does this shift unfold? If it is 10 per cent or less, this is within the margin of error of a conventional cost-benefit analysis of a transport project. In contrast, if the share is about 50 per cent, a conventional cost-benefit analysis is insufficient and must be supplemented by new econometric tools borrowed from regional and urban economics. Second, if small differences in accessibility can have a large impact on the location of economic activity, where is this more likely to happen? And third, how can we make sure that the right

transport investments are selected? For example, the EU has been promoting HSR for medium-distance travel, but the selected investments were far from optimal. Another related issue is to make sure that the capacity we currently have is used efficiently.

7. At present, *most interregional road, rail, inland waterways, and air networks are not priced efficiently.* European rail and air networks are still run largely by national monopolies that fail to comply with the principles of European integration. Furthermore, as member countries and regions do not take into account the full benefits of international and transit traffic, they are incentivized to charge too much for networks used intensively by foreign companies.

Acknowledgements

We thank F. di Comite, G. Duranton, M. Lafourcade, F. Robert-Nicoud, J. Süde-kum, A. Turrini, K. Van Dender, E. Viladecans-Marsal, as well as R. Lindsey, J-Cl. Prager, E. Quinet, K. Small, R. Evers, and C-M. Fung for their comments on previous drafts. We are grateful to M. Ivaldi, W. Leininger, and M. Paasi for their encouragement and the organization of the COEURE and DG-REGIO workshops, and acknowledge the funding by the FP7/320300 grant under the FP7 SSH research programme.

Notes

1. See Boldrin and Canova (2001), Midelfart-Knarvik and Overman (2002), and Puga (2002) for early critical assessments of the EU regional policies.
2. We follow the literature and view market integration as a gradual reduction in the costs of shipping goods and services.
3. See Baldwin et al. (2003), Fujita and Thisse (2013), and Zeng (2014) for a discussion of the HME in different set-ups.
4. Using a simple NEG model, a dataset including 250,000 randomly selected potential city locations, as well as all actual cities during the period 800–1800, Bosker and Buringh (2017) observe the two factors critical in explaining the location of cities: firstly, the proximity of waterways and land transport, and secondly, the relative position within the existing urban system. As suggested by NEG, being too close or far away from a large city reduces a place's chances to attract new activities.
5. See Fujita et al. (1999) and Baldwin et al. (2003) for more detailed analyses of NEG models.
6. See Fujita and Thisse (2013) for more details.
7. Rossi-Hansberg (2005) considers a set-up with a continuum of regions distributed along a one-dimensional space, several sectors, and positive transport costs. As transport costs decrease, firms become less sensitive to distance, which implies that peripheral locations will have better access to the core region and so will produce more than before. Thus, as in Helpman (1998), lowering transport costs fosters the geographical dispersion of activities. Desmet and Rossi-Hansberg (2014) propose

a dynamic version of this model in which technology diffuses across a continuous space to develop a spatial endogenous growth theory.

8. Intermediate goods represent 56 per cent of total trade in goods, while final consumption goods represent only 21 per cent of total trade in goods (Miroudot et al., 2009).

9. See Barrios and Strobl (2009) and Combes et al. (2011) and references therein.

References

Adler, N., Pels, E., and Nash, C. 2010. High-speed rail and air transport competition: Game engineering as tool for cost-benefit analysis. *Transportation Research Part B: Methodological*, **44**, 812–833.

Ahlfeldt, G. M., and Feddersen, A. 2015. From periphery to core: Measuring agglomeration effects using high-speed rail. *SERCDP0172. London, UK: Spatial Economics Research Centre, LSE.*

Anderson, J., and van Wincoop, E. 2004. Trade costs. *Journal of Economic Literature*, **42**, 691–751.

Aschauer, D. A. 1989. Is public expenditure productive? *Journal of Monetary Economics*, **23**, 177–200.

Bairoch, P. 1997. *Victoires et dboires. Histoire é conomique et sociale du monde du XVIe siĉcle ŕ nos jours*. Paris: Editions Gallimard.

Baldwin, R. E., Forslid, R., Martin, P., Ottaviano, G. I. P., and Robert-Nicoud, F. 2003. *Economic Geography and Public Policy*. Princeton, NJ: Princeton University Press.

Barbero, J., Behrens, K., and Zofio, J. L. 2015. *Industry location and wages: The role of market size and accessibility in trading networks*. CEPR Discussion Paper No. 10411.

Barrios, S., and Strobl, E. 2009. The dynamics of regional inequalities. *Regional Science and Urban Economics*, **39**, 575–591.

Behrens, K. 2005. Market size and industry location: Traded vs non-traded goods. *Journal of Urban Economics*, **58**, 24–44.

Behrens, K., and Thisse, J.-F. 2007. Regional economics: A new economic geography perspective. *Regional Science and Urban Economics*, **37**, 457–465.

Behrens, K., Gaigné, C., Ottaviano, G. I. P., and Thisse, J.-F. 2007. Countries, regions and trade: On the welfare impacts of economic integration. *European Economic Review*, **51**, 1277–1301.

Belleflamme, P., Picard, P., and Thisse, J.-F. 2000. An economic theory of regional clusters. *Journal of Urban Economics*, **48**, 158–184.

Beyer, R. C. M., and Smets, F. 2015. Labour market adjustments and migration in Europe and the United States: How different? *Economic Policy*, **30**, 643–682.

Boldrin, M., and Canova, F. 2001. Inequality and convergence in Europe's regions: Reconsidering European regional policies. *Economic Policy*, **16**, 206–253.

Bosker, M., and Buringh, E. 2017. City seeds: Geography and the origins of the European city system. *forthcoming in Journal of Urban Economics*.

Bosquet, C., and Overman, H. 2015. Home versus hometown: What do we mean by spatial sorting? *Paper presented at the RIETI Workshop on Spatial Economics, Tokyo, April 14, 2015*.

Breinlich, H., Ottaviano, G., and Temple, J. 2014. Regional growth and regional decline. In: Aghion, P., and Durlauf, S. N. (eds), *Handbook of Economic Growth*, vol. 2. Amsterdam: Elsevier, pp. 683–779.

Bröcker, J., Korzhenevych, A., and Schürmann, C. 2010. Assessing spatial equity and efficiency impacts of transport infrastructure projects. *Transportation Research Part B: Methodological*, **44**, 795–811.

Charlot, S., Gaigné, C., Robert-Nicoud, F., and Thisse, J.-F. 2006. Agglomeration and welfare: The core-periphery model in the light of Bentham, Kaldor, and Rawls. *Journal of Public Economics*, **90**, 325–347.

Cheshire, P., and Magrini, S. 2006. Population growth in European cities: Weather matters – but only nationally. *Regional Studies*, **40**, 23–37.

Cheshire, P., Nathan, M., and Overman, H. 2014. *Urban Economics and Urban Policy*. Cheltenham, U.K.: Edward Elgar Publishing.

Combes, P.-P., and Overman., H. 2004. The spatial distribution of economic activities in the European Union. In: Henderson, J. V., and Thisse, J.-F. (eds), *Handbook of Regional and Urban Economics*, vol. 4. Amsterdam: Elsevier, pp. 2845–2909.

Combes, P.-P., Lafourcade, M., Thisse, J.-F., and Toutain, J.-C. 2011. The rise and fall of spatial inequalities in France. A long-run perspective. *Explorations in Economic History*, **48**, 243–271.

Crozet, M. 2004. Do migrants follow market potentials? An estimation of a new economic geography model. *Journal of Economic Geography*, **4**, 439–458.

Dahl, M. S., and Sorenson, O. 2010. The migration of technical workers. *Journal of Urban Economics*, **67**, 33–45.

d'Aspremont, C., Gabszewicz, J. J., and Thisse, J.-F. 1979. Hotelling's 'Stability in Competition'. *Econometrica*, **47**, 1145–1150.

Davis, D. R., and Weinstein, D. E. 2003. Market access, economic geography and comparative advantage: An empirical test. *Journal of International Economics*, **59**, 1–23.

De Rus, G., and Nombela, G. 2007. Is investment in high speed rail socially profitable? *Journal of Transport Economics and Policy*, **41**, 3–23.

Desmet, K., and Rossi-Hansberg, E. 2014. Spatial development. *American Economic Review*, **104**, 1211–1243.

Di Comite, F., and Kancs, A. 2015. *Modelling of agglomeration and dispersion in RHO-MOLO*. Mimeo.

Dixit, A. K., and Stiglitz, J. E. 1977. Monopolistic competition and optimum product diversity. *American Economic Review*, **67**, 297–308.

Duranton, G., Martin, P., Mayer, T., and Mayneris, F. 2010. *The Economics of Clusters: Lessons from the French Experience*. Oxford: Oxford University Press.

Epifani, P., and Gancia, G. 2005. Trade, migration and regional unemployment. *Regional Science and Urban Economics*, **35**, 625–644.

Eurostat. 2015a. EU Transport in Figures – Statistical Pocketbook 2015. *Luxembourg: Publications Office of the European Union*.

Eurostat. 2015b. Regional Statistics. http://ec.europa.eu/eurostat/cache/RSI/#?vis=nuts2.economy.

Faber, B. 2014. Trade integration, market size, and industrialization: Evidence from China's national trunk highway system. *Review of Economic Studies*, **81**, 1046–1070.

Falck, O., Heblich, S., Lameli, A., and Südekum, J. 2012. Dialects, cultural identity, and economic exchange. *Journal of Urban Economics*, **72**, 225–239.

Fujita, M., and Thisse, J.-F. 2013. *Economics of Agglomeration: Cities, Industrial Location, and Globalization*. 2 edn. New York: Cambridge University Press.

Fujita, M., Krugman, P., and Venables, A. J. 1999. *The Spatial Economy: Cities, Regions, and International Trade*. Cambridge, MA: MIT Press.

Glaeser, E. L., and Kohlhase, J. E. 2004. Cities, regions and the decline of transport costs. *Papers in Regional Science*, **83**, 197–228.

Gramlich, E. M. 1994. Infrastructure investment: A review essay. *Journal of Economic Literature*, **32**, 1176–1196.

Harris, C. 1954. The market as a factor in the localization of industry in the United States. *Annals of the Association of American Geographers*, **44**, 315–348.

Head, K., and Mayer, T. 2004. The empirics of agglomeration and trade. In: Henderson, J. V., and Thisse, J.-F. (eds), *Handbook of Regional and Urban Economics*, vol. 4. Amsterdam: Elsevier, pp. 2609–2669.

Head, K., and Mayer, T. 2011. Gravity, market potential and economic development. *Journal of Economic Geography*, **11**, 281–294.

Head, K., and Mayer, T. 2013. What separates us? Sources of resistance to globalization. *Canadian Journal of Economics*, **46**, 1196–1231.

Helpman, E. 1998. The size of regions. In: Pines, D., Sadka, E., and Zilcha, I. (eds), *Topics in Public Economics: Theoretical and Applied Analysis*. Cambridge, UK: Cambridge University Press, pp. 33–54.

Henderson, J. V. 1997. Medium size cities. *Regional Science and Urban Economics*, **27**, 583–612.

Hirschman, A. O. 1958. *The Strategy of Development*. New Haven, CN: Yale University Press.

Hohenberg, P., and Lees, L. H. 1985. *The Making of Urban Europe (1000–1950)*. Cambridge, MA: Harvard University Press.

Hotelling, H. 1929. Stability in competition. *Economic Journal*, **39**, 41–57.

Ivaldi, M., and McCullough, G. 2008. Subadditivity tests for network separation with an application to U.S. railroads. *Review of Network Economics*, **7**, 1–13.

Klein, A., and Crafts, N. 2012. Making sense of the manufacturing belt: Determinants of U.S. industrial location, 1880–1920. *Journal of Economic Geography*, **12**, 775–807.

Knight, B. 2004. Parochial interests and the centralized provision of local public goods: Evidence from congressional voting on transportation projects. *Journal of Public Economics*, **88**, 845–866.

Koopmans, T. C. 1957. *Three Essays on the State of Economic Science*. New York: McGraw-Hill.

Krugman, P. R. 1980. Scale economies, product differentiation, and the pattern of trade. *American Economic Review*, **70**, 950–959.

Krugman, P. R. 1991. Increasing returns and economic geography. *Journal of Political Economy*, **99**, 483–499.

Krugman, P. R., and Venables, A. J. 1995. Globalization and the inequality of nations. *Quarterly Journal of Economics*, **110**, 857–880.

Magrini, S. 2004. Regional (di)convergence. In: Henderson, J. V., and Thisse, J.-F. (eds), *Handbook of Regional and Urban Economics*, vol. 4. Amsterdam: Elsevier, pp. 2741–2796.

Mandell, S., and Proost, S. 2016. Why truck distance taxes are contagious and drive fuel taxes to the bottom. *Journal of Urban Economics*, **93**, 1–7.

Mayer, T. 2008. Market potential and development. *CEPR Discussion Paper No. 6798.*

Mayer, T., and Ottaviano, G. I. P. 2007. *The Happy Few: The Internationalisation of European Firms. New Facts Based on Firm-Level Evidence.* Brussels: Bruegel Blueprint Series.

Melo, P., Graham, D. J., and Brage-Ardao, R. 2013. The productivity of transport infrastructure investment: A meta-analysis of empirical evidence. *Regional Science and Urban Economics*, **43**, 695–706.

Midelfart-Knarvik, K. H., and Overman, H. G. 2002. Delocation and European integration: Is structural spending justified? *Economic Policy*, **17**, 321–359.

Miroudot, S., Lanz, R., and Ragoussis, A. 2009. *Trade in intermediate goods and services.* OECD Trade Policy Working Paper No. 93, TAD/TC/WP(2009)1/FINAL, OECD.

Moretti, E. 2011. Local labor markets. In: Card, D., and Ashenfelter, O. (eds), *Handbook of Labor Economics*, vol. 4b. Amsterdam: Elsevier, pp. 1237–1313.

Nocke, V. 2006. A gap for me: Entrepreneurs and entry. *Journal of the European Economic Association*, **4**, 929–956.

Ohlin, B. 1967. *Interregional and International Trade.* Rev. ed. Cambridge, MA: Harvard University Press. (Originally published in 1933.)

Ottaviano, G. I. P., and Thisse, J.-F. 2002. Integration, agglomeration and the political economics of factor mobility. *Journal of Public Economics*, **83**, 429–456.

Ottaviano, G. I. P., and van Ypersele, T. 2005. Market size and tax competition. *Journal of International Economics*, **67**, 25–46.

Polése, M. 2009. *The Wealth and Poverty of Regions: Why Cities Matter.* Chicago: University of Chicago Press.

Pollard, S. 1981. *Peaceful Conquest: The Industrialization of Europe 1760–1970.* Oxford: Oxford University Press.

Porter, M. E. 1998. Clusters and the new economics of competition. *Harvard Business Review* (November-December), 77–90.

Proost, S., Dunkerley, F., van der Loo, S., Adler, N., Bröcker, J., and Korzhenevych, A. 2014. Do the selected Trans European transport investments pass the cost benefit test? *Transportation*, **41**, 107–132.

Puga, D. 1999. The rise and fall of regional inequalities. *European Economic Review*, **43**, 303–334.

Puga, D. 2002. European regional policies in the light of recent location theories. *Journal of Economic Geography*, **2**, 373–406.

Redding, S. J. 2011. Economic geography: A review of the theoretical and empirical literature. In: Bernhofen, D., Falvey, R., Greenaway, D., and Kreickemeier, U. (eds), *The Palgrave Handbook of International Trade*. London: Palgrave Macmillan, pp. 497–531.

Redding, S. J., and Sturm, D. 2008. The cost of remoteness: Evidence from German division and reunification. *American Economic Review*, **98**, 1766–1797.

Redding, S. J., and Turner, M.A. 2015. Transportation costs and the spatial organization of economic activity. In: Duranton, G., Henderson, J. V., and Strange, W. (eds), *Handbook of Regional and Urban Economics*, vol. 5. Amsterdam: Elsevier, pp. 1339–1398.

Redding, S. J., and Venables, A. J. 2004. Economic geography and international inequality. *Journal of International Economics*, **62**, 53–82.

Rossi-Hansberg, E. 2005. A spatial theory of trade. *American Economic Review*, **95**, 1464–1491.

Spulber, D. F. 2007. *Global Competitive Strategy*. Cambridge: Cambridge University Press.

Syverson, C. 2004. Market structure and productivity: A concrete example. *Journal of Political Economy*, **112**, 1181–1222.

Takahashi, T., Takatsuka, H., and Zeng, D.-Z. 2013. Spatial inequality, globalization, and footloose capital. *Economic Theory*, **53**, 213–238.

Thomas, I. 2002. *Transportation Networks and the Optimal Location of Human Activities: A Numerical Geography Approach*. Cheltenham, UK: Edward Elgar.

Van der Loo, S., and Proost, S. 2013. The European road pricing game: How to enforce optimal pricing in high-transit countries under asymmetric information. *Journal of Transport Economics and Policy*, **47**, 399–418.

Williamson, J. G. 1965. Regional inequality and the process of national development: A description of the patterns. *Economic Development and Cultural Change*, **13**, 1–84.

Zeng, D.-Z. 2014. The role of country size in spatial economics: A survey of the home market effects. *Journal of Economics and Business*, **32**, 379–403.

9   Skilled Cities and Efficient Urban Transport

Stef Proost and Jacques-François Thisse

Abstract

This chapter surveys the fundamental forces that drive the formation and size of cities. We discuss the different types of agglomeration economies generated by a dense web of activities, with special emphasis on the benefits associated with the clustering of highly skilled workers. The distribution of activities within cities results from the trade-off between commuting and housing costs. We show that in this trade-off commuting costs are the cause and land rent is the consequence. The land rent capitalizes the advantages associated with proximity to particular urban locations such as employment centres. We identify the main sources of inefficiency in various urban policies implemented in Europe. Special attention is paid to the regulation of the land market and the pricing of urban transport.

9.1   Introduction

The main distinctive feature of a city is the very high density of activities and population, which allows agents to be close to one another. Households and firms seek spatial proximity because they need to interact for a variety of economic and social reasons on a daily basis. For example, individuals want to be close to each other because they like to meet other people, learn from others, and have a broader range of opportunities. Hence, *the main reason for the existence of cities is to connect people*. This need is gravitational in nature in that its intensity increases with the number of agents set up nearby, and decreases with the distance between them. Contrary to an opinion widespread in the media, and despite the Internet and other new communication devices, face-to-face contact remains important, at least for a certain number of human and economic activities. To understand why this is so, one has to remember that information transferred through modern communication tools must be structured according to clearly defined schemes and codes known to all. Only formal and precise information can be transmitted this way. In contrast, information that is difficult to codify can often be conveyed only through face-to-face contact.

366

In the industrial era, cities have enabled transport costs between large and connected production plants to decrease substantially. Today, cities are the cradles of new ideas that benefit firms of very different sizes. But this is not new; cities are – and have been for centuries – the source of productivity gains as well as technological and cultural innovations (Hohenberg and Lees, 1985; Bairoch, 1985). To a large extent, it is fair to say that the agglomeration of economic activities in cities is the geographical counterpart of social and economic development. However, these positive effects come with negative ones: congestion, segregation, pollution, and crime. European cities are much older than American ones. While European cultural heritage is an advantage for economic and social development, it is also a major constraint when organizing and managing mobility within cities. This should not conflict with the fact that wealth is increasingly created in cities, a fact that holds for the European Union (EU) and, more generally, for developed and emerging countries alike. And, although no EU-level urban strategy exists (at least not yet), there is a growing recognition that many large European cities face similar social and cohesion problems.

The city has a spatial extension because economic agents consume land, which implies that consumers travel within the city. Therefore, an urban space is both the substratum of economic activity and a private good (land) that is traded among economic agents. The worldwide supply of land vastly exceeds the demand for land. As a consequence, the price of land should be zero. Yet, we all know that for reasons that do not depend on the quality of the housing structure, housing costs vary enormously with the size of cities. Therefore, the price of land reflects the scarcity of 'something' that differs from land per se.

The main objective of urban economics is to explain why cities – understood here as metropolitan areas that extend beyond the core city limits – exist and how they are organized; that is, to explain why jobs are concentrated in a few employment centres and how consumers are spatially distributed within the city according to their incomes and preferences. Central to the workings of a city is the functioning of its land market, which allocates both economic agents and activities across space, as well as the quality of the transport infrastructure used by commuters and shoppers. Equally important are various types of social networks that operate within very short distances. For example, informational spillovers affect positively the productivity of the local R&D sector, whereas neighbourhood effects are often critical to sustaining criminal activities in particular urban districts. To understand cities, we must view them not simply as places in space but as anchored systems of market and nonmarket interactions.

Looking at cities through the lens of microeconomics sheds new light on issues that are often poorly understood otherwise. Many prosperous regions are city-regions or regions that accommodate a dense network of medium-sized cities; an example is the Randstad in the Netherlands. This is backed up by casual evidence: among the top 10 NUTS-2 regions of the EU in terms of gross domestic product (GDP) per capita, 8 are formed by or organized around a major capital city. Figure 9.1 shows the range of the distribution of regional GDP per capita within each EU country; in most cases, the top position is occupied by the capital regions. In the US, the 20 largest metropolitan areas produce about half of the American GDP. This suggests that interregional systems should be studied in relation to urban systems.

In this chapter, we start by analyzing the fundamental forces that drive the formation and size of cities, that is, the agglomeration economies generated by a dense web of activities and the trade-off between commuting and housing costs. Afterwards, we discuss more specific issues with a special emphasis on residential segregation and urban transport.

9.2   Agglomeration Economies

Humans have a strong drive to form and maintain lasting relations with others. Cities may thus be viewed, at least in the first order, as the outcome of the interplay between social interactions and competition for land. Isolation allows an individual to consume more land but makes interactions with others more costly. To study this trade-off, Beckmann (1976) assumes that the utility of an individual depends on the average distance to all individuals and on the amount of land bought on the market. In equilibrium, the city exhibits a bell-shaped population density distribution supported by a similarly shaped land rent curve. In other words, *the natural gregariousness of human beings turns out to be a sufficient motivation for them to gather within compact areas*. However, while relevant, this explanation is not sufficient to explain the existence of urban agglomerations with millions of inhabitants.

It is well known that consumers in large metropolises pay high rents, have a longer commute, live in a polluted environment, and face high crime rates. So why would they choose to live in such places? It is because they get much better pay in large cities than in small towns. But why do firms in larger cities pay higher wages to their employees? If firms do not bear lower costs and/or earn higher revenues in large cities, they should rather locate in small towns or the countryside where both land and labour are much cheaper. The reason why firms set up in large cities is now well documented: *the productivity of labour is higher in larger cities than in smaller ones*. Or to put it bluntly, after controlling for unemployment and participation, wages and employment (both levels and rates) move together. This does not mean the demand for labour is upward-sloping. Instead, the reason for this urban wage premium is found in what economists call 'agglomeration economies'.

Whereas economists have long acknowledged the benefits associated with integrating international markets, it took them much longer to understand that there are similar benefits associated with dense and thick markets – such as

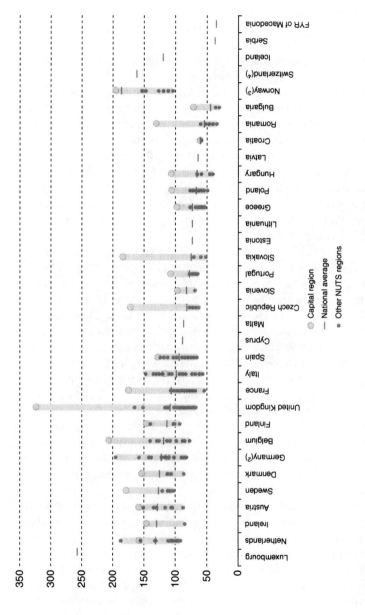

(1) The light grey shaded bar shows the range of the highest to lowest region for each country. The dark grey bar shows the national average. The light grey circle shows the capital city region. The dark grey circles show the other regions.
(2) Only available for NUTS level 1 regions.
(3) Only available at national level.
(4) 2012.
Source: Eurostat (online data codes: nama_10r_2gdp and nama_10_pc).

Figure 9.1 The distribution of GDP per capita within EU countries (Eurostat, 2015).

those in large cities. Starting with the highly influential work of Glaeser et al. (1992), Henderson et al. (1995), and Ciccone and Hall (1996), research on city size, employment density, and productivity has progressed enormously during the last two decades. An ordinary least squares (OLS) regression of the logarithm of the average wage on the logarithm of the employment density across cities yields an elasticity that varies from 0.03 to 0.10 (Rosenthal and Strange, 2004). However, this result could be explained by the fact that some econometric problems have not been properly addressed.

First, using a simple reduced form omits explanatory variables whose effects could be captured by employment density. For example, overlooking variables that account for differences in, say, average skills or amenities is equivalent to assuming that skills or amenities are randomly distributed across cities and are taken into account in the random term. This is highly implausible. One solution is to consider additional explanatory variables but, in so doing, we face a familiar situation of adding an endless string of control variables to the regressions. Instead, if we use city/region and industry fixed effects, we can control for the omitted variables that do not vary over time. However, time-varying variables remain omitted.

Second, the correlation of the residuals with explanatory variables – which also biases OLS estimates in the case of omitted variables – can also result from endogenous location choices. Indeed, shocks are often localized and thus have an impact on the location of agents, who are attracted by cities that benefit from positive shocks and repelled by those suffering negative shocks. These agents' relocation has an impact on cities' level of economic activity and, consequently, on their density of employment. Employment density is correlated with the dependent variable and, therefore, with the residuals. To put it differently, there is reverse causality: an unobserved shock initially affects wages and thus density through the mobility of workers, not the other way around. This should not come as a surprise; once it is recognized that agents are mobile, there is a two-way relationship between employment density and wages. The most widely used solution to correct endogeneity biases, whether resulting from omitted variables or reverse causality, involves using instrumental variables. This consists of finding variables that are correlated with the endogenous explanatory variables but not with the residuals.

Caution is therefore needed when measuring the impact of employment density on labour productivity. Using advanced econometric methods and taking into account additional explanations of workers' productivity (such as nonobservable individual characteristics or the impact of previous individual locational choices on current productivity), urban economists have obtained more accurate estimations of agglomeration gains. There is now a broad consensus that, everything else being equal, the elasticity of labour productivity with respect to current employment density is about 0.03 (Combes et al., 2012). This elasticity measures the static gains generated by a higher employment density. For example, doubling the employment density in Greater Paris would generate an increase in labour productivity that would be twice as large as it would be in the least populated 'départements' of France.

9.2.1 The Nature and Magnitude of Agglomeration Economies

Increasing returns are crucial to understanding the formation of the space-economy. The most natural way to think of increasing returns is when a plant with minimum capacity has to be built before starting production. This gives rise to overhead and fixed costs, which are typically associated with mass production. In this case, scale economies are *internal* to firms. Increasing returns may also materialize in a very different form, in which they are *external* to firms but specific to the local environment in which firms operate. Their concrete manifestation can vary considerably from one case to another, but the basic idea is the same: *each firm benefits from the presence of other firms*. In other words, even when individual firms operate under constant returns, there are increasing returns in the aggregate. In a nutshell, the whole is greater than the sum of its parts.

Duranton and Puga (2004) have proposed gathering the various effects associated with agglomeration economies into the following three categories: sharing, matching, and learning.

1. **Sharing** refers primarily to local public goods provided to consumers and producers. When seeking a reason for the existence of cities, one that comes most naturally to mind is the variety and quality of public services, as well as the availability of efficient and large infrastructures. This includes local public goods that contribute to enhancing firms' productivity, such as facilities required by the use of new information and communication technologies and various transport infrastructures, but it also includes public services that increase consumers' well-being. The large number of people and firms facilitate the provision of public goods. These public goods could hardly be obtained in isolation because they would then be supplied at a level below the critical mass permitting the goods to deliver their full impact. In other words, the efficiency of many public services rises when they are supplied to a dense population of users.

Sharing also refers to the supply of intermediate or business-to-business services available in large markets. Even though firms outsource a number of activities to countries where labour is cheap, they also use specialized services available only where they are produced, namely in big cities.

2. **Matching** means that the quality of matches between workers and firms in the labour market is higher in a thick market than in a thin one because of the greater number of opportunities for agents when they operate in a denser

labour market. But the strength of this effect remains an open question. However, sticky workers living in small cities operate in markets with few potential employers, thereby allowing firms to exploit their monopsony power and to pay lower wages.[1] In contrast, workers living in large cities do not have to move to search for jobs provided by other potential employers, which makes them more prone to change jobs. Consequently, workers having the same individual characteristics will earn higher wages in larger cities than in smaller ones because firms have less monopsony power in thicker than in thinner labour markets (Manning, 2010).

3. **Learning** asserts that different agents own different bits of information. Therefore, getting the agents together allows informational spillovers that raise the level of knowledge, thus improving firms' and workers' productivity. Spillovers stem from specific features of knowledge; in particular, knowledge is a nonrivalrous and partially excludable good. The role of information in modern cities has long been emphasized by economic historians. In the words of Hohenberg and Lees (1985), 'urban development is a dynamic process whose driving force is the ability to put information to work. After 1850, the large cities became the nurseries as well as the chief beneficiaries of an explosion in knowledge-centred economic growth.' Cities are the places where people talk. Of course, much of this talk does not generate productivity gains. However, the higher the number of people, the more likely the talk will lead to innovations, increasing productivity. For example, D'Costa and Overman (2014) find that rural workers with past experience in cities enjoy a wage growth premium, thus suggesting that people build knowledge and experience in cities.

Education generates an externality – the knowledge spillovers from skilled workers to other skilled workers – that did not attract much attention until recently. Moretti (2004) has convincingly argued that the social productivity of education exceeds its private productivity. In other words, acquiring human capital enhances not only the productivity of the worker who acquires it but also the productivity of others because we learn from others. What is important for the economic performance of cities is that skilled workers seem to benefit more from the presence of other skilled workers than unskilled workers. Evidently this effect is stronger in the case of regular, easy contacts between skilled workers. For example, Charlot and Duranton (2004) find that workers in larger and more educated cities exchange information more than in cities populated by less-skilled workers. These authors show that such communications explain between 13% and 22 per cent of the urban premium paid to high-skilled workers. In the same spirit, Bacolod et al. (2009) observe that the urban wage premium associated with large cities stems from cognitive skills rather than motor skills. Therefore, everything seems to work as if the marginal productivity of a worker endowed with a certain type of skill increased with the number of skilled workers working or living around him or her. It is no surprise, therefore, that specific workers tend to sort across space according to their skills.

In the US, Moretti (2012) observed that college graduates living in the richest cities, which are typically knowledge-based metropolitan areas, earn wages 50 per cent higher than college graduates living in the bottom group of cities. In France, about half the spatial disparities in income are explained by the different locations of skilled and unskilled workers (Combes et al., 2008), while between 85 and 88 per cent of spatial wage disparities in the United Kingdom are explained by individual characteristics (Gibbons et al., 2014). The concentration of human capital and high-value activities in large cities is a marked feature of developed and emerging economies. In other words, *spatial inequalities tend more and more to reflect differences in the distribution of skills and human capital across space.*[2] This has significant implications for the organization of the space-economy: cities specializing in high-tech activities attract highly skilled workers, who in turn help make these places more successful through other agglomeration economies and better amenities. To put it differently, *workers tend to be spatially sorted by skills* (Behrens et al., 2014, Davis and Dingel, 2015). The downside of spatial sorting is the existence of stagnating or declining areas that display high unemployment rates, or are specialized in industries that pay low wages and are associated with a small number of local businesses.

To a large extent, this evolution is enabled by the low transport and communication costs prevailing today. Although these reduced costs allow standardized activities to be located in remote, low-wage countries, big cities remain very attractive for those activities where access to information and advanced technologies is of prime importance. Firms operating in industries that undergo rapid technological changes must be able to react quickly to market signals and to design specialized and sophisticated products that require a skilled labour force, especially when competition is intensified by low transport costs. In a knowledge-based economy where information moves at an increasingly rapid pace, the value of knowledge and information keeps rising. This eventually increases the need for proximity for activities involving firms' strategic divisions, such as management, marketing, finance, and R&D, as well as specialized business-to-business (advertising, legal, and accounting services) and high-tech industries.

If the existence of informational and knowledge spillovers is indisputable, measuring their magnitude is hard as the spillovers are not observable. Different strategies have been proposed to figure out their importance. One of the most original approaches is that of Arzaghi and Henderson (2008), who study the networking effects among geographically close advertising agencies in Manhattan. Advertising is an industry in which creativity matters greatly and where new ideas are quickly obsolete. The authors find there is an extremely rapid spatial decay in the benefits of having close neighbours. They also show that firms providing high-quality services locate close to other high-quality firms because they do not want to waste resources on discovering which neighbours have valuable information or on establishing communication links with low-quality firms.

It is worth stressing that the geographical concentration of similar firms, such as advertising agencies on Madison Avenue in New York, shows the strength of the various agglomeration effects. Indeed, industrial organization provides evidence that competition between similar firms is a strong dispersion force that tends to push them away from one another (d'Aspremont et al., 1979, Tirole, 1988).

All the agglomeration effects discussed above may be intrasectoral as pointed out by Marshall (1890) or intersectoral as argued by Jacobs (1969). Regardless of their origin, the existence of these positive effects on firms' productivity is unquestionable. However, several issues remain unclear (Puga, 2010, Combes and Gobillon, 2015). First, different industries agglomerate for different reasons. Therefore, what is the relative importance of the various types of agglomeration economies in cities that specialize in different activities? Second, are agglomeration economies stronger in high-tech industries than in traditional sectors that are typically less information-based? Third, the geographical distribution of human capital explains a large share of spatial inequalities. However, it is not clear how much of the human capital effect is explained by the distribution of individual workers, and how much by the presence of human capital externalities across highly skilled workers. Last, how does city size affect the nature and magnitude of agglomeration economies? For example, in a specialized city, a negative shock to the corresponding industry affects its workers negatively. In contrast, in a city endowed with many different types of industries, workers may expect to find a job in firms belonging to other industries. In other words, a diversified – and probably large – city acts as an insurance device. For example, large French cities have been less affected by the Great Recession than other territories (Borzic and Le Jeannic, 2014). In the same vein, unplanned interactions allow firms belonging to one sector to benefit from the presence of another firm located in the same city.

In a recent comprehensive study, Faggio et al. (2014) give a qualified answer to these questions. They confirm the presence of the various effects discussed above but stress that *agglomeration is a very heterogeneous phenomenon*. For example, low-tech industries do benefit from spillovers but high-tech industries benefit more. Both intrasectoral and intersectoral external effects are at work, but they affect industries to a different degree. Firm size also matters: agglomeration effects tend to be stronger when firms are smaller. In other words, specialized and vertically disintegrated firms would benefit more from spatial proximity than larger ones. Despite the wealth of valuable new results, if we want to design more effective policies for city development and redevelopment, we need a deeper understanding of the drivers behind the process of agglomeration. Furthermore, the interactions across agents are driven by the accessibility of an agent to the others. Although geographers and transport economists consider employment density as a rather crude proxy for accessibility, the question of how to define and measure accessibility in econometric studies of agglomeration economies has been mostly ignored.

Another striking difference across cities lies in their ability to innovate. Based on the success of Silicon Valley, the conventional wisdom among political decision-makers holds that the presence of large university labs is necessary (and, hopefully, sufficient) for a city to become the cradle of new high value added products and processes. Armchair evidence shows that this is not a sufficient condition for boosting innovation productivity. A few decades ago, the experience of Italian industrial districts led some analysts to maintain that a dense network of small and medium-sized businesses (SMEs) was the best environment for innovating. A recent study by Agrawal et al. (2014) suggests a possible reconciliation between these two tenets. Studying American MSA-level patent data during the period 1975–2000, these authors find that the combination of large research labs and a wide array of SMEs is likely to be the friendliest environment for innovation. Although studying the various aspects of entrepreneurship and innovation within the framework of urban economics seems a very promising avenue for research, more work is called for before making solid policy recommendations.

9.2.2 Cities as Consumption Centres

The usual cliché is that big cities are bad for consumers. But the authors of anti-city pamphlets forget two things: (i) all over the world, free people vote with their feet by moving to cities; and (ii) cities are not just efficient production centres but are also great places for consumption, culture, and leisure (Glaeser et al., 2001). Consumers living in large cities enjoy a wider range of goods, services, and contacts as the number of shops, cultural amenities, and opportunities for social relations all increase with city size. Even if dating on the Internet tends to be more and more pervasive, one day the two parties have to meet physically. While the steady decline in transport costs and the progressive dismantling of tariff barriers have vastly improved access to foreign goods, models in industrial organization show that the concomitant increase in competition incentivizes both incumbent and new firms to restore their profit margins by supplying higher-quality goods as well as more differentiated products. Because both taste and income ranges are wider in bigger cities, and because larger cities also allow for more varieties to cover their fixed production costs, more goods and services are available in such markets (Picard and Okubo,

2012). In sum, consumers living in larger cities enjoy a broader range of goods and business-to-consumer services.

Even though, as shown below, housing is more expensive in large cities than in small ones, tradable goods need not be more expensive. Since a larger city provides a larger outlet for consumption goods, there is more entry, which intensifies competition; such cities also attract the most efficient retailers that benefit from agglomeration economies and better logistics. Again, as suggested by industrial organization theory, market prices tend to be lower in larger than in smaller cities and the number of varieties of a base product is greater. Calculating the first theoretically based urban price index for 49 US cities, Handbury and Weinstein (2015) show that prices will fall by 1.1 per cent when the population doubles, while the number of available products will increase by 20 per cent. These consumption benefits become even more pronounced once it is recognized that the hierarchy of public services is often the mirror image of the urban hierarchy. In particular, the congregation of a large number of people facilitates the provision of public services that could not be obtained in isolation. Health care and educational facilities are good cases in point.

Notwithstanding many qualifications, the empirical evidence strongly suggests that cities are likely to remain one of the main engines of modern economic growth. Agglomeration economies are not disappearing but their nature and concrete form are changing. But even so, if agglomeration economies are that strong (at least in some sectors), why do cities have a finite size and why are there so many of them? As we are going to see, agglomeration economies have their dark side that restricts the process of city growth and leads to the emergence of a system of cities.

9.3   The Trade-Off between Commuting and Housing Costs

In addition to the idea of agglomeration economies, two other fundamental concepts lie at the heart of urban economics: (i) *people prefer shorter trips to longer trips*, and (ii) *people prefer having more space than less space*. Since activities cannot be concentrated on the head of a pin, they are distributed across space. The authoritative model of urban economics is the monocentric city model developed by Alonso (1964), Mills (1967), and Muth (1969). Treading in these authors' footsteps, economists and regional scientists alike have developed the monocentric model in which a single and exogenously given central business district (CBD) accommodates all jobs. In this context, the only spatial characteristic of a location is its distance from the CBD. The main purpose of this model is to study households' trade-off between housing size – approximated by the amount of land used – and their accessibility to the CBD, measured by the inverse of commuting costs.

Commuting and housing are the two main consumption items in household budgets. Housing and transport represent respectively 26 per cent and 17 per cent of French household expenditures (INSEE). In Belgium, they account for 26 per cent and 13 per cent, respectively (Statistics Belgium). The expenditure share for transport, which takes into account some outlays unrelated to commuting, disregards consumers' time costs and the disutility associated with commuting. The opportunity cost of time spent in commuting accounts for three to six weeks of work a year for a Manhattanite and, on average, four weeks of work for a resident in Greater Paris. These are big numbers, which confirm that commuting costs and traffic congestion are issues that policy-makers have neglected for far too long. Commuting is also perceived as one of consumers' most stressful and unpleasant activities (Kahneman and Krueger, 2006).

9.3.1 The Monocentric City Model

Ever since the early 1970s, urban economics has advanced rapidly and shows no sign of abating. The reason for this success is probably that the monocentric city model is based on a competitive land market.[3] This assumption can be justified on the grounds that land in a small neighbourhood in any location belonging to a continuous space is highly substitutable, thus making the competition for land very fierce. By allocating a plot of land near the CBD to some consumers, the commuting costs borne by other consumers are indirectly increased as they are forced to set up farther away. Hence, determining where consumers are located in the city is a general equilibrium problem. In equilibrium, identical consumers establish themselves within the city so as to equalize utility. In such a state, the land rent at a particular location is equal to the largest bid for that location. Since people are willing to pay more to be closer to their workplace in order to save time and money on commuting costs, the urban land rent decreases with the distance from the CBD. In turn, since land is cheaper, the population density decreases with distance from the CBD because consumers can afford to buy more land. In sum, *the land rent reflects the differential in workers' accessibility to jobs*.

To illustrate, consider a featureless plain with a dimensionless CBD located at $x = 0$ and a population of consumers who share the same income and the same preferences $U(z, s)$ where z is the consumption of a composite good, chosen as the numéraire, and s the amount of space used. In this set-up, the essential quality which the CBD possesses is physical proximity, or accessibility, to all parts of the urban area. For this reason, consumers compete to be as close as possible to the workplace, but the amount of land available in the vicinity of the CBD is too limited to accommodate the entire population. How, therefore, do consumers distribute themselves across locations? This is where the land market comes into play. The formal argument is disarmingly simple. Denoting by $R(x)$ the land rent prevailing at a distance x from the CBD and by $T(x)$ the commuting cost borne by a consumer residing at x, the budget constraint of this consumer is given by $z(x) + s(x) \cdot R(x) = I(x) \equiv Y - T(x)$, where consumers have, by assumption, the same income Y.

Let $V(R(x), I(x))$ be the indirect utility of a consumer at x. Since the highest utility level attainable by consumers is invariant across locations, the derivative of $V(R(x), I(x))$ with respect to x must be equal to zero:

$$V_R \cdot R'(x) + V_I \cdot I'(x) = 0.$$

Using Roy's identity and the equality $I'(x) = -T'(x)$, we obtain the Alonso-Muth equilibrium condition:

$$s(x) \cdot R'(x) + T'(x) = 0.$$

Since a longer commute generates a higher cost, this condition holds if and only if the land rent $R(x)$ is downward sloping. As a consequence, *a marginal increase in commuting costs associated with a longer trip ($T'(x) > 0$) is exactly compensated for by the income share saved on land consumption.* In other words, people trade bigger plots for higher commuting costs. If commuting costs were independent of the distance ($T'(x) = 0$), the land rent would be flat and constant across locations. In other words, *commuting costs are the cause and land rents the consequence.*

Furthermore, the lot size occupied by a consumer must increase with the distance from the CBD. Indeed, although a longer commute is associated with a lower net income $Y - T(x)$, the spatial equilibrium condition implies that the utility level is the same across all consumers. As a consequence, in equilibrium, the consumer optimization problem yields a compensated demand for land that depends on the land rent and the endogenous utility level. The utility level is treated as a given by every consumer who is too small to affect it. With housing being a normal good, a lower price for land therefore implies higher land consumption. In other words, as the distance to the CBD increases, the lot size rises, whereas the consumption of the composite good decreases.

Note that housing costs are higher than the land rent because the former account for the quality of housing, which may be higher in the suburbs as units are often older and smaller in the core city. For example, Albouy and Lue (2015) show that, in US metropolitan areas, rent differences due to housing quality are considerable but smaller than differences due to location. All of this implies that *housing rents*, unlike the land rent, *do not necessarily decrease with the distance to the CBD.*

The monocentric city model also explains how the development of modern transport methods (cars and mass transport) has generated both suburbanization and a flattening of the urban population density, an evolution known as urban sprawl. The monocentric city model has thus produced results that are consistent with some of the main features of cities. However, it remains silent on why there is a district where all jobs are concentrated. So we are left with the following question: *Do cities emerge as the outcome of a trade-off between agglomeration economies and commuting/housing costs?*

9.3.2   Why Do Employment Centres Emerge?

The first answer to this question was provided by Ogawa and Fujita (1980) in a fundamental paper that went unnoticed for a long period of time.[4] They combine consumers and firms in a full-fledged general equilibrium model in which goods, labour, and land markets are perfectly competitive. Informational spillovers act as an agglomeration force. Indeed, the value of a firm's location depends on its proximity to other firms because informational spillovers are subject to distance-decay effects. As before, workers are keen to minimize commuting costs. The clustering of firms increases the average commuting distance for workers, which in turn leads workers to pay a higher land rent. Therefore, firms must pay workers a higher wage as compensation for their longer commutes to work. In other words, the dispersion force stems from the interaction between the land and labour markets in firms' optimization programme. The equilibrium distribution of firms and workers is the balance between those opposing forces. Note the difference with the monocentric model in which the CBD is given: interactions among agents make the relative advantage of a given location for an agent dependent on the locations chosen by other agents.

Ogawa and Fujita show that, in equilibrium, *the city may display different configurations*, implying that the city may be polycentric. First, when commuting costs are high in relation to the distance-decay effect, the equilibrium involves a full integration of business and residential activities. To put it differently, land use is unspecialized. As commuting costs fall, two employment centres, themselves flanked by a residential area, are formed around an integrated section. Eventually, when commuting costs are low enough, the city becomes monocentric. In this configuration, land use is fully specialized. This seems to concur with the evolution in the spatial organization of cities that has been observed since the beginning of the revolution in transport. Activities were dispersed in pre-industrial cities when people moved on foot, whereas cities of the industrial era were often characterized by a large CBD. Modern cities retain a large CBD, but city centres now accommodate land-intensive activities performed in offices rather than factories that are big consumers of space. Other forces, such as traffic congestion and the development of new information and communication technologies, foster the emergence of secondary employment centres.

Although the process of nonmarket interaction between firms (or workers) is typically bilateral, firms care only about their role as 'receivers' and neglect their role as 'transmitters'. A comparison of the equilibrium and optimum densities shows that the former is less concentrated than the latter. This suggests that, from the social standpoint, the need to interact results in an insufficient concentration of activities around the city centre. Therefore, contrary to general belief, firms and consumers would not be too densely packed.

In the next two subsections, we briefly discuss housing and residential segregation. Both are fundamental issues that would require longer developments.

9.3.3   Land Capitalization and Housing

The choice of a residence implies differential access to the various places visited by consumers. Therefore, it should be clear that the same principle applies when consumers are sited close to locations endowed with amenities and/or providing public services such as schools and recreational facilities. As a consequence, if the general trend is a land rent that decreases as the distance from the CBD increases, the availability of amenities and public services at particular urban locations within the city affects this trend by generating rebounds in the land rent profile (Fujita, 1989). For example, everything else being equal, if the quality of schools is uneven, the price of land is higher in the neighbourhood of the higher-quality schools. Likewise, dwellings situated close to metro stations are more expensive than those farther away. All of this has a major implication: *in a city, the land rent value at any specific location capitalizes* (at least to a certain extent) *the benefits* (and sometimes the costs) *associated with the distance to the workplaces, as well as the accessibility of various types of facilities and amenities.* This value is created by community growth through actions taken by firms, households, and local governments, but not much value (if any) is created by landlords.

As a first approximation, the value of a residential property may be viewed as the sum of two components: the value of the land on which the structure sits, plus the value of the structure. The value of the residential structure has to belong to the agent responsible for its construction. In contrast, the land rent value depends on the proximity to jobs and on public service providers financed by local or federal governments. Therefore, a laissez-faire policy allowing the landlord to capture the land rent is like an implicit transfer from the collectivity to the landlord. Evidently, for the land capitalization process to unfold, land prices must be free to react to consumers' residential choices.

Stiglitz (1977) has shown that the land capitalization process is a very powerful instrument with which to finance the provision of public goods: the aggregate land rent equals the level of public expenditure if, and only if, the population size maximizes the utility level of the city's residents. Under these circumstances, public services can be financed by taxing the land rent. When there are too many consumers, this leads to higher land rents, generating a total land rent that exceeds public expenditure. In contrast, when public expenditure exceeds the aggregate land rent, the population is below the optimal size. On this occasion, it is worth recalling that the gigantic transformation of Paris under the direction of Georges-Eugéne Haussmann in the second half of the nineteenth century was financed by 'the money ... borrowed against future revenues that would result from the increased property values created by the planned improvements' (Barnett, 1986). What was possible then should be possible today, allowing our cities to finance – at least up to a certain threshold – the investments made to improve urban life.

Equally important, a better understanding of the land market allows shedding light on an ongoing heated debate in many European countries, namely rent control and land-use planning. Contrary to a belief shared by the media and the public, past and current rise in housing costs in many European cities is driven mainly by excessive, rather than insufficient, regulation of the housing and land markets. Public policies typically place a strong constraint on the land available for housing. By instituting artificial land rationing, these policies reduce the price elasticity of housing supply; they also increase the land rent and inequality that go hand in hand with the growth of population and employment. For example, the evidence collected by Glaeser and Gyourko (2003) in the US suggests that 'measures of zoning strictness are highly correlated with high prices', while Brueckner and Sridhar (2012) find large welfare losses for the building height restrictions in Indian cities. The beneficiaries of these restrictions are owners of existing plots and buildings. Young people and new inhabitants, particularly the poorest, are the victims of these price increases and crowding-out effects, which often make their living conditions difficult. In a detailed study of the causal effect of land use regulation in the US, Turner et al. (2014) find that the implications of regulatory constraints for land prices and welfare can be decomposed in three parts: (i) how land in specific plots is used, (ii) how land nearby is used, and (iii) the overall supply of developable land. Due to lost residential land, the first effect has a negative and substantial impact on welfare, while the third one induces losses for residents that are almost offset by land owners' gains. The estimates are not precise enough to determine the sign of the second effect.

By restricting population size, the implementation of urban containment hurts new residents by reducing their welfare level or motivates a fraction of the city population to migrate away. In addition, such policies prevent the most productive cities from fully exploiting their potential agglomeration effects. Admittedly, environmental and esthetic considerations require green space. However, the benefits associated with providing such spaces must be measured against the costs they impose on the population. For example, housing land in southeast England was worth 430 times its value as farmland (Cheshire et al., 2014). Under such circumstances, the land rent level also reflects the 'artificial scarcity' of land stemming from restrictive land use regulation. It is worth stressing here that, in many EU countries, land made available for housing depends on municipal governments. Therefore, it is hardly surprising that decisions regarding land use vary with political parties (Solé-Ollé and Viladecans-Marsal, 2012).

High housing prices make the city less attractive. This may deter young entrepreneurs and skilled workers from settling there, which weakens the city's economic engine. Freezing rents – one of the most popular instruments used by political decision-makers in Europe – renders the housing supply function more inelastic. Subsidizing tenants does not work either because the money transferred to the tenants tends to end up in landlords' pockets when the elasticity of the housing supply is weak. *Providing affordable housing through the adoption of market-savvy land and construction policies is one of the keys to the future economic success of cities.*

Housing markets play a critical role in the workings of a city with an important impact on the global economy. Hsieh and Moretti (2015) show that lowering regulatory constraints in highly productive cities like New York, San Francisco, and San Jose to the level of the median city would expand those cities' workforce and increase GDP in the US by 7.5 per cent. Various housing supply constraints act as impediments to a more efficient spatial allocation of labour, which lowers the income and welfare of all US workers. Even though European workers are less mobile than Americans, these effects could very well be important within European countries too. *Smart land and housing policies are a key instrument for regional and urban development.* How to design such policies is an issue that cannot be underestimated, but going into further discussions would take us beyond the scope of this chapter. Note, however, that the literature on housing and cities is blossoming in the US but is still in its infancy in Europe.

9.3.4   Residential Segregation

The allocation of land across consumers may be viewed as the outcome of a competitive process in which consumers bid against others to occupy a specific plot. In other words, everything works *as if* consumers had a *bid rent function* that specifies their willingness to pay for one unit of land at different locations. The market then selects consumers who offer the highest bid. The bid rent function reflects the trade-off between commuting and housing costs at the individual level, while the land rent is the maximum of the individual bid rent functions (Fujita, 1989). This simple mechanism shows that residential segregation leads to the sorting of individuals within cities through the respective values of their bid rents. For example, when consumers share the same preferences but have different incomes, the same income group will occupy the city neighbourhood where it outbids other groups. This has a far-reaching consequence: consumers' income differences translate into spatial segregation. To put it differently, *consumers are sorted within the city through the working of the housing/land market*. As a consequence, the city is segmented into neighbourhoods in which consumers have similar characteristics.

Although some American core cities have rich enclaves, high-income residents in US urban areas tend to live in the suburbs. This pattern is often reversed in the EU. Brueckner et al. (1999) have proposed an amenity-based theory that predicts a multiplicity of location patterns across cities. Europe's longer history provides an obvious reason why its core cities offer more amenities, such as buildings and monuments of historical significance, than do their US counterparts. When the centre has a strong amenity advantage over the suburbs, the bid rent function can be used to show that the rich are likely to live in central locations. When the centre amenity advantage is weak or negative, the rich are likely to live in suburbs. In other words, superior amenities make the core city rich, while weak amenities make it poor.

In the same vein, when the urban space is not featureless, the rich can afford to set up in locations with better amenities, which may be exogenous or endogenous, and with more transport options than the poor. In particular, decentralizing the supply of schooling may exacerbate initial differences between people by allowing the rich to afford better education for their children. This in turn tends to increase differences in human capital among young people and worsen income inequality between individuals and neighbourhoods within the same city. Besides income and preferences, spatial segregation as an equilibrium outcome can also be based on culture, race, and language. However, it is worth stressing that, *regardless of the attributes that determine the bid rent that consumers are willing to pay for particular locations, the above sorting mechanism keeps its relevance.* Furthermore, through nonmarket interactions, the gathering of people sharing the same characteristics may generate different types of externalities. As in the foregoing, we end up with more homogeneous districts, but more heterogeneity between districts (Bénabou, 1993).

What makes spatial segregation a robust outcome is that, even in the absence of externalities, similar people competing on the land market will choose independently to be close to each other. This segmentation is the unintentional consequence of decisions made by a great number of consumers acting in a decentralized environment. The bid rent mechanism suggests that 'causation runs from personal characteristics to income to the characteristics of the neighbourhood in which people live' (Cheshire et al., 2014). This probably explains why many public policies that promote social mixing within cities fail to reach their objective.

Whether and how neighbourhood effects have an impact on individual characteristics is an important topic, as European cities tend to become more polarized and segregated. Topa and Zenou (2015) stress the importance of understanding the causality links and of distinguishing between neighbourhood effects and network effects. Neighbourhood effects mean that better access to jobs increases the employment prospects of the poor. This can be addressed by housing, transport, or neighbourhood regeneration policies. For example, distressed urban areas can be more or less isolated. This helps to explain why place-based policies, like the French enterprise zone programmes, may increase the employment rate of the poor in well-connected areas, but not in rather isolated areas (Briant et al., 2015). Network effects have to do with the poor quality of the socio-economic group to which they belong. In this case, transport policy is useless and specific social integration and human capital policies are needed. Topa and Zenou (2015) point to empirical evidence for Sweden and Denmark that suggests ethnic enclaves can have positive effects on labour market outcomes and the education level of immigrants, especially for the unskilled. The dark side is that such enclaves seem to have a positive impact on crime, as growing up in a neighbourhood with many criminals around has a long-term effect on the local crime rate.

To sum up, even though urban land use patterns reflect a wide range of possibilities, the way the bid rent functions vary with places' and residents' characteristics allows us to understand what kind of residential pattern emerges. The bid rent function, because it relies on a fundamental principle that guides consumers' spatial behaviour, is likely to be useful in designing market-savvy policies fostering less segregation.

9.4   More Cities or Bigger Cities?

Agglomeration economies explain why human activities are concentrated in cities. However, because commuting and housing costs rise along with the population size, they – along with negative externalities generated by the concentration of people in small areas – act as a strong force to put a brake on city growth. In accordance with the fundamental trade-off of spatial economics, *the size of cities may then be viewed as the balance between these systems of opposite forces.* Finding the right balance between agglomeration economies and diseconomies is at the heart of the urban problem.

Not all cities are alike. The existence of very large cities in different parts of the world at different time periods is well documented (Bairoch, 1985). Cities have very different sizes and form an urban system that is hierarchical in nature: *there are few large cities and many small cities*, together with an intermediate number of medium-sized cities. The stability of the urban hierarchy over decades or even centuries is remarkable (Eaton and Eckstein, 1997, Davis and Weinstein, 2002). All cities provide private goods that are nontradable (e.g., shops) and a variable range of public services (e.g., schools, day care centres). To a certain extent, the urban system reflects the administrative hierarchy of territorial entities. Because public services are subject to different degrees of increasing returns, cities accommodate a variable number of governmental departments and agencies, hospitals, universities, museums, and the like. More importantly, cities have a different industrial composition. In the past, cities produced a wide range of goods that were not traded because shipping them was expensive. Once transport costs decreased sufficiently, medium-sized and small cities became specialized in the production of one tradable good. This increased specialization often leads to significant labour productivity gains but makes cities vulnerable to asymmetric shocks. Today, only a few urban giants accommodate several, but not all, sectors.

Unlike specialized cities, *diversified* cities are better equipped when confronted with asymmetric shocks. Besides spillover effects between sectors, the coexistence of different sectors may also reduce the uncertainty associated with the initial phases of the product cycle (Duranton and Puga, 2001). For example, the preliminary stages in the development of a new technology or product require repeated contacts among those involved, which are much easier when these people are in close proximity. Information becomes a spatial externality because, as it circulates within the local cluster of firms and workers, it inadvertently contributes to aggregate productivity. However, as shown by Helsley and Strange (2014), potentially beneficial clusters do not necessarily emerge, while the co-agglomeration that does occur in diversified cities may not be that which creates the greatest productive benefits.

Henderson (1974, 1988) has developed a compelling and original approach that allows us to describe an urban system that involves an endogenous number of specialized cities trading goods. The second-generation models explore both the sorting of workers and the composition of population across cities, which are consistent with recent empirical evidence (Behrens et al., 2014, Eeckhout et al., 2014). Davis and Dingel (2015) observe that in the US the hierarchy of skills is highly correlated to the urban hierarchy. Specifically, these authors have proposed a new modelling strategy that suggests that 'the most skilled individuals in the population live only in the largest city and more skilled individuals are more prevalent in larger cities'. What makes these new models especially appealing is their ability to capture what we know from urban economics about the role of human capital externalities in the formation of cities.

However, in this strand of literature, cities produce the same good or, equivalently, different goods traded at zero cost. These models do not recognize that cities are anchored in specific locations and embedded in intricate networks of trade relations that partially explain the cities' size and industrial mix. In sum, they put aside the fact that *location matters because trade is costly* (see Chapter 8). Allowing for a large number of potentially asymmetric locations while trade between any two locations is subject to bilateral costs, Allen and Arkolakis (2014) and Redding (2015) explore a new line of research whose aim is to assess the role of locations in the geographical distribution of activities. This approach relies on the calibration of Ricardian spatial models that permit the study of counterfactuals. For example, the analysis undertaken by Allen and Arkolakis (2014) suggests that about 20 per cent of the spatial variation in income across the US can be explained by pure locational effects. These new models bring together ideas borrowed from trade and urban economics, but they use particular functional forms whose effects remain unexplored. Therefore, it seems fair to say that the dust has not yet settled.

It is also worth noting the work of Desmet and Rossi-Hansberg (2013), who decompose the determinants of the city size distribution into the following three components: efficiency, amenities and frictions. Higher efficiency and more amenities lead to larger cities but generate greater frictions (congestion). This model may be used to simulate the effects of reducing variations in efficiency and amenities, which makes it a relevant tool for designing regional and urban policies. Averaging the level of the above three components across cities and allowing the population to relocate leads to large population relocations but generates low welfare gains in the US. Using the same model for China, the authors find much bigger welfare gains.

The number of large metropolitan areas in the US is proportionally much higher than in the EU. Therefore, it is tempting to follow *The Economist* (13 October 2012), which argues that European cities are too small and/or too few for the European economy to benefit fully from the informational spillovers lying at the heart of the knowledge-based economy. A more rigorous analysis has been developed by Schmidheiny and Südekum (2015). Using the new EC–OECD functional urban areas dataset, they show that, unlike the US urban system, the EU city distribution does not obey the Zipf Law. The reason for this discrepancy is that the largest European cities are 'too small'. Undoubtedly, many European governments were not – and several of them are still not – aware of the potential offered by their large metropolitan areas to boost economic growth. Both in Europe and the US, '*urbaphobia*' has led governments to design policies deliberately detrimental to their large metropolises. In this respect, France is a good (or bad) case in point. For a few decades, Paris was considered 'too big' and public policies were designed to move activities toward other French regions. By French standards, Paris is big. Yet, on the international marketplace, Paris competes with a great many comparable or larger cities. However, in view of the productivity shown by the dense network of large/medium and well-connected German cities, it is not clear whether new and large metropolitan areas (10+ million people) are necessary to enhance European competitiveness.

9.5   The Organization of Metropolitan Areas

As the spread of new cities in Europe came to an end long ago, for a long time the European landscape has been dominated by a wide array of monocentric cities. European cities, probably because they were smaller than their American counterparts, undertook a structural transformation illustrated by the emergence of polycentric metropolitan areas. Indeed, the burden of high housing and commuting costs may be alleviated when secondary employment centres are created. Such a morphological change in the urban structure puts a brake on the re-dispersion process and allows big cities to maintain, to a large extent, their supremacy (Glaeser and Kahn, 2004). Among other things, this points to the existence of a trade-off between within-city *commuting costs* and between-cities *transport costs*, which calls for a better coordination of transport policies at the urban and interregional levels.

Urban sprawl and the decentralization of jobs have given rise to metropolitan areas that include a large number of independent political jurisdictions providing local public goods to their residents and competing in tax levels to attract jobs and residents. A few facts documented by Brülhart et al. (2015) suggest the magnitude of this evolution. Metropolitan areas with more than $500,000$ inhabitants are divided, on average, into 74 local jurisdictions, while local governments in the OECD raise about 13 per cent of total tax revenue. Therefore, a cost-benefit analysis of an urban agglomeration cannot focus only on the core city. Indeed, the metropolitan area is replete with different types of externalities arising from its political fragmentation. As a consequence, what matters is what is going on in the metropolitan area as a whole.

The efficient development of a metropolitan area requires a good spatial match between those who benefit from the public goods supplied by the various jurisdictions and the taxpayers (Hochman et al., 1995). This is not often the case because a large fraction of commuters no longer live in the historical centre. In other words, the administrative and economic boundaries of jurisdictions usually differ within metropolitan areas. Since constituencies are located inside the jurisdictions, local governments tend to disregard effects of economic policies that are felt beyond the political border, an issue that also arises at the international level. In addition to spillovers in the consumption of public goods, this discrepancy is at the origin of business-stealing effects generated by tax competition, which are studied in local public finance. However, this literature has put aside the spatial aspects that play a central role in the working of metropolitan areas. For example, the huge Tiebout-based literature leaves little space for urban considerations.

To the best of our knowledge, urban economics is not used as a building block in models studying the workings of a metropolitan area. Thus, research needs to be developed that recognizes the importance of the following aspects of the problem. First, agglomeration economies within core cities represent a large share of metro-wide agglomeration economies. This in turn implies that the CBD still dominates the metropolitan area's secondary business centres and attracts cross-commuters from the suburbs. As a consequence, agglomeration economies being internalized (even if partly) in wages, the economy of the CBD generates some wealth effects that go beyond the core city to positively impact suburban jurisdictions. Moreover, owing to the attractiveness of the CBD, the core city's government is incentivized to practise tax exporting through the taxation of nonresident workers. As a consequence, the structure of the metropolitan area is inefficient as firms and jobs are too dispersed for agglomeration economies to deliver their full potential (Gaigné et al., 2016).

Second, suburbanites who work in the CBD benefit from public services provided in the core city but do not pay for them. This is a hot issue in cities like Berlin, Brussels or Hamburg, which are also legal regional entities. Third, the metropolitan area is formed of local labour markets that are poorly integrated and coexist with pockets showing high and lasting unemployment rates. Fourth, and last, as cities grow, spatial segregation and income polarization tend to get worse. While the social stratification of cities seems to be less of a political issue in the US, it ranks high on the agenda of many EU politicians and is a major concern for large segments of the European population.

The political fragmentation of metropolitan areas has other unsuspected consequences. For example, establishing new malls on the city outskirts benefits suburbia but diverts consumers from visiting downtown retailers. This in turn leads to a contraction of the central commercial district through the exit of retailers, which makes this shopping area even less attractive. The overall effect is to further reduce the number of customers, which cuts down the number of retailers once more. By making the core city less attractive, this amenity-destructive process is likely to be damaging the productivity of the metropolitan area (Ushchev et al., 2015).

9.6   Managing Traffic and Congestion

People travel within metropolitan areas for a wide array of reasons, such as commuting to work, dropping children off at schools, shopping in the CBD or suburban malls, and attending various family and social events. Even trade is much localized, thus implying a large flow of local shipments.

The origin and destination of a trip, as well as the choice of a transport mode, are decisions users make. Economists study these decisions in a supply-and-demand context. The supply side is given by the transport infrastructure (roads, rail, airports), the transport service (bus, metro, taxi), and a price charged to the users (road user charge, parking fees, public transport prices). Users also supply personal inputs to their trips: cars, fuel, bicycles, insurance, and most importantly, their own time. On the demand side, for every origin-destination pair, people travel for different reasons and have different opportunity costs of time. Since the supply of infrastructure is limited, the precise timing of trips also matters. It is, therefore, the total user cost of a trip (including money, time and discomfort) that ultimately determines an individual's demand for trips by time of day, by mode of travel, and by route.

Most American cities (exceptions include New York, Washington D.C. and San Francisco) rely on car transport, whereas public transport accounts for a significant fraction of trips in most European cities. This duality is reflected in the topics studied in the academic literature. In the US, where road pricing seems to be banned from public debate, there is more focus on the pricing of parking and optional varieties of road pricing like pay lanes. In the EU, even though some European cities have pioneered new congestion pricing schemes, national and local governments alike favour other policies such as high gasoline and diesel prices, as well as investments and subsidies in public transport.

Urban transport issues can be studied from a short-run or a long-run perspective. In the short run, the origins and destinations (residences, workplace and shops) as well as the transport infrastructures (roads, rail and subway) are exogenous, and thus policy options are restricted to pricing (road pricing, parking and rail tickets) and regulation (speed limits, pedestrian zones). Passengers can react via the number and timing of trips, as well as the type of transport mode. In the long run, locations are endogenous, as is the city size. By implication, users of the transport system have more options because they may change destinations (workplace, school, shopping) and origins (residence). The set of policy options is also much wider in the long run: one can add transport infrastructure and regulate the use of land (housing permits, type of activities). Most of transport economics focuses on the case where locations are given: how the current infrastructure is used (choice of mode, network equilibrium) and how the policy-maker can improve the use of existing infrastructures. Several types of externalities exist, thus there is no satisfactory market mechanism to guarantee the best use of existing capacity. In addition, most road infrastructure can be accessed freely.

In what follows, we first consider the case in which locations and infrastructure are exogenous and focus mainly on passenger transport. To be precise, we first define and discuss the estimation of external costs associated with transport trips for given origins and destinations. We then look at public policies that can be used to address the various market failures associated with the supply and demand for trips. In the next section, we discuss the policy issues when locations and transport infrastructure are endogenous. This will bring us back to the core question in urban economics of how to understand the organization of cities and the location of different activities.

Table 9.1 *External costs by order of magnitude*

	Costs in euro cents	
External costs	Cars[a]	Public transport[b]
Climate costs	0.8	2.1 (bus)
Environmental costs	4.3	21.4 (bus)
Accident costs	0.3	
Congestion costs	0.6 to 242.6	0 to 576.3 (bus)
Wear-and-tear infrastructure costs	0.8	2.7 (bus)

[a] By passenger-kilometre.
[b] By vehicle-kilometre.

9.6.1   External Costs of Urban Transport

Urban transport accounts for some 20 per cent of total passenger-kilometres, where a passenger-kilometre is defined as one passenger who is carried one kilometre. In European cities, cars are the dominant transport mode (70 per cent), while public transport (rail, metro and bus) accounts for the remaining share. External costs of urban transport are difficult to measure because they result from decisions made by a myriad of individuals who do not pay the full cost that their decisions impose on other users. One therefore has to rely on indirect measurements using connected markets (e.g., the variation of housing values as a function of traffic nuisances) or constructed markets (experiments and surveys). In the *Handbook of External Costs* published by the European Commission (2014), five types of external costs are considered: climate costs, environment costs, accident costs, congestion costs, and wear and tear on infrastructure. In Table 9.1, we document the relative importance of these costs for cars and public transport (PT) in the EU. Although the emission of greenhouse gases is proportional to the type and quantity of fossil fuels used, an open question remains about how to evaluate the damage generated by one ton of greenhouse gases, which is the same across industries, power generation, and the residential sector. In Table 9.1, the climate damage generated by one vehicle-kilometre is evaluated at €25/ton of CO_2. In industry, the cap on greenhouse emissions has resulted in prices for tradable pollution permits varying between 5 and €30/ton of CO_2. As the place and sector of climate emissions does not matter, efficient pollution policies call for reducing greenhouse gases where it is cheapest. Above all, Table 9.1 confirms *the sizable impact and variability of congestion costs compared with other external costs.*

Road congestion costs are the most important external costs generated in urban areas, but they also vary substantially across space and time. The marginal external cost generated by traffic congestion is the additional time, schedule delay, and resource costs borne by other road users when one additional user decides to travel by car. This type of external cost is poorly understood by the general public, probably because car drivers experience their own time loss. Drivers internalize this time loss, but they do not take into account the additional time loss that others incur. In the simplest formulation, the average time cost of a road trip is given by $AC(X) = a + bX$, where X is the volume of traffic on a given road. If the total time cost is given by $TC(X) = aX + bX^2$, the marginal social cost (MSC) is given by $MSC(X) = a + 2bX$. The marginal external cost is then equal to $MSC(X) - AC(X) = bX$. Since the road capacity is constant over the day, the marginal external cost is expected to vary greatly with the intensity of the traffic flow.

For PT, positive density economies arise when the frequency of service increases with demand. Higher frequency decreases the expected waiting time for passengers who arrive at the bus stop randomly and decreases the schedule delay time for nonrandomly arriving passengers. PT by bus also contributes to congestion on the road. Because an additional passenger has to fit into the fixed capacity of the PT vehicles, there is also a negative discomfort external cost.

9.6.2   The Difficult Road to First-Best Pricing of Congestion

First-best pricing means that all transport activities are priced (or subsidized) so that the marginal user cost equals the marginal resource cost plus the marginal external costs. As there are different types of external costs, this requires different types of instruments. The easiest external cost to internalize is damage to the climate because this cost is proportional to the consumption of fossil fuel. A fuel excise tax on gasoline and diesel is sufficient to provide the right incentive to save fuel and, therefore, to reduce carbon emissions. That said, the most important marginal external cost of car use is congestion.

Congestion

Ever since the pioneering works of Vickrey (1969), economists have agreed that *the ideal instrument to tackle urban road congestion is congestion pricing*. The idea is easy to grasp. Many road transport externalities are strongly place- and time-dependent and, therefore, can hardly be tackled by using instruments such as fuel taxes or vehicle ownership or purchase taxes, whereas congestion pricing is based on the ongoing traffic. The first successful implementation of a congestion charge was in Singapore (1976). European cities that have introduced similar pricing instruments include London (2003), Stockholm (2007), Milan (2012) and Göteborg (2014).

There have been heated debates in a large number of cities about adopting congestion pricing. The application of road pricing is currently limited to only a few cities. Thus, the question to why implementing such a welfare-enhancing instrument fails is challenging. Of course, implementation of the pricing system and the transaction costs can eat away 10 to 20 per cent of toll revenues but technology is making big progress on this front. De Borger and Proost (2012) analyse the political economy of road pricing by means of a model of policy reform. They show that the majority of population may vote against road pricing ex ante because the expected gain of almost all drivers is negative, whereas some of the drivers may support this policy after implementation.

Congestion pricing has been studied intensively in transport economics. Two lessons can be drawn. First, the design of the road pricing system is very important for the magnitude of the net welfare effect. For example, Stockholm was more efficient than London because the Stockholm system had lower transaction costs and more finely differentiated charges for different times of the day. Indeed, time differentiation is crucial for capturing the full gains of congestion pricing. In the more detailed bottleneck model where homogeneous drivers trade off queuing costs and schedule delay costs by selecting a departure time, an appropriate toll scheme with strong time differentiation can transform all queuing costs into revenue. The result would be an unchanged user cost for the total trip and an unchanged total number of car trips, but departure times would be better distributed, and the local government would end up with extra tax revenues (Arnott et al., 1993). A simple differentiation of peak/off-peak times, as in London, foregoes a large part of these gains and has to rely mainly on reducing the total number of peak trips to alleviate congestion. A more finely tuned pricing scheme narrows the gap between social benefits and toll revenues. This is important for the political acceptability of peak pricing. For example, in London, toll revenues may be a factor five higher than the net benefits, which generate strong lobbying against peak pricing or on the way of sharing the collected toll revenues. More generally, *smart pricing of a bottleneck can transform queuing into toll revenue, bring about important time and productivity gains, and be a sensible alternative to building new and expensive transport infrastructures.*

A second striking feature is that only a small proportion (35 per cent or less) of the suppressed car trips were replaced by PT; the rest of the trips disappeared due to more car sharing, combining trips, or simply foregoing the trip (Eliasson et al., 2009). Having only one or more of the lanes as toll lanes can be effective only if there is a sufficient difference in time values among users, and it does require a careful design of the tolls (Small and Verhoef, 2007).

First-best pricing of public transport is comparatively easy to implement because every passenger has to enter a bus or metro and can be asked to pay. The resource costs and external costs of PT are complex but are known and vary strongly as a function of the density of demand and occupancy of the vehicle. For an almost empty bus, the cost of an additional passenger is limited to the additional time cost for the driver, plus the delay for the existing passengers and the other road users. There is also a positive externality when additional passengers increase the frequency of the bus service and decrease the expected waiting time at the bus stop. In most urban areas, the largest external cost of public transport is probably the discomfort imposed by additional passengers in the peak period when the PT-system is close to capacity. First-best pricing would then require higher prices in the peak than in the off-peak time.

Finally, it is worth stressing the importance of a major trade-off between boosting the productivity of the Metropolitan Area (MA) through a stronger concentration of jobs in the CBD and reducing congestion and the emission of greenhouse gases in the central city. Indeed, whereas subsidizing commuters may boost the productivity of the MA by fostering a better exploitation of agglomeration economies, road pricing policies, which aim to reduce the discrepancy between the social and the private costs of commuters' trips, have the nature of a tax. Arnott (2007) shows that, in the presence of agglomeration economies, the optimal congestion toll should be lower than the marginal external congestion cost, unless other instruments (e.g., subsidies to firms) are used to correct the agglomeration externalities. Moreover, if fine-tuned road pricing implies only small shifts in working hours, then agglomeration externalities are not very much affected. Note also that the recommendation of a bigger CBD need not necessarily conflict with the objective of lower emissions within the MA. Indeed, when the central city provides a denser and a more energy-efficient public transport system than the suburban jurisdictions, increasing the attractiveness of the CBD may be justified both for economic and environmental reasons, as car use typically increases at the expense of public transport when secondary business centres grow. Clearly, more work is called for to understand how to design better policies under the above trade-off.

Parking

Besides traffic, parking is another major source of urban congestion. Parking space in a city takes up a lot of valuable urban land that could be used for housing and economic activities. A car is parked 95 per cent of the time and often requires a parking spot at both the origin and the destination. Parking supply is divided into parking available for everybody and long-term contracted parking.

One of the main changes over the last 20 years has been the privatization of enforcement of on-street parking. Enforcement has become much more effective and the net revenues have increased. New technologies allow the regular update of prices for on-street parking. For example, in San Francisco, sensors keep track of the occupancy rate per block, which allows for the regular adjustment of parking fees. On-street parking is often provided for free, which worsens the unpriced congestion externalities. There have been many proposals to abolish these fringe benefits. A well-known example is the cash-out parking proposal where employers are forced to offer the option of receiving the cash equivalent of free parking instead of free parking itself. As parking largely determines the role of cars in urban transport (compare Los Angeles and New York), more research is needed on the effect of parking pricing and regulation in EU cities.

Most economic research has focused on pricing, while most policy interventions focus on regulations and allocation of space. Optimizing transport flows requires the right combination of rules (for example, speed limits), prices, and the allocation of space (for example, bus lanes, and on-street parking).

9.6.3   The Patchwork of Policy Instruments

In practice, we are far from first-best pricing schemes in urban transport. When it comes to transport policies, the division of responsibilities among member countries and among regional and city authorities leads to a complex and knotty patchwork. The EU uses mainly regulation (car emissions, safety standards and the like), while taxation power belongs to the member states. Cities have limited authority: parking fees, local traffic regulations and subsidies for PT.

The main tax instrument used to tax externalities of road use is the *fuel tax*. Even though this tax was probably established to raise public income (the average total revenue is 1.4 per cent of the EU GDP), it is de facto the main tax instrument affecting the use of cars. If one considers the fuel tax on cars as the main instrument for correcting externalities, the tax should have the following second-best structure where the tax is equal to all external costs associated with the consumption of a litre of fuel (Parry and Small, 2005):

Fuel tax/litre $=$ carbon damage/litre
$$+\gamma \cdot (\text{kilometre/litre}) \cdot (\text{other external costs/kilometre}).$$

The first term of this expression is the carbon damage that is proportional to the combustion of fossil fuel. When climate damage is assessed at €25/ton of CO_2, a low excise tax per litre (10 cents/litre) is sufficient. When there is no specific instrument used to price congestion, and other externalities are related to distance driven rather than to fuel consumed, the only way to 'price' these externalities is by adding an extra excise tax to the carbon tax for road use. This tax should equal the average other (nonclimate) externalities related to road use, which explains the term (kilometre/litre) (other external costs/kilometre) in the above expression. To compute the tax per litre, one needs information on the other external costs per car-kilometre and the number of kilometres per litre. Finally, one needs a correction factor (γ) that takes into account the share of fuel reduction accounted for by reduced road traffic, not by more fuel-efficient cars. Indeed, because congestion and accident externalities are related to distance rather than fuel use, it is the amount of driving that the second component of the fuel tax aims to reduce, not the use of fuel itself.

To fix ideas, assume that a 20 per cent increase in fuel tax leads to a reduction in fuel consumption of 10 per cent, of which 5 per cent comes from a more fuel-efficient car and 5 per cent from less driving. Then, the factor (γ) equals 0.5. Assume, furthermore, that the other external costs per kilometre are on average €0.10 and that the car consumes 5 litres per 100 km (see Table 9.1 for other orders of magnitude). Under these circumstances, we obtain a second-best fuel tax equal to €0.10 per litre + 0.5 · (20 kilometre per litre) · (€10 per litre) = €1.10 per litre.

It is worth stressing that *there is an inherent conflict in using the fuel tax to internalize both fuel-related externalities* (climate change) *and mileage-related externalities* (congestion, accidents). For climate-damage reasons, we want a car to be more fuel efficient (up to a marginal cost of €25/ton of CO_2). But to make car drivers take into account the other externalities, we want them to keep paying the same tax per kilometre. As the main objective of the fuel tax is probably to collect tax revenue, using this tax as an instrument to solve all problems amounts to squaring the circle.

It is not only the pricing of petrol that has gone wrong; the pricing of diesel fuel for cars is also problematic as low diesel excise taxes have led to the massive introduction of diesel cars in most of Europe. Diesel cars have a small carbon emission advantage but are more damaging to health when we rely on real world emission results rather than on the results of the test cycle (ICCT (International Council on Clean Transportation) (2014)). The US has taken another route and has almost no diesel cars.

One of the most effective additional instruments to control the environmental externalities of car use is the regulation of emissions of traditional air pollutants. The Auto-Oil programme of the EU regulated the emissions of new cars and the quality of fuel. This was efficient in tackling traditional pollutants (NOx, SO_2, particulates). By installing additional equipment (catalytic converter, lower sulfur content of fuels) at relatively low cost, emissions could be reduced by a factor of 5 to 20 (Proost and Van Dender, 2012). As for petrol, the EU could benefit from the American and Japanese experience and technologies, which was not the case for diesel.

A complement to stricter air pollution regulations is the use of low-emission zones. In a low-emission zone, only the cleanest cars are allowed to move freely, while 'dirtier' ones have to pay a charge or, if they get caught, a fine. As air pollution damage is directly proportional to population density, it makes sense to have an additional instrument for dense urban areas. The EU ambient air quality regulation sets a maximum for the concentration of air pollutants and, when this maximum is exceeded, city or national governments have to take action. More than 50 German cities have experimented with different policy measures. The overall conclusion was that improvements in public transport were not effective, but access restrictions for dirty cars were (Wolff, 2014). This type of instrument is less effective at present because, over time, all cars will comply with the latest EU emission standards. But as attention to conventional air pollution in cities is increasing and as the marginal cost of greening cars is growing, this instrument could again become more useful. It allows for the differentiation of requirements for urban road traffic and nonurban road traffic. Instead, one could think of banning diesel cars and even petrol cars in dense cities.

Using fuel-efficiency regulation for cars in order to reduce greenhouse gas emissions is costly as transport already has a high carbon tax in the form of a gasoline tax. One possible justification is the possible myopia or fuel-efficiency gap. If consumers systematically underestimate the future fuel costs, a fuel-efficiency regulation would help consumers and better signal the external costs. But the empirical evidence for consumer myopia is very weak for EU car buyers. Grigolon et al. (2014) have analysed car buyer behavior in the EU and found that consumers take 90 per cent of future fuel costs into account when they select a car. When this is combined with a fuel tax that is more related to mileage externalities than to fuel-related externalities, imposing more fuel-efficient cars is not an efficient policy measure. The EU is a world leader in terms of fuel-efficiency standards. If the aim is also to successfully transfer technology, we may need to reorient our technology standards toward less ambitious targets because other countries have less ambitious climate objectives and do not want to pay for elaborate super-efficient technologies (Eliasson and Proost, 2015). Note also that many countries have used vehicle purchase and ownership taxes as additional instruments to reduce CO_2 emissions. The Netherlands, Denmark, Sweden, and France have used vigorous policies to achieve significant carbon emission reductions but there is evidence that these policies are very costly and not effective.

9.6.4   Public Transport Pricing

In the EU, PT accounts for a significant share of commuters. In most European cities, the recovery of operational costs is low (below 50 per cent), while the peak demand is close to the rail and metro capacity. Implementing low prices for PT in cities is often presented as a good illustration of second-best pricing. But is such a recommendation well grounded? In the expression given below, the optimal PT price, $\mathbf{P}_{PT}(peak)$, is equal to the social marginal cost of PT, $\mathbf{MC}_{PT}(peak)$, corrected by the gap between the price, $\mathbf{P}_{CAR}(peak)$, and the social marginal cost of car use, $\mathbf{MC}_{CAR}(peak)$. Computing the social marginal cost of a PT trip is not simple. Indeed, it requires taking into account on-board scale economies (using available seats in the metro or bus) and negative discomfort economies when vehicles are crowded. It must also account for the following positive economies: even when buses or metros are not full, it is optimal to raise frequency as this allows one to reduce waiting time (Mohring, 1972). In the absence of congestion pricing, the price of car use in the peak period is lower than its social marginal cost, so a subsidy for PT is efficient insofar as this subsidy is able to make car users switch to PT. For this, we need the fraction φ of new PT users who would, in the absence of the subsidy, be car users:

$$\mathbf{P}_{PT}(peak) = \mathbf{MC}_{PT}(peak) + \varphi \cdot [\mathbf{P}_{CAR}(peak) - \mathbf{MC}_{CAR}(peak)].$$

Parry and Small (2009) have found that a subsidy of close to 90 per cent of the average operational costs for urban rail transport is socially desirable when $\varphi = 0.5$, which seems to ground the proposal of strongly subsidized PT. These authors find the subsidy efficient for two reasons. First, there are important scale economies, which are the most important element to justify subsidies in the off-peak period. Second, there are significant unpriced car congestion externalities, which are the main reason for justifying subsidies in the peak period.

However, some empirical studies find values for φ that are smaller than 0.2 (van Goeverden et al., 2006). In this case, the optimal subsidy for the peak falls from 90 to 10 per cent, thus casting serious doubt on the relevance of subsidizing the use of PT. In a numerical study for London as well as Santiago de Chile, Basso and Silva (2014) compare the pricing of car and bus combined with other instruments (bus subsidies, dedicated bus lanes, and congestion pricing). They find that dedicated bus lanes can be a much more efficient instrument than PT subsidies and are, in terms of efficiency, almost as efficient as road pricing for Santiago de Chile. Results tend to be city-specific as they depend on the current modal shares and the ease of substitution.

Current marginal prices for PT in the EU are often zero as most users pay a monthly subscription price, which allows them to travel when and as much as they want, giving rise to massive congestion problems in PT systems of big EU cities (London, Paris). There is a need to look for more efficient pricing systems that account for the differences in cost between peak and off-peak trips and in function of area and distance travelled, and for the congestion levels of car transport. As long as attention is paid to who pays for the PT subsidies, there is not necessarily a conflict between more appropriate PT fares and redistribution policies (Mayeres and Proost, 2001).

In the last 20 years, the United Kingdom has experimented with privatized PT services. In London, bus services were tendered to private companies but one central bus authority remained as the decision-maker for schedules and prices. The end result was a significant reduction in costs. Outside of London, bus services were fully privatized with the private companies deciding on the number of companies offering services, scheduling and prices. There are only limited and targeted subsidies. As each bus company offers services at different times of the day, there is a clear tendency to offer higher service frequencies. By offering a time schedule that closely matches the timetable of a competitor, a company could steal passengers from other companies, but this did not turn out to be in the interest of passengers. The end result was lower costs, higher prices, higher frequencies, and less competition (Gwilliam et al., 1985). Contracting out the operation is more common for buses than for rail and has led to important efficiency gains when the contracts are well designed (Gagnepain et al., 2013).

Opponents of congestion pricing put forward the argument that labour (therefore commuters) is already heavily taxed in the EU. Parry and Bento (2001) find that charging the full external congestion cost to commuters remains the best policy as long as additional tax revenues are used to reduce the existing labour tax. Moreover, in many EU countries, employers offer a company car as an untaxed fringe benefit, which amounts to subsidizing high-income commuters and leads to excessive car use, while some employers also pay for all public transport expenses of their employees (Harding, 2014). All of this shows *the need for a global assessment of commuting expenses in relation to income taxes.*

9.7   The Benefits of New Transport Infrastructure

9.7.1   *Does New Infrastructure Reduce Congestion?*

To the public and to many decision-makers, the answer seems obvious and positive. However, things are not that simple. First, when origins and destinations are given, more capacity leads to more car users. Hence, the time benefit of road extensions in the presence of unpriced congestion is reduced by this induced demand (Cervero, 2003). This already suggests that the standard approach to controlling congestion – forecast traffic growth and build enough roads to accommodate it – is likely to be ineffective. Second, Arnott (1979) shows that improving transport in a congested monocentric city leads to a new residential equilibrium in which congestion increases everywhere compared with the initial equilibrium. In other words, once it is recognized that consumers respond to changes in commuting costs, building new transport links loses a great deal of its appeal.

Duranton and Turner (2011) observe that those who argue in favour of a new transport infrastructure forget the simultaneity problem that we encountered when studying agglomeration economies: the supply of roads and the density of traffic are interdependent phenomena. When the number of vehicles on the road is given, additional capacity decreases the density of traffic and makes trips faster. However, a higher capacity attracts more traffic, and thus density increases. All this implies that it is a priori unclear how the causality runs. This has led Duranton and Turner to study the congestion problem in American cities for the years 1983, 1993, and 2003, using modern econometric techniques. Their conclusions cast serious doubt on the merits of infrastructure-based congestion policies. First, Duranton and Turner confirm that new roads and public transport generate more traffic. What is less expected, but more important, is that in the absence of road pricing and for some types of roads, 'new road capacity is met with a proportional increase in driving'. But where do the additional travellers come from? Again, the answer is not the one that comes immediately to mind: 'the law of traffic congestion reflects traffic creation rather than traffic diversion'. New cars and new trucks share the responsibility for the extra trips almost equally. Last, whenever the road capacity is extended and road use is not appropriately priced, the road extension will attract PT passengers back to driving cars. This reduces frequency in the use of PT, a vicious circle that may lead to the disappearance of the PT alternative.

In sum, work by Arnott, Duranton, Turner and others have a major implication that runs against standard policy recommendations: *when road pricing is not implemented, building new roads might not be the appropriate policy to reduce traffic congestion.* Therefore, congestion pricing is back to centre stage as the main tool to curb urban congestion. Despite the lack of enthusiasm of public policy-makers for this instrument, the impressive number of results obtained by urban transport economics should encourage governments and other authorities to evaluate new transport projects against smart pricing schemes.

Whenever we consider extending current road or PT infrastructure, we should keep in mind that new technologies may enhance the effective capacity of the existing transport system (Winston and Mannering, 2014). For example, the capacity of the current road infrastructure may be enhanced by software applications that facilitate ridesharing. In the long run, vehicle-to-vehicle communication may increase the capacity of a road network by coordinating conflicting traffic flows and by using the stock of cars more intensively, freeing urban space from parking. In the case of public transport, new technologies may also lead to a better use of existing capacity. For example, better software may generate 'on demand' collective transport. When there is a capacity shortage, pricing is crucial to using capacity optimally, while road pricing also stimulates the development of new technologies.

9.7.2   The Wider Benefits of Urban Transport Projects and New Developments in Assessment Methods

There is growing empirical evidence that big urban transport projects lead to changes in the city form. García-López et al. (2015) have looked into the effects of highways on urbanization patterns in Spain. They have found that a highway leading from a central city caused an 8 to 9 per cent decline in the central city population between 1960 and 2011. In addition, a highway ramp fostered a 20 per cent population growth in the suburban municipalities where ramps were located. Finally, each additional kilometre closer to the nearest highway ramp increased municipal density growth by 8 per cent. This provides strong evidence for the role of highway capacity on the population distribution within the urban area.

It is, therefore, important to understand the full impact of a large transport project (or important traffic regulation) on the welfare of the metropolitan population, including efficiency as well as equity aspects. Planners typically have little faith in the efficiency or equity of market-determined outcomes, and advocate detailed land-use planning. Yet, as argued in the foregoing, *market forces drive land use to its most productive use if markets are corrected for the most important externalities*. However, care is needed in selecting which externalities to correct. For example, compact cities are often promoted to reduce carbon emissions generated by private transport. However, in the EU, we have seen that carbon is already overtaxed via the gasoline tax. What is more, 30 years from now, standard cars might well be electric battery cars. Consequently, climate considerations are not a good motivation for compact cities.

Economists have developed cost-benefit analysis (CBA) techniques that aim to assess transport projects, be they new infrastructures, new pricing or new regulations. In the EU member countries, they are now widely used, but not necessarily followed by decision-makers. CBA techniques have progressed over the last 50 years from the Dupuit consumer surplus measures to methods that correct for externalities, as well as for market imperfections and the opportunity cost of public funds. Quinet and Raj (2015) review the advances made in assessment methods and distinguish among three approaches: (i) the basic CBA method focusing on changes in the transport market, corrected for externalities and side effects on other markets; (ii) the econometric analysis of causality effects; and (iii) a detailed spatial modelling embedded in land-use planning models. For nonmarginal projects, such as large transport network extensions, there is a need to use them all.

Land-use planning models have been around for a long time. However, there is a need for operational models that integrate both land use and transport (LUTI). Indeed, new transport infrastructures often increase the demand for land, while there is often a new demand for infrastructures when new land is made available for urban activities. Given the long-run implications of decisions made about land use and transport infrastructure, the market alone cannot solve all problems. Accordingly, *cities need to be planned*. For this, different agents (developers, firms, governmental agencies) pursuing different, and sometimes conflicting, objectives must coordinate their actions. Furthermore, coordination requires commitment on the part of some agents, which is not always possible. Finally, it would be futile to seek a model based on a unified theory of cities that would appeal equally to economists, geographers, architects and urban planners. Therefore, developing LUTI models is a formidable challenge. It is only recently that researchers have tried to build such models in line with the basic principles of urban economics (de Palma et al., 2015).

In principle, LUTI models help us understand the effect of one particular policy intervention and ultimately answer the important question of the ideal urban form. We begin to understand the different mechanisms that come into play: agglomeration economies, congestion, environmental externalities, as well as the impacts of policy instruments (land use, buildings regulation, transport, and parking pricing and capacity). However, our knowledge is still partial, as most studies focus on only one or two mechanisms and on only one instrument at a time. Moreover, most analyses focus on an ideal government planner, while in the real world, political authority is dissipated over sometimes overlapping jurisdictions. The new LUTI model developed by the Netherlands CPB (Bureau for Economic Policy Analysis) provides a good example of what can be accomplished in terms of a detailed understanding of the effects associated with a given policy (Teulings et al., 2014).

9.8   Where Do We Stand?

1. Cities – but not all of them – have been and still are the main engines of cultural, economic, and social development. By encouraging social interactions and the exchange of ideas, cities allow for a finer division of labour and the quick adoption of innovations. As new ideas are often a new combination of old ideas, connecting people remains crucial for the Schumpeterian process of innovation to unfold. As human capital is the main production factor in knowledge-based economies, ignoring the role played by cities often leads governments to design policies that are harmful (not on purpose, of course!) to the economic fabric of their countries.

Not all cities are equally affected by innovation and growth; inequality cuts through the urban system. History tells us that in each period of time there are vibrant as well as dormant cities. If anything else, the development of human capital should be the main target of urban policies. As accurately argued by Glaeser (2011), the oversupply of structures and infrastructures is the hallmark of stagnating and declining cities. Rather than spending billions of euros on large infrastructures and fancy buildings, local governments should facilitate movement in cities by means of congestion pricing and promote the supply of affordable housing.

What is more, *housing and transport markets are intimately intertwined with local labour markets.* As a consequence, European or national employment policies that ignore the urban environment in which jobs are created and destroyed are unlikely to be able to deliver their full potential. Similarly, if international immigration policies must be coordinated at the EU level, migrants typically have an impact on particular local economies. Moreover, understanding how land capitalization works might help finance local public goods and services, thus alleviating the need to reduce city budgets because of macroeconomic fiscal constraints. In a nutshell, as Cheshire et al. (2014) argue, 'urban policy informed by economic insights can help improve policy-making for individual cities and urban systems as a whole', hence the whole economy.

2. All regions benefit from the agglomeration effects arising in large cities through interregional and interpersonal transfers. For example, in 2012, the Île-de-France (Paris) produced 30.1 per cent of French GDP but received only 22 per cent of the disposable income. In other words, 8 per cent of the GDP is redistributed toward other French regions. Greater London's share of the GDP in the United Kingdom is 23.1 per cent, while its share of the UK's disposable income is about 16.7 per cent. In Belgium, the contrast is even more striking. The NUTS-2 region Brussels-Capital produces 20.6 per cent of the Belgian GDP but receives only 10.3 per cent of disposable income; thus, more than 10 per cent is redistributed towards the other two regions of Belgium. Very much like some American cities, Brussels attracts high-income commuters as well as poor residents.

3. Urban policies are probably more important for economic growth and social cohesion than regional policies. This is in contrast with the EU's role in designing regional policies and its absence from urban policies. Social tensions between urban neighbourhoods are strong and income discrepancies within large cities are wide, and both are growing. Investments in human capital and housing are needed to counter this evolution, but they will not be sufficient. Several aspects of urban policy suffer from the fragmentation of policy areas. This holds for public finance, spatial segregation and housing. Urban transport is characterized by many negative externalities, but the present policy orientations are far from optimal, as they do not address the most important externality, that is, congestion. Even though more work is called for, we understand better how cities work and what policies they need. By contrast, due to the relative absence of in-depth studies of the subject matter in Europe, we still have a fairly poor knowledge of what the effects of people's mobility across the European space-economy are and could be in the future.

4. For the research agenda proposed in chapters 8 and 9 to be carried out, we need data that are often available in the US but not necessarily in the EU. First, for comparative studies across cities to be meaningful, member countries should agree on the same geographical definition of what a metropolitan area is, as in the US where the concept of 'statistical metropolitan area' is widely used. Similarly, local data about employment, transport,

GDP, human capital, physical attributes (buildings, roads), environmental quality (air quality, soil) and cultural amenities should be made available for more countries. European economists quite often study American cities rather than European cities because very good data are available in the US, but not in the EU. There is also a need for data at a fine spatial scale about what is going on within cities. For example, such data are needed to study how firms and households choose their locations. New technologies of data collection can help to overcome the data gaps and definitional problems in Europe.

Acknowledgements

We thank F. di Comite, G. Duranton, M. Lafourcade, F. Robert-Nicoud, J. Südekum, A. Turrini, K. Van Dender, E. Viladecans-Marsal, as well as R. Lindsey, J-Cl. Prager, E. Quinet, K. Small, R. Evers, and C-M. Fung for their comments on previous drafts. We are grateful to M. Ivaldi, W. Leininger, and M. Paasi for their encouragement and the organization of the COEURE and DG-REGIO workshops, and acknowledge the funding by the FP7/320300 grant under the FP7 SSH research programme.

Notes

1. This and the low value of land explain why many manufacturing firms have relocated their production plants from large to small cities.
2. See, for example, Glaeser and Maré (2001) and Moretti (2012) for the US; Combes et al. (2008) for France; Mion and Naticchioni (2009) for Italy; and Groot et al. (2014) for the Netherlands.
3. The best synthesis of the results derived with the monocentric city model remains the landmark book by Fujita (1989).
4. Only a limited number of papers have tackled the endogenous formation of employment centres. They are surveyed in Duranton and Puga (2004) and Fujita and Thisse (2013).

References

Agrawal, A., Cockburn, I., Galasso, A., and Oettl, A. 2014. Why are some regions more innovative than others? The role of small firms in the presence of large labs. *Journal of Urban Economics*, **81**, 149–165.

Albouy, D., and Lue, B. 2015. Driving to opportunity: Local rents, wages, commuting, and sub-metropolitan quality of life. *Journal of Urban Economics*, **89**, 74–92.

Allen, T., and Arkolakis, C. 2014. Trade and the topography of the spatial economy. *Quarterly Journal of Economics*, **129**, 1085–1140.

Alonso, W. 1964. *Location and Land Use*. Cambridge, MA: Harvard University Press.

Arnott, R. 1979. Unpriced transport congestion. *Journal of Economic Theory*, **21**, 294–316.

Arnott, R. 2007. Congestion tolling with agglomeration externalities. *Journal of Urban Economics*, **62**, 187–203.

Arnott, R., de Palma, A., and Lindsey, R. 1993. A structural model of peak-period congestion: A traffic bottleneck with elastic demand. *American Economic Review*, **83**, 161–179.

Arzaghi, M., and Henderson, J. V. 2008. Networking off Madison Avenue. *Review of Economic Studies*, **75**, 1011–1038.

Bacolod, M., Blum, B. S., and Strange, W. C. 2009. Skills in the city. *Journal of Urban Economics*, **65**, 136–153.

Bairoch, P. 1985. *De Jéricho á Mexico. Villes et économie dans l'histoire*. Paris: Éditions Gallimard. English translation by C. Braider, *Cities and Economic Development: From the Dawn of History to the PresentChicago: University of Chicago Press, 1988*.

Barnett, J. 1986. *The Elusive City: Five Centuries of Design, Ambition and Miscalculation*. New York: Harper and Row.

Basso, L. J., and Silva, H. E. 2014. Efficiency and substitutability of transit subsidies and other urban transport policies. *American Economic Journal: Economic Policy*, **6**, 1–33.

Beckmann, M. J. 1976. Spatial equilibrium in the dispersed city. In: Papageorgiou, Y. Y. (ed), *Mathematical Land Use Theory*. Lexington, MA: Lexington Books, pp. 117–125.

Behrens, K., Duranton, G., and Robert-Nicoud, F. 2014. Productive cities: Sorting, selection, and agglomeration. *Journal of Political Economy*, **122**, 507–553.

Bénabou, R. 1993. Workings of a city: Location, education, and production. *Quarterly Journal of Economics*, **108**, 619–652.

Borzic, M., and Le Jeannic, T. 2014. En matière d'emploi, les métropoles ont davantage résisté à la crise. *INSEE Premiére No. 1503*. https://insee.fr/fr/themes/document .asp?reg_id=99&ref_id=ip1503.

Briant, A., Lafourcade, M., and Schmutz, B. 2015. Can tax breaks beat geography? Lessons from the French enterprise zone experience. *American Economic Journal: Economic Policy*, **7**, 88–124.

Brueckner, J. K., and Sridhar, K. S. 2012. Measuring welfare gains from relaxation of land-use restrictions: The case of India's building-height limits. *Regional Science and Urban Economics*, **42**, 1061–1067.

Brueckner, J. K., Thisse, J.-F., and Zenou, Y. 1999. Why is central Paris rich and downtown Detroit poor? An amenity-based theory. *European Economic Review*, **43**, 91–107.

Brülhart, M., Bucovetsky, S., and Schmidheiny, K. 2015. Taxes in cities. In: Duranton, G., Henderson, J. V., and Strange, W. (eds), *Handbook of Regional and Urban Economics*, vol. 5. Amsterdam: Elsevier, pp. 1123–1196.

Cervero, R. 2003. Road expansion, urban growth, and induced travel: A path analysis. *Journal of the American Planning Association*, **69**, 145–163.

Charlot, S., and Duranton, G. 2004. Communication externalities in cities. *Journal of Urban Economics*, **56**, 581–613.

Cheshire, P., Nathan, M., and Overman, H. 2014. *Urban Economics and Urban Policy*. Cheltenham, U.K.: Edward Elgar Publishing.

Ciccone, A., and Hall, R. E. 1996. Productivity and the density of economic activity. *American Economic Review*, **86**, 54–70.

Combes, P.-P., and Gobillon, L. 2015. The empirics of agglomeration economies. In: Duranton, G., Henderson, J. V., and Strange, W. (eds), *Handbook of Regional and Urban Economics*, vol. 5. Amsterdam: Elsevier, pp. 247–348.

Combes, P.-P., Duranton, G., and Gobillon, L. 2008. Spatial wage disparities: Sorting matters! *Journal of Urban Economics*, **63**, 723–742.

Combes, P.-P., Duranton, G., Gobillon, L., Puga, D., and Roux, S. 2012. The productivity advantages of large cities: Distinguishing agglomeration from firm selection. *Econometrica*, **80**, 2543–2594.

d'Aspremont, C., Gabszewicz, J. J., and Thisse, J.-F. 1979. On Hotelling's 'Stability in Competition'. *Econometrica*, **47**, 1145–1150.

Davis, D. R., and Dingel, J. I. 2015. The comparative advantage of cities. Columbia University, mimeo.

Davis, D. R., and Weinstein, D. E. 2002. Bones, bombs, and break points: The geography of economic activity. *American Economic Review*, **92**, 1269–1289.

D'Costa, S., and Overman, H. 2014. The urban wage growth premium: Sorting or learning? *Regional Science and Urban Economics*, **48**, 168–179.

De Borger, B., and Proost, S. 2012. A political economy model of road pricing. *Journal of Urban Economics*, **71**, 79–92.

de Palma, A., Bierlaire, M., Hurtubia, R., and Waddell, P. 2015. Future challenges in transport and land use modeling. In: Bierlaire, M., de Palma, A., Hurtubia, R., and Waddell, P. (eds), *Integrated Transport and Land Use Modeling for Sustainable Cities*. Lausanne: EPFL Press, pp. 513–530.

Desmet, K., and Rossi-Hansberg, E. 2013. Urban accounting and welfare. *American Economic Review*, **103**, 2296–2327.

Duranton, G., and Puga, D. 2001. Nursery cities: Urban diversity, process innovation, and the life cycle of products. *American Economic Review*, **91**, 1454–1477.

Duranton, G., and Puga, D. 2004. Micro-foundations of urban agglomeration economies. In: Henderson, J. V., and Thisse, J.-F. (eds), *Handbook of Regional and Urban Economics*, vol. 4. Amsterdam: Elsevier, pp. 2063–2117.

Duranton, G., and Turner, M. A. 2011. The fundamental law of road congestion: Evidence from US cities. *American Economic Review*, **101**, 2616–2652.

Eaton, J., and Eckstein, Z. 1997. Cities and growth: Theory and evidence from France and Japan. *Regional Science and Urban Economics*, **27**, 443–474.

Eeckhout, J., Pinheiro, R., and Schmidheiny, K. 2014. Spatial sorting. *Journal of Political Economy*, **122**, 554–620.

Eliasson, J., and Proost, S. 2015. Is sustainable transport policy sustainable? *Transport Policy*, **37**, 92–100.

Eliasson, J., Hultzkranz, L., Nerhagen, L., and Rosqvist, L. Smidfelt. 2009. The Stockholm congestion charging trial 2006: Overview of effects. *Transportation Research A*, **43**, 240–250.

European Commission. 2014. *Update of the Handbook on External Costs of Transport*. Final Report for the European Commission: DG Move. Ricardo-AEA/R/ED57769. London, UK: Ricardo-AEA. https://ifr.uni-kiel.de/de/forschung/handbook-external-costs-transport-2014.pdf.

Eurostat. 2015. Regional statistics. http://ec.europa.eu/eurostat/statisticsexplained/index.php/GDP_at_regional_level.

Faggio, G., Silva, O., and Strange, W. C. 2014. Heterogeneous agglomeration. SERC Discussion Papers, SERCDP0152. Spatial Economics Research Centre (SERC), London School of Economics and Political Science.

Fujita, M. 1989. *Urban Economic Theory: Land Use and City Size.* Cambridge, MA: Cambridge University Press.

Fujita, M., and Thisse, J.-F. 2013. *Economics of Agglomeration: Cities, Industrial Location, and Globalization.* Cambridge University Press.

Gagnepain, P., Ivaldi, M., and Martimort, D. 2013. The cost of contract renegotiation: Evidence from the local public sector. *American Economic Review*, **103**, 2352–2383.

Gaigné, C., Riou, S., and Thisse, J.-F. 2016. How to make the metropolitan area work? Neither big government, nor laissez-faire. *Journal of Public Economics*, **134**, 100–113.

García-López, M-Á., Holl, A., and Viladecans-Marsal, E. 2015. Suburbanization and highways: When the Romans, the Bourbons and the first cars still shape Spanish cities. *Journal of Urban Economics*, **85**, 52–67.

Gibbons, S., Overman, H. G., and Pelkonen, P. 2014. Area disparities in Britain: Understanding the contribution of people vs. place through variance decompositions. *Oxford Bulletin of Economics and Statistics*, **76**, 745–763.

Glaeser, E. L. 2011. *Triumph of the City.* London: Macmillan.

Glaeser, E. L., and Gyourko, J. 2003. The impact of building restrictions on housing affordability. *Federal Reserve Bank of New York Economic Policy Review*, **9**, 21–39.

Glaeser, E. L., and Kahn, M. E. 2004. Sprawl and urban growth. In: Henderson, J. V., and Thisse, J.-F. (eds), *Handbook of Regional and Urban Economics*, vol. 4. Amsterdam: Elsevier, pp. 2481–2527.

Glaeser, E. L., and Maré, D. 2001. Cities and skills. *Journal of Labor Economics*, **19**, 316–342.

Glaeser, E. L., Kallal, H. D., Scheinkman, J. A., and Shleifer, A. 1992. Growth in cities. *Journal of Political Economy*, **100**, 1126–1152.

Glaeser, E. L., Kolko, J., and Saiz, A. 2001. Consumer city. *Journal of Economic Geography*, **1**, 27–50.

Grigolon, L., Reynaert, M., and Verboven, F. 2014. Consumer valuation of fuel costs and the effectiveness of tax policy: Evidence from the European car market. CEPR Discussion Paper No. DP10301.

Groot, S. P. T., de Groot, H. L. F., and Smit, M. J. 2014. Regional wage differences in the Netherlands: Micro evidence on agglomeration externalities. *Journal of Regional Science*, **54**, 503–523.

Gwilliam, K. M., Nash, C. A., and Mackie, P. J. 1985. Deregulating the bus industry in Britain – (B) the case against. *Transport Reviews*, **5**, 105–132.

Handbury, J., and Weinstein, D. 2015. Goods prices and availability in cities. *Review of Economic Studies*, **82**, 258–296.

Harding, M. 2014. Personal tax treatment of company cars and commuting expenses: Estimating the fiscal and environmental costs. OECD Taxation Working Papers no. 20. Paris: OECD Publishing.

Helsley, R. W., and Strange, W. C. 2014. Coagglomeration, clusters, and the scale and composition of cities. *Journal of Political Economy*, **122**, 1064–1093.

Henderson, J. V. 1974. The sizes and types of cities. *American Economic Revie*, **64**, 640–656.

Henderson, J. V. 1988. *Urban Development. Theory, Fact, and Illusion*. Oxford: Oxford University Press.

Henderson, J. V., Kuncoro, A., and Turner, M. 1995. Industrial development in cities. *Journal of Political Economy*, **103**, 1067–1090.

Hochman, O., Pines, D., and Thisse, J.-F. 1995. On the optimal structure of local governments. *American Economic Review*, **85**, 1224–1240.

Hohenberg, P., and Lees, L. H. 1985. *The Making of Urban Europe (1000–1950)*. Cambridge, MA: Harvard University Press.

Hsieh, C.-T., and Moretti, E. 2015. Why do cities matter? Local growth and aggregate growth. Mimeo, http://eml.berkeley.edu//~moretti/papers.html.

ICCT (International Council on Clean Transportation). 2014. *European Vehicle Market Statistics Pocketbook 2014*. Berlin: ICCT. http://eupocketbook.theicct.org.

Jacobs, J. 1969. *The Economy of Cities*. New York: Random House.

Kahneman, D., and Krueger, A. B. 2006. Developments in the measurement of subjective well-being. *Journal of Economic Perspectives*, **20**, 3–24.

Manning, A. 2010. The plant size-place effect: Agglomeration and monopsony power in labour markets. *Journal of Economic Geography*, **10**, 717–744.

Marshall, A. 1890. *Principles of Economics*. 8th edn. London: Macmillan, 1920.

Mayeres, I., and Proost, S. 2001. Marginal tax reform, externalities and income distribution. *Journal of Public Economics*, **79**, 343–363.

Mills, E. S. 1967. An aggregative model of resource allocation in a metropolitan area. *American Economic Review*, **57**, 197–210.

Mion, G., and Naticchioni, P. 2009. The spatial sorting and matching of skills and firms. *Canadian Journal of Economics*, **42**, 28–55.

Mohring, H. 1972. Optimization and scale economies in urban bus transportation. *American Economic Review*, **62**, 591–604.

Moretti, E. 2004. Estimating the social returns to higher education: Evidence from longitudinal and repeated cross-sectional data. *Journal of Econometrics*, **121**, 175–212.

Moretti, E. 2012. *The New Geography of Jobs*. Boston: Houghton Mifflin Harcourt.

Muth, R. F. 1969. *Cities and Housing*. Chicago: University of Chicago Press.

Ogawa, H., and Fujita, M. 1980. Equilibrium land use patterns in a nonmonocentric city. *Journal of Regional Science*, **20**, 455–475.

Parry, I., and Bento, A. 2001. Revenue recycling and the welfare effects of road pricing. *Scandinavian Journal of economics*, **103**, 645–671.

Parry, I., and Small, K. A. 2005. Does Britain or the United States have the right gasoline tax? *American Economic Review*, **95**, 1276–1289.

Parry, I., and Small, K. A. 2009. Should urban subsidies be reduced? *American Economic Review*, **99**, 700–724.

Picard, P., and Okubo, T. 2012. Firms' locations under demand heterogeneity. *Regional Science and Urban Economics*, **42**, 961–974.

Proost, S., and Van Dender, K. 2012. Energy and environment challenges in the transport sector. *Economics of Transportation*, **1**, 77–87.

Puga, D. 2010. The magnitude and causes of agglomeration economies. *Journal of Regional Science*, **50**, 203–219.

Quinet, E., and Raj, A. 2015. Welfare and growth effects in transport and trade – a practitioner's point of view. Report prepared for the World Bank.

Redding, S. J. 2015. Goods trade, factor mobility and welfare. Princeton University, mimeo.

Rosenthal, S. S., and Strange, W. C. 2004. Evidence on the nature and sources of agglomeration economies. In: Henderson, J. V., and Thisse, J.-F. (eds), *Handbook of Regional and Urban Economics*, vol. 4. Amsterdam: Elsevier, pp. 2119–2171.

Schmidheiny, K., and Südekum, J. 2015. The pan-European population distribution across consistently defined functional urban areas. *Economics Letters*, **133**, 10–13.

Small, K. A., and Verhoef, E. T. 2007. *Economics of Urban Transportation*. London: Routledge.

Solé-Ollé, A., and Viladecans-Marsal, E. 2012. Lobbying, political competition, and local land supply: Recent evidence from Spain. *Journal of Public Economics*, **96**, 10–19.

Stiglitz, J. 1977. The theory of local public goods. In: Feldstein, M. S., and Inman, R. P. (eds), *The Economics of Public Services*. London: Macmillan, pp. 273–334.

Teulings, C. N., Ossokina, I. V., and de Groot, H. L. F. 2014. Welfare benefits of agglomeration and worker heterogeneity. CESifo Working Paper Series No. 4939.

Tirole, J. 1988. *The Theory of Industrial Organization*. Cambridge, MA: MIT Press.

Topa, G., and Zenou, Y. 2015. Neighborhood and network effects. In: Duranton, G., Henderson, J. V., and Strange, W. (eds), *Handbook of Regional and Urban Economics*, vol. 5. Amsterdam: Elsevier, pp. 561–624.

Turner, M. A., Haughwout, A., and Van Der Klaauw, W. 2014. Land use regulation and welfare. *Econometrica*, **82**, 1341–1403.

Ushchev, P., Sloev, I., and Thisse, J.-F. 2015. Do we go shopping downtown or in the 'burbs'? *Journal of Urban Economics*, **85**, 1–15.

van Goeverden, C., Rietveld, P., Koelemeijer, J., and Peeters, P. 2006. Subsidies in public transport. *European Transport / Trasporti Europei*, **32**, 5–25.

Vickrey, W. S. 1969. Congestion theory and public investment. *Papers and Proceedings of the Eighty-first Annual Meeting of the American Economic Association*, 251–260.

Winston, C., and Mannering, F. 2014. Implementing technology to improve public highway performance: A leapfrog technology from the private sector is going to be necessary. *Economics of Transportation*, **3**, 158–165.

Wolff, H. 2014. Keep your clunker in the suburb: Low emission zones and adoption of green vehicles. *Economic Journal*, **124**, F481–F512.

10 Fiscal and Monetary Policies after the Crises

Charles Brendon and Giancarlo Corsetti

Abstract

We review the recent literature on macroeconomic stabilization policy, with a particular focus on two major challenges that are particular to the post-crisis landscape. These are, first, how to provide meaningful economic stimulus when the zero lower bound on nominal interest rates is binding. Second, how to design a stabilization policy for the Eurozone that will remedy the large macroeconomic imbalances among member states.

10.1 Introduction

European policy-makers are currently facing formidable policy challenges. First, while many other economic regions in the world have shown tangible signs of economic recovery already in 2014, the Eurozone as a whole slipped into a downturn with high unemployment and current and expected inflation falling well below the 2 per cent target. Monetary policy will be constrained by the zero lower bound for the foreseeable future, giving the European Central Bank (ECB) little alternative to engaging in policy experimentation such as quantitative easing. Second, the progress towards the correction of internal imbalances has been very slow, with the questionable exception of the reversal of previous current account deficits, essentially driven by large and costly recessions in the high debt countries. Reform efforts have been frustrated by low economic activity and financial fragility, forcing governments in need of change to implement costly initiatives with scarce tax and financial resources. The inward-looking precautionary approach to fiscal policy adopted by surplus countries has ensured that the overall fiscal stance of the currency area is contractionary, at an inappropriately tight level for the Eurozone as a whole. Third, the Eurozone as an incomplete monetary union needs to ensure its sustainability via institutional development that requires strong political cohesion. Lack of sufficient institutional development has undermined timely and intense policy responses to the crisis, and created mistrust and conflict over viable solutions, as policy-makers are having to design stabilization mechanisms, at the same time as reaching agreement on the fundamental contracts and mutual insurance rules governing banking union, monetary backstops for public debt, and the credibility of the no-bailout principle. The process of overcoming the insufficient institutional development during a severe crisis has exacerbated policy credibility problems at country and union-wide level, and arguably created room for destabilizing speculative behaviour. Last but not least, growth rates across the Eurozone are disappointingly low, at the same time as the income and wealth distributions have become more concentrated. On the one hand, demographic and structural factors weigh on the dynamics of these economies, suggesting a far-reaching reassessment of the stability of their public finance and welfare state institutions is needed. On the other hand, the low growth rates may themselves have resulted from past policy choices regarding investment in human capital and knowledge. More recently, they reflect the accumulation of public and private debt. Assessing changes in the long-run trends is bound to have a first-order impact on the design of stabilization policy.

This chapter provides a compact survey of the academic and policy debate on fiscal and monetary policy after the crisis, in and outside the Eurozone, with the goal of identifying areas of policy research that can directly contribute to addressing the three main challenges mentioned above: (a) economic stabilization at the zero lower bound constraint on monetary policy; (b) correction of imbalances; and (c) the complementarity of stabilization policy and reforms. The survey is meant to be neither exhaustive, nor technical. Yet we have tried where possible to structure the arguments around a common stylized analytical framework, so as to obtain a clearer understanding of the questions and issues that require further analytical and empirical work.

In doing this, we make sure to relate the policy debates before and after the eruption of the global crisis, trying where possible to account for the complexity of these debates, and for the heterogeneity of ideas and models that are currently being deployed. The crisis has naturally led to a very deep reconsideration and redevelopment of the pre-crisis consensus regarding stabilization policy, bringing forward lines of research that were previously marginal to that consensus. Simultaneously, innovation and experimentation in the design of practical stabilization policy have become both necessary and desirable. This is particularly true of policy in the Eurozone, where it is now evident that there are important gaps in the ability of policy-makers to deal with asymmetric economic performances among countries. Academic research in Europe and beyond provides many important insights into the direction that policy reform should take in light of these new challenges. Rather than allowing a new consensus to form around experimental decision making, it would be far more preferable to incorporate this literature actively into the reform agenda. The aim of this survey is to take a helicopter view over the most important insights that current academic research has to offer.

We are fully aware that many issues raised by the crisis have not, so far, found a satisfactory answer in theory and policy-making. Yet our focus is on what the academic literature does provide, rather than what it does not. Even allowing for this, space constraints have forced us to interpret our remit narrowly, and two omissions should be singled out upfront. First, while we analyse the consequences of sovereign risk crises for the design of stabilization policy, we do not delve into a comprehensive analysis of debt sustainability and issues in debt default. Second, we do not go in detail on the specific roots of the financial crisis, although we devote a long section to stabilization policy in the wake of such a crash.

The chapter is structured as follows. Section 10.2 synthesizes the academic debate predating the crisis, documenting substantial heterogeneity in views and theories at odds with popular media accounts. Section 10.3 provides the macroeconomic context for the crisis and briefly introduces key challenges to the design of stabilization policy. A long section follows with an account of the debate on what has caused policy rates to fall to, and be constrained at, their zero lower bounds, and how to stabilize the economy via forward guidance, fiscal policy, or central bank purchases of assets. In Section 10.5 we account for models and mechanisms that have been recently proposed, to account for large and persistent periods of low economic activity and inflation. Section 10.6 focuses on issues that are specific to the Eurozone, including low risk sharing, the role of fiscal policy and economic reforms.

10.2   The Pre-Crisis Consensus, and Heterogeneity

Our starting point is the strengthening consensus among policy-makers, up to the eruption of the global crisis, that the most important questions relating to macroeconomic stabilization were essentially resolved. Developed economies were benefitting from the steady, low-inflationary period of growth known as the 'Great Moderation', with improved monetary policy-making widely believed to have been a contributory factor in engineering this.[1] The launch of the euro, the greatest monetary experiment in recent history, went far more smoothly than even optimistic observers were expecting. The newly created European Central Bank appeared to be able to steer the European economy in the *'uncharted waters'* of the newly created economic space defined by the common currency without substantial problems. Possible issues foreshadowed by the body of literature loosely referred to as Optimum Currency Area theory did not seem to materialize. More generally, the ongoing process of rapid trade and financial globalization, with the growth in supply chain and global and international banking, did not seem to alter in any substantive way the best practice of monetary and fiscal stabilization, essentially focused on inward-looking objectives such as inflation and the output gap at the national level. Of course there was considerable debate on the emergence of large current account imbalances, and/or financial vulnerability. But the experience of the Greenspan era – and particularly the ease with which the world economy endured the dot-com collapse of the early 2000s – suggested there was a tried and tested strategy for maintaining macroeconomic stability even in the wake of significant financial turbulence.

At the level of academic research, the policy literature was similarly tranquil. Macroeconomists had devised a suite of interconnected Dynamic Stochastic General Equilibrium (DSGE) models that could account for observed, calmer business-cycle dynamics, and monetary policy, in turn, played a crucial controlling role in these models.[2] It would have been clear even to an outsider that important disagreements remained in the academic discipline, for instance over the role of sticky-price New Keynesian models in explaining the business cycle,[3] but these did not have the same direct connection with day-to-day stabilization policy as, say, the debates surrounding monetarism in the 1970s and 1980s. From the late 1990s on, few academic macroeconomists publicly advocated – or analysed the implications of – major innovations in the conduct of stabilization policy. It is easy to see how, from a policy-maker's perspective, academic research was seen as formalizing what was already widely considered to be best practice.

The crisis has, by contrast, placed policy innovation at the centre of the political agenda. As we will argue, this is partly a product of necessity: monetary policy has become less effective as nominal interest rates have approached their apparent lower bound of zero. But it is also partly a product of the apparent inadequacies of pre-crisis conduct. In order to understand the forces driving innovation, it is useful to sketch the pre-crisis 'consensus' regarding stabilization policy. This is necessarily an exercise in simplification, and some policy-makers would no doubt consider their pre-crisis views as departing from it, but the aim is to capture the essence of mainstream opinion. We would argue that this ran roughly as follows:[4]

1. Monetary policy should play the primary role in economic stabilization.
2. The appropriate monetary policy instrument is the short-term nominal interest rate.
3. Policy should pursue a modestly positive, stable rate of inflation, to the exclusion of other goals.
4. Active fiscal policy is of limited additional usefulness.
5. Financial crises should be addressed via provision of abundant liquidity to contain the propagation of financial instability into macroeconomic instability.

Importantly the connections between these consensus views and formal theoretical modelling ran in both directions. Some components were certainly a product of earlier developments in the academic literature. The emphasis on price stability as a policy objective, for instance, ultimately derived from the work of Milton Friedman and Edmund Phelps on inflation dynamics and the natural rate of unemployment, subsequently updated to a New Keynesian setting for the purposes of policy analysis.[5]

What we want to stress, however, is that in other regards the focus of research arguably followed from the received policy wisdom. This was particularly noticeable in the development of a theory of optimal interest-rate setting, which replaced the more traditional focus in the academic literature on the money supply as the object of policy choice. The switch in focus was popularized by the work of Woodford (2003), who argued that monetary policy could meaningfully be analysed in 'cashless' settings, where money was used as a unit of account but not actively traded. Thus the money supply was no longer viewed as a relevant policy variable, and outcomes could be controlled by interest rates alone.[6] This was an important development from the perspective of the third part of the consensus too, because optimal policy in models *with* money very often required the central bank to induce permanent deflation, consistent with the so-called Friedman rule – a conclusion plainly out of line with actual central bank choices. Optimal interest-rate rules in a cashless setting instead stressed the merits of low – but non-negative – inflation.[7] In both regards, however, these developments in the theoretical literature took place after the associated developments in policy-making. Interest-rate setting had already become the dominant instrument of monetary policy conduct in OECD economies by the late 1980s, and by the late 1990s a large number of central banks had already moved to formal inflation targeting regimes – a trend that was reinforced in 1999 when the new European Central Bank was given a mandate that gave principal emphasis to price stability. Whilst the monetary framework of the European central bank, initially based on the 'two pillars' of monetary and economic analysis, could in principle have stimulated work developing an alternative theoretical and institutional paradigm, this was not considered a relevant priority in the contemporary intellectual environment.

The Great Moderation thus generated a clear symbiosis between the priorities of policy-makers and the academic work *that attained prominence in policy-making circles*, but this work was not necessarily representative of developments in the subject as a whole. Many of the innovative post-crisis modelling developments that we survey have built on pre-crisis work that was widely discussed in academic circles, but sat apart from any pre-crisis 'consensus'. Thus the common view that macroeconomics entered 2008 as an excessively homogenized discipline is, at best, an over-simplification.

10.3   The Context and Challenges Posed by the Crisis

The purpose of this section is to revisit in simple form the basic facts of the crisis, laying out in very broad terms what any new academic analysis of stabilization policy should be seeking to address. Focusing on the headline macroeconomic trends in leading OECD economies over the past decade, we will draw attention both to the initial homogeneity of experiences across countries, and to substantial differences in their subsequent performances (particularly stark in outcomes across Eurozone members).

10.3.1   Headline Macroeconomic Trends

The ultimate purpose of stabilization policy is to ensure steady growth, low unemployment and stable prices. Any diagnosis of the problems that the crisis has raised must start with these aggregates.

Output

The consequences of the crisis for global production are well known, though no less striking for it. 2009 remains the only year since the Second World War in which gross world output fell in real terms. This fall was particularly severe for advanced economies, though the growth rates of emerging market and developing economies also slowed very substantially.

Looking across developed economies, what was particularly unusual about the crisis was the uniformity with which its effects were felt. Of the 34 OECD members, 29 saw lower real output in 2009 than 2008. Poland was the only EU member state to see output grow that year. In this regard 2008–2009 was by far the most synchronized downturn since the 1930s. Even Canada, which did not see any major domestic financial crisis, suffered a year-on-year contraction of around 2.7 per cent during this period.

But if the early post-crisis years were distinctive for the *similarity* of experiences across countries, the years since 2009 are far better characterized by their differences. Some contrasts stand out across the G7 economies. By the end of 2014 real output in the US was around 8 per cent above its pre-crisis peak, and in Canada more than 10 per cent. In Italy a long period of stagnation has instead left GDP 10 per cent below its level in early 2008.

With respect to the Eurozone member countries, the story is both one of divergence within the bloc, and relative stagnation by comparison with other leading economies. It has become common to draw a distinction between northern and southern members when discussing the problems of the currency area.[8] Yet whilst it is true that the group of five countries most commonly grouped together as the 'South' – Greece, Ireland, Italy, Portugal and Spain – have performed far worse than most others since the crisis, there are also important laggards in the North – notably Finland and the Netherlands, whose production levels remain stuck below the pre-crisis peak at the time of writing. Overall, it is notable that no Eurozone country has yet experienced a recovery in aggregate production of a similar magnitude to that of the US and Canada.

Germany, the zone's best-performing large economy, had exceeded its pre-crisis real GDP level by a little under 4 per cent by the end of 2014.

Alongside this, the Greek crisis has operated on a different scale from problems elsewhere. Greece's real output in the second quarter of 2015 remained more than 25 per cent below its pre-crisis peak, the effects of the bitterly-contested July 2015 bailout agreement still to be felt. In proportional terms the magnitude of this contraction is almost identical to the estimated decline in GDP in the US between 1929 and 1933, through the worst years of the Great Depression. In terms of lost output, the Greek depression is unrivalled in its magnitude and duration among advanced economies throughout the postwar era.

Unemployment

A similar overall picture emerges from viewing unemployment data – that is, of a common economic shock during the 2008–2009 period, followed by very diverse dynamics as some economies recovered from the crisis and others saw their difficulties compound. Yet labour market outcomes also indicate important new disparities. For instance, measured in terms of unemployment Spain's post-crisis experience stands out as much as that of Greece among Eurozone states, both countries having experienced long periods during which the headline unemployment rate exceeded 25 per cent. By contrast, Germany's performance stands out as a far clearer success – particularly when viewed over the entire decade since 2005. Its unemployment rate has fallen by more than half over the Merkel years, from a peak of over 11 per cent to less than 5 per cent at the time of writing – moving from the highest to the second-lowest rate in the G7.

It is also striking just how far the dispersion of unemployment rates across Eurozone countries has increased by comparison with the immediate pre-crisis period. In January 2008 the lowest rate among the original 12 members of the currency area was the Netherlands' 3.8 per cent, and the highest was Spain's 9 per cent. By July 2015 the equivalent range ran from 4.6 per cent in Germany to 25 per cent in Spain. If it was possible to argue prior to 2008 that stabilization policy need only be designed for the currency area as a whole, the case is insupportable now.

Inflation

Turning next to prices, there was again a very clear correlation between consumer-price inflation rates across G7 economies during the initial months of the crisis. In July 2008 all seven economies were experiencing year-on-year inflation rates in excess of 2 per cent, with US annual price increases approaching 7 per cent. By July 2009 all bar the UK were experiencing deflation. These aggregate price trends were driven in part by large simultaneous changes in commodity prices, particularly oil prices. Since 2009 there has been less apparent divergence in inflation rates than output levels, with a particularly notable downward trend in headline inflation rates across OECD economies since 2012 – with the result that the Eurozone, US and UK were all flirting with negative inflation rates over the course of 2015. Indeed, it was the common Eurozone trend towards deflation that justified the ECB's decision to embark on quantitative easing in January 2015.

Greece is once more an outlier when it comes to post-2008 inflation trends, though to a lesser extent than in output and unemployment data. Consumer prices in Greece have been falling since early 2013, whereas the Eurozone as a whole did not experience deflation until December 2014. The Greek year-on-year inflation rate has been one to two percentage points below the Eurozone average persistently since early 2012.

10.3.2   Market Impairment and the Transmission of Stabilization Policy

Matching these headline trends in macroeconomic aggregates have been important developments in the operation and scope of conventional stabilization policy. The first relates to the transmission of monetary policy to the wider economy. This transmission is heavily dependent on the smooth working of the interbank markets. Before August 2007 a large share of interbank transactions involved unsecured loans, but risk premia nonetheless remained low. This meant there was a tight link between headline policy interest rates and interbank rates.

This changed radically with the crisis, in two steps. First, between August 2007 and August 2008 significant risk premia emerged in interbank lending markets, caused by a mixture of liquidity and default risks. There was some reduction in the quantity of unsecured interbank lending. However, there was not yet a mass exodus to secured interbank lending. The default and liquidity risks were perceived to be bank-specific concerns, with lenders judging the creditworthiness of a borrowing counterparty on a case by case basis.

Second, the failure of Lehman Brothers in September 2008 resulted in *systemic* default and illiquidity risk emerging as a significant concern across financial systems in mature economies. This change led to an effective closure of unsecured interbank markets in both the Eurozone and the US: the quantity of unsecured interbank lending fell significantly. Investors sought safer and more liquid assets. Banks sought refuge in secured interbank markets and recourse to central bank lending and deposit facilities.

Following the initial market panic, central banks effectively substituted themselves for the core of the interbank market, offering lending and deposit facilities to banks that would not otherwise be able or willing to trade bilaterally with one another. This succeeded in reducing risk premia, and placed significant downward pressures on a range of interest rates, particularly the short-term cost to private banks of obtaining funding.

Yet these initial improvements were set back in Europe by the sovereign debt crises that set in from 2010 onwards. These triggered significant fragmentation in money markets in the Eurozone. A particular source of difficulties was the link that emerged between fears for the solvency of a country's banking sector, and fears for its sovereign. The national focus of banking sectors in Eurozone states meant that private banks tended to have large holdings of their domestic sovereign's debt. Concerns about the sovereign thus led directly to questions about the health of the banking sector. But the early experience of the crisis worldwide had been one of domestic sovereigns providing an ultimate backstop to the financial sector in times of turmoil. Thus an impaired banking sector increased the likely liabilities of the state. The result was a vicious circle that affected Greece, Ireland, Portugal, Spain and Cyprus in turn, the flow of credit to the private sector becoming severely impaired in these states as a consequence.

The associated financial turmoil and deterioration of the economic outlook led the European Central Bank to embark on a range of unconventional policy measures to overcome perceived financial market illiquidities. These included in particular the Securities Markets Programme (SMP), launched in May 2010, the three-year maturity Long Term Refinancing Operations (LTROs) of December 2011, and the Outright Monetary Transactions (OMT) programme announced in August 2012. Together these measures appeared to have reduced funding costs both for private-sector banks in most of the impaired southern European states, and for the domestic sovereigns whose debt these banks bought. The one exception has again been Greece, where fears of default and even a much-hyped Eurozone 'exit' necessitated capital controls to prevent a collapse of the banking sector in the summer of 2015. At the time of writing conditions for Greek banks appear to have improved, but remain precarious.

10.3.3   The Zero Bound on Nominal Interest Rates

At the same time as the usual transmission mechanism from central bank interest rates to the wider economy became impaired, a more direct constraint has come to limit conventional monetary policy: the zero – or near-zero – lower bound on nominal interest rates. This arguably poses the most universal, global challenge for stabilization policy at present. Where exactly the lower bound on nominal interest rates falls is the subject of ongoing debate and policy experimentation,[9] but there is near-unanimous agreement that there is some limit to savers' willingness to pay depository institutions for the privilege of holding their funds. This is ultimately due to the availability of cash as an alternative savings instrument, with a guaranteed zero rate of return.[10] The policy instrument that was considered the most important stabilization device prior to the crisis – the nominal interest rate – no longer seems capable of injecting additional stimulus, despite continued economic weakness. Policy innovation is the only possible response to this, and a large part of this survey is concerned with the theoretical and empirical literatures that are emerging to understand (a) why the zero bound has come to matter – in a way that was not foreseen before the crisis (outside of Japan) – and (b) what channels stabilization policy can now exploit.

The Japanese experience is particularly noteworthy from the perspective of part (a) of this. As we shall see, in large parts of the macroeconomic literature it is common to treat the zero bound as a temporary concern, driven by a short-term desire by consumers to delay purchases for some particular reason. This perspective is very difficult to reconcile with the fact that Japan's zero bound episode has now lasted two decades, and shows no signs of ending soon. The central hypothesis of the fast-growing '*secular stagnation*' literature – that global long-term real interest rates are now permanently lower – provides an intriguing alternative.[11]

Our survey will focus principally elsewhere, reflecting the majority of the post-crisis academic literature to date. But we do wish to highlight here that a central concern for ongoing research should be to ask whether Japan will remain an outlier, or whether other OECD economies are following in its path.

10.4   The Zero Lower Bound: Implications for Stabilization Policy

This section provides a detailed analysis of the literature analysing the policy implications of the zero bound on nominal interest rates. There is a substantial body of work suggesting that if interest rates are constrained from falling, this may have a causal role in worsening economic conditions. A number of different mechanisms have been proposed in this regard. They hinge on the idea that the zero lower bound may interfere with an adjustment process that would otherwise ensure an efficient level of production. In particular, it may not be possible to provide individual consumers with the incentives to spend an adequate fraction of their current incomes. This will depress aggregate demand relative to the production capacity of the economy, as a decline in income becomes the only means for the economy to adjust to the low level of consumer spending. We will examine both the alternative mechanisms that have been identified as potential causes of depressed output, and the alternative policy options that are available for stimulating the economy in the face of these dynamics. Where possible, we try to frame the main contributions to the literature through the lens of the workhorse equation at the heart of modern dynamic macroeconomics, the consumption Euler equation. This is not intended as a particular endorsement of the Euler condition, whose empirical relevance has often been challenged.

It simply proves the easiest device for unifying and understanding the key theoretical contributions that have so far been made to the academic debate on post-crisis stabilization policy.

10.4.1   Savings Decisions and Nominal Interest Rates

We start, then, by revisiting the savings decision of a consumer in an environment where interest rates may be constrained by a zero bound. This is well summarized by the famous consumption Euler equation:

$$\frac{u'(C_t)}{p_t} = \beta_t (1 + i_t) \mathbb{E}_t \frac{u'(C_{t+1})}{p_{t+1}}, \tag{10.1}$$

where $u'(C_t)$ is the marginal subjective loss to the consumer at time t from reducing their period-t consumption, C_t, by a unit; p_t is the monetary price of a standardized unit of consumption in period t; i_t is the nominal interest rate that is paid on savings between t and $t + 1$; and β_t is the subjective discount factor that consumers attach to welfare in period $t + 1$ as distinct from period t.[12] If the consumer values current welfare more than future welfare, $\beta_t < 1$ will hold. The nominal interest rate is set by the central bank.

The theoretical literature on the zero bound generally studies stochastic economies that last for an indefinite amount of time, but the main distinctions among the different contributions can be well understood by placing alternative restrictions on this two-period condition.[13] To keep the discussion simple we can assume for now that the only source of aggregate demand in the economy is consumption – that is, investment, government spending and the trade balance are all zero. Under this assumption, and to the extent that (10.1) captures (if only in a stylized way) the process governing *aggregate* consumption choice in the economy, then we can rewrite the equation in terms of per-capita output, using the GDP identity that aggregate expenditure and aggregate income must be equal:

$$u'(Y_t) = \beta_t (1 + i_t) \mathbb{E}_t \frac{1}{1 + \pi_{t+1}} u'(Y_{t+1}) \tag{10.2}$$

where Y_t is realized per-capita output in period t, and π_{t+1} is inflation in period $t + 1$. Alongside the actual level of production Y_t, there is a 'full capacity' production level $\bar{Y}_t$, which would be obtained in the event that all productive resources in the economy were used efficiently. There is also an optimal level of inflation in each time period, which minimizes the distortions that are induced by price changes. We can treat this as fixed in all periods, equal to some value π^*. The exact process that determines inflation will depend on how the supply side of the economy is assumed to work; for now we remain agnostic on this.

Suppose first that there were no zero bound on the nominal interest rate. Absent any other complications, the policy problem in period t amounts to setting i_t so that the following equation is true:

$$u'\left(\bar{Y}_t\right) = \beta_t \left(1 + i_t\right) \mathbb{E}_t \frac{1}{1 + \pi_{t+1}} u'\left(Y_{t+1}\right). \tag{10.3}$$

That is, given what consumers expect to observe tomorrow in terms of inflation and output, and given the value of the discount factor β_t, the nominal interest rate should be set so that it is just optimal for consumers to want to spend $\bar{Y}_t$ in the current time period. Notice that the question of what exactly consumers expect in period $t + 1$ can largely be left to one side here. So long as inflation and output expectations do not depend significantly on the current choice of i_t, there will exist a current nominal interest rate that clears the market for goods – setting $C_t = \bar{Y}_t$.

The problem comes from the fact that this market-clearing nominal interest rate may be negative. This could happen for a number of different reasons, and policy conclusions hinge critically on the exact mechanism at work. A number of important disagreements in the literature rest on the precise causal mechanisms that are operational in Equation (10.2). We first follow the bulk of the New Keynesian literature, in assuming that the force driving the economy to the zero bound is an exogenous shock to the 'natural' real rate of interest that equilibrates the economy. Having outlined this device, we consider the main stabilization options that are available to address it. We then turn to alternative approaches for understanding the source of the zero bound problem.

10.4.2   Shocks to the 'Natural' Rate of Interest

The simplest analytical device for ensuring a zero bound is to assume that current consumers have an unusually high desire to save, for some subjective reason whose cause lies outside of the model.[14] Following the terminology of Woodford (2003), this is commonly referred to as a fall in the 'natural' interest rate that equilibrates the economy – that is, a fall in the real interest rate that would set aggregate savings equal to aggregate investment, in a world without any monetary imperfections.[15] The resulting policy problem involves important trade-offs that would be absent if the zero bound could be ignored, but these trade-offs are generated by factors (i.e., a forcing process) not directly explained by the model. This is to be distinguished from the possibility of an endogenous '*expectations trap*' with multiple equilibria, which we will discuss in more detail later.

In the present setting the 'exogenous shock' approach essentially means assuming the value of β_t – the intrinsic value placed on future welfare – is unusually high for a random length of time. This mode of analysis was first adopted by Eggertsson and Woodford (2003), in a major early contribution to the current literature. The influential papers by Eggertsson (2011), Christiano et al. (2011), Werning (2012), Wieland (2014) and Cochrane (2015) all follow such an approach, as does the work of Eggertsson et al. (2014) – which focuses specifically on the implications of proposed structural reforms in Europe when the zero bound is binding.

The basic argument starts from the observation that if β_t is sufficiently large, the following inequality can hold:

$$u'\left(\bar{Y}_t\right) < \beta_t \frac{1}{1+\pi^*} \mathbb{E}_t u'\left(\bar{Y}_{t+1}\right). \tag{10.4}$$

What this implies is that there cannot be a market equilibrium in which (a) output is equal to its efficient level in both t and $t + 1$, and (b) inflation is equal to the target value in $t + 1$. At least one of these desirable goals will have to be missed. The basic problem is that if consumers expect only modest future inflation and value the future highly, they will usually want to hold a sizeable share of their current earnings in cash. But this willingness to hold cash would constrain aggregate demand below productive capacity: unspent earnings imply unsold production. Some adjustment mechanism needs to overcome this demand deficiency.

The key question is whether the mechanism can be expected to operate through changes in prices – in particular the rate of inflation at $t + 1$ – or changes in current production. With the notable exception of Cochrane (2015), most papers in the literature treat the latter as a 'benchmark' case, in the absence of any active policy to the contrary. This relies on a view that once normal times return to an economy there need not be any effect of prior outcomes on current price-setting, and thus inflation at $t + 1$ should be fixed independently of whether a zero bound was encountered at t.

The implication of this is that the real interest rate on savings from t to $t + 1$ is fixed at $-\pi^*$. Consumers would remain too willing to save at this interest rate if pre-tax incomes were to equal $\bar{Y}_t$, meaning that the only way for current aggregate demand to equal output is for output to fall. The realized production level Y_t occurs where the Euler condition is satisfied with equality:

$$u'\left(Y_t\right) = \beta_t \frac{1}{1+\pi^*} \mathbb{E}_t u'\left(\bar{Y}_{t+1}\right). \tag{10.5}$$

Under the standard assumption of diminishing marginal utility, this equality will hold for $Y_t < \bar{Y}_t$. Thus there is a temporary recession that ensures the path of production mirrors the desired path for consumption: higher in the future than in the present. But this is not an optimal outcome as it comes at the cost of unrealized current production.

10.4.3   Forward Guidance as a Solution?

The focus of the literature is then on the policy options that might help mitigate the recession, as well as highlighting those that could unexpectedly do damage. An important starting point is that there does appear to be a relatively painless alternative to a current recession, namely a higher future inflation rate. The anticipation of this inflation should reduce the expected real returns to saving in zero-interest instruments, raising current demand. Policies that are found to be good potential stimulus devices often operate more or less explicitly through such a channel.

The most direct approach is for monetary policy explicitly to promise future inflation above target. The early work of Eggertsson and Woodford (2003) suggested that a central bank could reduce the output gap by several percentage points if it committed to holding interest rates low over an extended period of time *after* underlying economic conditions had recovered from the shock to savings. The widely-cited contribution by Werning (2012) also suggests such a strategy would be optimal. The approach has come to be known as '*forward guidance*', with Campbell et al. (2012) adding the adjective '*Odyssian*' to draw attention to the binds that are placed on the choices of the monetary authority in the future.[16] If there has been a consensus in the recent theoretical literature behind any form of policy innovation, it is not quantitative easing, structural reform, or fiscal stimulus, but this.

This begs the question why experiments with forward guidance have been much tamer than experiments with various forms of quantitative easing. A number of central banks have sought to do more to communicate a likely future path for policy – most notably in the cases of the Federal Reserve and Bank of England, both of which informed market participants to expect low rates until the unemployment rates in the US and UK respectively fell below critical thresholds. But none has gone so far as to make an explicit commitment for a rate of *inflation* above target for an extended period of time, even after recovery has taken hold. The unemployment thresholds used were 6.5 per cent in the US, and 7 per cent in the UK – both of which are still above standard estimates of the 'natural rate', or full employment conditions.

One explanation for the disparity between research and practice is that this sort of guidance is time-inconsistent. It requires the central bank to overshoot its inflation target *ex-post*, at a time when the economy may be operating close to full capacity. Since the benefits from acting in such a manner will already have accrued, the credibility of the plan is questionable.[17] Indeed, some policy-makers have gone so far as to suggest that their experiments with forward guidance should not be seen as binding. Speaking in December 2013, during the period when the Bank of England's forward guidance policy was in operation, one member of its Monetary Policy Committee (MPC) stated: 'I find it inconceivable that, without forward guidance, I, or any of my colleagues, would have already voted to raise Bank Rate and that the only thing that has stopped us is forward guidance.'[18] The strong implication is that past commitments are not to be treated as binding.

Another possibility, noted by Campbell et al. (2012), is that to promise high future inflation would violate formal price stability mandates. Indeed, the same policy-maker, Martin Weale, noted that the MPC had been 'keen to implement forward guidance *in a way which did not take risks with inflation expectations*".[19] Yet to do so is to undermine the most important mechanism through which the strategy is predicted to work. In this regard it seems that the pre-crisis consensus in favour of inflation targeting has itself generated an institutional bias that prevents more effective stimulus. With the notable exception of the Federal Reserve, most independent central banks have some form of price stability objective as their primary delegated goal; this is true of all states within the EU. The most influential justification for granting independence to monetary policy-makers is, in turn, that doing so ensures a credible commitment to inflation stability. Allowing central banks actively to use inflation as a stabilization tool is not easy to square with an inflation-fighting mandate, and no doubt many central bankers would find it hard to justify to themselves.

From a theoretical perspective, however, it seems important for the literature to take a more practical turn. If legal constraints do indeed rule out inflation promises as stimulus devices, are there other sorts of guidance that could be useful at the zero bound? How far do the potential gains from forward guidance *rely* on the ability of policy-makers to increase inflation expectations? What are the implications for the economy if and when forward guidance is misinterpreted? It would be a shame if a form of intervention that receives wide support among academic macroeconomists were to be discarded because the gap between theoretical assumptions and practical constraints could not be bridged.

A particularly understudied question theoretically is how gains could best be achieved from state-contingent forward guidance – that is, linking nominal interest rates to observed economic outcomes. This is despite the experiments that have been taken with such an approach, and the attention that it has received in policy discussions.[20] Campbell et al. (2012) provide the most detailed analytical investigation. They consider the economic implications of unemployment-contingent rate increases, of the form tried by the Bank of England and the Federal Reserve. Yet their choice both of thresholds and of critical values was relatively arbitrary: why the unemployment rate, and why 6.5 or 7 per cent? In the event the recovery in unemployment in both the US and the UK has been far stronger than the recovery in real output, and this has meant the attempted guidance has proved redundant. It is clear that further experiments with the approach will be limited unless a more coherent case can be made in favour of specific, implementable rules, and this should be a focus of the literature.

An alternative to state-contingent forward guidance is to promise that nominal interest rates will remain at a specified level over a specified period of time – an approach the Federal Reserve experimented with in 2011 and 2012. Yet as Woodford (2012) has argued, a risk associated with this is that it may be misinterpreted by market participants as a signal that the central bank is more pessimistic about the future evolution of the economy than previously believed. This may in turn induce greater uncertainty about the variables that matter – output and employment – than in the absence of such 'guidance'. The more uncertain is future income, the higher are the marginal benefits from saving, and the natural rate shock is exacerbated rather than mitigated.[21] Practical measures for ensuring guidance operates as intended ought to be a focal point for future research.[22]

An issue of specific relevance to the Eurozone is the interaction between exchange rate policy and the effects of forward guidance. Corsetti et al. (2011) and Cook and Devereux (2014) have drawn attention to the similarities between the role played by future rate commitments in the canonical Eggertsson-Woodford framework, and the impact on future price expectations of membership of a currency union. Suppose that a small, open economy were to be affected by a negative natural rate shock, of the sort discussed above. So long as demand remains suppressed, the likely effect of this shock is to keep domestic inflation below levels elsewhere. If the country is a member of a currency union, however, the gradual effect of low *current* inflation is to raise consumer beliefs about the rate of price growth that must obtain when normal times return – and domestic prices return closer to the levels of other countries within the union. This high expected price growth is precisely what forward guidance in a closed economy is seeking to engineer. Thus in theory a commitment to be – and remain – a member of a currency union should help in placing a limit on the deflationary consequences of negative natural rate shocks. Of course, an obvious question raised by this research is why southern countries in the Eurozone, in particular Greece, do not appear to have benefitted from this automatic cushion. A likely possibility is that Greece was widely perceived to have had an overvalued real exchange rate prior to the crisis, and thus consumer expectations are far from the point where relatively high inflation is seen as a likely consequence of continued membership of the currency area – quite the opposite.

We end the discussion of forward guidance on a more cautionary note, which has been sounded by the recent work of McKay et al. (2015). These authors emphasize that the overwhelming share of research advocating forward guidance as a normative option has been conducted in New Keynesian models, assuming that financial markets are complete and households are perfectly able to insure themselves against future income shocks. McKay et al. (2015) instead assume that households face uninsurable, idiosyncratic income risk (the income risk associated with unemployment, for instance), together with credit constraints that limit their capacity to borrow. In such an environment, long-run promises about the level of nominal interest rates once normal times return are dominated by short-run fears about income risk.

More specifically, McKay et al. (2015) show that the usual mechanism by which the economy responds to forward guidance in a complete markets New Keynesian setting is through a reduction in household savings as confidence in the future grows. When there is idiosyncratic income risk, however, the scope for this to happen is more muted. In terms of the Euler condition (10.5), at the household level earnings in $t + 1$ are substantially more variable than aggregate income, Y_{t+1}. This variability gives households an incentive to retain a '*buffer stock*' of savings, which they can run down in the event that they are unfortunate enough to draw a low income shock in the future. The sensitivity of this buffer stock to promised changes in future nominal interest rates is generally quite low, and this reduces the scope for forward guidance to work.

It should be stressed that these results remain contingent on the particular experiment considered by McKay et al. (2015). In particular, their paper does not attempt to analyse an *optimal* forward guidance strategy in the manner of Eggertsson and Woodford (2003) or Werning (2012). Thus it is possible that more effective stabilization could be achieved by a policy better tailored to the circumstances. Overall, forward guidance remains the 'ideal' strategy for addressing natural rate shocks in the literature, but it remains an open question whether – and how best – its gains can be obtained through clear, practicable policy rules.[23]

10.4.4   Fiscal Stimulus as a Solution?

The other major policy option at the zero bound that is given emphasis in the theoretical literature is fiscal stimulus. Numerous papers have shown that the multipliers associated with increased government spending are potentially much larger when the zero bound is binding than during normal times. Eggertsson (2011), for instance, found that if the fraction of government spending in GDP were increased by 1 percentage point, GDP would rise by 2.3 per cent. Similar results go through in the influential paper by Christiano et al. (2011), and Coenen et al. (2012) confirm the point in a meta-analysis of seven influential macroeconomic models, including the ECB's NAWM model and a version of Smets and Wouters (2007). Importantly, all of the main contributions that take shocks to desired savings as their starting point find that multipliers are substantially higher when the zero bound binds than when it does not.[24]

What exactly is the mechanism at work here? Again it is useful to start from the consumption Euler equation, augmented now for the fact that we must allow for government spending to be a feature of the economy – consuming some of the final output good. This implies that consumption will equal output less government spending: $C_t = Y_t - G_t$. Unlike the simpler exposition of forward guidance, we will also now assume that the economy will only recover from the savings 'shock' in $t + 1$ with some positive probability. Thus it is possible that the economy will remain at the zero bound in the future, and be faced with the same policy dilemmas. Policy decisions made today may be mirrored in the future, if the 'state of the world' remains bad.

When nominal interest rates are zero the Euler condition will now read:

$$u'(Y_t - G_t) = \beta_t \mathbb{E}_t \frac{1}{1 + \pi_{t+1}} u'(Y_{t+1} - G_{t+1}). \tag{10.6}$$

The basic argument for the effectiveness of fiscal stimulus runs as follows. Suppose that government spending, G, were increased both in period t and in all 'bad' states of the world in $t + 1$ – that is, those for which the zero bound remained binding. If consumers' savings rates have returned to normal by $t + 1$, so can government spending.[25] The central policy problem is that when the zero bound binds, output is below capacity. It follows that it should be *technologically* possible to raise Y_t one-for-one with G_t, at least for low enough increases in government spending, keeping C_t constant throughout. Simple resource feasibility is not an issue if demand starts out below productive capacity.

Suppose a joint increase in G_t and Y_t of this kind were to happen. If inflation at $t + 1$, π_{t+1}, were to remain unaffected across all states of nature, then by construction Equation (10.6) would remain satisfied. Thus we would have constructed an alternative feasible equilibrium, with aggregate consumption unchanged, but higher output and higher government spending. Whether this is a desirable change ultimately depends on whether consumers value the extra government spending more than the extra resources that are used to produce it. Presumably this is more likely to be true if the higher total output comes from employing workers who would otherwise lack jobs, but in any event it is not a given. Notice that the government expenditure multiplier, $\frac{dY_t}{dG_t}$ would be exactly one in these circumstances.

What Eggertsson (2011), Christiano et al. (2011) and others *additionally* show, however, is that there will be a beneficial pricing effect from the fiscal expansion. Higher government spending implies higher output, and this in turn puts some upward pressure on firm costs: the labour market will become tighter, for instance, increasing real wages relative to their level without the fiscal expansion. These higher costs will be passed through to consumer prices, meaning that inflation will be higher with the fiscal expansion than without it. Since the higher public spending is expected to last into $t + 1$ with some probability – whenever desired savings remain high – the result is a higher ex-ante expected value for inflation at $t + 1$. This reduces the real interest rate in period t, meaning C_t will also rise, and Y_t will increase still further with it. Symmetrically, higher expected consumption can be expected in 'bad' states at $t + 1$, and this further reduces the benefits from saving in t: in mathematical terms, the value of $u'(C_{t+1})$ is no longer so high in expectation. This feeds back into still more consumption and output in period t. The overall consequence is a multiplier, $\frac{dY_t}{dG_t}$, that is significantly greater than one. It is not just employment and public consumption that rise – private consumption does so too.

An important lesson from this is that the theoretical case for high multipliers at the zero bound – that is, multipliers in excess of one – relies on an inflation expectations channel. Without the effect of higher G_{t+1} on π_{t+1}, a rise in G_t could increase Y_t but not C_t – at least in our basic setting. Yet large fiscal stimulus packages seem a very blunt instrument for increasing inflation expectations. It may be the case that *conditional on underemployment*, resources are better used by the public sector than standing idle, but this seems too readily to give up on the idea that output could be restored to the level of productive capacity by other means.[26] Given that the political direction of travel in EU states at present seems to be towards reduced fiscal deficits, the headline results on the multiplier – though important – have perhaps attracted more attention than is now warranted.

Fiscal Stimulus in Stressed Economies

Indeed, a number of authors have highlighted that the benefits to fiscal expansion could easily be undone if the fiscal solvency of the government comes to be questioned – an issue that is of obvious relevance to southern European countries at present. The paper by Corsetti et al. (2013) explores theoretical mechanisms that would generate a spread between the nominal interest rate set by the central bank and the nominal rate that is of relevance to consumer saving and borrowing decisions. Their framework allows for multiple countries and multiple consumers, some of whom borrow and some save.[27] But the essential point can again be made by reference to the Euler equation. The nominal interest rate faced by consumers is now $i_t^c = i_t + \omega_t$, where i_t is again the central bank rate and ω_t measures the period-t interest rate spread. This spread is in turn assumed to depend positively on the size of the fiscal deficit: higher deficits raise the interest rate spread, and the marginal effect of the current deficit on the spread is in turn increasing in the existing size of outstanding government debt. Returning to the Euler condition, and assuming that the central bank's interest rate is zero, we will have:

$$u'(Y_t - G_t) = \beta_t \mathbb{E}_t \frac{1 + \omega_t (G_t - \tau Y_t)}{1 + \pi_{t+1}} u'(Y_{t+1} - G_{t+1}), \qquad (10.7)$$

where τ is a marginal income tax rate, capturing the idea that the total fiscal deficit, $G_t - \tau Y_t$, will tend to rise in recessions due to a fall in tax collection.

If the effect of a higher government deficit on ω_t exceeds the effect on future inflation expectations, π_{t+1}, higher government spending will tend to raise real interest rates at the zero bound rather than lower them. This in turn will feed back into a multiplier that is lower than one: C_t falls when G_t rises. This can rationalize the notion that countries whose fiscal position is initially strong will benefit from government spending at the zero bound, but countries where the deficit starts at a high level could do better from budgetary discipline instead.

What Corsetti et al. (2013) additionally show is that this sort of framework is conducive to multiple equilibria. Suppose there is a bout of pessimism regarding the future level of output, Y_{t+1}, in 'bad' states at $t + 1$. In general this should raise the incentives to save in period t, contracting aggregate demand and thus output, Y_t. Lower output, in turn, implies lower tax revenue, and a higher current budget deficit. This raises the spread, contracting Y_t still further. If this effect is sufficiently large, the lower level of output can be supported as an equilibrium in all 'bad' states of the world, now and in the future, and this justifies the initial pessimism.

An implication of this logic is that there may be a case for asymmetries across countries in the cyclical properties of fiscal policy. Those that start with a high level of debt are likely to see more responsiveness of interest-rate spreads to the current budget deficit. Other things being equal, they will therefore be more susceptible to self-fulfilling pessimism bouts. Those countries that start with low levels of debt, by contrast, will be far less vulnerable: ω_t will respond only slightly to a recession-induced reduction in tax revenues. Thus high-debt economies will be better advised to follow pro-cyclical fiscal policies, contracting spending as the economy shrinks, and thereby mitigating the impact of the recession on spreads. Low-debt economies, by contrast, will benefit from the more conventional expansionary effects of fiscal expenditure at the zero bound analysed by Eggertsson (2011), Christiano et al. (2011) and others.

Corsetti et al. (2013) calibrate their model to the Eurozone economy in 2012, divided into two regions: '*stressed economies*' (Cyprus, Greece, Ireland, Italy, Portugal, Slovenia and Spain), and others. Their results confirm that procyclical fiscal policy for the stressed economies, and countercyclical for the rest, should indeed be sufficient to avoid self-fulfilling bouts of pessimism.

Fiscal Stimulus, Tax Evasion and Corruption

Recent work by Pappa et al. (2015) has considered a further practical dimension to the use of fiscal policy from the perspective of southern European countries. This is how best to choose among different fiscal instruments in economies that are subject to widespread tax evasion. This question is particularly relevant to

Greece and Italy: the shadow economy exceeded 25 per cent of GDP on average in both of these countries from 1999 to 2010,[28] whilst the modalities of fiscal consolidation remain an important issue for both. To what extent should the scope for (a) tax evasion and (b) corruption in the public sector influence the optimal balance to strike between achieving consolidation through tax increases and through government spending cuts?

Pappa et al. (2015) start by presenting empirical evidence that economies with high levels of corruption and tax evasion appear to differ in their responses to tax increases and expenditure cuts, relative to other economies of a comparable size. Tax increases in particular seem to be associated with higher output losses when corruption and tax evasion are high. Italian data on employment in the informal sector additionally indicate that there are important reallocation effects of fiscal policy, with more workers being driven into the '*black economy*' the higher income taxes are.

The authors then construct a theoretical model to rationalize these effects. In their setting, higher taxes have larger negative effects on productivity when evasion is high, because higher evasion implies that an ever-larger burden of any consolidation must fall on the subset of workers that have chosen not to evade taxes. Those in the official sector thus face large tax disincentives to work, and this only serves to increase further the relative merits from working in the informal sector instead – by assumption at a lower level of efficiency. Spending cuts, by contrast, allow for lower taxes that raise consumers' disposable income, and this increases production and employment in the official sector. The presence of corruption in the government expenditure process reinforces the relative merits of expenditure reductions. The multipliers associated with tax-based consolidations are thus far larger than spending-based consolidations.

Of course, these results raise the question of whether tax evasion and corruption ought to be treated as fixed features of the economic landscape, or outcomes that policy has the scope to change. At the time of writing, heavy emphasis is being given to the importance of reducing tax evasion as a means to remedy Greece's fiscal difficulties. There remains an important gap in the macroeconomic literature for thinking through the implications of this for the wider economy. A further issue, central to our wider discussion, is that the analysis of Pappa et al. (2015) does not incorporate a zero lower bound on nominal interest rates. As discussed below, Eggertsson (2011) and Eggertsson et al. (2014) have shown that 'conventional' results about the efficacy of different stimulus instruments can fail to go through at the zero bound, due to the perverse implications that they can have for inflation expectations. Similar logic may well apply in the setting that Pappa et al. (2015) adopt, in which case tax increases may not be so detrimental in the short run. This would be a useful area for further work to explore.

Government Expenditure or Taxation as an Instrument?

Returning to the specific problem of providing stimulus at the zero bound, an insightful paper by Correia et al. (2013) suggests an alternative stimulus strategy to the use of headline government spending, based on manipulating consumption taxation. Their main argument relies on the observation that if consumer goods are taxed at proportional rate τ_t^c in period t, the inflation rate in $t + 1$ will satisfy the following relationship:

$$(1 + \pi_{t+1}) = \frac{1 + \tau_{t+1}^c}{1 + \tau_t^c} (1 + \hat{\pi}_{t+1}), \tag{10.8}$$

where $\hat{\pi}_{t+1}$ is the rate of inflation in pre-tax prices. If the concern is that inflation in period $t + 1$ is too low to incentivize consumption at t, an obvious strategy is to raise τ_{t+1}^c relative to τ_t^c. This strategy for escaping a liquidity trap had been previously advocated by Feldstein (2002) for the Japanese case. The contribution of Correia et al. (2013) has been to clarify that the policy can go all the way to eliminating the problems caused by the zero bound, provided there are appropriate offsetting changes in other tax instruments. Most notably this means a cut in the labour income tax rate, so that the overall tax burden on workers is unaffected. Importantly, an appropriately-designed policy of this form can be revenue-neutral – the cuts to the labour income tax and the increase in the sales tax offset one another. This seems a substantial advantage in the current European context.

Yet it is vital to this argument that the correct tax instruments should be chosen, with the explicit aim in mind of generating future inflation so as to stimulate current demand. When taxation is used imprudently as a stimulus device, it could have very detrimental consequences – a point highlighted by Eggertsson (2011). Suppose that a government were to try to conduct fiscal stimulus by cutting the marginal tax rate on labour income, in an economy constrained by the zero bound and a high desire to save. The main consequences can again be understood through the Euler condition. For simplicity we can now revert to ignoring government spending in this condition, giving:

$$u'(Y_t) = \beta_t \mathbb{E}_t \frac{1}{1 + \pi_{t+1}} u'(Y_{t+1}). \tag{10.9}$$

Suppose that the income tax rate were to be reduced in period t, and in all 'bad' states of the world in $t + 1$ – symmetrically to the analysis of higher government spending above. In 'good' states at $t + 1$ outcomes would remain essentially unaffected: there is no change to the income tax rate, and desired savings are sufficiently low to keep the economy away from the zero bound. But in 'bad' states – where the desire to save remains high – the incentives for would-be workers to seek employment are higher than they would be without the tax cut. This is likely to put downward pressure on the real wage: the lower the marginal tax rate, the lower the pre-tax wage that workers will be willing to work for. If the real wage is lower, this will reduce firms' costs, which in turn should put downward pressure on inflation. This will increase the real returns to holding cash in period t, further contracting aggregate demand so long as β_t remains high.

Again, therefore, any programme for engineering a stimulus when interest rates are at the zero bound must be designed with proper regard to its effects on the real interest rate. Tax cuts that may well be expected to stimulate the economy in normal times could have the opposite effect at the zero bound. It would be particularly harmful, for instance, for policy-makers to take from the Correia et al. (2013) paper the idea that labour taxes should be cut relative to consumption taxes, but to believe that this could be done by cutting labour taxes up front, and waiting until a recovery has 'taken hold' before introducing the offsetting consumption tax increases. At the zero bound, stimulus comes from engineering increases in inflation expectations, and a credible promise that consumption taxes are on the rise can be a very expansionary device.

Transfers or Government Purchases?

An important feature of the 'headline' studies of fiscal multipliers conducted by Eggertsson (2011), Christiano et al. (2011) and others is that government expenditure increases are modelled as increases in government purchases of final goods. Expansionary fiscal policy thus consists of classic 'public works' style projects, directly responsible for generating employment. Yet, as Oh and Reis (2012) have argued, the large wave of fiscal stimulus packages that were rolled out across OECD countries between 2007 and 2009 were dominated by increases in targeted transfers – these comprised 64 per cent of the increase in expenditure in the median case. A large body of empirical work has documented evidence that suggests fiscal multipliers and marginal propensities to consume out of such transfers are large, but the theoretical literature is only gradually providing ways to model this process satisfactorily. The interaction between transfer policy and the zero bound remains particularly understudied.

Recent empirical work provides a strong motivation for more theoretical analysis of the decisions of illiquid households in particular. Studies of the US fiscal stimulus payment episodes of 2001 and 2008 suggest not only that, overall, households spend a non-negligible share of a cash transfer on nondurable goods, but there is significant heterogeneity in consumption responses due to differences in wealth liquidity and the degree of indebtedness of homeowners. Misra and Surico (2014), for instance, find a large propensity to consume out of the US tax rebates among homeowners with high mortgage debt. More generally, the evidence points to large consumption responses from transfer payments. In their study of the 2001 tax rebate, Johnson et al. (2005) estimate the cumulative change in expenditures on nondurable goods during the quarter of the tax rebate and the subsequent three-month period to be roughly 70 per cent of the amount rebated. Between 20 and 40 per cent of the rebate is spent in the quarter when funds are received. In regard to the 2008 episode, Parker et al. (2013) and Broda and Parker (2014) find that the share of the stimulus payment spent on nondurable goods is large in the quarter in which it is paid out, in line with the estimates for the 2001 stimulus. Furthermore, there is also a significant increase in spending on durable goods.

This US evidence is consistent with analyses of European data – where again there appear important interaction effects with the degree of household liquidity. For instance, Jappelli and Pistaferri (2014) find that the MPC out of rebate cheques in Italy is 0.65 for the lowest cash-on-hand households, and 0.30 for the highest.

The basic difficulty in incorporating these sorts of effects in a theoretical model is that for transfers to have a significant impact, there must be some device for overcoming Ricardian equivalence. In any representative-agent macroeconomic model, higher government transfers to consumers today will raise their tax liabilities in the future, so that total wealth is left unaffected – as are broader economic outcomes. The theoretical research agenda has thus increasingly focused on environments with multiple types of consumers, usually with a subset facing a liquidity restriction of some kind. Transfers can enhance the liquidity of constrained households, and this raises overall aggregate demand. This is the approach taken by Oh and Reis (2012), who argue that transfers operate through two distinct channels. The first, which they label a 'neoclassical' channel, is due to the fact that higher transfers imply a redistribution away from more productive workers. This generates a negative income effect, raising the willingness of more productive agents to work, which in turn raises output. The second channel is a 'Keynesian' one. Transfers tend to redistribute income from wealthier individuals, whose marginal propensity to save is high, to poorer individuals, whose marginal propensity to save is low. The overall effect is that aggregate willingness to save falls, and aggregate demand is increased. In terms of the discussion above, it is as if the natural rate of interest has increased.

Oh and Reis (2012) thus show that higher targeted transfers can increase private consumption and investment, but they ultimately struggle to generate a fiscal multiplier of the same order of magnitude to those obtained by Eggertsson (2011) and Christiano et al. (2011): they obtain an overall increase in GDP of $0.06 for every dollar increase in transfers. Yet they do not consider the possibility that aggregate output could be inefficiently low due to the zero bound, and given the nature of their 'Keynesian' effect this seems an important extra dimension to consider. When the basic stabilization problem is that the natural rate is too low, transfers ought to be an effective policy device for increasing it.

Another perspective on the transfer issue is provided by Kaplan and Violante (2014). These authors are motivated by the fact that the increases in household consumption observed in response to fiscal stimulus packages are too widespread to be accounted for by the relatively small fraction of low-wealth consumers that are conventionally assumed to be liquidity-constrained in heterogeneous-agent consumption analyses.[29] In their setting, households with a large fraction of their wealth in illiquid assets (such as housing) are labelled '*wealthy hand-to-mouth*': though their wealth is significant, its illiquidity stops the households from using it to smooth their consumption response to economic shocks such as unexpected job loss. Using data from the Survey of Consumer Finances, Kaplan and Violante (2014) document that these households are substantial in number, and their consumption indeed responds significantly to transitory income shocks – their focus being on the 2001 US tax rebates. Again, this was not a period in which the zero bound was binding, and the authors do not consider its potential role in the response of consumption to transfer spending.

Related evidence is provided by Surico and Trezzi (2015), who exploit the unexpected redesign of the municipal tax on residential and nonresidential properties in Italy at the peak of the Sovereign risk crisis (the 'IMU' tax) as an effective increase in transfers *away* from households. They find an average 25-cent reduction in spending per euro of tax increase overall, but with vast differences across groups with different degrees of wealth liquidity. The consumption of owner occupiers with a mortgage and just one residential property dropped by 90 per cent of the tax. The effects on richer households – real estate owners with multiple properties – were instead negligible.

10.4.5 Central Bank Asset Purchases as a Solution?

The policy area that has arguably seen the most innovation since the crisis is the use of large-scale asset purchases, both by central banks and national governments, to try to influence macroeconomic outcomes. This has taken two forms. First, central banks have experimented with '*quantitative easing*' as a substitute for cuts to nominal interest rates once the zero bound has been reached. This was the justification for the European Central Bank's decision to embark on a programme of asset purchases in January 2015, mirroring earlier programmes by the Federal Reserve and Bank of England. Second, governments and central banks have shown willingness to buy up problem assets, in attempts to calm erratic movements in financial markets – sometimes known as '*credit easing*'. This was the reasoning behind the ECB's Outright Monetary Transactions programme, announced in August 2012, as well as the US government's $700 billion Troubled Asset Relief Programme of 2008. The main distinction between the two approaches is that the first is perceived to be effective even when the assets purchased are widely perceived to be risk free – effects come from the expansion of the central bank's balance sheet *per se* – whereas the second is specifically targeted at problems associated with risky debt. We will consider both in turn.

Quantitative Easing

What is most remarkable about the widespread experiments with '*quantitative easing*' is the absence of a widely-agreed-upon mechanism through which such a policy should work. Woodford (2012) provides a useful discussion of the main candidates. These are, first, that an expansion of the central bank balance sheet is equivalent to an increase in the money supply, and a higher money supply should – according to various versions of the traditional quantity theory – stimulate an increase in nominal expenditure in the economy, and hence inflation. Higher expected future inflation reduces the current real interest rate, stimulating spending. Second, there is the possibility of a so-called '*portfolio balance effect*'. If central banks purchase large quantities of long-term assets, issuing short-term debt (or money) as a counterpart, the relative scarcity of long-term assets should drive up their price. This lowers the long-term interest rate even whilst the short-term rate is stuck at zero, potentially stimulating investment and current consumption.[30]

Yet both of these arguments encounter conceptual difficulties. The problem with the quantity theory channel is that it is unclear why raising the supply of one zero-interest asset (money) whilst contracting that of another (nominal bonds, which pay $i_t = 0$ when the zero bound binds) should make any difference to the economic decisions of consumers. The textbook case for a higher money supply raising the price level relies on the idea that consumers wish to hold money only for short-term, transaction purposes. This is because in normal times bonds dominate money in rate of return. Any increase in the money supply can only be absorbed if there is an increase in the demand for money for transaction purposes, and this can occur through an increase in the price level. But if money and bonds are paying an equivalent rate of return, the logic breaks down. A higher supply of money can be absorbed without requiring an increase in transactions demand. This is precisely the case when the zero bound binds. It follows that there need not be any direct pass-through from the money supply to the price level.

The difficulty with the portfolio balance channel comes when trying to square it with modern asset pricing theory, as applied in macroeconomics. Since Lucas (1978) the conventional approach has been to treat financial assets as claims on future consumption, priced according to the present value of this consumption in terms of some numeraire. This delivers asset pricing formulae in which values reflect market outcomes, but do not have a significant role in determining them. The price of long-term assets falls in recessions, for instance, because demand for future consumption is low relative to current consumption. But these demand patterns follow from production and preference patterns in the real economy, not asset market developments. The result is that the value of any given asset can be determined without knowing its overall net supply. In other words, demand is perfectly elastic. It follows from this that any active intervention to change the relative supplies of short-term and long-term assets ought not to change their prices, nor have any significant impact on overall economic allocations. Wallace (1981) was the first to show the irrelevance of the central bank balance sheet as an instrument in such circumstances.

It should be stressed that this is a far more contingent argument than the case against a quantity theory channel, as it relies on the particular conclusion that the demand for assets should be perfectly elastic. This is a property that is common to all models in which financial markets are 'complete', in the sense that all conceivable gains from financial trade are being realized – a convenient assumption for modelling purposes, but hardly a realistic one. A number of authors have therefore built models in which large-scale asset purchases have an impact because of limitations on the set of trades available to consumers and/or financial firms. These can deliver some successes in linking the price of long-term assets to their relative supply. Chen et al. (2012), for instance, explore a setting in which different households face differing restrictions on their capacity to purchase long- and short-term bonds. A contraction in the supply of long-term assets causes a reduction in an assumed 'transaction premium' associated with purchasing long-term assets, driving up their price. This lowers the long-term real interest rate. When estimated on US data, they show that the model is capable of delivering some impact on the real economy from large-scale asset purchases, but of a relatively small magnitude. Expanding the Federal Reserve's balance sheet by $600 billion should, according to their formulation, have less of an effect on the US economy than a 25 basis point cut in the short-term nominal interest rate (were this available).

Similar stories based on segmentation of the markets for long- and short-term assets are explored in Vayanos and Vila (2009), Harrison (2011), Harrison (2012), and Ellison and Tischbirek (2014). Yet there remains no widely-accepted conceptual approach for understanding why a portfolio balance effect might deliver meaningful stimulus. Woodford (2012) concluded that such a mechanism could *conceivably* be a way for central bank asset purchases to affect the real economy, but that this does not follow from 'hypotheses that seem likely to be true'. A number of empirical papers have nonetheless found apparent effects of the US and UK quantitative easing programmes on the respective countries' term premia – suggesting that there is some pass-through from central bank actions to prices in practice.[31] There is a real gap in the policy literature for a model that can rationalize this on the basis of more appealing hypotheses about the functioning of financial markets.

There is a final transmission mechanism for quantitative easing that gains significant support in the empirical literature. This is the so-called '*signalling channel*', by which large-scale asset purchases are found to reduce expected future short-term interest rates. Work by Krishnamurthy and Vissing-Jorgensen (2011), Christensen and Rudebusch (2012), Bauer and Rudebusch (2014) and Lloyd (2015) all find significant evidence of these expectational changes, with Lloyd (2015) attributing 70 per cent of the fluctuations in yield on announcement days to signalling.

It is straightforward to tell a heuristic story that captures this result. Since the work of Clarida et al. (2000), numerous researchers have observed persistence in the nominal interest rates chosen by central banks, in the sense that the interest rate in period t, i_t, satisfies a relationship of the form:

$$i_t = \rho i_{t-1} + (1 - \rho) i_t^*, \tag{10.10}$$

where i_t^* can be thought of as an optimal nominal rate given current economic conditions alone, and ρ is a parameter between 0 and 1. What this means is that whenever ρ is positive, any reduction to nominal interest rates today will imply lower expectations for nominal interest rates over the immediate future – since future policy-makers will inherit a lower lagged rate.

Suppose now that the nominal interest rate reaches the zero bound, so that the central bank is constrained from setting the negative nominal rate that it would ideally like. It may be that it is nonetheless able to convey a signal about its desired rate to market participants through its asset purchase policy. Market participants will infer that the desired nominal interest rate is lower, the larger the asset purchase programme is. If a recursion of the form (10.10) applies not just to the actual rate when the zero bound does not bind, but also to the desired rate when it does, any decision to embark on quantitative easing (QE) provides a signal for the market that desired rates have fallen, and thus to expect the desired short-term rate to remain low for longer. This lengthens the period of time over which rates can be expected to remain at zero, delivering the sort of expectational stimulus implied by forward guidance.

In more practical terms, by taking a decision to embark on an asset purchase programme the central bank generally ensures that the next meeting of its rate-setting committee will debate whether or not to continue with that programme, rather than whether or not to increase nominal interest rates. Policy rates thus remain near zero for longer.

Whether this or some other story best captures the exact dynamic, the very fact that QE may operate principally through a signalling channel is troubling. As Woodford (2012) notes, 'the signal would seem more likely to have the desired effect if accompanied by explicit forward guidance, rather than regarded as a substitute for it'. The balance sheet of the ECB is increasing at a rate of €60 billion per month at the time of writing, as a consequence of the quantitative easing programme announced in January 2015. If the principal mechanism by which this will have an impact on the economy is by reducing expectations of future policy rates, there seem far more direct means to the same end – namely forward guidance.

Credit Easing

The alternative form for large-scale asset purchases to take is so-called '*credit easing*', whereby the government or central bank purchases private-sector securities from markets that are widely considered to be malfunctioning. An example from the recent crisis is the Federal Reserve's Term Asset-Backed Securities Loan Facility (TALF), launched in November 2008, under which the US central bank purchased $71 billion-worth of private-sector securities backed by small business loans, automobile loans, credit card loans and similar. These actions reflected fears of substantial liquidity problems in markets for asset-backed securities following the subprime crisis and collapse of Lehman Brothers. The ECB's Securities Markets Programme (SMP), launched in May 2010, was motivated by similar concerns, though it also allowed for the purchase of public-sector debt as part of its remit.

Unlike quantitative easing, the purpose of these interventions was not to substitute for broader monetary policy operations at the zero bound, but rather to intervene in markets that were suffering from specific malfunctionings. In this regard they could be viewed as following the famous prescription of Bagehot (1873), who advocated central bank assistance to private-sector banks that were illiquid but not insolvent. The twist was that entire markets were perceived to be facing liquidity problems – not just individual institutions.

On one level this could be seen as the 'microeconomic' functioning of the central bank, and thus of little relevance to stabilization policy. But when impaired credit markets are affecting funding conditions for a large share of potential investment projects in the economy, it is clear that there could be wider macroeconomic effects. Gertler and Karadi (2011) consider just such a case. They assume that there are frictions in the private provision of credit to productive investment projects, driven by the fact that financial intermediaries are limited in the leverage positions that they are able to take.[32] This means a large spread can exist between the interest rate paid to households on deposits and the interest rate at which investors are able to obtain funding for projects. The larger this spread, the more productive investment projects are inefficiently curtailed through lack of funding – despite the fact that their expected returns exceed the interest rate households are willing to accept on their savings.

Direct intervention by the central bank can reduce this friction. If the monetary authority promises to conduct direct purchases of asset-backed securities issued by financial intermediaries, it ensures banks have an incentive to create more new loans at the margin: they now know that these loans need not enter on to their balance sheets, and so will not cause them any difficulties with the maximum leverage ratio. Gertler and Karadi (2011) consider a scenario in which the net worth of financial intermediaries is negatively affected by an exogenous reduction in the quality of the assets they hold, providing them with a need to reduce leverage and restrict loans – an attempt to capture the main features of the subprime crisis. They show that an aggressive policy of credit easing by the central bank is capable of substantially reducing the depth of the associated recession.

One advantage of this policy is that it is not impeded by the zero bound constraint. The higher the price that the central bank pays to buy loans securitized by private-sector banks, the lower the nominal interest rate faced by borrowers. There is no economic reason why the interest rate for borrowers need not turn negative. As discussed above, difficulties come when *savers* face a negative rate, and instead switch to holding cash. The central bank may be losing money on asset holdings that pay a negative nominal return, but this could simply be understood as the price of more effective stabilization. Provided the central bank is only willing to purchase securities backed by real investment projects, the scope for arbitrage should be limited.

Yet Gertler and Karadi's mechanism has received some criticism, since it implicitly grants the central bank greater technological capacity to operate in financial markets than the private sector. The essential point is the following: why should leverage restrictions constrain the ability of private banks to channel funding to borrowers, but not the central bank?[33] Ongoing work by Gaballo and Marimon (2015) explores a channel through which credit easing can have an effect without relying on asymmetries of this form – operating instead through the impact of policy on information about investment conditions.[34] Their framework is one in which firms have a choice between risky and safe investment projects. Because of limited liability, the relative benefits of risky investment increase in the interest rate that banks charge firms. Intuitively, when required repayments are high, it is better to gamble on a high return than to obtain a near-zero profit margin for sure. But the interest rate that banks charge firms to borrow is, in turn, increasing in the perceived riskiness of the investment projects that the firms will embark upon.

Gaballo and Marimon (2015) show that this setting is consistent with the existence of a '*self-confirming*' equilibrium, in which investment is inefficiently risky and output inefficiently low. Banks observe that the typical investment projects undertaken in the economy are risky, and for this reason they only offer high interest rates to borrowers. Borrowers respond to this by selecting riskier projects. A central bank policy of credit easing can '*break the spell*' by making banks willing to offer (and sell on to the monetary authority) lower-cost loans, which in turn incentivize investing firms to embark on safer projects. According to this theory, the role of credit easing is to provide an informational benefit to the wider market, demonstrating that low-cost loans can indeed be profitable. The private sector lacks the incentives to carry out similar experimentation with low-cost lending given competition in the banking sector, because a successful innovation in lending behaviour will soon be mimicked by rival firms, reducing the profits it delivers. Gaballo and Marimon argue that this mechanism can account for the successes of the TALF in the US. What remains unclear is how far the gains from such a policy are a '*one-off*' benefit from credit easing, or whether they could provide the basis for an alternative approach to stabilization policy when the zero bound is binding.

10.4.6   The Benefits and Risks of Structural Reform

Structural reform is often viewed as a complement to 'demand-side' measures – such as fiscal policy or unconventional monetary policy – as an adjustment instrument. The recent paper by Müller et al. (2015), for instance, analyses the role that such reforms could play in the context of the sovereign debt problem facing Europe at present. They predict an interesting nonmonotonic relationship between reforms and the scale of outstanding debt: when debt levels increase from low levels, countries have higher incentives to reform in the face of a recession. This is because reforms speed up recovery. But at high debt levels, reform efforts merely increase the welfare of creditors, without debtor countries gaining much at all. This reduces the incentives to embark upon reforms in the first place.

In the context of the zero bound problem, however, work by Eggertsson et al. (2014) has questioned whether structural reforms would increase the speed of recovery at all. This is based on a very similar argument to that of Eggertsson (2011). The specific measures that Eggertsson et al. (2014) consider are those intended to raise the degree of competition in product and labour markets. In the long run they concur that these are likely to raise output – largely by reducing the inefficiencies that come with market power. In terms of the Euler condition, this is equivalent to an increase in the economy's productive potential, $\bar{Y}$. But again, whether this increase in productive *potential* will be passed through into actual output will depend on its implications for consumers' desire to save. There are two channels at work. First, the long-run improvement in productivity should give consumers greater confidence in their lifetime income trajectories, reducing their need to save. In terms of the Euler condition, this can be viewed as an increase in expectations of Y_{t+1} for states of the world in $t + 1$ that are 'good'. The implication will be an increase in aggregate demand at t, and hence in Y_t.

Against this is the risk of a negative effect operating through expected inflation. Reforms to labour and product markets make it likely that price and wage inflation will be lower, for any given level of current output. If desired savings remain high at $t + 1$ – that is, the economic state remains 'bad' – π_{t+1} is likely to be lower for any given level of Y_{t+1}. Intuitively, an increase in productive potential reduces inflation pressure. But once more, lower expected inflation implies a higher real interest rate when the nominal rate is constrained at zero, and this serves to reduce aggregate demand.

Eggertsson et al. (2014) calibrate their model to match salient features of the Eurozone economy, and find that the second of these effects dominates when the zero bound is binding. The long-run implications of structural reforms remain positive: output in reforming countries increases by as much as 5 per cent as a consequence, with positive spillovers additionally felt by the wider region. The short-run consequence, however, is a worsening of the recession.

Fernández-Villaverde et al. (2014) place a slightly different emphasis on a similar result. They show that supply-side reforms can help the economy to emerge from a zero-bound trap, provided these reforms are only implemented *after* the zero bound has ceased to bind. This overcomes the negative pricing effect, so that current demand is affected only by an income effect. Here too, the lesson for policy design is that crucial attention must be given to pricing dynamics. There are beneficial effects to be had from structural reforms, just as there may be from lower labour income taxes, but these can easily be dominated if an effort is not made to offset deflationary consequences.

10.4.7   Empirical Evidence on the 'Expectations Channel'

Coming in to the crises, very few economies had recent experience of the policy trade-offs implied at the zero bound, of the sort that could be brought to bear on the choice among alternative instruments. It is for this reason that much of the debate has centred around theoretical exercises. Wieland (2014) provides one of the few empirical attempts to understand whether the policy models – particularly the New Keynesian framework – make the right predictions. He studies the observed dynamics of output and inflation at the zero bound, based on a combination of post-2008 data from the US, Eurozone, UK, Canada and Sweden, and post-1995 data from Japan. His motivation is to investigate whether 'negative supply shocks' – that is, unanticipated reductions in economies' productive potential – are expansionary at the zero lower bound. This is one of the counterintuitive predictions that emerges in the New Keynesian framework, and it operates for very similar reasons to those that mean structural reforms can be contractionary. A negative shock to an economy's productive capacity, such as an earthquake or an oil price shock, will tend to reduce long-run income, and this ought to have a negative impact on aggregate demand. But at the same time there will be a positive effect on expected future inflation so long as the zero bound binds: for any given level of actual output, Y_{t+1}, a lower level of productive capacity will mitigate disinflationary pressure. Wieland (2014) shows that this pricing effect can dominate dynamics at the zero bound, causing negative supply shocks to be expansionary, so long as the zero bound episode is expected to last sufficiently long.

The paper then asks whether there is empirical support for this paradoxical outcome. This is of interest beyond the positive question of how best to analyse supply shocks, because the dynamics that cause supply shocks to be expansionary in theory are identical to those that imply structural reform could be contractionary in Europe. Indeed, they constitute the central mechanism in the New Keynesian literature on policy at the zero bound: the interaction between expected future inflation on current aggregate demand. The results of Wieland's study sound a cautionary note. In a first exercise he extracts a data series of international oil price shocks, and shows that these shocks do indeed generate increases in expected inflation, but are nonetheless associated with short-run increases in unemployment and reductions in production – contrary to the prediction that economic activity should expand. A second part of the analysis draws similar conclusions from the economic developments that followed the Japanese earthquake in 2011.

These results certainly present challenges for the New Keynesian framework, though there are different ways to read them. The analysis is complicated by the presence of two simultaneous economic shocks. First, there is a shock to desired savings, which takes the form of a higher value for β_t in Equation (10.4). Second, there is a shock to productive capacity. The overall outcome will depend on whether the income effect of lower capacity dominates the effect due to expected inflation increasing. As Wieland (2014) shows, this hinges on which of the two shocks will have a longer duration. The supply shock is only guaranteed to be expansionary if its duration is known to be shorter than the shock to desired savings. More generally, the theoretical predictions can go either way. Wieland's data have not falsified the inflation expectations channel per se – just the contention that this channel ought to dominate the effects of oil price shocks and earthquakes on the macroeconomy.

Complementary to this work is the paper by Bachmann et al. (2015). These authors use US micro data to examine the link between expected inflation and consumers' willingness to spend on durable goods. During 'normal' times, when the zero bound does not bind, they find no significant relationship – though this can easily be explained by the fact that monetary policy responds endogenously to higher inflation, preventing the real interest rate from being significantly affected. More worryingly for the theoretical literature, the data do point to a significant *negative* effect of inflation expectations on durables spending when interest rates are constrained at zero. This is the opposite of what theory would predict, as lower future inflation should lower the relative benefits to holding cash.

Ongoing work by Bahaj and Rendahl (2015) partially reinforces these conclusions. Using data from the US Survey of Professional Forecasters, these authors study the role of inflation expectations in the macroeconomic transmission of fiscal policy. As discussed above, the New Keynesian mechanism adopted by Eggertsson (2011) and Christiano et al. (2011) posits that higher spending is associated with higher future inflation, which reduces the *ex ante* real interest rate and raises current output more than one-for-one with the increase in G_t. Bahaj and Rendahl instead find evidence that unanticipated increases in government spending are associated with *decreases* in inflation. This means that the inflation expectations channel works against stabilization: the real interest rate is higher when future government spending is expected to be higher. Consequently, Bahaj and Rendahl show that the fiscal multipliers would be higher without the inflation expectations channel. Unlike Wieland (2014), these results do rely on data from periods when the zero bound was not binding, and for this reason they cannot be viewed as a direct contradiction to the New Keynesian mechanism. It is possible that expectations react differently during a liquidity trap, due to the role of monetary policy counteracting any fiscal stimulus. Nonetheless, strong evidence in favour of the New Keynesian mechanism remains notably absent.

Given the central role of inflation expectations in the policy conclusions surveyed above, this is an area where further contributions are urgently needed. If it *is* the case that changes in inflation expectations do not deliver large inducements to spend, or if the empirical relationship between real economic developments and inflation expectations departs from the New Keynesian model, conclusions ranging from the size of the fiscal multipliers to the role of forward guidance will need to be rethought. This would not rule out the possibility of, for instance, fiscal multipliers being higher at the zero bound than during normal times, but it may have very important implications for the appropriate ranking of policies. When the inflation expectations channel is weak, forward guidance in particular does not appear such a useful option.

10.5   Policies and Diagnoses of the Crisis

In keeping with the bulk of the literature, our analysis so far has assumed that the main reason for nominal interest rates reaching their zero bound is an exogenous increase in the willingness of consumers to save. This is often interpreted as a reduction in the 'natural' real rate of interest that equates aggregate savings and aggregate investment in the economy, but it is unclear what economic phenomenon could be driving such a drop. A more recent literature has sought to account for this development in a more detailed manner.

10.5.1   *What Causes 'Savings Shocks'?*

Work by Guerrieri and Lorenzoni (2015) has formalized the idea that large increases in aggregate net savings rates could be driven by a need for households to deleverage when faced with a tightening of their borrowing constraints. They take as their motivation the detailed evidence of Mian and Sufi (2011), who showed that a contraction in the borrowing capacity of US households in the wake of the subprime crisis, mainly driven by declining house prices, was largely responsible for the large fall in US consumer spending in 2008–2009.

Guerrieri and Lorenzoni (2015) highlight that if consumers face uninsurable income risk, an unanticipated reduction in their borrowing capacity affects far more households than the fraction whose borrowing is directly required to fall to meet the limit. This is because a precautionary motive tends to drive the net asset position of households above its lower limit, so that when a worker is laid off there will remain some scope to incur extra borrowing (or run down savings) and prevent consumption from falling one-to-one with labour income. This additional precautionary motive provides precisely the increase in desired savings that was proxied above by increases in β_t. The consequence is a lower equilibrium real rate of interest. If nominal rigidities additionally mean that the zero bound matters, Guerrieri and Lorenzoni (2015) show that a reduction in borrowing capacity associated with a 10 per cent fall in the economy-wide debt-to-GDP ratio will induce a drop in output of the order of 1 to 2 percentage points. Effects can be much larger if the model is expanded to allow for durable goods and variable credit spreads.

Similar logic has been applied by Eggertsson and Krugman (2012) in a model that abstracts from the insurance motive for saving. They focus instead on a setting where some consumers are simply more impatient than others, and seek to borrow as a consequence. The imposition of tighter borrowing constraints again raises the effective level of desired savings in the economy as a whole, but it does more than this. Eggertsson and Krugman work in a setting with nominal debt, and this allows for changes in the current price level to affect spending, independently of the expectations channel – a 'Fisherian' debt deflation effect. The argument can be seen heuristically by considering the budget constraint of a typical household:

$$p_t C_t + B_{t+1} = (1 + i_{t-1}) B_t + p_t Y_t, \qquad (10.11)$$

where p_t is the nominal price level and B_t is the quantity of nominal assets that the household carries forward from t to $t + 1$. In addition to this, a borrowing constraint limits the expected *real* value of debt that the household will be scheduled to repay at $t + 1$. This can be treated as placing a lower bound on the value of $\frac{B_{t+1}}{p_t}$:

$$\frac{B_{t+1}}{p_t} \geq -D, \qquad (10.12)$$

where D is some positive value, capturing the household's long-run capacity to repay its obligations.

Suppose that the household enters period t with outstanding nominal debt, so that B_t is negative. The maximum level of consumption available to it in t will be given by substituting (10.12) into (10.11), assuming the inequality is binding:

$$C_t = D + Y_t + (1 + i_t) \frac{B_t}{p_t}. \tag{10.13}$$

If the zero lower bound binds in t and Y_t is below full capacity, a mechanistic fall in consumption must follow. The additional effect that Eggertsson and Krugman highlight is that unexpectedly low output in t generally implies a low value for p_t, relative to past expectations. This raises $\frac{B_t}{p_t}$ in absolute value, and since $B_t < 0$ this in turn implies a further fall in consumption. The result is that households who are borrowing-constrained reduce their consumption more than one-for-one with the fall in their incomes. The only way for aggregate demand to be restored to the level of productive potential would be for unconstrained households to run down their savings, but with the real interest rate kept high by the zero bound there is no policy scope to engineer this.

Thus the impact of borrowing limits on the analysis of stabilization policy is twofold. First, they provide a possible explanation for the 'natural' rate of interest in the economy falling: as credit conditions worsen, mechanistic and precautionary motives drive would-be borrowers to accumulate assets instead. Second, they suggest policy-makers should be concerned about falling prices not just to the extent that these imply lower expectations for *future* inflation, but also for the impact on current debt repayments. Eggertsson and Krugman (2012) show that this second implication has important knock-on effects for the merits of expansionary fiscal policy. As we saw above, in the influential studies by Christiano et al. (2011), Eggertsson (2011) and Werning (2012), fiscal policy was particularly effective at the zero lower bound because it raised expectations of inflation – thus lowering the real interest rate. With nominal debt constraints, higher government spending can have additional beneficial effects by mitigating current price falls, keeping the value of outstanding debt more manageable in real terms. Eggertsson and Krugman show that this effect can imply a significant reduction in the length of time that the economy spends at the zero bound.

Other papers have sought to embed these mechanisms in large models of the economy, so as to conduct more realistic policy experiments. Notable is Benigno et al. (2014), who study the optimal conduct of monetary and fiscal policy in a generalized version of the Eggertsson-Krugman setting. They consider the best response to an unanticipated requirement for borrowers to deleverage, and show that an optimal strategy should induce a high initial inflation rate, gradually falling back to target from above. Again, this serves both to lower the real interest rate through its effect on π_{t+1}, and to deflate the real value of outstanding debt. The effect of the latter is to reduce net savings incentives, and thus raise the natural rate of interest, relative to an inflation-targeting policy regime.

Importantly, optimal policy in the Benigno et al. (2014) setting is qualitatively different from a case in which the natural rate of interest is exogenous, as in the original contribution by Eggertsson and Woodford (2003). There, it is best to promise above-target inflation after the exogenous negative shock to the natural rate (positive shock to β_t) has disappeared, but not before. This suggests some care should be taken in interpreting optimal policy results from papers that treat the natural rate as exogenous. Few observers would attribute the fundamental cause of Europe's current weakness to a psychological shift in preferences towards saving – though higher net savings rates may have followed from disruption in financial and real estate markets. More work is needed to understand exactly what the mechanisms driving a reluctance of consumers to spend are, and how best to overcome them.

10.5.2 The Possibility of Secular Stagnation

Yet even when allowing for these richer explanations for 'savings shocks', there is a growing concern in the literature that an account of low equilibrium interest rates dependent on *shocks* to the natural rate is, by its very nature, too temporary. As highlighted above, the nominal interest rate has now been near zero for more than six years in the US and much of Europe, and for around two decades in Japan. It is extremely hard to account for such long-lasting episodes by reference to a transitory disturbance, whether a deleveraging process or a short-term shock to individuals' willingness to save. The challenge that the incipient secular stagnation literature is attempting to meet is how to explain long-lasting liquidity traps.[35]

The central secular stagnation thesis is that a binding zero bound can be explained by long-term ('secular') downward pressures on the equilibrium real rate of interest, rather than transitory shocks. Among the candidate explanations for this downward trend are: (1) a lower population growth rate; (2) a permanent tightening of credit conditions; (3) a decline in the relative price of investment goods; and (4) a decline in the relative supply of safe assets. The paper by Eggertsson and Mehrotra (2014) treats the first three of these, whilst the work by Caballero and Farhi (2015) addresses the fourth. In both cases the modelling approach departs from the common assumption of infinitely-lived consumers, in order to allow for meaningful variations in consumers' demand for assets over the life cycle.

Eggertsson and Mehrotra (2014) consider a simplified economy in which individuals belong to three distinct generations: young, middle-aged and old.

Knowing their income will be higher in later life, the young have an incentive to borrow to finance their initial consumption. Middle-aged consumers repay these early loans, and save for retirement. For simplicity it is assumed that the old leave no bequests.

An implication of this structure is that at any given point in time there will be a meaningful credit market. Middle-aged consumers seek profitable investment vehicles for their savings, whilst young consumers look to borrow. Firms may also borrow to carry out capital investment projects. The main results that Eggertsson and Mehrotra obtain really hinge on changes in the relative importance of these groups in the savings and loans market. A reduction in the population growth rate, for instance, has the effect of reducing the total demand for funds from the young. This corresponds to a reduction in investment opportunities for middle-aged savers, and – in line with the logic of intertemporal substitution captured by the Euler condition – the equilibrium response of the market real interest rate is to fall. This contracts the supply of loanable funds in line with the lower demand.

A tightening of credit conditions has a similar effect. The assumption is that young consumers face limits on their ability to borrow against their future earnings, due to a lack of collateral. A tightening of lending conditions implies a reduction in the quantity of funds they are able to borrow at any given point in time, without significantly influencing the desire of middle-aged workers to save.[36] The same consequences play out, pulling down the equilibrium real rate.

The contrast here with deleveraging shocks of the Eggertsson and Krugman (2012) or Guerrieri and Lorenzoni (2015) form is instructive. In both of these cases a tightening of credit conditions only necessitated a temporary adjustment in consumers' borrowing and savings patterns. In the case of Guerrieri and Lorenzoni (2015), for instance, consumers were required to build up a higher '*buffer stock*' of savings to elevate themselves sufficiently above their new, tighter borrowing limits. With this accumulation completed, the real interest rate could be restored close to its prior equilibrium level. Credit constraints in the Eggertsson and Mehrotra setting, by contrast, imply a permanent reduction in the demand for funds on the part of the young. There is no endogenous dynamic that gradually mitigates the effect of the tighter constraints on the savings market, akin to the gradual building up of assets in Guerrieri and Lorenzoni (2015).

Finally, Eggertsson and Mehrotra (2014) show that a fall in the relative price of investment goods pushes the equilibrium real interest rate down. The basic idea here is that if investment goods are cheaper, a given quantity of real capital investment will absorb a lower stock of savings, again leaving a glut that must be accommodated by a lower real interest rate. Eichengreen (2015) has highlighted a significant fall in the relative price of investment goods in the

US at least since the 1980s, making this an important candidate explanation for what has occurred.

An important policy implication of Eggertsson and Mehrotra's work is that an exogenous increase in the demand for loanable funds can be a way to restore equilibrium at a positive real interest rate in the savings and loans market. This is notable because precisely such a role can be provided by government debt. If the public sector expands its borrowing requirements at the same time as demographic, credit market or investment price factors cause the demand for funds elsewhere to fall, this may be enough to stop the zero bound from binding. Since around 2010 there has been a very noticeable shift in government attitudes towards fiscal policy, away from the stimulus injections of the early post-crisis years and towards fiscal consolidation and debt reduction. If Eggertsson and Mehrotra are correct in their account of low real interest rates, this may have been a very significant error.

A similarly stylized approach to the problem of low real interest rates is provided by Caballero and Farhi (2015). These authors construct a model with a sharp distinction between 'safe' and 'risky' assets, the former constructed by 'tranching' the losses on an underlying risky prospect. They allow for a corresponding binary distinction between risk-neutral and (extremely) risk-averse savers,[37] with the risk-averse only willing to hold safe assets. Caballero and Farhi (2014) provide evidence to suggest that the supply of safe assets dropped significantly in the US from 2007 to 2011, and this is the underlying motivation for analysing a similar contraction in their full model. They focus their analysis on long-run steady states, and show that the safe and risky real interest rates must depend on the size of the two groups in the population, relative to the supplies of safe and risky assets.

When the supply of safe assets is low relative to the share of risk-averse savers, some mechanism must prevent excess demand for safe assets. The equilibrium outcome that would usually ensure this, according to Caballero and Farhi's model, is for risk-averse savers to end up holding a relatively low share of total wealth in the economy. This arises in the long run when there is a low average rate of return on safe assets relative to risky, meaning risk-neutral savers earn a premium – and come to be the largest source of asset demand.

Yet, as Caballero and Farhi show, this mechanism may rely on the real interest rate on safe assets turning negative. When this is not possible, because of a zero bound, some 'disequilibrium' dynamic must play out: the demand for safe assets from risk-averse savers will otherwise exceed its supply. In the usual Keynesian tradition, the authors allow for total output to play the role of adjustment, in lieu of a price channel. A permanently low production level arises, at the level where incomes of all agents have fallen by enough to choke off the excess safe asset demand. Caballero and Farhi show that in these circumstances a quantitative easing policy may be successful, in contrast with the usual irrelevance results. This is because QE can increase the relative supply of safe assets available to savers, thus raising the output level at which their safe asset demand equals safe asset supply (at a zero real interest rate).

It is indicative of the early character of the secular stagnation literature that both of the papers surveyed here remain very stylized exercises, and it is unclear how far their insights can be generalized. In the case of Eggertsson and Mehrotra (2014), a possible objection to the model is that it cannot explain how a permanent zero (or negative) real interest rate can coincide with perpetual assets, such as land. When future income is negatively discounted by the market, such perpetuities ought to be of infinite value. Either their model must be one in which stagnation is secular but still temporary – a perfectly reasonable hypothesis – or there are some risk factors affecting 'perpetual' assets that are outside of their model. In the case of Caballero and Farhi (2015) the modelling device used to generate relative asset demands is deliberately tailored to ensure changes in the risky interest rate cannot entice risk-averse savers to place some of their savings in these instruments. This may be justifiable if regulatory constraints limit risky investments, but it seems an important restriction to relax if their analysis is to fit into larger macroeconomic models. These are promising starts, but there is much work to be done if secular stagnation is to become established as a central macroeconomic phenomenon of our age.

10.5.3   Dynamic Interactions through the Labour Market

A small but growing literature has emerged since the crisis reinvestigating the fundamental role played by aggregate demand in macroeconomic models, and particularly the possibility that aggregate production may be impaired because of demand-side confidence crises or excessive uncertainty about the future. Much, though not all, of this work is based around the idea that search frictions may impede the functioning of goods or labour markets, with wider macroeconomic implications.[38] Perhaps more fundamentally, the literature divides between papers that allow self-fulfilling bouts of pessimism to generate recessions by themselves – suggesting policy could have a useful coordinating role – and papers that instead emphasize the *amplification* role for uncertainty and search frictions, given an exogenous disturbance to the economy. Examples of the former type include Farmer (2013, 2014), Chamley (2014), Kaplan and Menzio (2015), Michaillat and Saez (2015), and Heathcote and Perri (2015).[39] Examples of the latter include Ravn and Sterk (2013), den Haan et al. (2014) and Rendahl (2015). The last of these places particular focus on amplification effects due to the zero lower bound, and how an expansionary fiscal policy can best exploit these. This makes it of particular interest in the present context.

The main point made by Rendahl (2015) is again well understood by reference to the Euler condition, with the zero bound imposed:

$$u'(Y_t) = \beta_t \mathbb{E}_t \frac{1}{1 + \pi_{t+1}} u'(Y_{t+1}). \tag{10.14}$$

Suppose, as before, that some shock causes an increase in consumers' desire to save – that is, a higher value for β_t. To keep matters as simple as possible we can imagine that this shock will last only for the current period. In $t + 1$ a return to 'normal times' is guaranteed. If π_{t+1} were to equal some target value π^*, and Y_{t+1} equal to a full capacity output level $\bar{Y}_{t+1}$, we would be back to the starting point for our discussion: Y_t is determined by the demand side of the economy alone, and will generically be below $\bar{Y}_t$. The dynamic that Rendahl (2015) emphasizes is that if Y_t is below $\bar{Y}_t$, fewer unemployed workers will find jobs in period t, and some existing hires will be laid off. These additional unemployed workers will take time to find new jobs, and many will not have been successful in doing so by the time the liquidity trap has ended (here, period $t + 1$). If this is true, the 'full capacity' level of output in $t + 1$ will itself be reduced by the fact that there is an abnormally large pool of unemployed workers, not yet matched to an appropriate job. Heuristically, it is as if $\bar{Y}_{t+1}$ is given by a weighted average of Y_t and some fixed, steady-state output level $\bar{Y}$. This reduction in expected income at $t + 1$ raises the marginal benefits from saving still further, worsening the initial unemployment problem. The end result is a more substantial recession than would be predicted if the labour market were neglected.

As in the paper by Eggertsson and Krugman (2012), the addition of this extra recessionary dynamic strengthens the benefits from expansionary fiscal policy. A higher level of government spending does not just put upward pressure on inflation at $t + 1$: it additionally increases the total level of hiring in period t, and this means that the labour market will have far less slack once the liquidity trap has been exited. This means workers in period t are much more confident about their prospects for $t + 1$, and this reduces their overall desire to save – through a fall in $u'(Y_{t+1})$. Rendahl (2015) shows that the government spending multiplier can be well above 1 for conventional calibrations of the model's parameters – implying that consumption indeed rises as government spending increases.

Given the dependence of Christiano et al. (2011) and Eggertsson (2011) on an inflation expectations channel to generate large fiscal multipliers, and given that clear evidence for this channel at the zero bound remains elusive, Rendahl's results are an important contribution. There is a vast empirical literature on the size of the fiscal multiplier, some of which finds that output increases more than one-for-one with government spending, some of which points to a smaller response.[40] If it *is* the case that higher government spending raises aggregate consumption, but this does not operate through an inflation expectation channel, an important open question is why it does occur. Dynamic propagation through the labour market seems an important possibility. Moreover, the precise reason for fiscal expenditure's effectiveness could have important implications for the way policy should be conducted – and, indeed, whether government spending is the best instrument to use at all. If the main purpose of a stimulus policy is to raise inflation expectations, government spending would seem a very indirect means to achieve this. A promised increase in future consumption taxation, as proposed by Correia et al. (2013), is a far more targeted instrument. If instead the purpose is to sustain employment and prevent unnecessary separations in the labour market, public spending could be much better suited to the job.[41]

10.5.4   *Deflation Traps, Self-Fulfilling Dynamics and Equilibrium Selection*

For all that there are substantial differences in the theoretical treatments of the zero bound discussed so far, they share one common methodological thread. The basic thought experiment is that some exogenous shock has forced the 'natural' rate of interest in the economy to be lower than normal, and this implies there is no equilibrium such that $i_t > 0$, future inflation and output are at their target levels, and a current recession is avoided. But it has long been recognized that 'fundamental' shocks of this kind might not be the only cause of a zero bound episode. Influential work by Benhabib et al. (2001) highlight the risk of self-fulfilling 'deflation traps'. The basic mechanism works as follows: Suppose that, for some reason, consumers are pessimistic about the future state of the economy, expecting a low level of output and inflation at $t + 1$. *By itself* this will tend to imply a low level of current demand, as both forms of pessimism should increase the benefits to current consumers from saving. Without the zero bound this should not be a problem: the nominal interest rate can be cut sufficiently far to raise demand by an offsetting amount.[42] When the zero bound interferes with this policy, however, there is no means left for stimulating aggregate demand. The economy could be forced to stay at a lower level of output and inflation, both now and in the future. This justifies the initial pessimism.

Benhabib et al. (2001) show that if the central bank followed standard feedback rules when setting nominal interest rates, there were two possible long-run inflation rates that could rise.[43] The first was the central bank's target rate π^*, implying a nominal interest rate i^* that satisfies the Euler equation:

$$u'\left(Y^*\right) = \beta \frac{1 + i^*}{1 + \pi^*} u'\left(Y^*\right), \tag{10.15}$$

where $Y_t = Y_{t+1} = Y^*$ is the level of output associated with this long-run equilibrium. This collapses simply to:

$$\beta^{-1} = \frac{1 + i^*}{1 + \pi^*} \tag{10.16}$$

which is a version of the well-known Fisher equation – linking expected inflation and the nominal interest rate to the real interest rate, here β^{-1}.

The second alternative long-run inflation rate, $\tilde{\pi}$, will satisfy the same Euler
condition, but with $i = 0$. This implies:

$$u'\left(\tilde{Y}\right) = \beta \frac{1}{1 + \tilde{\pi}} u'\left(\tilde{Y}\right) \tag{10.17}$$

where $\tilde{Y}$ is the level of output associated with this long-run equilibrium. Again,
this simplifies:

$$\beta^{-1} = \frac{1}{1 + \tilde{\pi}} \tag{10.18}$$

Provided consumers are somewhat impatient, preferring current consumption
to future, we will have $\beta^{-1} > 1$. This implies $\tilde{\pi} < 0$: there is deflation at a rate
equal to the steady-state real interest rate. According to some analyses, this may
be desirable. It is consistent with the famous '*Friedman rule*' that stipulates that
the opportunity cost of holding money, i, should optimally be driven to zero.[44]
This derives from a view that money matters because it adds an extra dimension
to households' portfolio choice problems. Purchasing goods requires holding
cash in advance. If holding cash means foregoing interest on alternative assets,
consumption demand will be negatively affected by this. Driving the nominal
interest rate to zero is a way to iron out this needless inefficiency.

Against this, however, is the New Keynesian approach linking inflation rates
to output, and overall economic efficiency. Broadly speaking, this posits that a
positive relationship will exist between the steady-state inflation rate in an economy and the steady-state level of production. Thus deflation equal to $\tilde{\pi}$ could
only occur if $\tilde{Y} < Y^*$. This derives from an explicit link between firms' price-
setting decisions and the aggregate state of the economy. If output is below its
full capacity level, wage pressure in the economy will be low, limiting firms'
marginal costs and causing price-setters to exercise restraint. High output, by
contrast, drives up real marginal costs and the prices of those firms that reset.
Instead of low inflation causing high money holdings and high consumption
demand, it is inefficiently low output that causes low inflation (or deflation).

This self-fulfilling dynamic has particular appeal in accounting for recent
trends in Europe and beyond, because it implies that the nominal interest rate
should remain at zero for an extended length of time. The 'fundamental' story,
with the exception of the secular stagnation literature, assumes interest rates
must fall to equilibrate domestic savings and investment, given an increase in
consumers' intrinsic readiness to save. But there is a limit to how long desired
savings can be expected to remain high. If the shock to savings rates is ultimately driven by a tightening of borrowing constraints, as analysed by Eggertsson and Krugman (2012), Benigno et al. (2014) and Guerrieri and Lorenzoni

(2015), it will take some time for the economy to adjust to the more restrictive credit conditions, but this dynamic should last no longer than a few quarters. This contrasts with the practical experience of Japan in particular, where nominal interest rates have been at or near zero since 1995. The experiences of the UK, US and Eurozone, where rates have been very close to zero since 2009, are likewise becoming difficult to account for by the 'fundamental' approach.[45]

If the reason for nominal interest rates being at zero is simply that consumers and firms are pessimistic, expecting low inflation (or deflation) and low output in the future, there is no reason to believe that this should be a short-term outcome. Indeed, it is precisely an expectation that the deflationary trap will persist that causes it to arise in the first place. The longer nominal interest rates remain at or close to zero in major developed economies, the more it seems possible that the underlying problem is a confidence trap, not a shock to the natural rate.

Crucially, the monetary policy options for escaping from this sort of trap are limited, even via forward guidance. Low current output is caused by a self-fulfilling perception that there will be low future output and inflation. This is not easily overcome by issuing the sort of policy promise that Eggertsson and Woodford (2003) advocate – that is, to raise inflation above its target value for an extended period of time even after 'normal' times have returned. Such an approach does not address the central confidence problem, which is that consumers do not believe circumstances *will* return to normal with a sufficiently high likelihood any time soon. In addition, the relationship between stimulus policy and pessimism about future economic outcomes may not be a straightforward one. It is quite possible, for instance, that an announcement of unconventional forward guidance policy by the central bank may reinforce a belief on the part of consumers that deflation will persist.

Recent work by Mertens and Ravn (2014) has investigated whether fiscal policy offers a viable alternative for expanding the economy in such circumstances. In particular, they investigate whether fiscal multipliers ought to be as large when the main economic problem is a pessimism crisis, as they are when the problem is that the natural rate is too high. They show quite the opposite.[46] Provided the fiscal expansion does not alter the likelihood of the confidence trap persisting, higher government spending at the zero bound will tend to be deflationary, and output will increase less than one-for-one with the increase in government spending. Their setting is a little more complex than the original analysis of Benhabib et al. (2001), as they allow for the evolution of confidence in the economy to be random – meaning that a current pessimism crisis always has some probability of ending tomorrow. Again, the result is best seen by reference to the Euler condition:

$$u'(Y_t - G_t) = \beta \mathbb{E}_t \frac{1}{1 + \pi_{t+1}} u'(Y_{t+1} - G_{t+1}). \qquad (10.19)$$

Suppose that there is a commitment to increase government spending for as long as pessimism – and thus a zero nominal interest rate – persists. As in the case of natural rate shocks, a good starting point for analysing the consequences is to suppose that Y_t increases one-for-one with G_t, leaving the marginal utility of consumption unaffected. If this were to happen, the higher value for Y_{t+1} in 'bad' $t + 1$ states would tend to put upward pressure on π_{t+1}, as firms are faced with a comparatively tight labour market. This is familiar: it was precisely this effect that generated a higher fiscal multiplier when the zero bound episode was driven by a shock to the natural rate, as higher π_{t+1} implies a lower real interest rate in t. But in the present setting it is not possible for π_{t+1} to increase without undermining the confidence trap. The very reason that output is below its efficient level is that there are expectations of substantial future deflation. The only way to make sure that the confidence trap persists is for output to increase less than one-for-one with government spending. This will reduce the inflationary pressure at $t + 1$, though it will also imply that aggregate consumption, $Y - G$, will fall in both periods.

For very similar reasons, Mertens and Ravn additionally show that supply-side policies such as cuts in labour income tax rates should be expansionary, where they are contractionary under natural rate shocks. This is because lower marginal tax rates in future periods raises workers' willingness to find jobs, putting downward pressure on inflation. The confidence trap now needs a higher output level to be consistent with deflation at the required rate.

Thus the deflationary effects of fiscal spending obtained by Mertens and Ravn (2014), as well as the low multipliers that are associated with them, follow quite subtly from the exercise they conduct. They ask what the effects of fiscal policy would be were the economy automatically to adjust to that fiscal policy, so as to leave the confidence trap intact in all states of the world where it previously existed. What this does not address, therefore, is the possibility that expansionary fiscal policy could itself reduce the likelihood of pessimism persisting. When the logic behind the Mertens and Ravn result is considered, this seems an intuitive alternative: their model predicts that output will adjust to remain consistent with (unchanging) sentiments, rather than changing sentiments being an important driving force behind output adjustment. The latter possibility has some recent empirical support: Bachmann and Sims (2012) show that at times of economic slack, fiscal expansions tended to have important positive effects on consumer confidence – in contrast with the negative effects implicit in Mertens and Ravn (2014).

To summarize, it seems ever more plausible that Mertens and Ravn (2014) are drawing attention to the relevant *problem* for stabilization policy. Interest rates have been at or near zero for so long, particularly in Japan, that the notion of a natural rate shock is harder and harder to endorse. A pessimism crisis seems a sensible alternative way to rationalize the zero-bound episode. Where further work would be of great use is in clarifying the complex relationship that exists between changes in policy and the state of expectations. This is an intrinsically difficult issue, with theory providing very little guidance. By their nature, self-fulfilling crises occur for no reason other than that they do. Additional empirical work building on Bachmann and Sims (2012) seems the obvious direction to take.

An alternative multiplicity argument is explored in ongoing work by Brendon et al. (2015). These authors take as their starting point the observation that potential output, $\bar{Y}$, has proved very difficult to measure in many developed economies since the crisis. This matters for monetary policy, because interest rates must generally be set based on some estimate for how much inflationary pressure is implied by the 'output gap', $Y - \bar{Y}$. If potential output is unknown, or measured only with great uncertainty, policy-makers may instead look to an alternative measure of current economic conditions, such as the growth rate.

What Brendon et al. (2015) show is that this can be a dangerous strategy, given the zero bound constraint. Suppose there were a collapse in output in period t, driving the nominal interest rate to the zero bound in response. At some point a recovery will follow, during which output grows back to trend. But if monetary policy is designed to feed back on growth rather than the output gap, this recovery will immediately induce policy tightening, which in turn will put downward pressure on the rate of inflation. When growth feedback is sufficiently high, the result is that consumers in t can reasonably expect low future inflation, conditional upon a collapse in Y_t. This means the real interest rate in t will be high, conditional upon a collapse in Y_t – given that i_t is constrained at the zero bound. A high real interest rate is enough to cause the collapse in output in the first place.

In an empirical exercise based on an estimated model of the US economy with housing and leveraged borrowing by some consumers,[47] Brendon et al. (2015) show that the likelihood of exposure to this form of crisis is around two-thirds, given the observed strength of policy feedback. When interest rates respond to an estimate of the output gap rather than output growth, the likelihood of exposure instead falls below 10 per cent. The main lesson is broader though: if monetary policy-makers give the impression that large recessions will cause them to revise downwards their future estimate of *'full capacity'* output, this can reinforce a state of pessimism that drives the economy to collapse in the first place.

A final important paper on the problem of equilibrium selection at the zero bound is Cochrane (2015). This work revisits the standard framework of Eggertsson and Woodford (2003), in which the zero bound binds because of an exogenous increase in consumers' desire to save – that is, a high value for β_t in the Euler condition:[48]

$$u'(Y_t) = \beta_t \frac{1 + i_t}{1 + \pi_{t+1}} u'(Y_{t+1}).$$

(10.20)

Cochrane starts by asking what the response to such a shock would look like if there were no pricing frictions in the economy whatsoever – essentially the textbook case of a vertical 'aggregate supply' curve. When this is true, aggregate demand below capacity can never be an equilibrium outcome. We can treat it as implying $Y_t = Y_{t+1} = \bar{Y}$ for some constant capacity output level $\bar{Y}$. The result is a version of the Fisher equation:

$$\beta_t \frac{1 + i_t}{1 + \pi_{t+1}} = 1. \tag{10.21}$$

As before, if the shock to β_t is sufficiently large, this equation may not be possible to satisfy for a positive value of i_t and an inflation rate equal to the central bank's target, π^*. Once i_t has reached zero, the only possibility is for expected inflation to exceed its target.

Taken on its own terms this is a perfectly benign outcome. Output remains at the level of productive capacity, and aggregate welfare is not substantially affected. Of course, this occurs by construction: it is not possible for output to depart from $\bar{Y}$ when investigating a frictionless Walrasian general equilibrium. Cochrane's main point, however, is that a very similar equilibrium remains a possibility in the New Keynesian model studied by Eggertsson and Woodford (2003) and numerous subsequent authors. That is, it is quite possible for a rise in consumers' desire to save to be associated with an increase in inflation expectations, and an output level that departs very little from its capacity level. The assumption that rules this out in the New Keynesian literature is that the rate of inflation tomorrow should depend only on the state of the economy tomorrow – not any past outcomes, such as consumers' historic willingness to save. This essentially means that π_{t+1} is fixed at π^* in expectation, and only output is available to adjust to the savings shock – as analysed at length above. Whether this is an appropriate assumption remains very debatable. As we have seen, empirical evidence on the relationship between economic conditions and inflation expectations is very partial, particularly for periods when the zero bound is binding. A number of the policy prescriptions of the New Keynesian model at the zero bound appear counterintuitive, as the work of Eggertsson et al. (2014) on structural reforms highlights. If nothing else, Cochrane's paper reiterates still further the importance of more empirical work on the expectations channel.

10.6   Risk Sharing and Fiscal Policy in a Monetary Union

So far we have been discussing the debate on macroeconomic stabilization of economies hit by large shocks, that cause policy rates to be constrained by their zero lower bound, impairment and/or malfunctioning of financial markets, and the emergence of disruptive sovereign risk crises. We now focus our discussion on issues that are specific to stabilization of the Eurozone.

10.6.1   *Imbalances and Imperfect Risk Sharing*

The birth of the euro gave rise to a fast integration of the money market and large cross-border banking flows. While these developments at the time were considered positive steps towards increasing cross-border risk sharing, financial markets remained insufficiently developed at the union level, and cross-border risk remained severely limited. In light of modern theory and the experience from the crisis, we are now in a better position to understand the implications.

Under perfect risk sharing, markets allocate financial funds up to the point that a unit of currency has the same marginal utility across agents and countries under any circumstances. Since agents in different countries consume different baskets of goods, the same unit of currency tends to be more valuable where, over the business cycle, prices are relatively low, that is, the real exchange rate is depreciated. A key implication of perfect insurance is therefore that, under mild conditions on preferences, consumption tends to rise more in countries where domestic inflation is relatively low. In other words, a domestic consumption boom, causing an external deficit, cannot occur simultaneously to a hike in relative inflation, causing real appreciation.

Consider an exogenous unexpected increase in the *future* demand for services produced in a country, say, tourism, raising the profitability of domestic firms supplying these services. If markets in the union are perfect, there are enough instruments for domestic and foreign households in the union to achieve perfect risk diversification. By way of example, through a well-diversified equity portfolio, both the residents in the country and the residents in other areas of the union can share the benefits from the higher stock market value of these firms. As a result, wealth and demand tend to move symmetrically across countries in response to the shock: more demand moves domestic and foreign prices in the same direction.

Conversely, if markets are not perfect (diversification is low), the higher profitability of domestic firms will tend to benefit mainly domestic residents. By consumption smoothing, these will borrow to raise their current expenditure consistent with their new perceived level of wealth, feeding an external deficit. Domestic demand rises asymmetrically with respect to the rest of the union, driving domestic inflation above foreign inflation. Hence the country will simultaneously experience a widening of the external deficit and a loss of competitiveness. Ex-post, the accumulation of noncontingent debt instruments will in turn increase the vulnerability of the country to adverse shocks – if, for instance, the demand for tourism services turn out to be weaker than initially anticipated.

Recent work by Brunnermeier and Sannikov (2014) and Heathcote and Perri (2015), or the results by Corsetti et al. (2010), suggest examples of incomplete market economies in which trade in more assets is actually welfare-reducing. 'Demand' or 'pecuniary' externalities are the ultimate cause of these results. These models are typically read as theoretical justifications for limiting capital flows and introducing some form of capital controls, if only as a consequence of desirable regulation.[49]

But overall the arguments in this subsection provide a strong motivation, from a macroeconomic perspective, to improve cross-border risk sharing in (well supervised and regulated) capital markets. While the mechanism just described is active whether or not the nominal exchange rates can adjust, it is especially relevant in a currency union.

10.6.2   Complete Markets are not a Substitute for Risk Sharing via Transfers

Complete markets and efficient risk sharing address an important source of inefficiency in a monetary union, but are not sufficient to prevent undesirable business cycle movements at the national level. In particular in the presence of nominal rigidities that prevent adjustment to asymmetric business cycle shocks, contingent financial flows from efficient markets do not provide enough redistribution of income and demand for smoothing out recessions and overheating. Market-based risk sharing is no substitute for cross-border transfers compensating for lack of demand at national level.

Recent work has reconsidered the mechanism by which cross-border transfers can overcome insufficiency of aggregate demand in part of the union. Fahri and Werning (2014) build on the following argument. When prices are sticky in nominal terms, and the exchange rate cannot adjust, the relative price of tradable goods in terms of nontradable goods is sticky in real terms, at least in the short run. If preferences are homothetic, given this relative price stickiness, any change in overall consumption demand will move the demand for both goods in proportion. This means that if one country transfers tradable resources to another, the consumption of this transfer will have a 'multiplier' effect on local output, via a rise in the demand for nontradables. Domestic aggregate demand will increase more than one-to-one relative to the size of the transfer.

This elegant example clarifies a key requisite for the transfer programme to work: the resources transferred across borders must be immediately spent, feeding current demand at given relative prices. To the extent that the transfer is partly saved and spent in the future, and price adjustment takes place over time, the multiplier effect will be smaller. Indeed, in the simulations proposed by Fahri and Werning, and according to a vast body of quantitative literature developed in academic and policy institutions, transfers are more consequential, the more persistent (the shock and) the transfers are. Temporary transfers have a limited effect on current consumption of tradables, since they do not imply a significant increase in permanent income. The multiplier is correspondingly muted.

The overall message is nonetheless worth repeating: well-functioning financial markets, generating state-contingent financial flows that accrue to regions hit by adverse output or price shocks, do not dispose of the need for setting up some mutual insurance mechanism working through a common budget or a nonmarket allocation mechanism. Whether or not markets are complete, agents do not completely internalize the effects of their spending and saving decision on the level of demand and economic activity. There are demand externalities associated with nominal rigidities and an inflexible exchange rate. With this in mind, an important practical subject for current research is how best to design an insurance system of contingent transfers at the Eurozone level. Ongoing work by Ábrahám et al. (2015) is making important steps in this direction, paying particular attention to the need to structure future transfers in a way that gives all countries an ex-ante incentive to participate in the scheme.

10.6.3   Fiscal Devaluation

In the traditional approach, national fiscal policy is seen as a regulator of the level of spending on final goods and services (as discussed in the previous sections). Recent literature has, however, proposed a new approach, more in line with the theory of monetary policy, stressing the need to identify welfare-reducing distortions (or wedges) and design instruments to correct them. A leading example is the work by Correia et al. (2008, 2013), showing that taxes and subsidies can completely compensate for nominal price and wage rigidities, making monetary policy de facto irrelevant. Building on this early contribution, the elegant model by Fahri et al. (2014) establishes the conditions under which exchange rate adjustment may be completely replaced by 'fiscal devaluation'.

An effective fiscal devaluation may have demanding informational and administrative requirements. The government needs to collect timely information about fundamental shocks and the state of the economy, and have the administrative capacity to vary tax and subsidy rates for firms to dispose of the need to alter production prices. The interventions need to alter the relative valuation of nontraded and traded goods enough to facilitate a shift in resources and economic activity across sectors. They need to influence incomes enough to correct undesirable consequences on the trade balance. The tax and subsidy regime must be put in place credibly, such that, in each period, agents can formulate their investment and consumption plans under reasonable expectations that there will also be efficient stabilization in the future – under the constraint that debt and the deficit are sustainable.

The benefits from fiscal devaluation are often interpreted in a narrow sense, as a correction of the international price of a country's output and the internal price of its nontradables, to restore 'competitiveness'. It is appropriate to stress, however, that as long as risk sharing is not perfect, a fiscal devaluation, like any exchange-rate movement, also has strong income effects. Real depreciation not only tends to make domestic firms more competitive and imports more expensive. It also reduces domestic residents' relative income.[50]

Recent empirical work substantiates this point. Bems and di Giovanni (2014) study the 'internal devaluation' experiment carried out by Latvia, where at the height of the crisis (2008–2009) the government cut public wages, resulting in a drop in private wages and, among other effects, in a large current account adjustment. These authors document that consumption demand expenditure switched from expensive imports into cheaper local goods, with little change in their relative prices. They conclude that 'the conventional price channel plays little role' by comparison with income effects.[51]

Finally for this section, we should note an important issue raised by the work both on transfer unions and on fiscal devaluations. This is whether stabilization policy should be seen as a substitute for market adjustment or as a facilitator of it. By way of example, the transfers analysed by Fahri and Werning (2014) are effective in redressing insufficient domestic demand to the extent that transfers are quite persistent. But should a monetary union rely on persistent transfers to address business cycle shocks that are by their nature transitory? By the same token, a systematic resort to fiscal devaluation would require a reform of the tax code and the welfare state, setting up a consistent system of state-contingent taxes and subsidies by which a country would dispose of the need for relative price adjustment. Should countries permanently adapt their welfare state in light of this goal? A word of caution is clearly necessary in this area. For one thing, the literature has long clarified that lack of price flexibility may be only one of the distortions that prevent an efficient reallocation of resources in response to shocks (say, from nontradables to local tradables). In practice this shift may also be hampered by administrative and bureaucratic constraints, and may be particularly difficult in the absence of smooth financial support by intermediaries. Intervening on these distortions would require quite a different set of instruments to the ones underlying fiscal devaluation.

Recent contributions have indeed focused on how to design a stabilization problem in conjunction with reforms facilitating market-based adjustment. Instances are provided by Cacciatore et al. (2016), who analyse stabilization strategies to accompany product and labour market deregulation, or Müller et al. (2015), focusing on structural reforms under the threat of a sovereign debt crisis.

10.7   Conclusions

The new economic questions that surfaced during the recent crises have profoundly challenged existing economic and policy theory. In this chapter, we have identified what we see as some of the most important developments in the academic debate on stabilization policy since 2008 – a debate that has seen the roles for, and boundaries between, fiscal and monetary policy fundamentally redefined by comparison with the pre-crisis consensus. On the one hand, fiscal policy can be expected to play a much larger role in macroeconomic stabilization than previously envisioned, but at the same time it has also become more closely interconnected with financial stability. On the other hand, monetary theorists and policy-makers are currently reflecting on a radically redefined role for central banking, in which balance sheet policies are bound to play a much larger role than in the past.

Given its central role in motivating a departure from 'business as usual' in macroeconomic stabilization, we have devoted a large section of our survey to the design of policies at the zero lower bound. In spite of the accumulated experience and evidence we have reviewed, a fair conclusion from our survey is that vast, uncharted economic waters lie ahead of us. Many critics may find the theoretical models most commonly deployed in the current policy debate not appropriate to capture observed outcomes, particularly the length of time that the zero bound has now remained binding. Models of secular stagnation that could account for persistently low real interests remain very much in their infancy, and the appropriate policy conclusions to take from them are not yet clear. One trend that does emerge is a noticeable tendency since the crises for theoretical work to deploy quite stylized assumptions, tailored to the particular effect that is being demonstrated. This can be very useful for illustrating the central driving force behind particular results, but the cost can sometimes be a lack of generalizability. A priority for future work must surely be to identify robust policy recommendations that could be expected to work well independently of the specific models employed in their analytical formulation.

Acknowledgements

The task of surveying the academic literature on fiscal and monetary policy since the crisis has been a daunting one, particularly given the sheer number of topics that could fall under this umbrella. Although our text includes an extensive list of works, space limitation made it impossible to provide a satisfactory account of the many papers, topics and ideas relevant to our subject.

A draft of this chapter was presented at the COEURE workshop 'Fiscal and Monetary Policies after the Crises' at the European University Institute, Florence, on 5 June 2015. We thank participants for comments and suggestions, and particularly our discussants John Hassler, Isabel Correia and Benedict Clements. We are very grateful to Yildiz Akkaya, Simon Lloyd and Anil Ari for assisting in the process of compiling this work. All errors are ours.

Notes

1. Stock and Watson (2002) first coined the term Great Moderation to describe the characteristics of the US business cycle since 1984.

2. The canonical policy model remains that developed by Smets and Wouters (2003, 2007). This built on the New Keynesian idea that macroeconomic fluctuations were propagated and amplified through wage and price rigidities, adding numerous additional frictions so as better to capture the properties of observed data series. Unlike previous authors in the DSGE literature, Smets and Wouters were able to estimate their model directly, applying Bayesian statistical techniques. Variants upon this model remain commonly used by central banks for forecasting purposes: examples include the ECB's NAWM model, the Bank of England's COMPASS model and the Riksbank's RAMSES model.

3. See Chari et al. (2009), for instance.

4. See Blanchard et al. (2010) and Mishkin (2011) for fuller discussions of the pre-crisis view.

5. In a widely-cited piece applying the textbook New Keynesian model, Blanchard and Galí (2007) confirm that price stabilization *requires* output to be stabilized at an augmented version of the natural rate, describing this as a '*divine coincidence*'.

6. This latter conclusion remains controversial. Cochrane (2011) has argued that the nominal interest rate should not be considered as effective an instrument as Woodford claims.

7. See Schmitt-Grohé and Uribe (2011) for a comprehensive analysis of the optimal rate of inflation.

8. Ireland is a geographical anomaly among the latter.

9. The interest rate paid by the ECB on overnight deposits by financial institutions is slightly negative at the time of writing. The central banks of Denmark and Switzerland also charge negative deposit rates, whilst the Swedish Riksbank has successfully cut its main policy rate to -0.25 per cent.

10. Some authors have therefore considered the relative merits of abolishing cash, or changing its properties in a manner that removes the impediment. Buiter (2009) considers the relative merits of different proposals.

11. See Baldwin and Teulings (2014) for a collection of nontechnical pieces on the idea of secular stagnation.

12. The operator $\mathbb{E}_t$ simply denotes that the consumer's expectation across possible outcomes in $t + 1$ is relevant to choice.

13. This fact was first exploited by Krugman (1998), in a piece widely acknowledged to have launched the modern literature on policy options at the zero bound.

14. We discuss endogenous mechanisms that can generate this 'shock' below.

15. The term 'natural rate' derives from Wicksell (1898).

16. Campbell et al. distinguish this from '*Delphic*' forward guidance, whereby the monetary authority may influence outcomes by issuing forecasts for the future evolution of the economy, but without these forecasts having any binding influence on future policy.

17. Svensson (2001) attempts to address this problem by proposing a '*foolproof*' mechanism for institutionalizing the desired commitment, including a short-term commitment to an (increasing) price-level target in place of any inflation target, and

a currency devaluation. Such a complete – albeit short term – overhaul of the central bank's objective has not been engineered in any major country since the crisis.

18. See Weale (2013).

19. See Weale (2013).

20. See, in particular, Evans (2011) and Woodford (2012).

21. This is captured mathematically by fact that greater dispersion in Y_{t+1} raises the term $\mathbb{E}_t u'(Y_{t+1})$ in the Euler condition (10.5).

22. Related work by Akkaya (2014) considers the role for forward guidance in reducing uncertainty about future interest rates. Yet for similar reasons it is unclear whether this also implies reduced uncertainty about key policy variables – particularly output and inflation. This point is modelled explicitly in recent work by Andrade et al. (2015).

23. Del Negro et al. (2012) stress a problem with DSGE monetary models in accounting for forward guidance. These models tend to predict unreasonably large responses of key macroeconomic variables to central bank announcements about future interest rates. This phenomenon is labelled the '*forward guidance puzzle*'.

24. Again, Cochrane (2015) is an exception.

25. Recall that the underlying 'shock' is an unusually high value for β_t, which captures a subjective preference for later consumption.

26. Once there, the appropriate level of government spending may of course be high or low: this is a matter for democratic choice. The issue here is whether resource misallocation – relatively low employment, and relatively high government spending – is the least-bad option when the zero bound binds.

27. This builds on Cúrdia and Woodford (2009), who develops a simple device for incorporating financial frictions between borrowers and savers into an otherwise traditional New Keynesian model.

28. These estimates are based on Schneider and Buehn (2012).

29. See Heathcote et al. (2009) for a survey of heterogeneous-agent consumption models.

30. Such a mechanism was identified by MPC member David Miles (2009), for instance, as a justification for the Bank of England's first experiment with quantitative easing.

31. See, for instance, the widely-cited study by Gagnon et al. (2011) for the US, and Joyce et al. (2011) for the UK case. Bauer and Rudebusch (2014) argue that these studies rely on a decomposition of the yield curve that is biased in favour of finding too high a portfolio rebalancing effect.

32. In Gertler and Karadi's model this leverage restriction is generated by an information friction: households are reluctant to entrust assets to financial firms without believing these firms have an incentive to manage them well. A large enough capital buffer gives intermediaries '*skin in the game*', ensuring good practice. It would be easy to rewrite the model to allow for the leverage ratio to be a direct regulatory choice.

33. Given the precise way that Gertler and Karadi motivate their credit friction, the fundamental difference between the central bank and private-sector financial institutions is that the central bank can credibly commit not to steal depositors' funds. It is not clear where this difference in commitment technology derives from, nor that it truly accounts for the significant difference between the two types of institution that undoubtedly exists.

34. This work is part of a growing literature in macroeconomics that links aggregate fluctuations to information problems at the microeconomic level. Important contributions include Lorenzoni (2009), Angeletos and La'O (2013) and Hellwig and Venkateswaran (2014). Similar investment-information dynamics are analysed by Straub and Ulbricht (2014).

35. A very readable introduction to the secular stagnation literature is provided by Baldwin and Teulings (2014).

36. If anything the supply of savings may be expected to increase, since middle-aged workers do not inherit such large debts from their early years. This leaves them with a larger stock of funds to save.

37. Strictly, these are *'ambiguity-averse'* consumers, who assess future prospects according to the worst-case outcome.

38. Such frictions were pioneered by Diamond (1982) and Mortensen and Pissarides (1994).

39. Related is the work of Beaudry and Portier (2013), who show that changes in perceptions about *future* economic outcomes can generate changes in production in the present. (This is not quite a self-fulfilling dynamic, due to the difference in timing.) Their paper provides an alternative theory for the source of fluctuations in aggregate demand, with the property that these fluctuations have relatively little impact on inflation rates. Beaudry and Portier argue that this property is important in accounting for recent US business cycle dynamics.

40. Papers that obtain an increase in aggregate private consumption as government spending rises, and thus a multiplier above one, include Fatas and Mihov (2001) and Ravn et al. (2012). Ramey and Shapiro (1998) and Ramey (2011) find multipliers below one. See Hall (2009) for a full survey of the multiplier literature.

41. This is a nuanced area, however. It is true that the effectiveness of fiscal policy does not *depend* on the inflation expectations channel in Rendahl's model, but this does not mean that inflation expectations can have no impact on equilibrium outcomes. It should be equally possible to generate stimulus in his setting through promised changes in expected future prices – that is, forward guidance. This may provide a superior solution to the stabilization problem: private-sector consumption could be restored to more normal levels without government purchases being distorted by pure stimulus motives.

42. This claim brushes over some important technicalities, including whether the policy-maker has the ability to feed back on inflation expectations or just realized inflation. Cochrane (2011) provides a critical take on the literature that assumes feedback on current inflation is sufficient.

43. 'Long-run' here is used as shorthand for a situation in which output and inflation are constant.

44. Friedman (1969) was one of the first to see potential merits in this outcome.

45. Guerrieri and Lorenzoni (2015)'s main exercise exploring the zero bound predicts just a 5-quarter stay at zero. Benigno et al. (2014) prescribe a stay of up to 24 quarters under an optimal policy response, but this is associated with output and inflation levels that are above their normal values, which makes this an unlikely positive explanation for why rates have stayed low for so long. Rates rise faster under automatic policy rules. None of these cases can account for the 20-year episode of near zero rates that Japan has witnessed.

46. Similar results are established by Aruoba, Cuba-Borda and Schorfheide (2016), who analyse the effects of a fiscal expansion that is calibrated to the 2009 American

Recovery and Reinvestment Act, comparing outcomes between fundamental and self-fulfilling equilibria.

47. This model is due to Iacoviello and Neri (2010).

48. As before, for simplicity we assume that all production is used for private consumption. We also suppose outcomes at $t + 1$ are known with certainty, in line with Cochrane's own assumptions.

49. See Benigno et al. (2012) for a more sceptical interpretation of the scope for capital controls.

50. See Corsetti et al. (2008, 2013).

51. See also Burstein et al. (2005) on this issue.

References

Ábrahám, A., Carceles-Poveda, E., Liu, Y., and Marimon, R. 2015. On the Optimal Design of a Financial Stability Fund. Manuscript.

Akkaya, Y. 2014. Uncertainty of Interest Path as a Monetary Policy Instrument. Manuscript.

Andrade, P., Gaballo, G., Mengus, E., and Mojon, B. 2015. Forward Guidance and Heterogeneous Beliefs. Manuscript.

Angeletos, G. M., and La'O, J. 2013. Sentiments. *Econometrica*, **81**, 739–779.

Aruoba, S. B., Cuba-Borda, P., and Schorfheide, F. 2016. Macroeconomic Dynamics at the ZLB: A Tale of Two Equilibria. Manuscript.

Bachmann, R., and Sims, E. R. 2012. Confidence and the Transmission of Government Spending Shocks. *Journal of Monetary Economics*, **59**, 235–249.

Bachmann, R., Berg, T. O., and Sims, E. R. 2015. Inflation Expectations and Readiness to Spend at the Zero Lower Bound: Cross-Sectional Evidence. *American Economic Journal: Economic Policy*, **7**, 1–35.

Bagehot, W. 1873. *Lombard Street: A Description of the Money Market*. Henry S. King & Co.

Bahaj, S., and Rendahl, P. 2015. Deconstructing the Fiscal Multiplier. Manuscript.

Baldwin, R., and Teulings, C. 2014. *Secular Stagnation: Facts, Causes and Cures*. published at https://voxeu.org.

Bauer, M. D., and Rudebusch, G. D. 2014. The Signaling Channel for Federal Reserve Bond Purchases. *International Journal of Central Banking*, **10**, 233–289.

Beaudry, P., and Portier, F. 2013. Understanding Non-Inflationary Demand Driven Business Cycles. Manuscript.

Bems, R., and di Giovanni, J. 2014. Income-Induced Expenditure Switching. CEPR Discussion Paper 9887.

Benhabib, J., Schmitt-Grohé, S., and Uribe, M. 2001. The Perils of Taylor Rules. *Journal of Economic Theory*, **96**, 40–96.

Benigno, G., Chen, H., Otrok, C., Rebucci, A., and Young, E. R. 2012. Capital Controls or Exchange Rate Policies? A Pecuniary Externality Perspective. Centre for Economic Performance Discussion Paper No 1160.

Benigno, P., Eggertsson, G. B., and Romei, F. 2014. Dynamic Debt Deleveraging and Optimal Monetary Policy. NBER Working Paper 20556.

Blanchard, O., and Galí, J. 2007. Real Wage Rigidities and the New Keynesian Model. *Journal of Money, Credit, and Banking*, **39**, 35–65.

Blanchard, O., Dell 'Ariccia, G., and Mauro, P. 2010. Rethinking Macroeconomic Policy. *Journal of Money, Credit and Banking*, **42**, 199–215.

Brendon, C., Paustian, M., and Yates, A. 2015. Self-Fulfilling Recessions at the Zero Lower Bound. Manuscript.

Broda, C., and Parker, J. A. 2014. The Economic Stimulus Payments of 2008 and the Aggregate Demand for Consumption. NBER Working Paper 20122.

Brunnermeier, M. K., and Sannikov, Y. 2014. A Macroeconomic Model with a Financial Sector. *American Economic Review*, **104**, 379–421.

Buiter, W. H. 2009. Negative Nominal Interest Rates: Three Ways to Overcome the Zero Lower Bound. *The North American Journal of Economics and Finance*, **20**, 213–238.

Burstein, A., Eichenbaum, M., and Rebelo, S. 2005. Large Devaluations and the Real Exchange Rate. *Journal of Political Economy*, **113**, 742–784.

Caballero, R. J., and Farhi, E. 2014. On the Role of Safe Asset Shortages in Secular Stagnation. In: Baldwin, R., and Teulings, C. (eds), *Secular Stagnation: Facts, Causes and Cures*. published at https://voxeu.org.

Caballero, R. J., and Farhi, E. 2015. The Safety Trap. Manuscript.

Cacciatore, M., Fiori, G., and Ghironi, F. 2016. Market Deregulation and Optimal Monetary Policy in a Monetary Union. *Journal of International Economics*, **99**, 120–137.

Campbell, J. R., Evans, C. L., Fisher, J. D. M., and Justiniano, A. 2012. Macroeconomic Effects of Federal Reserve Forward Guidance. *Brookings Papers on Economic Activity*, **44**, 1–80.

Chamley, C. 2014. When Demand Creates Its Own Supply: Saving Traps. *Review of Economic Studies*, **81**, 651–680.

Chari, V. V., Kehoe, P. J., and McGrattan, E. R. 2009. New Keynesian Models: Not Yet Useful for Policy Analysis. *American Economic Journal: Macroeconomics*, **1**, 242–266.

Chen, H. V., Cúrdia, and Ferrero, A. 2012. The Macroeconomic Effects of Large-Scale Asset Purchase Programmes. *Economic Journal*, **122**, F289–F315.

Christensen, J. H. E., and Rudebusch, G. D. 2012. The Response of Interest Rates to US and UK Quantitative Easing. *Economic Journal*, **122**, F385–F414.

Christiano, L., Eichenbaum, M., and Rebelo, S. 2011. When is the Government Spending Multiplier Large? *Journal of Political Economy*, **119**, 78–121.

Clarida, R., Galí, J., and Gertler, M. 2000. Monetary Policy Rules and Macroeconomic Stability: Evidence and Some Theory. *Quarterly Journal of Economics*, **115**, 147–180.

Cochrane, J. H. 2011. Determinacy and Identification with Taylor Rules. *Journal of Political Economy*, **119**, 565–615.

Cochrane, J. H. 2015. The New-Keynesian Liquidity Trap. Manuscript.

Coenen, G., Erceg, C. J., Freedman, C., Furceri, D., Kumhof, M., Lalonde, R., Laxton, D., Lindé, J., Mourougane, A., Muir, D., and Mursula, S. 2012. Effects of Fiscal Stimulus in Structural Models. *American Economic Journal: Macroeconomics*, **4**, 22–68.

Cook, D., and Devereux, M. B. 2014. Exchange Rate Flexibility under the Zero Lower Bound. CEPR Discussion Paper 10202.

Correia, I., Nicolini, J. P., and Teles, P. 2008. Optimal Fiscal and Monetary Policy: Equivalence Results. *Journal of Political Economy*, **116**, 141–170.

Correia, I., Farhi, E., Nicolini, J. P., and Teles, P. 2013. Unconventional Fiscal Policy at the Zero Bound. *American Economic Review*, **103**, 1172–1211.

Corsetti, G., Dedola, L., and Leduc, S. 2008. International Risk Sharing and the Transmission of Productivity Shocks. *Review of Economic Studies*, **75**, 443–473.

Corsetti, G., Dedola, L., and Leduc, S. 2010. Optimal Monetary Policy in Open Economies. Chap. 16 of: Friedman, B. M., and Woodford, M. (eds), *Handbook of Monetary Economics*, vol. 1. Elsevier, pp. 861–933.

Corsetti, G., Kuester, K., and Müller, G. 2011. Floats, Pegs and the Transmission of Fiscal Policy. In: Cespedes, Luis Felipe, and Gali, Jordi (eds), *Fiscal Policy and Macroeconomic Performance*. Santiago, Chile: Central Bank of Chile.

Corsetti, G., Martin, P., and Pesenti, P. 2013. Varieties and the transfer problem. *Journal of International Economics*, **89**, 1–12.

Cúrdia, V., and Woodford, M. 2009. Credit Spreads and Monetary Policy. *NBER Working Paper 15289*.

David Miles. 2009. Money, Banks and Quantitative Easing. *Speech given at the 14th Northern Ireland Economic Conference, Belfast, 30 September 2009*.

Del Negro, M., Giannoni, M., and Patterson, C. 2012. The Forward Guidance Puzzle. Federal Reserve Bank of New York Staff Report No. 574, Revised May 2013.

den Haan, W. J., Rendahl, P., and Riegler, M. 2014. Unemployment (Fears), Precautionary Savings, and Aggregate Demand. Manuscript.

Diamond, P. A. 1982. Aggregate Demand Management in Search Equilibrium. *Journal of Political Economy*, **90**, 881–894.

Eggertsson, G. B. 2011. What Fiscal Policy is Effective at Zero Interest Rates? *NBER Macroeconomics Annual*, **25**, 59–112.

Eggertsson, G. B., and Krugman, P. R. 2012. Debt, Deleveraging, and the Liquidity Trap: A Fisher-Minsky-Koo Approach. *Quarterly Journal of Economics*, **127**, 1469–1513.

Eggertsson, G. B., and Mehrotra, N. R. 2014. A Model of Secular Stagnation. NBER Working Paper 20574.

Eggertsson, G. B., and Woodford, M. 2003. The Zero Interest-Rate Bound and Optimal Monetary Policy. *Brookings Papers on Economic Activity*, **1**, 139–211.

Eggertsson, G. B., Ferrero, A., and Raffo, A. 2014. Can Structural Reforms Help Europe? *Journal of Monetary Economics*, **61**, 2–22.

Eichengreen, B. 2015. Secular Stagnation: The Long View. *American Economic Review: Papers & Proceedings 2015*, **105**, 66–70.

Ellison, M., and Tischbirek, A. 2014. Unconventional Government Debt Purchases as a Supplement to Conventional Monetary Policy. *Journal of Economic Dynamics and Control*, **43**, 199–217.

Evans, C. L. 2011. The Fed's Dual Mandate Responsibilities and Challenges Facing US Monetary Policy. *Speech delivered at the European Economics and Financial Centre Distinguished Speaker Seminar, London, September 7, 2011*.

Fahri, E., and Werning, I. 2014. Fiscal Unions. Manuscript.

Fahri, E., Gopinath, G., and Itskhoki, O. 2014. Fiscal Devaluations. *Review of Economic Studies*, **81**, 725–760.

Farmer, R. E. A. 2013. Animal Spirits, Financial Crises and Persistent Unemployment. *Economic Journal*, **123**, 317–340.

Farmer, R. E. A. 2014. The Evolution of Endogenous Business Cycles. *Macroeconomic Dynamics*, 1–14.

Fatas, A., and Mihov, I. 2001. The Effects of Fiscal Policy on Consumption and Employment: Theory and Evidence. CEPR Discussion Paper 2760.

Feldstein, M. 2002. Rethinking Stabilization. Manuscript.

Fernández-Villaverde, J., Guerrón-Quintana, P., and Rubio-Ramirez, J. F. 2014. Supply-Side Policies and the Zero Lower Bound. *IMF Economic Review*, **62**, 248–260.

Friedman, M. 1969. *The Optimum Quantity of Money*. London: Macmillan.

Gaballo, G., and Marimon, R. 2015. Breaking the Spell with Credit-Easing: Self-Confirming Credit Crises in Competitive Search Economies. Manuscript.

Gagnon, J., Raskin, M., Remache, J., and Sack, B. 2011. The Financial Market Effects of the Federal Reserve's Large-Scale Asset Purchases. *International Journal of Central Banking*, **7**, 3–43.

Gertler, M., and Karadi, P. 2011. A Model of Unconventional Monetary Policy. *Journal of Monetary Economics*, **58**, 17–34.

Guerrieri, V., and Lorenzoni, G. 2015. Credit Crises Precautionary Savings and the Liquidity Trap. Manuscript.

Hall, R. E. 2009. By How Much Does GDP Rise If the Government Buys More Output? *Brookings Papers on Economic Activity*, **10**, 183–231.

Harrison, R. 2011. Asset Purchase Policies and Portfolio Balance Effects: A DSGE Analysis. In: Chadha, J. S., and Holly, S. (eds), *Interest Rates, Prices and Liquidity: Lessons from the Financial Crisis*. Cambridge: Cambridge University Press, pp. 117–143.

Harrison, R. 2012. Asset Purchase Policy at the Effective Zero Lower Bound for Interest Rates. Bank of England Working Paper 444.

Heathcote, J., and Perri, F. 2015. Wealth and Volatility. Manuscript.

Heathcote, J., Storesletten, K., and Violante, G. 2009. Quantitative Macroeconomics with Heterogeneous Households. *Annual Review of Economics*, **1**, 319–354.

Hellwig, C., and Venkateswaran, V. 2014. Dispersed Information, Sticky Prices and Monetary Business Cycles: A Hayekian Perspective. Manuscript.

Iacoviello, M., and Neri, S. 2010. Housing Market Spillovers: Evidence from an Estimated DSGE Model. *American Economic Journal: Macroeconomics*, **2**, 125–164.

Jappelli, T., and Pistaferri, L. 2014. Fiscal Policy and MPC Heterogeneity. *American Economic Journal: Macroeconomics*, **6**, 107–136.

Johnson, D. S., Parker, J. A., and Souleles, N. S. 2005. Household Expenditure and the Income Tax Rebates of 2001. *American Economic Review*, **96**, 1589–1610.

Joyce, M. A. S., Lasaosa, A., Stevens, I., and Tong, M. 2011. The Financial Market Impact of Quantitative Easing in the United Kingdom. *International Journal of Central Banking*, **7**, 113–161.

Kaplan, G., and Menzio, G. 2015. Shopping Externalities and Self-Fulfilling Unemployment. *forthcoming in Journal of Political Economy*.

Kaplan, G., and Violante, G. L. 2014. A Model of the Consumption Response to Fiscal Stimulus Payments. *Econometrica*, **82**, 1199–1239.

Krishnamurthy, A., and Vissing-Jorgensen, A. 2011. The Effects of Quantitative Easing on Interest Rates: Channels and Implications for Policy. *Brookings Papers on Economic Activity*, **43**, 215–287.

Krugman, P. R. 1998. It's Baaack: Japan's Slump and the Return of the Liquidity Trap. *Brookings Papers on Economic Activity*, **1998**, 137–206.

Lloyd, S. P. 2015. Unconventional Monetary Policy and the Interest Rate Channel: Signalling and Portfolio Rebalancing. Manuscript.

Lorenzoni, G. 2009. A Theory of Demand Shocks. *American Economic Review*, **99**, 2050–2084.

Lucas, R. E. Jr. 1978. Asset Prices in an Exchange Economy. *Econometrica*, **46**, 1429–1445.

McKay, A., Nakamura, E., and Steinsson, J. 2015. The Power of Forward Guidance Revisited. NBER Working Paper 20882.

Mertens, K., and Ravn, M. O. 2014. Fiscal Policy in an Expectations-Driven Liquidity Trap. *Review of Economic Studies*, **81**, 1637–1667.

Mian, Atif, and Sufi, Amir. 2011. House Prices, Home Equity-Based Borrowing, and the US Household Leverage Crisis. *American Economic Review*, **101**, 2132–2156.

Michaillat, P., and Saez, E. 2015. Aggregate Demand, Idle Time, and Unemployment. *Quarterly Journal of Economics*, **130**, 507–569.

Mishkin, F. 2011. Monetary Policy Strategy: Lessons from the Crisis. NBER Working Paper 16755.

Misra, K., and Surico, P. 2014. Consumption, Income Changes, and Heterogeneity: Evidence from Two Fiscal Stimulus Programs. *American Economic Journal: Macroeconomics*, **6**, 84–106.

Mortensen, D. T., and Pissarides, C. A. 1994. Job Creation and Job Destruction in the Theory of Unemployment. *Review of Economic Studies*, **61**, 397–415.

Müller, A., Storesletten, K., and Zilibotti, F. 2015. Sovereign Debt and Structural Reforms. CEPR Discussion Paper 10588.

Oh, H., and Reis, R. 2012. Targeted Transfers and the Fiscal Response to the Great Recession. *Journal of Monetary Economics*, **59**, S50–S64.

Pappa, E., Sajedi, R., and Vella, E. 2015. Fiscal Consolidation with Tax Evasion and Corruption. *forthcoming in Journal of International Economics*.

Parker, J. A., Souleles, N. S., Johnson, D. S., and McClelland, R. 2013. Consumer Spending and the Economic Stimulus Payments of 2008. *American Economic Review*, **103**, 2530–2553.

Ramey, V. A. 2011. Can Government Purchases Stimulate the Economy? *Journal of Economic Literature*, **49**, 673–685.

Ramey, V. A., and Shapiro, M.D. 1998. Costly Capital Reallocation and the Effects of Government Spending. *Carnegie-Rochester Conference Series on Public Policy*, **48**, 145–194.

Ravn, M. O., and Sterk, V. 2013. Job Uncertainty and Deep Recessions. Manuscript.

Ravn, M. O., Schmitt-Grohé, S., and Uribe, M. 2012. Consumption, Government Spending, and the Real Exchange Rate. *Journal of Monetary Economics*, **59**, 215–234.

Rendahl, P. 2015. Fiscal Policy in an Unemployment Crisis. Manuscript.

Schmitt-Grohé, S., and Uribe, M. 2011. The Optimal Rate of Inflation. In: Friedman, B. M., and Woodford, M. (eds), *Handbook of Monetary Economics*, vol. 3B. Elsevier, pp. 653–722.

Schneider, F., and Buehn, A. 2012. Shadow Economies in Highly Developed OECD Countries: What Are the Driving Forces? IZA Discussion Papers 6891, Institute for the Study of Labor (IZA).

Smets, F., and Wouters, R. 2003. An Estimated Dynamic Stochastic General Equilibrium Model of the Euro Area. *Journal of the European Economic Association*, **1**, 1123–1175.

Smets, F., and Wouters, R. 2007. Shocks and Frictions in US Business Cycles: A Bayesian DSGE Approach. *American Economic Review*, **97**, 586–606.

Stock, J. H., and Watson, M. W. 2002. Has the Business Cycle Changed and Why? *NBER Macroeconomics Annual*, **17**, 159–230.

Straub, L., and Ulbricht, R. 2014. Endogenous Uncertainty and Credit Crunches. Manuscript.

Surico, P., and Trezzi, R. 2015. Consumer Spending and Property Taxes. Finance and Economics Discussion Series 2015-057, FRB.

Svensson, L. E. O. 2001. The Zero Bound in an Open Economy: A Foolproof Way of Escaping from a Liquidity Trap. *Monetary and Economic Studies*, **19**, 277–312.

Vayanos, D., and Vila, J.-L. 2009. A Preferred-Habitat Model of the Term Structure of Interest Rates. NBER Working Paper 15487.

Wallace, N. 1981. A Modigliani-Miller Theorem for Open-Market Operations. *American Economic Review*, **71**, 267–274.

Weale, M. 2013. Forward Guidance and its Effects. *Speech given to the National Institute for Economic and Social Research, London, 11 December 2013*.

Werning, I. 2012. Managing a Liquidity Trap: Monetary and Fiscal Policy. Manuscript.

Wicksell, K. 1898. *Interest and Prices*, English translation by R.F. Kahn. London: Macmillan.

Wieland, J. 2014. Are Negative Supply Shocks Expansionary at the Zero Lower Bound? Manuscript.

Woodford, M. 2003. *Interest and Prices: Foundations of a Theory of Monetary Policy*. Princeton: Princeton University Press.

Woodford, M. 2012. Methods of Policy Accommodation at the Interest-Rate Lower Bound. Manuscript.

11   Financial Regulation in Europe: Foundations and Challenges

Thorsten Beck, Elena Carletti and Itay Goldstein

Abstract

This chapter discusses recent regulatory reforms and relates them to different market failures in banking, based on the recent theoretical and empirical literature with focus on insights from the recent crisis. We also provide a broader discussion of challenges in financial sector regulation, related to the regulatory perimeter and financial innovation as tools financial market participants use to evade tighter regulatory frameworks. We argue for a dynamic view of regulation that takes into account the changing nature of risk-taking activities and regulatory arbitrage efforts. We also stress the need for a balanced approach between complex and simple tools, a strong focus on systemic in addition to idiosyncratic regulation, and a stronger emphasis on the resolution phase of financial regulation.

11.1   Introduction

The recent crisis has given impetus not only to an intensive regulatory reform debate, but also to a deeper discussion on the role of financial systems in modern market economies and the role of financial innovation. While the pre-crisis consensus on the financial system had been that finance serves as the engine for modern market economies, this has been questioned since the recent crisis experience. The fragility risks of finance have claimed a much more important space in the public debate than before the crisis. The pendulum has swung from focus on self-regulation and reliance on market forces to a debate on reducing implicit subsidies and the range of permissible activities for banks.

Historically, the banking system has been one of the most regulated sectors in the economy. As we will discuss further below, this is due to market failures resulting in the external costs of the failure of a specific bank for the rest of the financial system and the real economy. Regulation thus has the task of minimizing the risk of bank failure and its negative effects. On the other hand, there are concerns of overregulation imposing unnecessary costs on financial service providers, reducing their efficiency and ultimately undermining economic

470

growth. The right balance of reducing fragility and maximizing the efficiency of financial intermediation has been thus at the core of regulatory debates over the past decades, with observers pointing to regulatory super-cycles. Regulatory regimes are often tightened after major crises, with heavy emphasis on restrictions and regulatory oversight and then relaxed over time, with more emphasis on market forces and self-regulation.

The recent crises have raised doubts not only about the right regulatory balance, but more generally, about the nature of bank regulation. The experience over the past few years has shown that focusing on the stability of individual financial institutions is insufficient to understand the fragility of the overall financial system. The recent credit boom–bust cycle has also shed doubt on the separation of monetary and prudential policy, a founding principle of inflation targeting. The recent fragility and taxpayer support for many financial institutions has raised questions about the activities regulated banks should be permitted to undertake and about a financial safety net that minimizes bail-out risks for taxpayers across the globe. Finally, the global nature of the recent crises has underlined the need for better cooperation mechanisms between regulators, and pointing to the need to match the geographic footprint of individual financial institutions with a corresponding regulatory perimeter. These new debates have partly arisen from the crisis experience, but partly also from underlying changes in the nature of financial intermediation over the past decade: more market-based, more interconnected, more global.

The recent crises have consequently led to an array of regulatory reform efforts, on the national, European and global level, ranging from tighter capital requirements over activity restrictions to new bank resolution frameworks. Beyond these individual reforms, however, there looms a larger challenge: how to construct a regulatory system which is safe to regulatory arbitrage. Regulatory reforms following crises often aim at preventing the last crisis, closing loopholes and addressing sources of fragility that caused that particular crisis. Ample experience, however, has shown that new regulation leads to evasion efforts by financial market participants and shifting of risky activities outside the regulatory perimeter. This feedback loop and catch-up process of regulators raises the more fundamental question of how regulation can adapt to the dynamic nature of the financial system.

On a more general level, behind the debate on the optimal degree of regulation is the growth-fragility trade-off in the financial system. On the one hand, providing liquidity transformation, creating private information and operating in payment systems make banks and markets critical for modern economies and economic growth. On the other hand, the same activities make banks and other institutions fragile, as they force a high degree of interconnectedness and create substantial externalities from the failure of an individual institutions. Importantly, this suggests that the growth benefits are not obtainable without a certain degree of fragility and risk-taking in the financial system. Thus, the focus should be more on the optimal degree of risk-taking and – what is more feasible – on minimizing the repercussions of bank failure for the overall financial system and the real economy. Critically, financial stability is not an objective in itself, but rather a condition for the sustainability of an efficient and market-supporting financial system.

The remainder of the chapter is structured as follows. The next section presents the different regulatory reforms enacted and planned in Europe after the recent crises. Section 11.3 discusses the market failures in banking as micro-foundation for bank regulation and maps them to the regulatory reforms presented in Section 11.2. Section 11.4 focuses on the regulatory perimeter and efforts by regulated financial intermediaries to use financial innovation to move risky activities outside this perimeter. Section 11.5 discusses regulatory challenges specific to Europe, including the overreliance on banks, challenges related to the banking union and the governance structure more generally. Section 11.6 draws policy conclusions from our analysis and concludes by looking forward to new research challenges.

Before proceeding, we would like to point to a couple of areas that we are unable to cover in this survey, given space constraints. One such area is compliance risk, which has featured prominently in recent years with high penalty payments either being imposed by regulators or negotiated between regulators and banks. Another area is that of corporate and regulatory governance. While we will refer to the new supervisory architecture in Europe in the context of the discussion on the banking union, we will be unable to go in depth into this. Similarly, the issue of taxation will not be covered in depth. Another area is that of the relationship between competition and stability, where ambiguous theoretical predictions have given rise to a large number of empirical studies. Finally, we will focus primarily on the banking system, where regulation has traditionally been centred, but we will discuss the need for and challenges in expanding the regulatory perimeter.

11.2   Recent Financial Reforms in Europe

The main financial reforms introduced after the 2007 Global Financial Crisis are contained in the new Basel III regulatory standards. The new accord introduces a stricter definition of capital, a higher quality and quantity of capital, two dynamic capital buffers, a minimum leverage ratio, and two minimum liquidity ratios. The Basel III accord is implemented in Europe through the Capital Requirement Directive IV (CRD IV), whose objective is to create a level playing field across countries. The package contains a directive and a regulation. Key aspects of the Basel III accord such as the new definition of capital and the liquidity requirements are included in the regulation and will thus be directly applicable in the Member States. Others such as capital buffers, enhanced governance and other rules governing access to deposit-taking activities are included in the directive and will therefore need to be transposed into national laws with the usual discretion left to the national regulators to implement more stringent rules (Department for International Development, 2013).

Other important reforms in Europe concern the new rules for the resolution of banks and the creation of the Banking Union.

We will discuss each area of regulatory reform in turn. Specifically, we will present regulatory reforms of (i) capital requirements, (ii) liquidity requirements, (iii) bank resolution reforms, including bail-in rules, (iv) banking union and (v) activity restrictions. As we will point out, one theme throughout these reforms is a stronger focus on systemic rather than idiosyncratic bank risk.

11.2.1 Capital Requirements

As in the Basel III standards, the CRD IV leaves the minimum capital requirements unchanged at 8 per cent of risk-weighted assets (to which the capital buffers have to be added) but, as in the international accord, it requires banks to increase the Common Equity Tier 1 (CET 1) from the current 2 per cent to 4.5 per cent of risk-weighted assets. The regulation defines CET 1 instruments using 14 criteria similar to those in Basel III and mandates the European Banking Authority to monitor the capital instruments issued by the financial institutions. Banks are also required to maintain a nonrisk-based leverage ratio that includes off-balance sheet exposures as a way to contain the risk-based capital requirement as well as the build-up of leverage.

To address the problems related to systemic risk and interconnectedness, the CRD IV also introduces size restrictions in line with the prescriptions of the Basel Committee and the Financial Stability Board. In particular, it prescribes mandatory capital buffers for global systemically important institutions (G-SIIs) and voluntary buffers for other EU or systemically important domestic institutions. G-SIIs will be divided in five sub-categories, depending on their systemic importance. A progressive additional CET 1 capital requirement, ranging from 1 per cent to 2.5 per cent, will be applied to the first four groups, while a buffer of 3.5 per cent will be applied to the highest sub-category. Each Member State will maintain flexibility concerning the stricter requirements to impose on systemically important domestic institutions (D-SIIs). This means that the decision on the supplementary capital requirements for larger institutions will be left to the discretion of the respective supervisors, with potential distortions in terms of the level playing field.

Further, the CRD IV package contains a capital conservation buffer in the form of an additional common equity for 2.5 per cent of risk-weighted assets, as well as of a countercyclical buffer requiring a further range of 0-2.5 per cent of common equity when authorities judge that credit growth may lead to an excessive build-up of systemic risk. Banks that do not maintain the conservation buffer will face restrictions on dividend payouts, share buybacks and bonuses.

Member States have some flexibility in relation to the above mentioned capital buffers and also with respect to macroprudential tools such as the level of own funds, liquidity and large exposure requirements, the capital conservation buffer, public disclosure requirements, risk weights for targeting asset bubbles in property bubbles, etc. For these tools Member States have the possibility, for up to two years (extendable), to impose stricter macroprudential requirements for domestic institutions that pose an increased risk to financial stability. The Council can however reject, by qualified majority, stricter national measures proposed by a Member State.

Note also that the CRD IV leaves the possibility for European banks to have zero risk weight for all sovereign debt issued in domestic currency (Hay, 2013), while it assigns capital requirements depending on the risk of the sovereign for non-Euro denominated bonds. This is the same situation as in the US currently, where Basel I, under which the sovereign debt of developed countries enjoys zero-risk weighting, still holds. Discussions are ongoing at the moment as to whether to change the favourable prudential treatment of European sovereign bonds following, in particular, the recent ESRB report (ESRB, 2014).

In summary, tighter capital requirements aim both for higher quantity and higher quality of capital. However, they also complement the originally purely micro-prudential approach with a macroprudential approach, both related to the cross-sectional dimension (SIFIs) and to the time-series dimension (capital buffers) of systemic risk.

11.2.2   Liquidity Requirements

In addition to changes in the capital requirements, the CRD IV package also introduces global liquidity standards. Following again the Basel accords, two ratios are envisaged: a Liquidity Coverage Ratio (LCR) to withstand a stressed funding scenario and a Net Stable Funding Ratio (NSFR) to address liquidity mismatches. The LCR is a measure of an institution's ability to withstand a severe liquidity freeze that lasts at least 30 days. Liabilities are categorized in terms of the degree of difficulty in rolling them over. Each category is assigned a percentage representing the portion of the liability that remains a source of funding during the next 30 days or is replaced by funds in the same category. Assets are also sorted into categories with each category being assigned a percentage haircut representing the loss that would be incurred if the asset were to be sold in the middle of a severe financial crisis. The LCR is defined as the ratio of High Quality Liquid Assets (HQLA) to total net cash outflows over the next 30 calendar days and should exceed 100 per cent so that the financial institution can survive at least 30 days.

By contrast, the NSFR is designed to reveal risks that arise from significant maturity mismatches between assets and liabilities and takes therefore a longer-term approach. It is the ratio of the available amount of stable funding to the required amount of stable funding over a one-year horizon. Stable funding includes customer deposits, long-term wholesale funding, and equity. The required amount of stable funding is calculated by weighting assets (longer-term assets receive higher weights but assets which mature within one year do not necessarily receive a zero weight). Again, the idea is that the ratio exceeds 100 per cent.

The liquidity requirements are to be introduced over an extended period of time and the exact implementation and thus effectiveness will be a function of the classification of different funding sources.

11.2.3   Resolution Framework and Bail-In Instruments

During the Global Financial Crisis, the lack of effective bank resolution frameworks was one major impediment to effectively intervening into failing financial institutions, which left most countries with the option to either bail-out or close and liquidate banks through the corporate insolvency process. Many countries have therefore introduced or reformed their bank resolution frameworks in recent years. While there are important differences across different jurisdictions in Europe, consistent with different legal traditions and institutional arrangements of the financial safety net, the Bank Recovery and Resolution Directive (BRRD) sets minimum standards, with the objective of creating consistency across borders within the European Union. These include recovery and resolution plans to be drawn up by national resolution authorities, providing authorities with a set of early intervention powers and resolution mechanisms, including the power to sell or merge the business with another bank, to set up a temporary bridge bank to operate critical functions, to separate good assets from bad ones and to convert to shares or write down the debt of failing banks. The directive also foresees the establishment of national resolution funds, to be financed by bank contributions to cover up to 5 per cent additional losses beyond the capital buffers of failing banks.

One important dimension of the post-crisis bank resolution reforms has been the move from bail-out to bail-in. After the crisis, politicians pledged to 'never' have tax payers have to pay for bank losses again, and bail-in regimes are therefore being introduced as an additional buffer to offset losses in worst-case scenarios. The directive therefore foresees bail-in of an additional 8 per cent of liabilities to be converted to equity capital in case equity funding is exhausted.

In the discussion of the additional loss absorption capacity to enable such a bail-in, two concepts have to be distinguished. Specifically, the total loss absorbing capacity (TLAC) for 30 G-SIBs, as recommended by the Financial Stability Board (FSB) and the minimum requirement of own funds and eligible liabilities (MREL) for all EU banks in line with the Bank Recovery and Resolution Directive (BRRD) requirements for all EU banks and investment firms, and set by resolution authorities. In addition to own funds, this can include the needed recapitalization amount according to a resolution plan plus an estimate of possible losses to the deposit insurance fund if the bank were to be liquidated.

The TLAC is part of the pillar 1 requirements of Basel III and is defined in terms of RWA and leverage. Specifically, the proposed minimum TLAC requirements for G-SIBs is 16–20 per cent of a group's consolidated risk-weighted assets. The TLAC should consist of instruments that can be written down or converted into equity in case of resolution, including capital instruments (Common Equity Tier 1 (CET1), Additional Tier 1 (AdT1) and Tier 2 (T2)), and long-term unsecured debt. It is to be applied starting in 2019. The MREL is defined relative to total liabilities and own funds and starts in 2016 with a four year transition period. The exact amount of the MREL is to be determined by the relevant resolution authorities.

11.2.4   Banking Union

One major financial reform in Europe concerns the creation of a banking union. This comprises a single supervisory mechanism (SSM), a Single Resolution Mechanism, a Single Rulebook and a harmonized (but, importantly, still decentralized) deposit insurance scheme. The rationales for a banking union are various: (i) break the adverse feedback loop between sovereigns and the financial system; (ii) act as a pre-condition for bank recapitalization through the European Stability Mechanism (ESM); (iii) create more distance between banks and regulators, thus preventing forbearance and regulatory capture; and (iv) improve the effectiveness of supervision through the implementation of a '*single rulebook*'.

The SSM, which is hosted by the European Central Bank (ECB), started its functioning on 4 November 2014. In brief, the SSM is now the supervisor of all banks operating in the Euro area. It supervises directly the 133 largest banks, accounting for approximately 85 per cent of the assets of the banks operating in the Euro-area, and, indirectly, the other remaining banks. Banks in other European Member States may voluntarily decide to be supervised by the SSM. Moreover, the SSM should conclude Memorandums of Understanding with national authorities of nonparticipating Member States to set the general terms of cooperation.

The SSM operates as any other normal supervisor in that it is empowered with the supervisory tasks that can ensure the coherent and effective implementation of the prudential supervision of credit institutions, in particular concerning the application of the single rulebook for financial services. For example, the ECB has the power: to grant and withdraw banks' license authorizations, although in compliance with national laws and subject to specific arrangements reflecting the role of national authorities; assess the suitability of the purchase of significant stakes in credit institutions; monitor and enforce compliance with capital regulation rules, limits to the size of exposures to individual counterparties and disclosure requirements on a credit institution's financial situation; require credit institutions to dispose of sufficient liquid assets to withstand situations of market stress; and limit leverage.

Other measures like additional capital buffers, including a capital conservation buffer, a countercyclical capital buffer and global and other systemic institution buffers and other measures aimed at addressing systemic or macroprudential risk remain under the control of national authorities. The SSM can request stricter requirements and more stringent measures than the ones proposed by the national authorities. These rules apply only for the macroprudential tools for which there is a legal basis, which implies that at the moment all the instruments that are not included in the CRD IV package such as loan-to-value ratios, that is, the ratio of a loan to the value of an asset purchased, remain with the national authorities, without the ECB having any possibility to intervene. This can turn out to be an important shortcoming, which we will discuss in more detail.

The SSM retains powers to ensure that credit institutions have proper internal governance arrangements, and if necessary, impose specific additional own funds, liquidity and disclosure requirements to guarantee adequate internal capital. Moreover, the SSM has the tasks and the power to intervene at an early stage in troubled credit institutions in order to preserve financial stability. This should, however, not include resolution powers. Other tasks like consumer protection or supervision of payments services remain with national authorities.

Specific governance structures have been put in place to maintain full separation and avoid conflicts of interest between the exercise of monetary policy and supervisory tasks within the ECB. In particular, the SSM's Supervisory Board plans and carries out the SSM's supervisory tasks and proposes draft decisions for adoption by the ECB's Governing Council. Decisions are deemed adopted if the Governing Council does not object within a defined period of time that may not exceed ten working days. The Governing Council may adopt or object to draft decisions but cannot change them. A Mediation Panel has been created to resolve differences of views expressed by the NCAs concerned regarding an objection by the Governing Council to a draft decision of the Supervisory Board.

The second pillar of the banking union concerns the Single Resolution Mechanism (SRM). The objective is to manage resolution efficiently with minimal costs to taxpayers and the real economy. As for the SSM, the SRM applies to all banks in the Euro Area and other Member States that opt to participate within the SRM, the Single Resolution Board (SRB) and the Single Resolution Fund (SRF). The former, which started to operate on 1 January 2015 but will be fully operational from January 2016, is the European resolution authority for the Banking Union. It works in close cooperation with the national resolution authorities of participating Member States in order to ensure an orderly resolution of failing banks according to the rules contained in the Bank Recovery and Resolution Directive (BRRD). These include harmonized rules concerning acquisitions by the private sector, creation of a bridge bank, separation of clean and toxic assets and bail-in creditors.[1]]

The SRB is in charge of the SRF, a pool of money constituted from contributions by all banks in the participating Member States. The SRF has a target level of €55 billion (approximately 1% of all banks' assets of participating Member States) but has the possibility to borrow from the markets based on Board decisions. It will reach the target level over 8 years.

The resolution process is quite complicated and includes various institutions. The decision to resolve a bank will in most cases start with the ECB notifying the Board, the Commission, and the relevant national resolution authorities that a bank is failing. The Board will then adopt a resolution scheme including the relevant resolution tools and any use of the Fund. Before the Board adopts its decision, the Commission has to assess its compliance with state aid rules and can endorse or object to the resolution scheme. In case of disagreement between the Commission and the SRB, the Council will also be called to intervene. The approved resolution scheme will then be implemented by the national resolution authorities, in accordance with national law including relevant provisions transposing the Bank Recovery and Resolution Directive.

11.2.5   Activity Restrictions and Other Reforms

Another important set of reforms or proposals for reforms includes activity, size and bonus restrictions. For the sake of brevity, we describe them very briefly here and refer to Allen et al. (2013) for a more detailed discussion. The enactment and implementation of these reforms has proceeded at a much slower pace than the reforms described above.

The proposals on activity restrictions in Europe are contained in two reports, the Vickers report in the UK and the Liikanen report in Europe. Both the Vickers proposal and the Liikanen proposal aim at making banking groups safer and less connected to trading activities so as to reduce the burden on taxpayers. However, the two approaches present significant differences. The Vickers approach suggests ring-fencing essential banking activities that may need government support in the event of a crisis. In contrast, the Liikanen approach suggests isolating in a separate subsidiary those activities that will not receive government support in the event of a crisis but will rather be bailed-in. Moreover, the two proposals differ in terms of what activities have to be separated/ring-fenced. For example, deposits from and loans to large corporations have to be given permission not to be ring-fenced according to the Vickers approach, while they do not have to be separated according to the Liikanen approach. Also, trading activities need to be separated under the Liikanen approach only if they amount to a significant share of a bank's business, while they are never permitted within the ring-fence in the Vickers approach.

While ring-fencing is being implemented in the UK, to date no structural reforms have been formally introduced in Europe. Following the Liikanen report, in January 2014 the Commission put forth a proposal for a regulation on structural reforms but this has not yet been approved. Some individual countries, on the other hand, have been moving ahead with their national approaches, including the UK.

A final area of reforms has been financial sector taxation, though not much progress has been made. Based on the observation that taxation of the financial system is lower than its contribution to the economy and the idea that taxation can influence risk-taking behavior as well as volatility in financial markets, additional taxes such as financial transaction taxes have been proposed. Political resistance from several large players in the European Union, most prominently the UK, however, has so far prevented such plans from moving forward. Finally, there has been an array of regulatory reforms in the nonbank sector, which we will not discuss here (see Allen et al., 2013).

11.3   Microfoundations for Financial Reforms

11.3.1   Basic Failures in the Financial System

Financial regulation is designed to address market failures in the financial system. We now review the different failures that have been proposed by the literature and then link them to the financial reforms enacted in Europe to assess the microfoundations behind these reforms. We discuss three types of failures that have been widely discussed and studied:
1. Coordination problems and panics
2. Moral hazard and incentives
3. Interbank connections and contagion.

Coordination Problems and Panics
Banking crises have been observed for many years in many countries. One of their typical features is the massive withdrawal of deposits by depositors, often referred to as bank run. A leading view in the academic literature is that runs

are driven by panics or self-fulfilling beliefs. The formal analysis goes back to Bryant (1980) and Diamond and Dybvig (1983).

In these models, agents have uncertain needs for consumption in an environment in which long-term investments are costly to liquidate. Banks provide useful liquidity services to agents by offering demand deposit contracts. But these contracts lead to multiple equilibria. If depositors believe that other depositors will withdraw, then all agents find it rational to redeem their claims and a panic occurs. Another equilibrium exists where everybody believes no panic will occur and agents withdraw their funds according to their consumption needs. In this case, their demand can be met without a costly liquidation of assets.

Banking panics are inefficient. Hence, a common theme behind government intervention in the financial system is to prevent panics and help agents coordinate towards an efficient equilibrium. Going back to Diamond and Dybvig (1983), various tools have been considered in the literature for this purpose, with deposit insurance being perhaps the main one. One issue, however, is that the traditional theory is silent on which of the two equilibria will be selected in what circumstances. Hence, policy analysis that addresses costs and benefits of different tools becomes hard to conduct given that the exact benefits of policies in terms of reducing the likelihood of crises are hard to assess.

Challenging the panic-based approach to bank runs, a second set of theories has emerged, proposing that crises are a natural outgrowth of the business cycle. An economic downturn will reduce the value of bank assets, raising the possibility that banks will be unable to meet their commitments. If depositors receive information about an impending downturn in the cycle, they will anticipate financial difficulties in the banking sector and try to withdraw their funds, as argued by Chari and Jagannathan (1988) and Jacklin and Bhattacharya (1988). This attempt will precipitate the crisis. According to this interpretation, crises are not random events but depositors' response to the arrival of sufficiently negative information on the unfolding economic circumstances.

One strand of the business cycle explanation of crises stresses the role of information-induced runs as a form of market discipline. In particular, Calomiris and Kahn (1991) and Diamond and Rajan (2001) suggest that the threat of bank liquidation induced by depositors' runs can prevent the banker from diverting resources for personal use or can ensure that loans are repaid. In this view, not only may run crises prevent the continuation of inefficient banks, but may also help provide bankers better incentives, thus inducing better investment choices and better equilibrium allocations.

The global-games literature offers a reconciliation of the panic-based and fundamental-based approaches to bank runs. This literature goes back to Carlsson and van Damme (1993), who show that the introduction of slightly noisy information to agents in a model of strategic complementarities and self-fulfilling beliefs can generate a unique equilibrium, whereby the fundamentals uniquely determine whether a crisis will occur or not. Goldstein and Pauzner (2005) take the global-games approach to a bank-run setting. First, they show how the fundamentals of the bank uniquely determine whether a crisis will occur in a model that matches the payoff structure of a bank-run model, which is quite different from other global-games models. They also link the probability of a crisis to the banking contract, showing that a crisis becomes more likely when the bank offers greater liquidity. The bank then takes this into account, reducing the amount of liquidity offered, so that the cost of runs is balanced against the benefit from liquidity and risk sharing.

This approach is thus consistent with the panic-based and fundamental-based views. Here, crises occur because of self-fulfilling beliefs, that is, agents run just because they think that others are going to run. But, the fundamentals uniquely determine agents' expectations and thus the occurrence of a run. Thus, the approach is consistent with empirical evidence pointing to the element of panic and to those pointing to the link to fundamentals. In the first line of work, analysing the period 1867–1960, Friedman and Schwartz (1963) argued that the crises that occurred then were panic-based. In the second line of work, Gorton (1988) shows that in the US in the late nineteenth and early twentieth centuries, a leading economic indicator based on the liabilities of failed businesses could accurately predict the occurrence of banking crises. Goldstein (2012) surveys the differences between panic-based and fundamentals-based approaches and the ways of testing the hypotheses in the data.[2]

The global-games approach also lends itself to more extensive policy analysis, whereby a policy tool, such as deposit insurance, can be evaluated taking into consideration costs (e.g., creating a moral hazard for the bank and/or having to pay the bank in case of failure) and benefits (e.g., reducing the probability of runs). In a recent paper, Allen et al. (2014) use the global-games framework exactly for this purpose.

A final important remark is due here. Some argue that modern banking systems have increased in complexity over the last two decades; thus the literature à la Diamond and Dybvig, with its focus on bank runs by retail depositors, is no longer applicable to today's financial institutions. We argue that this is not the case. Despite running off-balance sheet vehicles or using various financial instruments to transfer credit risk, banks have remained as sensitive to panics and runs as they were at the beginning of the previous century. As Gorton (2008) points out, in the summer of 2007 holders of short-term liabilities refused to fund banks, expecting losses on subprime and subprime-related securities. As in the classic panics of the nineteenth and early twentieth century, there were effectively runs on banks. The difference is that modern runs typically involve the drying up of liquidity in the short-term capital markets (a wholesale run) instead of or in addition to depositor withdrawals. This also implies a much stronger interplay between financial institutions and financial markets in modern financial systems, as we shall stress later in the chapter. In summary, problems of runs and panics, and ways of reducing their likelihood are important, as is the challenge of the regulatory perimeter, as funding and thus sources of contagion can easily move outside the traditional banking system. The changing nature of bank runs also reflects the dynamic and rapidly changing nature of financial systems.

Moral Hazard and Incentives

The put-option character of banking provides incentives to bank owners to take aggressive risk (see, for example, the discussion in Carletti, 2008). Specifically, bank owners participate only in the upside of their risk decisions, while their losses are limited to their paid-in capital. This moral hazard problem is exacerbated by guarantees provided by governments targeted at avoiding the coordination problems and panics discussed above, which in turn might encourage bad behavior and excessive risk-taking. Knowing that the government is concerned about panics (described above) and/or contagion (described below), and will take steps to make sure that banks do not fail, banks might internalize less the consequences of their risk-taking, and so bring the system to a more fragile state. Hence, governments typically have to supplement any guarantees policy with restrictions on bank policies to curtail any incentive for excessive risk-taking. Such restrictions include, for example, imposing capital requirements on banks, reducing their risk taking incentives. Another important restriction to excessive risk-taking would be to allow banks to fail, thus forcing risk takers to face losses.

But moral hazard, incentive problems, and excessive risk-taking are not only the result of government guarantees. Allen and Gale (2000a) study the interaction between incentives in the financial system and asset prices. The idea is that many investors in real estate and stock markets obtain their investment funds from external sources but the ultimate fund providers are unable to observe the characteristics of the investment. This leads to a classic asset-substitution problem, which increases the return to investment in risky assets and causes investors to bid up prices above their fundamental values. A crucial determinant of asset prices is thus the amount of credit provided by the financial system. By expanding the volume of credit and creating uncertainty about the future path of credit expansion, financial liberalization can interact with the agency problem and lead to a bubble in asset prices. When the bubble bursts, either because returns are low or because the central bank tightens credit, there is a financial crisis.

This is indeed consistent with the vast evidence that a banking crisis often follows collapse in asset prices after what appears to have been a 'bubble'. This is in contrast to standard neoclassical theory and the efficient markets hypothesis, which precludes the existence of bubbles. The global crisis that started in 2007 provides a stark example. In numerous countries, including the US, Ireland, the UK and Spain, real estate prices were steadily rising up to 2007 and the financial crisis was triggered precisely when they collapsed. Numerous other crises show a similar pattern of events. As documented, among others by Kaminsky and Reinhart (1999) and Reinhart and Rogoff (2011), a common precursor to most crises is financial liberalization and significant credit expansion. These are followed by an average rise in the price of stocks of about 40 per cent per year above that occurring in normal times. The price of real estate and other assets also increases significantly. At some point the bubble bursts and the stock and real estate markets collapse. Given that banks and other intermediaries tend to be overexposed to the equity and real estate markets, typically a banking crisis starts about one year after the bubble burst.

There is a substantial literature attempting to understand how shocks, and in particular negative shocks, are amplified through the system and generate negative bubbles. Some theories rely on the so-called financial accelerator (Bernanke and Gertler, 1989, Bernanke et al., 1996). The idea is that negative shocks to borrowers' wealth are amplified because of the presence of asymmetric information and of an agency problem between borrowers and lenders. In a similar spirit but focusing on the role of collateral, Kiyotaki and Moore (1997) suggest that a shock that lowers asset prices may lead to a crisis. The reason is that by lowering the value of collateral, lower asset prices imply less borrowing and thus further reduction in asset prices and borrowing capacity, and triggering a downward spiral. Geanakoplos (1997, 2003, 2009) and Fostel and Geanakoplos (2008) push this analysis further by investigating the effect of asset prices on collateral value and borrowing capacity in more general equilibrium settings.

From a regulatory framework perspective, there are important lessons to be learnt about asset price cycles. Specifically, there are common trends and exposures of financial institutions; while these might make individual institutions look safe and sound when assessed on a stand-alone basis, they could also mask an increase in systemic risk. Overall, this calls for the regulatory framework to use capital requirements and other regulatory tools not just on the individual bank-level but also as a system-wide tool.

Interbank Connections and Contagion

One important source of market failures in the financial system is due to banks exerting externalities on each other. The fact that they do not internalize externalities implies that there is a need for government intervention to try and push the system towards a more efficient outcome.

Inefficiencies of this kind have been discussed in the context of interbank markets, which play a key role in financial systems. Their main purpose is to redistribute liquidity in the financial system from the banks that have cash in excess to the ones that have a shortage. Their smooth functioning is essential for maintaining financial stability. The problem is that there are externalities in the liquidity provision by banks, and so the equilibrium will typically not feature the optimal amount of liquidity provision. There are market breakdowns and market freezes that lead to insufficient liquidity provision due to the externalities among banks.

Bhattacharya and Gale (1987) provide a model where individual banks face privately observed liquidity shocks due to a random proportion of depositors wishing to make early withdrawals. Since liquidity shocks are imperfectly correlated across intermediaries, banks co-insure each other through an interbank market by lending to each other after the liquidity shocks are realized. In the absence of aggregate uncertainty and frictions concerning the structure of the interbank market or the observability of banks' portfolio choices, the co-insurance provided by the interbank market is able to achieve the first best solution. By contrast, as soon as a friction is present, the interbank market no longer achieves full efficiency. For example, given that liquid assets have lower returns than illiquid ones, banks have incentives to under-invest in liquid assets and free-ride on the common pool of liquidity.

Similarly, interbank markets appear to be inefficient also when they do not work competitively. Acharya (2012), for example, analyse the situation when in times of crisis, in addition to moral hazard, interbank markets are characterized by monopoly power. They show that a bank with surplus liquidity has bargaining power vis-à-vis deficit banks that need liquidity to keep funding projects. Surplus banks may strategically provide insufficient lending in the interbank market in order to induce inefficient sales of bank-specific assets by needy banks, which results in an inefficient allocation of resources.

Full efficiency is also not achieved by interbank markets when banks are subject to aggregate uncertainty concerning their liquidity needs. The reason is that banks set their portfolio choice before the realization of the liquidity shocks. When the shocks realize, banks can obtain additional liquidity from other banks or from selling their long-term assets. As long as the liquidity shocks are idiosyncratic and independent across banks, the market works well in relocating liquidity from banks in excess to banks in shortage of liquidity. When the uncertainty concerning liquidity shocks is aggregate, the internal mechanism of liquidity exchange among banks fails. When the system as a whole faces a liquidity shortage, banks are forced to satisfy their liquidity demands by selling their long-term assets. This leads to fire sales, excessive price volatility and, possibly to runs by investors, when asset prices are so low that banks are unable to repay the promised returns to their depositors.

The malfunctioning of interbank markets provides a justification for the existence of a central bank. For example, in contexts of asymmetric information, the central bank can perform an important role in (even imperfectly) monitoring banks' asset choices, thus ameliorating the free riding problem among banks in the portfolio allocation choice between liquid and illiquid assets. When surplus banks have bargaining power over deficit banks, the role of the central bank is to provide an outside option to the deficit bank for acquiring the liquidity needed. In contexts of aggregate liquidity risk, the central bank can help alleviate the problem of excessive price volatility when there is a lack of opportunities for banks to hedge aggregate and idiosyncratic liquidity shocks. By using open market operations to fix the short-term interest rate, a central bank can prevent fire sales and price volatility and implement the constrained efficient solution (Allen et al., 2009b). Thus, the central bank effectively completes the market, a result in line with the argument of Goodfriend and King (1988) that open market operations are sufficient to address pure liquidity risk on the interbank markets.

Other works relate the possibility of market freezes to problems of asymmetric information. For example, Heider et al. (2015) show that interbank market freezes are possible in extreme situations when banks invest in risky long-term investments and there is asymmetric information on the prospects of these investments. This is because the existence of counterparty risk increases interbank market spreads and, in extreme situations, leads to nonviable spreads. A similar mechanism but based on banks' desire to avoid fire sales is presented by Bolton et al. (2011). The idea is that they may prefer to keep assets whose value they have private information about in their portfolios rather than placing them on the market in order to avoid having to sell them at a discount. The problem, however, is that by keeping the assets on their portfolios, banks run the risk of having to sell them at an even lower price at a later stage if the crisis does not cease before they are forced to sell. This so-called '*delayed trading equilibrium*' in which intermediaries try to ride out the crisis and only sell if they are forced leads to a freeze of the market for banks' assets but may be Pareto superior.

A related phenomenon to the interbank market freeze is a freeze in the credit market, whereby externalities among banks prevent the efficient provision of credit to the real economy. A freeze can arise when there are strategic complementarities among banks in the decision to provide credit. This has been analysed by Bebchuk and Goldstein (2011). Suppose that the success of banks' projects depends on how many banks invest in them. This can occur due to network externalities in the real economy, for example. Then, the expectation that other banks are not going to invest will make it optimal for an individual bank not to invest, thus making this a self-fulfilling belief. Bebchuk and Goldstein (2011) use this framework to compare various types of government policy aimed at assisting the financial sector and analyse which one is more effective under what circumstances.

While the above papers analyse how externalities across banks lead them to inefficient decisions, another concern is of direct contagion across banks, whereby shocks spread from one bank to another, leading to the possibility of systemic crises. Empirically, crises indeed appear to be quite systemic. This is a typical justification for central bank and government intervention to prevent the bankruptcy of large/important financial institutions so that they will not cause a chain of failures in other institutions. This was, for example, the argument the Federal Reserve used for intervening to ensure Bear Stearns did not go bankrupt in March 2008 (see Bernanke, 2008).

Contagion requires an idiosyncratic shock affecting one individual or a group of intermediaries and a propagation mechanism that transmits failures from the initially affected institutions to others in the system. Various forms of propagation mechanisms have been analyzed ranging from information spillovers (Chen, 1999) and interbank connections via interbank deposits (Allen and Gale, 2000b) or payment systems (Freixas and Parigi, 1998, Freixas et al., 2000), to portfolio diversification and common exposures (Goldstein and Pauzner, 2004, Wagner, 2011), common assets and funding risk (Allen et al., 2012), transmission of fire sales prices through interdependency of banks' portfolios (Allen and Carletti, 2006) or the use of mark-to-market accounting standards (e.g., Allen and Carletti, 2008). The academic literature on contagion is vast and, for reasons of brevity, it is not fully described here. Rather, we will limit ourselves to explaining only a few key mechanisms of contagion in more detail. Interested readers may turn to more comprehensive surveys, such as Allen et al. (2009a).

In looking for contagious effects via direct linkages, early research by Allen and Gale (2000b) shows how the banking system responds to liquidity shocks when banks exchange interbank deposits. The first important result is that the connections created by swapping deposits allow banks to insure each other against idiosyncratic liquidity shocks but, at the same time, they expose the system to contagion as soon as some frictions, such as a small aggregate liquidity shock, emerge. The second important result is that the resiliency of the system depends on the network structure of interbank deposits. In particular, incomplete networks, that is networks where all banks are connected but each bank exchanges deposits only with a group of other banks, turn out to be more prone to contagion than complete structures. The intuition is that better connected networks are more resilient since the losses in one bank's portfolio are transferred to more banks through interbank agreements. Similar results concerning the resiliency of more complete networks are present also in Freixas et al. (2000) and more recently in Acemoglu et al. (2015), where the resiliency of different networks is analyzed also as a function of the size of shocks.

A related question concerns the issue of network formation, that is, how banks choose to connect when they anticipate contagion risk. Based on the intuition as in Allen and Gale (2000b) that better connected networks are more resilient to contagion, Babus (2016) predicts that banks form links with each other up to a certain connectivity threshold above which contagion does not occur. In other words, banks choose the network that prevents the risk of contagion, but given that forming links is costly, they do not wish to go beyond such a connectivity threshold.

Another channel of contagion based on direct linkages among banks is based on financial innovation. The idea is that financial products, like for example credit risk transfer, allow banks to insure each other against certain risks but at the same time, under certain conditions, they may expose banks to failures and contagion. For example, credit risk transfers are beneficial as a way to insure different intermediaries or different sectors that are subject to independently distributed liquidity shocks. However, when some intermediaries are forced to sell the assets, say for idiosyncratic liquidity reasons and there is price volatility and fire sales in some states of the world, then the presence of credit risk transfers may be detrimental as they may generate contagion across intermediaries or sectors (Allen and Carletti, 2006). Similar results on the benefits and risks of financial innovations are obtained by Shin (2009) and Parlour and Winton (2013), among others. This dynamic nature of risk management and shifting poses additional challenges for the regulation and supervision of financial institutions and markets.

The second approach to modelling contagion focuses on indirect balance-sheet linkages. One possible contagion mechanism works through portfolio readjustments (Lagunoff and Schreft, 2001, De Vries, 2005, Cifuentes et al., 2005). The basic idea is that the return of a bank's portfolio depends on the portfolio allocations of other banks. This implies that the decision of some banks to readjust their portfolios in response to some shocks produces negative externalities in that it reduces the returns of other banks' portfolios. This may induce other banks to abandon the investments as well. This may happen either gradually as losses propagate through the system, or more rapidly in an attempt to avoid future contagion of losses.

Portfolio readjustments may also generate contagion if they happen at the level of investors holding claims on different banks. Such mechanisms have been analyzed by Kodres and Pritsker (2002), Goldstein and Pauzner (2004) and others. In the case analysed by Goldstein and Pauzner (2004), for example, investors hold deposits in two different banks. The crisis in one bank reduces their wealth, and so makes them more risk averse (under the common assumption of a decreasing absolute risk aversion utility function). Then, investors are more likely to run in the other bank, generating the contagion between the two banks.

In summary, there are multiple sources from which systemic risk may arise. These risks might not be obvious from analysing individual financial institutions. They only transpire from a systematic approach, focusing on the aggregate risk, distribution of risk and linkages between different market participants. It is important to realize that these linkages and thus sources of contagion might change over time, reflecting the dynamic nature of the financial landscape. If there is one common trend, it is the increasing complexity of the banking world, a theme we will return to below.

11.3.2   Mapping between Basic Failures and the Reforms Enacted in Europe

In this section, we review the recent regulatory reforms described in Section 11.2 in light of the basic failures in the financial system described above. Our main question is what problem(s) each specific reform tries to address and what potential challenges still remain for financial stability. Given the complexity of the issues, we restrict ourselves to the main regulatory reforms: capital and liquidity requirements, banking union and resolution regime. Although we make use of the existing empirical evidence, our discussion is mostly of a theoretical nature.

Capital Requirements

Capital performs various functions and helps to alleviate the three basic failures in the financial system that we have discussed before. It absorbs unanticipated losses, thus reducing the risk of insolvency for a financial institution and contagion through the financial system. Moreover, by protecting uninsured investors, capital helps maintain confidence in the financial system. Finally, capital is an important tool to provide incentives to bank managers and shareholders not to expose the bank to excessive risks.

The academic literature has mostly focused on capital as a way to reduce the problem of limited liability and excessive risk taking due to high leverage and the (implicit or explicit) support of financial institutions through widespread deposit insurance and bailouts. The general idea is that because banks have access to low cost funds guaranteed by the government, they have an incentive to take significant risks. If the risks pay off, they receive the upside, whereas if they do not, the losses are borne by the government. Capital regulation that ensures that shareholders will lose significantly if losses are incurred is needed to offset the incentive for banks to take risks. One way of capturing this is to model the effects of capital on banks' monitoring incentives (Holmström and Tirole, 1998). Using this framework, Dell'Ariccia and Marquez (2006) and Allen et al. (2011) have shown that capital regulation does improve banks' incentives to monitor, although its effectiveness depends on the presence and design of deposit insurance, credit market competition etc. Overall though, this literature supports a positive role of capital and thus of capital regulation in ameliorating banks' incentives to monitor borrowers, thus reducing the credit risk of individual banks. In this sense, the new Basel accord and its greater emphasis on bank capital is certainly a positive reform.

The focus on the macro effects of capital regulation seems to be particularly relevant. Up to the recent crisis, capital regulation was much more focused on micro-prudential considerations, the idea being that it was enough to protect the stability of the individual financial institutions to guarantee the stability of the financial system as a whole. However, the crisis has clearly shown that this presumption is incorrect. As pointed out by several economists (see for example, Brunnermeier et al., 2009), there is a *'fallacy of composition'* in that it is not possible to make the system as a whole safe by making sure that individual banks are safe. The reason for this paradox is that in trying to make themselves safer, banks can behave in ways that collectively undermine the system. For example, when selling assets on the financial markets, banks disregard the impact their sales will have on asset prices and the possibility of fire sales, thus on the solvency of other financial institutions holding similar assets. The same applies to diversification: Banks choose their diversification strategies taking account of their own individual risk sharing and hedging motives, disregarding the potential effects of increasingly more correlated portfolios on systemic risk. In other words, there are a number of externalities that individual banks do not consider when taking their decisions. For this reason, it is important to introduce regulation and, in this case, capital requirements that also take account of the potential externalities that the actions or the failure of one particular institution may have on the rest of the system. Setting capital requirements on the basis of bank size is certainly an important step in this direction. The question remains as to whether the levels envisaged in Basel III and the various forms of TLAC and MREL are sufficient in guaranteeing the stability of the overall system.

Unfortunately, the academic literature on the macro effects of capital regulation is still in its infancy. Going forward, it is essential to develop new theories of capital regulation based on preventing contagion and systemic risk. In general, as we argue further below, there is a need for a deeper analysis of the appropriate design of macroprudential regulation. Attempts in this direction have been made by Rochet (2004) and Acharya (2012), but much more work is needed in this area, also to provide insights and possibly useful calibrations.

The discussion on the appropriate levels of capital for macroprudential purposes and, more generally, also of macroprudential tools is especially relevant for the European Union, and even more so for the newly established banking union. While the SSM can use macroprudential tools covered under the CRR and CRD IV, it cannot use other macroprudential tools, which will remain exclusively under national authority (Sapir, 2014). Given that not only micro- but also macroprudential decisions have externalities beyond national borders, this seems an important gap in the regulatory framework constructed under the banking union. The ESRB, which does not have any formal powers beyond issuing warnings and recommendations, cannot completely fill this gap.

While it is difficult to predict the effects of the new capital regulation, we can make use of existing empirical literature studying the general effects of capital. The first question is the extent to which capital buffer helps reduce moral hazard and bank fragility. A rich empirical literature has gauged this question. Recently, Laeven and Levine (2009) have shown that the effect of higher capital requirements on risk-taking decisions might vary with the ownership structure of banks, and higher capital requirements might not always lead to lower risk. This is because of the various effects capital has on the relationships between management and shareholders and between these two groups and depositors.

Another important discussion in the empirical literature has been on the role of risk-weights for computing capital requirements. The Basel II and III accords include different models to risk-weigh assets, based on the conclusion that Basel I equalized weights for assets of very different risk profiles, inviting banks to focus on the riskiest asset classes for a given risk weight. Risk-weighted capital-asset ratios try to force banks to hold capital buffers appropriate for their level of risk-taking. The question is whether giving banks the option to calibrate these risk weights with the internal risk-based approach invites manipulation to under-report riskiness of assets, thus to overstate regulatory capital. For example, Mariathasan and Merrouche (2014) show on a sample of 115 banks from 21 OECD that the reported riskiness of asset declines upon regulatory approval of the IRB approach, an effect that is stronger among weakly capitalized banks. On a more general level, Haldane and Madouros (2012) argue for less complex rules, pointing to the costs of complexity and their limited benefits. The leverage ratio, on the other hand, can be seen as a back-stop, a rather simplistic tool, but one that cannot be easily circumvented. In this sense, the reintroduction of the leverage ratio in Basel III is also welcome.

Evidence based on the recent crisis has demonstrated that unweighted risk-capital ratios before the crisis were a better predictor for banks' performance during the crisis than risk-weighted capital-asset ratios. Specifically, Demirguc-Kunt et al. (2013) show that while capital ratios predicted the stock market performance of banks during the crisis, this relationship was driven by non-weighted rather than weighted capital-asset ratios and by higher quality capital elements, including tier 1 capital and common equity.

Liquidity Regulation

As discussed above, Basel II and the corresponding CRD IV package in Europe introduce liquidity requirements in the form of a Liquidity Coverage Ratio and a Net Stable Funding Ratio. Although there is practically no academic literature on the effects of liquidity regulation, it is plausible to argue that liquidity regulation will help mitigate the problem of fire sales, as banks will have more liquid assets in their portfolio and will therefore be in a better position to withstand liquidity shocks without resuming to the premature liquidation of longer term assets. This will help alleviate the contagion and negative externalities across financial institutions. It can also help alleviate panic in any individual institution because investors will be less concerned about runs by others if they do not lead to costly liquidation.

However, introducing liquidity requirements may also have some negative effects. The problem is that requiring banks to hold more liquid assets may reduce the longer-term profitability of banks, as more liquid and shorter-term assets are usually associated with lower profitability in the long run. This may become a source of concern as it may induce bank managers to take more risk in order to foster profitability and may also induce investors to respond more quickly, prompting more easily fundamental-based runs. Finally, it is also important to understand how liquidity and capital regulation interact. In fact, while capital requirements are mostly intended to preserve financial stability in the longer run, they may also represent a form of loss absorption in the shorter run and thus interact with liquidity regulation in important ways. As we will discuss below in more detail, this is certainly an important avenue for future research.

Banking Union and Resolution

As we have already mentioned, the banking union has been the response to important shortcomings that emerged during the crisis. In particular, the creation of the banking union was an attempt to break the adverse loop between sovereign stability and bank stability, curb the link between national supervisors and large financial institutions, thus reducing the risk of forbearance, and a way to address some of the externalities stemming from cross-border banking in the Eurozone.

The banking union seems well structured to address some of these issues, such as the risk of forbearance and the internalization of externalities. The possibility of setting regulatory tools at the central level and considering the banking business in its entirety should foster the focus on the system as a whole rather than a more micro-approach to regulation, despite the problems described above concerning the setting of macroprudential tools. The lower risk of forbearance should provide better incentives to bank managers, thus reducing the problem of excessive risk taking. Finally, the central supervisor should also be better positioned to internalize the spillovers across banks, and thus taking into account issues such as contagion risk in its policy decisions.

Despite all positive developments, some aspects of the banking union remain problematic. Most prominently, only supervision has been completely centralized, while resolution is only partly centralized and there are only limited centralized funding tools. Deposit insurance schemes remain national as of now, although the coverage and other aspects are better harmonized than in the past. In spite of the Single Rule book, the Eurozone still operates with different banking laws and bank resolution regimes whose harmonization is not easy. Most importantly, despite the creation of the Single Resolution Board, the common funding scheme for resolution remains limited as described above.

The appropriate size of the resolution fund, and more generally, the need for guaranteeing fiscal backstops are important issues for various reasons. First, an appropriate fund is necessary to maintain confidence in the financial system. The idea is not that banks should continue to be bailed out or not resolved, but it is important that the system is able to guarantee an orderly restructuring as to to maintain investors' confidence and also avoid problems of financial contagion. Second, whereas it is true that the new regulatory regime introduces a system of bail-in rather than bail-out so that losses will have to be imposed on bank creditors rather than on taxpayers, we think that the application of bail-in will be difficult in practice since its application still may in itself generate panic runs and adverse systemic effects, especially as it is unclear who will hold the bail-in-able debt. Third, the lack of appropriate funds to resolve banks may also lead to important incentive distortions for all agents involved in the process. We are not arguing that moral hazard considerations are not important, and therefore, bank managers and investors should not bear losses in case of bank failure. However, the separation of supervision and resolution authorities coupled with a lack of appropriate fiscal capacity at the central level may introduce distortions in the supervisory process, possibly reintroducing conflicts of interests and/or forbearance risks.

One last important issue concerns the misalignment between the Eurozone and the European Union. While the externalities on cross-border banking are especially strong within the Eurozone and the possibilities to move towards closer regulatory cooperation are larger, many of the regulatory reform initiatives introduced above have been taken on the level of the European Union and are thus also relevant for non-Eurozone countries.

Overall, research on banking unions and the challenges they pose is still in its infancy. Considerably more research is needed to better evaluate the optimal design and size of such unions.

11.4   Moving beyond Banks and Traditional Activities: The Regulatory Perimeter

11.4.1   The Regulatory Perimeter

The crisis has revealed gaps in the regulatory perimeter, as risk has been shifted outside regulated banks into shadow banks, partly connected to regulated banks and partly stand-alone. Some of this risk-shifting has been the result of long-term changes in the intermediation process and landscape of financial systems, some of it has been the result of deliberate decisions of bank management to maximize the use of existing capital and increase profitability.

To a large extent, other financial entities operating in financial markets, such as mutual funds, hedge funds, and money-market funds, etc. have been left unattended by financial-stability regulation. The idea was that they are different from banks, as they do not have the peculiar structure of demand deposit contracts and they do not have the system of vast connections among institutions, so they do not put the system at risk. A common theme is that prices should be allowed to fluctuate, people should be allowed to take risks, and institutions should be allowed to fail as long as there is no severe externality that they do not internalize, which might threaten the system. This line of thinking, however, has proven to be incomplete.

Over the years, other financial institutions have started taking on bank-like features. Perhaps the most striking example is the Long Term Capital Management (LTCM) hedge fund which failed in 1998. LTCM exposed itself to huge leverage in an attempt to enhance returns to shareholders. While doing that, it also generated large risks, and indeed collapsed in 1998. Hence, the thinking that deposit-type risk does not exist in such institutions was shown incorrect. Moreover, after that, people realized that LTCM was also at the heart of a network of vast connections to other institutions, so its failure put the system at the risk of systemic failure. Indeed, it took considerable effort on the side of US regulators to have all parties agree to a resolution to stabilize the system. The failure of Lehmann Brothers in 2008, an investment bank outside the regulatory perimeter of the Federal Reserve and FDIC, although different from LTCM in many respects, carried some similar lessons.

More generally, the fact that banks have been so heavily regulated has limited their ability to provide credit and liquidity leading to the emergence of other institutions that had many features similar to banks, but were not treated like banks or regulated like banks. The common name for such institutions is '*shadow banking*', for which the definition is somewhat unclear. It probably covers everything that is not a traditional bank. Indeed, one of the key lessons from the last crisis is that shadow banking has to be looked at and that the regulation of the financial system has to take an integrative approach and consider the potential fragility of banks alongside shadow banks rather than banks in isolation. The idea is that if you regulate only banks, other institutions will emerge and take over their functions, thus it is important to prevent such a regulatory arbitrage and regulate the system with a holistic view.

A case in point is the money-market mutual funds. These are funds that invest in bonds, treasuries, and other such assets and have a liability structure that is very similar to banks. Specifically, they promise investors the right to withdraw a fixed amount. This is known as a fixed net asset value (NAV), whereby the net asset value promised to investors upon withdrawal is fixed. Due to this feature, investors have been treating their claims in money-market funds as very safe, using them like money for different transactions. This entity emerged to a large extent as a response to regulation in the banking system: the limitations on the returns that banks can offer led investors to demand this kind of vehicle that will offer a bank-like claim with a higher return. As regulation did not treat money-market funds like banks, they were free to do many of the things banks could not.

Over the years, money market funds did not experience many problems and the perception that they are safe was validated in reality. But in the years leading to the crisis, they started investing in riskier securities, exposing themselves to the mismatch between very liquid liabilities and less liquid assets, just like banks. This whole structure led to a crisis in the fall of 2008 when, following the collapse of Lehmann Brothers, one money market fund could not honor its liabilities to investors (this is known as 'breaking the buck'). This almost unprecedented event led to massive runs in the industry across other money market funds. (For empirical evidence, see Schmidt et al., 2014, and for a discussion on regulatory implications, Rosengreen, 2014.)

The events in the money-market funds led regulators in the US and other countries to realize that regulation should not target just entities called 'banks', but more broadly other entities that look like banks or offer services like banks. One of the conclusions has been that the fixed-NAV structure is not sustainable and money market funds are thus moving into a structure of floating NAV, which resembles the one used in other mutual funds. According to this structure, investors are not promised a fixed amount when they withdraw, but rather the market value of their underlying assets as of the day of redemption. This will surely decrease the extent to which money market funds look like banks and the extent to which they should be regulated like banks.

However, the shift to a model of floating NAV does not prevent runs and panics. Recall that runs are generated by the presence of a first mover advantage. Investors want to demand their money when they think others will do so if the liability structure is such that some investors' redemption reduces the value to those who do not redeem. This is certainly the case with fixed deposits or money market funds that have fixed NAV: Investors withdrawing early get the fixed amount, which reduces whatever is left for the remaining investors. But, Chen et al. (2010) have provided empirical evidence that such first-mover advantage exists also in floating NAV funds.

The idea is that when investors take their money out of a mutual fund, they get the last updated market value of the underlying assets. However, following large redemptions, the fund will have to take action and adjust the portfolio in the following days, which will affect the value that remaining investors can get. The problem is particularly severe in funds that hold illiquid assets. These are the funds that provide the liquidity transformation (in the spirit of banks), and for them the costs of portfolio adjustments following redemptions will be more pronounced. Indeed, Chen et al. (2010) have shown that there is a very different pattern in funds holding illiquid assets compared to those holding liquid assets. The former exhibit much stronger sensitivity of outflow to negative performance, indicating that investors are more likely to take their money out fearing redemptions by others.

This force has recently shifted attention to bond funds. These are funds that invest in corporate, government, and other types of bonds. They have grown tremendously in the US over the last few years. This is again likely to be a response to the tightened regulation of banks. As banks find it more difficult to lend, firms are issuing more bonds to address their financing needs, and mutual funds are holding these bonds. The problem with bonds, especially corporate bonds, is that as they are much more illiquid than equity, the liquidity mismatch for funds that hold corporate bonds is more severe. Goldstein et al. (2015) show in a recent paper that corporate bond funds indeed exhibit different flow-performance sensitivity that leads to more outflows upon poor performance and is consistent with the fact that they lead to greater first-mover advantage and fragility. They also show that this is amplified in times of aggregate illiquidity.

If indeed corporate bond funds create the trigger for panic, this can put pressure on the financial system and the real economy in times of crisis. Vast evidence from the empirical literature on financial markets has shown that outflows from mutual funds create persistent price pressure (e.g., Coval and Stafford, 2007, Ellul et al., 2011 and Manconi et al., 2012) and that these price impacts can have real effects on firms' activities (e.g., Edmans et al., 2012 and Hau and Lai, 2013). Recently, Gilchrist and Zakrajšek (2012) have verified an effect of market-driven credit spread on real economic outcomes.

In summary, financial regulation should view the system as a whole and consider the fact that regulating certain parts of the system is likely to shift activity to other parts putting them at the risk of fragility. An integrative approach, which is now attempted by the Financial Stability Oversight Council (FSOC) in the US, is welcome with more of this approach to be implemented worldwide. Fragility should be measured based on the activity that is being pursued rather based on the entity pursuing it.

11.4.2   Financial Innovation

New bank-like financial institutions and deposit-like financial products are one form of financial innovation. However, financial innovation is a broader concept and can be generally defined as new financial products and services, new financial intermediaries or markets, and new delivery channels.[3] Examples abound, ranging from the introduction of the ATM/cash machine in the 1970s and mobile phone based financial services in the 2000s, the introduction of money market funds as an alternative to bank deposits and the emergence of venture capital funds, to structured financial products. The intermediation platforms of peer-to-peer lending and crowdfunding also fall under the category of financial innovation. Goetzmann and Rouwenhorst (2005) identify 19 major financial innovations, grouped into innovations that (i) facilitate the transfer of value through time (e.g., savings accounts), (ii) enhance the ability to contract on future values (e.g., venture capitalists) and (iii) increase the negotiability of contracts (e.g., securitization).

The traditional *innovation-growth view* posits that financial innovations help reduce agency costs, facilitate risk sharing, complete the market, and ultimately improve allocative efficiency and economic growth, thus focusing on the bright side of financial innovation. Laeven et al. (2015) quote several historical examples where financial innovation has been critical in allowing major technological innovation to be adopted on a broad scale. For example, in the nineteenth and twentieth centuries specialized investment banks emerged to facilitate the construction of vast railroad networks across North America and Europe, screening and monitoring borrowers on behalf of dispersed and distant investors. In the second half of the twentieth century, venture capital funds arose to finance IT start-ups, characterized by limited, if any, tangible assets that could be used as collateral, thus requiring patient investment capital, and close screening and monitoring as well as technical advice. In recent decades, financial innovation has supported bio technology. Lerner and Tufano (2011) undertake a counterfactual exercise, a 'counterfactual historiography', comparing real development with hypothetical development in a world without (i) venture capital and private equity, (ii) mutual funds and exchange-traded funds and (iii) securitization. Their analysis points to the overall positive effects of these innovations that might not have been achieved with alternative arrangements. There is also empirical evidence of the importance of financial deepening for innovation (Amore et al., 2013, Chava et al., 2013) as well as of financial innovation for economic growth (Laeven et al., 2015). Beck et al. (2016) show that countries with higher innovative activity in the banking system experience faster growth in industries with higher needs for external finance and higher growth opportunities.

The *innovation-fragility view*, on the other hand, focuses on the 'dark' side and has identified financial innovations as the root cause of the recent Global Financial Crisis, by leading to an unprecedented credit expansion that helped feed the boom and subsequent bust in housing prices (Brunnermeier, 2009), by engineering securities perceived to be safe but exposed to neglected risks (Gennaioli et al., 2012), and by helping banks and investment banks design structured products to exploit investors' misunderstanding of financial markets

(Henderson and Pearson, 2011). Several authors have pointed to distortions introduced by financial innovations, such as securitization and new derivative securities, demonstrating how they have contributed to aggressive risk taking, reduction in lending standards and thus fragility (e.g., Rajan, 2006, Keys et al., 2010 and Dell'Ariccia et al., 2012).

Financial innovation has often been used for purposes of regulatory arbitrage or to get around regulatory restrictions. For example, Euro-accounts were established in reaction to Regulation Q, which prohibited payment of interest on sight accounts in the US. Another example is the use of Special Purpose Vehicles (SPV), investment trusts to which banks off-loaded loan portfolios, in return for securities issued by the SPV and often rated AAA. In total, banks set up conduits to securitize assets worth $1.3 trillion, insuring the securitized assets with explicit guarantees (Acharya, 2012). The objective of such securitization operation was to save capital, as guarantees were structured in a way to reduce regulatory capital requirements. Acharya (2012) show that the losses on these conduits had to be taken back on banks' balance sheets during the crisis as a consequence of wholesale runs.

Taking a broader view, Freixas et al. (2015) argue that financial innovation is one of the key drivers of systemic risk. Financial innovation allowing for better risk management and sharing might reduce idiosyncratic risk, that is, the risk of individual financial institutions considered on a stand-alone basis, while at the same time increase systemic risk, as larger parts of the financial system are exposed to the same systematic or aggregate risk and/or increasing the appetite and capacity to take on risk. This is developed further by Wagner (2010), who shows theoretically that as banks become more similar due to diversification of risks, systemic risk increases.

Empirical research on the use of financial innovation at the bank level has provided somewhat ambiguous results. On the one hand, Norden et al. (2014) show that the use of credit derivatives reduced corporate loan spreads in the US, suggesting that banks passed on benefits of risk management. The benefits were even stronger during the recent crisis, when banks with higher holdings of such derivative positions cut lending by less. On the other hand, Nijskens and Wagner (2011) show that even before the crisis the share price beta of banks trading credit default swaps (CDS) or issuing collateralized loan obligations (CLOs) increased, suggesting higher risk from the use of these risk management tools. This effect is driven by higher correlation with the market while volatility actually decreases, suggesting that while these risk management tools serve to reduce idiosyncratic bank risk, they actually increase systemic risk.

Financial innovation might also affect the incentives of financial intermediaries. Wagner (2007a,b) shows that financial innovation that reduces asymmetric information can actually increase risk-taking due to agency problems between bank owners and managers, or because of lower costs of fragility. Keys et al. (2011), for example, show how reduced incentives to screen borrowers in the US due to the possibility of being able to securitize loans contributed to higher loan losses.

In summary, both theory and empirical work suggest that financial innovation can bring benefits but also increased risks both by the design of products and through changing incentives. While financial innovation is thus critical for the development of the financial system, it also poses significant challenges for regulators. Regulatory frameworks are designed in light of existing products and providers. They are mostly rule-based (and intermediary-based), for example, for liquidity requirements only specific clearly-defined assets are considered. Rule-based regulatory regimes have the clear advantage of providing clarity, and reduce the room for supervisory overreach. They also guarantee certain independence for supervisors, given the limited degree of freedom for interpretation. On the other hand, rule-based regulatory systems are less adequate in reacting to new products and markets, as existing rules do not refer to them. A principle-based regime is more flexible in this context, but might be more open to arbitrage possibilities.

While regulation might give rise to certain financial innovations, regulators in turn will try to catch up with innovation, a process that Kane (1977) refers to as 'regulatory dialectic'. Compared to the financial sector, regulators are at a disadvantage, as regulation (especially rule-based regulation) refers to specific institutions, products and markets. Risk-based supervision would imply regulating and supervising all financial intermediaries that offer the same products under the same regime. For example, all institutions offering deposit services should be subject to the same prudential regulation.

11.4.3   Complexity

One striking phenomenon over the past decades has been a clear trend towards more complex financial institutions, which results in serious challenges for regulators. Specifically, Cetorelli and Goldberg (2014) report that while in 1990 only one US bank holding company had more than 1000 subsidiaries, in 2012 at least half a dozen did. Using data both for US and non-US banks with branches in the US, they show that many of the leading banks have hundreds if not thousands of subsidiaries, making it very hard for supervisors to properly monitor them. Complexity can take on different forms, reflected not just in the number of subsidiaries, but also in the expansion across different financial activities, including investment banking, insurance, mutual funds, and even nonfinancial activities. In addition, banks have organized their increasing variety of activities often in multi-tiered ownership relations, with up to ten levels of ownership links. Cetorelli and Goldberg (2014) also show that while the number of affiliates and the share of nonbank activity are positively correlated with the size of the parent bank, measures of business and geographic complexity are not. Complexity is thus a bank characteristic, which is not completely correlated with size; in addition to the challenge of too-big-to-fail, there is thus the challenge of too-complex-to-resolve.

Not just financial institutions, but also the regulatory framework has grown in complexity over the past decade, with the Basel II capital regime being a watershed. Hakenes and Schnabel (2014) use a theoretical model to show that it is in banks' interest to push complex regulation, in what they refer to as 'regulatory capture by sophistication'. Specifically, in a world where regulators are less well paid than bankers and with a variation in skills across regulators, regulators might be swayed to rubber-stamp banks' risk models in order not to have to admit that they do not understand these risk models. This allows banks to hold less capital than required. This trend towards sophistication and the resultant capture have been exacerbated by the Basel II regulatory framework, which allowed the use of banks' internal risk model to compute risk weights for different asset classes. However, this phenomenon becomes more critical if the regulator has discretionary power, such as under pillar II of Basel II. It is important to note that this type of regulatory capture by sophistication is somewhat different from the regulatory capture due to conflict of interest, social connection (rotating door), political interference or lobbying activity by banks.

Related to the trend towards complexity is the increasing globalization of banks, with leading global banks active across a large number of regions and countries. In addition, over the past decade there has been a trend towards regional banks, that is, Latin American and African banks reaching out across their respective regions. This poses additional challenges for supervisors in terms of cooperation across borders. While this topic is somewhat outside the current survey, it is important to be flagged.

Overall, the financial sector and, with it, the financial regulation are becoming more and more complex over time. The two phenomena are related, as greater the complexity of the financial sector calls for the greater complexity of regulation, but are also driven by additional separate factors. There is also a vicious circle in that complexity of regulation leads to complexity of financial services, which leads to more complexity of regulation, and so on. This trend is not conducive for effective regulation and efficient financial systems and needs to be considered by policy-makers when going forward.

11.5   Special Issues in Europe and How they Affect Future Regulation

Many of the regulatory issues discussed in this paper concern all advanced countries if not the emerging/developing world as well. However, some of the challenges have a larger impact on Europe, especially on the Eurozone. This has to do with the delayed crisis resolution in many European countries, especially many peripheral Eurozone countries, the biased financial structure, also referred to as 'bank bias', in Europe compared to other advanced economies, and the political economy challenges facing a monetary and economic union. While this survey does not have sufficient space to go in depth into these political economy challenges, they are related to the fact that the allocation of losses after the recent crisis had a geographic distributional dimension because creditors were concentrated in the *'core'* and debtors in the *'periphery'* countries of the Eurozone. In addition, being able to rely on a common lender of last resort for a country's banks may result in a 'tragedy of commons' problems, as it is in the interest of every member government with fragile banks to *'share the burden'* with other members.

11.5.1   Crisis Resolution and Macro-Management in a Monetary Union

While not synchronized or similarly pronounced across all European countries, large parts of the European Union and the Eurozone went through a credit bubble in the first decade of the twenty-first century, followed by a bust in the wake of the Global Financial Crisis. Unlike the US, most European countries have been very slow at recognizing losses incurred during the crisis and forcing or supporting banks in their recapitalization. The sluggish credit recovery over the past years has been the backdrop on which the ECB has moved towards quantitative easing, though much later than other leading economies, including the US, UK and even Japan, a delay partly explained by political considerations.

There is an ongoing debate about the extent the current credit crisis reflects supply or demand side constraints. It seems that the recent crises have resulted in both supply constraints as well as demand reduction in the bank lending market. In spite of recapitalization by governments and through private markets and investors, seven years after the Global Financial Crisis, Europe's banking system continues to be in a rather weak position, at least compared to that of the US.

Overall, the much slower recovery can be partly explained with distributional repercussions of crisis resolution and the lack of a centralized financial safety net and macro-management. While the Eurozone has made substantial progress in building a common financial safety net in the form of the banking union (with the caveats discussed above), other elements to make the monetary union sustainable are still missing and the same political economy challenges will delay their construction in the near future (e.g., Wyplosz, 2016). One other reason for the slow recovery, which we will discuss more below, is the unbalanced nature of Europe's financial systems.

11.5.2   Financial Structure: Does Europe Suffer from a Bank Bias?

Beyond concerns about the recovery of different components of the financial system across Europe, the current discussion on the Capital Market Union has again put in the forefront the discussion on the financial structure in Europe, not only within the Eurozone. While previous research has shown the irrelevance (on average) for economic growth of the degree to which a financial system was bank- or market-based, more recent research has shown that Europe's relative strong reliance of Europe on bank intermediation (both in absolute and relative terms) might explain the underperformance in growth and the stronger impact of the recent crisis (e.g., Langfield and Pagano, 2015). This comes in addition to the observation that certain segments of the financial system critical for financing young and small enterprises are underdeveloped in most European countries, including the private equity industry, venture capital and angel financing. These findings also serve as motivation for a stronger focus on building sources of equity finance/capital markets in Europe, including the Capital Market Union initiative.

Contrasting markets and banks, however, might be wrong. Most finance today is intermediated, even if it goes through public markets, such as public debt and equity markets. Institutional investors, including insurance companies, pension and mutual funds play a critical role in financial markets, which is also reflected in the prominent role of institutional investors in the ownership structure of publicly listed firms. Financial intermediaries and markets also have other complementarities. Securitization is an important link between intermediaries and markets in the cross-section. IPOs of companies financed by venture capitalists are an important connection over time, between financial intermediaries and public markets.

The question, therefore, is not necessarily the contrast of the two specific segments, but rather the fact of having a diversified, if not complete, financial system. It is in this context that the focus should be on specific segments of the financial system that play less of a role in Europe in than other developed regions of the world, including private equity funds, venture capital funds, and corporate bond markets.

It is also important to take note of the new emerging players, including nonintermediated forms of bringing savers and entrepreneurs together, such as peer-to-peer lending and crowd-funding platforms, players who we cannot easily assign to either the bank- or market components of the financial system. These platforms work with many borrowers and lenders, with only a limited role for the platform provider, building on other social media models. Rather than building on private information acquisition, these new models of financial intermediation often rely on Big Data collected on potential borrowers based on social media. As discussed before, the emergence of new players is an important dimension of financial innovation and contributes to the process of financial deepening. However, these new players will eventually pose the question about the regulatory perimeter.

There is an array of policies and institutions that can help enhance the development of the nonbanking part of Europe's financial system, some of which have been laid out in the recent Green Paper by the European Commission. They include (i) the revival of securitization markets (including the creation of standards; creation of platforms; and the important interaction with liquidity requirements under the new Basel III regulatory regime); (ii) increase in liquidity by linking corporate bond markets – where segmented insolvency laws are one major barrier; (iii) creating linkages between different stock exchanges to increase liquidity, while maintaining competition, and (iv) creating a EU-wide second tier capital market/private placement market. There are also important demand-side policies, aiming at getting more firms to accept market finance, which includes corporate governance reforms, but also reducing cost barriers, as for example, lowering prospectus costs.

It is important to understand, however, that these policies and institutions cannot work over night. They are aimed at long-term structural changes in the financial system. They certainly will not contribute to leading Europe out of the current crisis, but might contribute to long-term higher sustainable growth rate through more efficient resource allocation.

11.6   Summary, Policy Lessons and Directions for Future Research

In this chapter, we have described the main ingredients of the new financial policies in Europe following the global financial crisis. We have evaluated them on the background of the vast theoretical literature of market failures in the financial system, explaining the goals of different regulations and their limitations. We have highlighted some important tensions in light of the need to expand the regulatory perimeter and address the ongoing financial innovation and the ever-increasing complexity of the financial system. We have also discussed special challenges in Europe given the sluggish recovery, the particular structure of the financial system and the political issues surrounding the European Union and the Eurozone.

In conclusion, we would like to emphasize four policy lessons going forward that are directly related to our analysis so far. These policy lessons are broad and forward looking as they point to future analysis as much as they are based on past experience.

The first policy lesson is related to the tension between complexity and simplicity. As the financial system is increasingly complex and sophisticated, there is a tendency to make regulation more complex to address some of the newly emerging issues. This might backfire, however, for two reasons. First, increasing the complexity of the financial regulation might provide the industry players with stronger incentives to make their institutions more complex. Second, complex financial regulation opens the door for the manipulation of rules by financial institutions and investors. For example, when capital requirements introduced risk weights, banks could have more discretion in how they measure and report risk, and this might have led to greater risk-taking. Similarly, forcing banks to hold additional capital or impose higher risk-weights for specific activities that expose the bank to higher risks and/or are not considered central to financial service provision is a pricing-based tool, whereas outright prohibition of certain activities (e.g., trading on own account) is a simpler tool to achieve the same. While a pricing-based tool might be better to balance social benefits and costs, complete prohibition might be better in case of uncertainty about (the distribution of) costs and benefits. Hence, in our view, it is important to complement ever-increasing complex regulation with some simple rules. For example, going back to a simple leverage ratio in the new Basel accord in addition to risk-weighted capital requirements is a step in the right direction.

The second policy lesson has to do with the new emphasis on macroprudential policies, as opposed to the traditional micro-prudential policies. As the recent crisis made us realize, making sure that individual institutions are sound may not be enough, as they all may be taking action to secure themselves, but these can make the system as a whole less secure. New policy measures such as bank stress tests and capital requirements that depend on the aggregate state of the economy are steps in the right direction in trying to take the systemic risk aspect into account. But, a considerable amount of work is still needed for measuring systemic risk, and assessing the effectiveness of macroprudential policy measures more precisely.

The third policy lesson has to do with the required focus on resolution. The chaos that came with the failure of leading financial institutions was arguably an important factor in how deep the global financial crisis was. It is thus critical to have frameworks in place to resolve financial intermediaries in a way that minimizes disruptions for the rest of the financial system and the real economy, while allocating losses according to creditor ranking. An incentive-compatible resolution framework has therefore not only important effects ex-post, that is, in the case of failure, but also important ex-ante incentive effects for risk-decision takers. This implies that a lot of attention and preparation is needed now before the actual failure of big and complex institutions. Imposing living wills and requiring bail-in strategies in case of failures are indeed important steps that will make institutions think more about the event of the failure and internalize better the risks that they are imposing on the system. But again much more work on the effectiveness of resolution mechanisms and the legal aspects of what can and cannot work is needed.

The fourth policy lesson is that we need to have a dynamic and forward looking approach to regulation. The problem with regulatory reforms in the past was that it always addressed the regulatory gaps exposed in the most recent crises. But, as regulators tightened restrictions on institutions that have had problems before, activity and risk-taking shifted to other institutions and markets. Then, new crises always caught regulators unprepared, as they happened in places outside the regulatory perimeter at the time. It is thus important to think about the system as a whole and understand new innovations as they happen. It is important to remember that regulating one type of institution will lead to the emergence of others and to design regulation in a forward-looking way. This would imply that the regulatory perimeter has to be adjusted over time and that the focus of prudential regulation (both micro- and macroprudential) might have to shift over time as new sources of systemic risks arise.

In preparing for the future and designing the new financial playing field, research has a vital role, including in exploring in more depth the four broad conclusions discussed above. First, theoretical research is critical in thinking about the underlying mechanisms and how new policy measures will affect the system in light of these mechanisms. In this context, it is important to move from partial to general equilibrium analyses. Second, as new policies are implemented and new data is collected, empirical research will also be crucial to better understand in real time how policies are affecting markets and their effectiveness. An array of new data sources will become available over the next years that might support some of this research. The SSM in Frankfurt has access to detailed data from both the directly supervised financial institutions, and other institutions within the Eurozone. In addition, there are attempts to link the different credit registries across Europe (some of which are still to be established), which will provide a wealth of information on the loan level for researchers. However, too often data across countries are not comparable, which impedes consistent cross-country comparison even within closely integrated regions such as the Eurozone. And in too many instances, researchers have no direct access to supervisory data sources due to confidentiality barriers that are higher in Europe than in other parts of the world. We should also not underestimate the methodological challenges going forward, such as moving from documenting correlations to establishing causality. The new research agenda also requires work across strict borders of sub-disciplines, such as between macroeconomics and financial economics.

The years since the crisis have seen an enormous increase in theoretical and empirical explorations in both (idiosyncratic and systemic) risk measurement and micro- and macroprudential regulation. The overhaul of regulatory frameworks across the globe was not only the result of lessons learned from the recent crises but was also accompanied by extensive academic work. We have become better at measuring risk and designing regulatory tools to reduce the build-up of systemic risk and manage it more effectively. Having said this, much of the discussion has been dominated by the last crisis – as always: regulatory reforms after a crisis are designed to prevent the last but not the next crisis. We have thus become better at analyzing the known unknowns; this, however, leaves us with the unknown unknowns, including financial innovation leading to new business models and new structures in the financial system and thus new and future sources of financial fragility. As the financial system develops, research and analysis (both academic and within central banks and regulatory authorities) have to adapt to the dynamic nature of the financial system.

Acknowledgements

We would like to thank Andrea Amato and Marco Forletta for excellent research assistance. We are grateful to participants, especially Jean-Edouard Colliard and Evren Ors, attending a workshop in Florence for useful comments and suggestions.

Notes

1. There has been an intense debate on the coordination between the provisions concerning bail-in in the BRRD directive and those contained in the new state aid regulation. On this matter, see Kerle (2014) and Micossi et al. (2014).
2. Other related surveys on the origins of financial crises are provided by Bhattacharya and Thakor (1993), Gorton and Winton (2003), Allen and Gale (2007) (Chapter 3), Freixas and Rochet (2008), Rochet (2008), Allen et al. (2009a) and Degryse et al. (2009).
3. One can also refer to this as production, process and organizational innovation.

References

Acemoglu, D., Ozdaglar, A., and Tahbaz-Saleh, A. 2015. Systemic Risk and Stability in Financial Networks. *American Economic Review*, **105**, 564–608.

Acharya, V. 2012. A Theory of Systemic Risk and Design of Prudential Bank Regulation. *American Economic Journal; Macroeconomics*, **4**(2), 184–217.

Allen, F., and Carletti, E. 2006. Credit Risk Transfer and Contagion. *Journal of Monetary Economics*, **53**, 89–111.

Allen, F., and Carletti, E. 2008. Mark-to-Market Accounting and Liquidity Pricing. *Journal of Accounting and Economics*, **45**, 358–378.

Allen, F., and Gale, D. 2000a. Bubbles and Crises. *Economic Journal*, **110**, 236–255.

Allen, F., and Gale, D. 2000b. Financial Contagion. *Journal of Political Economy*, **108**, 1–33.

Allen, F., and Gale, D. 2007. *Understanding Financial Crises*. Clarendon Lecture Series in Finance, Oxford: Oxford University Press.

Allen, F., Babus, A., and Carletti, E. 2009a. Financial Crises: Theory and Evidence. *Annual Review of Financial Economics*.

Allen, F., Carletti, E., and Gale, D. 2009b. Interbank Market Liquidity and Central Bank Intervention. *Journal of Monetary Economics*, **56**, 639–652.

Allen, F., Carletti, E., and Marquez, R. 2011. Credit Market Competition and Capital Regulation. *Review of Financial Studies*, **24**, 983–1018.

Allen, F., Babus, A., and Carletti, E. 2012. Asset Commonality, Debt Maturity and Systemic Risk. *Journal of Financial Economics*, **104**, 519–534.

Allen, F., Beck, T., and Carletti, E. 2013. Structural Changes in European Financial Systems: The Impact of the Regulatory Framework on Investment in the European Union. In: Bank, European Investment (ed), *Investment and Investment Finance in Europe*, pp. 243–275.

Allen, F., Carletti, E., Goldstein, I., and Leonello, A. 2014. Government Guarantees and Financial Stability. Working paper, Bocconi and University of Pennsylvania.

Amore, M. D., Schneider, C., and Žaldokas, A. 2013. Credit Supply and Corporate Innovation. *Journal of Financial Economics*, **109**, 835–855.

Babus, A. 2016. The Formation of Financial Networks. *The Rand Journal of Economics*, **47**(2), 239–272.

Bebchuk, L. A., and Goldstein, I. 2011. Self-fulfilling Credit Market Freezes. *Review of Financial Studies*, **24**, 3519–3555.

Beck, T., Chen, T., Lin. C., and Song, F. 2016. Financial Innovation: The Bright and the Dark Sides. *Journal of Banking and Finance*, **72**, 28–51.

Bernanke, B. 2008. Reducing Systemic Risk: A Speech at the Federal Reserve Bank of Kansas City's Annual Economic Symposium, Jackson Hole, Wyoming, August 22, 2008. *Speech 429, Board of Governors of the Federal Reserve System (U.S.)*.

Bernanke, B., and Gertler, M. 1989. Agency Costs, Net Worth, and Business Fluctuations. *American Economic Review*, **79**, 14–31.

Bernanke, B., Gertler, M., and Gilchrist, S. 1996. The Financial Accelerator and the Flight to Quality. *The Review of Economics and Statistics*, **78**, 1–15.

Bhattacharya, S., and Gale, D. 1987. Preference Shocks, Liquidity and Central Bank Policy. In: Barnett, W., and Singleton, K. (eds), *New Approaches to Monetary Economics*, pp. 69–88.

Bhattacharya, S., and Thakor, A. 1993. Contemporary Banking Theory. *Journal of Financial Intermediation*, **3**, 2–50.

Bolton, P., Santos, T., and Scheinkman, J. 2011. Inside and Outside Liquidity. *Quarterly Journal of Economics*, **126**, 259–321.

Brunnermeier, M. 2009. Deciphering the Liquidity and Credit Crunch 2007-08. *Journal of Economic Perspectives*, **23**, 77–100.

Brunnermeier, M. K., Crockett, A., Goodhart, C. A., Persaud, A., and Shin, H. S. 2009. The Fundamental Principles of Financial Regulation. Vol. 11. London: Centre for Economic Policy Research.

Bryant, J. 1980. A Model of Reserves, Bank Runs, and Deposit Insurance. *Journal of Banking and Finance*, **4**, 335–344.

Calomiris, C., and Kahn, C. 1991. The Role of Demandable Debt in Structuring Optimal Banking Arrangements. *American Economic Review*, **81**, 497–513.

Carletti, E. 2008. Competition and Regulation in Banking. *Handbook of Financial Intermediation and Banking*, 449–482.

Carlsson, H., and van Damme, E. 1993. Global Games and Equilibrium Selection. *Econometrica*, **61**, 989–1018.

Cetorelli, N., and Goldberg, L. S. 2014. Measures of Global Bank Complexity. *Economic Policy Review, Federal Reserve Bank of New York*, 107–126.

Chari, V.V., and Jagannathan, R. 1988. Banking Panics, Information, and Rational Expectations Equilibrium. *Journal of Finance*, 749–761.

Chava, S., Oettl, A., Subramanian, A., and Subramanian, K. V. 2013. Banking Deregulation and Innovation. *Journal of Financial Economics*, **109**, 759–774.

Chen, Q., Goldstein, I., and Jiang, W. 2010. Payoff Complementarities and Financial Fragility: Evidence from Mutual Fund Outflows. *Journal of Financial Economics*, **97**, 239–262.

Chen, Y. 1999. Banking Panics: The Role of the First-Come, First-Served Rule and Information Externalities. *Journal of Political Economy*, **107**, 946–968.

Cifuentes, R., Ferrucci, G., and Shin, H. 2005. Liquidity Risk and Contagion. *Journal of European Economic Association*, **3**, 556–566.

Coval, J., and Stafford, E. 2007. Asset Fire sales (and Purchases) in Equity Markets. *Journal of Financial Economics*, **86**, 479–512.

De Vries, C. G. 2005. The Simple Economics of Bank Fragility. *Journal of Banking and Finance*, **29**, 803–825.

Degryse, H., Ongena, S., and Kim, M. 2009. *Microeconometrics of Banking Methods, Applications, and Results*. Oxford University Press.

Dell'Ariccia, G., and Marquez, R. 2006. Lending Booms and Lending Standards. *Journal of Finance*, **61**, 2511–2546.

Dell'Ariccia, G., Igan, D., and Laeven, L. 2012. Credit Booms and Lending Standards: Evidence from the Subprime Mortgage Market. *Journal of Money, Credit and Banking*, **44**, 367–384.

Demirguc-Kunt, A., Detragiache, E., and Merrouche, O. 2013. Bank Capital: Lessons from the Financial Crisis. *Journal of Money, Credit and Banking*, **45**, 1147–1164.

Department for International Development. 2013. *Global Financial Sector Regulatory Reform: Understanding the Impact on Developing Countries*. Tech. rept. London.

Diamond, D., and Dybvig, P. 1983. Bank Runs, Deposit Insurance, and Liquidity. *Journal of Political Economy*, **91**, 401–419.

Diamond, D., and Rajan, R. 2001. Liquidity Risk, Liquidity Creation and Financial Fragility: A Theory of Banking. *Journal of Political Economy*, **109**, 2431–2465.

Edmans, A., Goldstein, I., and Jiang, W. 2012. The Real Effects of Financial Markets: The Impact of Prices on Takeovers. *The Journal of Finance*, **67**, 933–971.

Ellul, A., Jotikasthira, C., and Lundblad, C. 2011. Regulatory Pressure and Fire Sales in the Corporate Bond Market. *Journal of Financial Economics*, **101**, 596–620.

ESRB. 2014. Is Europe Overbanked? Report of the Advisory Scientific Committee, Number 4, available at https://esrb.europa.eu/pub/pdf/asc/Reports_ASC_4_1406 .pdf.

Fostel, A., and Geanakoplos, J. 2008. Leverage Cycles and the Anxious Economy. *American Economic Review*, **98**, 1211–1244.

Freixas, X., and Parigi, B. 1998. Contagion and Efficiency in Gross and Net Interbank Payment Systems. *Journal of Financial Intermediation*, **7**, 3–31.

Freixas, X., and Rochet, J. 2008. *The Microeconomics of Banking*. 2nd edn. Cambridge: MIT Press.

Freixas, X., Parigi, B., and Rochet, J. 2000. Systemic Risk, Interbank Relations and Liquidity Provision by the Central Bank. *Journal of Money, Credit and Banking*, **32**, 611–638.

Freixas, X., Laeven, L., and Peydro, J.-L. 2015. *Systemic Risk, Crises, and Macroprudential Regulation*. MIT Press.

Friedman, M., and Schwartz, A. J. 1963. *A Monetary History of the United States, 1867–1960*. Princeton University Press for NBER.

Geanakoplos, J. 1997. Promises, Promises. In: Arthur, B., Durlauf, S., and Lane, D. (eds), *The Economy as an Evolving Complex System II*. Reading, MA: Addison-Wesley, pp. 285–320.

Geanakoplos, J. 2003. Liquidity, Default, and Crashes: Endogenous Contracts in Equilibrium. In: Dewatripont, M., Hansen, L., and Turnovsky, S. (eds), *Advances in Economics and Econometrics: Theory and Applications, Eighth World Congress*, vol. II, pp. 278–283.

Geanakoplos, J. 2009. The Leverage Cycle. *2009 NBER Macroeconomics Annual*, **24**, 1–65.

Gennaioli, N., Shleifer, A., and Vishny, R. 2012. Neglected Risks, Financial Innovation, and Financial Fragility. *Journal of Financial Economics*, **104**, 452–468.

Gilchrist, S., and Zakrajšek, E. 2012. Credit Spreads and Business Cycle Fluctuations. *American Economic Review*, **102**, 1692–1720.

Goetzmann, W., and Rouwenhorst, K. 2005. *The Origins of Value: The Financial Innovations that Created Modern Capital Markets*. Oxford University Press, number 9780195175714, March.

Goldstein, I. 2012. Empirical Literature on Financial Crises: Fundamentals vs. Panic. In: Caprio, G. (ed), *The Evidence and Impact of Financial Globalization*. Elsevier.

Goldstein, I., and Pauzner, A. 2004. Contagion of Self-fulfilling Financial Crises Due to Diversification of Investment Portfolios. *Journal of Economic Theory*, **119**, 151–183.

Goldstein, I., and Pauzner, A. 2005. Demand-Deposit Contracts and the Probability of Bank Runs. *Journal of Finance*, **60**, 1293–1327.

Goldstein, I., Jiang, H., and Ng, D. T. 2015. Investor Flows and Fragility in Corporate Bond Funds. Working paper.

Goodfriend, M., and King, R. G. 1988. Financial Deregulation, Monetary Policy, and Central Banking. *Economic Review, Federal Reserve Bank of Richmond*, 3–22.

Gorton, G. 1988. Banking Panics and Business Cycles. *Oxford Economic Papers*, **40**, 751–781.

Gorton, G. 2008. *The Panic of 2007*. Tech. rept. Jackson Hole Conference Proceedings, Federal Reserve Bank of Kansas City.

Gorton, G., and Winton, A. 2003. Financial Intermediation. Chap. 8, pages 431–552 of: Constantinides, G., Harris, M., and Stulz, R. (eds), *Handbook of the Economics of Finance*, vol. 1A. North Holland, Amsterdam.

Hakenes, H., and Schnabel, I. 2014. Bank Bonuses and Bail-Outs. *Journal of Money, Credit and Banking*, **46**, 259–288.

Haldane, A., and Madouros, V. 2012. The Dog and the Frisbee. *Bank of England. In Speech given at the Federal Reserve Bank of Kansas City's 36th economic policy symposium, 'The Changing Policy Landscape', Jackson Hole, Wyoming*, **31**.

Hau, H., and Lai, S. 2013. Real Effects of Stock Underpricing. *Journal of Financial Economics*, **108**, 392–408.

Hay, G. 2013. Regulators Must Grab Chance to Bin EU Capital Ruse. Reuters Breaking News, http://blogs.reuters.com/breakingviews/2013/01/15/regulators-must-grab-chance-to-bin-eu-capital-ruse/.

Heider, F., Hoerova, M., and Holthausen, C. 2015. Liquidity Hoarding and Interbank Market Spreads: The Role of Counterparty Risk. *Journal of Financial Economics*, **118**, 336–354.

Henderson, B. J., and Pearson, N. D. 2011. The Dark Side of Financial Innovation: A case study of the pricing of a retail financial product. *Journal of Financial Economics*, **100**, 227–247.

Holmström, B., and Tirole, J. 1998. Private and Public Supply of Liquidity. *Journal of Political Economy*, **106**, 1–40.

Jacklin, C. J., and Bhattacharya, S. 1988. Distinguishing Panics and Information-based Bank Runs: Welfare and Policy Implications. *Journal of Political Economy*, **96**, 568–592.

Kaminsky, G. L., and Reinhart, C. M. 1999. The Twin Crises: The Causes of Banking and Balance-of-Payments Problems. *American Economic Review*, **89**, 473–500.

Kane, E. J. 1977. Good Intentions and Unintended Evil: The Case against Selective Credit Allocation. *Journal of Money, Credit, and Banking*, **9**, 55–69.

Kerle, C. 2014. Burden-sharing Under State Aid Rules: Evolution, State of Play and the Way Ahead. In: Allen, F., Carletti, E., and Gray, J. (eds), *Bearing the Losses from Bank and Sovereign Default in the Eurozone*, pp. 99–112.

Keys, B., Mukherjee, T., Seru, A., and Vig, V. 2010. Did Securitization Lead to Lax Screening: Evidence from Subprime Loans. *Quarterly Journal of Economics*, **125**, 307–362.

Keys, B., Barr, M. S., and Dokko, J. K. 2011. Exploring the Determinants of High-Cost Mortgages to Homeowners in Low-and Moderate-Income Neighborhoods. In: Wachter, S., and Smith, M. (eds), *The American Mortgage System: Rethink, Recover, Rebuild*. University of Pennsylvania Press.

Kiyotaki, N., and Moore, J. 1997. Credit Chains. *Journal of Political Economy*, **99**, 220–264.

Kodres, L., and Pritsker, M. 2002. A Rational Expectations Model of Financial Contagion. *Journal of Finance*, **57**, 769–799.

Laeven, L., and Levine, R. 2009. Bank Governance, Regulation and Risk Taking. *Journal of Financial Economics*, **93**, 259–275.

Laeven, L., Levine, R., and Michalopoulos, S. 2015. Financial Innovation and Endogenous Growth. *Journal of Financial Intermediation*, **24**, 1–24.

Lagunoff, R., and Schreft, S. 2001. A Model of Financial Fragility. *Journal of Economic Theory*, **99**, 220–264.

Langfield, S., and Pagano, M. 2015. Bank Bias in Europe: Effects on Systemic Risk and Growth. *Economic Policy*, **31**(85), 51–106.

Lerner, J., and Tufano, P. 2011. The Consequences of Financial Innovation: A Counterfactual Research Agenda. *Annual Review of Financial Economics*, **3**, 41–85.

Manconi, A., Massa, M., and Yasuda, A. 2012. The Role of Institutional Investors in Propagating the Crisis of 2007–2008. *Journal of Financial Economics*, **104**, 491–518.

Mariathasan, M., and Merrouche, O. 2014. The Manipulation of Basel Risk-weights. *Journal of Financial Intermediation*, **23**, 300–321.

Micossi, S., Bruzzone, G., and Cassella, M. 2014. Bail-in Provisions in State Aid and Resolution Procedures: Are They Consistent with Systemic Stability? *CEPS Policy Briefs, 318.*

Nijskens, R., and Wagner, W. 2011. Credit Risk Transfer Activities and Systemic Risk: How Banks Became Less Risky Individually but Posed Greater Risks to the Financial System at the Same Time. *Journal of Banking and Finance*, **35**, 1391–1398.

Norden, L., Silva Buston, C., and Wagner, W. 2014. Financial Innovation and Bank Behavior: Evidence from Credit Markets. *Journal of Economic Dynamics and Control*, **43**, 130–145.

Parlour, C. A., and Winton, A. 2013. Laying off Credit Risk: Loan Sales versus Credit Default Swaps. *Journal of Financial Economics*, **107**, 25–45.

Rajan, R. G. 2006. Has Finance Made the World Riskier? *European Financial Management*, **12**, 499–533.

Reinhart, C. M., and Rogoff, K. S. 2011. From Financial Crash to Debt Crisis. *American Economic Review*, **101**, 1676–1706.

Rochet, J. C. 2004. Macroeconomic shocks and banking supervision. *Journal of Financial Stability*, **1**, 93–110.

Rochet, J. C. 2008. *Why Are There So Many Banking Crises?* Princeton, NJ: Princeton University Press.

Rosengreen, E. S. 2014. Our Financial Structures – Are They Prepared for Financial Instability? *Journal of Money, Credit and Banking. Supplement to*, **46**, 143–156.

Sapir, A. 2014. Europe's Macroprudential Policy Framework in Light of the Banking Union. In: Schoenmaker, D. (ed), *Macroprudentialism*. VoxEU e-book.

Schmidt, L., Timmerman, A., and Wermers, R. 2014. Runs on Money Market Mutual Funds. University of Maryland working paper.

Shin, H. S. 2009. Securitisation and Financial Stability. *The Economic Journal*, **119**, 309–332.

Wagner, W. 2007a. Aggregate Liquidity Shortages, Idiosyncratic Liquidity Smoothing and Banking Regulation. *Journal of Financial Stability*, **3**, 18–32.

Wagner, W. 2007b. The Liquidity of Bank Assets and Banking Stability. *Journal of Banking and Finance*, **31**, 121–139.

Wagner, W. 2010. Diversification at Financial Institutions and Systemic Crises. *Journal of Financial Intermediation*, **19**, 373–386.

Wagner, W. 2011. Systemic Liquidation Risk and the Diversity-Diversification Trade-Off. *The Journal of Finance*, **66**, 1141–1175.

Wyplosz, C. 2016. The Eurozone after Stress Testing. *Economic Policy, forthcoming.*

12   Inequality and Welfare: Is Europe Special?

Alain Trannoy

In Memoriam of Tony Atkinson

Abstract

This chapter reviews the literature about inequality and welfare with a particular focus on whether Europe has a special sensitivity to these matters or specific outcomes. It is argued that both statements are likely to be true, which raises the possibility of a causal link. Europe has relatively good results in terms of inequality and welfare in comparison with other continents and more specifically America, because these issues matter for European people. Still, research needs to be fostered in at least 5 areas that are detailed at the end of this review. Specific attention is devoted to the contribution of other social sciences and natural sciences (cognitive science) to the development of our knowledge for the field of inequality and welfare.

12.1   Introduction

Distribution and redistribution issues have never left the European stage either in public debate or on the research agenda in economics and other social sciences. The novelty comes from the US where public opinion is changing dramatically. While for a long time inequality was not considered a hot topic, and correlatively a benign-neglect public policy seemed to be in force, rising inequality is attracting the attention of the media, of the public and of politicians in the US, as testified by the huge success of Piketty's masterpiece *Capital in the Twenty First Century*. Since to some extent the political agenda of each society is reflected in the scientific agenda of researchers through inclination and public funding, it is not surprising that Europe is challenging the US in many areas regarding inequality and welfare. Having said that, our understanding of the dynamics of inequality does not match the needs required by well-calibrated economic and social policies.

This chapter will be structured around the points mentioned in COEURE's call for expression of interest. All issues may be encompassed in a broader

511

question: is Europe special? Special because of the issues raised at a social or political level or because of the nature of the contribution made by European economists. As Angela Merkel likes to say, 'Europe represents 7% of the world's population, 25% of the global GDP and 50% of the total social spending at the world level.' These figures tell us first that Europe is small and rich. In terms of revealed collective preference, it also tells us that European societies, as diverse as they are, care more on average about the distribution of welfare than other parts of the globe. Various reasons may allow us to explain such a pattern: European societies are rich, they are getting older (the median age in Germany is almost ten years higher than in the US, China, Australia and Russia), and in democratic societies this high social spending should also reflect the preference of the citizens and tax payers. The above words of the German Chancellor convey the fear – and this feeling is likely widespread – that social spending is so much higher in the EU than in other parts of the world that it is undermining Europe's competitiveness. Notwithstanding that inequality and social welfare are prerogatives of nation states, European institutions to some extent play the role of a lifeguard station. The coordination of social security rights for mobile workers, standards for health and safety in the workplace, some EU directives on workers' rights (maximum weekly hours of work for instance), and a legal basis for enforcing nondiscrimination among EU citizens can be viewed as the first steps of a more coordinated and developed policy in the social realm as called for by some recent policy reports (Vandenbroucke, 2014, Vandenbroucke and Vanhercke, 2014, Friends of Europe, 2015).

This chapter falls into eight parts. I will start by setting the scene in defining the concepts of inequality and welfare and the links that economists establish between them. Next, I will proceed by showing that these two concepts raise issues involving several sciences (social and hard). I will then outline Europe's inequality pattern vis-à-vis the US and the rankings of Europe nation states according to various concepts of welfare. It turns out that Europe is at the forefront of research in many subfields and this will be the topic of the fourth part. After the diagnosis, comes advice for action. I will develop the fact that data are improving, but remain largely incomplete when looking at more sophisticated issues. Section 12.6 argues that among the most interesting and important issues regarding inequality and welfare, some are at the intersection of several topics surveyed by the different PI. I then zoom in on the most cutting edge research issues in this field in my opinion. Among these issues some are more specific to Europe and this is the focus of the last part. I will end by making recommendations on ways to gear research in Europe about inequality and welfare toward forefront issues.

I should also mention that there is another motive to redistributing income; risk-aversion. There are many social risks such as illness, ageing, handicap, long-term care, and unemployment that will partially or fully reduce the earning capacity of an individual. Risk aversion leads people to insure against these risks. Social insurance will also redistribute income across individuals. However, from a purely conceptual point of view, the main motive of insurance redistribution is not between individuals, but for the same individual at different periods or across different states in the world. Due to clear constraints, I cannot review the literature about this insurance redistribution which is somewhat difficult to disentangle from the pure vertical distribution from rich to poor in empirical analysis. This is an important omission since risk preferences are important to understand the magnitude of public health expenditures, social security and public education. These public expenditures help to mitigate inequality of well-beings as well as vertical redistribution, but their interplay is quite complex to understand. For instance, Moene and Wallerstein (2001) build a model where redistribution is an inferior good, whereas insurance motive is a normal good.

I have tried to maintain the technicalities at a minimum so that this survey can be read by a larger audience. There are no equations in the main text.

12.2 Inequality and Welfare: Two Interconnected Notions

Inequality and welfare are two catch-all terms, and a natural way to get into the substance is to describe how economists and, more generally, social scientists have approached these two notions. This section is more conceptual than the others, but there is no short cut to avoid misleading interpretations here.

12.2.1 Inequality

The word inequality refers to the distribution of some measurable (in a cardinal sense) quantity. In economics, there are many quantities whose distribution one may be interested in. Earnings, disposable income, consumption, savings, wealth, working hours, leisure time, longevity, number of years of schooling, etc. are just a few examples. A fundamental difference comes in when one asks whether inequality should be assessed ex-post or ex-ante.

The former means that all the different processes have occurred. The various processes refer to the production phase, the consumption phase, price determination and also government intervention through taxes, expenditures and transfers, depending whether we want to look before or after the government intervention. Another way to term this ex-post inequality is to say that we are interested in the inequality of outcomes. A natural way to do this is to look at the distribution of the outcome in a statistical sense and to adopt simple or sophisticated measures of the dispersion of this outcome. The initial conceptual steps regarding measuring inequality date back to the beginning of the twentieth century. They were put forward by Vilfredo Pareto with his Pareto Law, by Max Lorenz with the Lorenz curve, by Corrado Gini with the Gini index, and by the British economist and member of the House of commons, Dalton (1920) (see Atkinson and Brandolini, 2015 for an appraisal of his contribution) with the Pigou-Dalton principle of transfers. This principle states that inequality decreases when one performs a transfer from a richer individual to a poorer individual which does not reverse the ranking of the individuals, other things being equal. It is interesting to note that the period of the founding fathers of the measurement of inequality of income occurred at a time where, in many industrialized countries, the income and wealth inequalities were probably at a peak (see Figure 12.8 below).

Basically no cutting-edge innovation took place during the next 50 years except Kuznet's (1955) discovery of the inverse U-shape curve between income inequality and growth. As countries experience economic growth, income inequality first increases and then decreases. And indeed this was the case with the period 1930–1970 corresponding to a period of decreasing inequality in the US and in many Western countries. At the beginning of the 1970s, a second wave of innovations in the field of the measurement of inequality was initiated with the seminal works of Kolm (1969), Atkinson (1970), and Sen (1973) making crystal clear why the use of the Lorenz curve should be at the cornerstone of inequality measurement. Afterwards, many further developments came with measures which deal with the appraisal of multidimensional inequality (Atkinson and Bourguignon, 1982, 1987). The main novel issue was to cope with the relation between the different attributes (income, health, leisure etc.), whether they are substitutes or complements (Bourguignon and Chakravarty, 2003). If the different dimensions are thought to be substitutes for one another, then a decorrelation of the distribution of the different dimensions may decrease inequality, while if they are thought to be complements, a decorrelation can only increase inequality. A multidimensional setting seems particularly adapted to measuring poverty when looking at empirical distribution data censored to the poverty line in each dimension (Alkire and Foster, 2011). A major difference between Europe and the US is that it is defined in relative terms (50% or 60% of the median) in Europe, whereas it is defined in absolute terms in the US (in monetary terms). Adam Smith already argued in favour of a relative poverty line. Since the 1970s the study of ex-post inequality and poverty has not left the stage in economics literature, with a greater emphasis since the 1990s when it became apparent that inequality was on the rise, at least in the US and in the UK, as well as elsewhere in many (but not all) other industrialized countries, invalidating the optimism delivered by the prediction of the Kuznets curve.

At the same time, at the beginning of the 1970s, economists' attention was progressively drawn to the work of political philosophers who pointed out that ex-ante inequality was as important as ex-post inequality and maybe more important than inequality of outcome from a normative perspective. Since John Rawls's major opus (see Rawls, 1971), all the subsequent flow of political philosophy (Sen, 1980, 1985, Dworkin, 1981a, Arneson, 1989, Cohen, 1989) argue in one way or another that the focus on inequality of outcomes in the economic and social science literature is ill-conceived since some inequality can be considered as legitimate. The surfer in Malibu example (Van Parijs, 1991) is emblematic of the argument. Suppose that someone living in LA, and being a college graduate,[1] after having paid low fees at one of the campuses of the University of California, chooses to spend most of his time surfing. California is known to be a good place to find surfing spots as well as jobs, except in downturn periods. In addition, he can count on the skill premium if he decides to go to the labour market. He is doing some part-time job just to cover his bare-bone subsistence needs. Looking at the distribution of disposable income ex-post, this guy would be at the bottom part of the earnings distribution. Is the income inequality between him and his friend who is employed with the same degree in some movie studio in LA legitimate? Van Parijs (1996) and most post-Rawls philosophers argue that in terms of possibility sets, the Malibu surfer has got the same possibility set as the other graduates of the same university and that the discrepancy between ex-post incomes just reflect differences in preference. As a matter of fact, they result from differences of choices within the same opportunity set. The philosophers claim that these differences are legitimate and should not be compensated by public policy. This idea has been developed in many different ways because measuring ex-ante inequality is much more complex than measuring ex-post inequality. Inequality of opportunity sets, of capability sets, and of opportunity refer to different objects. Economists and other social scientists under the impulse of Sen (1985), Nussbaum and Sen (1999), Roemer (1993), Roemer (1998), Fleurbaey (2008) have tried to cope with conceptual difficulties and paucity of data.

Attitudes towards inequality depend on the source of inequality. According to questionnaires or experiments, most individuals like inequalities when they are based on merit, but much less when they are based on luck. It is therefore important to recognize that the evolution of inequality does not necessarily describe the evolution of unfairness.

12.2.2 Welfare

While inequality is purely positive, welfare belongs to the normative realm and then it does not come as a surprise that it can be viewed from outside of economics as a muddling topic, where there is large variation of view-points among economists and more generally social thinkers. As a matter of fact, it can also be viewed within economics as a shaky notion. Robbins (1935) is notorious for having defended the view that the level of happiness is neither measurable nor comparable across a population, a standpoint that is maintained in the segment of the profession which has a quite narrow view of economics and which thinks that the less economists talk about welfare, the better. But even beyond them, very recently, two prominent economists who are deeply interested in redistribution issues, Emmanuel Saez from Berkeley and Stéphanie Stancheva from Harvard, in a paper devoted to optimal income taxation (Saez and Stantcheva, 2016) argue in favour of an approach which completely bypasses the construction of a social welfare function, which has been the cornerstone of welfare economics since the seminal article of Bergson (1938). Politics or maybe political science is replacing political philosophy. The priorities devoted to different groups are just a matter of political opinions retrieved from questionnaires and these opinions are then plugged in the abbreviated formula of optimal marginal income tax. This line of research suggests that it is not the business of economists to tackle the murky issue of trying to do more than taking political opinions for granted.

Welfare may be defined both at an individual and at a collective level. In its common sense, welfare refers to the well-being and happiness of an individual. By extension, it also designates social benefits to the poor or socially disabled in tune with the fact that the government's objective in a welfare state is to provide assistance to those in need. Collective welfare is by extension the well-being of a group of people. GDP or GDP per capita has been used as a measure of the standard of living at a country scale. It is a rather crude measure of collective welfare and indeed it has been challenged since the very beginning. Simon Kuznets, one of the founding fathers of the national income account, declared in 1934 that 'the welfare of a nation can scarcely be inferred from a measure of national income'. On the other side of the Atlantic, John Hicks and Nicholas Kaldor proposed as a measure of national welfare something close to the GDP adjusted for leisure and pollution (Hicks, 1946). Basically, the GNI (Gross National Income) per capita suffers from two weaknesses. First, it ignores negative externalities on the environment generated by economic activity, and it neglects other important dimensions that matter for welfare such as health, knowledge, and leisure. Second, distribution issues are missed by using a per capita measure. Well before the Stiglitz-Sen-Fitoussi report (2009) report, the index of human development (HDI) produced by the UNDP (United Nations Development Program) attempted to address the first weakness by incorporating two additional dimensions, health and education, on top of per capita GNI. The health indicator is the life expectancy at birth. The education indicator is made up of variations around the mean years of schooling. The three indicators are normalized on a (0, 1) scale by the average of a lower and upper bounds. The dispersion of the three elementary indicators across the population of a country is ignored in the traditional HDI. Alkire and Foster (2010) (based on Foster et al., 2005) helped to build an IHDI (inequality of human development index) which accounts for inequality in each dimension. As will become clear below, there is a presumption that inequality reduces social welfare. The construction of such indicators is far from obvious and requires many assumptions:

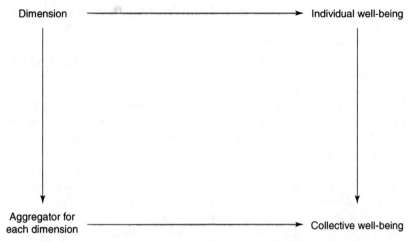

Figure 12.1 The two routes for aggregating welfares in a multidimensional setting.

some are technical, others are more normative. Consequently, the robustness of the country ranking according to these indicators is all but warranted.

12.2.3 Aggregating Welfare

There are basically two routes to construct such indices. The basic information structure can be illustrated by the following matrix where the profiles of individuals are represented in rows according to various dimensions that are featured in columns. The typical element of this matrix is the allocation of individual i in good j, x_i^j:

$$\text{Individuals} \quad \begin{pmatrix} \overset{\text{Dimensions}}{x_i^j} \end{pmatrix}$$

The HDI or IHDI illustrates (see Figure 12.1) a first alternative where each dimension is first aggregated into a specific aggregator (for instance the GNI per capita for the income dimension) and then we have to solve the problem of how to add carrots and tomatoes. It is important to recognize that with this first route, collective welfare does not aggregate individual welfare, which is not defined as such. This way of proceeding bypasses computing individual welfare and hence it ignores the correlation between the different distributions.

The other route is deeply imbedded in the social choice literature which deals with the principles of aggregation of preference. The main concept is the Bergson-Samuelson social welfare function, which dates back to Bergson (1938). This concept has been enlarged by Sen to functional, namely, a function of functions aggregating the various individual utility functions which are numerical representations of individual preferences over the various dimensions into a function, that is, a numerical representation of collective choices. The crucial role of the informational basis of social choice introduced by Sen (1970) in his book *Collective Choice and Social Welfare* was perfectly understood by d'Aspremont and Gevers (1977) to offer some escape to the Arrow impossibility theorem (see Arrow, 1963). The important distinctions are between the requirements of:

- *Level comparability* where the levels of each individual well-being indicator[2] are made comparable. The worst-off in a society need to be defined, as in the maxmin solution. This kind of comparison is, for instance, necessary when one has to decide who most deserves social benefits.
- *First-difference comparability*. The differences (gains and losses) in well-being indicators are comparable across individuals. This sort of comparability is needed to compute the sum of utilities, or to compute the total welfare gain of a tax-transfer policy measure.
- *Ratio-scale comparability*. The ratio of individual well-being indicators is comparable. The ratio-scale comparability requires each individual well-being indicator to have a common and natural 0. For instance, the Nash Bargaining solution (defined as a product of utilities gains with respect to some status quo) has to be computed, or each individual has to report his happiness on a common scale between 0 and 10, as is quite common in all happiness studies.

This second route allows for the correlation between attributes to matter in computing social welfare. To some extent, this second approach is preferable to the first one, but obviously the construction of an individual well-being indicator represents a major challenge. There again, two routes may be followed, a normative one trying to build an individual well-being indicator on sound properties, a route followed by Fleurbaey (2009) or a more positive route built on happiness literature (Layard, 2011). One may also want to combine both, an attempt proposed by Fleurbaey and Maniquet (2011). Of course, even if it were proved that one can strictly measure individual well-being on an objective basis, it remains a normative choice to select this objective measure of well-being as the measure of individual welfare that will be used in collective choice.

12.2.4   The Relationship between Inequality and Welfare

It arises from the previous developments that inequality and welfare are closely related. And yet, it is far from obvious that the two words and concepts, inequality and welfare, are intimately related in the mind of the layman, as they are in the economist's. In the history of economic thought they have been linked since Edgeworth (1897). He put forward the idea that even if you are interested in total welfare defined as the sum of individual happiness, as advocated by Jeremy Bentham and John Stuart Mill, you should favour egalitarianism, and in particular you should agree to progressive income taxation. This reasoning is important because the conclusion is paradoxical. Even if one only cares about the sum of welfare across the population,[3] one should look carefully at income distribution. Of course, the conclusion that the more equal a society, the greater the collective welfare defined as a sum, does not hold without assumptions. More precisely, if the marginal utility of income is the same for each individual and is decreasing, then the bliss point is reached for an equal distribution of income. The result is valid, absent any cost of redistributing income and in particular any behavioral responses. Obviously, one can immediately find people who would object to fully confiscating individual incomes. However, the important point is not there. This framework has been the point of departure of the optimal income taxation à la Mirrlees (1971), who reintroduced behaviour responses but who kept intact the two major assumptions set up by Edgeworth. The model represents the canonical model of the welfarist tradition of optimal income taxation and then of welfarist redistribution before the attempt of Saez and Stantcheva (2016) to replace it by another paradigm.

12.2.5   Two Assumptions about Individual Welfare

Let us have a look at each assumption which underlies Edgeworth's reasoning. The decreasingness of marginal utility of income, after having been postulated by Bentham, has been recently tested thanks to happiness surveys (Layard et al., 2008) and is confirmed by empirical evidence. Apparently, the utility that fits the date the most is logconcave, that is, marginal utility declines more rapidly than it decreases with a log utility function.

On the other hand, it seems obvious that the similarity assumption could be violated by the data. The similarity assumption is normative, but is important to understand it in depth before rejecting it. The critics of this assumption are often misguided. Obviously, there is no particular reason to think that a € 1000 additional income given to two individuals who have already the same base income would make them equally happier. However, suppose that they are equally the same from all objective characteristics that can be gathered in any household survey. They are the same age, they grew up in the same family, school and neighborhood background, they are in good physical and mental health, they have the same jobs and so on. Obviously even if they are similar from all objective perspectives, it does not mean that they are going to assess an income gain in the same way. So, another way of formulating this assumption is to say that unless there is some objective characteristic that is measurable and can be certified at the bar of political justice, in a parliament for instance, the marginal utility associated to a gain or a loss of income from a given level of income is assumed to be the same. That is, the burden of proof falls on those who claim that some categories of people need specific treatment. The fact that you are grumpy, for instance, will not pass the bar of social justice unless you demonstrate that it is related to some external objective cause. This discussion is partly linked to the question of expensive/cheap tastes in the philosophical literature about social justice.

Normative social choice theorists learnt to cope with what is known as the expensive taste problem. Expensive tastes play an important role in rejecting the use of a subjective indicator of welfare in prominent theories of social justice: in Scanlon (1975) when adopting an objective criterion of well-being, in Rawls's account of primary goods (Rawls, 1982), in Dworkin (1981b)'s advocacy of equality of resources rather than welfare, in Arneson (1989) when he made equality of opportunity for welfare more appealing than equality of welfare. The prevalent view is that expensive tastes should not play a role in the redistributive policy unless they are correlated to some objective cause. This standpoint concerns utility levels. We would add an additional point when the discussion brings about comparing gains and losses in utility induced by transferring income from one individual to another, as in the Pigou-Dalton principle of transfers.

This kind of comparison is common practice and I would like to illustrate the contrast between an acceptable point to discriminate and a case which might be viewed as unpalatable. Family needs provide the right case and the distinction wage earners/self-employed the wrong case.

Figure 12.2 illustrates the dilemma faced by a redistributive policy which looks at the redistribution around the allocation coming out from the markets, which may have the property of a status quo. If there is no social agreement, then no redistribution takes place. For the sake of illustration we only graph a first-order approximation of a local change of income around the status quo.[4] It is simpler to consider that all categories of individuals get the same market income, even if the reasoning can be extended a little bit beyond that.

Let us suppose that there are two kinds of persons, those who are more sensitive to pain and pleasure (plain line), and those who are less sensitive to pain and pleasure (dotted line). The situation can also be contrasted in terms of the elasticity of marginal utility to income around some initial allocation, if we accept the ratio-scale comparison assumption. This elasticity gives the relative change in marginal utility gained from an increment in consumption of 1 per cent.

Family size provides a first example of such a differentiation and it is largely admitted that an additional gain will bring more happiness to a couple with two kids than to a single household. This kind of assumption has been put forth by Atkinson and Bourguignon (1987) in their extension of the Lorenz criterion to

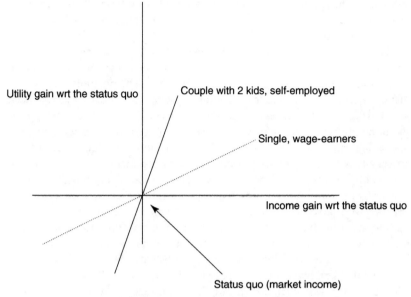

Figure 12.2 Comparing gains and losses around the status quo.

households who differ in needs and in particular in family size. Tax treatments in all advanced countries provide specific provisions for family composition and size for the benefit of families and at the expense of singles. Social benefits are also greater for families than for singles. Then, we have an example of largely accepted transfers between groups, which is welfare-enhancing when welfare is computed as the sum of objective differences in well-being at the margin.

Now consider the case of the tax treatment of self-employed with respect to wage earners. It is more speculative to assume that self-earners are more marginal-utility elastic than wage-earners. They self-select as self-employed and it is very likely that this self-selection process bears selection bias in terms of preference. Risk attitude, being one's own master and love of freedom, ambition, less work disutility come to mind as dimensions of preference with a potential selection bias. However, all these aspects miss the point that we want to emphasize, which is that they may embark on self-employment because they aspire to become rich in a way that wage-earners do not. Empirical evidence consistent with this supposition is the fact that all empirical studies find a higher labour elasticity and a higher reported elasticity of taxable income to the net-of-tax rate for self-employed than for wage earners (Saez et al., 2012). Optimal income tax theory recommends a specific lower tax treatment, something that has not been granted even if the latter may occasionally benefit from specific advantageous tax deductions for business expenses. It is then interesting to investigate why they have not benefited from a more advantageous treatment on a large scale.

There are basically three reasons[5] that can be invoked to explain that it has not happened yet. The first one is that the taste for money is not verifiable and then at this stage highly manipulable. Still, it could be verifiable in the near future thanks to the rapid advances in the neuroscience of happiness (see Kringelbach and Berridge, 2010). The second reason may be that there is a large heterogeneity in the preference for money by the self-employed, while everyone agrees that taking care of a kid represents additional expenses. The magnitude of heterogeneity among the self-employed is an empirical matter that could also be unveiled by the progress of neuroscience. The third reason is ethical. Suppose that we get to learn that all self-employed are suffering from a greater utility sacrifice to be taxed than all wage earners. It will not be enough to convince MPs to grant them a specific tax treatment because of the widespread opinion that people should be held responsible for their preferences and should not be compensated for. This political stance is advocated by the philosophers of responsibility and by economists like Marc Fleurbaey and François Maniquet (Fleurbaey and Maniquet, 2011). May look reasonable, except that the same reasoning applies to children for it is difficult to defend that in western societies the presence of children in a family does not testify their parents' preferences.

This kind of comparison of first differences in utility is also made in optimal income tax theory when establishing the optimal marginal tax formula with the use of a small perturbation à la Saez (2001). We are looking at a small tax change (tax and transfer payment since tax reform is budget neutral) and we compute the first-order welfare changes (including behavioral responses and tax revenues) for all individuals impacted by the change. Basically the analogue of Figure 12.2 illustrates the marginal gains and losses associated to the tax perturbation with the status quo figuring out the optimal allocation. If the initial allocation is locally optimal, then the net collective welfare gain introduced by any tax perturbation should be zero. The computation is just a little bit less crude than the one we have previously described since the marginal individual welfare changes are weighted by social weight describing the society concern for fairness. Saez and Stantcheva (2016) nested the standard welfarist approach in a more general one with generalized marginal social welfare weights which represents the value that society puts on providing an additional € 1 of consumption to any individual.

Making stock of what we want to communicate as the main message here is that a small departure from utilitarianism by assuming that individuals in a homogenous society have the same marginal utility allows us to conclude that an extra income is more valuable to the poor than to the rich, and that inequality means a loss in collective welfare. This idea was immensely influential in the

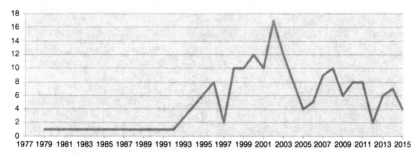

Figure 12.3 Stylized trends in the economic literature about inequality: number of inequality articles (title or keywords) in selected economics journals: *AER, QJE, JPE, RES, Econometrica, J Pub Econ* and *EJ* (Scopus).

Anglo-Saxon world and in fact was the idea pioneered by Dalton (1920) to measure inequality. This idea of an ethical measure of inequality was brought into the full view of the economics profession and beyond by Atkinson (1970) in his seminal paper with his equally distributed equivalent income (EDE). It is defined as the equal distribution of income which gives the same total welfare as the actual welfare. The reduction of average income in the EDE in proportion to the actual average income gives a measure of the waste of resources induced by the inequality of the income distribution.[6]

The second message is that departing from the identity assumption of the well-being indicator is hazardous and should not be undertaken except in some well identified cases such as family size, handicap, etc. Here, I fully agree with the following quote from Saez and Zucman (2014): 'Redistribution based on marginal utility is socially acceptable if there are objective reasons a person has higher needs, such as having a medical condition requiring high expenses, or a large family with many dependents.'

12.3   Normative and Positive Issues Involving Several Sciences

Maybe the first important observation that is important to convey to a large public is that inequality and welfare are far from being at the heart of the discipline. Figures 12.3 and 12.4 illustrate[7] the trend in publication in comparison with articles devoted to detection of causal phenomena. One can see that from the late 1970s to the early 1990s it was a topic that had no particular appeal to economists. Afterwards following the inequality increase in the US and the UK in the 1980s and 1990s, there was a surge of economists' interest in this issue. In 1997, Antony Atkinson gave his presidential address to the Royal Economic Society titled 'Bringing Income Distribution in from the Cold'. The inequality plateaued in both these countries at the beginning of the millennium

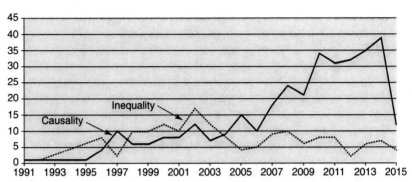

Figure 12.4 Stylized trends in the economics literature: Comparison causality and equality (Scopus). Same journals as in Figure 12.3.

and the interest is fading again. In Section 12.2, we already noted a positive correlation between peaks of inequality and interest by social scientists in the field earlier in the twentieth century. Regarding Piketty's shock on the economic literature, it is still to be confirmed. Even when it was rocketing, the expression of interest from economists in inequality seems quite moderate in comparison with the interest in causality that has become a central topic in the field (see Figure 12.4).

Fortunately, economists can rely on other colleagues of other disciplines. I am here giving some examples of interaction between economics and other sciences. Distribution and redistribution are and should be described in a purely positive manner. However, people are very interested in these issues because they are likely to have a representation of what should be a just or fair distribution issuing from markets and a just redistribution process involving various public policies. They will compare what they see, to what they think, and if the discrepancy is too high they will declare that the situation is unfair. Obviously, differences in opinions are present and are shaped by political stances and economic environments. So they are only partly endogenous to economic variables and economists need the contribution of other social sciences to understand how ideas emerge and then spread due to social or economic conditions.

12.3.1   Political Philosophy

I have already mentioned the deep influence that political philosophers since John Rawls have had on the evolution of thinking among economists about the normative approach to social justice. They helped to structure ideas which have been around in a consistent way and it clarifies the opposition and the incompatibility between the different stances. Utilitarianism, which had long been the leading ethics inspiring economics, was challenged by the works of John Rawls, Amartya Sen, Ronald Dworkin and many others. It has pervaded the work of economists dealing with economic inequality by suggesting that the normative judgment about the fairness of an allocation depends as much on the process leading to inequality as on the resulting inequality level. Political philosophy continues to fuel economics with new ideas regarding equality and attention needs to be paid to how they cope with new problems. I will drop a few names whose thesis has received widespread attention among economists and social scientists. Robert Nozick with his 1974 book *Anarchy, State, and Utopia* (see Nozick, 1974) expressed a libertarian viewpoint in a rejoinder to John Rawls, Parfit (1984) with the repugnant conclusion of utilitarianism when applied to population ethic problems, Barry (1994) and Van Parijs (1996) for their support of the universal basic income, Elster (1992) for studying how institutions allocate rights and goods to cope with social justice, Dworkin (1981a,b), Scanlon (1986), Cohen (1989) and Arneson (1989) for focusing on the issue of responsibility, the former two where individuals are held responsible for preferences as long as they identified with them, the latter two where individuals are responsible for what they control. All these ideas have been brought into the full view of the economic profession by the textbook of Roemer (1996) on distributive justice, where the axiomatic method is used to understand the prerequisite of each normative ethic in depth by the choice of some primitive principle. They also fuse political philosophy and modern economic thinking with their own proposals on equality of opportunity, Roemer (1993), Roemer (1998) and Fleurbaey (2008) following the example of their elders, Sen (1985) with his capability approach and Serge-Christophe Kolm, when he was promoting envy-free allocations (Kolm, 1972) or the 'Equal Labour Income Equalisation' (ELIE), (Kolm, 2005).

12.3.2   History

If philosophy is helpful on the normative side, *History* or maybe more accurately the use of historical data in departments of economic history, has been extremely helpful on the positive side to give a sense of the degree of magnitude of income or wealth inequality nowadays in comparison to the past. I here give the example of the extraction rate a simple but meaningful concept by Milanovic (2006). It is computed as the ratio between the actual Gini of some income distribution and the maximum feasible Gini. It is defined as the Gini which will prevail if almost all the population except a tiny fraction of the population received an income just allowing them to struggle with life. The subsistence level has been defined nearly as $1 a day (in purchasing power parity terms) for all periods. The original '$1 a day' line was a typical line amongst low-income countries in the data available in the 90s.[8] A tiny fraction of the population receives all the surplus of the economy. Ancient Egypt comes to mind as a typical example. The inequality possibility frontier (IPF) (see Figure 12.5) delineates two regions. Above the frontier, we should not observe

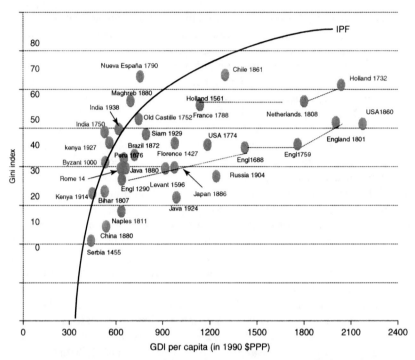

Figure 12.5 Estimated Gini coefficients and the Inequality Possibility Frontier (pre-industrial economies, Milanovic, 2013). Updated from Milanovic et al. (2011).

any society unless some fraction of the population is going to starve and the population is going to decrease. Then above the frontier, it cannot be a steady state. Below the frontier, we observe societies where either the exploiters are not a tiny group or the exploited are going to get an income higher than the subsistence level or both.

The graph extracted from Milanovic (2013) based on Milanovic et al. (2011) in Figure 12.5 is absolutely fascinating. It provides the most damning indictment of colonization of the rest of the world by Europeans. All the regions above the IPF are colonized regions except Byzantium and the Moghul Empire (India, 1750). It proves that the colonial regimes were just regimes of total extraction of the surplus to the benefit of the colonizers. Latin America is still trying to cope with this daunting legacy in terms of inequality. Rome in the beginning of the first century or England in the late thirteenth century performed a little bit better, but it is quite amazing how the slow growth of England from that century onwards was pro-poor. The same went for Holland. In contrast, on the eve of Revolution, France was extraordinarily unequal with modern current deep consequences for the way the French view any form of inequality.

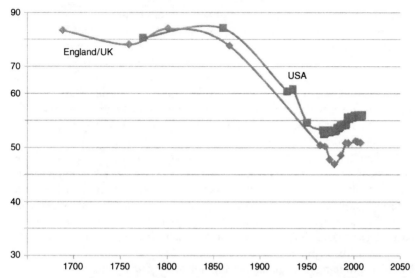

Figure 12.6 UK and US historical inequality extraction ratios (elasticity of the social minimum with respect to mean income = 0.5, Milanovic, 2013).

What is also amazing is that restricting the focus on just the US and the UK, this movement of going away from the IPF stopped since the mid-70s and even reversed. The concept of minimal subsistence level has been adapted by Milanovic (2013) to take into account the fact that the basic need requirement is going to increase with the average income in developed societies. The elasticity of the social minimum with respect to mean income has been estimated at around 0.5. We have to admit as robust empirical evidence that in the Anglo-Saxon world growth has failed to be pro-poor since the last quarter of the twentieth century. However we cannot say that *from the point of view of the worst-off* we are back to the eve of World War I as Piketty can rightly argue for the wealth share of the top 1 per cent. It is also slightly reassuring that the rise in the extraction ratio has been at a standstill since the beginning of the third millennium (Figure 12.6).

12.3.3 Sociology and Political Science

Sociology and political science are bringing their expertise in carrying out representative surveys within and across countries on opinions on various matters. A very good example of their expertise in Europe is provided by the European Social Survey (n.d.) (ESS) which is an academically driven cross-national survey that has been conducted every two years across Europe since 2001. This representative survey measures the attitudes, beliefs and behavior patterns of diverse populations in more than 30 European nations. In comparison with other surveys conducted all over the world, the distinctive feature of the ESS is the high quality of comparative data provided. Survey respondents were selected using strict random probability sampling, with a minimum target response rate of 70 per cent, to try and ensure that representative national samples were obtained. The ESS's high-quality translation of questions and systematic international sampling approach enables reliable cross-country comparisons to be made. In the next section, we will use their survey results about well-being across Europe's nations.

Another domain where sociological studies have been extremely influential on the economists' research agenda even implicitly was social mobility and more specifically the reproduction of social disadvantage at school. Well before it became fashionable in economics, sociologists of education have explored the degree to which family, environmental characteristics, and genetics influence educational achievement. For instance, the *Coleman Report* in 1966 found that student background and socioeconomic status are much more important in determining educational outcomes than measured differences in school resources. In the same vein, the work of Richard Breen and John Goldthorpe in the UK, and Pierre Bourdieu and Jean-Claude Passeron in France come to mind.

Another important sociological idea has pervaded the debate about the inequality of opportunity among economists. Sociologists have been divided about the relative importance of social structure vs autonomy (human agency in the sociological jargon) in determining individual behavior but they all agree that the former factor is important. In contrast, a corner stone of neoclassical economics is that preferences are stable and make an individual what he is. How the preferences came to be formed was outside of economics. John Roemer has contended that the rank of the student in the distribution of, let's say, school effort (if it can be measured) among all students sharing the same background characteristics provides a measure of the autonomy of the individual. This profound idea is clearly reminiscent of the sociological debate about determinism versus voluntarism. The fact that this distribution is not reduced to a spike implies that there is some room for voluntarism.

Political science sheds light about why western democracies have not fully reacted to counterbalance the increase of market-income inequality. Regarding the emblematic US case, Bonica et al. (2013) provide very useful insights. It is fascinating that the great inequality moderation during the period 1930–1970 corresponds to a period where the ideological opposition between Republicans and Democrats on the liberal-conservative dimension was minimal. From the 1970s, the average political opinions in each party fell apart, Democrats becoming more and more liberal (in the American sense) and Republicans more and more conservative. As Figure 12.7 shows, most of the polarization has been produced by a rightward movement of Republicans. Since the American political

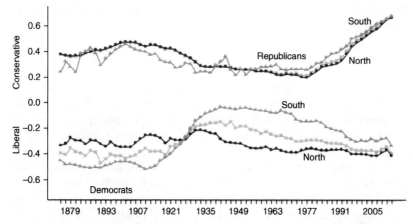

Figure 12.7 Republican–Democrat distance on Liberal–Conservative Dimension for the US House of Representatives, 1879–2012 (Bonica et al., 2013).

system requires to some extent a consensus, or at least moderate representatives from the other political side (because of the bicameral legislature with a filibuster) to pass laws, the polarization has created a policy gridlock preventing the US system from adopting redistributive policies to maintain disposable inequality in a moderate range.

The next issue is to understand why such of polarization happens and why after all redistribution policies become less popular. It is maybe the most difficult issue of social sciences to establish some causal relations about why political stances are becoming more or less popular. John Roemer (Roemer et al., 2007) hypotheses that instead of being one dimensional (more or less welfare state), the political agenda is nowadays bi-dimensional, where the second political axis is how open the society should be to people originating from other ethnicities. The choice along this second dimension interferes with the choice over the redistributive dimension and changes the equilibrium of the political game. If people of the ethnic majority have the feeling (maybe it is untrue) that the welfare recipients come in a disproportionate fraction from the minorities, some voters will be against an extension of the welfare state and even for a reduction of the welfare state because of their mixed feelings vis-à-vis the minority. The authors estimate that if all voters held nonracist views, liberal and conservative parties alike would have proposed levels of redistribution 10–20 per cent higher than they did. On European data (ESS), Senik et al. (2009) found that natives that hold negative views about immigrants tend to be less supportive of the welfare state independently of the perceived presence of immigrants. To the extent that the racial issue used to be less intense in Europe than in the US, it may explain the distinctive choice of the US political system regarding the degree of powerfulness of the welfare state.

12.3.4   Psychology

Psychology helps to understand how to design experiments to assess the fairness of a situation and the different feelings like happiness induced by a given situation or a change in situation. Psychologists are particularly useful to help us understand the traps that the scientist has to bypass to get an adequate answer to some questionnaire.

There is a huge wave of studies about happiness, but the work of psychologists, such as Daniel Kahneman (Kahneman and Riis, 2005), shows that individuals approach this concept in various ways. They cannot think straight about well-being. People are confused about how they feel in their life and how happy they are *about* their life. The former view corresponds to emotional states, whereas the latter view is closer to what people think of their life. Depending on what you are asking, the emotional-self or the cognitive-self, the answers will be different and the correlation is not higher than 0.4–0.5. To illustrate, when people are asked about how their feelings vary with income, the emotional-self (Gallup polls for the US in a study conducted by Kahneman and Deaton, 2010) reports a completely flat curve beyond an annual income of $75,000, whereas the remembering-self reports a life evaluation which rises steadily (approximately linearly with the log of income). These authors conclude that money buys life satisfaction but not happiness, whereas a lack of money exacerbates the bad feeling associated with ill health, divorce and being alone. At this stage, it is still not clear how we can use these figures to design public policies, but this issue represents a clear challenge for the future years.

A second distinction refers to the emotional quality of an individual. The experienced-self knows about the present, while the remembering-self keeps records and maintains the story of his/her life. The remembering-self is a storyteller. What we keep in memories helps us to build a story. Discrepancies can occur between the experiencing-self and the remembering-self. When a colonoscopy experience ending with a pain peak is extended with some moments of further lower pain, the patient keeps in mind a lower pain although the pain experienced by the patient lasts longer and is at least as great in the extending clinical test as in the initial test.[9] Any social scientist who fails to make the distinction between these two notions is going to mess up the study of emotional happiness.

12.3.5   Neurosciences: Happiness in the Twenty-First Century

And what if Jeremy Bentham was right with his invention of happiness? I am referring here to the famous quote 'Nature has placed mankind under the governance of two sovereign masters, pain and pleasure'. One century later, Sigmund Freud was of the opinion that people strive for happiness. Nowadays, according to Ken Berridge[10] from Michigan University (Kringelbach and Berridge, 2010), we do have a few insights to understand the brain mechanism of hedonic states, even if we do not have a full-fledged neuroscience of happiness as we have for memory or vision. The Aristotelian distinction between Eudemonia and Hedonia is still useful. Hedonic feelings are generated deep in the brain and all rewards arise from the same brain circuit (network), which is quite fragile, whereas the prefrontal cortex is just a coding region. Abstract pleasure such as art and music or social pleasure such as meeting children or friends activate the same brain region as sensory pleasures such as food and sex, raising the hypothesis, extrapolating from what we know, that the same brain circuit is generating a sustainable sense of well-being embracing both eudemonia and hedonia. The brain region for pleasure wanted is separate from the region for pleasure liked and it opens the possibility to wanted pleasure that is not liked. Apparently this is what happens with addiction, which is a recipe for unhappiness. Hedonic feelings arise within us as testified by the example of paraplegics, who can report very high feelings of hedonic feelings despite constraint conditions. The role of some neurotransmitters, such as dopamine, is better understood. Neuroscientists use neuro imaging such as functional magnetic resonance imaging (fMRI) to determine which areas of the brain are the most active during particular tasks. We can thus detect happiness in the brain through different techniques and happiness is not a pure invention of moral philosophy. Can we measure happiness by a somewhat physical scale in the brain by correlating existing chemical levels with different responses of subjects on some scale? Can we imagine measuring happiness directly by physiological assessment alone? A first step has been made by measuring thermal pain in a controlled lab experiment (see Brown et al., 2011, Wagner et al., 2013). Cerebral circuitry is far from having revealed all its secrets, but we can hope for major progress in this century.

Another important domain where development psychology and neurosciences can help is the study of cognitive and noncognitive development of infants in relation to their family background. It is fascinating to learn (Gopnik et al., 2001, Dehaene, 2013[11]) that the same mechanisms used by scientists to develop scientific theories are used by children to develop causal models of their environment. The cognitive development of children in early life is made possible by three factors: innate knowledge, advanced learning ability (Bayesian learning), and the evolved ability of parents to teach their offspring. It is this third factor that may be linked to the familial and early-school roots of equality of opportunity.

In the US, the gap between blacks and whites in terms of equality of opportunity continues to be a pressing political issue. In particular, it is important to dismiss the idea that children growing up in poor families cannot achieve good educational outcome due to low innate talent. On tests of intelligence, young adult blacks systematically score less than whites although the gap is diminishing. However, incentives partly determine scores on IQ tests. The black-white gap in IQ completely vanishes by giving candies for correct answers (the evidence is summarized in Borghans et al., 2008 and Almlund et al., 2011). Using a newly available nationally representative data that includes a test of mental functions for children aged eight to twelve months, Fryer and Levitt (2013) reveal new insights on the social construction of this cognitive capacity gap. They find only minor racial differences in test outcomes (0.06 standard deviation units in the raw data) that disappear with the inclusion of a limited set of controls. Interestingly, when introducing SES, higher SES black children perform better but the effect is small (a top-quintile SES child outscores a bottom-quintile child by 0.08 of a standard deviation) and the deviation is not robust with respect to the introduction of other controls. Black children, however, lose ground in the first years of schooling (Fryer and Levitt, 2004, 2006). Differences emerge as early as age two, and by the time black children enter kindergarten they lag behind whites by 0.64 of a standard deviation in maths. The gap continues to grow as children advance in schooling. According to these authors, there is suggestive evidence that differences in school quality may be an important part of the explanation for this widening in test scores. Both neuroscience, psychological and economic studies support Heckman (2012)'s political stance that if we want to raise equality of opportunity, the sooner the public intervention, the better, with respect to the age of children. This should be fully understood by all decision makers if we want to build more pro-active social states.

This survey will not be useless if it helps to get a sense that cutting-edge research programmes on inequality and welfare should mix researchers from different fields. As an example of how to do this, one can look at the International Panel of Social Progress.[12] For each field brings up some specific skills that, due to the division of labour, will be very hard for economists to develop in a few months.

12.4   Europe's Inequality Pattern vis-à-vis the US

I will now review how Europe and the US differ in many ways regarding both the pattern and the evolution of inequality. As suggested by the previous insights, it is important to distinguish results in terms of inequality of outcome from those capturing inequality of opportunities. Next, I will move to attitudes to income inequality and I will end up with what we know about welfare comparisons.

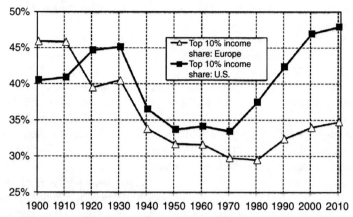

Figure 12.8 Income inequality: Europe and the US (Piketty and Saez, 2014).

12.4.1   Inequality of Income

Even if the situation is contrasted across European countries, it is fair to say that, with respect to the US, inequality increase has been contained in Europe as a whole. The redistributive power of the welfare state has not been reduced globally. Of course, these statements should be qualified. It remains to be seen how the Great Recession will affect the current state of affairs on the long run. At this point, a cautionary note is in order. The picture may depend to some extent on the measure of inequality one is using. The share of top 1 per cent, the share of top 10 per cent in total income, or the Gini index do not deliver exactly the same message, the same ranking, although the correlation between all these measures is high. Due to page constraints, we focus on the main robust messages and the figures presented here should be merely viewed as illustrations.

The graph for pre-tax and pre-transfer income inequality in Figure 12.8 provides a long-run perspective from which we can see that inequality in the US and Europe (defined arbitrarily by Piketty and Saez (2014) as the arithmetic mean of the situation prevailing in France, Germany, Sweden and the UK) has followed different paths. We can distinguish three periods. In the first period, 1900-1930, inequality fell in Europe while it rose in the US. World War I and its consequences levelled down both output and inequality in Europe. In a second period, 1930-1970, inequality fell sharply in both continents and the trends are remarkably parallel. In the last period, 1970-1980, inequality rose steadily in the US and moderately in Europe. As a matter of fact, the rise in Europe did not occur before the 80s. The first decade of this millennium shows a slowing down of the inequality rise in both regions.

In looking at this chart, we have focused on the changes over time. We will not speculate on the levels up to the 70s for the stark construction of the graph for Europe. Nevertheless, the huge gulf in 2010 between the US and Europe in terms of inequality levels is confirmed by all studies, whether we look at market-income inequality or at disposable income inequality and the chosen inequality index. For instance, the LIS dataset,[13] whose purpose is to make distributional data comparable between countries, delivers the message that the Gini index for the 2010 disposable income is higher in the US than in the 23 European countries present in this dataset.

However, the heterogeneity in Europe remains large with the best student in the European (and likely world) class being Sweden with a Gini index of 0.237, closely followed by all Nordic countries. Most countries of continental Europe (plus Ireland) follow next, with the Netherlands leading the pack, the other Benelux and Alpine countries, the countries which used to belong to the former Austro-Hungarian Empire (Slovenia, Slovakia, the Czech Republic, Hungary), Germany and France (0.289) and Ireland (0.294) closing the march. All these countries have a Gini index lower than 0.3. The somewhat outliers in Europe are the Mediterranean countries (Italy, Spain, Greece) with a Gini of about 0.330, the UK with around the same degree of inequality, Poland being somewhat in between the pack and the outliers (0.31). On the whole, Europe can be described as the continent of depressed or contained inequality in the developed world, the other zone of quite low inequality being Japan, South Korea and Taiwan, but still with Gini values slightly above 0.3. The former British dominions, Canada, Australia are quite close to their mother country, the Eastern former communist countries Russia, Serbia and Estonia are in the same league as the Mediterranean countries. The US, Israel and Uruguay share a different vision of inequality with a Gini index in the range 0.37–0.38. It is notable for the further development of the European Union towards a more integrated area in the post-brexit period that the UK is in a midway position between the US and continental Europe.

Of course, the inequality between all citizens of the European Union is far larger than the inequality in each member state, for it takes into account the per-capita-GDP discrepancy between the different countries.[14] What is amazing is that the inequality in Europe viewed as a unified country is as high as the inequality in the US (Milanovic, 2012). This means that in the US–Europe comparison, the between-country inequality term offsets the within-country inequality term. From this we can draw that the convergence policies directed toward enhancing growth in the lowest-GDP members are as important nowadays as they were in the past.

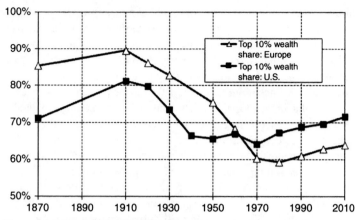

Figure 12.9 Wealth inequality: Europe and the US (Piketty and Saez, 2014).

12.4.2   Forces behind the Increase in Gross-Income Inequality

We do know much more about the reasons behind the evolution of inequality in the US than for any European country. The US benefit from a size effect in applied research to their economy (a kind of economies of scope). There are many more US economists working on a given applied subject than colleagues from any other country. A side effect is that there is more competition and the emulation raises the quality of the studies.

Primary income comes from two factors, capital, or more exactly wealth,[15] and labour. Piketty (2014) entertains the idea that capital-income inequality was partially responsible for the rise of inequality, whereas the main bulk of research has been mainly focused on labour income. Here, we consider a somewhat restrictive issue which is the potential impact of wealth inequality in the divergence between Europe and the US in the inequality pattern since the 70s. The empirical evidence points in two opposite directions. On the one hand, the wealth-income ratio is higher in Europe than in the US (see Figure 3 in Piketty and Saez (2014)), meaning that if the rate of return were the same, the share of capital income should be higher in Europe than in the US. On the other hand, the following chart (Figure 12.9) shows that wealth has been more concentrated in the US since the end of the Vietnam War than in Europe. Moreover, the speed of concentration is somewhat higher in the US than in Europe. We conclude that at this stage, it is far from obvious that the divergence between Europe and the US mainly comes from capital income.

A labour-inequality pattern is the usual suspect for the growing transatlantic divergence. Autor (2014) provides a very well-documented review of the reasons which may explain the dramatic increase in earning inequality in the US since the end of the Vietnam War. According to Goldin and Katz (2008), about two-thirds of the overall rise of earnings dispersion between 1980 and 2005 is approximately accounted for by the increased premium associated with schooling in general and postsecondary education in particular. The skill premium in the US has more than doubled over the past three decades. The magnitude of the impact of this phenomenon on the earning inequality is four times as large as the increase share of the top 1 per cent. The US labour economists, following Golding and Katz, favour an explanation through the demand and supply forces on the labour market. There is a race between education and technology, namely, if the supply of college graduates does not keep pace with a persistent outward shift in demand for skills, the skill premium will rise. Many factors may explain the upward shift of the demand for college graduates. The so-called skill-biased technological change is one of them, and it is not debatable that the ITC revolution has increased the demand for high cognitive skills at the expense of people with only physical stamina. On top of this, the falling barriers on international trade have increased the potentiality of outsourcing. In terms of the international division of labour, the western countries up to now managed to keep the design and the marketing of products, while the production processes were partially or totally outsourced to low-wage countries. For some reason that we will not try to explain here, the American educational system was not able to produce enough college graduates in the period 1982–2004. The top panel of Figure 12.10 underscores that the pace of increase lowered during this period and the bottom panel shows how the college-graduate deficit for this period is associated with impressive surge in the skill premium well fitted by the labour market model.

While there has been a lot of debate about the skill premium evolution in the US among labour economists, this issue has received less attention in Europe. Crivellaro (2014) represents a first attempt at filling the gap. As a matter of fact, we do not have a beautiful simple story as in the US case. We can make the premise that the same market-driven forces are at work in each European country. However, the labour demand shift towards skilled labour may be less pronounced in European countries than in the US because of the lower importance of multinational firms or because European countries have been mainly followers in the ICT revolution. Bertola and Ichino (1995) report a lack of high-skill intense sectors in Europe. Regarding the supply effect, this is governed by national conditions and particularly by national education institutions and the dynamics of college enrollment. There is no particular reason to believe that the US example is going to be replicated everywhere. Apparently, according to this study, the wage premium was flattening or slightly decreasing in all European countries surveyed except the UK. It seems that

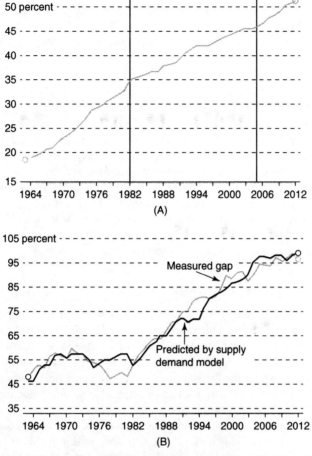

Figure 12.10 The supply of college graduates and the US college/high school premium, 1963–2012. **A**: College share of hours worked in the US, 1963–2012: All working-age adults. **B**: The fit of a simple labour market model to explain the evolution of the skill premium (Autor, 2014, *Science*).

in most European countries, the supply of college graduates keeps up with demand.

On top of market-driven forces, there are obviously other factors such as the role of public policies, (tax and transfer, minimum wages), the labour-market institutions (labour legislation, union density, more of less decentralized wage-bargaining) that play a role and which can influence for better or worse the interaction of supply and demand. Apparently, this has also occurred in Europe (see Machin and Van Reenen, 2010), but we need further research here.

Now, regarding the dramatic increase of the share of the top 1 per cent in the US which has not been experienced at this scale by any other country, one can also elaborate a driven-market explanation which would be based on the superstar story (Rosen, 1981). The competition game in the ICT sector is often a winner-take-all game. The bandwagon effect generated by the network of consumers means that the first firm which succeeds in driving consumer mindshare will be in a position of natural monopoly. The US, because of their technological leadership and market size, would be the place where this bandwagon effect occurs more often and the leader on the US market will have a decisive competitive advantage over its foreign competitors. We deduce that the density of winner-takes-all in the US should be higher than in any other Western country. It would be strange if this feature were not related to the share of top 1 per cent in the US. On top of that, the importance of the finance industry in the US (in the UK too) cannot be dismissed (see Bivens and Mishel, 2013).

At this stage, it can be concluded that it would be quite hazardous to put on the same footing labour income inequality and wealth inequality as potential culprits of the great transatlantic divergence in terms of inequality.

12.4.3   Convergence Process in Europe

The inequality of primary income can be more or less reduced through the system of tax and transfers organized at the household level. We have already mentioned that many European countries share a relatively low level of disposable-income inequality (Gini lower than 0.3). What is fascinating, and this feature has been overlooked in the literature, is that a convergence process across European states is underway, both in terms of disposable income inequality and in terms of the redistributive power of the state.

The top panel in Figure 12.11 illustrates the former feature and the bottom panel the latter over the period 1985–2010. The starting period is when the internal market was set out by the Single European Act. The convergence process in terms of disposable income has been mainly obtained by a catching-up of low-inequality countries (Nordic countries), while the inequality in the high-inequality countries has been contained (UK, Italy, Poland). The mid-way countries (Germany, France and the Netherlands) follow the path of a slight upward trend of inequality. This lower dispersion has been obtained at the cost of a levelling-up, which may entail mixed feelings.

Still, it would be false to deduce that the tax and transfer system across member states has not become less redistributive over these years as shown by bottom panel. Indeed, there also seems to be a convergence amongst EU Member states on the extent of redistribution. The system has become less redistributive in Nordic countries and the Netherlands, but more so in Italy, the UK and

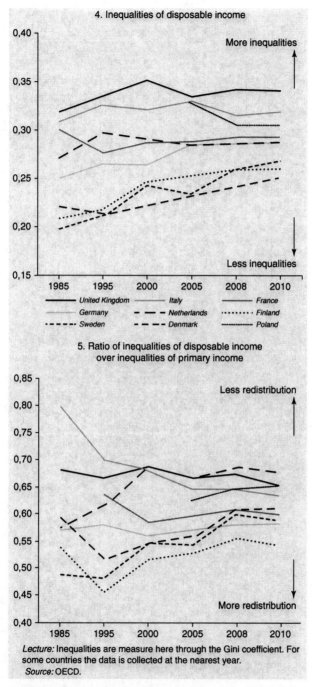

Figure 12.11 Convergence in Europe of the redistributive power of the state. Left Panel: Inequalities (Gini) of disposable income. Right Panel: Ratio of inequalities (Gini disposable income/Gini primary income, OECD and Bénassy et al., 2014).

Poland. In France and Germany, the tax-and benefit system has achieved an amount of redistribution which remains more or less constant along the period. In 2010, the ratio of after- to pre-tax inequalities ranged from 0.54 to 0.68, while it belonged to the 0.48–0.80 band in 1985.

The redistributive powerfulness of the state is lower in other advanced countries, 0.69 in Japan, 0.71 in Australia, 0.72 in Canada and 0.76 in the US: EU countries have seemed to converge to a degree of redistribution that is higher than in other advanced regions. This is quite good news for the promotors of a building up of a 'European Union of social states' since it points out through a revealed preference argument that the redistributive preferences of citizens in different European countries are getting closer. This is an important building step in the movement to a more integrated Europe and it is interesting to note that this trend is not limited to countries belonging to the Eurozone. On a more cautionary note, it remains to be seen whether the current crisis in the Eurozone will undermine this convergence process. The reforms of the welfare state which are underway in Britain can reverse the current trend for this country. Once again, it should be added that a constant redistributive power has not been enough to prevent an increase in inequality in Europe. It can be argued, however, that the system should have become more redistributive to countervail the rise in primary income inequality.

12.4.4   Inequality of Opportunity and Intergenerational Mobility

Intergenerational mobility and equality of opportunity are related concepts. We begin by reporting empirical evidence about the former concept for which we have accumulated more results. The global picture appears to be the following. The US has long had the reputation of being the land of opportunities. When looking at the data, the current situation is much less impressive. Nordic countries clearly perform better; Southern European countries perform not much better than the US; continental European countries are in between. At first glance, the ranking of countries is not so different from the ranking in terms of income inequality and indeed the correlation is high, but still the scattered diagram in the space income inequality, intergenerational mobility is far from being lined up as illustrated by Figure 12.12. The comparison of Canada, Australia and France is instructive in this respect. Although they were in the same league in 1985 for disposable income inequality (Gini index), Figure 12.12 reveals that these three countries are in a very different position in terms of intergenerational mobility. This concept is approached by the intergenerational income elasticity, which measures the extent to which offspring income levels reflect those of their parents. More precisely, it shows how a marginal gain of parent income (usually the father) is translated 30 years later in a marginal gain in descendant income (usually the son). The value of this elasticity is low

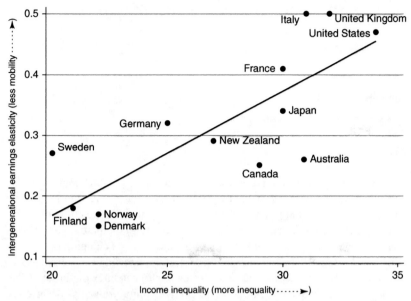

Figure 12.12 The Great Gatsby curve: More inequality is associated with less intergenerational mobility (Corak, 2013). Income inequality is measured as the Gini coefficient, using disposable household income for about 1985. Intergenerational economic mobility is measured as the elasticity between paternal earnings and a son's adult earnings, using data on a cohort of children born, roughly speaking, during the early to mid 1960s and measuring their adult outcomes in the mid to late 1990s.

in Nordic countries (Denmark) around 0.20, meaning that 20 per cent of the parental income advantage is passed on the following generation. Canada is not far behind with an elasticity of 0.25, but now for France the figure is as high as twice the value reported for Denmark. In Italy, the United Kingdom, and the US, the situation is even worse and roughly 50 per cent of any advantage or disadvantage of the past generation is passed on.

There is a strong relationship between inequality of opportunity and intergenerational immobility. Roughly speaking, inequality of opportunity measures how the outcome inequality in the offspring generation is linked to the inequality in the parent generation. The inequality in the offspring generation refers to some outcome such as education, income, occupation, wealth, health, longevity etc. The inequality in the parent generation refers to the same variables, which are called *circumstances* in the terminology that comes from Roemer (1993). These circumstances are certainly exogenous to the offspring destiny. For pedagogical purposes, suppose that we are only interested in income for both generations, that is, income as a circumstance, and income as an

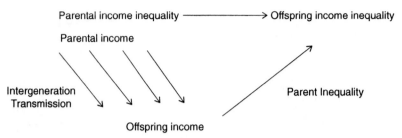

Figure 12.13 The decomposition of inequality of opportunity.

outcome. It is quite limitative but at the same time, parental income is an omnibus measure catching up many different advantages that can be passed onto offspring. We want to know the extent to which income inequality in the offspring generation is due to the income inequality in the parent generation. Figure 12.13 reveals that the inequality of opportunity is a chaining process in which the output of the intergeneration transmission mechanism (computed as the intergenerational income elasticity for example) becomes the input of the parental income inequality process. The intergeneration transmission mechanism is applied to each parental income to obtain the income fraction of the offspring related to that of their parent and then we allocate the inequality of the parental distribution to the obtained distribution.[16]

Under some assumptions, one can obtain a simple formula for this composition operation. Lefranc et al. (2007) show that inequality of income opportunity can be described as the product of the intergenerational elasticity of income times the parental income inequality.

The pattern of inequality of opportunity then depends on two forces, the evolution of parental distribution inequality and the trend in the intergenerational income elasticity. This leads to the following key-observation. The evolution of inequality of opportunity nowadays, that is, for the current generation in the age group 30–50, depends on events which took place deep in the past. The transmission phenomena mostly lasts from the cradle to college attendance, namely, for the youngest of the age group of interest in 1985–2005 and for the oldest in 1965–1985 (in the data used in Figure 12.12). The parental income inequality that matters is therefore that prevailing in the period 1965–1985, assuming correctly that parents had their first child when they are 30.

The French example (see Lefranc et al., 2007) illustrates the legacy of the past in terms of inequality of opportunity. This was reduced over the period 1977–1993 solely because of the wage compression that occurred after the events of 1968. The intergenerational elasticity has been at best constant if not increasing. In contrast, one can deduce in the US example that the dramatic increase of earning inequality in the US observed in the period

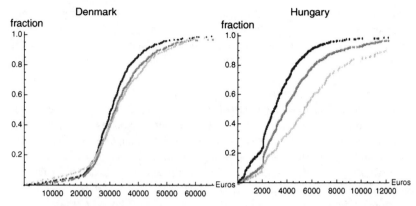

Figure 12.14 Distribution of chances to get an annual earning (male) according to three different parental educations (primary, secondary and tertiary education, Roemer and Trannoy, 2015).

1970–2010 will strongly hurt equality of opportunity in the period 2000–2040, assuming that the findings of Chetty et al. (2014) of a more or less constant intergenerational earnings elasticity are empirically correct. Inequality of opportunity displays a strong hysteresis which does not favour political action in democratic governments because the incumbents will never see and benefit from popular recognition in this domain.

Another way to look at the distribution of results from the point of view of inequality of opportunity is to draw the distribution of outcome conditional on some feature of the parental background. Figure 12.14 contrasts the extent of equality of opportunity in Denmark and Hungary. The distribution of earnings of male offspring conditional on a stark description of the educational advantage of the family background (primary, secondary and tertiary education) reveals than in Denmark the cumulated probability to obtain any income are quite close. The curves are almost mixed-up except in the upper part of the income distribution, meaning that even in Denmark to get a high-paid job, it is better to have grown up in a family with high educational capital. The Hungarian case does not need to be inspected for long to realize that the Hungarian situation is at the opposite end to the Danish one. The chance of ending up with an annual earning of at most € 4000 is only about 30 per cent when parents have tertiary education. It culminates at 70 per cent in the case the parents have only completed primary education. There is a gulf in the Hungarian offspring's prospects depending on background luck, while they are roughly similar in Denmark. We have described Europe as a continent of depressed inequality of outcomes. Regarding equality of opportunity, a divided Europe should be a rather adequate description of the reality as Figure 12.12 already illustrates.

Obviously, it is rather crude to condition the outcome of offspring only on parental education. Björklund et al. (2012a) provide a fine-grained typology (1152 types), which partitions the sample of 35 per cent of Swedish men born between 1955 and 1967 into types based upon parental income quartile group (four groups), parental education group (three groups), family structure/type (two groups), number of siblings (three groups), IQ quartile groups (four groups), body mass index (BMI) quartile group at age 18 (four groups). The outcome is an average of pre-fisc income over 7 years (age group: 32-38). 'Social' circumstances account for between 15.3 per cent and 18.7 per cent of the overall Gini between the descendant generations. In the counterfactual situation where the only factors of inequality would be these social circumstances, the Gini coefficient would attain a modest value of 0.043 for the oldest cohort! The contribution of IQ represents about 12 per cent of the overall Gini. (16% for cognitive and noncognitive skills).

The great Gatsby curve is not a causal relationship and mainly describes an association. The studies (see Corak, 2013, for a review) looking at causal linkages point in various directions. First much of the variation in children's outcomes emerges before they enter the labour market. This suggests that there is a positive correlation between high return to schooling and lower intergenerational earnings mobility. In the US, the college education attendance is an archetypical example of unequal opportunities (see Figure 12.15). If there were equal opportunity according to Roemer's definition of equal opportunity, the probability of attendance conditioned on family background should be equal. However, at the eve of the last decade of the 20th century the hope of good prospects for offspring of a low income background were rather bleak (see Figure 12.15). About one third of children of parents of the first quintile could hope to attend college. The figure for the last percentile was about 90 per cent. However, there are many causes that can impact educational achievement. Chetty et al. (2014) step in starting to identify the main factors by exploiting the substantial variation of income mobility that exists across the US metropolitan areas. Indeed the big surprise is that the US exhibits a very large dispersion of income mobility, some towns such as Salt Lake City, Boston, San Francisco, San Diego, or even New York or Los Angeles have rates of mobility comparable to European levels, while southern cities such as Atlanta or Charlottesville have lower rates of mobility than any developed country for which data are available. The two main factors that affect children when they grow up are racial segregation and family structure, measured by the fraction of single parents in the area. Both these factors do not matter purely for their impact at the individual level. Offspring of a poor white family with two parents will also bear the negative consequences of living in segregated communities with many single parents. High levels of social capital indices at the community level are also positively associated with upward mobility. All this said, even in the

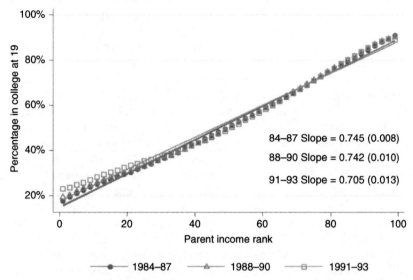

Figure 12.15 College attendance rates vs. parent income rank by cohort (Chetty et al., 2014).

Nordic countries, the top income earners seem to resist equalizing opportunity policy. Everywhere, the elite finds a way to overcome egalitarian policies and to pass on its advantages to the next generation (see Björklund et al., 2012b to cite just one example).

12.4.5 Attitudes to Inequality

If Americans see the inequality pattern with rose-coloured glasses, good for them even if this is a disturbing state of affairs for some economists. Alesina et al. (2004), for instance, found that inequality reduces reported subjective well-being among Europeans but not Americans. The authors suggest greater (perceived) social mobility in the US as one potential explanation of this difference. A systematic bias in the perception of reality is difficult to analyse with simple tools of rational choice and needs to be understood with the help of other social scientists (see the use of cognitive dissonance by Bénabou and Tirole, 2006). Take for example the POUM hypothesis formulated by Bénabou and Ok (2001). The 'prospect of upward mobility' hypothesis is the idea that those with lower incomes are not strong advocates of redistributive policies because of the belief that they, or at least their children, are likely to climb up the income ladder. In other words, the American Dream is a reason why US citizens have been willing to tolerate a good deal more inequality of outcomes than citizens of European countries. The POUM hypothesis could have had an empirical validation in the nineteenth century and even in the first half of the twentieth century, in the light of Piketty and Saez (2014)'s comparison of European and American inequality. Wealth concentration was lower in the US up to the 1960s and income inequality was of the same magnitude. So we can speculate that the intergenerational transmission of inequality was somewhat lower or at least not greater in the US than in continental Europe up to the 1960s. Indeed, according to Aaronson and Mazumdar (2008)'s estimations, the intergenerational earnings elasticity was below 0.4 from 1940 to 1980, before exceeding 0.5 afterwards. So why do Americans fail to realize that upward mobility has been reduced? After all, Grosfeld and Senik (2010) find that Poles changed their minds after 1996. Before that date, inequality and well-being satisfaction went hand in hand, whereas the correlation became negative afterwards. This finding may be brought closer by the observation that Poland was on a slightly negative inequality trend in the first decade of this century (see the top panel of Figure 12.11). Kuklinski et al. (2003) find that providing (accurate) information on the demographic composition of welfare recipients and the share of the federal budget dedicated to welfare payments has no effect on respondents' preferences, despite the fact that their initial beliefs are largely incorrect. Or maybe it is the other way round. Instead of choosing their best social policy on the basis of informed knowledge, individuals choose their social beliefs that support their political prejudice. As has been emphasized nicely by Bénabou and Tirole (2006)[17] 'Ethnographic studies of the working and middle classes reveal that people do not come to views as dispassionate statisticians. On the contrary, they constantly struggle with the cognitive dissonance required to maintain and pass on to their children the view that hard work and good deeds will ultimately bring a better life, despite that life may not always be that fair.' Indeed, according to the randomized survey experiments of Kuziemko et al. (2015) most social preferences about redistribution policies are hard to move through manipulation of the information given to the subjects. Or another reason would be that their concept of fairness is just different from equality of outcomes. It is here that it is important to focus on normative social preferences as done for instance by a recent study by Almås et al. (2015). Using identical economic environments and a spectactor design,[18] they indeed find much higher inequality acceptance in the US than in Norway. However, they do not find that Americans are more meritocratic than Norwegians or that Americans place more emphasis on efficiency than Norwegians. This suggests that less support for redistribution in the US than in Scandinavia does not reflect a greater concern for merit or efficiency, but rather greater acceptance of inequality caused by luck (figure 12.16).

Normative preferences, attitudes or opinions about inequality should be distinguished from comparative statements where the individual is part of the

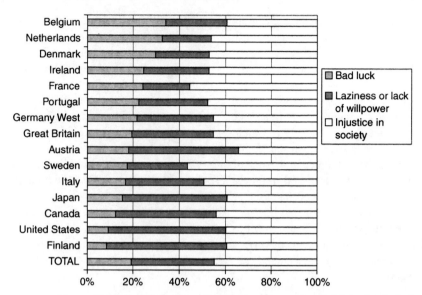

Figure 12.16 Beliefs in the role of luck, effort and social injustice in bad economic outcomes. Answers to the question: 'Why are there people living in need?'. Authors' computations excluding the following answers: It is an inevitable part of modern progress; None of these; Don't know (Lefranc et al., 2009 and World Values Survey 1990).

distribution (see Clark and D'Ambrosio, 2014). Here we focus on the former in relation to fairness issues, which can be elicited through direct questioning, experimental approaches or inference from observed behaviours. Yaari and Bar-Hillel (1984) were the first to use questionnaires, Frohlich and Oppenheimer (1992) the first to use experiments in the field of social justice. In the wake of these two pioneering studies, there has been a burgeoning literature which is surveyed by Gaertner and Schokkaert (2012). It appears that there is large agreement on the subject all around the world about the prerequisites of equality of opportunity. People should be held responsible for at least something in the process generating their income. Obviously, people may disagree about the extent to which they should be held responsible. The failure to take into account this normative background, for instance in the questionnaire sent to subjects by Kuziemko et al. (2015), may explain their difficulty to elicit preferences over a full domain of parameters. Indeed the US opinions as expressed in the World Value Survey are clearly different from the average European one, but the main information is the heterogeneity among the countries of the European Union. The difference between Finland and Denmark see Figure 12.16 is especially telling since they appear quite close, both from the point of view of income inequality and income mobility (see Figure 12.12). France is the country for which effort seems to play the least important role according to respondents. This may be related to the quite low level of income mobility (see Figure 12.12 and the difference with Germany). It may cast light on the role played by France in the last episode of the Greek drama. According to the French press, the responsibility played by the Greeks in the crisis is limited, which is not the view of the Finnish or German media, not to mention politicians. Managing a social welfare state at a European level may be quite challenging in view of the difference in social representations across the people of Europe. At least it can explain the difference in the size of the welfare state (see Alesina et al., 2001, Alesina and Glaeser, 2004). France's social expenditures are also the highest of the Union in proportion of GDP.

Still, a lot of Europeans have the feeling that luck and unfairness are pervasive in their real life and it may be unclear whether this feeling is the result of a greater sensitivity to inequality or a greater injustice in situations that are not detected by actual data so far. With respect to the US, the first answer seems to be favoured.

12.4.6   Well-Being and the Size of the Welfare State

There have been thousands of studies on cross-country comparison of well-being and it is difficult to pick one of them. I chose the one done by the ESS because of their expertise in handling surveys across Europe and because the results are recent. We should keep in mind that people have been surveyed during the current crisis and that the results may reflect its impact and not the long-standing level of life satisfaction (Ireland, Portugal). The distinction between happiness and eudomenia well-being does not seem to matter much since the country ranking is remarkably similar for both notions. Taken at face value, the general picture (see Figure 12.17) is that the most affluent and competitive countries in Europe are also those where people are happier. The award goes to Denmark, but the nominees are the Nordic countries with Switzerland and the Netherlands being close followers. It is impossible to also miss the fact that these countries are also the least unequal and the most mobile (see Figure 12.12).

At the other extreme, Eastern and some Mediterranean countries (Portugal) perform poorly. Inequality and heritability of economic advantages across dynasties reach comparatively high levels in all these countries. Bulgarians are the least happy of the league and it might be corroborated by the most recent demographic projection of the UN for 2050. The population decline in this country would be the steepest (28% from 7.2 to 5.2 million inhabitants) and it is really a staggering figure. On the other hand, the Scandinavian countries and Switzerland are the countries with the rosiest projection (increase of 28% in

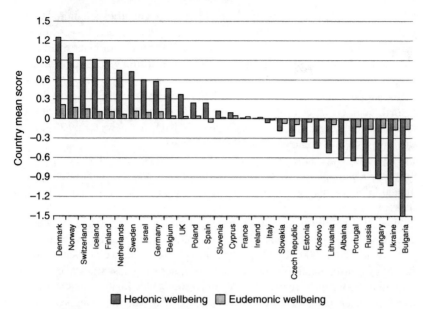

Figure 12.17 Hedonic and eudemonic well-being across Europe by country (ESS 2012–2013).

Norway, 21% in Sweden, 21% and Switzerland). We might expect that if people are happier they should be inclined to reproduce and to attract people from other countries. To date, the relationship between migration and happiness is relatively unexplored in the literature, and in particular the economics literature (see Simpson, 2011).

However, we should avoid introducing causality statements. What can be said is that economic performance and social performance in terms of well-being seem to go together. There are good news and bad news here. Commonicity is good news in the sense that economic performance is not against social performance. The bad news is that the lagging countries should act on all aspects at once. There is no magic solution to climbing the happiness (Cantril) ladder.

Something of a curse of large countries can be detected. Big European countries (Germany, UK, Poland, Spain, France, Italy in this order) stood in the middle. It is also relatively true for the US which, according to the Gallup World Poll, ranks ninth after the Scandinavian countries, Canada, The Netherlands, Switzerland, and New Zealand. The quite high level of inequality and income heritability do not seem to significantly alter the well-being of Americans, showing by contrast that they are rather indifferent to these issues. All in all, scale effects cannot be detected in terms of life satisfaction. Two factors may explain this state of affairs. First, large countries are more hetero-geneous and people in general trust more those who appear to be similar to them.[19] It indeed turns out that trust is an important determinant of life sat-isfaction. Second, political problems in big countries may be harder to solve. Or put differently, we need more gifted politicians to cope with problems – including problems linked to a greater heterogeneity – in a big country than in a small country. Indeed the correlation between average satisfaction with life and democratic performance is very high (0.79). It is bad news for the Eurozone in view of the mismanagement of the Euro crisis.

The quite remarkable ranking of Poland should be noticed. Poland was the only European country to go through the Great Recession without a drop in annual GDP and we have noted a slight downward move of inequality level in recent years.

Now, if the size of the welfare state and particularly of the social welfare state were a key-determinant of life satisfaction, then France[20] should come first. Veenhoven (2000) found no association between the welfare state and the degree of well-being. Before throwing away either happiness studies or the wel-fare state two caveats are in order. The first refers to habituation and the second to rivalry. It may be the case that well-being went up when welfare state or some measures of welfare state were introduced. However, progressively peo-ple get used to it and then it makes little difference. If the tax system is globally progressive, welfare state increases the well-being of many at the expense of some. However, this is true if people do not have a reference group. Happiness studies show that individual life satisfaction increases to the extent that the gap between the individual income and the reference group income widens. If the reference group of poor people is only composed of poor people, the levelling-up of the situation of all deserving people will not improve their well-being satisfaction. However, it is doubtful whether we should base our reflection on the evolution of the welfare state on this kind of feelings. For one can guess that the loss in well-being will be huge, if we threaten people with giving up some part of the welfare state. This is reminiscent of the deviation that exists between the willingness to accept and the willingness to pay.

12.4.7   Partial Conclusion

Summing up the findings so far, one can answer our main question with some pieces of empirical evidence. Europe is special because of the low level of inequality of outcome compared with other industrialized countries. The speed of convergence up to the Great Recession among European countries, in terms of the powerfulness of the redistributive tax and transfer instruments, was also quite striking. However, the results also reveal a deep division between countries which have been able to sustain a high level of social mobility and the others. In terms of equality of opportunity or happiness, Europe is very heterogeneous. These results, specifically in Northern Europe, could not have been obtained if people in Europe did not care about inequality. This social concern is also reflected in the importance of the field in Europe.

12.5   Europe Is at the Forefront of Research on Many Topics

Some empirical evidence is provided by the affiliation of the chapter authors of the three volumes of the *Handbook of Income Distribution*, edited by Atkinson and Bourguignon, which constitutes an invaluable source of information. 60 per cent of the authors report an affiliation in a European University. 50 per cent of the papers submitted or accepted at the *Journal of Economic Inequality* were written by scholars of European Universities. Nobody has forgotten the contribution of European economists to the methodological issues raised by the measurement of inequality with the initial impulse given at the end of the 1960s by Antony Atkinson, Serge-Christophe Kolm and Amartya Sen (who at that time worked in the UK). This was followed by the decomposition of inequality indices with the work of François Bourguignon, Frank Cowell and Tony Shorrocks etc.

More recently, the issues of fairness and distributive justice have received a lot of attention from European economists with leading propositions formulated by Marc Fleurbaey and François Maniquet (Fleurbaey, 2008, 2009 and Fleurbaey and Maniquet, 2011), the inventive experimental approach to social justice of the NHH team (Cappelen et al., 2007, Almås et al., 2010, Cappelen et al., 2013), just to give a few examples.

The contribution of European economists to empirical issues also cannot be dismissed and Anthony Atkinson, well before it became fashionable, did much to expand our knowledge of income distribution for the UK and elsewhere. Thomas Piketty was a pioneer in the 90s on focusing his research on the upper tail of the distribution and to realize that the share of the top 1 per cent was a good 'sufficient statistics' in many cases and in particular in the study of wealth inequality. His work with Emmanuel Saez (Piketty and Saez, 2003) has received widespread media and web attention. It may not be by chance that the booming of the pre-tax income share of top 1 per cent (from 9.0 per cent in 1970 to 22.4 per cent by 2012) or the surge of the wealth share of top 0.1 per cent (from 8 per cent in the mid-1970s to 22 per cent in 2012) was brought into full view of the economics profession by French economists working in the US and in France (Saez and Zucman, 2014). Anthony Atkinson did a great deal to extend the focus of this research all over the world and the construction of the world top income data base is really a European initiative and is supported by institutions on both sides of the Atlantic.

Another field where European economists are on the top of the list is the study of happiness which is connected to welfare, although, as has been argued previously, should not be mixed up with it. Even if happiness studies started with Easterlin's paradox (Easterlin, 1974 and Easterlin et al., 2010), they became very popular with the works of David Blanchflower, Andrew Clark, Bruno Frey, John Layard, Andrew Oswald, and many others, at the intersection of economics and psychology. As noted by Clark and D'Ambrosio (2014) three of the four top-cited articles published in the *Economic Journal* over the past 20 years have the word happiness in their title. Britain remembers that it was the homeland of Jeremy Bentham.

So there is a lot of expertise in the field of inequality and welfare in Europe but still they are some domains where the US took the lead. The most important is the understanding of the process of how social inequality deepens 'natural inequality' in childhood and teenage years with the impressive centre at the University of Chicago around James Heckman, the *Center for Economics of Human Development*.[21] There is no analogue in Europe to understand the fabric of inequality of opportunity. Once again, one can detect an influence of the society on the research priority at a country level. The phantom of the American dream continues to haunt the minds of American economists. In the same vein one can point out 'the Equality of Opportunity Project' of Emmanuel Saez and Raj Chetty, a research study conducted by Harvard University and the University of California at Berkeley using big data.[22]

In a nutshell, it is maybe possible to describe the research forces in the Transatlantic world by saying that American economists might have produced deeper understanding of the process of inequality linked to education and the labour market, while European economists have taken the lead in measuring and collecting data and about how to interpret it in a normative way. But obviously this kind of statement should be qualified.

Without understanding the causes, social scientists cannot propose remedies to enhance equality of opportunity. The social and legal contexts are different on both sides of the Atlantic. It is not because Americans will understand the process generating inequality of opportunity in their country that automatically the solutions can be transposed to this side of the Atlantic. There is quite a broad political support in Western democracies (even among people who are more inclined to support equality of outcome) for fighting inequality of opportunity due to differences in initial background. The way to proceed does not appear to be simple and in particular it is not clear that it can be achieved on a large scale without lowering inequalities among the previous generation.

In the best interest of citizens of each European nation, we advocate the launching of a network of economists and other social scientists to understand the fabric of equality of opportunity at the European scale. This is our *first research proposal*. This encompasses many theoretical and empirical specific issues. For instance, although most normative theory suggests that people should only be held morally responsible for factors within individual control, economic experiments have shown that most people also view inequalities due to talent as fair, despite the fact that talent to a large degree is the result of a genetic lottery. Understanding this discrepancy between normative theory and what people actually think could be important for understanding what drives support for different welfare policies.

12.6 Data Are Improving but Remain Largely Incomplete when Looking at More Specific Issues

Data in Europe on income and wealth distributions are improving rapidly but are still insufficient to cope with the study of poverty and inequality of opportunity. We have already mentioned the remarkable effort to build the world top incomes database[23] managed by Facundo Alvaredo, Anthony Atkinson, Thomas Piketty and Emmanuel Saez (Alvaredo et al., 2013) and which gathered more than 30 researchers all around the world. Another remarkable enterprise supported by both institutions in Europe and the US is the Luxembourg Income Study, which helps to build a data archive and research centre dedicated to cross-national analysis. LIS is home to two databases, the Luxembourg Income Study Database, and the Luxembourg Wealth Study Database.[24]

We should also talk about the European Survey of Income and Living Condition (EU-SILC) and the European Community Household Panel (ECHP) to assess earnings inequality in Europe from 1994 to 2009. The ECHP is a survey of 15 countries in the European Union from 1994 up to 2001. The EU-SILC is a collection of timely and comparable multidimensional micro data covering EU countries, starting in 2004 and ending in 2009, for a total of six waves. These surveys share many features, which makes it possible to harmonize the variables of interest. One advantage of these data is that they provide information for an overall period of 15 years within which we can observe a total of 12 European countries: Austria, Belgium, Germany, Denmark, Spain, Finland, France, Greece, Ireland, Italy, Portugal and the United Kingdom.

However, when looking at equality of opportunity, the lack of good data is widespread, except in Nordic countries where inequalities, including those linked to initial background, have been a social and political issue for a very long time.[25] One can say that there is a kind of paradox: In countries where the concern is high regarding inequality, we have good data, and to some extent, inequalities and inequalities of opportunity are low, while it is the opposite in countries where the social concern for inequality is weak. So we have good data for countries where the issue is almost fixed. A point should be raised about the fact that in most databases, measures of cognitive skills (such as IQ) and of noncognitive skills are missing. This hampers good identification of the impact of the social background on the destiny of offspring.

Nevertheless, the lack of good knowledge of the bottom part of the distribution is likely to be the most important handicap for our understanding of the evolution of inequality and poverty.[26] And yet, the poorest people in society should be those with the highest social welfare weight. For many reasons, the surveys are missing either the people or the income of the people in the bottom segment of the distribution. Typically, people consume more than their income in the first decile but respondents are quite shy when talking about their incomes.

To fill the gap, I propose to build a European Panel dedicated to the study of the dynamics of poverty, to study how people get out of poverty. People will not be asked to report income but only consumption, as well as health problems (mental and physical), housing conditions, employment, family conditions and social relations. This is our *second research proposal*.

12.7   Inequality and Welfare as Transversal Issues

The most interesting and important issues are at the intersections of several topics. Here are some examples of themes that are in a sense worldwide (see below for more specific European themes), but that are also meaningful in the European context.

Gender inequality. We know more and more about the levers for promoting gender equality. Nordic countries and the Netherlands are the high performers,[27] whereas most Mediterranean and eastern countries do not perform very well. Cultural barriers are important here.

Inequality and global warming. It is far from obvious that coordination between national states will avoid the bad scenario of an increase in temperature of 2°C or more and more frequent extreme episodes. The consequences in terms of distribution of welfare are not fully understood.

Inequality and migration. It is likely that Europe will remain a continent of immigration. The societies that have not developed specific institutions to level the playing field will not be immune to an increase in inequality. Even in societies that are really concerned with equality of opportunity, immigration may result in higher inequality for a while. The full process of integration, and how it interferes with the existing institutions and generates new inequalities, needs to be further studied. Notice, there is a strong link between the migration issue and the sustainability of the nationwide welfare state (see below). For instance, three quarters of the increase in poverty in Belgium in the age bracket 25–54 in recent years is accounted for adults not born in Belgium.[28]

Inequality and growth. The genuine question is to know whether less inequality impedes a faster growth. The empirical answer at the continental scale is no. The per capita growth rates in Western Europe and in the US have been the same since 1970 and up to the Great Recession. The common wisdom nowadays is that policies enhancing EOP are good for growth and this consensus extends to the case of reducing outcome inequality at least in the US case (see the recent policy reports of the IMF and OECD). One possible mechanism could be that equality increases trust, which again increases growth, creating a possible causal channel between equality and growth.

Inequality and ageing. What are the consequences of ageing on inequality? Maybe a better formulation would be: What would be the redistributive consequences of a longer life cycle? What would be the redistributive consequences of a retirement age increasing with productivity?

Inequality and borrowing. A small bunch of papers investigate the causal links between the increase in inequality and increase in borrowing in the case of the US economy before the crisis. This issue can be raised as well in a few European countries.

Inequality and technical progress. There is quite a consensus that the ICT revolution has had adverse effects in terms of inequality, in the sense that it has disproportionately increased the opportunities and therefore the market income of college graduates, that is, those who have been trained to be able to stock, understand and benefit from information. Will the next scientific revolution (to be less dependent on fossil energy) be more neutral in distributional terms?

Inequality and globalization. This is also an old issue that needs to be revisited. To some extent, as long as Asia becomes richer, the downward pressure for low-skilled wage in the developed world will become less strong and maybe it will open the way to a more equal distribution of the productivity gains in the firm in the old industrialized countries. However, globalization cannot be reduced to the free-trade dimension. The other dimension is the fact that production factors and particularly, capital and skilled labour, are freer to go from one zone to another. The consequences of factor moves on economic inequalities are still to be fully understood.

Inequality and social insurance. Although from a policy perspective it is often hard to distinguish the social insurance motive from the redistributive motive, studying the role of risk preferences in explaining welfare policies and the relationship between risk preferences and social preferences could also be part of a fruitful research agenda.

On all these subjects, broadly speaking, we have data, we have models, but generally we lack good calibrated models, particularly at the macroeconomic level.

12.8 Cutting Edge Research Issues

I see four issues that are not settled, the fourth one being quite new.

First, in the wake of Thomas Piketty's latest book, *Capital in the Twenty First Century*, the role of wealth distribution on the increase of inequalities has been addressed by many scholars. Piketty challenges the previous view that the increase in inequalities in the US was mainly due to the increasing returns of college graduates, while the returns of other qualifications had suffered from different causes (adverse technical progress, trade liberalization, and immigration of low-skilled workers). Not all economists agree with Piketty's demonstration and this issue should remain on the research agenda.

Second, the increasing gulf between CEOs pay in large companies and the earnings of other employees remains puzzling. Some economists (Gabaix and Landier, 2008 and Gabaix et al., 2014) argue that it simply reflects the increasing size of the companies and the increasing risk associated with bad decisions by managers. Other economists such as Atkinson (2015) argue that it comes from the change in social norms. Clearly more research in this direction is needed.

Third, the digitalization of many services to consumer (sometimes depicted as '*uberization*') raises new challenges. A growing part of the labour force may become self-employed, and their social protection may be reduced with respect to a world of homogeneous employees. The empirical evidence here is not straightforward since the evolution of the labour market points in the US and in the UK towards two divergent directions. There is the fear that this intermediation reorients market forces in a way that is more inequality prone. This research programme can be viewed as an outgrowing of the linkage between technical progress and inequality.

Fourth, the happiness literature, and more specifically John Layard, draws attention to the fact that most of the worst unhappiness is caused by mental disorders, especially depression and schizophrenia. According to John Layard 'Roughly 25 per cent of us experience serious mental illness during our lives, and about 15 per cent experience major depression.'

More importantly, there is much evidence on the correlation between different dimensions of deprivation during younger age and outcomes later in life, and that social deprivation correlates with both personality features and with mental health later in life. Here, I see an important missing relationship between equality of opportunity and mental disorders that opens possible new vistas for research.

In particular, for people of working age, mental or emotional health problems may lead an individual to leave his job, to be fired or to make him difficult to get out of unemployment. His saving or borrowing decisions may be inappropriate and as long as he has to take care of children, this can be detrimental to their development. Addiction can go along with mental health problems and affected people can even plunge into extreme poverty and become homeless. *As long as a person can switch from an economic and social status to a lower status because of mental health problems, or involves someone else to follow a downward path (mainly children), mental health problems demand some action from the public authorities.* The gist of the argument is about the bad dynamics with potential externalities entailed by mental health problems. Social policy can be preventive or curative, but any adequate public expenditure in this domain should have a high social return. It will not replace any other existing public policy, activation of the labour market, social benefits and so on. I will view all these actions as complementary, not as substitutes. I do not claim that there should be a trade-off between any mental health public policy and other existing public policies, even if an efficient mental health policy may lead to saving money on other social programmes.

For children, taking care of mental health problems is their parents' responsibility, and if they do not care, social policy has to compensate for parents' deficiencies. This is a direct consequence of an equality of opportunity policy, whereas for adults, it is a different inspiration to some extent. It can be termed a '*standing-up policy*', to help people to cope with the difficulties of life in a complex and competitive society. Not all people are well-equipped, and some may be severely handicapped in that matter. Dworkin (1981b) would have probably supported such a policy since it can be viewed as a lack of internal resources of a specific kind that should be compensated by external resources. Following this line of reasoning will lead to include retirees into the social programme improving mental health. A research programme into what could be the goals and the ways to build up a standing-up policy is our *third research proposal*.

12.9   Issues More Specific to Europe

Two issues seem to be more specific to Europe as an emerging fiscal federation. On the one hand, mobility of capital and labour result from country differences in tax regimes and are induced by the fact that tax matters remain the symbol of national sovereignty, and, on the other hand, mobility undermines this tax sovereignty.

- *Tax competition on capital*. Capital is more mobile than labour and the concern is about the impact of capital mobility on the possibility to tax capital, in the first place. Tax competition seems to have induced a race to the bottom, both in statutory and effective tax rates. Corporate tax rates are indeed higher in the US than in most European countries. There is a concern that it will be more difficult to tax capital at the national level, unless more coordination or harmonization is effectively implemented.
- *The sustainability of the nationwide welfare state in the Eurozone*. The second issue is more specific to the Eurozone and is related to the sustainability of the nationwide welfare state. This is under threat both from an internal and external perspective. The internal challenge with all welfare systems is that they are vulnerable to mistakes. Two common mistakes are related to false positives and false negatives: respectively, giving support to those who do not deserve it and not giving support to those who do. A fundamental question in the design of welfare policies, then, is to determine how one should make

the trade-off between false positives and false negatives. This is challenging as even individuals who may agree about what is fair may disagree about this trade-off. External shocks such as migration and globalization, technical progress and macroeconomic downturns may change voter minds about the divide between those who deserve and those who do not. This will then affect the perception of the false positives and false negatives and then undermine the welfare state, if, for some reasons, it does not adapt to the changing mood.

Many economists believe that it is good to ease migration of labour within the Eurozone to help countries that have been hurt by an asymmetric shock. A more unified labour market seems desirable, but at the same time this raises the question of the sustainability of the welfare state designed at the national level. Sinn (2003) was right in pointing out this issue as threatening the European construction well ahead. Migration of labour undermines the funding of social security systems, specifically pay as you go systems in emigrating countries, if some countries should become emigration countries forever. Mobility of capital and labour call for redesigning tax policies and welfare institutions on a broader scale than the national one. Otherwise, there will be adverse consequences in terms of inequality and social insurance in emigrating countries. A pan-European welfare state (at least for some branches) should be thought of as a natural evolution to cope with these issues.

But the scope of the problem should not be limited to within-Europe problems. The problem can be restated more generally between Europe and other economic zones. More specifically, the US is part of the problem and strengthened transatlantic links through the Transatlantic Treaty should make the problem more acute. If many European entrepreneurs, in particular in the high-tech industry, are going to the US to benefit from a more business-oriented climate and lower taxes, then the European income distribution will be censored to the right with a lower share of the cake for the top 1 per cent who will be in the US! Any change of the US attitude vis-à-vis the tolerance to inequality and in particular to the top income share may have dramatic influence on the sustainability of the welfare state on the European continent.

This second issue calls for specific research and funding at the European level. It is our *fourth research proposal*.

12.10   Conclusion

We have covered a lot of ground. We have surveyed the recent economic literature on inequality and welfare with a glimpse at the contribution of other social sciences. We can now answer the question raised in the title of this chapter.

Yes, Europe has a specific relationship with equality that may not be shared widely all across the world. It may be called some kind of inequality aversion, a term coined 45 years ago by Anthony Atkinson. This is witnessed by the common interest in equality all around Europe and reflected by the rather low level of inequality on the continent. The convergence of the degree of redistribution among member states before the Great Recession is also telling.

Europe is also special because the issue of inequality and welfare is also specific to each country. The Nordic countries and the Netherlands have achieved a low degree of inequality and a high level of income mobility. The challenge for Europe would be to manage to coach the Southern countries so that they catch up with the Northern countries, both in terms of standard of living and distributional achievements. Such an agenda cannot be reached through massive transfers from the North to the South because indeed Northern countries did not achieve their social performance with the help of massive transfers from abroad (see Barth et al., 2014 for an interpretation of the Scandinavian model). The convergence process will be a long-term process involving a gradual change of institutions and social preferences. What has been neglected in the research agenda at least by economists, however, is that institutions also shape preferences. An important question, then, is to understand how institutions may change preferences. For Hungary to converge to the Danish template, it will take 30 or 40 years. The issue of convergence should be at the heart of any social policy meant at the continent scale. It is far from obvious that belonging to the same monetary zone is going to speed up the convergence process. We have also noted the curse of big states in terms of social achievements. Denmark, with a small and relatively homogenous population, may not be a template for large demographically diverse countries, like France or Italy.

We have identified five areas where further research would help European policy-makers.

1. A network of researchers in economics and social sciences to understand the fabric of equality of opportunity.
2. The building up of panel data specific to studying the dynamics of poverty, how people are getting in, how people are getting out.
3. To prepare the ground for a standing-up policy to fight poverty and promote equal opportunities.
4. To look at the sustainability of nation welfare states in an environment where capital and labour are mobile.
5. The issue of the convergence of Southern societies to the social model of Northern societies.

Let me end up with a more general remark regarding the respective place of growth and inequality and welfare on the political agenda on both sides of the Atlantic. Robert Lucas and other macroeconomists have expressed the view that growth is the best way to improve the situation of the poor and of the middle class. They were clearly right in a world growing at a fast rate, as we experienced during the twentieth century (except war periods). That said, if the grim predictions of Robert Gordon are correct about the slowing down of the rate of growth for the most advanced economies, raising social welfare through a policy addressing distributional issues may come at the top of the political agenda more quickly than we can imagine. In addition to this, among the headwinds listed by Gordon we have to face when reaching for faster growth, inequality is conspicuous.

Acknowledgements

This is a revised version of a preliminary draft that was discussed at the COEURE workshop, *Inequality and Welfare: The State of the Art, Policy Challenges and a Research Agenda for Europe* at the Université Libre de Bruxelles, on 3 September 2015. I thank all the participants of this workshop and in particular, Ingvild Almas, Alexander Cappelen, Marc Fleurbaey, Lucinda Glover, Ingar Haaland, Marte Gerhardsen, Peater Neary, Karl Moene, Erik Shokkaert, Frode Steen and Frank Vandenbroucke for their comments that helped me to improve the first version. The usual caveat applies.

Notes

1. I have changed the story a little bit so it becomes also compatible with the equality of opportunity requisite.
2. At this stage, I prefer not to use the word utility which I reserve for naming subjective well-being.
3. Of course, it is all but obvious that we should choose the sum or the average of individual welfare to define collective well-being. It is only for pedagogical purposes that the discussion focuses on the sum.
4. A kink at the status reflecting a ratchet effect might be more realistic. Anyway, the important feature is the fact that the two curves cross.
5. The expensive taste argument cannot be used here, because those who have expensive tastes on the tax side have cheap tastes on the transfer side and vice-versa.
6. Dalton measured inequality by W_e/W, where W_e is the welfare that would be obtained if everybody received the average income. This measure is generally not invariant with respect to equi-proportional changes in all incomes. By contrast, Atkinson measured equality by EDE/average income is invariant to equi-proportional changes in all incomes.
7. I am grateful to Pedro Rosa-Dias from Sussex University for sending me these graphs that he prepared for his talk about causality and inequality for the conference in honour of John Roemer in Queen Mary's, London, June 2015.
8. See the 1990 Word Development Report of the World Bank.
9. It might have been anticipated by the French philosopher Bergson (1889) who contended in his doctoral dissertation that people's conscience fails to record duration.
10. Aspen conference https://www.youtube.com/watch?v=8f-T7lgdLPI.
11. http://www.college-de-france.fr/site/stanislas-dehaene/course-2013-01-08-09h30 .htm.

12. http://www.ip-socialprogress.org/.
13. LIS key figures: http://www.lisdatacenter.org/data-access/key-figures/download-key-figures/ downloaded 4 August 2015.
14. By the way, international inequality, that is, inequality of living standards between countries, raises some difficult measurement issues (see for instance, Neary, 2004).
15. An important part of wealth, mainly housing, is not a production factor.
16. Mathematically, the inequality of opportunity is a function of the distribution of parental income obtained as a composite function $I(f(y_p))$ where y_p is parental income, f the intergenerational process and I the inequality of parent distribution.
17. The Benabou-Tirole model allows for two equilibria, one of the American type with low taxes and welfare state and one of the European type with high taxes and generous welfare state. Thanks to the work of Piketty and Saez (2014) we have now understood that during the period 1930–1970, the American equilibrium was in fact of the European type. The US switched from the European type equilibrium to the American type on the eve of the 1980s. Can we calibrate the Benabou-Tirole model to exhibit the external parameters that cause that switch? It is an open but daunting question.
18. In the experiment, there are two kinds of subjects, the workers and the spectators. The workers are recruited through an online market place (mturk) and the spectators are representative samples of the US and Norwegian population. The spectators are asked about the compensation scheme of the workers.
19. On inter-area data for the US see Alesina and La Ferrara, 2000. At the experimental level, Harvard students are less likely to behave in a trusting and trustworthy way towards members of other nationalities or ethnic groups (Glaeser et al., 2000).
20. Cultural dimensions also explain the responses to happiness questions. Claudia Senik has documented the case of the French collective depression (Senik, 2014).
21. https://heckman.uchicago.edu/page/about-cehd.
22. http://www.equality-of-opportunity.org/.
23. The World Top Incomes Database, http://topincomes.g-mond.parisschoolof-economics.eu/.
24. http://www.lisdatacenter.org/about-lis/.
25. See however the new initiative of "Equal chances" launching a new databasis "The world data base of equal opportunity and social mobility: www.equalchances.org
26. For instance, the Economic and Social Developments in Europe, (http://ec.europa.eu/social/main.jsp?catId=738&langId=en&pubId=7684), in spite of being a useful source of interesting analyses on poverty, uses the EU-SILC database, which is not sufficiently oversampled on the bottom part of the distribution.
27. http://eige.europa.eu/gender-statistics/gender-equality-index/2012/.
28. Source: Eurostat and personal communication with Frank Vandenbroucke. See also for a similar study of increase of poverty among children Vandenbroucke (2013).

References

Aaronson, D., and Mazumdar, B. 2008. Intergenerational Economic Mobility in the United States, 1940 to 2000. *Journal of Human Resources*, **43**, 139–172.
Alesina, A., and Glaeser, E. 2004. *Fighting Poverty in the US and Europe: A World of Difference*. Oxford, UK: Oxford University Press.

Alesina, A., and La Ferrara, E. 2000. Participation in Heterogeneous Communities. *The Quarterly Journal of Economics*, **115**, 847–904.

Alesina, A., Glaeser, E., and Sacerdote, B. 2001. Why Doesn't the US Have a European-Type Welfare State? *Brookings Papers on Economic Activity*, **2**, 187–277.

Alesina, A., Di Tella, R., and McCulloch, R. 2004. Inequality and Happiness: Are Americans and Europeans Different? *Journal of Public Economics*, **88**, 2009–2042.

Alkire, S., and Foster, J. 2010. Designing the Inequality-Adjusted Human Development Index (IHDI). Human Development Research Paper 2010/28.

Alkire, S., and Foster, J. 2011. Counting and Multidimensional Poverty Measurement. *Journal of Public Economics*, **95**, 476–487.

Almlund, M., Duckworth, A. L., Heckman, J. J., and Kautz, T. 2011. Personality Psychology and Economics. In: Hanushek, E., Machin, S., and Woessman, L. (eds), *Handbook of the Economics of Education*, vol. 4. Amsterdam: Elsevier, pp. 1–181.

Almås, I., Cappelen, A. W., øO. Søorensen, E., and Tungodden, B. 2010. Fairness and the Development of Inequality Acceptance. *Science*, **328**, 1176–1178.

Almås, I., Cappelen, A. W., øO. Søorensen, E., and Tungodden, B. 2015. Are Americans More Meritocratic and Efficiency-seeking than Scandinavians. *forthcoming working paper NHH*.

Alvaredo, F., Atkinson, A. B., Piketty, T., and Saez, E. 2013. The Top 1 Percent in International and Historical Perspective. *J. Econ. Perspect*, **27**, 3–20.

Arneson, R. 1989. Equality and Equal Opportunity for Welfare. *Philosophical Studies*, **56**.

Arrow, K. 1963. *Social Choice and Individual Values*. 2 edn. Yale University Press.

Atkinson, A. B. 1970. On the Measurement of Inequality. *Journal of Economic Theory*, **2**, 244–263.

Atkinson, A. B. 2015. *Inequality. What Can Be Done?* Harvard University Press.

Atkinson, A. B., and Bourguignon, F. 1982. The Comparison of Multi-dimensioned Distributions of Economic Status. *Review of Economic Studies*, **49**, 183–201.

Atkinson, A. B., and Bourguignon, F. 1987. Income Distribution and Differences in Needs. in: Feiwel, G. R. (ed), *Arrow and the Foundation of the Theory of Economic Policy*. Macmillan, London, pp. 350–370.

Atkinson, A. B., and Brandolini, A. 2015. Unveiling the Ethics behind Inequality Measurement: Dalton's Contribution to Economics. *Economic Journal Article*.

Autor, D. H. 2014. Skills, Education and the Rise of Earnings Inequality among the 'Other 99 Percent'. *Science*, **344**, 843–851.

Barry, B. 1994. Justice, Freedom, and Basic Income. in: Siebert, H. (ed), *The Ethical Foundations of the Market Economy*. Ann Arbor: University of Michigan Press, pp. 61–89.

Barth, E., Moene, K. O., and Willumsen, F. 2014. The Scandinavian Model. An Interpretation. *Journal of Public Economics*, **117**, 60–72.

Bénabou, R., and Ok, E. A. 2001. Social Mobility and the Demand for Redistribution: the Poum Hypothesis. *Quarterly Journal of Economics*, **116**, 447–487.

Bénabou, R., and Tirole, J. 2006. Belief in a Just World and Redistributive Politics. *The Quarterly Journal of Economics*, 699–746.

Bénassy, A., Trannoy, A., and Wolf, G. 2014. Tax Harmonization in Europe: Moving forward. *Note CAE n. 14*.

Bergson, A. 1938. A Reformulation of Certain Aspects of Welfare Economics. *Quarterly Journal of Economics*, **52**, 310–334.

Bergson, H. 1889. *Essai sur les données immédiates de la conscience. Translation. Time and Free Will: An Essay on the Immediate Data of Consciousness*. 2001 Dover Publications.

Bertola, G., and Ichino, A. 1995. Wage Inequality and Unemployment: United States versus Europe. in: *NBER Macroeconomics Annual 1995*, vol. 10. NBER Chapters, NBER, Inc., pp. 13–66.

Bivens, J., and Mishel, L. 2013. The Pay of Corporate Executives and Financial Professionals as Evidence of Rents in Top 1 Percent Incomes. *J. Econ. Perspect*, **27**, 57–78.

Björklund, A., Jäntti, M., and Roemer, J. 2012a. Equality of Opportunity and the Distribution of Long-run Income in Sweden. *Social Choice & Welfare*, **39**, 675–696.

Björklund, A., Roine, J., and Waldenström, D. 2012b. Inter-generational Top Income Mobility in Sweden: Capitalist Dynasties in the Land of Equal Opportunity? *Journal of Public Economics*, **96**, 474–484.

Bonica, A., McCarty, N., Poole, K. T., and Rosenthal, H. 2013. Why Hasn't Democracy Slowed Rising Inequality? *J. Econ. Perspect*, **27**, 103–124.

Borghans, L., Duckworth, A. L., Heckman, J., and Weel, B. T. 2008. The Economics and Psychology of Personality Traits. *J. Human Resources*, **43**, 972–1059.

Bourguignon, F., and Chakravarty, S. 2003. The Measurement of Multidimensional Poverty. *Journal of Economic Inequality*, **1**, 25–49.

Brown, J. E., Chatterjee, N., Younger, J., and Mackey, S. 2011. Towards a Physiology-Based Measure of Pain: Patterns of Human Brain Activity Distinguish Painful from Non-painful Thermal Stimulation. *PLoS One*, **6**.

Cappelen, A. E., Konow, J., øO Søorensen, E., and Tungodden, B. 2013. Just Luck: An Experimental Study of Risk Taking and Fairness. *American Economic Review*, **103**, 1398–1413.

Cappelen, A. W., Hole, A. D., øO. Søorensen, E., and Tungodden, B. 2007. The Pluralism of Fairness Ideals: An Experimental Approach. *American Economic Review*, **97**, 818–827.

Chetty, R., Hendren, N., Kline, P., and Saez, E. 2014. Where is the Land of Opportunity? The Geography of Intergenerational Mobility in the United States. *Quarterly Journal of Economics*, **129**, 1553–1623.

Clark, A. E., and D'Ambrosio, C. 2014. Attitudes to Income Inequality: Experimental and Survey Evidence. In: Bourguignon, F., and Atkinson, A. (eds), *Handbook of Income Distribution*, vol. 2A. Elsevier, pp. 1148–1208.

Cohen, G. A. 1989. Ethics. *On the Currency of Egalitarian Justice*, **99**, 906–944.

Corak, M. 2013. Income Inequality, Equality of Opportunity, and Intergenerational Mobility. *J. Econ. Perspectives*, **27**, 79–102.

Crivellaro, E. 2014. College Premium over Time: Trends in Europe in the Last 15 years. *WP03 University of Foscari*.

Dalton, H. 1920. The Measurement of the Inequality of Incomes. *Economic Journal*, **30**, 348–361.

d'Aspremont, C., and Gevers, L. 1977. Equity and the Informational Basis of Collective Choice. *Review of Economic Studies*, **44**, 199–209.

Dehaene, S. 2013. Les principes Bayésiens de l'apprentissage: sommes-nous des scientifiques dès le berceau? http://college-de-france.fr/site/stanislas-dehaene/course-2013-01-08-09h30.htm.

Dworkin, R. 1981a. What Is Equality? Part 1: Equality of Welfare. *Phil.& Pub.Affairs*, **10**, 185–246.

Dworkin, R. 1981b. What Is Equality? Part 2: Equality of Resources. *Phil.& Pub.Affairs*, **10**, 183–234.

Easterlin, R. A. 1974. Does Economic Growth Improve the Human Lot? Some Empirical Evidence. In: David, P. A., and Reder, M. W. (eds), *Nations and Households in Economic Growth: Essays in Honor of Moses Abramovitz*. New York: Academic Press, pp. 89–125.

Easterlin, R. A., Angelescu McVey, L., Switek, M., Sawangfa, O., and Smith Zweig, J. 2010. The Happiness-Income Paradox Revisited. *PNAS Early Edition*, **107**, 22463–22468.

Edgeworth, F. 1897. The Pure Theory of Taxation. *Economic Journal*, **7**, 46–70.

Elster, J. 1992. *Local Justice: How Institutions Allocate Scarce Goods and Necessary Burdens*. Russell Sage.

European Social Survey. Measuring and Reporting on Europeans' Wellbeing: Findings from the European Social Survey. http://esswellbeingmatters.org.

Fleurbaey, M. 2008. *Fairness, Responsibility, and Welfare*. Oxford University Press.

Fleurbaey, M. 2009. Beyond GDP: The Quest for a Measure of Social Welfare. *J. Econ. Lit*, **47**, 1029–1075.

Fleurbaey, M., and Maniquet, F. 2011. Compensation and Responsibility. Chap. 22 of: Arrow, K., Sen, A., and Suzumura, K. (eds), *Handbook of Social Choice and Welfare*, vol. 2. Elsevier.

Foster, J., Lopez-Calva, L., and Szekely, M. 2005. Measuring the Distribution of Human-Development: Methodology and an Application to Mexico. *Journal of Human Development*, **6**, 5–29.

Friends of Europe. 2015. Unequal Europe: Recommendations for a More Caring EU. Final Report of the High-study Group.

Frohlich, N., and Oppenheimer, J. A. 1992. *Choosing Justice: An Experimental Approach to Ethical Theory*. Berkeley University of California Press.

Fryer, R., and Levitt, S. 2004. Understanding the Black-white Test Score Gap in the First Two Years of School. *Rev. Econ. & Stat.*, **86**, 447–464.

Fryer, R., and Levitt, S. 2006. The Black-white Test Score Gap through Third Grade. *Amer. Law & Econ. Rev.*, **8**, 249–281.

Fryer, R., and Levitt, S. 2013. Testing for Racial Differences in the Mental Ability of Young Children. *Amer. Econ. Rev.*, **103**, 981–1005.

Gabaix, X., and Landier, A. 2008. Why Has CEO Pay Increased So Much? *The Quarterly Journal of Economics*, **123**, 49–100.

Gabaix, X., Landier, A., and Sauvagnat, J. 2014. CEO Pay and Firm Size: An Update After the Crisis. *The Economic Journal*, **124**, F40–F59.

Gaertner, W., and Schokkaert, E. 2012. *Empirical Social Choice: Questionnaire – Experimental Studies on Distributive Justice*. Cambridge: Cambridge University Press.

Glaeser, E. L., Laibson, D., Scheinkman, J., and Soutter, C. 2000. Measuring Trust. *Quarterly Journal of Economics*, **115**, 811–846.

Goldin, C., and Katz, L. F. 2008. *The Race Between Education and Technology*. Harvard Univ. Press, Cambridge, MA.

Gopnik, A., Meltzoff, A. N., and Kuhl, P. K. 2001. *How Babies Think: The Science of Childhood*. 2nd edn. Phoenix.

Grosfeld, I., and Senik, C. 2010. The Emerging Aversion to Inequality. Evidence from Poland. *Economics of Transition*, **18**, 1–26.

Heckman, J. 2012. *Giving Kids a Fair Chance*. Cambridge, MIT Press, Cambridge. Mass.

Hicks, J. R. 1946. *Value and Capital: An Inquiry into Some Fundamental Principles of Economic Theory*. 2nd edn. Oxford: Clarendon Press.

Kahneman, D., and Deaton, A. 2010. High Income Improves Evaluation of Life but Not Emotional Well-being. *Proceedings of the National Academy of Sciences of the United States of America*, **107**, 16489–16493.

Kahneman, D., and Riis, J. 2005. *The Science of Well-Being*. eds: F. A. Huppert and N. Baylis and B. Keverne. Oxford University Press, Oxford.

Kolm, S.-C. 1969. The Optimal Production of Social Justice. In: Margolis, J., and Guitton, H. (eds), *Public Economics*. London: Macmillan, pp. 145–200.

Kolm, S.-C. 1972. *Justice et Equité*. CNRS.

Kolm, S.-C. 2005. *Macrojustice, The Political Economy of Fairness*. Cambridge, Cambridge University Press.

Kringelbach, M. L., and Berridge, K. C. (eds). 2010. *Pleasures of the Brain*. Oxford: Oxford University Press.

Kuklinski, J. H., Quirk, P. J., Jerit, J., Schwieder, D., and Rich, R. F. 2003. Misinformation and the Currency of Democratic Citizenship. *Journal of Politics*, **62**, 790–816.

Kuziemko, I., Norton, M., Saez, E., and Stantcheva, S. 2015. How Elastic are Preferences for Redistribution? Evidence from Randomized Survey Experiments. *American Economic Review*, **105**, 1478–1508.

Kuznets, S. 1955. Economic Growth and Income Inequality. *American Economic Review*, **45**, 1–28.

Layard, R. 2011. *Happiness: Lessons from a New Science*. Penguin, Second Edition.

Layard, R., Nickell, S., and Mayraz, G. 2008. The Marginal Utility of Income. *Journal of Public Economics, Special Issue: Happiness and Public Economics*, **92**.

Lefranc, A., Pistolesi, N., and Trannoy, A. 2007. Une réduction de l'inégalité des chances dans l'inégalité du revenu salarial en France? *Revue d'Economie Politique*, **117**, 91–117.

Lefranc, A., Pistolesi, N., and Trannoy, A. 2009. Equality of Opportunity and Luck: Definitions and Testable Conditions, with an Application to Income in France. THEMA Working Papers 2009.

Machin, S., and Van Reenen, J. 2010. *Inequality: Still Higher, But Labour's Policies Kept it Down*. Centre for Economic Performance, London.

Milanovic, B. 2006. An Estimate of Average Income and Inequality in Byzantium Around Year 1000. *Review of Income and Wealth*, **3**, 449–470.

Milanovic, B. 2012. Income Inequality in Europe and the US.: Regional vs. Social-Class Inequality. *World Bank - Inequality in Focus, The World Bank*, **1**, 5–8.

Milanovic, B. 2013. The Inequality Possibility Frontier: Extensions and New Applications. *Policy Research Working Paper Series 6449, The World Bank*.

Milanovic, B., Lindert, P., and Williamson, J. 2011. Pre-industrial Inequality. *Economic Journal*, 255–272.

Mirrlees, J. A. 1971. An Exploration in the Theory of Optimum Income Taxation. *The Review of Economic Studies*, **38**, 175–208.

Moene, K., and Wallerstein, M. 2001. Inequality, Social Insurance and Redistribution. *American Political Science Review*, **95**, 859–874.

Neary, P. 2004. Rationalising the Penn World Table: True Multilateral Indices for International Comparisons of Real Income. *American Economic Review*, **94**, 1411–1428.

Nozick, R. 1974. *Anarchy, State, and Utopia*.

Nussbaum, M., and Sen, A. (eds). 1999. *The Quality of Life*. Oxford: Oxford University Press.

Parfit, D. 1984. *Reasons and Persons*. Oxford: Clarendon Press.

Piketty, T. 2014. *Capital in the Twenty First Century*. Cambridge MA: Harvard University Press.

Piketty, T., and Saez, E. 2003. Income Inequality in the United States, 1913–1998. *Quarterly Journal of Economics*, **118**, 1–41.

Piketty, T., and Saez, E. 2014. Inequality in the Long Run. *Science*, **23**.

Rawls, J. 1971. *A Theory of Justice*. Cambridge, MA: Harvard University Press.

Rawls, J. 1982. Social Unity and Primary Goods. In: Sen, A., and Williams, B. (eds), *Utilitarianism and Beyond*. Cambridge: Cambridge University Press.

Robbins, L. 1935. *An Essay on the Nature and Significance of Economics*. 2nd revised edn. London: Macmillan.

Roemer, J. 1993. A Pragmatic Theory of Responsibility for the Egalitarian Planner. *Phil. & Pub. Affairs*, **22**, 146–166.

Roemer, J. 1996. Equality versus Progress. *Nordic Journal of Political Economy*, **23**, 47–54.

Roemer, J. 1998. *Equality of Opportunity*. Harvard University Press.

Roemer, J., and Trannoy, A. 2015. Equality of Opportunity. In: Bourguignon, F., and Atkinson, A. (eds), *Handbook of Income Distribution*, vol. 2A. Elsevier, pp. 217–300.

Roemer, J., Van der Straeten, K., and Lee, W. 2007. *Racism, Xenophobia and Distribution: Multi-issue Politics in Advanced Democracies*. Cambridge: MA, Harvard University Press and Russell Sage Foundation.

Rosen, S. 1981. The Economics of Superstars. *The American Economic Review*, **71**, 845–858.

Saez, E. 2001. Using Elasticities to Derive Optimal Income Tax Rates. *Review of Economic Studies*, **68**, 205–229.

Saez, E., and Zucman, G. 2014. Wealth Inequality in the United States since 1913: Evidence from Capitalized Income Tax Data. National Bureau of Economic Research Working Paper 20625.

Saez, E., and Stantcheva, S. 2016. Generalized social marginal welfare weights for optimal tax theory. *The American Economic Review* **106**(1), 24–45.

Saez, E., Slemrod, J., and Giertz, S. H. 2012. The Elasticity of Taxable Income with Respect to Marginal Tax Rates: A Critical Review. *Journal of Economic Literature*, **50**, 3–50.

Scanlon, T. 1975. Preference and Urgency. *Journal of Philosophy*, **72**.

Scanlon, T. 1986. Equality of Resources and Equality of Welfare: A Forced Marriage? *Ethics*, **97**, 111–118.

Sen, A. K. 1970. *Collective Choice and Social Welfare*. Holden-Day,San Francisco.

Sen, A. K. 1973. *On Economic Inequality*. Oxford: Oxford University Press.

Sen, A. K. 1980. Equality of What? In: McMurrin, S. (ed), *The Tanner Lectures on Human Values*. Salt Lake City: University of Utah Press.

Sen, A. K. 1985. *Commodities and Capabilities*. North-Holland.

Senik, C. 2014. Why Are the French so Unhappy? The Cultural Dimension of Happiness. *Journal of Economic Behavior and Organization*, **106**, 379–401.

Senik, C., Stichnoth, H., and Van der Straeten, K. 2009. Immigration and Natives' Attitudes towards the Welfare State: Evidence from the European Social Survey. *Social Indicators Research*, **91**, 345–370.

Simpson, N. B. 2011. Happiness and Migration. In: Zimmerman, K., and Constant, A. (eds), *International Handbook on the Economics of Migration*. Edward Elgar.

Sinn, H. W. 2003. *The New Systems Competition*. Blackwell.

Stiglitz-Sen-Fitoussi report. 2009. Report by the Commission on the Measurement of Economic Performance and Social Progress.

Van Parijs, P. 1991. Why Surfers Should Be Fed: The Liberal Case for and an Unconditional Basic Income. *Philosophy & Public Affairs*, **20**, 101–131.

Van Parijs, P. 1996. *Real Freedom for All*. New York: Oxford University Press.

Vandenbroucke, F. 2013. *The Active Welfare State Revisited*. Brugge, Die Keure.

Vandenbroucke, F. 2014. The Case for a Social Union: From Muddling to a Sense of Common Purpose. *Policy Papers Euroforum n. 18, KU Leuven*.

Vandenbroucke, F., and Vanhercke, B. 2014. A European Social Union '10 Tough Nuts to Crack'. Background Report of the High-level Study Group. Friends of Europe.

Veenhoven, R. 2000. Well-being in the Welfare State. *Journal of Comparative policy analysis*, **2**, 91–125.

Wagner, T. D., Atlas, L. Y., Lindquist, M. A., Roy, M., Woo, C. W., and Kross, E. 2013. An fMRI-Based Neurologic Signature of Physical Pain. *N. Engl. J. Med.*, **368**, 1388–1397.

World Bank. 1990. *World Development Report 1990: Poverty*. New York: Oxford University Press.

Yaari, M., and Bar-Hillel, M. 1984. On Dividing Justly. *Social Choice & Welfare*, **1**, 1–24.

13 Developments in Data for Economic Research

Roberto Barcellan, Peter Bøegh Nielsen, Caterina Calsamiglia, Colin Camerer, Estelle Cantillon, Bruno Crépon, Bram De Rock, László Halpern, Arie Kapteyn, Asim I. Khwaja, Georg Kirchsteiger, Vigdis Kvalheim, Julia Lane, Markus Mobius, Luke Sibieta, Joseph Tracy, Frederic Udina, Gugliemo Weber and Lisa Wright

Abstract

There has been a steep increase in empirical research in economics in the past 20–30 years. This chapter brings together several actors and stakeholders in these developments to discuss their drivers and implications. All types of data are considered: official data, data collected by researchers, lab experiments, randomized control trials, and proprietary data from private and public sources. When relevant, emphasis is placed on developments specific to Europe. The basic message of the chapter is that there is no single type of data that is superior to all others. We need to promote diversity of data sources for economic research and ensure that researchers are equipped to take advantage of them. All stakeholders – researchers, research institutions, funders, statistical agencies, central banks, journals, data firms, and policy-makers – have a role to play in this.

13.1 Introduction

The past 20–30 years have witnessed a steady rise in empirical research in economics. In fact, a majority of articles published by leading journals these days are empirical, in stark contrast with the situation 40 or 50 years ago (Hamermesh, 2013). This change in the distribution of methodologies used in economic research was made possible by improved computing power but, more importantly, thanks to an increase in the *quantity, quality* and *variety* of data used in economics.

This chapter brings together several actors and stakeholders in these changes to discuss their drivers and implications.[1] *All* types of data are considered. When relevant, emphasis is placed on developments specific to Europe. Sections 13.2 and 13.3 deal with official microdata. Section 13.2 focuses on the level of access to microdata in Europe and its determinants. Section 13.3 focuses on cross-country data harmonization. Section 13.4 then switches gears entirely and discusses the benefits and costs of large-scale data collection efforts led by researchers, instead of statistical offices. Section 13.5 discusses data produced by researchers, either in the context of lab experiments or in the context of randomized control trials. Both types of data have led to major advances; for the first one in our understanding of human behaviour and the robustness of economic institutions; for the second in our understanding of the impact of policies and the mechanisms underlying them. The chapter closes by discussing new forms of collaborations that researchers are developing with private- and public-sector organizations, with the benefit of access to data of very high quality, as well as the opportunity to contribute to product and policy designs, and what it implies for how research is organized, evaluated and funded.

The basic message of the chapter is that there is no single type of data that is superior to all others. Each type of data is unique and has advantages over the others for a given research question. In many cases, they even complement one another. We need to promote this diversity and ensure researchers are equipped to take advantage of them. All stakeholders – researchers and their institutions, funders, statistical agencies, central banks, journals, data firms, policy-makers – have a role to play in this.

13.2   Organizing Access to Microdata

By Roberto Barcellan, Caterina Calsamiglia, Estelle Cantillon, Vigdis Kvalheim, Luke Sibieta and Frederic Udina

Microdata, that is, data at the individual, household, firm or establishment level, are a rich source for economic research. Their granularity allows researchers to get a better understanding of the heterogeneity of behaviour and outcomes in the population of interest, and thus yields better insights into the potential mechanisms at play. Two types of microdata are of particular interest to economists: survey data, which cover a representative sample of the population of interest and usually follows them over time (for example the Labour Force Survey in Europe), and administrative data, which are collected for administrative purposes.

Survey data were at the forefront of important empirical developments in economics in the 1980s, 1990s and 2000s. The current frontier now is administrative data. Administrative data have many advantages over survey data. They cover a broader set of activities and outcomes. They cover the entire population and track it over time, instead of providing a snapshot on a population sample. Their quality is high: they do not suffer from the kind of attrition, nonresponse and measurement errors that can plague survey data. They are cheap (they already exist) and recent advances in computing power and data management techniques have made them easier to extract, manipulate and analyse. Last but not least, the possibility of linking different administrative datasets (for example, crime history and education history at the individual level) opens up endless possibilities for new research questions.

But microdata are sensitive. Individuals have the right to have their privacy protected. Firm-level data can contain competition-sensitive information that firms may not want to become public. Providing secure access to microdata and linked microdata is also resource-intensive. These factors make the option of not providing any access attractive for risk-averse or resource-constrained statistical systems. This section describes the legal environment and practical solutions that the European Union and the different Member States have put or are putting in place to reconcile the need for data protection and the promotion of data access for research purposes.

13.2.1   Legal and Technical Background

The European framework for data protection relies on two principles: the protection of personal data as a basic right, and the promotion of the free flow of personal data as a common good.[2] These principles necessarily go hand in hand: data subjects will not accept to have data collected on them if they cannot trust data owners to ensure their confidentiality. In turn, opt out clauses, which are unavoidable if trust is low, reduce the value of the data produced.

Existing European regulations allow (but do not require) Member States to grant access to microdata without the consent of the data subjects (which is typically the case for administrative data) when such data are essential for the pursuit of research and on the condition that they are de-identified.[3] De-identification involves the removal of personal identifiers such as national IDs or names, but can also involve the removal or blurring of other quasi-identifiers such as the address or date of birth.

De-identification does not necessarily remove all privacy concerns, however. Users of the data may be able to use combinations of variables (such as workplace and employment history to re-identify the individuals in the data). This risk of re-identification is heightened with linked microdata. Protocols need to be in place to ensure that confidentiality is preserved. These protocols regulate *who* can access the data and *how* this access is organized.

Under European regulations, access is granted in two steps. First, the institution to which the researcher is affiliated needs to be recognized as a research institution. This is important because it is the institution that eventually guarantees that proper safeguards are in place and the data will remain confidential. Second, access is only granted on a project-by-project basis. Each project (data request) is evaluated on its scientific merit and the necessity for the confidential data.

Three forms of access are common: secure physical transfer of the data to the researchers, virtual access, and data enclaves (dedicated secure environments). Data enclaves are the safest form of access because the data never leave the room. They are also the most constraining for researchers who need to be able to set aside blocks of time during office hours to go to the data enclave. Virtual access is a remote desktop connection to the institution hosting the data. The data analysis is carried out on the remote desktop and the output is checked before it is sent to the researcher.[4] Secure transfer of the data to the researcher is of course the most convenient form of access for researchers, but it requires trusted researchers and a careful assessment of risks.

Despite a common legal framework at the European level, there are important variations across Europe in laws, and in legal and technical practices for access to microdata. These can be seen as the result of differences in cultural traditions and norms, public attitudes towards research, and quality and resources of local statistical systems. The following Table 13.1 taken from Castellani and Koch (2015) reporting on a comprehensive inventory exercise of data on indicators of competitiveness (the MAPCOMPETE project, described in greater detail in the next section) illustrates the existing heterogeneity in the legal conditions for data access. The indicators of competitiveness reported in this table all need to be built up from firm-level data. The table shows whether the data needed to construct the indicator are available without restriction (++), whether access is possible under some conditions (+) or whether access is impossible (−). The symbol '?' indicates cases where the authors could not get the information on access.[5]

In addition (and not reported in Table 13.1), there are also great differences in nonlegal barriers to access, such as lengthy approval procedures, overly restrictive interpretations of what constitutes '*necessity for research*', and time-consuming or inconvenient access. On this front, revealed preferences by researchers are the best indicators. Nordic countries stand out clearly on this dimension.

13.2.2   *The Nordic Leadership*

Nordic countries are world leaders in providing access to microdata for research. Their success is partly based on a long tradition of collecting data for administrative and statistical purposes. Virtually all interactions with the government or publicly funded service providers are covered. For individuals, this means for example family composition, medical records (including prescriptions and care), education history, employment status and employer identity, income, and social benefits. For firms, the available data include tax and other

Table 13.1 *Accessibility of selected indicators of competitiveness across EU countries (excerpt from Table 2.4 of Castellani and Koch, 2015)*

	Labour productivity[a]		
	All firms	Exporters	Foreign-owned firms
Austria	–	–	?
Belgium	++	–	–
Bulgaria	+	+	+
Croatia	?	?	?
Czech Rep.	+	+	+
Denmark	+	+	?
Estonia	+	+	+
Finland	+	+	+
France	+	+	+
Germany	+	+	?
Hungary	+	+	?
Ireland	+	+	+
Italy	+	+	–
Latvia	+	+	?
Lithuania	–	–	–
Malta	+	+	–
Netherlands	+	?	?
Poland	+	+	?
Portugal	+	+	?
Romania	–	–	–
Slovakia	–	–	–
Slovenia	+	+	+
Spain	–	–	–
Sweden	+	+	+
UK	+	+	+

[a] Average, median, other moments.

financial statements, sales, ownership, and employee identities and salary histories. Individuals and firm establishments are uniquely identified in all of these administrative registers, making linking possible. Some of the data series start in the early twentieth century. Very few, if any, statistical systems in the world match the comprehensiveness of the Nordic statistical systems.

Data availability and quality are only part of the explanation, however. Ensuring and organizing access to these data is essential too. Trust is the key word here. Nordic countries combine some of the highest levels of protection of personal and business data with the highest levels of access. Projects are screened for their societal interest and to ensure that the data request is legitimate given the research question. Researchers must be affiliated with a pre-approved research institution (usually in the country), which takes responsibility for any violation of the confidentiality agreement by the researcher. The flip side of these high standards is the shared understanding and public support for securing access to data for researchers. Laws contain provisions to secure legitimate access to data for research purposes. Statistics Finland, Statistics Norway, and the Norwegian Social Science Data Services (NSD), a go-between organization between researchers and data owners, have among their mandates to service researchers.

There is no single '*Nordic model*', however. While all Nordic countries have comprehensive population and business registers that they make available to the research community, research arrangements and organization practices differ.[6] One dimension in which the countries differ concerns how access to data is provided. In Denmark, virtual access prevails. Norway hands out data to researchers but is currently developing virtual access as well. In Sweden, virtual access and physical transfer of data coexist. On-site access is the default option in Finland, but virtual access is also possible. Because these different modes of access entail different risks in terms of data confidentiality and integrity, some data may only be accessible through one channel and not the other.

Irrespective of how access is granted, direct access prevails: the data owners (data registers) are those providing access to the data and thus screening the projects for their compliance with the law and approving researchers. When the data request involves several data registers (for example: education data and employment data), the national office of statistics performs the data merger and its de-identification.

Norway is special among Nordic countries in that it also offers mediated access. The Norwegian Social Science Data Services (NSD) acts as an intermediary between the research institutions and Statistics Norway to provide access to researchers. The NSD screens projects, provides guidance to researchers, negotiates research use and access, and hands out the prepared data to the researchers. The main advantage of mediated access for researchers is its efficiency: Access is fast and free. Not all data can be accessed through NSD, however. NSD focuses on scientific use files (such as surveys) for which the risk of identification is appropriately reduced and simple data requests. With 1200–1400 projects serviced per year, these represent the bulk of microdata requests.[7] Data requests that involve data owners other than Statistics Norway, cover the entire population, or require very detailed and thus identifiable personal information must go through Statistics Norway (direct access).

Despite their success, statistical offices and other data stakeholders in Nordic countries are continuing to push for greater access (including from abroad), while keeping the same high standards of data protection. One of the ongoing projects seeks to develop research on cross-Nordic administrative data. Such research is still rare. The absence of common descriptors (metadata) is a major obstacle. Other hurdles include a lack of data harmonization, independent and sometimes lengthy application procedures to get access, and organizational constraints with some countries still restricting access on-site or to researchers based in the country. In 2012, NordForsk, the platform for joint Nordic research and infrastructure cooperation, funded a feasibility study on how to enhance cross-Nordic register cooperation. The report (NORIA-net, 2014) advocated the development of a common metadata framework, a common application procedure and a model of joint access to Nordic microdata through the existing remote access systems. This model for cross-Nordic register data access is currently being developed for social data. Economic and medical data will follow.

13.2.3   Improving Data Access: Two Case Studies

Beyond Nordic countries, there is also a clear trend in several European countries towards facilitating access to administrative data for researchers. Individual researchers are playing a key role in these developments by leveraging existing laws and working through them to get access and set precedents for other researchers. It would be wrong, however, to view existing developments as being only demand-driven. The UK and the Autonomous Community of Catalonia (Spain) provide two contrasting examples of transition towards greater access in countries that do not a priori benefit from the favourable conditions of Nordic countries. The two cases illustrate the different drivers of this evolution and the form that the transition can take.

A Top Down Initiative with a Central Role for the Research Funding Agency

Two factors drive the current push in the UK for greater access to administrative data. First, recent research using this type of data has changed policies and shown the societal value of such access. For example, the creation of the National Pupil Database, which tracks all pupils in state-funded schools starting from 2002 has led to a better understanding of the drivers of students' outcomes, and to more reliable estimates of the effects of policies. Using this database, Dustmann et al. (2011) and Wilson et al. (2011) have for example shown that ethnic minorities tend to outperform pupils from White-British backgrounds. This changed the way policy-makers view the relationship between ethnicity and student outcomes. The database is also widely used to evaluate the impact of different educational interventions as part of randomized control trials (see Section 13.5).[8] Linking these data to higher education records has shed new light on the policy debate on access to higher education by showing that access is not so much driven by socio-economic characteristics (raising concerns about socially biased admissions) than by prior academic performance (Chowdry et al., 2013). As another example, Best and Kleven (2015) have used data on housing transactions to document the distortionary impact of several features of the housing tax in the UK, with the policy subsequently changed.

The second driver of change is the concern that the UK may be falling behind in research if it does not grant its researchers access to data.[9] Access to quality data is essential for high-quality research and, worldwide, access to administrative data tends to be limited to researchers based in nationally accredited institutions. Therefore, providing access to UK-based researchers is critical to ensure their ability to carry out research at the highest level. However, access has been variable and difficult to date. There are legal barriers, of course (such as determining whether data access requires consent by the individuals that the data cover). There have also been cultural barriers, such as unwillingness to hand over data even when it is legal to do so, or institutional barriers, such as lack of human resources, preventing the extraction and preparation of the data for research. In addition, intrinsic data limitations, such as the inexistence of national IDs, make linking difficult in the UK.

The UK Administrative Data Research Network (ADRN) was set up in 2014 as a partnership between universities, government departments and agencies, statistical agencies, funders and researchers to foster access to linked de-identified administrative data.[10] It is funded by the Economic and Social Research Council (ESRC) and relies on two building blocks: an administrative data service (ADS) and four administrative data centres (ADRCs).

Ensuring the ethical and lawful use of data and building trust are at the core of the architecture put in place: projects are screened, researchers are trained, the data are de-identified, access is provided in secure environments and all outputs are screened to ensure identification is not possible. The model being put in place is a variation on the mediated access model. The Administrative Data Service helps researchers prepare their proposals and trains them for accreditation to use de-identified administrative data. It also negotiates access to data with the different statistical agencies. Once a proposal is approved and data owners have agreed to provide access, the ADRCs then provide secure access to the data, either on-site or virtual, depending on the preferences of the data owners.

The ADRN is new but it has already received a large number of applications from researchers. This is promising. Challenges remain, however. The existing legal framework for access to confidential data in the UK is fragmented. By law, the data must be destroyed 5 years after the start of the project, raising concerns about replicability. Changes are under way and the ADRN is contributing to the efforts by identifying remaining legal barriers. The main challenge, however, is to increase acceptability by the wider public and data owners. Privacy concerns remain pervasive and understanding of the societal value of research on administrative data is not largely shared.

Partnerships Between the Statistical Agency and Universities
Driving Change

Developments in Catalonia illustrate the power of bottom-up initiatives as a source of change when other conditions are ripe to leverage them. The push for greater data access there came from a request received in 2010 by Idescat, the Statistical Office of Catalonia. Two researchers, Caterina Calsamiglia and Maia Guëll, had collected data on school choice (submitted preferences) and school enrolment from the city of Barcelona. The fact that they had obtained these data was in itself remarkable, and the result of lengthy trust-building with the department of education of the city of Barcelona. The researchers had identified interesting patterns in the school application behaviour of Barcelona families and consequently raised the interest of the Department of Education to understand the impact of socio-economic background on this behaviour. This required linking the data with census data.

The data request came at a good time for Idescat. The institute was transitioning from the traditional (stove pipe) linear model of data collection and production of statistics, where different databases covering different aspects of the same statistical object are kept distinct, to an integrated model, where common descriptors in different databases allow for their integration, and new data are seamlessly integrated with preexisting data as they arrive. Moreover, the culture of the organization was receptive to change: the institute is a relatively young and small organization and it had just appointed a new director, Frederic Udina, with a prior career in academia.

The data request was used by Idescat to learn about protocols for secure data access elsewhere (notably Norway and Denmark) and develop them in collaboration with the two researchers. A contract was eventually signed between Idescat and the Barcelona Graduate School of Economics (GSE), to which the two researchers were affiliated. The linking and de-identifying were carried out by Idescat for the researchers.

The contractual and logistical arrangements used for this first exercise served as a template for other data requests. It eventually led to the signature of a framework agreement between the Barcelona GSE and Idescat. The agreement establishes a partnership between the two organizations, where Idescat links and de-identifies the data (possibly first negotiating access with third party owners) and Barcelona GSE provides technical support and some manpower. A scientific committee with representatives from both the Barcelona GSE and other leading research institutions screens data requests and projects and oversees rules. The form of access is decided on a case-by-case basis depending on the re-identification risk that the data contain. Partnerships between Idescat and other research institutes are being developed alongside the same model.

13.2.4 Concluding Remarks

Microdata, and in particular linked microdata, are a goldmine for research. Several chapters in this volume allude to their potential to generate significant research breakthroughs in their respective fields. The good news is that progress is happening, not only in the countries that have traditionally been at the forefront of giving access to researchers, but also elsewhere. When progress takes place, there is usually a common understanding that making data available to researchers generates useful knowledge for policy and society, and provides a leading edge to domestic researchers. Researchers have an important role to play in testing the laws, opening doors, and showing the societal value of the research produced with this type of data. The current European legislative framework for access to microdata is adequate, but, at the time of writing, there are concerns that the new data protection regulation at the EU level could significantly restrict access to personal data. History will tell.

Of course, providing access is costly. In addition, there exist risks of breach of data confidentiality. These factors can lower the appetite of data owners to grant access, with high nonlegal barriers to access as consequences. From this perspective, the creation of a data mediator, such as NSD in Norway or ADS in the UK, whose main mandate is to service data requests by researchers, is particularly attractive. This model also seems particularly scalable in the presence of multiple data owners. Clearly, however, each country will need to develop its own variant that is compatible with the current organization of their statistical system and the incentives in place.

13.3 Data Standards and Cross-Country Datasets

By Roberto Barcellan, Peter Bøegh Nielsen, Bram De Rock, László Halpern, Joseph Tracy, and Lisa Wright

This section discusses the challenges and recent progress towards greater cross-country data harmonization and integration. Cross-country variations in data standards and data definitions are big obstacles to multi-country research. Comparative analyses are nevertheless crucial for better understanding the scope for replicability of policies across borders (i.e., is the experience of country X relevant for country Y?). Moreover, the recent economic crisis highlighted the high degree of interconnection of world economies and financial markets, and the inability of purely national databases to render an accurate picture of their operations.

Improvements in cross-country data are taking place at two levels.[11] First, there is a policy push in response to the crisis to increase cooperation among central banks and statistical offices to *produce better and more reliable* macroeconomic indicators at the global level. We discuss how the G20 Data Gaps initiative is driving change at this level. Data access for researchers will, however, be limited to macro indicators, at least in the foreseeable future.

Second, there are efforts to harmonize and link *existing microdata* across different countries. The challenges there are enormous. We start by reporting on the FP7-funded project MAPCOMPETE, which aimed to produce an inventory of indicators of competitiveness, and assess the data accessibility and availability to compute them. We then discuss several ongoing initiatives among statistical agencies in Europe to create harmonized, cross-country, linked microdata. Among other things this will demonstrate that creating the data of the future is not a job that can be done by a few statistical agencies or a small group of researchers. Private data firms also have a role to play in the research landscape to harmonize, link and repackage publicly available data from different sources and countries. We discuss the experience of Bureau Van Dijk, a publisher of global business information, from this perspective.

13.3.1   *The Lessons of the Financial Crisis for the Data Environment*

While the recent economic crisis did not necessarily result from a lack of proper economic and financial statistics, it nonetheless caught supervisors, policy-makers and investors unprepared to understand its development and impacts in key areas poorly covered by existing datasets. For example, policy-makers and supervisors were unable the weekend before the Lehman Brothers bankruptcy to obtain information on aggregate exposures by each large bank. Banks could not provide this information, partly because of a lack of internal appropriate data systems, but also partly because Lehman consisted of thousands of legal entities. This complicated the planning for the possible Lehman bankruptcy.

The Lehman example illustrates two important challenges for business and economic data. First, firms operate in complex settings but the data structure does not always capture this complexity. This makes it, for instance, very hard to have a precise idea on the aggregate exposure of a given bank or firm. Second, even when the data exist at the micro level, it is essential to be able to link these datasets across countries, time, and legal entities.

Importantly, the data gap identified by the Lehman bankruptcy was not necessarily a problem of *quality* of economic and financial statistics. The problem was the combination of the lack of comparability across countries with the presence of interconnections amongst economies and financial institutions. This combination implied that exposures taken through complex instruments and cross-border linkages of financial institutions were *not* covered by existing data.

The lack of relevant and comparable data, available in a timely fashion, brought statistical authorities under scrutiny. It was clear that they did not have the capacity to accurately detect, assess and forecast the consequences of the financial crisis. This profoundly impacted the way official statistics are organized. The rest of this section describes several initiatives that were taken in response. The bulk of these initiatives are policy-driven, but the greater awareness for the need to have better and more comparable data also benefits researchers through greater data harmonization and improved linking opportunities.

13.3.2   The G20 Data Gaps Initiative

After the crisis, the G20 countries became fully aware of the need to set up an international framework to address the challenges faced by statistical offices. They called on the International Monetary Fund (IMF) and the Financial Stability Board (at the time called Financial Stability Forum) 'to explore gaps and provide appropriate proposals for strengthening data collection'. This resulted in the report 'The Financial Crisis and Information Gaps', in which the IMF and the Financial Stability Board identified data gaps and presented a set of 20 recommendations to be implemented in the years to come.[12] The 20 recommendations are divided into four different, albeit interconnected groups: built-up risk in the financial sector, cross-border financial linkages, vulnerability of domestic economies to shocks, and improving communication of official statistics. Most of these recommendations concern financial stability indicators, but some of them relate directly to real economic indicators. The objective is to collect policy-relevant data that can, when needed, lead to early warnings.

In parallel, the Inter-Agency Group on Economic and Financial Statistics (IAG) was established to coordinate statistical issues and strengthen data collection. The IAG comprises the Bank for International Settlements (BIS), the European Central Bank (ECB), Eurostat, the IMF, the Organisation for Economic Co-operation and Development (OECD), the United Nations, and the World Bank. The IAG may be seen as a global facilitator. It coordinates international agencies to limit the duplication of efforts at the international level as much as possible. As the crisis had demonstrated a need to enhance communication, the IAG also promotes data provision and dissemination, particularly among the G20 economies. A website, www.principalglobalindicators .org, provides access to comparable economic and financial indicators for the G20 economies and the FSB countries.

The work undertaken by the Financial Stability Board with respect to two of the G20 data gaps' recommendations, namely Global Network Connections (R8) and Systematically Important Global Financial Institutions (R9), provide a good illustration of the challenges involved in the task. As the Lehman example made clear, the financial system is increasingly global. It is also less bank-centric, with other increasingly important nonbank intermediaries. However, the pre-crisis data environment was largely domestic and bank-focused. There was almost no data sharing across national supervisors. This created an increasing mismatch between the reality of financial markets and data structures.

In the middle of the Lehman crisis, national supervisors decided to start collecting risk exposure data for their large banks. In the US, the Federal Reserve Bank of New York cleaned and analysed the data before producing anonymized reports for the supervisors. With time, the accuracy and frequency of the data reports improved, but the anonymized nature of the reports limited their usefulness.

The work of the Financial Stability Board under the Data Gaps Initiative formalizes and expands on these early efforts, with four differences. First, the data now flow from the banks to their home supervisors on to a hub at the Bank of International Settlement. This is a crucial difference since global exposure can only be assessed from merging the data from all supervisors. Second, coverage was expanded to nearly all global systemically important banks. Third, the range of data collected was also expanded, from risk exposure of global systemically important banks in phase I of the project, to funding relationships and indicators for both micro and macro-prudential regulation by the last phase. Fourth, banks and counterparties' identities are not masked in internal reports (subject to jurisdiction confidentiality restrictions). The last phase of the project is scheduled for 2016.[13]

A critical challenge faced by the Financial Stability Board was to set up a multilateral framework for data sharing that would overcome the national supervisors' reluctance to share their data. The agreed upon framework relies on three principles: data ownership by national supervisors, reciprocity (supervisors do not receive reports unless they share their data) and unanimity (all supervisors agree on procedures). Only reports are shared by supervisors; there is no direct access to the pooled data. Given that the ultimate goal is to aid macro-prudential surveillance and regulatory design, the BIS, the IMF and the Financial Stability Board will likely have access to (some of) the data, but access arrangements are still under discussion at the time of writing. Access to researchers is not discussed.

A second important challenge was to properly assess the structure and interconnections in the global financial network in order to adequately identify the risks and vulnerabilities of the system. Special attention was devoted to assessing the links between global systemically important banks but also nonbank intermediaries, and institutions that may not be systemic but are deeply interconnected with several global systemically important institutions. These links can be due to ownership relationships, funding dependencies or other sources of spill-over. Data collection integrates both the exposure side and the funding side for both the consolidated and connected entities, thereby avoiding the earlier biases and gaps due to reporting groups' organizations.

There was also an interesting trade-off with respect to the frequency of data collection, between monitoring requirements (for which monthly data are enough) and crisis management (for which daily data are more adequate). The view held at the time was that if banks designed their data systems for normal reporting, they would not necessarily be able to accommodate daily reporting when needed. A weekly reporting frequency was selected, with the side benefit of forcing banks to significantly improve their internal data analytic capabilities.

13.3.3   Linking Existing Microdata

There is no doubt that the G20 Data Gaps Initiative is leading to better, more comparable, and more timely cross-country data. However, access to researchers is limited to the macro-indicators. In this section, we evaluate existing initiatives and prospects for harmonizing and linking existing microdata across countries.

Data Issues Assessed by MAPCOMPETE

The analysis of the competitiveness of firms is mostly done on the basis of macro-indicators (i.e., measured at the national level). This is partly because these macro data are easy to communicate and the measures can be computed relatively straightforwardly. However, competitiveness of a country (or a sector) is an idle concept, since competitiveness is related to the ability of firms (in a given country or sector) to efficiently produce goods and services. As such, it is crucial to start the analysis from the firm level and take firm heterogeneity into account, in order to fully grasp the impact of, for instance, the financial crisis.

This was the starting point of the FP7-funded project MAPCOMPETE (www .mapcompete.eu). The objectives of MAPCOMPETE were to study and compare existing firm data from 25 European countries and produce new micro (i.e., bottom-up) indicators related to productivity, firm dynamics, international activities and other aspects related to competitiveness. When possible, these micro indicators were linked to available macro indicators. All this allows for the replacement of the macro indicators by the more informative (because they take firm heterogeneity into account) micro indicators.

Although the benefits of these new and comparable micro indicators should be obvious, it is impossible, in the current data environment, to construct them for many countries. MAPCOMPETE identified several reasons for this (Castellani and Koch, 2015). First, there are important differences across countries in terms of availability and accessibility of the data, as well as data definitions (including different units of observations or timing). Second, it is often simply impossible to uniquely link existing datasets inside a given country. Finally,

not all European countries are equally convinced about the potential and benefits of creating these micro indicators of competitiveness. This is problematic
because, in the absence of a centralized and coordinated view on data collection, policy recommendations will, by construction, remain seriously limited.

Establishing Internationally Harmonized Statistical Databases

As European business statistics are to a large extent based on common EU regulations, the central business or economic statistics (such as, e.g., structural
business statistics, international trade in goods or services statistics and R&D
statistics) are de facto harmonized and thus in principle comparable across the
28 member states of the European Union. However, due to the stove pipe production process of official statistics, i.e., each statistic is produced in isolation
from one another, these micro data all focus on a limited number of aspects of
the firm. To fully analyse the impact of the financial crisis on European firms,
or simply get a full picture of firms or sectors, we need to be able to link these
existing datasets.

Eurostat has recently funded a series of micro data linking (MDL) projects in
order to 'modernize' the European enterprise and trade statistics (the MEETS
programme). The basic driver behind this development is twofold. On the one
hand, the analysis of cause and effect requires linking micro data, which in
turn implies breaking the traditional stove pipe model of statistical production.
On the other hand, there is the practical argument of minimizing respondent
burden. This not only increases the return on investment from these existing
detailed micro datasets, it also means that the statistics can be more adequately
used to guide policy-makers. In this sense, these micro data linking projects
are clearly complementary to initiatives such as the G20 Data Gaps Initiative,
which focus more on new and aggregate indicators.

Figure 13.1 shows the methodology developed for these projects.[14] One of
these projects covers, for example, the international organization and sourcing
of business functions of firms in nine European countries, for which harmonized datasets based on input data from five different statistical sources in each
country were compiled for the period 2008–2012. The resulting data will be
used to conduct micro-level economic analyses of essential questions related to
social and economic conditions, for example, which factors generate economic
growth or how international activities of enterprises influence their economic
or job creating performance.

These projects, as well as others such as the project described in Section
13.2 to link administrative datasets across Nordic countries, show the potential of micro data linking for the development of statistical information on the
international dimension. Micro data linking serves as an appropriate method
to analyse typical research questions on cross border activities ('what kind of
enterprise is trading?' instead of 'what do countries trade?'), firm heterogeneity

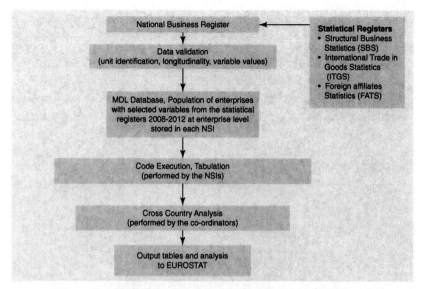

Figure 13.1 Typical organization of micro data linking (MDL) projects.

in systems of national accounts ('what kind of enterprises contribute to GDP?') and the organization of cross-border production processes ('what parts of the business organization move up or down the value chain?').

However, implementing micro data linking to a full extent, both across countries and within countries, is resource-intensive. It also requires coordination amongst and the cooperation of all national statistical offices. As such it is fair to conclude that we still have a long way to go.

The Role of Private Data Firms in Producing Harmonized Firm Data

Statistical offices are not alone in their efforts to harmonize cross-country data. Private data firms have long been involved in collecting, harmonizing and repackaging publicly available business data. Bureau van Dijk (BvD) is one of them. BvD is an established commercial company, collecting financial and Merger and Acquisition (M&A) data on more than 150 million firms worldwide, and a prime example that it is indeed possible to gather, and link, timely available micro data.

The M&A database produced by BvD illustrates some of the challenges involved in creating reliable and harmonized data from publicly available data. An M&A transaction involving two public companies does not pose any difficulties because it follows formal disclosure rules set by the stock exchanges.

Transactions involving privately held firms are trickier. To construct their international M&A database, BvD relies on several data sources, such as official company filings, data from stock exchanges and regulatory bodies, but also news services and M&A advisor data. The main added value of BvD comes from linking all these data sources in a standardized way. This requires the creation of unique identifiers, a mapping of local regulations to international standards and a harmonization of financial formats to allow for international comparisons. All this is done by local experts who understand the local specificities (and languages) and more than 100 specialists active in different fields (company data, scoring companies, stock market info, etc.). This network of experts, combined with the raw data, ensures that the resulting database is both reliable and accurate.

The business model of these private data firms is, of course, not comparable to those of statistical offices. It is nevertheless interesting to note that their work both complements the work of national statistical offices (by covering more data sources and linking them), and substitutes for them (when they sell access to their linked data to researchers). The message to statistical offices should be clear. On a daily basis, and even in the pre-crisis era, data firms like BvD show that it is possible to gather harmonized firm and financial data required for adequately advising policy-makers.

13.3.4   Towards a New Data Environment

The financial crisis has made it clear that the pre-crisis data environment was not capable of adequately informing regulators and policy-makers. As a response, statistical agencies have changed their data collection drastically. This is based on two essential ingredients. The first ingredient is a centralized view on data gathering. Firms and banks operate more and more in a global and interconnected world. To improve the comparability across countries and, equally importantly, to better grasp the complexity of markets, data standards should be the same across countries. The second ingredient, which is related to the previous one, is data warehousing. There already exist many high-quality databases, but one cannot fully exploit their potential because it is simply impossible to link them to each other in a consistent and country-comparable way. In a setting where institutions are often reluctant to share private information, the new data architecture will need a new governance system, such as the one put in place by the Financial Stability Board in the context of the G20 Data Gaps Initiative.

The data environment of the future will require some central coordination and guidelines. The Inter-Agency Group is a nice example of this (and it should continue its efforts). Equally important is to ensure structural funding for this type of data collection and linking.

A final recommendation is related to collaboration with academic researchers. An important motivation for the G20 Data Gaps Initiative was to develop data to enable policy-makers to analyse the impact of the financial crisis. However, the ultimate goal should, of course, be to prevent the next financial crisis (or at least to be able to provide early warnings). As markets keep evolving, researchers can play a crucial role in identifying new indicators of interest and new ways to use the data to better grasp the complexities of financial systems and markets.

13.4 Researcher-Generated Databases

By Bram De Rock, Arie Kapteyn, Julia Lane and Gugliemo Weber

Partly in response to frustration with the poor cross-country comparability of data, restricted access to data and/or simply the lack of collected data on issues of interest to them, a number of researchers have been involved in large-scale data collection, which they have turned into databases publicly available for the entire research community. This section describes three such highly successful data collection projects and the experiences of the researchers, amongst whom three of the authors, who played leading roles in their creation.

The chosen data projects provide a sample of the diversity in approaches and designs, but also of the challenges that such projects face. The first data project is the Measurement and Experimentation in the Social Sciences (MESS) project, an internet-based survey panel database created by Arie Kapteyn, and Marcel Das and Arthus van Soest from Tilburg University. Kapteyn has in the meantime led other internet-survey panel data projects including the American Life Panel and the Understanding America study. This first case study highlights the advantages of module-based internet surveys.

The second data project is the UMETRICS programme, a large-scale data project involving hundreds of partners in the US to better understand the impact of research funding. Julia Lane is one of the masterminds of UMETRICS to which she is contributing her extensive experience with other data projects, including the Longitudinal Employer-Household Dynamics (LEHD) programme in the US, and the NORC/University of Chicago data enclave. This second case study illustrates the added value of bringing several partners together to tackle large-scale data collection projects.

Our last case study is the Survey of Health, Ageing and Retirement in Europe (SHARE). In contrast to the MESS project, SHARE is a more traditionally organized social survey. The distinguishing feature of SHARE is that data are gathered in 21 countries and one region. SHARE is recognized as a European Research Infrastructure Consortium (ERIC). Guglielmo Weber is country team leader for Italy and deputy director of the SHARE Consortium. This case study illustrates the challenges linked to organizing such multinational data projects when funding is done at the national level.

The first three sections will, for each specific context and its corresponding objectives, shed light on the benefits and costs of researcher-generated databases. In the final section we discuss the general lessons learned from these projects and provide some recommendations for future data collection.

13.4.1   Measurement and Experimentation in the Social Sciences Project

The MESS project was developed in the Netherlands during the period 2006–2013 with funding from the NWO, the Dutch national research council. It was a collaboration between 8 of the 13 universities in the Netherlands to develop a very innovative and rich social survey on a panel of Dutch households. MESS resulted in the core Longitudinal Internet Studies for Social Sciences (LISS) panel (www.lissdata.nl), containing relatively standard household demographics, to which several modules with specific questions or experiments were added.

Given that the traditional way of collecting household data is time-consuming, and thus expensive, it was decided to save costs in two specific ways. First, the data are collected via the Internet and via innovative tools such as time use apps and internet bathroom scales. These features save time and provide convenience for respondents. They also remove the need for interviewers, which hugely reduces the cost of collecting this type of data. For instance, the cost per interview for the Panel Study of Income Dynamics (PSID) and the Health and Retirement Study (HRS) is between 1,200 and 1,500 US dollars. Data collection in the LISS panel is four times cheaper. It is also two to three times cheaper than traditional social surveys in the Netherlands.

Second, the dataset is constructed in modules. The LISS panel is the core module. It contains the household information typically available in social surveys. In addition, researchers from around the world could suggest extra modules, with for example, extra questions or an experiment. These extra modules were, of course, motivated by the specific research questions of these researchers who hoped to derive a publication from it, but, by design, the collected data were made immediately available to the whole research community. This innovative and flexible system optimally avoids overlap between several questionnaires, thereby reducing the marginal cost of each extra module. Moreover, data from different modules can be linked, allowing researchers to leverage rich data on many dimensions of household behaviour.

The MESS project was highly successful: 131 projects and experiments were conducted during the project, involving 85 different universities and institutes around the world. Unfortunately, it did not receive funding from NWO for the second phase of the project (2013–2023) and was therefore discontinued. The motivations for the funding decision were twofold. MESS had received infrastructure funding and there was an understanding that the infrastructure should be ready after seven years. In addition, collecting this type of data was no longer a priority. This decision illustrates that funding decisions do not always fully reflect the infrastructure needs of social sciences. In social sciences, collecting data is the main type of needed infrastructure. To capture all dimensions of life, it is crucial to follow individuals and households over a long period. This implies that collecting data is a long term, and actually a 'never-ending' project. While at some point the Netherlands was at the frontier of collecting household data, stopping the funding no longer allowed maintaining the LISS panel and its corresponding modules. A large and attractive infrastructure is wasted.

13.4.2 The UMETRICS Programme

The objective of the UMETRICS programme (iris.isr.umich.edu) is to construct an integrated dataset to measure the impact of public funding on research in the US. The ultimate goal is to answer questions such as 'how much is spent in each discipline and do we get value for money?', or 'does demand for funding by potential science performers imply a shortage of funding or a surfeit of other performers?'.

Although there are several datasets available containing useful information related to the impact of research funding in the US, no single dataset covers all relevant dimensions of both inputs and outputs of research. UMETRICS brings together several US partners (including statistical offices, more than 100 universities and researchers from different disciplines) in order to properly combine existing datasets and/or to create new data. For instance, new text mining approaches and automatic data creation methods were designed in order to create new measures on the impact of 'research output'.

UMETRICS shows that collaboration between research stakeholders can be highly effective. This process starts by identifying the existing gaps (i.e. existing datasets that are not linked or simply missing data). Consequently, funders, universities and the research community need to be convinced to build coalitions to fill these gaps. Building coalitions is essential to obtain the necessary funding and the access to existing data. Finally, a team of dedicated and flexible collaborators has to be assembled to carry out the project. This requires visionary researchers, designing for instance new data mining methods, as well as operational producers implementing these algorithms or adapting existing ones.

Visibility and exchanging ideas were two crucial ingredients during this process. In the development phase, this was done through newsletters, research workshops, and presentations. Subsequently, several user-friendly products, such as dashboards, short reports and data access, were developed.

UMETRICS has resulted in a unique data source, including novel impact measures, frequently used by researchers and policy-makers. It has generated research published in leading academic journals, such as Science, containing answers to questions similar to the ones mentioned above. It has the potential to be a major source of innovation and evidence-based policy recommendations on how to (re)design research funding schemes.

13.4.3   The Survey of Health, Ageing and Retirement in Europe

Population ageing is one of the important challenges of the twenty-first century for which we need to understand the individual, social and economic impact. SHARE (www.share-project.org) is an ambitious social survey that gathers, in 21 European countries and one region, data on health variables, socio-economic status and social participation for a representative sample of individuals aged 50 or more. Moreover, since ageing is a historical process, the same individuals are also followed through time. As of 2015, 6 waves of data which are, in principle, perfectly comparable across countries, have been completed.

The funding for the first three waves of the SHARE data was mainly provided by the European Commission. Then, in 2011, SHARE was recognized as a European Research Infrastructure Consortium (ERIC). This means that the main funding had to be provided by each individual country. This decentralized system put the sustainability of the SHARE project under severe pressure. For instance, in 2015, 65 different sources had to be combined and four countries did not obtain enough funding to continue to fund the project.

The SHARE data are frequently used by both researchers and policy-makers. Since the start of SHARE in 2005, more than 1,200 papers have been written on the basis of the collected data in one or more countries. SHARE has also provided evidence to support policy in Member States (e.g., retirement age and work conditions in France), at the European level (e.g., longterm projections of the costs of population ageing for DG EcFin) and at the international level (e.g., (re)migration corridors and social support for the World Bank).

The popularity and usefulness of the SHARE dataset are due to its interdisciplinary nature (it involves economists, sociologists, epidemiologists, geriatrics and psychologists) and its multinational and longitudinal aspects. Data that are comparable across countries are important to deal with big societal challenges, such as ageing. Otherwise it is impossible to compare, for instance, the different welfare state policies or to link individual decisions to institutional background variables. Given the many different languages in Europe and the sensitivity of many of the questions in the survey to their actual wording, this is of course not straightforward to implement. The same holds for the longitudinal aspect, which requires either convincing individuals to keep on participating and/or a complex tracking of individuals. However, the many academic and policy papers convincingly demonstrate the relevance of gathering this type of data.

13.4.4   Lessons from Successful Researcher-Led Databases

We briefly presented three very successful examples of researcher-generated databases. An important common feature of all these data projects is that they are governed by scientists. This ensures the quality of the data and, even more importantly, the relevance of the data. For instance, allowing researchers from around the world to add well-motivated questions and experiments to the core modules of the LISS panel increased its impact and take-up by scientists. Of course, data collection projects should be subjected to scientific review, but experience shows that giving researchers the opportunity to design their own databases can stimulate innovation in research and increase the returns on investment from data collection.

Another important feature in all three examples, and in many other large-scale researcher-led data collection projects, is that the collected data are made freely accessible as soon as possible for researchers. To some extent this should be obvious, since the data gathering is often supported by public funds. But, if we look for instance at the output that the SHARE data generate, it is also clear that this open access policy is essential to stimulate academic research and maximize the return on investment of the funds.

Researcher-led data collection does not, of course, minimize the role of statistical offices. On the contrary, statistical offices play at least two crucial and complementary roles. First, their role in setting data standards is vital in ensuring quality and international comparability. As discussed in Section 13.3, there is a need for central coordination in this respect. Second, there are huge benefits from linking the data gathered by statistical offices to these researcher-generated databases. The Nordic countries and the UMETRICS programme discussed above provide convincing examples that demonstrate that such linking is not only feasible, but boosts the research value of researcher-generated databases.

Data is the main infrastructure for most disciplines in social sciences. However, the nature of this infrastructure is in sharp contrast with, for instance, the natural sciences. Data gathering is, so to speak, a never ending project. This does not mean that one should keep on investing in a specific database, in particular if the data loses its relevance. But, it does imply that funders need a long-term vision and realize that, if one stops funding a database, it often automatically reduces significantly the value of the existing infrastructure. Funding mechanisms for social sciences should take this into account and not tie funding to today's policy problems. Instead, there should be clear guidelines for review panels analysing renewal requests.

Relatedly, and as the experience of SHARE shows, decentralized funding schemes are a serious threat to the sustainability of longitudinal and international databases. Not all national governments are equally interested in evidence-based research, which implies that it is almost impossible to obtain funding in these countries. This pleads for centralized funding for this type of international data collection projects.

Private funding can play a crucial role during the earlier stages of large-scale data collection projects. In contrast to public sources of research funding, private foundations are more flexible. They are more mission and people-oriented, and are therefore willing to take more risks and accept longer time horizons. Private funding has played a crucial role in the success of UMETRICS. Likewise, the US Longitudinal Employer-Household Dynamics programme (LEHD) had been funded for 20 years by private funds before becoming a national (publicly funded) statistical programme in 2008.

13.5   Data Generation in Controlled Environments

By Colin Camerer, Bruno Crépon, and Georg Kirchsteiger

For a long time, economics has been considered a nonexperimental science, and empirical work was done only with field data. This has changed drastically during the last four decades when more and more economists have begun to conduct experiments. One can distinguish between two types of economic experiments: Laboratory experiments and randomized control trials (RCTs) in field settings. This section describes both methods, their contributions to economics and recent developments in methods and applications of these two kinds of experiments.

13.5.1   Laboratory Experiments

The basic idea of a lab experiment is simple: Participants are put into an artificially-designed and controlled economic situation in which they make decisions. The canonical experimental design creates endowments and induced preferences over outcomes, and specifies a set of rules which compile participants' choices into outcomes. The rules can be very simple, in decision-making experiments, or specify a game-theoretic or market structure in more complicated experiments. The target of discovery is what choices people actually make.

Lab experimental situations are 'real' in the sense that the participants' decisions have an impact on the rewards they receive for participation in the experiment. Monetary reward is typically used because almost everyone is motivated to earn more money, and marginal reward is positive (there is no satiation, as might occur with points, public reports of success, or other non-monetary rewards). In order to test economic theories, the actual decisions of the participants are recorded and compared to the decisions predicted by economic theory. Careful control of endowments and preferences, and explanation of the rules determining outcomes, create conditions under which theoretical predictions should apply. Experimental results contradicting established economic theories are also used to guide the development of new, better theories.

Experimental data generated in a carefully designed and controlled environment have many advantages compared to field data. First of all, the researcher observes directly the variables of interest – no proxies are needed. All relevant variables can either be induced by design, or measured. One can also easily compare the results of treatments differing only in one aspect of the experiment. This allows for a direct test of a causal relationship. Experiments can also be purely replicated – that is, replicated with the intent of reproducing original experimental conditions as closely as possible. Pure replication checks whether the results of the initial experiment were a false positive, are robust to inevitable small changes, or resulted from biases in investigator reporting or journal selection practices. To allow for replications, experimental papers typically include the written instructions given to the participants. Going even further, it is common practice, and is also required by some leading journals, that researchers make their experimental data and analysis code available for the purpose of making replication easy. Note that RCTs in field sites typically require access to a group of participants, and may be more difficult to purely replicate in comparison to lab experiments.

Two major concerns about results of lab experiments are the robustness and the generalizability of experimental findings. Fortunately, robustness can be easily checked by doing experiments using theoretically motivated variations of the initial experimental design. Indeed, robustness explorations have been done in many areas, particularly when initial results contradicted received theory. Another important concern is whether lab results generalize to particular field settings. First note that most lab experiments test theories which purport to apply generally to many field settings. And since field settings differ on many dimensions, if one desired to maximize generalizability of a lab experiment there is no obvious metric for doing so. However, in many cases, lab designs have taken special care to match corresponding field settings as closely as possible. In general, when the design in the lab closely matches the conditions in the field, observed behaviour is usually very similar, as judged by responses to changes in variables such as prices or description (Camerer, 2015).

Ideally, there is a dynamic complementarity between field data, experimental data research, and economic theory. Take 'gift exchange' as an example:

Akerlof's 1982 theory of involuntary unemployment assumed that workers and firms are prone to exchange gifts, in which firms pay higher wages and workers repay the wage gift with high effort. In theory, this mechanism is used by firms to induce workers to provide reciprocal effort in situations otherwise characterized by moral hazard. This hypothesis was confirmed by many experiments (beginning with Fehr et al., 1993), which in turn led researchers to develop theories to explain reciprocity (e.g., Dufwenberg and Kirchsteiger, 2004) and to look for similar kinds of reciprocity in the field (see e.g., Falk, 2007). The interplay between the lab and field data can also go the other way. For example, the winner's curse was first observed in field data on oil-lease bidding (Capen et al., 1971). It was then extensively analysed in lab experiments (summarized by Kagel and Levin, 2002).

Lessons from Lab Experiments

During the last 30 years, lab experiments have become well-established and central to economics research. This is reflected by the number of articles reporting experimental results that are published in economic journals. Between 2006–2010, about 100 experimental papers were published in leading general journals (*American Economic Review, Econometrica, Journal of Political Economy, Quarterly Journal of Economics, Review of Economic Studies*, and *Economic Journal*), and more than 350 papers were published in specialized journals (such as *Games and Economic Behavior, Journal of Economic Behavior and Organization*, and *Experimental Economics*).[15]

While there are also some experimental studies in macroeconomics and political economy, the huge majority of the papers (about 95%) investigate four broadly defined fields: Individual decisions, social preferences, markets, and games. This reflects the close relation of lab experiments with (micro)economic theory. Most of the experimental findings are quite robust up to plausible variations of the experimental design. These robust findings include:

Markets. In market experiments with induced supply and demand for a homogenous good, observed prices and quantities converge quickly to the market clearing equilibrium, in particular when trade is organized in a centralized manner ('double auctions'). This result holds for very thin markets (even with only three traders on each market side), for a huge variety of different demand and supply conditions, for multiple connected markets operating at the same time, for different subject pools, etc. (for an overview see part 1 of Plott and Smith, 2008).

Games. In many experimental games, the observed outcome coincides with the Nash equilibrium prediction. Systematic deviations from the Nash equilibrium prediction have induced the development of level-k and quantal response theory, which can (most of the time) explain the observed deviations from Nash.

Auctions. In experimental auctions, one typically observes the winner's curse in common value auctions, and overbidding in auctions where bidders' values are privately known and unaffiliated.

Social preferences. Participants do not simply care about their own earnings. Fairness, reciprocity motives and social image motivations also have an impact on their behaviour (see e.g., Fehr et al., 1998).

Public goods. In games of voluntary provision of public good, participants typically start with a contribution level of 50 per cent of their endowment. This is followed by a decrease of the contributions to 10 per cent. If participants have the opportunity to punish each other at a personal cost, contributions start and stay at high levels because low contributions are sometimes punished, with important cultural variations (Herrmann et al., 2008).

Monopoly. In experimental markets with a monopolist, the actual price demanded by the monopolist is below the monopoly price because buyers withhold demand, which disciplines the monopolist to lower prices.

In all these cases the experiments were typically replicated 10–100 times, either as pure replications or with an initial replication followed by changes to the original design to test the robustness of the findings. A typical example is provided by the public good experiments, with and without punishment opportunities (see Herrmann et al., 2008).

On the other hand, some experimental findings are not as robust, due to endogenous expectations, local norms, or other reasons. An example of this is provided by experimental financial markets. Some, but not all, of these markets experience price bubbles and, when bubbles occur, their size differs substantially.

Lab experiments are also used in teaching economics. More and more introductory classes in economics use experiments to bring theoretical concepts like the impact of incentives, or market equilibration, or social dilemmas, to life. This increasing use of simple economic experiments arises from the fact that the results are reliable. The dependability of economic experiments is similar to other experimental demonstrations, such as visual illusions that are used to teach principles of perception in cognitive psychology, and chemical reactions used in basic chemistry. On the other hand, experimental economics still has limited influence on the core courses in economics graduate training. Even at institutions such as Caltech, where most economics faculty do some experiments, PhD students can graduate without knowing anything at all about the methods or findings.

New Developments and Outlook for Lab Experiments
A new development in lab experiments is the use of biomedical tools. This started with the use of eye-tracking tools and the measurement of response

time. functional magnetic resonance imaging (fMRI), electroencephalograms (EEG), and causal administration of bioactive substances have also been used (typically in co-operation with neuroscientists) to get a better understanding of the detailed biological mechanisms underlying the observed behaviour, and of individual differences (e.g., Camerer, 2013). So far, the impact of this research on mainstream economics has been limited. It is unlikely that the economics profession will begin to use these new tools as enthusiastically as it has taken up 'conventional' (choice-based) lab experiments. However, as for the impact of psychology experiments, biological evidence may have some impact on theory, in understanding emotions, self-control, addiction, and other topics, even if those data are collected by noneconomists (or in occasional collaborations with economists).

Another important development is the use of advanced technology to recruit volunteer participants outside of the usual constraints of a college campus. Why should participants have to come to a physical lab, when modern technology enables them to participate remotely, perhaps even on mobile phones? To this end, a large number of experiments increasingly use online 'labour markets' such as Amazon Mechanical Turk (*'Mturk'*). An even more dramatic step is to conduct abstract experiments outside of the places where the researchers work, a method called lab-in-the-field (pioneered in economic anthropology, for example, Henrich et al., 2005 and see Haushofer et al., 2014). Lab-in-the-field experiments can address the important concern that experimental social science has traditionally oversampled highly educated and rich subjects from industrialized countries while striving to make generalizations about everyone on earth (Henrich et al., 2010).

13.5.2   *Randomized Control Trials*

Economic experiments can also be used to evaluate the impact of (proposed) policy measures. The basic idea of such Randomized Control Trials (RCTs) is the following. A policy measure is proposed in order to achieve a certain goal. Before the measure is implemented broadly, randomly chosen potential 'recipients' of the measure receive the measure ('treatment group'). Some other randomly chosen potential recipients do not get the measure, but are observed with respect to the variable(s) of interest ('control group'). Since the treatment and the control group are randomly selected, there is no systematic difference between the two groups except for being subject to the policy measure or not. Therefore, any observed difference between the two groups, after the measure has been implemented, can be attributed *causally* to the policy measure and the result is an unbiased predictor of the impact of the proposed measure. This allows assessing the impact and efficiency of the measure and to improve its design before it is rolled out generally.

The provision of summer jobs to disadvantaged teenagers in order to reduce their criminality provides an illustration of the approach. Some disadvantaged youngsters (the treatment group) get summer jobs, while others do not (the control group). To assess the efficiency of this programme, the crime rates of both groups are compared. To make sure that the observed differences in the crime rates are indeed due to the summer job, and not due to other systematic differences between the two groups, both groups are randomly chosen. In an RCT study conducted among 1634 disadvantaged high school youth in Chicago, Heller (2014) found that such a programme reduced violence by 43 per cent over a period of 16 months and 3.95 fewer violent-crime arrests per 100 youth.

RCTs have some important advantages over field data to evaluate the impact of policy measures. The main advantage is the ability to establish and assess the causal link between the policy measure and the outcome of interest. Results are obtained in a clear, understandable and transparent framework. The policy decision is a complicated and long process. Thanks to the transparency and palpable scientific rigour surrounding their use, RCTs provide results which can inform the policy-making process efficiently about the right programmes and their impacts.

Lessons from RCTs

There has long been a demand by policy-makers and institutions for scientific evidence about the impact of policies. The first RCTs were implemented in the US to this effect by large nonprofit consultancies. Famous examples include employment programmes or changes in the unemployment insurance system (for an overview, see Meyer, 1995) or, more recently, changes in the health insurance system (the Oregon experiment, see Finkelstein et al., 2015). In some cases the results of these RCTs have led to major changes in policy, for example, the National Job Training Partnership Act Study (see Bloom et al., 1997).

Use of RCTs is not restricted to the US, however. In France, anonymous resumes have been proposed as a measure against discrimination on the job market. Behaghel et al. (2014) used an RCT to measure its potential impact and found it resulted in worsened outcomes for minorities. This led the French employment agency to abandon the idea. Martin Hirsch, the French High Commissioner for Youth, set up an 'Experimental Fund for Youth' in 2008, to encourage innovative programmes for youth as well as their rigorous testing and evaluation. In the context of this fund a large number of RCTs have been launched to address youth policy questions in education, health, housing, and employment.[16] The impact of RCTs on policy implementation has been strongest in developing countries. There also, there is a high demand for evidence. This has given rise to close co-operation between researchers, NGOs, and aid donors, with RCTs used to evaluate programmes in fields like health, education, gender and agriculture.

The development of RCTs has achieved several outcomes. One first outcome of RCTs is their ability to update and, when needed, correct beliefs about the effectiveness of different policies. Education in developing countries is an example. Measured by additional years of schooling per 100$ spent, policies informing parents about the returns on schooling and policies on deworming of primary school children have turned out to be far more effective than other measures like cash transfers, merit scholarships, or free school uniforms.[17]

Microcredit provides another example where RCTs have led to a shift in beliefs about which policies are effective. Due to the widespread belief that microcredit is a strong tool to alleviate poverty, politicians as well as aid donors in many parts of the world have supported microcredit institutions. However, RCTs conducted in six countries (Bosnia and Herzegovina, Ethiopia, India, Mexico, Mongolia and Morocco) have found that while microcredits have a positive impact on the scale of activities, they do not significantly improve earnings of beneficiaries (Bauchet et al., 2011). These results changed beliefs about the promises of microcredit. Microcredit should be seen as one tool, among many others, to fight poverty.

Another outcome of RCTs is that, in some instances, it has been possible to test important aspects of economic theories. One example is the issue of cost-sharing. Many programmes involve some cost-sharing, where the recipient of a certain programme has to share some of the costs. Bed nets, which are one of the most effective tools to fight malaria, are one such example. They are usually sold at a subsidized price. The reason for the subsidy is the belief that otherwise many people would not buy it, so the demand would be too small. On the other hand, bed nets are not given for free because of the belief that people have to pay something to value a product. So the question is twofold: Is the demand price-elastic? If yes, does giving the bed nets for free reduce their use? To answer these questions, Cohen and Dupas (2010) ran an RCT where participants were first asked whether they were willing to buy the bed net at a price that was randomly determined. This allowed the researchers to determine the price-elasticity of the demand. In the second step, some participants received their bed nets for free, and use of the bed nets was compared between those who paid for it and those who received it for free. The results were clear-cut: the answer to the first question is yes, demand is highly price-sensitive. This replicates other studies looking at the price-elasticity of water disinfectant (Ashraf et al., 2010) or deworming drugs (Kremer and Miguel, 2007). And, interestingly, the answer to the second question is no: the use of bed nets was not influenced by whether it was given for free or not.

A second example of the use of RCTs for testing theories concerns displacement effects in labour markets. A concern about active labour market policies, that is, policies used to bring unemployed back to the labour market, is that the benefits obtained by the beneficiaries of these policies come at the expense of workers who do not have access to these programmes. This concern has been around for long but, until recently, the presence of this effect or its magnitude had not been measured. Crépon et al. (2013) developed and implemented an experiment to address this question. The design was based on a double randomization. In a first step, markets were selected to develop or not the programme, generating 'test' and 'control' markets. In a second step, a fraction of the potential participants in test markets were randomly assigned to the programme and some to a control group. Comparing potential participants in the control group in test markets and control markets has shown that there is indeed a displacement effect and that it is substantial. Results showed a substantial improvement in the employment situation of beneficiaries, but no improvement of potential participants in test markets as a whole compared to control markets.

A final example is related to price incentives. One general belief is that for a price policy to have an impact, it has to substantially change financial incentives. For example, if it comes to subsidizing a product, the subsidy has to be large. RCTs have shown that this is not necessarily the case: large impacts can be obtained from very small incentives. One example is immunization programmes. These programmes often face the challenge that participation is low. Too few people start the immunization and/or too many drop out. In the context of an immunization programme for children in rural India, Banerjee et al. (2010) found that even a reward as small as one kilo of lentils considerably increases participation. The authors tested two different treatments. In 30 villages they installed reliable immunization camps and in 30 other villages they installed the same type of immunization camp combined with small incentives (one kilo of lentils for each child for each show-up). 74 villages served as control group. The authors found that twice as many children finished the immunization programme when it was combined with small incentives relative to when it was not.

New Developments and Outlook for RCTs

Faced with a policy design question, policy-makers have many ways to try to answer it. All these potential answers are based on ideas about mechanisms at play and on views about what matters or not. Simultaneously, there is a demand from policy-makers to learn about the impact of their programmes. RCTs are increasingly used to meet this demand. They have shown that not all the solutions work, that some beliefs about programme efficiency and underlining mechanisms are incorrect. They have also shown that the consequences of mistakes can be of first order importance.

RCTs allow accumulating two types of knowledge: about programmes that work or not, but also about mechanisms at work or not. This knowledge enriches the information set of policy-makers when thinking about new policies. Because of their versatility and ease of implementation, RCTs have also allowed policy-makers to test new ideas and policies cheaply and are therefore contributing to innovative policies.

Challenges remain, however, regarding their external validity. This is an active and interesting area of current research. One external validity challenge for RCTs is that the selection into the treatment or the control group might have a direct impact on the behaviour of subjects (the so-called '*Hawthorne and John Henry effect*') and this might therefore lead to biased estimates of the policy impact. Aldashev et al. (2015) show how such effect can be minimized by a careful communication about the randomness of the selection process. Another concern is that a general introduction of a policy measure might trigger general equilibrium effects that cannot be captured by RCTs. The likelihood of such effects is small when the policy measure concerns only a small fraction of the population and/or has a relatively minor impact on the recipients. Most of the RCTs fulfil one or the other of the two conditions.

An open question for many RCTs is the generalization of findings found in one country to other countries, contexts and cultures. While some of the studies discussed in this section are cross-country, most of the RCTs concentrate on a single country and context. Replication in other countries would be desirable, but is often not possible due to financial constraints. Another open question concerns the (absence of) corruption. When a treatment is tested, the researchers make sure that the rules are followed and that no corruption occurs. But when the policy is rolled out to the general public, corruption, for example, of the civil servants involved, might actually reduce the effectiveness of the tested programmes relative to the results found in the RCTs. The next section will return to some of these issues.

13.6   The Changing Face of Public and Private-Sector Collaborations in Economic Research

By Estelle Cantillon, Liran Einav, Asim I. Khwaja and Markus Mobius

An emerging trend in economic research is the development of new forms of collaboration between researchers and private- and public-sector organizations. One form that such collaborations have taken is closer relationships with private firms for access to their proprietary data. A complementary form has been collaborations between researchers and policy-makers, where the focus is not only on data, but also on helping design and recalibrate policy interventions. In both cases, these collaborations are providing researchers with unmatched data access and data quality, as well as opportunities to investigate novel research questions or existing open questions in new ways.

Figure 13.2, taken from Einav and Levin (2014), illustrates some of these trends. The figure shows the percentage of papers published in the American Economic Review (AER) that obtained an exemption from the journal's data availability policy, as a share of all papers published by the AER that relied on some form of data (excluding simulations and lab experiments). Almost 50 per cent of empirical papers published in the past two years benefited from an exemption, a big jump from the situation less than 10 years earlier. Of course, proprietary data include other types of data than those obtained through close collaborations with public and private organizations, but it does provide a sense of the speed at which these changes are taking place.[18]

This section describes several examples of fruitful public and private research collaborations, and uses them to discuss their potential and their implications for how we organize, evaluate and fund research in economics.

13.6.1   New Private-Sector Collaborations in Economic Research

More and more data are generated by private firms. Firms now routinely collect data on their interactions with customers, on the activities of their employees, or on their suppliers. These data are often stored in electronic format reducing the cost of their retrieval and handling. For some of these firms (the 'data-driven' firms), the management and exploitation of these data are at the core of their business. Examples include Google, Microsoft, or Yahoo!, to name some of the most famous. For others, data represent a way to tailor their marketing efforts, optimize their pricing, or simply improve their organization. For yet some others, these sources of data are left unexploited for lack of expertise or awareness of their potential.

The richness of these data is a goldmine for researchers. Data that cover the internal workings of firms offer a chance to understand their operations like nothing before. For example, Tucker (2008) examined the roll out and the determinants of adoption of a new video messaging technology in an investment bank, using data on their employees and the 2.4 million calls that they made over a three year period. The data contain information about the hierarchical relationships between employees as well as their position within the informal communication network. This allowed the researcher to measure 'whose adoption matters' for the decision of an employee to adopt.

Because their coverage is different from other data sources, private proprietary data also allow researchers to look at new issues. For example, Adams et al. (2009) used transaction-level data from a US auto sales and financing company to document consumer behaviour in the subprime market. This unique dataset, covering 500,000 applicants and 150,000 loans originated between 2001 and 2004, as well as subsequent payments, default, and recovery outcomes, provides a great lens into the behaviour of the poor and unstable (e.g., undocumented workers), who are often under-represented in survey or

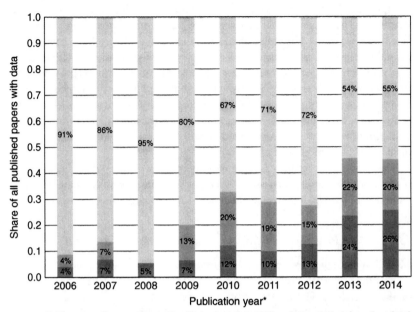

Figure 13.2 The rising use of nonpublicly available data in economic research (Einav and Levin, 2014).

administrative data. The data allowed the researchers to document the level of adverse selection and moral hazard in this understudied market that happened to be important in the outset of the subprime crisis in 2007.

A third advantage of these data is that their higher granularity can be useful to identify natural experiments arising from micro-level variations, thereby providing stronger identification. For example, Einav et al. (2014) used detailed browsing and purchase data on the population of eBay customers in the US to study the effect of sales taxes on internet commerce. In the US, online retailers must collect sales taxes only on purchases by residents of the same state. No taxes are collected for interstate purchases. The authors identified thousands of items and millions of browsing sessions in which individuals clicked on an item only to find out whether they were subject to the sales tax (if they lived in the same state as the seller). The difference in behaviour between the two groups of buyers then allowed the researchers to estimate the tax elasticity in a way that would be hard to measure from aggregate data.

These data have their own issues, however. They are collected for the needs of the business, not for research. As a result, the data may not cover all the variables one would ideally want. Their format may not be optimized for research use, and in fact can rapidly change over time as internal IT systems are upgraded. The data may not be kept for a long time, reducing the potential time-span that one can study. Documentation is occasionally poor. Last but not least, they can be highly sensitive for the firm.

This means that access to these data tends to be more effort intensive, and involve a longer and riskier process than other sources of data.[19] Relationships are crucial here. Successful projects have often had a cheer-leader inside the firm. Relationships are crucial at the beginning of the project because a minimum level of trust needs to be established between the researchers and the firm giving them access to its data. They are crucial during the project because the firm will often need to continue to devote time and internal resources to provide access to the data, explain the data, and/or extract additional data, and because preliminary results may force the researchers and the firm to reorient the research question. Finally, they are crucial at the end of the project because the firm will often request to first clear the paper before it is circulated publicly.

Data-driven firms are special in the context of private-sector collaborations with researchers. Data form the core of their business and they already make heavy use of data scientists to put them to good use. However, they are often interested in research that can help better harness the power of their data and inform the design of their products. To foster research on questions of relevance for them, many of these firms – including Microsoft, Yahoo! and eBay – have experimented over time with different forms of engagement with researchers. This has gone from sponsoring papers and conferences on selected themes to establishing their own research labs that recruit economists on the academic job market and have a visitor programme to encourage academic economists to work on issues of relevance to them. Athey and Mobius (2012), Celis et al. (2014), and Blake et al. (2015) are examples of empirical research papers that have grown out of these collaborations.

An interesting aspect of these data-intensive firms is their ability to experiment with different product designs or prices easily and at a low cost. In fact, many online platforms already routinely carry out experiments on a small share of their operations and then implement the successful ones. It is a small step to the development of carefully crafted field experiments for research purposes (in the spirit of RCTs discussed in Section 13.5). Blake et al. (2015) designed such an experiment to measure the returns on paid keyword search in search engines and found them to be much lower than previously understood.

13.6.2 New Public-Sector Collaborations in Economic Research

New forms of collaborations are also developing between academics and policy-makers. The drivers there are different: this is not just about greater data availability – though that is often part of this as well – but more about a genuine interest, on both sides, to go beyond the traditional interactions that characterize consulting relationships or policy evaluations towards a deeper collaboration where researchers can directly contribute to policy design.

This form of collaboration has been particularly salient in developing and emerging economies which, often lacking internal research capacities, have been relatively more willing to engage researchers in this manner. The Evidence for Policy Design (EPoD) research group at the Harvard Kennedy School has been at the forefront of these developments. The group is involved in long-term policy research engagements with government agencies in several developing countries, including Pakistan (education, taxation, and reform of the civil service), India (air pollution), and Indonesia (welfare programmes). Their early experience served to develop a systematic '*Smart Policy Design*' approach to such policy research engagements. In this approach, researchers and policy-makers start by identifying questions of common interest, then jointly diagnose the underlying factors that are at play. Next, they use theory to collaboratively design potential mechanisms that could address these factors, followed by empirically testing the assumptions and implications of these mechanisms as the policies are rolled out, and finally use these feedback loops to carry out regular policy recalibrations.

The research upside of this approach is significant. The joint definition of the research question ensures its policy relevance and thus the potential impact of the research. The ability to carry out large-scale policy experiments addresses existing concerns about the scalability and external validity of 'standard' randomized control trials (see Section 13.5). The continuity of the relationship allows researchers to address the dynamic aspects of policy-making, including the need to recalibrate based on new information, which are often absent in 'standard' research.

Like for private-sector collaborations, relationships are crucial. Trust is built over a long period of time, through engagement at multiple levels of governments and agencies, where researchers have to demonstrate the value they can bring. In the case of the Smart Policy Design programme, early institutionalization between faculty members at Harvard and the relevant administrations and agencies, as well as the development of executive education programmes targeted at senior civil servants in these countries contribute to further trust.

One example of the potential of such work is an ongoing multi-year (now in its sixth year) collaboration between researchers at Harvard, LSE and MIT and the Excise & Taxation department in Punjab (Pakistan). The researchers have been involved in three distinct projects to date. The first was the design and testing of different pay for performance schemes for tax collectors (Khan et al., 2014). The second is using merit-based transfers and posting as a way of rewarding civil servant performance. The third project involves credibly linking property tax payments to better provision of local public goods and services in order to rebuild tax morale and the citizen's social compact with the state. Each of these projects arose from specific questions that were of interest to both policy-makers and researchers, introduced policy mechanisms that were informed by theory, and involved large scale RCTs in order to produce plausible causal estimates of the impact of these mechanisms. Each project started with a pilot phase where initial design was recalibrated using small-scale experiments. Access to proprietary data (tax collector level collection rates etc.) was also critical. The projects were natural follow-ups to one another. Such an intense, theory and data driven process would not have been feasible without having built the trust and mutual interest needed for a long-term relationship.

Duflo et al. (2014) provide another example. Their research builds on a long-term relationship between the researchers and the Gujarat Pollution Control Board (GPCB) in the Indian state of Gujarat. Their paper combines an RCT approach designed to change environmental auditors' choice and frequency of the firms to audit, with 5 years of administrative records of correspondence between regulated firms and GPCB. The implementation of the RCT changed GPCB's financial resources dedicated to environmental audits as well as some staffing and managerial processes, in a way that would not have been possible without the full backing and active involvement of GPCB. The data allowed the researchers to estimate the cost of regulation in this setting and quantify the benefits of discretion in the selection of the firms to audit.

Other applications, this time to the design of welfare programmes, include the work of Alatas and coauthors with the Indonesian government on the re-design of their social welfare programmes (Alatas et al., 2012a, Alatas et al., 2012b, Alatas et al., 2016) or Muralidharan's collaboration with the state of Andhra Pradesh (India) on the use of biometric identification cards for enhancing the effectiveness of welfare payments (Muralidharan et al., 2015).

13.6.3   Risks, Challenges and Outlook

We have so far mostly outlined the research benefits of these new forms of collaboration between researchers and private firms or governments. They are not without risks, however.

A significant risk for researchers is that the collaboration breaks down, after much effort has been expended, but before the research outputs are cleared and the results published. A common reason for such break-down is staff turnover. A manager or department head, who was initially supporting the project, changes jobs or moves firms/departments, leaving the project without an inside cheer-leader. Another reason is that the results are too sensitive. Adams et al.'s 2009 work on the subprime market described above is an example. The paper was first circulated during the outset of the subprime crisis and drew much attention in the trade journals of subprime lending. Given the regulatory risks associated with the results, the firm that gave them the data froze the dissemination of follow-up work for two years, after which the authors managed to negotiate a 'termination' deal and got their results published (Einav et al., 2012 and Einav et al., 2013).

Maintaining trust and interest, over the long run, is therefore essential. Identifying research questions that are of interest to both parties is useful. A suitable definition of the research question may also prevent tensions ex-post when the results turn out to be unacceptable – for regulatory, public relations, or competitiveness reasons. Designing the relationship for multiple research outputs is another (complementary) solution. Initial research outputs build appetite for the following ones, reduce the risks borne by researchers who can already publish some results, and alleviate the tension between the short-term horizons of policy-makers and firms, and the longer-run horizons of researchers. More generally, successful collaborations require a change of mindset from researchers, who need to be more problem-driven (identifying a question of relevance to the other party) than solution-driven (identifying a dataset that best suits the effect the researchers are interested in).

An important hurdle for many researchers is nondisclosure agreements (NDAs) which not only involve them and the data owners, but also their institutions. Given the sensitivity of their data, data owners often require stringent conditions to guarantee confidentiality and high penalties in case of breach, which legal offices of research institutions are reluctant to accept.[20] Over time, best practices that are acceptable to all will emerge based on the more successful experiences.

An obvious risk arising from such a necessarily close relationship between the researchers and the data owners is the risk of conflict of interest and the loss of scientific integrity that comes with it. The nondisclosure of the data only exacerbates this risk (though going through a rigorous academic review process does help). Financial independence is useful here. It frames the relationship as one between equals, rather than consulting, and provides credible walk-off threat points.[21] Several leading journals in economics are now requesting authors declare any financial interests, including funding, related to their research before it is published.

In the end, however, the risk for scientific integrity is probably not much higher than for other empirical work. Biased reporting (due to conflict of interest) may be a bigger issue but, on the other hand, the involvement of parties with a direct interest in the research actually provides greater discipline against other types of scientific fraud, such as cooking the results. Indeed, the firm or department will not continue the research or policy reform without being convinced about its usefulness. The difficulty of replication may not be such a big issue either. Even when data are available, pure replications are rare in economics because the culture of replication does not exist (Sebransk et al., 2010).

If the results are sufficiently important, similar databases can be used as a substitute for replication. Moreover, to the extent that the implications coming out of the work get adopted by the private or policy partner, this may allow for an even higher level of continuous testing and field 'replication'.

A final challenge is the complexity of handling and analysing data produced by some of the data-intensive firms for which the standard statistical software packages are inadequate. Most economists do not have the programming skills and technical training (aggregation algorithms, machine learning, etc.) to take advantage of some of these data. In fact, some of the projects reported here have data scientists as coauthors for exactly these reasons. Things are changing. Some graduate programmes in economics now offer courses on statistical learning and other methods for 'Big Data'. In the UK, the Economic and Social Research Council (ESRC) is sponsoring the development of doctoral courses to handle new forms of data such as internet data, satellite and aerial imagery, and geolocation and other tracking data.

Scientific disciplines always adapt to scientific opportunities and practices. New forms of research collaborations will be no different. Journals will continue to adapt their practices to the needs of the profession as they have done in the past for rules on collaborative work, data sharing and financial interest disclosure. Likewise, larger and possibly multi-disciplinary teams of researchers are likely to eventually impact how we organize and fund research in economics, and how we evaluate individual contributions for co-authored research.[22]

Despite these risks and challenges, we are optimistic regarding the research potential of these new forms of research collaboration. There is a lot of terrific information lying in private hands or simply outside of official data and much of it does not have good publicly available substitutes. The possibility of jointly designing and recalibrating policies can catalyse really exciting and novel work. We should simply be aware of the constraints and optimize around them.

13.7   Concluding Comments

An easy prediction to make is that economics will be more data-intensive in the future, and that both existing and new sources of data will continue to contribute to significant research breakthroughs. This chapter covered many different types of data and argued that each has its unique benefits. It is important for economic research to acknowledge the benefits of this diversity and the potential complementarity among data producers.

Each data type comes with its own constraints and challenges. They were described in detail in the corresponding section. If one general message stands out it is that all stakeholders have a role to play in improving the production, quality and accessibility of data for economic research. **Researchers** are, of course, at the heart of this. They can build trust and support for greater data access by showcasing the value of their research based on these data. They can contribute to data innovation when they act as academic entrepreneurs in large-scale data collection efforts. They can develop new methods to generate and leverage data that can increase our understanding of human behaviour and the economy. **Funders** need to design flexible funding instruments that meet the needs of the diversity and specificity of data in economics. They can also play a role in federating researchers' interests for training and promoting data access. **Statistical agencies and central banks** are essential to ensure the quality of data, define standards, and develop metadata to promote data harmonization and linking across countries. **Data firms** will continue to provide value by harmonizing and linking firm data that lie outside of the scope of official data. **Research institutions** need to establish protocols to guarantee the integrity of the data entrusted to their researchers and build the required ethical and legal expertise to support their researchers' ventures into new data sources. **Journals** are important to maintain the highest standards of scientific integrity. The leading journals in the profession have in the past accompanied changes in the way research is organized and produced. They should continue to do so. Last but not least, **governments and policy-makers** are essential because they provide the political impetus that makes changes possible. Their leadership will be determining for the likely developments in key areas for research such as access to microdata, cross-country data harmonization and linking, and research funding for data infrastructure. At the European level, this means:

1. ensuring that the current revision of the Data Protection Directive does not reduce access to personal data for researchers,
2. promoting the introduction of legal provisions in European and national legislations to secure legitimate access to data for researchers, as in done in several Nordic countries,
3. promoting the introduction of mandates for statistical offices, including Eurostat, to service researchers,
4. clarifying the legal framework for the access of confidential data across borders,
5. mandating data harmonization and linking of existing business data across Member States, and developing access to such data for researchers,
6. reforming the current funding mechanism for data infrastructure to meet the needs of data infrastructure in the social sciences, including securing stable European-level funding for cross-national data collection efforts.

Notes

1. This explains why this chapter has an unusual number of coauthors. It is based on the presentations made and discussions that took place at the COEURE workshop on 'developments in data and methods for economic research' in July 2015. Authors of individual sections are indicated under the title of the section. Reference to this

chapter can be made to the chapter as a whole by citing all the authors or to an individual section by citing only the authors and the title of that section. This chapter represents the views of the authors and not of their institutions.

2. The main legal texts at the EU level are regulation 45/2001 on data protection, and regulations 223/2009 and 557/2013 on the access to confidential data for scientific purposes, as well as their translation into national laws and regulations.

3. At the time of writing this text, the Data Protection Directive of 1995 is being revised with ongoing discussions between the Council, the European Commission and the European Parliament. Some of the proposed changes risk restricting access to personal data without consent. See, for example, the position statement issued by the Wellcome Trust with the backing of hundreds of European research agencies and academic associations: http://www.wellcome.ac.uk/stellent/groups/corporatesite/ @policy_communications/documents/web_document/wtp059364.pdf.

4. A less user-friendly version of virtual access, sometimes referred to as remote execution, requires researchers to send their codes without seeing the data; the codes are applied to the data and the output is checked for risk of confidentiality breach before it is sent to the researchers.

5. Castellani and Koch (2015) also identify barriers in terms of the ability to link different datasets. This is not reported here.

6. Annex II of the NORIA-net (2014) report describes the legal and organizational conditions under which access to microdata including biobanks and register data is organized in Nordic countries.

7. As a point of comparison, Eurostat services about 300–400 survey-based projects per year.

8. See https://educationendowmentfoundation.org.uk/evaluation/.

9. This echoes a similar concern in the US for facilitating access to administrative data. See, for example, Card et al. (2010).

10. The ADRN is one component of the Big Data Network initiative (http://www.esrc .ac.uk/research/our-research/big-data-network/). A second component is the Business and Local Government Data Research Centre that seeks to make data collected by business and local government available to researchers. A third component focuses on the third sector and social media data.

11. Because of its motivation, the focus of this section is on business data.

12. 'The Financial Crisis and Information Gaps', October 29, 2009, available at: https:// www.imf.org/external/np/g20/pdf/102909.pdf.

13. See http://www.financialstabilityboard.org/what-we-do/policy-development/ additional-policy- areas/addressing-data-gaps/ for details.

14. An online Handbook on Methodology of Modern Business Statistics available at http://www.cros-portal.eu/content/handbook-methodology-modern-business-statistics was developed and serves as a template for future exercises. Funded projects are described at http://ec.europa.eu/eurostat/statistics-explained/index .php/MEETS_programme_-_towards_more_efficient_enterprise_and_trade_ statistics.

15. See Charles Noussair's website: www.slideshare.net/charlies1000/ laboratory-experiments.

16. See http://www.experimentation.jeunes.gouv.fr/.

17. See http://www.povertyactionlab.org/policy-lessons/education/student-participation.

18. Proprietary data also include data that the researcher had to purchase from a commercial data vendor and administrative data.
19. There are also occasional data dumps where firms give out data to researchers because they know one of the researchers personally or through contacts (Cohen and Einav, 2007 is one such example). Access in this case is fast and easy but the one-shot nature of the relationship prevents any follow-up or additional data extraction based on initial results and is not free of legal risk about data disclosure.
20. One of us was involved in a NDA that required her research institution to accept responsibility for any accident or death caused by her presence on the firm's premises.
21. Interestingly several funding agencies are moving towards demanding that the data collected as part of funded projects be publicly available, in sharp contrast with the funding needs for the type of research described in this section.
22. In an analysis of articles published in three leading economics journals (*American Economic Review, Journal of Political Economy, Quarterly Journal of Economics*), Hamermesh (2013) noted a steady increase in the number of coauthors over time with the first four-author paper published in 1993 and the first five-author and six-author papers published in 2011. Currently, there is very little penalty for publishing coauthored papers in economics.

References

Adams, W., Einav, L., and Levin, J. 2009. Liquidity Constraints and imperfect Information in Subprime Lending. *American Economic Review*, **99**, 49–84.

Akerlof, G. 1982. Labor Contracts and a Partial Gift Exchange. *Quarterly Journal of Economics*, **97**, 543–569.

Alatas, V., Banerjee, A., Chandraskhar, A., Hanna, R., and Olken, B. 2012a. Network Structure and the Aggregation of Information: Theory and Evidence from Indonesia. NBER Working Paper 18351.

Alatas, V., Banerjee, A., Hanna, R., Olken, B., and Tobias, J. 2012b. Targeting the Poor: Evidence from a Field Experiment in Indonesia. *American Economic Review*, **102**, 1206–1240.

Alatas, V., Banerjee, A., Hanna, R., Olken, B., Purnamasari, R., and Wai-Poi, M. 2014. Self-targeting: Evidence from a Field Experiment in Indonesia. *Journal of Political Economy*, **124**, 371–427.

Aldashev, G., Kirchsteiger, G., and Sebald, A. 2015. Assignment Procedure Biases in Randomized Policy Experiments. *forthcoming, The Economic Journal.*

Ashraf, N., Berry, J., and Shapiro, J. 2010. Can Higher Prices Stimulate Product Use? Evidence from a Field Experiment in Zambia. *American Economic Review*, **100**, 2383–2413.

Athey, S., and Mobius, M. 2012. The Impact of News Aggregators on Internet News Consumption: The Case of Localization. Mimeo available at http://markusmobius .org/sites/default/files/localnews.pdf.

Banerjee, A., Banerji, R., Duflo, E., Glennerster, R., and Khemani, S. 2010. Pitfalls of Participatory Programmes: Evidence from a Randomized Evaluation in Education in India. *American Economic Journal: Economic Policy*, **2**, 1–30.

Bauchet, J., Marshall, C., Starita, L., Thomas, J., and Yalouris, A. 2011. Latest Findings from Randomized Evaluations of Microfinance, Access to Finance Forum, Report by CGAP and its Partners. Available at: http://povertyactionlab.org/publication/latest-findings-randomized-evaluations-microfinance.

Behaghel, L., Crépon, B., and Le Barbanchon, T. 2014. Unintended Effects of Anonymous Resumes. IZA Discussion Paper 8517.

Best, M., and Kleven, H. 2015. Housing Market Responses to Transaction Taxes: Evidence from Notches and Stimulus in the UK. Mimeo London School of Economics.

Blake, T., Nosko, C., and Tadelis, S. 2015. Consumer Heterogeneity and Paid Search Effectiveness: A Large Scale Field Experiment. *Econometrica*, **83**, 155–174.

Bloom, H., Orr, L., Bell, S., Cave, G., Doolittle, F., Lin, W., and Bos, J. 1997. The Benefits and Costs of JTPA Title II-A Programmes: Key Findings from the National Job Training Partnership Act Study. *The Journal of Human Resources*, **32**, 549–576.

Camerer, C. F. 2013. Goals, Methods and Progress in Neuroeconomics. *Annual Review of Economics*, **5**, 425–455.

Camerer, C. F. 2015. The Promise and Success of Lab-Field Generalizability in Experimental Economics: A Reply to Levitt and List. In: Frechette, G., and Schotter, A. (eds), *The Methods of Modern Experimental Economics*. Oxford Univ. Press, 2015.

Capen, E. C., Clapp, R. V., and Campbell, W. M. 1971. Competitive Bidding in High-Risk Situations. *Journal of Petroleum Technology*, **23**, 641–53.

Card, D., Chetty, R., Feldstein, M., and Saez, E. 2010. Expanding Access to Administrative Data for Research in the United States. In: Schultze, C. L., and Newlon, D. (eds), *Ten years and Beyond: Economists Answer NSF's Call for Long-Term Research Agendas*. National Science Foundation.

Castellani, D., and Koch, A. 2015. Mapping Competitiveness with European Data. *BRUEGEL blueprint 23*.

Celis, E., Lewis, G., Mobius, M., and Nazerzadeh, H. 2014. Buy-it-Now or Take-a-Chance: Price Discrimination through Randomized Auctions. *Management Science*, **60**, 2927–2948.

Chowdry, H., Crawford, C., Dearden, L., Goodman, A., and Vignoles, A. 2013. Widening Participation in Higher Education: Analysis using Linked Administrative Data. *Journal of the Royal Statistical Society Series A, Royal Statistical Society*, **176**, 431–457.

Cohen, A., and Einav, L. 2007. Estimating Risk Preferences from Deductible Choice. *American Economic Review*, **97**, 745–788.

Cohen, J., and Dupas, P. 2010. Free Distribution or Cost-Sharing? Evidence from a Randomized Malaria Prevention Experiment. *Quarterly Journal of Economics*, **125**, 1–45.

Crépon, B., Duflo, E., Gurgand, M., Rathelot, R., and Zamora, P. 2013. Do Labor Market Policies have Displacement Effects? Evidence from a Clustered Randomized Experiment. *The Quarterly Journal of Economics*, **128**, 531–580.

Duflo, E., Greenstone, M., Pande, R., and Ryan, N. 2014. The Value of Regulatory Discretion: Estimates from Environmental Inspections in India. NBER working paper 20590.

Dufwenberg, M., and Kirchsteiger, G. 2004. A theory of Sequential Reciprocity. *Games and Economic Behavior*, **47**, 268–298.

Dustmann, C., Machin, S., and Schoenberg, U. 2011. Ethnicity and Educational Achievement in Compulsory Schooling. *The Economic Journal*, **120**, F272–F297.

Einav, L., and Levin, J. 2014. Economics in the Age of Big Data. *Science*, **346**, 715–721.

Einav, L., Jenkins, M., and Levin, J. 2012. Contract Pricing in Consumer Credit Markets. *Econometrica*, **80**, 1387–1432.

Einav, L., Jenkins, M., and Levin, J. 2013. The Impact of Credit Scoring on Consumer Lending. *RAND Journal of Economics*, **44**, 249–274.

Einav, L., Knoepfle, D., Levin, J., and Sundaresan, N. 2014. Sales Taxes and Internet Commerce. *American Economic Review*, **104**, 1–26.

Falk, A. 2007. Gift Exchange in the Field. *Econometrica*, **75**, 1501–1511.

Fehr, E., Kirchsteiger, G., and Riedl, A. 1993. Does Fairness Prevent Market Clearing. *Quarterly Journal of Economics*, **108**, 437–459.

Fehr, E., Kirchsteiger, G., and Riedl, A. 1998. Gift Exchange and Reciprocity in Competitive Experimental Markets. *European Economic Review*, **42**, 1–34.

Finkelstein, A., Hendren, N., and Luttmer, E. 2015. The Value of Medicaid: Interpreting Results from the Oregon Health Insurance Experiment. Mimeo MIT.

Hamermesh, D. 2013. Six Decades of Top Economics Publishing: Who and How? *Journal of Economic Literature*, **51**, 162–172.

Haushofer, J. et al. 2014. A Methodology for Laboratory Experiments in Developing Countries: Examples from the Busara Center. Mimeo available at https://princeton.edu/~joha/publications/Haushofer_Busara_2014.pdf.

Heller, S. 2014. Summer Jobs Reduce Violence among Disadvantaged Youth. *Science*, **346**, 1219–1223.

Henrich, J., Boyd, R., Bowles, S., Camerer, C.F., Fehr, E., Gintis, H., McElreath, R., Alvard, M., Barr, A., Ensminger, J., Hill, K., Gil-White, F., Gurven, M., Marlowe, F., Patton, J.Q., Smith, N., and Tracer, D. 2005. Economic Man in Cross-Cultural Perspective: Behavioral Experiments in 15 Small-Scale Societies. *Behavioral and Brain Sciences*, **28**, 795–855.

Henrich, J., Heine, S. J., and Norenzayan, A. 2010. The WEIRDest People in the World? *Behavioral and Brain Sciences*, **33**, 61–83.

Herrmann, B., Thöni, C., and Gächter, S. 2008. Antisocial Punishment across Societies. *Science*, **319**, 1362–1367.

Kagel, J. H., and Levin, D. 2002. *Common Value Auctions and the Winner's Curse*. Princeton: Princeton University Press.

Khan, A., Khwaja, A. I., and Olken, B. 2014. Tax Farming Redux: Experimental Evidence on Performance Pay for Tax Collectors. *Quarterly Journal of Economics*, **131**, 219–271.

Kremer, M., and Miguel, E. 2007. The Illusion of Sustainability. *The Quarterly Journal of Economics*, **122**, 1007–1065.

Meyer, B. D. 1995. Lessons from the U.S. Unemployment Insurance Experiments. *Journal of Economic Literature*, **33**, 91–131.

Muralidharan, K., Niehaus, P., and Sukhtankar, S. 2015. Building State Capacity: Evidence from Biometric Smartcards in India. Mimeo University of California at San Diego.

NORIA-net. 2014. Joint Nordic Registers and Biobanks, A Goldmine for Health and Welfare Research. NordForsk Policy Papers 5.

Plott, C., and Smith, V. 2008. *Handbook of Experimental Economic Results*. Elsevier.

Sebransk, N., Young, L., Kelner, K., Moffit, R., Thakar, A., Raddick, J., Ungvarsky, E., Carlson, R., Apweiler, R., Cox, L., Nolan, D., Soper, K., and Spiegelman, C. 2010. Make Research Data Public? – Not always so Simple: A Dialogue for Statisticians and Science Editors. *Statistical Science*, **25**, 41–50.

Tucker, C. 2008. Identifying Formal and Informal Influence in Technology Adoption with Network Externalities. *Management Science*, **54**, 2024–2038.

Wilson, D., Burgess, S., and Briggs, A. 2011. The Dynamics of School Attainment of England's Ethnic Minorities. *Journal of Population Economics*, **24**, 681–700.

14   Big Data in Economics: Evolution or Revolution?

Christine De Mol, Eric Gautier, Domenico Giannone, Sendhil Mullainathan, Lucrezia Reichlin, Herman van Dijk and Jeffrey Wooldridge

Abstract

The Big Data Era creates a lot of exciting opportunities for new developments in economics and econometrics. At the same time, however, the analysis of large datasets poses difficult methodological problems that should be addressed appropriately and are the subject of the present chapter.

14.1   Introduction

'*Big Data*' has become a buzzword both in academic and in business and policy circles. It is used to cover a variety of data-driven phenomena that have very different implications for empirical methods. This chapter discusses some of these methodological challenges.[1]

In the simplest case, '*Big Data*' means a large dataset that otherwise has a standard structure. For example, Chapter 13 describes how researchers are gaining increasing access to administrative datasets or business records covering entire populations rather than population samples. The size of these datasets allows for better controls and more precise estimates and is a bonus for researchers. This may raise challenges for data storage and handling, but does not raise any distinct methodological issues.

However, '*Big Data*' often means much more than just large versions of standard datasets. First, large numbers of units of observation often come with large numbers of variables, that is, large numbers of possible covariates. To illustrate with the same example, the possibility to link different administrative datasets increases the number of variables attached to each statistical unit. Likewise, business records typically contain all consumer interactions with the business. This can create a tension in the estimation between the objective of 'letting the data speak' and obtaining accurate (in a way to be specified later) coefficient estimates. Second, Big Data sets often have a very different structure from those we are used to in economics. This includes web search queries, real-time

612

geolocational data or social media, to name a few. This type of data raises questions about how to structure and possibly re-aggregate them.

The chapter starts with a description of the '*curse of dimensionality*', which arises from the fact that both the number of units of observation and the number of variables associated with each unit are large. This feature is present in many of the Big Data applications of interest to economists. One extreme example of this problem occurs when there are more parameters to estimate than observations. In this case, standard estimators (such as ordinary least squares) do not yield a unique solution. The section, which borrows heavily from De Mol et al. (2008), describes the econometric problems raised by the curse of dimensionality. It describes some of the methodological solutions called regularization methods that have been proposed.

Section 14.3 then discusses recent research on recovering policy effects using Big Data. In many fields of economics, we are interested in measuring a (causal) relationship between some variable of interest (for example, a policy) and its effects. In other words, although there might be many variables, some of them (related to a specific policy) are of special interest to the researcher. The section describes current efforts to develop methods that combine the ability of regularization methods to harness the information contained in these richer datasets with the possibility to identify the impact of specific policy relevant effects.

Section 14.4 turns to prediction problems. Here we are not interested in specific coefficients per se but in our ability to forecast a variable of interest, for example, inflation, growth or the probability of default. Forecasting has a long tradition in macroeconomics and the greater availability of highly granular microdata is creating renewed interest in prediction problems also at the microeconomic level. A priori, regularization methods are well-suited for this type of problem. However, 'off-the-shelf' regularization methods are agnostic regarding the data generation process. On the basis of the experience with macro forecasting models, the section argues for the need to develop regularization methods that account for the specificities of the data generation processes in economics, such as serial correlation or mixed frequencies.

Recent progress in computing power and storage capacities has allowed researchers to handle and analyse increasingly big datasets. For some of the Big Data (e.g., high frequency trading data, browsing data), this may not be enough. Section 14.5 discusses how simulation-based methods can be refined to leverage the potential of parallel computing.

Section 14.6 concludes. The availability of unprecedented amounts of data offers exciting research opportunities in economics. While researchers will be able to exploit some of the methods developed in other fields, such as statistics and computer science, it is essential that some of these methods be tailored to the specificities of economic research questions and economic data. On these fronts, there is still much to be done.

14.2   The Curse of Dimensionality and Regularization

An early occurrence of the term '*Big Data*' in economics is to be found in a discussion by Diebold (2003, 2012). To quote, 'I stumbled on the term Big Data innocently enough, via discussion of two papers that took a new approach to macro-econometric dynamic factor models (DFMs), Reichlin (2003) and Watson (2003), presented back-to-back in an invited session of the 2000 World Congress of the Econometric Society.'

The two authors referenced above were presenting their research on factor models in high-dimensional time series (Forni et al., 2000, Stock and Watson, 2002), which mainly consisted in deriving asymptotic results for the case where both the number of time samples and the cross-sectional dimension, that is, the number of time series, tend to infinity. The approach relied on a factor model dating back to Chamberlain and Rothschild (1983) in finance, but generalized to take serial correlation into account. Stock and Watson (2002) considered so-called '*static*' factor models, whereas Forni et al. (2000) derived asymptotics in the case of '*dynamic*' factor models. The estimators they used are based on a few principal components either in the time domain for the static case or in the Fourier domain for the dynamic case. This factor-model literature was probably the first in economics to address the difficulties arising from the high dimensionality of the data, albeit under rather strong assumptions (namely factor models) on the data generating process.

In statistics, the difficulties pertaining to the analysis of high-dimensional data are well-known issues, often referred to as the '*curse of dimensionality*'. Some of the facets of this curse can be explained using the familiar example of the linear regression model. To introduce some background notation useful for our discussion, let

$$\mathbf{Y} = \mathbf{X}\beta + \mathbf{U}, \tag{14.1}$$

where $\mathbf{X}$ is a $n \times p$ matrix containing the observed predictors (covariates), $\mathbf{Y}$ is the outcome or $n \times 1$ vector of the observed responses and $\mathbf{U}$ is an unobserved zero-mean error or nuisance term. The $p \times 1$ vector β contains the regression coefficients. In the case of time series, n is the number of time samples and p is the number of time series used for prediction. In the case of cross-section data, n is the number of observations and p is the number of covariates. In the discussion in this section, we will consider the matrix $\mathbf{X}$ as deterministic.

Depending on the application under study, two different problems can be highlighted. The first is prediction (also referred to as 'generalization' by the machine-learning community), in which case one is only interested in estimating the outcome for future times or new examples to come. This requires the estimation of the regression parameters, but only as an auxiliary step to the estimation of the outcome. The second problem, the identification of the model, pertains more to the vector β of regression coefficients itself, in the linear regression example in (14.1). This is essential for interpreting the estimated coefficients in terms of their relevance in predicting the response. For example, some coefficients can be zero, indicating that the corresponding predictors are not relevant for this task. The determination of these zeroes, hence of the relevant/irrelevant predictors, is usually referred to as '*variable selection*'.

As is well known, the most straightforward solution for the linear regression problem is Ordinary Least Squares (OLS). The OLS estimator for β in (14.1) minimizes the least-squares loss

$$\Phi(\beta) = \|\mathbf{Y} - \mathbf{X}\beta\|_2^2 , \tag{14.2}$$

where $\|\mathbf{Y}\|_2 = \sqrt{\sum_{i=1}^n |Y_i|^2}$ is the L_2-norm of the vector $\mathbf{Y}$. It is given by

$$\hat{\beta}_{ols} = (\mathbf{X}'\mathbf{X})^{-1}\mathbf{X}'\mathbf{Y} \tag{14.3}$$

($\mathbf{X}'$ denotes the transpose of the matrix $\mathbf{X}$).

For the OLS estimator, expression (14.3), to make sense we need the $p \times p$ matrix $\mathbf{X}'\mathbf{X}$ to be of full rank, hence invertible. This cannot be the case in high-dimensional situations where the number of coefficients, p, is larger than the number of observations, n.[2] In that case, the minimizer of the least-squares loss is nonunique, but uniqueness can be restored by selecting the so-called '*minimum-norm least-squares solution*', orthogonal to the null-space, that is, by ignoring the subspace corresponding to the zero eigenvalues.

Notice that although this remedy may work well for prediction, the identification problem remains hindered by this nonuniqueness issue. An additional difficulty arises when the matrix $\mathbf{X}'\mathbf{X}$ has eigenvalues that are close to zero, or more precisely, when its '*condition number*', that is, the ratio between the largest and the smallest of its nonzero eigenvalues, becomes large. This situation prevents a stable determination of the least-squares (or minimum-norm least-squares) estimator: small fluctuations in the outcome vector $\mathbf{Y}$ will be amplified by the effect of the small eigenvalues and will result in large uncontrolled fluctuations (high variance/volatility) on the estimation of β, again preventing meaningful identification.

The pathologies described above contribute to what is often referred to as the '*curse of dimensionality*' or else the '*large p, small n paradigm*' in high-dimensional statistics. As early as in the 1950s, Stein (1956) introduced a 'high-dimensional' surprise in statistics by showing that the maximum-likelihood estimator of the unknown mean vector of a multivariate Gaussian distribution is not 'admissible' in a dimension higher than three, that is, that it is outperformed by '*shrinkage*' estimators. Heuristically, 'shrinking' means that a naive estimate is improved by combining it with other information or priors.

Many remedies have been proposed to address these pathologies under the common designation of '*regularization methods*', which provide in one form or

---

Box 14.1: Principal Component Regression (PCR)

The Principal Component Regression consists in estimating β by

$$\hat{\beta}_{pcr} = \sum_{i=1}^{k} \frac{\langle \mathbf{X'Y}, \mathbf{V}_i \rangle}{\xi_i^2} \mathbf{V}_i \qquad (14.4)$$

where the $\mathbf{V}_i$'s are the eigenvectors of $\mathbf{X'X}$ with eigenvalues ξ_i^2, and $\langle \cdot, \cdot \rangle$ denotes the scalar product.

---

another the dimensionality reduction necessary to reduce the variance/volatility of unstable estimators, or in other words, to avoid '*overfitting*'. Overfitting refers to the fact that, when using a model with many free parameters (here the *p* components of β), it is easy to get a good fit of the observed data, that is, a small value for the residual (14.2), but that this does not imply that the corresponding (unstable) value of β will have a good predictive power for responses corresponding to new observations. For time series, good in-sample fit does not imply good out-of-sample forecasts.

One of the simplest regularization methods is principal component regression (PCR), a statistical procedure that transforms the possibly correlated variables into a smaller number of orthogonal new variables (the components, see Box 14.1). The truncation point *k* for the number of components, usually much smaller than the true rank of $\mathbf{X'X}$, has to be carefully chosen to overcome instabilities. In this method, also referred to as '*Truncated Singular Value Decomposition*' (TSVD), the truncation introduces a bias in order to reduce variance.

Until recently alternative estimators were less well known in econometrics. Other regularization methods introduce constraints or penalties on the vector β of the regression coefficients. Probably the oldest penalized regression method is '*Ridge regression*' (see Box 14.2), due to Hoerl and Kennard (1970). This method is also known in the applied mathematics literature as Tikhonov's regularization. It consists in adding to the least-squares loss a penalty proportional to the size of β, measured by its squared L_2-norm. As for the truncation point in PCR, the regularization parameter has to be chosen carefully in order to provide a proper balance between the bias introduced by shrinkage, and the variance of the estimator and its value is usually determined by cross-validation.

Ridge regression introduces a form of linear '*shrinkage*', where the components of $\hat{\beta}_{ols}$ are shrunk uniformly towards zero, as can be easily seen in the case of orthonormal regressors (i.e., for $\mathbf{X'X} = \mathbf{I}$), where $\hat{\beta}_{ridge} = \frac{1}{1+\lambda_2} \mathbf{X'Y}$. More generally, quadratic penalties provide estimators which depend linearly on the response $\mathbf{Y}$ but do not allow for variable selection, since typically all regression coefficients are different from zero.

Box 14.2: The Ridge Regression Estimator

The ridge regression estimator is given by

$$\hat{\beta}_{ridge} = \text{argmin}_\beta \left[\|\mathbf{Y} - \mathbf{X}\beta\|_2^2 + \lambda_2 \|\beta\|_2^2 \right]$$
$$= (\mathbf{X}'\mathbf{X} + \lambda_2 \mathbf{I})^{-1} \mathbf{X}'\mathbf{Y} \tag{14.5}$$

where $\mathbf{I}$ is the identity matrix and $\lambda_2 > 0$ is the so-called '*regularization parameter*', which, as seen from (14.5), reduces the impact of the smallest eigenvalues of $\mathbf{X}'\mathbf{X}$, at the origin of the instability of the OLS estimator.

An alternative to quadratic penalties that allows for variable selection by enforcing sparsity, that is, the presence of zeroes in the vector β of the regression coefficients, has been popularized in the statistics and machine-learning literature under the name of '*Lasso regression*' by Tibshirani (1996). It consists in replacing the L_2-norm penalty used in ridge regression by a penalty proportional to the L_1-norm of β (see Box 14.3).

In the case of orthonormal regressors, it is easily seen that the Lasso penalty provides a nonlinear shrinkage of the components of $\hat{\beta}_{ols}$, which are shrunk differently according to their magnitude, as well as sparsity, since the jth coefficient $[\hat{\beta}_{lasso}]_j = 0$ if $|[\mathbf{X}'\mathbf{Y}]_j| < \lambda_1/2$. Unfortunately, there is no closed-form expression for $\hat{\beta}_{lasso}$ in the case of general matrices $\mathbf{X}$, and the Lasso estimator has to be computed numerically as the solution of a (nonsmooth) convex optimization problem.

The previous estimators can be given a Bayesian interpretation, since $\hat{\beta}_{ols}$ can be viewed as the maximum (log-)likelihood estimator for a Gaussian error term and the penalized maximum likelihood estimators $\hat{\beta}_{ridge}$ and $\hat{\beta}_{lasso}$ can be interpreted as maximum a posteriori (MAP) estimators, the penalty resulting from a prior distribution for the regression coefficients. In Ridge regression, it corresponds to a Gaussian prior whereas in Lasso regression it is a Laplacian or double-exponential prior.

The regularization techniques described above are paradigmatic since they convey the essential ideas in dealing with high-dimensional settings. There are however numerous extensions and generalizations. For example, more general types of penalties can be used such as $\|\beta\|_\gamma^\gamma = \sum_{j=1}^p |\beta_j|^\gamma$, *i.e.*, the L_γ-norms used in '*bridge regression*' (Frank and Friedman, 1993). Notice that in this family, though, only the choice $\gamma = 1$ yields both convexity and sparsity. Moreover, weights or even a nondiagonal coupling matrix can be introduced in the penalty to cover the case of non i.i.d. (independent and identically distributed) regression coefficients. Composite penalties are also used, for example, in elastic-net or group-lasso regularization. Finally, different loss functions can be considered such as those used in robust statistics, logistic regression, etc. A good pointer to this variety of techniques is the book by Hastie et al. (2009).

Box 14.3: The Lasso Regression Estimator

Lasso consists in replacing the L_2-norm penalty used in ridge regression by a penalty proportional to the L_1-norm of β, that is, to the sum of the absolute values of the regression coefficients, $\|\beta\|_1 = \sum_{j=1}^{p} |\beta_j|$, yielding the estimator

$$\hat{\beta}_{lasso} = \mathrm{argmin}_\beta \left[\|\mathbf{Y} - \mathbf{X}\beta\|_2^2 + \lambda_1 \|\beta\|_1 \right], \tag{14.6}$$

In the special case of orthonormal regressors ($\mathbf{X}'\mathbf{X} = \mathbf{I}$), the Lasso estimator is easily seen to be given by

$$[\hat{\beta}_{lasso}]_j = S_{\lambda_1}([\mathbf{X}'\mathbf{Y}]_j)$$

where $S_{\lambda_1}(x)$ is the *'soft-thresholder'* defined by

$$S_{\lambda_1}(x) = \begin{cases} x + \lambda_1/2 & \text{if } x \leq -\lambda_1/2 \\ 0 & \text{if } |x| < \lambda_1/2 \\ x - \lambda_1/2 & \text{if } x \geq \lambda_1/2. \end{cases}$$

Let us remark that global variable selection methods, preferably convex to facilitate computation, such as the Lasso and its relatives, are essential to deal with high-dimensional situations. Indeed, considering all possible submodels and selecting the best among them, for example according to the Akaike Information Criterion (AIC) proposed by Akaike (1974) or the Bayesian Information Criterion (BIC) proposed by Schwarz (1978), leads to a complexity growing exponentially with the number of variables involved and renders the methods totally unpractical. To paraphrase the title of a paper by Sala-I-Martin (1997): 'You cannot just run two million regressions!' (and, incidentally, two million would not even suffice for $p \geq 22$).

As concerns asymptotic and consistency results, the settings have to go beyond the classical scheme of keeping the number of parameters p constant (and usually small), while letting the number of observations n of the dependent variable tend to infinity. In high-dimensional situations, both n and p may tend to infinity, while assuming or not some relationship between their respective growth rates. The theory is more subtle in this case and is still developing. This question has been studied for principal component regression for time series under a factor model assumption. Results in this line for the case of penalized regression, and in particular of Ridge regression, have been derived by De Mol et al. (2008, 2015). The first paper also contains an empirical part where predictive accuracy of PCR, Ridge and Lasso regression is evaluated based on a dataset of about 100 time series. It is shown that all three methods perform similarly and that results of Lasso are uninformative when used for applications where, as is typically the case for macroeconomics, data are cross-correlated. Moreover, in that case Lasso is unstable in selection.

14.3   Policy Analysis and Causal Inference

In the actual big data activity sphere, in parallel with the developments of powerful machine-learning techniques, the emphasis is on predictive rather than causal models. As we shall further discuss in the next section, successful predictive algorithms are rapidly developing in response to the increasing demand coming from all kinds of applications. These algorithms convert large amounts of unstructured data into predictive scores in an automatic way and often in real time.

Whether this trend is desirable may be a matter of debate but it is clear that it implies a significant shift from the single-covariate causal-effect framework that has dominated much empirical research, especially in microeconomics. Being nonstructural, predictive models are subject to the Lucas critique (Lucas, 1976) and their success should not obscure the fact that many economic applications are about inference on a causal effect. In microeconomics, for example, a successful literature has developed methods to assess the effectiveness of a given policy or treatment.

In the case where the intervention is binary in nature, we define a binary variable, W, equal to unity for the treatment group and zero for the control group. We typically have in mind a counterfactual setting, where it makes sense to think of potential outcomes for each unit in the control and treated states. These outcomes are often denoted $Y(0)$ and $Y(1)$, and then we observe the treatment status, W, and the outcome under the corresponding treatment status, $Y = (1 - W)Y(0) + WY(1) = Y(0) + W[Y(1) - Y(0)]$. For unit i in the population, the treatment effect is $Y_i(1) - Y_i(0)$ – which is not observed. Instead, attention typically centres on the average treatment effect, $\tau = E[Y(1) - Y(0)]$, or the average over an interesting subpopulation (such as those actually receiving the treatment). A special case is when the treatment effect is constant, in which case we can write $Y = \tau W + Y(0)$, and the $Y(0)$ plays the role of the unobserved factors affecting Y.

The potential outcomes setting can be extended to cases where the policy variable, W, is not binary. If the policy effect is constant across units and across levels of the treatment, we can write a simple regression equation

$$Y = \tau W + R, \tag{14.7}$$

where Y, W and R are random variables and τ is a scalar coefficient of interest. We (eventually) observe data on Y and W. The variable R includes unobserved factors – $Y(0)$ in the simplest setting – affecting Y.

In medicine and the experimental sciences, truly randomized experiments can be carried out, which means the treatment level W can be made independent of R. For example, when W is binary, we can randomly assign individuals into the treatment and control groups. In such cases, (14.7) can be estimated using simple regression, which delivers an unbiased and consistent estimator of τ. In economics, random assignment is much less common, and in general one has access only to so-called observational – not experimental – data. Hence, several strategies, when randomized assignment is not available have been developed. Here we review a few of those strategies, highlighting how high-dimensional regression methods can be applied to estimating causal effects. Good pointers to part of the relevant work in this field are the review papers by Belloni et al. (2013, 2014a).

A traditional and still commonly used method to handle nonrandom treatment assignment is regression adjustment, where one assumes the availability of covariates that render the policy assignment appropriately 'exogenous'. Let X be a $1 \times p$ vector of covariates. Then, if X is thought to predict both Y and the treatment assignment, W, we can 'control for' X in a multiple regression analysis. This leads to a linear model,

$$Y = \tau W + X\beta + U, \tag{14.8}$$

where now $R = X\beta + U$ and, if the elements of X suitably control for the nonrandom assignment, the treatment and covariates satisfy the exogeneity conditions

$$E[WU] = 0, \ E[XU] = 0. \tag{14.9}$$

If p, the number of control variables, is large and the $p \times 1$ vector β is sparse, the model can be estimated by means of a Lasso regression, as described in the previous section. However, one has to know in advance the right vector X such as, under the usual exogeneity conditions (14.9), there are no more confounding variables and one recovers the marginal effect τ, holding fixed everything else.

One can relax the linearity assumption in X and just assume

$$E[R|W, X] = E[R|X], \tag{14.10}$$

which yields

$$Y = \tau W + g(X) + U, \tag{14.11}$$

where $g(X) = E[R|X]$ and $U = R - E[R|W, X]$ is such that $E[U|W, X] = 0$. Model (14.11) is a so-called partially linear model and g is generally a nonparametric function. Belloni et al. (2014b) use Lasso-type methods to nonparametrically partial out X from both Y and W. They approximate the mean functions $E[Y|X]$ and $E[W|X]$ using functions of the form $\sum_{j=1}^{p} \beta_j \phi_j(X)$, for a large dictionary of functions $(\phi_j)_{j=1}^{p}$, and build a confidence interval around τ. This method is particularly appealing as it does not require one to chose a bandwidth to estimate the nonparametric conditional mean functions. If the approximations $\sum_{j=1}^{p} \beta_j \phi_j(X)$ are sparse, then the method selects the significant $\phi_j(X)$ for each of $E[Y|X]$ and $E[W|X]$. As shown in Belloni et al. (2014a), using the union of the functions selected from the methods in a standard regression analysis with Y as the response variable and W as the other regressor, the usual heteroscedasticity-robust standard error produces valid t statistics and confidence intervals. It should be emphasized that, while the approach works well for selecting functions of X that appear in the conditional mean, it does not select the variables X such as (14.10) holds; the researcher is assumed to have already selected the appropriate controls.

When (14.9) or (14.10) do not hold, we can rely on instrumental variables, namely, assume to have at our disposal a vector of random variables Z, called instrumental variables, such as in (14.7),

$$\text{Cov}[Z, R] = 0. \tag{14.12}$$

This yields the relation

$$\text{Cov}[Z, Y] = \tau \text{Cov}[Z, W]. \tag{14.13}$$

If Z is a scalar, (14.13) identifies τ when $\text{Cov}[Z, W] \neq 0$. When we have more than one instrumental variable for W, two stage least squares (2SLS) is a common estimation approach. However, 2SLS only uses the linear projection of W on Z in forming instruments. If we strengthen the exogeneity requirement to $E[R|Z] = 0$, 2SLS is asymptotically inefficient if $E[W|Z]$ is nonlinear or $\text{Var}[R|Z]$ is not constant. If we assume homoscedasticity in (14.7), that is, $\text{Var}[R|Z] = \text{Var}[R]$, then the optimal instrument for W is given by $E[W|Z]$, the best mean square predictor of W. Belloni et al. (2012) propose to use Lasso-type methods to estimate the regression function $E[W|Z]$ using a large dictionary of approximating functions, and they show how to conduct inference on τ using a heteroscedastic-robust standard error.

Gautier and Tsybakov (2011) propose an instrumental variables method to make inference for high-dimensional structural equations of the form

$$Y = X\beta + U \tag{14.14}$$

where the dimension of X is large (and may include exogenous and endogenous variables). This occurs, for example, in large demand systems, or when treatment variables are interacted with (exogenous) group dummies. In the latter case, the policy might have an effect on only certain groups, and the policy-maker would like to determine for which group the policy has an effect. The instrumental variables literature has identified various problems: (i) the instrumental variable candidates, Z, might not be exogenous; (ii) the instrumental variables can be 'weak' and estimating in a first-stage a reduced form equation can yield multimodal and non-normal distributions of the parameter estimates, even with very large sample size, so that asymptotic theory is not reliable; (iii) in the presence of many instrumental variables, estimating in a first-stage a reduced form equation can give rise to a large bias. Gautier and Tsybakov (2011) rely on a new method which is robust to (ii) and (iii) in order to treat the more challenging case of a high-dimensional structural equation. Confidence sets can be obtained for arbitrary weak and numerous instrumental variables, whether or not the condition $\text{Cov}[Z, U] = 0$ gives rise to a unique β. Therefore, it is also possible to handle the case where the dimension of Z is smaller than the dimension of X, which can yield the identification of β under sparsity of the structural Equation (14.14) or other shape restrictions. To deal with the possibility of (i), a high-dimensional extension of the Sargan and Hansen method is developed.

There is much interest in the literature on heterogeneous treatment effects, and variable selection methods can also be applied in such cases. For example, variable selection methods can be applied to estimating the propensity score when the treatment variable takes on a small number of levels. Moreover, variable selection methods can be applied to both propensity score estimation and regression function estimation to obtain so-called *doubly robust* estimators. Unlike the linear, additive Equation (14.11), methods that weigh by the inverse of the propensity score allow for heterogeneous treatment effects. See, for example, the papers by Farrell (2015) and Athey and Imbens (2015).

Besides these high-dimensional problems, let us mention another important issue which arises in connection with the availability of big datasets, namely, to determine whether the accumulation of data, say, over an entire population, affects the precision of estimates. Abadie et al. (2014) analyse how to compute uncertainty in empirical situations where the sample is the entire population and where the regression function is intended to capture causal effects. Other contributions on *Causal Inference* in a big data setting use machine-learning methods. A recent example is the work by Athey and Imbens (2015). There are many open challenges in this area, pointers to recent progress are available from the site of the Sackler Colloquium on 'Drawing Causal Inference from Big Data', organized in March 2015 at the US National Academy of Science in Washington.[3]

The previous discussion has focused on cross-sectional data, but empirical researchers attempting to estimate causal effects often rely on panel data that exploit changes in policies over time. An important component of panel data models is allowing for time-constant, unobserved heterogeneity. Belloni et al. (2014a) propose first differencing a linear unobserved effects equation to remove additive heterogeneity, and then using variable selection methods, such as Lasso, to allow for correlation between unobserved heterogeneous trends and unknown functions of observed covariates – including the policy variable or variables being studied. The approach seems promising. So far, such methods have been applied to linear models with relatively few sources of heterogeneity.

14.4   Prediction

Despite recent advances in identification and causality in big data settings, which we have just reviewed, it is fair to say that the literature in the field is mainly focused on prediction. Using the same notation as above, the problem consists in computing the conditional expectation

$$E(Y|W, X). \tag{14.15}$$

Forecasting has a long tradition in economics, especially in macroeconomics. Indeed, many economists in the private sector and policy institutions are employed for this task. In forecasting, robustness is typically tested in out-of-sample validation studies, a perspective typically ignored in empirical microeconomics. For desirable out-of-sample performance, models must respect the principle of parsimony (i.e., contain a rather small number of free parameters) to avoid overfitting. However, the curse of dimensionality problem naturally arises from lags, nonlinearities, and the presence of many potentially relevant predictors.

The recent literature has suggested methods to deal with the curse of dimensionality issue in dynamic models. Here we should mention dynamic factor models cited earlier and, more recently, large Bayesian vector autoregressive models. Following the work of De Mol et al. (2008), Banbura et al. (2010) have shown empirically how to set priors to estimate a vector autoregressive model with large datasets. The idea is to set the degree of 'shrinkage' in relation to the dimension of the data. Intuitively this implies to set priors so as to avoid overfitting, but still let the data be informative. Giannone et al. (2015) have developed a formal procedure to conduct inference for the degree of shrinkage. These models have many applications in economics beyond pure forecasting and can be used to design counterfactuals for policy analysis and identification of exogenous shocks and dynamic propagation mechanisms. Large data allow to better identify exogenous shocks since they can accommodate for realistic assumptions on agents' information set (for an analysis on this point, see Forni et al. (2009)).

One very successful application of the large models described above (if measured by impact on modelling in policy institutions and the financial industry) has been '*now-casting*'. Now-casting is the forecast of the present (present quarter or present month) based on data available at different frequencies (daily, weekly, monthly and quarterly). A now-cast produces a sequence of updates of predictions in relation to the publication calendar of the data. This allows to exploit the timeliness of certain data releases to obtain an early estimate of those series which are published with a delay with respect to the reference quarter such as GDP or the reference month such as employment (see Giannone et al., 2008 and subsequent literature). Empirical results show that exploiting survey data, which are published earlier than hard data, allows to obtain an accurate early estimate at the beginning of the quarter and, as new data are released through time, the estimates become more accurate (see Banbura et al., 2013 for a review of the literature). In principle, nonstandard data such as Google queries or twitters, due to their timeliness, could be exploited in this context. However, once the details of the problem (mixed frequency, nonsynchronous data releases) are appropriately modelled and relevant timely indicators considered, there is no evidence that Google indexes used successfully in a simpler setup by Choi and Varian (2012) and Scott and Varian (2014) have any additional predictive value (see Li, 2016), but more research is needed on this topic.

It has to be noted that most of the applied work on the methods mentioned have concerned traditional time series (macroeconomic variables, possibly disaggregated by sectors or regions, financial variables and surveys) and rarely with dimension above 150. Empirical results show that, in general, forecasts of macroeconomic variables based on datasets of medium dimension (of the order of 20) are not outperformed by forecasts based on 100 or more variables although the dimension helps especially in now-casting where successful results rely on the use of timely information. Moreover, as mentioned in Section 14.2, Lasso regressions provide unstable variable selection due to the near-collinear feature of macroeconomic data. Important empirical issues are also related to robustness with respect to variable transformation such as deseasonalization or detrending as well as nonlinearity. Potentially, machine-learning type of techniques could be useful in this setup but this is open to future research. The literature is at too early stage to provide a definitive answer on the potentials of new data and new methods in this context but it is our view that any successful applications have to incorporate the detailed micro-structure of the problem. In now-casting, for example, this implies taking care of mixed frequency, the nonsynchronicity of releases and other details.

In microeconometrics the emphasis on predictions and out-of-sample is newer than in macro but studies using big data are more numerous. Predictions based on a large cross-section of data have been successfully obtained for various problems. Examples can be found in papers by Varian (2014), by Einav and Levin (2014) and by Kleinberg et al. (2015b), as well as in the references therein. The last paper discusses a problem of health economics, namely the prediction of whether replacement surgery for patients with osteoarthritis will be beneficial for a given patient, based on more than 3000 variables recorded for about 100,000 patients. Another policy decision based on prediction is studied by Kleinberg et al. (2015a), who show that machine-learning algorithms can be more efficient than a judge in deciding who has to be released or go to jail while waiting for trial because of the danger of committing a crime in the meanwhile. Another application would be to predict the risk of unemployment for a given individual based on a detailed personal profile.

It should be remarked that machine-learning algorithms present several advantages: they focus on a best-fit function for prediction, possibly handling very rich functional forms, and have built-in safeguards against overfitting so that they can handle more variables than data points. Moreover, they do not require too many assumptions about the data generating process as it is the case in classical econometrics. We should be aware, however, that precisely because of their great generality and versatility, they may not be optimally tailored for the specificities of a given problem.

Another trend is to make use not only of more data, but also of new types of data. Many types of data are nowadays passively collected and are largely unexploited, such as those provided by social networks, scanner data, credit card records, web search queries, electronic medical records, insurance claim data, etc. They could complement more traditional and actively collected data or even be a substitute for them. The mining of language data, such as online customer reviews, is also a challenge and can be used for so-called '*sentiment analysis*' (see e.g., Pang et al., 2002).

Returning to the issue of causality discussed in the previous section, it should be noted that prediction algorithms also provide new ways to test theories. Indeed, we can see how well we can predict the output Y with all variables but X and/or how much the inclusion of a given variable (or a group of variables) X helps improving the prediction. We should be cautious, however, in drawing conclusions: the fact that a variable is not among the best predictors does not necessarily mean that it is not 'important'. For example, when Varian (2014) discusses differences in race in mortgage applications, saying that race is not among the best predictors is not the same as saying that evidence of discrimination does not exist.

In addition, the completeness of a given theory could be tested by confronting its prediction abilities against an atheoretical benchmark provided by machine learning.

14.5   Computational Issues

The collection and analysis of bigger and bigger datasets obviously pose methodological as well as computational challenges. Nevertheless, since there has been at the same time a tremendous increase in computing capabilities, researchers can handle larger and larger datasets using standard software and desktop computers. For example, up to the late 90s maximum-likelihood estimation of dynamic factor models could be performed only with a small set of variables (Stock and Watson, 1989), while recent research has shown how these models can be easily estimated in a high-dimensional context (Doz et al., 2012, Jungbacker and Koopman, 2015). In parallel with this increase in computing power, significant progress has been made in the development of fast and reliable numerical algorithms which scale well with dimension. In particular, considerable research effort has been dedicated to improving the speed and performance of algorithms for Lasso regression.

In many situations, however, computational capability still represents an important constraint on our ability to handle and analyse big datasets. Methods that can handle thousands of variables may become inappropriate when moving to millions of variables. Moreover, some procedures can be particularly demanding in terms of computational complexity when applied to more than a handful of data. This is the case, for example, for complex latent variable models for which closed-form solutions are not available. In this context there is a demand for extra computing power. Unfortunately, the growth rate in computational capability of integrated circuits (CPU microchips) seems to be slowing down. However, thanks to technological progress driven by the video-game industry, new and fast growing computational power is coming from so-called graphics processing units (GPU), which allow for parallel computation and are easy to program. The general idea is that it is often possible to divide large problems into smaller independent tasks, which are then carried out simultaneously.

Splitting large problems into small ones is particularly natural in simulation-based Bayesian methods, which have recently attracted growing interest (see e.g., Hoogerheide et al., 2009, Lee et al., 2010, Durham and Geweke, 2013). In Bayesian methods, the reduction in dimensionality is made by assuming prior distributions for the unknown parameters to infer and, whereas the computation of the so-called MAP (Maximum a Posteriori) estimator requires solving an optimization problem, the computation of conditional means and covariances only requires integration, but in a high-dimensional space. For this task stochastic simulation methods and artificially generated random variables are used. Since the early days of Monte Carlo methods, there has been substantial development of new more sophisticated Sequential Monte Carlo and Particle Filter methods, allowing us to deal with complex posterior distributions and more flexible econometric models.

Examples of successful applications of simulation-based Bayesian methods are reported by Billio et al. (2013a,b) and Casarin et al. (2013, 2015). The paper by Casarin et al. (2015) deals with the problem of conducting inference on latent time-varying weights used to combine a large set of predictive densities for 3712 individual stock prices, quoted in NYSE and NASDAQ, using 2034 daily observations from 18 March 2002 to 31 December 2009. The authors find substantial forecast and economic gains and also document improvement in computation time achieved by using parallel computing compared to traditional sequential computation. Another application to nowcasting is discussed by Aastveit et al. (2014), who show that a combined density now-cast model works particularly well in a situation of early data releases with relatively large data uncertainty and model incompleteness. Empirical results, based on US real-time data of 120 leading indicators, suggest that combined density now-casting gives more accurate density now-casts of US GDP growth than a model selection strategy and other combination strategies throughout the quarter, with relatively large gains for the first two months of the quarter. The model also provides informative signals on model incompleteness during recent recessions and, by focusing on the tails, delivers probabilities of negative growth, that provide good signals for calling recessions and ending economic slumps in real time.

14.6   Conclusions

Data are essential for research and policy. Definitely there is a trend towards empirical economics, and from this perspective, the advent of big data offers an extraordinary opportunity to take advantage of the availability of unprecedented amounts of data, as well as of new types of data, provided that there is easy access to them, in particular for academic research.

In this chapter, we have focused on some methodological aspects of the analysis of large datasets. We have argued that many of the issues raised by big data are not entirely new and have their roots in ideas and work over the past decades. On the applied side, applications with truly big data are still rare in economics although in recent years more research has been devoted to the use of relatively large but traditional datasets.

While in many problems the focus is shifting from identification towards prediction, which is a more '*revolutionary trend*', causality is still considered important and this duality is a matter for interesting debates in econometrics.

As concerns algorithmic and computational issues, the field of '*machine learning*', a popular heading covering very different topics, is and will remain helpful in providing efficient methods for mining large datasets. However, we should be careful rather than blindly import methodologies from other fields, since economic data structures have their own specificities and need appropriately designed research tools.

Undoubtedly, this research area calls for a lot of new, exciting and perhaps unexpected developments within and outside the framework sketched here, and if the datasets are big, the challenges ahead are even bigger, in optimally exploiting the information they contain.

Notes

1. This chapter is based on the presentations given by the authors at the COEURE workshop on 'Developments in Data and Methods for Economic Research' held in Brussels in July 2015. The presentations took place in two sessions of the workshop: 'Big Data: Definition, challenges and opportunities', chaired by Christine De Mol, and 'How will Big Data change econometrics?' chaired by Domenico Giannone. Christine De Mol coordinated and integrated the authors' presentations to the chapter.
2. Since this implies the existence of a nontrivial null-space for $\mathbf{X}'\mathbf{X}$, with at least $p - n$ zero eigenvalues.
3. See   http://www.nasonline.org/programs/sackler-colloquia/completed_colloquia/ Big-data.html.

References

Aastveit, K. A., Ravazzolo, F., and van Dijk, H. K. 2014 (Dec). *Combined Density Now-casting in an Uncertain Economic Environment*. Tinbergen Institute Discussion Papers 14-152/III. Tinbergen Institute. Accepted for publication in *Journal of Business Economics and Statistics*. http://tandfonline.com/doi/abs/10.1080/07350015 .2015.1137760

Abadie, A., Athey, S., Imbens, G. W., and Wooldridge, J. M. 2014 (July). *Finite Population Causal Standard Errors*. Working Paper 20325. National Bureau of Economic Research.

Akaike, H. 1974. A New Look at the Statistical Model Identification. *IEEE Transactions on Automatic Control*, **AC-19**(6), 716–723.

Athey, S., and Imbens, G. W. 2015. Machine Learning Methods for Estimating Heterogeneous Causal Effects. *ArXiv e-prints*, Apr.

Banbura, M., Giannone, D., and Reichlin, L. 2010. Large Bayesian Vector Auto Regressions. *Journal of Applied Econometrics*, **25**(1), 71–92.

Banbura, M., Giannone, D., Modugno, M., and Reichlin, L. 2013. Now-Casting and the Real-Time Data-Flow. In: Elliott, G., and Timmermann, A. (eds), *Handbook of Economic Forecasting, Volume 2, Part A*. Elsevier-North Holland, pp. 195–237.

Belloni, A., Chen, D., Chernozhukov, V., and Hansen, C. 2012. Sparse Models and Methods for Instrumental Regression, with an Application to Eminent Domain. *Econometrica*, **80**(6), 2369–2429.

Belloni, A., Chernozhukov, V., and Hansen, C. 2013. Inference for High-Dimensional Sparse Econometric Modelling. In: Acemoglu, D., Arellano, M., and Dekel, E. (eds), *Advances in Economics and Econometrics, Tenth World Congress of the Econometric Society*, vol. 3. Cambridge University Press, pp. 245–295.

Belloni, A., Chernozhukov, V., and Hansen, C. 2014a. High-Dimensional Methods and Inference on Structural and Treatment Effects. *Journal of Economic Perspectives*, **28**(2), 29–50.

Belloni, A., Chernozhukov, V., and Hansen, C. 2014b. Inference on Treatment Effects after Selection among High-Dimensional Controls. *The Review of Economic Studies*, **81**(2), 608–650.

Billio, M., Casarin, R., Ravazzolo, F., and van Dijk, H. K. 2013a. *Interactions between Eurozone and US Booms and Busts: A Bayesian Panel Markov-switching VAR Model*. Working Papers 2013:17. Department of Economics, University of Venice 'Ca' Foscari'.

Billio, M., Casarin, R., Ravazzolo, F., and van Dijk, H. K. 2013b. Time-varying combinations of predictive densities using nonlinear filtering. *Journal of Econometrics*, **177**(2), 213–232.

Casarin, R., Grassi, S., Ravazzolo, F., and van Dijk, H. K. 2013. *Parallel Sequential Monte Carlo for Efficient Density Combination: The DeCo Matlab Toolbox*. Working Papers 2013:08. Department of Economics, University of Venice 'Ca' Foscari'.

Casarin, R., Grassi, S., Ravazzolo, F., and van Dijk, H. K. 2015 (July). *Dynamic Predictive Density Combinations for Large Data Sets in Economics and Finance*. Tinbergen Institute Discussion Papers 15-084/III. Tinbergen Institute.

Chamberlain, G., and Rothschild, M. 1983. Arbitrage, Factor Structure, and Mean-Variance Analysis on Large Asset Markets. *Econometrica*, **51**(5), 1281–304.

Choi, H., and Varian, H. 2012. Predicting the Present with Google Trends. *The Economic Record*, **88**(s1), 2–9.

De Mol, C., Giannone, D., and Reichlin, L. 2008. Forecasting Using a Large Number of Predictors: Is Bayesian Shrinkage a Valid Alternative to Principal Components? *Journal of Econometrics*, **146**(2), 318–328.

De Mol, C., Giannone, D., and Reichlin, L. 2015. Forecasting with High-dimensional Time Series. Oberwolfach Reports, No. 38/2015. European Mathematical Society.

Diebold, F. X. 2003. Big Data Dynamic Factor Models for Macroeconomic Measurement and Forecasting: A Discussion of the Papers by Reichlin and Watson. In: Dewatripont, M., Hansen, L., and Turnovsky, S. (eds), *Advances in Economics and Econometrics: Theory and Applications, Eighth World Congress of the Econometric Society*, vol. 3. Cambridge University Press, pp. 115–122.

Diebold, F. X. 2012 (Sep). *On the Origin(s) and Development of the Term 'Big Data'*. PIER Working Paper Archive 12-037. Penn Institute for Economic Research, Department of Economics, University of Pennsylvania.

Doz, C., Giannone, D., and Reichlin, L. 2012. A Quasi-Maximum Likelihood Approach for Large, Approximate Dynamic Factor Models. *The Review of Economics and Statistics*, **94**(4), 1014–1024.

Durham, G., and Geweke, J. 2013 (Apr.). *Adaptive Sequential Posterior Simulators for Massively Parallel Computing Environments*. Working Paper Series 9. Economics Discipline Group, UTS Business School, University of Technology, Sydney.

Einav, L., and Levin, J. 2014. Economics in the Age of Big Data. *Science*, **346**(6210).

Farrell, M. H. 2015. Robust Inference on Average Treatment Effects with Possibly More Covariates than Observations. *Journal of Econometrics*, **189**(1), 1 – 23.

Forni, M., Hallin, M., Lippi, M., and Reichlin, L. 2000. The Generalized Dynamic Factor Model: Identification and Estimation. *Review of Economics and Statistics*, **82**, 540–554.

Forni, M., Giannone, D., Lippi, M., and Reichlin, L. 2009. Opening the Black Box: Structural Factor Models with Large Cross Sections. *Econometric Theory*, **25**(10), 1319–1347.

Frank, I. E., and Friedman, J. H. 1993. A Statistical View of Some Chemometrics Regression Tools. *Technometrics*, **35**(2), pp. 109–135.

Gautier, E., and Tsybakov, A. 2011. High-dimensional Instrumental Variables Regression and Confidence Sets. *ArXiv e-prints*, May.

Giannone, D., Reichlin, L., and Small, D. 2008. Nowcasting: The Real-time Informational Content of Macroeconomic Data. *Journal of Monetary Economics*, **55**(4), 665–676.

Giannone, D., Lenza, M., and Primiceri, G. E. 2015. Prior Selection for Vector Autoregressions. *Review of Economics and Statistics*, **97**(2), 436–451.

Hastie, T., Tibshirani, R., and Friedman, J. 2009. *The Elements of Statistical Learning.* 2 edn. Springer-Verlag.

Hoerl, A. E., and Kennard, R. W. 1970. Ridge Regression: Biased Estimation for Nonorthogonal Problems. *Technometrics*, **12**(1), pp. 55–67.

Hoogerheide, L. F., van Dijk, H. K., and van Oest, R. D. 2009. Simulation-Based Bayesian Econometric Inference: Principles and Some Recent Computational Advances. In: *Handbook of Computational Econometrics*. John Wiley and Sons, Ltd, pp. 215–280.

Jungbacker, B., and Koopman, S. J. 2015. Likelihood-based Dynamic Factor Analysis for Measurement and Forecasting. *Econometrics Journal*, **18**, C1–C21.

Kleinberg, J., Lakkaraju, H., Leskovec, J., Ludwig, J., and Mullainathan, S. 2015a. *Human Decisions and Machine Predictions*. Harvard mimeo.

Kleinberg, J., Ludwig, J., Mullainathan, S., and Obermeyer, Z. 2015b. Prediction Policy Problems. *American Economic Review*, **105**(5), 491–495.

Lee, A., Yau, C., Giles, M. B., Doucet, A., and Holmes, C. C. 2010. On the Utility of Graphics Cards to Perform Massively Parallel Simulation of Advanced Monte Carlo Methods. *Journal of Computational and Graphical Statistics*, **19**(4), 769–789.

Li, Xinyuan. 2016. *Nowcasting with Big Data: Is Google Useful in the Presence of Other Information?* London Business School Mimeo.

Lucas, R. J. 1976. Econometric Policy Evaluation: A Critique. *Carnegie-Rochester Conference Series on Public Policy*, **1**(1), 19–46.

Pang, B., Lee, L., and Vaithyanathan, S. 2002. Thumbs up? Sentiment Classification Using Machine Learning Techniques. In: *Proceedings of EMNLP*, pp. 79–86.

Reichlin, L. 2003. Factor Models in Large Cross Sections of Time Series. In: Dewatripont, M., Hansen, L., and Turnovsky, S. (eds), *Advances in Economics and Econometrics: Theory and Applications, Eighth World Congress of the Econometric Society*, vol. 3. Cambridge University Press, pp. 47–86.

Sala-I-Martin, X. X. 1997. I Just Ran Two Million Regressions. *The American Economic Review*, **87**(2), pp. 178–183.

Schwarz, G. 1978. Estimating the Dimension of a Model. *The Annals of Statistics*, **6**(2), 461–464.

Scott, S. L., and Varian, H. R. 2014. Predicting the Present with Bayesian Structural Time Series. *International Journal of Mathematical Modelling and Numerical Optimisation*, **5**(1/2), 4–23.

Stein, C. 1956. Inadmissibility of the Usual Estimator for the Mean of a Multivariate Normal Distribution. In: *Proceedings of the Third Berkeley Symposium on Mathematical Statistics and Probability, Volume 1: Contributions to the Theory of Statistics*. Berkeley, Calif.: University of California Press, pp. 197–206.

Stock, J. H., and Watson, M. W. 1989. New Indexes of Coincident and Leading Economic Indicators. In: *NBER Macroeconomics Annual 1989, Volume 4*. NBER Chapters. National Bureau of Economic Research, Inc, pp. 351–409.

Stock, J. H., and Watson, M. W. 2002. Forecasting Using Principal Components from a Large Number of Predictors. *Journal of the American Statistical Association*, **97**, 147–162.

Tibshirani, R. 1996. Regression Shrinkage and Selection via the Lasso. *Journal of the Royal Statistical Society. Series B (Methodological)*, **58**, 267–288.

Varian, H. R. 2014. Big Data: New Tricks for Econometrics. *Journal of Economic Perspectives*, **28**(2), 3–28.

Watson, M. W. 2003. Macroeconomic Forecasting Using Many Predictors. In: Dewatripont, M., Hansen, L., and Turnovsky, S. (eds), *Advances in Economics and Econometrics: Theory and Applications, Eighth World Congress of the Econometric Society*, vol. 3. Cambridge University Press, pp. 87–115.

Index

CPSIA information can be obtained
at www.ICGtesting.com
Printed in the USA
LVOW09*1045020517
532984LV00009B/72/P